Instructor's Resource Manual

Psychology
Modules for Active Learning

TWELFTH EDITION

Dennis Coon

John O. Mitterer

Prepared by

David Topor
VA Boston Healthcare System
Harvard Medical School

WADSWORTH
CENGAGE Learning

Australia • Brazil • Japan • Korea • Mexico • Singapore • Spain • United Kingdom • United States

WADSWORTH
CENGAGE Learning

For product information and technology assistance, contact us at
Cengage Learning Customer & Sales Support,
1-800-354-9706

For permission to use material from this text or product, submit all requests online at **www.cengage.com/permissions**
Further permissions questions can be emailed to
permissionrequest@cengage.com

ISBN-13: 978-1-111-34355-2
ISBN-10: 1-111-34355-1

Wadsworth
20 Davis Drive
Belmont, CA 94002-3098
USA

Cengage Learning is a leading provider of customized learning solutions with office locations around the globe, including Singapore, the United Kingdom, Australia, Mexico, Brazil, and Japan. Locate your local office at: **www.cengage.com/global**

Cengage Learning products are represented in Canada by Nelson Education, Ltd.

To learn more about Wadsworth, visit
www.cengage.com/wadsworth

Purchase any of our products at your local college store or at our preferred online store
www.cengagebrain.com

READ IMPORTANT LICENSE INFORMATION

Printed in the United States of America
1 2 3 4 5 6 7 14 13 12 11 10

Contents

INTRODUCTION TO THE INSTRUCTOR'S RESOURCE MANUAL

The purpose of this manual is to support the unique features of **Psychology: Modules for Active Learning (12th ed.)** and to facilitate its use. Provided in the manual are survey questions, discussion questions, lecture enhancements with simple demonstrations, role-playing scenarios, value clarification statements, one-minute motivators, broadening cultural horizons, supplemental activities, journal questions and suggested readings. There are video and multimedia suggestions, CD-ROM topics, computer and Internet resources, Infotrac College Edition journal article recommendations with related discussion questions, a "psychology in the news" section and references for teaching psychology. The brief comments that follow will acquaint you with the text, its ancillaries, and the contents of this manual.

THE TEXT

The content and format of the text reflect a combination of goals. First and foremost, the text is written for students, not for instructors. It attempts to make the reader a **voluntary participant in learning**, rather than a passive and inattentive captive. To achieve this goal, chapters are structured around a unique study/reading format. Also, each chapter includes a section on **practical applications of psychological principles**. It is our hope that the extra effort taken to show students how to apply psychology gives the text an unusual degree of relevancy and impact.

The text consists of 16 topical chapters and a statistics appendix. In an introduction that precedes the first chapter various study skills are presented to students, including the reflective **SQ4R method**. This section is a key to the rest of the text and should be assigned. In addition to giving students a good start and some helpful suggestions, it explains the chapter format and shows how it is designed to foster active learning.

FORMAT

Perhaps the most distinctive aspect of the text is the chapter format, which guides students through an **active reading and information-processing experience**. Each chapter begins with an attention-arousing introduction of very high-interest material. This is followed by a list of **Modules** and **Survey Questions** for that chapter, key questions that guide the student through the topics in the chapter. These features are designed to augment the survey portion of an SQ4R reading approach, but they are no substitute for an actual chapter survey. Students should, therefore, be encouraged to study all topic headings in a chapter.

Throughout each chapter, the **Survey Questions** are repeated at appropriate places in the text to establish a feeling of dialogue and anticipate student questions. Following each module is a **Module Summary** outlining key points form the module. Following the module summary is a section called **Knowledge Builder**. These Knowledge Builders challenge the student to think, rehearse, relate and test their memory of information in the preceding module. Each of these sections includes subsections: **Relate**, a short question or questions helping the student relate the material of the previous section to their own lives and experiences; and **Recite** (brief self-quizzes). **Recites** offer immediate feedback and a chance to do some recitation while reading. Most students will find them helpful enough to use them voluntarily. However, students might be further encouraged if you include some questions on quizzes or tests and announce in class that you plan to do so. Also included as part of each **Knowledge Builder** are **Critical Thinking** questions. These questions challenge students to sharpen their thinking skills while pondering various conundrums related to the concepts they are studying. Answers to the **Knowledge Builder** material, are at the end of each of these sections. **Boldface type** indicates important terms and a **running glossary** contains precise definitions beside the text students are reading.

After core topics have been covered, each chapter has a **Psychology in Action Module** that discusses explicit applications of psychological principles. Alternatively, the Psychology in Action Modules offer added information of high personal relevance or practicality. The information presented in Psychology in Action is designed to meet the real needs of students and to bring psychology to life.

After reading the entire chapter, students should go back and read the point-by-point **Module Summary** again to increase comprehension and to consolidate what they have learned. Additionally, this edition includes and **Interactive Learning** section at the end of each chapter which directs students to Internet resources via the web, including **CengageNow,** and the Book Companion Website. Students should be strongly encouraged to utilize these additional resources to enhance their learning experience.

STUDY GUIDE AND OTHER STUDENT AIDS

STUDY GUIDE WITH LANGUAGE DEVELOPMENT GUIDE

The Study Guide, revised for this edition by Steven J. Hoekstra , is designed to help students learn information presented in the text. Students using the Study Guide will find it easy to review in great detail--something many find difficult to do without guidance. Students can also use the Study Guide to test themselves prior to taking in-class quizzes or tests. By using the Study Guide to review and quiz themselves, students can greatly improve the quality of their studying and their classroom performance. Each Study Guide chapter includes the following sections:

- ☞ **Chapter Overview**—This section is a concise chapter summary, easily incorporated into the SQ4R method of study.
- ☞ Survey Questions-These are meant to stimulate thinking and establish continuity throughout the chapter.
- ☞ **Recite and Review**—This is a survey of major terms and concepts. It allows students to assess text reading comprehension and recall of important ideas.
- ☞ **Connections**—This section consists of matching items Through it and the following sections, students will learn whether or not they really understand the concepts they have read about.
- ☞ **Check Your Memory**—This section consists of true-false items
- ☞ **Final Survey and Review**—This section consists of fill-in-the-blank items and provides a final detailed review of the text chapter.
- ☞ **Mastery Test**—This section contains multiple-choice questions similar to those used in the classroom testing.

Like the text, the study guide is designed to structure learning and to reinforce study skills. Instructors who assign the Study Guide, or who arrange for the campus book store to carry optional copies, will find it is a valuable aid to students. For many students, differences in language and culture prove to be a barrier to full comprehension. The *Language Development Guide* helps clarify idioms and special phrases, historical and cultural allusions, and challenging vocabulary found in the text. All terms and phrases in the **Guide** are page-referenced and clearly defined.

CONCEPT MODULES WITH NOTE-TAKING AND PRACTICE EXAMS

Created by Claudia Cochran and Shawn Talbot, this booklet includes a visual presentation of key concepts that parallel the text's modules, a place to take notes, and a practice exam of 20 multiple-choice questions.

MULTIMEDIA ANCILLARIES AND INTERNET RESOURCES

PowerLecture with JoinIn™ and ExamView® CD-ROM: A Microsoft® PowerPoint® Tool created by Corinne McNamara. This one-stop lecture and class preparation tool contains ready-to-use slides in Microsoft® PowerPoint®, and allows you to assemble, edit, publish, and present costume lectures for your course.
This one-stop lecture and class preparation tool contains ready-to-use Microsoft® PowerPoint® slides created by Corinne McNamara and other great tools—enabling you to assemble, edit, and present custom lectures for your course. With PowerLecture, you can bring together text specific lecture outlines and art from Coon and Mitterer's text, along with videos or your own materials-culminating in a powerful, personalized, media-enhanced presentation. PowerLecture also includes a full Instructor's Resource Manual and Test Bank in Microsoft® Word® format, ExamView® computerized testing, and JoinIn™ Student Response System.

Book Companion Website: Cengage Publishing Company has a website established for this text. It can be located at the following address on the Internet: academic.cengage.com/psychology/coon.

When you adopt this text, you and your students will have access to a rich array or teaching and learning resources that you won't find anywhere else. These outstanding site feature chapter-by-chapter outline tutorial quizzes, chapter-by-chapter web links, flashcards, and more!

Web Tutor: With Web Tutor you can easily create and manage your own custom course website. Web Tutor Advantage's course management tools give you the ability to provide virtual office hours, post syllabi, set up threaded discussions, track student progress, and more.

TEST BANK

The **Test Bank,** revised by Jeannette Murphey, contains more than four thousand multiple-choice questions. Items are organized to correspond to the learning objectives contained in this **Instructor's Resource Manual**. In addition, items are page-referenced and classified according to type (factual, conceptual, and applied).

THE INSTRUCTOR'S RESOURCE MANUAL

This instructor's resource manual provides resources that can enrich the experiences of the student and make it easier for the instructor to provide the variety that successful teaching requires. Since students come to psychology with varied backgrounds and learning styles, a single mode of presentation cannot adequately meet their needs. This manual provides, for each chapter, ideas for fruitful discussion, classroom exercises, role-playing suggestions, journal questions, and more. There are also suggestions for films and readings. The learning objectives provide the instructor and students with a detailed outline of each chapter.

Another goal of this manual is to foster interactive dialogue with and among students, rather than continuous professorial monologues. This engages the part of teaching that is an art. Interactive instruction can make teaching an emotional dialogue between you and your students. That is, instructors can be facilitators of change and insight, as well as disseminators of knowledge. When a course is maximally effective, students change cognitively, affectively, and behaviorally. The way that you teach will be affected by your goals for the class, by your skills, and by your students. Each chapter of this manual provides you with the following ten categories of ideas: **Survey Questions, Discussion Questions, Lecture Enhancements, Role-Playing Scenarios, Value Clarification Statements, One-Minute Motivators, Broadening Our Cultural Horizons, Supplemental Activities, Journal Questions, Suggestions for Further Reading, Video Suggestions, and Computer and Internet Resources.**

INSTRUCTIONAL MATERIALS

SURVEY QUESTIONS

DISCUSSION QUESTIONS

These questions ask your students to go beyond a description of the concepts covered in each chapter. Whether your class consists of hundreds of students in a large lecture hall or a dozen students in a small, cozy seminar lounge, these questions can be discussed by the class as a whole, in small groups, or by pairs of students. Select a few Discussion Questions that fit your goals, or duplicate all of the questions for students as "food for thought."

Students can learn from one another through discussion. Also, their thinking may be stimulated in an exchange with their peers. Planning and leading productive discussions requires skill; it doesn't just happen by itself. Some guidelines for planning and leading a discussion follow:

1. **One essential ingredient of productive discussion (over which instructors have little control) is the degree of preparation students bring to class.** If students have not read the material to be discussed, no amount of skill on the instructor's part is likely to produce an effective interchange. If a sizable portion of the students in a particular class do not seem to be keeping up with reading

   assignments, it might be wise to schedule a short quiz on days when you plan to devote class time to discussion. If the quiz is brief and "painless", students will then be ready and eager to discuss what they have learned.

2. **It is frequently useful to set the stage for discussion with an overview of the topics to be addressed.** In the case of an enthusiastic and usually well-prepared class, this can serve as an alternative to the quiz strategy described above.

3. **Numerous specific questions are often essential to maintain high content quality and to keep a discussion moving.** It is usually best to begin an extended discussion with a long list of questions or issues in hand. The Behavioral Objectives can be useful for generating questions.

4. **If at all possible, try to phrase questions so that they cannot be answered "yes" or "no."** Also avoid questions that call for a straight factual answer. Remember that the goal is discussion, not rote recall of the text. Even if the question or issue at hand is fairly factual, questions should be stated in a way that encourages elaboration.

   If students feel that what they say must be "right," they are often very hesitant to say anything at all. Try to use phrases like, "How did you feel about," "Do you agree with," "What do you find attractive or unattractive about," "Do you see any problems with," "What might happen if," "Who has had an experience that relates to," and so forth. Once discussion is underway, it is relatively easy to shift to more challenging questions or issues, but at first it is important not to intimidate students.

5. **Don't worry about getting to another question or topic if the group is interested, and the discussion is informative.** However, as soon as the quality of contributions begins to decline (i.e. they become redundant or irrelevant), change immediately to a new question or issue. This type of movement is what distinguishes a sparkling classroom discussion from the sort of session that students and instructors may perceive as a waste of time. It also makes clear to the students that the instructor is providing structure and leadership.

6. **It is wise to avoid revealing your own position early in the discussion of a particular topic or issue.** This allows you to play devil's advocate, and it avoids closing off expression of divergent viewpoints. Eventually students will want to know what you think, but save this for a summary statement and then move on to the next question. Specific misinformation can and should be corrected immediately. Beyond this, however, be sure to make a clear distinction between your opinions and more factual information.

7. **Try to make your interest in students visible and liberally compliment interesting and informative contributions.** If the initial participants in a discussion are treated in a reinforcing manner, others are more likely to join in. Try to make it "safe" to participate. If you strongly disagree, say so, but try to do it in a non-threatening way. Often you need only say, "I'm not sure I agree with that. Who can think of a reason why?" Then another student will correct the first. In this way you can avoid being the sole dispenser of disagreement or disapproval.

8. **Don't allow one or two individuals to monopolize the discussion even if they are articulate and what they say is interesting.** Strive to involve as many students as possible. This can often be done by simply saying, "(S)he says...Let's get another viewpoint." If no one volunteers, ask another student, "What do you think?" Or say, "Who agrees (or disagrees with (student's name)?" or, "Has anyone had a similar (or different) experience?" It is not unreasonable, of course, to return to particularly articulate students after others have had a chance to participate.

9. **Try to ensure that the entire group can hear questions and responses.** Whenever possible, try to prevent comments from becoming a conversation between you and an individual student. In larger classes a student who cannot be heard can be handled in several ways: **Restate** for the class what the student has asked or said and call for a response. **Compliment** the student on an interesting contribution and ask her or him to face the class and repeat it for others to hear. **Walk** to the far side of the class as the student speaks so that his or her voice must be raised and directed at the class.

10. **It is generally a good idea to move around the classroom during a discussion.** Also make a point of establishing eye contact with students in each section of the classroom once every few minutes. Sometimes, looking expectantly at students in a particular area can be as effective as a direct question for prompting a response. Remember, too, that posture and gestures can influence classroom atmosphere. If you approach students, sit or lean on front desks, etc., a casual tone is set. Standing at a greater distance or behind a lectern or desk imparts a more formal quality. By effectively manipulating such cues, you can communicate your intentions (lecture or discussion) to students. This can be more effective than saying, "Now let's discuss...," (which is often as ineffective as saying, "Be spontaneous"). If you simply begin, students will follow your lead.

11. **When working with large classes, or when performing demonstrations that preclude participation by the entire class** choose one or two students and have them come to the front of the class. In this way, other students will identify with the participants and will feel involved. Also, your interaction with the surrogate participants will add a dimension of spontaneity that will make the class more interesting for you as well as for the students.

LECTURE ENHANCEMENTS

Involving the students in the classroom activity increases motivation and enhances learning. The activities presented in this section are intended to promote learning and enthusiasm for the course. They can provide the substance for a change of pace in the classroom routine and serve as demonstrations of how psycho-gists observe behavior. **Most are simple demonstrations or discussions, requiring little preparation or equipment.** In every instance, it is important to tie in the activity with the material being studied in the course, and the relevance of conclusions arrived at should be underlined for maximum benefit to the students. It should never be assumed that the students will make the connections on their own or that they are self-evident.

ROLE-PLAYING SCENARIOS

The exercises in this section are designed to **facilitate perspective-taking**. These scenes can be used as lecture examples in a large lecture course. Students can be asked to think about ways of handling a specific situation. Talking about an issue often mainly changes how we think. Role-playing can change thoughts, feelings, and behaviors. For example, students may say that it is "terrible that some parents physically abuse their children." But if the student has to articulate the feelings of the abusive parent, usually there is an increase in sensitivity to the parent's frustration and anger.

It is wise to gradually introduce students to role-playing. The first few "scenarios" may be clumsy and filled with refusals and giggles. However, even when students hesitate to act out the roles, they will talk about the issues and learn a great deal. You will soon know which students want to be coaxed and which students do not want to participate. Each time you use this technique you will find students protesting less and volunteering more. With practice, you will learn to sense when the flow of insights starts to decline and the role-playing should end.

VALUE CLARIFICATION STATEMENTS

Controversial Value Clarification statements are included for each chapter. Ideally, the statements will prompt strong and diverse reactions from students. For example, the statement could be, "Children should be removed from the home of abusive parents." Four 8 X 20 signs are prepared. One sign says, "Strongly agree," another "Agree," another "Disagree," and finally "Strongly disagree." In a large lecture hall, students can simply raise their hands and express why they support any given position. After arguments are made for all views, students can vote again. A student can be appointed "teller" to record the number of votes for each view. Often it will only take a few votes before public opinion on the issue will shift.

A "silent" value clarification can take place in a large lecture hall. A controversial statement can be written on a 5 X 8 filing card. The card is passed down each row and students write whether they agree or disagree and why. The cards are collected and are read to the student audience.

In smaller classes, the four position signs are placed around the four sides of the room. Students are asked to stand in the center of the room. A statement is read and students literally move to the sign describing their viewpoint. Students are reminded that: feelings about issues are not right or wrong; they just are. ☞reactions to each statement depend on how the words are defined. Once all students have moved to a sign, a person from each side of the room will be asked to define terms and support his or her position.

We can reject a person's views on an issue without rejecting that person in general. Feelings toward issues change when we receive new information or process old information in a new way. Listen to each other. If someone convinces you to change your mind, move to that side of the room. There is no sign for "neutral" because a lack of a stance usually becomes a position in support of the more vocal majority. It will be difficult, but students must take a stand on all issues.

The instructor's role is to reinforce short responses, to encourage people to change their views and move to another side of the room, and to move on to another statement when the key points of one issue have been covered. After about 20-30 minutes, students are asked to complete the following pre-prepared anonymous form. They are also told that they will be reading each other's anonymous sheets.

> "I was pleased to learn that..."
> "I was surprised to learn that..."
> "I felt uncomfortable when someone said that..."
> "I wish I would have said that..."
> "I learned from this exercise that..."

Completed forms are passed to the right and each person silently reads the previous person's form. This continues until each student silently has read five or six forms. The instructor says, "Stop," and each student reads aloud one or two lines from the form in his or her hand. This feedback sheet has a powerful impact on both small and large classes.

Value clarification can be used with any topic. Usually students will be very open and direct about their feelings. The instructor may need to help students reword ideas so people disagree sensitively, and the instructor may need to support less "popular" views. Invariably, the most frequent student response at the end of this exercise is, "I was surprised to learn that we could still be friends after disagreeing so strongly." **Value clarification can help open up future class dialogues because students learn to feel that it is safe to disagree.**

ONE-MINUTE MOTIVATORS

Often it takes only a moment to motivate students to think about a topic, to feel the implications of an issue, or to make a commitment to change their behavior. One-minute Motivators are **quick demonstrations, examples, analogies, props, or challenges**. They need to flow into and out of your presentation; they should not seem contrived or artificial. These devices should be used as a way to change the pace of the class, not as ends in themselves. While they can diversify your presentation, they shouldn't serve as a substitute for meaningful analysis of the issues.

BROADENING OUR CULTURAL HORIZONS

Ideas from this section can be used to analyze bias in psychological research, to update lecture materials, to role-play diverse cultural values, or to change how we respond to individuals different from ourselves. Students seem to be fascinated by intercultural information and would enjoy bringing to their instructors articles that discuss their own roots or the backgrounds of others. If you would like to add to your own cultural knowledge, you will find a list of helpful journals in the Appendix of this manual.

SUPPLEMENTAL ACTIVITIES

There are two or more activities developed for each chapter in the text. These exercises are more elaborate than those described in the previous sections. **Each of the exercises has a rationale, an explanation of the purpose and procedure, a specific set of directions for carrying out the exercise, data sheets and worksheets for collecting information, and some points for discussion after the exercise is completed.**

The data sheets and worksheets should be copied for distribution to the class. Where appropriate, directions and supplementary information are provided for students and may be duplicated as well. Some of the exercises can be done in one session in the classroom. Others may take more than one class period and may require some work outside the classroom. Most of the exercises require students to work in groups, which should help to promote student interaction. It is important to change the groupings for each activity so that students will get to know each other and will not get into a rut.

JOURNAL QUESTIONS

Questions from this section can be used to trigger a large class discussion, sharing in a small group or a pair, or a private dialogue between you and your student. Even if time is not available for answering all of the questions, making the questions available to students can help them reflect on parts of their life relevant to chapter content. Answers to these questions should always be handled sensitively, respectfully, and confidentially.

SUGGESTIONS FOR FURTHER READING

A list of additional readings is provided for each chapter in the text. While a few of these references are older, those references are considered classics in the field and are included for that reason. All other references have been updated. Some care has been taken to find reading material that is accessible to students and interesting to read. Some of these could be assigned as enrichment for the class. Assignments to review articles or books for credit or extra credit could be made from this list. Some of the items are classic and should be introduced to serious students of psychology. Other readings are simply informative and/or entertaining.

VIDEO SUGGESTIONS

Videos are suggested for each chapter. No attempt has been made to provide a complete list. These are simply some suggestions of videos or CD-ROMs that have been found by instructors to be helpful in class. Every teacher of introductory psychology will have personal favorites and could add to the list provided.

COMPUTER AND INTERNET RESOURCES

In this section are several sources of CD-ROM and Internet materials pertaining to the chapter. *InfoTrac®* provides reference to specific journal articles and related questions for students. In addition, a section called *Psychology in the News* is provided. Although the web addresses listed in this manual were current at the time of preparation, web addresses have a tendency to change frequently, so no guarantee is made that these web addresses will be continue to be current. If you find a web address that is no longer active, simply type the name of the site into your web browser and the current URL should come up.

COURSE SYLLABUS OF INTRODUCTORY GENERAL PSYCHOLOGY
PSY 2200: Section 4A

Instructor: Janice Smith, Ph.D.
Office: SS 2201; Ph: 555-9797; email: jsmith@hometownuniversity.edu
Office Hours: SS 2201; Mon. & Fri. 4:00 – 5:00pm, or by appointment
Class Time & Room Mon., Wed., and Friday 10:00am – 11:00am; Lecture Hall 11

Graduate Teaching Assistant: To be named.

REQUIRED TEXT
Coon, D, John Mitterer. *Psychology: Modules for Active Learning, (11th ed.).* Belmont, CA: Cengage, 2008.

WEB RESOURCES
The text publisher (Wadsworth) offers an online resource center with practice multiple-choice quizzes and links to relevant sites for each chapter. Go to: academic.cengage.com/psychology/coon and follow the links.

COURSE OBJECTIVES:
(a) to provide students with and integrative overview of psychology's history and evolution to a modern day science;
(b) to familiarize students with the multiple theoretical perspectives in the explanation of human behavior;
(c) to illustrate an integrative view of research in the many disciplines and theoretical perspectives of human behavior;
(d) and, to discuss the biological, cultural, social and learning components to the development of human behavior.

ATTENDANCE AND SCHOLARLY CONDUCT
Attendance in class is required and excessive absences may affect your final course grade. It is the responsibility of the student to information presented in class from another student member. In order for you to do well on exams, you will need to attend class lectures as some of the material present in class lecture will not be found in your textbook.

EXAMS
There will be five exams. All exams are multiple choice and will cover materials covered in lectures, in-class videos, and assigned text readings. The first four exams will be 50 items long and will be given during regularly scheduled class time. The final exam will be 100 items and will be partly comprehensive. The **final exam is scheduled Friday, May 17, 10:30am-12: 30pm (LH11).**

MAKE-UPS
Please note that, except under extreme circumstances, no make-up exams will be given. You should make every effort to attend all exams, and/or otherwise contact the instructor ahead of time if an emergency arises.

EXTRA CREDIT

You may earn up to 20 pts. of extra credit that can be applied toward your final cumulative grade point total. A handout will be provided during the first class meeting outlining projects available for extra credit.

ACADEMIC DISHONESTY

Any student caught cheating on an exam; plagiarizing and/or altering extra credit assignments will receive an "F" for the course. Please consult your student handbook for a description of what constitutes academic dishonesty and possible expulsion.

SPECIAL NEEDS STUDENTS

Students with special needs or disabilities covered under the Americans with Disabilities Act (ADA) who may require special accommodations for this class should make this know to the instructor prior to class, if possible, but certainly during the first week of class.

COURSE GRADE

Your course grade will be based on the cumulative points you earn from all exams and any extra credit earned on or before the 4th regular exam. You can earn an A in this course without doing extra credit. Grades are not curved in calculating final grades. Final grades will be calculated according to the following grading rubrics:

A = 285 – 300+ pts.	C = 224 – 27 # pts.	Exam 1 = 50 pts.
A- = 270 – 284 # pts.	D = 180 – 209 # pts.	Exam 2 = 50 pts.
B+ = 258 – 269 # pts.	F = less than 180 # pts	Exam 3 = 50 pts.
B = 253 – 257 # pts.		Exam 4 = 50 pts.
A- = 240 – 252 # pts.		Final = 100 pts.
C+ = 228 – 239 # pts.		Total = 300pts.

ACKNOWLEDGMENTS

I would like to acknowledge the contributions of authors of previous editions of the Instructor's Manual who have provided much of the source material and inspiration for this current edition; namely, Saundra K. Ciccarelli, Kendra Jeffcoat, Carole Woodward, the late Michael C. Sosulski. I am grateful to these people for the tremendous amount of work they put into this manual before my own efforts to make the material more accessible and current. I would like to thank and express my deep appreciation to the textbook authors Dennis Coon and John Mitterer for this opportunity to provide material that I hope will help facilitate bringing his textbook to life in the classroom. I would also like to thank my students for their inspirations, my colleagues for their dedication to the education process, and my wife for her continued support. I express my deepest gratitude to Kelly Miller, Assistant Editor Psychology of Cengage/Wadsworth Publishing for her support and encouragement during this project. Lastly, I would like to thank Susan Weldon for her work on the last edition of this manual and for her contribution to the many ideas and exercises found in this book.

David Topor, Ph.D.

VA Boston Healthcare System

Harvard Medical School

CHAPTER 1

Introducing Psychology and Research Methods

Survey Questions
Discussion Questions
Lecture Enhancements
              Countering widespread student belief in astrology
              Examining the limits of "they say that…"
              Pseudopsychology meets research
              The limits of introspection
              Gestalt psychology
              Animal rights
              Thinking about our own behavior
              The nature of science
              Operational definitions
              Distinguishing beliefs from theories
              Naturalistic observation
              What's interesting?
              Recognizing independent and dependent variables
              Recognizing good and poor research
              Attitudes toward experimentation
              Sometime negative is "positive"
              Casual observation
              Pop psychology
              The nature of empiricism
              Evaluating TV commercials
              Internet hoaxes can cost you more than time

Role-Playing Scenarios
Value-Clarification Statements
One-Minute Motivators
              Self-observation and human behavior
              Demographics and sampling
              Anthropomorphizing in everyday life
              The diffusion of responsibility
              Principles of Gestalt psychology
              Psychological perspectives
              Human motivation and social desirability
              Cognitive psychology
              Perceptions about psychologists
              Psychological perspectives: the behaviorists
              The experimenter effect and self-fulfilling prophecies
              Placebo effects and control groups
              Representative sampling
              Biases in internet surveys
              Thinking critically about astrology
              Thinking critically about psychics
              Psychologists' qualifications

1

2

Module 1.1 The Science of Psychology

Survey Question: What is psychology and what are its goals?

Module 1.2 Critical Thinking and the Scientific Method in Psychology

Survey Question: What is critical thinking?

Survey Question: How does psychology differ from false explanations of behavior?

Survey Question: How is the scientific method applied in psychological research?

Module 1.3 History and Contemporary Perspectives

Survey Question: How did the field of psychology emerge?

Survey Question: What are the contemporary perspectives in psychology?

Module 1.4 Psychologists and Their Specialties

Survey Question: What are the major specialties in psychology?

Module 1.5 The Psychology Experiment

Survey Question: How is an experiment performed?

Survey Question: What is a double-blind experiment?

Module 1.6 Nonexperimental Research Methods

Survey Question: What nonexperimental research methods do psychologists use?

Module 1.7 Psychology in Action: Psychology in the Media

Survey Question: How good is psychological information found in the popular media?

3

➤ DISCUSSION QUESTIONS

1. What did you know about psychology and psychologists before reading Chapter 1? Did you think of psychology as a science? Has your image changed? How accurate are television and movie portrayals of psychologists? What psychological specialty do you consider most interesting at this point?

2. Why did you take a psychology course? Would you take it if it were not required? Do you think this course will be easy or difficult? What do you most want to learn in this course?

3. What are the benefits and possible disadvantages of studying psychology? Are there ever times when "ignorance is bliss"?

4. What do you see as the strengths and weaknesses of each of the schools of psychology? What specific human problems do you think psychologists should study? Which school of psychology would be most appropriate for the study of the problem you have identified?

5. Do you believe your behavior is controlled by the environment? Do you believe that you have free will? Is there any way to tell if an apparent "free choice" is really determined by your past?

6. Which of the following do you believe and why: astrology/horoscopes, graphology (hand-writing analysis), ESP, channeling or communicating with the dead, palm reading. Can you name additional systems of thought that you suspect are pseudopsychologies? What are their claims? Why do you think people believe in them?

7. During the Victorian era (a time of marked sexual repression), Freud treated a large number of women with sexual problems. What kinds of psychological problems do you believe are most common today? What kinds do you think will be most common 5, 10, or 15 years from now? Why?

8. Presently, a number of non physicians can prescribe certain medications under certain conditions. Examples include optometrists, nurse practitioners, and physician assistants. In your opinion, what are the advantages and disadvantages to psychologists being trained to prescribe mood-altering drugs?

9. Is science just a more formal version of "common sense"? Do you view scientific studies in psychology to be essential in determining the "truth" about human nature, or are most psychological studies likely just to confirm what we already know to be true?

4

10. What human problem or behavior do you think could most effectively be studied using naturalistic observation? For what behaviors would this approach be the least appropriate? Why?

11. What type of correlation would you expect to find between noise levels and productivity in an office? Between income and education? Between physical attractiveness and frequency of dating? Between class attendance and grades? Between use of alcohol by parents and their children? How would you demonstrate a causal link in any of these cases?

12. Give an example of a research hypothesis that you would like to investigate. What would you use as the independent variable? The dependent variable? What extraneous variables could distort your results? How would you try to control or eliminate these extraneous variables?

13. Many statements begin with the words "They say that…" Give examples of so-called facts that would actually be difficult or impossible to verify. How would psychology attempt to test some of these statements?

14. How should subjects be assigned to a control group and an experimental group in order to reduce systematic differences between the groups?

15. What confounding variables (i.e. variables outside of alcohol itself) might contribute to people getting into more accidents after drinking than when sober? How would a scientist design an experiment to test whether drinking and driving causes accidents? What factors would be held constant? Which operational definitions would be used? If all other factors were controlled, what do you think would be the results of such an experiment?

16. In your opinion, is it dishonest or unethical for a researcher to administer placebos to patients? Why or why not? Would it be unethical for a physician to give a patient a placebo? Why or why not?

17. Regarding self-fulfilling prophecies, how have the expectations of teachers, parents, or friends affected your expectations for yourself? What advantages and disadvantages do you see in an education system that has different levels of instruction (ie. remediation, accelerated, etc.) and how might these levels influence self-fulfilling prophecies?

18. What are the advantages and disadvantages of animal research? Under what conditions should animals be used instead of people? Most people anthropomorphize pets. How could this be a problem in the objective study of animals? What ethical guidelines do you feel should be followed in animal research?

19. Clinical cases are often described in the popular press. What could be the positive and negative effects of this kind of publicity? What factors might contribute to incomplete, inaccurate, or misleading descriptions of research in the news?

20. Have you ever taken part in a survey? On the basis of your participation, how accurate do you think surveys are? What are the flaws of typical "person on the street" surveys often done by local newspapers? What can be done to make survey data as accurate as possible?

21. Could the courtesy bias (social desirability) ever take place within a lab experiment? What do you suggest could be done to reduce the experimenter effect and the impact of self-fulfilling prophecy?

22. What are some of the ways to spot internet hoaxes? What are some of the common characteristics of internet hoaxes? If an email message quotes a source (e.g. Bill Gates, the government, some researcher, entertainers, etc.) what are some of the ways to determine whether that source actually made that statement?

➤ LECTURE ENHANCEMENTS

1. **Countering widespread student belief in astrology can be worth the class time and effort.** The inaccuracy of the system can be illustrated by use of the adjective checklist that follows. In class, have students check all of the adjectives that apply to their personalities.
   The adjectives in the following list were compiled by William Balch from 11 astrology books. They represent the most frequently mentioned characteristics for astrological "signs."

1) pioneering	13) extroverted	25) honest
2) enthusiastic	14) generous	26) impulsive
3) courageous	15) authoritative	27) optimistic
4) stable	16) critical	28) ambitious
5) stubborn	17) exacting	29) hard working
6) organized	18) intelligent	30) cautious
7) intellectual	19) harmonizing	31) original
8) adaptable	20) just	32) open minded
9) clever	21) sociable	33) independent
10) sensitive	22) secretive	34) kind
11) nurturing	23) strong	35) sensitive
12) sympathetic	24) passionate	36) creative

After students have made their responses, identify the signs corresponding to each group of three adjectives. They are: 1 to 3, Aries; 4 to 6, Taurus; 7 to 9, Gemini; 10 to 12, Cancer; 13 to 15, Leo; 16 to 18, Virgo; 19 to 21, Libra; 22 to 24, Scorpio; 25 to 27, Sagittarius; 28 to 30, Capricorn; 31 to 33, Aquarius; 34 to 36, Pisces. Next, call for a show of hands from those students who checked all three adjectives listed for "their sign." Follow this with a show of hands by students who checked all three adjectives for any other sign. You should, of course, get a roughly equal number of hands raised each time—showing that there is no compelling association between astrological signs and personality traits. (Adapted from Balch, W. R. 1980. "Testing the validity of astrology in class." *Teaching of Psychology, 7(4)*, pp. 247-250.)

2. **Examining the limits of "They say that…"** A number of well-known "facts" can be used to illustrate the problem of uncritical acceptance. For example, "They say that during one's lifetime, a person swallows x number of spiders while sleeping." Ask students to evaluate this statement. Problems with this statement include: Where does this statistic come from and how was it tested? Have any students had the personal experience of waking up with spiders in their mouths? Another example is the popular idea that if you dream that you are falling and you "hit bottom" you will die. Are there people who have dreamed of hitting bottom and survived? Do dead people tell us what they were dreaming about when they died? A similar effect is found in the misuse of statistics. If, say, 90 percent of plane crash survivors knew where the exits were (and that's why they survived), how do we determine—for comparison—what percent of the non-survivors knew the location of the exits?

3. **Pseudopsychology meets research.** The textbook includes an in-depth discussion of pseudopsychologies, astrology, and the Barnum Effect. Copy the "Personality Profile" from the text onto sheets of paper. Divide students into pairs or small groups and give each student a "kit" containing 12 copies of the profile. On the back of each copy, write a different astrological "sign" (Aries, Taurus, Gemini, Cancer, Leo, Virgo, Libra, Scorpio, Sagittarius, Capricorn, Aquarius, and Pisces). Send students out to test whether people are able to determine the validity of their sign's description. Groups should approach students at random, ask them their sign, and then hand them the description to read. (All participants will be getting the same description.) Each participant should be asked whether they believe in astrology and whether the personality description is accurate. Before leaving, each team should show the participant that all descriptions are the same, and record the participant's reaction.

a. Does participant believe in astrology?   Yes   No

b. What was participant's rating of the personality profile?

Very much like me   Somewhat like me   Somewhat unlike me   Very unlike me

c. What did the participant say when told that all profiles were the same?

7

Personality Profile:

You have a strong need for people to like you and admire you. You have a tendency to be critical of yourself. You have a great deal of unused energy, which you have not turned to your advantage. While you have some personality weaknesses, you are generally able to compensate for them. Your sexual adjustment has presented some problems for you. Disciplined and controlled on the outside, you tend to be worrisome and insecure inside. At times you have serious doubts as to whether you have made the right decision or done the right thing. You prefer a certain amount of change and variety and become dissatisfied when hemmed in by restrictions and limitations. You pride yourself on being an independent thinker and do not accept other opinions without satisfactory proof. You have found it unwise to be too frank in revealing yourself to others. At times, you are extroverted, affable, and sociable, while at other times, you are introverted, wary, and reserved. Some of your aspirations tend to be pretty unrealistic.

4. **The limits of introspection.** The limits of introspection as a method of observation can be demonstrated by a simple exercise. Ask students to identify the most basic taste sensations. With some help from you, they will come up with the four basic taste qualities: sweet, sour, salty, bitter. Now ask students to introspect by analyzing the taste of water (from memory or from a sample provided by you). They should identify which of the four basic tastes best describes the taste of water. Or if they prefer, a combination of two or more tastes may be listed. Students will arrive at a variety of answers, but mostly they will feel consternation because the task is nearly impossible. The difficulty of using introspection as a research method should be apparent.

5. **Gestalt psychology.** The day before talking about Gestalt psychology, ask everyone to wear a solid-color shirt or t-shirt to class. Assign the role of "artist" to one student. Have that person "arrange" members of the class as if they were splotches of paint. Of course, have your camera ready to create snapshots. Then ask another "artist" to rearrange students to create a different design. Obviously, the arrangement of the parts affects the whole picture that is created. Exhibit these pictures somewhere in the classroom.

6. **Animal rights.** You may want to invite a spokesperson from a local animal rights organization to come to class. Also, ask someone to attend who is engaged in animal research (a local research hospital or college animal laboratory are good sources). This person should be prepared to discuss the care that research animals are given and the rationale for animal research. Rather than force your visitors to debate, it is probably best to have each state his or her position, after which students can discuss or debate the issues. This can be a risky activity, so be certain that the spokesperson for each position is articulate, well informed, and aware of the other speaker's position.

7. **Thinking about our own behavior.** One ability that separates humans from other species is the ability to think about our own behavior. Students may better appreciate the importance of the cognitive perspective by completing the following examples. In each

8

example, students should write a positive statement and a negative statement that the person in the described situations could be thinking. What are the implications of such thoughts for the person's behavior?

    a. Mark does poorly on a test in spite of studying for many hours. He has another test in a week. He is probably thinking that…

    b. Shannon just bought a lottery ticket. She is probably thinking that…

    c. Rashana is newly married and is finding it difficult to adjust to being sexually active. She is probably thinking that…

8. **The nature of science.** A major theme of the second half of Chapter 1 is summarized by Bertrand Russell who said, "It is not what the man of science believes that distinguishes him, but how and why he believes it. His beliefs are tentative, not dogmatic; they are based on evidence, not on authority." (In the interest of using non-sexist language, it might be best to paraphrase this quotation, substituting "scientists" for "man of science" and using the plural pronoun "they.") This can be the start of a good discussion on what science is and how it differs from philosophy, mathematics, values, religion, magic, art, and so forth. It would also be important to discuss psychology as a science.

9. **Operational definitions.** Individually, have students create operational definitions for all variables in the following question: Do hungry rats learn to run a maze faster than non-hungry rats? Variables will be: time last fed in hours for each rat, type of rat (age, sex, breed, etc.), type of maze, and type of learning (speed or number of errors). Explain that for an experiment to be repeated (replicated) by another experimenter, the same definition must be used. To expand on the text, you may want to point out, however, that a conceptual replication occurs when different operational definitions of the same concepts or variables are used.

10. **Distinguishing beliefs from theories**. Students often think that a "theory" is either an educated guess, or a belief. Depending on the sensitivities of your students, you can use evolution (or some other theory) and religion (or some other belief). Make it clear to students that you respect their beliefs, and their right to believe whatever they want. Beliefs can be very powerful, and beliefs (religious or otherwise) give our lives meaning, purpose, and satisfaction. They affect our thoughts and behaviors and they are important. They are <u>not</u>, however, theories. Characteristics of theories are that they are based on empirical evidence, and they can be tested and replicated. Theories often differ in strength, such as Freud's theory versus evolutionary theory. Encourage students to avoid mixing and matching terms, such as creation *theory* and *belief* in evolution. Evolution is a theory, whereas creationism is a belief. In order to drive home the point that beliefs do have value, ask students to list other beliefs they have that make a difference in their lives. These could be political beliefs, beliefs about getting rich versus finding joy, beliefs about family, and so on. Examine each one to determine whether it qualifies as a theory.

9

11. **Naturalistic observation.** Allow students to practice naturalistic observation by showing an excerpt from the commercial film, *Gorillas in the Mist*. Ask each student to describe what the gorillas do. Have students compare their descriptions. Point out disparities in these descriptions to underscore the importance of systematic observation, where the experimenter decides in advance exactly what is to be observed and how it will be quantified.

12. **What's interesting?** Assign students to small groups. Ask them to think of a human or an animal behavior they would like to study experimentally. Ask them to develop a hypothesis, describe the variables they want to study, explain how they would assign subjects to the various groups, manipulate the independent variable or variables, control extraneous variables, and minimize various forms of bias. Present the proposed study to the class as a whole for discussion and evaluation.

13. **Recognizing independent and dependent variables.** Many students find it difficult to recognize dependent and independent variables in situations other than those provided in the text. To generalize these concepts, present the following descriptions and ask students to identify the independent and dependent variables in each.

    a. A biopsychologist injects several monkeys with male hormones and notes that by comparison to control animals, they display more aggressive acts in a testing situation.
    b. After being deprived of food for varying amounts of time, participants show a progressive decline in hand dexterity and steadiness.
    c. An educational psychologist finds no differences in the math achievement scores of elementary school students who have, or have not, been assigned to a special math education program.
    d. A social psychologist observes that participants tested in crowded rooms have slower reaction times than those tested individually.
    e. A psychologist decides to test the idea that you "can't teach old dogs new tricks." What would the dependent and independent variables be?

14. **Recognizing good and poor research.** To clarify the various elements of a carefully controlled experiment and to review problems such as the placebo effect and experimenter expectancies, describe the following experiment to students and have them identify the mistakes that have been made:

    Let's say that I am interested in the effects of caffeine on memory. In order to test the effects of caffeine, I divide the class in half. All the students on the right are given five cups of coffee to drink, and one hour later they are given a test of memory. The students on the left are dismissed. After the first group has been tested, the second group returns and is given the same memory test as the first group. The average scores are compared, and they show that the first group remembered more than the second group.

10

Major errors that students should note are: The experimental and control groups were not formed by random assignment; subjects were not tested at the same time of day; no placebo was used; subjects were probably aware of the experimenter's hypothesis; extraneous variables were not identified or controlled; pre-tests and post-tests were not given. Have students identify the impact these errors may have on the results of this experiment. How may confirmation bias influence this experiment and what could be done to reduce this?

15. **Attitudes toward experimentation.** Ask students to create a list of the conditions under which they would feel comfortable and uncomfortable participating in an experiment. Develop a list of conditions that would best protect the subject without making the research impossible or inaccurate.

16. **Sometimes negative is "positive."** Discuss with students the definition of positive and negative correlation. To illustrate that a negative correlation does not mean "bad" and a positive correlation does not mean "good," ask students to generate a list of variables that are either positively or negatively related to increased smoking. Examples of variables that are negatively related to increased smoking, but are good, include: money, health, lifespan, fresh breath, and lifespan. Examples of variables that are positively related to increased smoking, but are bad, include: cancer, heart disease, being broke, having smelly clothes, or risking a fire.

17. **Casual observation.** One way to illustrate the limitations of casual observation is to ask students to describe things in their environment that they "see" on a regular basis. The following questions regarding items that people observe all the time can serve as a starting point. Answers are indicated in parentheses. You may be surprised at how poor most students are at identifying things they have seen many times.

    a. Everyone knows that it's red with white letters, but what is the shape of a stop sign? (Octagon)
    b. Which way does Abe Lincoln face on a penny? (To his left, which means the viewer's right)
    c. In which hand does the Statue of Liberty hold her torch? (Her right hand)
    d. How many tines are on a standard dinner fork? (Four)
    e. Which two letters are missing on a standard telephone? (Q and Z)
    f. If a common pencil isn't cylindrical, how many sides does it usually have? (Six)
    g. On which side of their uniforms do police officers wear their badges? (Their left)
    h. On the back of a $5.00 bill is the Lincoln Memorial, and on the back of a $10.00 bill is the U.S. Treasury building. What is on the reverse side of a $1.00 bill? (the two sides of the great seal – the pyramid and the eagle)

18. **Pop psychology.** At some point in coverage of the first chapter, you might want to bring up the subject of pop psychology, especially as it is represented in self-help books and commercial therapies. As *The New York Times News Service* observed a few years ago:

If you were to believe the current dogma, happiness is getting rid of your erroneous zones, looking out for No. 1, asserting yourself, taking charge of your life, and learning to love every minute of it. It is clearing your psyche by screaming, rolfing, encountering, hallucinating, meditating, and levitating, tuning into your biorhythms, following your stars, getting in touch with your feelings, letting it all hang out, and teleporting yourself into an extrasensory universe.

19. **The nature of empiricism.** In addition to providing a good contrast to academic psychology, pop psychology can lead to a discussion of empirical and non empirical approaches. At the very least, the self-help books pale in comparison to Maslow's work on self-actualization. As Jonathan Freedman of Columbia University points out in the same article, "Most of the advice in the pop psych books and therapies is dangerously egocentric. It teaches people just to look out for themselves. Yet, to be happy, you have to care, to take responsibility. Egocentric, narcissistic types don't form relationships very easily or maintain them will."

20. **Evaluating TV commercials.** Ask students to watch three or four television commercials and to take notes on the "evidence" used to support the claims made in the commercials. Should these claims be believed? Why or why not? How can these claims be substantiated?

21. **Internet hoaxes can cost you more than time.** Break students into groups and ask them to brainstorm some of the ways that internet hoaxes create problems. Once students have compiled their lists, compare them to the major categories of hoaxes—e.g., charitable requests, "phishing," conspiracies, magical effects, chain letters (and supposed consequences of not forwarding), easy money, etc.

➤ ROLE-PLAYING SCENARIOS

1. **Divide the class into small groups.** Assign each group a "school of psychology." Ask students to discuss their assigned theory in detail and to select a representative who will voice their viewpoint. At the front of the room, form a panel made up of each of the representatives. Ask each representative to discuss his or her approach. Field questions from the class.

2. **Split the class into an even number of groups.** Designate half the groups "A" and half "B." The "A" groups should brainstorm as many ideas as they can produce to support the idea that the government should put more funding into psychology research. "B" groups should produce ideas supporting the idea that private funding should fuel psychological research. When both groups are done, have them switch perspectives and brainstorm for the other position. (This will eliminate order effects for the two main ideas.) Which perspective did they find easier to support and why? Are there any important concepts that are similar to both perspectives?

3. **Divide the class into small groups of five or six students.** Give each group the handout, "Differing Views of Animal Research," reproduced below. Ask students to enact each role described in the handout. Students should attempt to express in detail their thoughts and feelings as they assume each view. What evidence would each person probably use to support his/her view? Students may also want to role-play the different views as they try to persuade the "politician" to vote a certain way on impending legislation. This could be done in small groups or in front of the class.

4. **Differing views of animal research**
   a. Brenda is opposed to all animal research. She is active in animal rights organizations supporting legislation to stop animal research completely.
   b. Terri is a veterinarian who is in favor of some forms of research, as long as precautions are taken to prevent animals from experiencing excessive pain.
   c. Ruth is a diabetic who depends on animal research for the production of improved forms of insulin. She understands the importance of preventing unnecessary pain, but she also knows that the lives of many diabetics have been saved because of research on dogs.
   d. Patrick is a university researcher whose work on the visual system of cats has brought him worldwide recognition. He feels that the blindness that often must take place in cats is a small price to pay for the human sight that has been restored by his research.
   e. Frank is an AIDS victim who has volunteered to receive a highly controversial medication because protests over animal research have stopped research in this area.
   f. Mary is an accountant who hates dogs, cats, and rats. She is more concerned about the effect of costly animal research on her taxes than she is about the effect on animals.
   g. Geraldine is a politician who is reviewing legislation to limit animal research. She has mixed feelings and wants more information on this issue.

➤ VALUE-CLARIFICATION STATEMENTS

1. Psychology is just a more complicated version of "common sense."

2. Having students from fields such as business or engineering take a psychology course is a waste of time.

3. Most people with problems can get through them by themselves; our society has too many psychologists and psychiatrists.

4. Lab experiments are too expensive, artificial, and time-consuming to be very useful to our understanding of human behavior.

13

5. It is an invasion of privacy to observe public behavior systematically without first receiving the permission of people being observed.

6. Students in introductory psychology courses should be required to participate in psychological research.

7. Psychologists' emphasis on critical thinking in really just cynicism.

8. Any research that causes pain for animals should be banned, regardless of its value to humans.

9. A survivor of incest, alcoholism, or spousal abuse will always have emotional scars that will often affect his or her behavior.

➤ ONE-MINUTE MOTIVATOR

1. **Self-Observation and Human Behavior.** Ask one student to describe all of the things he or she did, thought, and felt during the last five minutes. Point out that human behavior is exceedingly complex and difficult to understand even for the person performing the behaviors!

2. **Demographics and Sampling.** Quickly collect demographic data from the class by a raise of hands. What kind of generalizations can be made about the "kind of people" in that specific class? Can these be scientifically tested?

3. **Anthropomorphizing in Everyday Life.** Generate a list of examples of the way humans talk to public telephones, vending machines, automatic bank tellers, automobiles, and computers when the machines are "moody." Is there anything wrong with this kind of anthropomorphizing?

4. **The Diffusion of Responsibility**. To demonstrate "diffusion of responsibility" as it relates to prosocial behavior, drop something and count the number of students who rush to help. Do the same thing on the way to class when only a few students are present and bring that data to class for discussion.

5. **Principles of Gestalt Psychology.** Add a slide or transparency to your lecture to show closure or figure/ground shifts to demonstrate the premise of Gestalt psychology.

6. **Psychological Perspectives.** The text lists three major perspectives in psychology— biological, psychological, and sociocultural. After you have explained the basic tenets of each of these, ask your students to rank order them in terms of how interested they are in each. Also ask them to indicate why their first choice was of greatest interest. Collecting their answers and quickly tabulating the results will give you a better idea of their areas of interest.

14

7. **Human Motivation and Social Desirability.** Intentionally slip some malapropisms into the lecture. See how many students notice, or did they unconsciously deny the presence of the errors to avoid embarrassing the instructor? How much human behavior is unconsciously motivated?

8. **Cognitive Psychology.** To demonstrate the tenor of cognitive psychology, say to students, "Imagine that I am going to give you a pop quiz. What thoughts would you have? What thoughts could help you do well?" Put these on the chalkboard. Suggest that writing similar coping statements on file cards could affirm that students are going to do well in this course.

9. **Perceptions About Psychologists.** The text discusses the concept of mental health professionals as "shrinks." Ask your students whether they would go to a psychologist or psychiatrist if they were depressed or anxious. Ask them why or why not. You will probably hear answers ranging from acceptance to rejection of "getting help." People often fail to seek help because they fear it makes them look weak, or because they think they can fix it on their own. You can round out the discussion by asking if they would seek assistance for other things in their lives, like buying a house, a medical ailment, managing debt, improving their game/sport, moving, finding a job, etc. Ask them how getting help with other parts of one's life is different than getting help with mental health problems, and why? Encourage students to think of mental health professionals as people who "stretch" rather than "shrink" your mind.

10. **Psychological Perspectives: The Behaviorists.** The text lists the four goals of psychology as description, understanding, prediction, and control. As the text states, "Control may seem like a threat to personal freedom." The text goes on to point out that control (altering behavior) has many positive benefits. The behaviorists go one step further and suggest that almost all of our behavior is "controlled" by the results it produces. Ask your students how much of their behavior—and even choices—is controlled. In Western, individualistic culture, students typically substantially underestimate how much we are "controlled," even in the scientific sense of the word.

11. **The Experimenter Effect and Self-Fulfilling Prophecies.** Ask for a female volunteer. Explain that you want to show that the reaction time of females is faster than that of males. You will drop a piece of paper. Her job is to catch it as quickly as possible. Ask another student to serve as timer.

   Before you start, say things like, "Are you relaxed? Do you understand what I want you to do? Are you ready?" Of course, she will catch the paper. Then ask for a male volunteer. Quickly say, "Ready, go." He invariably misses the paper. Conclude, "Thus you can see that female reaction time is faster than male reaction time." Ideally, as you start to move on, someone will say, "But that wasn't fair…"

15

12. **Placebo Effects and Control Groups**. Tell students the following: Let's do an experiment to see if the drug amphetamine (a stimulant) affects learning. Before studying, members of our experimental group take an amphetamine pill. Control group members get nothing. Later, we assess how much each subject learned. Does this experiment seem valid? **Answer:** Actually, it is seriously flawed because it fails to control for the placebo effect.

13. **Representative Sampling.** To demonstrate a representative sample, bring in two boxes of candy, one filled only with nut chocolates and the other with a blend. (Plain M&Ms and peanut M&Ms would also work for larger classes.) Ask students to sample one piece from each box and then draw a conclusion about the whole box. While we need more than a piece or two to gain confidence in our conclusions, we really don't have to eat the entire box to be fairly accurate.

14. **Biases in Internet Surveys.** Ask the students if any of them have ever participated in an Internet survey. Ask them to think about what kind of sample population is available to this type of survey and what kind of biases might exist within that sample. Ask them to think of how the purpose of the survey may have influenced how the designers of the survey structure the survey questions and answers.

15. **Thinking Critically About Astrology.** To quickly illustrate the fallacies of astrology, buy a bag of fortune cookies. Have each student read his or her fortune and then explain how it is "true" or "accurate" in some way. Discuss confirmation bias and its effects.

16. **Thinking Critically About Psychics.** A nice exercise in critical thinking involves asking students to think about the psychic hotlines advertised on television. Ask them to think about how common "psychic" abilities must be if all of those agencies employ enough psychics to operate the telephone lines. Why would the "psychic" take some basic information and then promise to call the person back in several minutes? What is the training necessary to be a psychic?

17. **Psychologists' Qualifications.** After describing the academic preparation of psychology professionals, ask, "What education and experience should a psychology professor have? Why?"

➤ BROADENING OUR CULTURAL HORIZONS

1.   **Cultural Orientations Toward Psychology.** Ask students to read a short selection from an encyclopedia on the culture of the former Soviet Union. Which school of psychology would a Russian most easily accept? Ask students to read about the Japanese culture. Which school of psychology would you guess would be most interesting to a person from Japan? Is it possible to have one valid psychology for all cultures?

2.   **Cultural Relativity.** Imagine that you are a psychologist. Your client Linda, who is a Native American, tells you that spirits live in the trees near her home. Is Linda suffering from a delusion? Is she abnormal? Obviously, you will misjudge Linda's mental health if you fail to take her cultural beliefs into account. *Cultural relativity* (the idea that behavior must be judged relative to the values of the culture in which it occurs) can greatly affect the diagnosis of mental disorders (Draguns, Gielen, & Fish, 2004). Cases like Linda's teach us to be wary of using inappropriate standards when judging others or comparing groups. A stimulating article to discuss is humorously entitled "The weirdest people in the world?" (Henrich, Heine, & Norenzayan, 2010). The authors use the acronym "weird" ("Western, educated, industrialized, rich, democratic") as a charming way to argue that WE are the odd people, not people from other cultures. For a quick summary see http://www.nationalpost.com/Westerners+World+weird+ones/3427126/story.html.

3.   **Psychology as Science?** Psychology is a system for explaining behavior. In western cultures psychology is approached as if it were a natural science, with great emphasis placed on empiricism and the scientific method. Is this a cultural preference? Or is it the most defensible approach to psychology, regardless of cultural values?

4.   **What Are Your Cultural Values?** Many people within the American culture highly value domesticated dogs and cats. There are other cultures where dogs are not treated as "family." How would research in psychology be different if dogs and cats were not valued as they are in our culture?

5.   **How Important Is Science?** Most western societies place a lot of importance on empirical proof, statistical data, and research in attempting to determine what "the truth" is. If there are students in your class from other cultures, ask them whether the emphasis on science is greater, lesser, or similar in their home culture. What other ways are there of "knowing" that are valued in those cultures? Is the world becoming increasingly westernized in what it emphasizes?

➤ SUPPLEMENTAL ACTIVITIES

Exercise 1.1: What Is Psychology?
The purpose of this exercise is to help students to learn what psychology is about and to impress on them the difference between the public perceptions of psychology and the science of the discipline. This exercise is set up on the following pages in such a way that it can be duplicated and distributed. Students may record responses and write their analysis directly on the form provided. This is intended to be a take-home exercise.

Exercise 1.2: Introspection
This exercise is a classroom activity that should generate discussion on methodology, particularly on the validity of self-reporting personal experiences as a method of understanding behavior. With a few simple materials you can involve students in this project. You can follow the directions using three pairs, with the rest of the class as observers, or you can divide the whole class in pairs of "experimenters" and "introspectionists."

Exercise 1.3: Positive and Negative Correlation
In this in-class exercise, students are asked to respond to a questionnaire that will provide the class with raw data to be plotted on a scattergram. The students are more likely to give correct responses to the questions if they do not have to identify themselves, so keep the responses anonymous. Collect the questionnaires. They will provide you with plenty of data. You can read the data and have the students plot a scattergram. After plotting several pairs of variables, they will soon see that relationships are not all the same. You will find that some of the relationships will be positive and some negative. Other variables will show little or no relationship.

Once the students see the relationships on the graph, it is important to discuss cause and effect. Does it exist? How can you tell? Copy and distribute the prepared data sheets and the diagrams provided for this exercise. Would the results be the same if students had to identify themselves on their questionnaires? Discuss the importance of clearly defining the variables (i.e., Are there multiple ways to define a party?) and how this might impact the results.

Exercise 1.4: "Scientific Marvels" in the News
Students should be able to evaluate reports of research using the principles of the scientific method discussed in this chapter. Students may find it fun to review some of the sensational reports found in the periodicals that are displayed in the grocery store checkout lines. That exercise should provide a clear demonstration of the absurdity of these reports when examined using scientific criteria.

18

Exercise 1.5: Independent and Dependent Variables

This exercise will allow students to better understand the difference between independent and dependent variables. Sample experiments are found on **Handout 1.5**. The answers are:

1. IV: number of bystanders
2. IV: type of diet (amount of carbohydrates)
3. IV: IQ
4. IV: gender
5. IV: seating position
6. IV: degree of similarity
7. IV: marital/family status
8. IV: personality type
9. IV: personality type
10. IV: length of tail

DV: probability of getting help
DV: IQ
DV: type of diet
DV: number of driving errors
DV: grade in class
DV: level of attraction
DV: amount of pet ownership
DV: susceptibility to flattery
DV: degree of risk for heart attack
DV: type of temperament

Exercise 1.6: On the Nature of Empiricism—Is the Earth Flat?

Students often have difficulty distinguishing between strongly held beliefs, factual knowledge, and empiricism. At the very heart of empiricism is the idea that empirical information can be measured and—most importantly—replicated. Inform your students that you belong to The Flat Earth Society, which actually exists, and whose members are quite sincere in their belief that the Earth is flat and that the idea of a round Earth is a secular attempt to replace traditional beliefs. (They also have a webpage.) Most of your students will giggle at your premise because it contradicts what they have always been taught.

But is your students' conviction that the Earth is round (spherical) a belief, or is it supported by empirical evidence? Have them either write down or say aloud their "proof" that the Earth is round. You will find that they have a long list of reasons. For each of their reasons, be prepared to counter with reasons of "your" own about the Earth being flat.

Examples include:

1.   We have pictures from outer space. **Retort**—how do you know they're real? They're fake and part of a government conspiracy to hide the truth. It's like seeing talking animals on TV. Just because you see a picture, doesn't mean that the picture is real.

2.   People don't fall off the edge. **Retort**—sure they do. People go missing all the time. They never did find Amelia Earhart. And what about the Bermuda Triangle?

The discussion will probably continue for some time and, with a bit of creativity, you can come up with an answer for each of their points. It should quickly become apparent that the discussion is starting to sound like different ideas/points of view, without any "real" proof offered by either side. Logic alone does not constitute empirical data.

If they do not come up with a truly empirical answer on their own, push them to give you evidence or design a way to measure the characteristics of the planet that is clearly empirical and can be replicated. Although the average person can't climb on board the space shuttle, they can set their watch on North American time using a 24-hour clock and then go to Japan, where it will be dark at "noon hour." Alternately, explain to them that if a person goes into a very tall building and watches the sunset, that person can then take the elevator to the top of the building and watch the sun set a second time. This shows that the surface of the Earth is curved, not flat, and, furthermore, this will work in any tall building, thus eliminating the explanation of hills and valleys. This can be measured and replicated by any number of people. The same is true about the age of dinosaur bones—any person can learn to do carbon dating and can carbon date the bones. This provides empirical evidence that the Earth is much, much older than 6,000 years.

Handout 1.1: WHAT IS PSYCHOLOGY?

TO THE STUDENT:

The purpose of this exercise is to help you understand what psychology is and how it differs from popular ideas that many people have about it. You probably had some of the same misconceptions before beginning this course. Begin by reading Chapter 1 of the text. Look for the definition of psychology and write it down so that you can complete this assignment. Then follow the directions, record responses, and discuss what you find.

1. Ask five people what they think psychology is. Ask each to give a brief statement about what it is or what psychologists study. Select a variety of people. They should be persons of various ages, genders, and educational levels.

2. Record pertinent data about each subject (gender, approximate age, and educational level) and the verbatim response to your question. Do not add to the response or try to clarify it.

3. After you have collected all your responses, do an analysis comparing what you were told by the respondents with the definition in the text. The questions that follow the data sheet should help you in your analysis.

Handout 1.1: WHAT IS PSYCHOLOGY? DATA SHEET:

Subject #1   Gender_____   Age (approx.)_____   Education_____

Subject #2   Gender_____   Age (approx.)_____   Education_____

Subject #3   Gender_____   Age (approx.)_____   Education_____

Subject #4   Gender_____   Age (approx.)_____   Education_____

Subject #5   Gender_____   Age (approx.)_____   Education_____

Handout 1.1: WHAT IS PSYCHOLOGY? ANALYSIS OF RESPONSES

A.   What are some of the common elements in the statements made by your subjects?

B.   How do the popular notions about psychology differ from the definition given in the text?

C.   What are some of the misconceptions that your subjects had about psychology?

Handout 1.2: INTROSPECTION

TO THE INSTRUCTOR:

The concept of structuralism as a philosophical underpinning to early psychological inquiry is sometimes difficult for students to comprehend. This is partly attributable to the difficulty students have with introspection, the methodology of structuralism. Many students perceive introspection to be a valid source of information and find it difficult to question findings from this methodology. (How many people doubt the truthfulness of their own sensory experiences?) The purpose of the following demonstration is to assist students in understanding the methodology of introspection, the inherent difficulties of relying on data generated with introspection, and what structuralists were trying to accomplish through the use of this method.

Equipment: Data sheets and several simple objects (e.g., apple, pencil, cup, an aromatic liquid)

Demonstration: Begin by exploring with the class what structuralists attempted to discover about the "mind." Be sure it is understood that structuralists were attempting to discover the "building blocks" of conscious experience. Next, discuss the methodology of introspection and its attendant language (reporting on a "pure" immediate sensory experience). Once this discussion is complete, you can begin the demonstration.

Have six students from the class volunteer to participate in the demonstration. Randomly assign three persons to be experimenters and three to be introspectionists. Divide them into three pairs, each with an experimenter and an introspectionist. Conduct the demonstration in the following manner:

1. Give one of the objects to each of the experimenters. The experimenter should present the object to the introspectionist briefly (about two seconds) then remove it from sight.

2. During the time the object is being presented, the introspectionist should say whatever comes to mind about the qualities of the object being considered. Allow students to determine for themselves what constitutes a basic quality or irreducible conscious element. Be sure the students do not report on emotional experiences but on their sensory experiences as objectively as possible. The experimenter should record the responses on the data sheet.

3. Have the experimenters repeat this procedure three to five times for the same object.

4. Rotate the objects among the pairs so that each pair introspects with each object.

5. After all of the objects have been "introspected," collect the data sheets and note the similarities and differences among the reports given to the experimenters. These should be listed on the chalkboard in the form of a table.

6. The instructor should, at the conclusion of the above demonstration, have the students respond to one or more of the questions on the data sheet. These may be used in small group discussions in class or as a take-home exercise.

(Adapted from a demonstration by Dr. William C. Titus, Arkansas Tech University.)

Handout 1.2: INTROSPECTION DATA SHEET

OBJECT	TRIALS				
	1	2	3	4	5
1.					
2.					
3.					
4.					

DISCUSSION QUESTIONS

A.   Should we rely on this methodology as a way of obtaining consistent and unbiased data? Why or why not?

B.   What problems exist with interpreting data based on this methodology?

C.   What problems exist with regard to studying certain types of psychological phenomena using the method of introspection (e.g., altruism, aggression, and psychopathology)?

D.   To what degree (or how) does this methodology violate the basic tenets of empiricism?

26

Handout 1.3: POSITIVE AND NEGATIVE CORRELATION

TO THE STUDENT:

Complete this questionnaire giving information about you. You do not need to put your name on this sheet, so your information will be confidential. If you are not sure, estimate what you think the response should be. Your responses will be collected, and the class will use the information to study correlation.

Age_____   Height_____

Weight_____   Shoe size_____

Grade point average_____

Number of members in your family_____

Number of hours of study per week_____

Number of hours of part-time or full-time work per week_____

Number of credit hours being taken by you this term_____

Number of courses from which you withdrew last term_____

Number of courses you completed last term_____

Number of movies attended per month_____

Number of parties attended per month_____

Number of sports in which you regularly participate_____

Number of books you read for pleasure per month_____

Handout 1.3: POSITIVE AND NEGATIVE CORRELATION

SCATTERGRAMS:

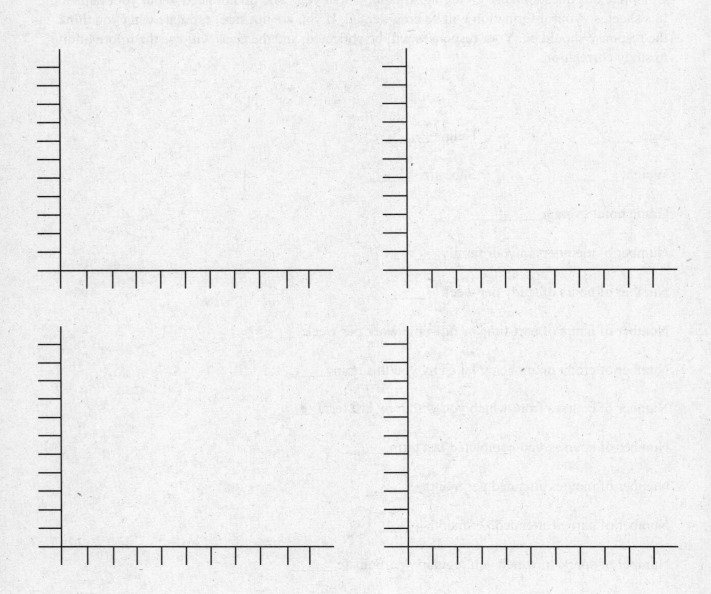

Handout 1.3: POSITIVE AND NEGATIVE CORRELATION

SCATTERGRAMS:

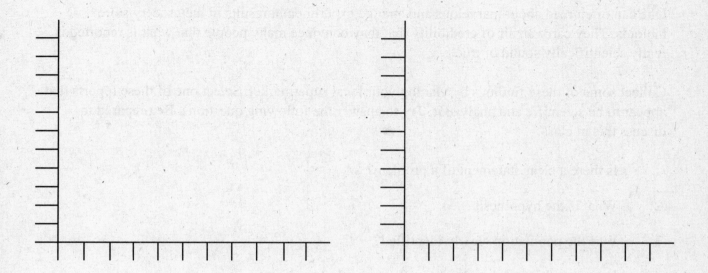

Handout 1.4: "SCIENTIFIC MARVELS" IN THE NEWS

TO THE STUDENT:

One can often read about marvelous and strange experimental results in the grocery store tabloids. They carry an air of credibility that may convince many people that what is reported is really scientifically sound or true.

Collect some of these findings by visiting your local supermarket. Select one of these reports that appear to be scientific and analyze it. Try to answer the following questions. Be prepared to discuss this in class.

1. Is there a clear statement of a problem?

2. What is the hypothesis?

3. Was the population clearly identified?

4. How was the sample selected, and was it adequate?

5. What was the independent variable?

6. What was the dependent variable?

7. Were all important extraneous variables identified?

8. How were extraneous variables controlled?

9. Was there a control group?

10. How were subjects selected for the experimental and control groups?

11. Was the method of observation adequate to test the hypothesis?

12. Was there any evidence of bias in the procedure?

13. Are the conclusions based on accurate measuring and reporting of data?

14. Are the conclusions warranted?

Handout 1.5: INDEPENDENT AND DEPENDENT VARIABLES

For each of the following, indicate the independent variable and the dependent variable:

1. Researchers have found that people in distress are more likely to receive help if there are fewer people present. The chances of receiving help decrease when there are more people present.

   IV: DV:

2. A researcher wants to discover whether children's diets affect adult intelligence. Twenty years later, he gives an IQ test to adults who as children ate a low-fat, low-carbohydrate diet and compared them with adults who as children ate a low-fat, high-carbohydrate diet.

   IV: DV:

3. A researcher wants to find out whether more intelligent people make healthier diet choices than less intelligent people.

   IV: DV:

4. Dr. Wilson wants to find out whether men or women are better drivers. She sets up an obstacle course and records the number of errors made by the drivers.

   IV: DV:

5. Harriet has a hypothesis that higher grades are achieved by students who sit at the front of the classroom. With the help of her colleagues, she gathers information about seating arrangements and classroom grades.

   IV: DV:

31

6. Researchers studying attraction and intimacy want to determine which statement about attraction is most true: "opposites attract" or "birds of a feather flock together."

IV: DV:

7. Jenny and Sarah are having an argument. Jenny thinks that single people are more likely to own pets, for companionship. Sarah thinks that pets are more likely to be adopted into a family because "pets and kids go together."

IV: DV:

8. A researcher is trying to determine whether introverted people are more susceptible to flattery than extroverted people.

IV: DV:

9. Researchers have consistently found that people who have a "Type A" personality are more likely to suffer heart attacks than people who have a "Type B" personality.

IV: DV:

10. Margaret is crazy about cats. She wants to know everything about them. She thinks that cats with longer tails are more relaxed than cats with shorter tails.

IV: DV:

➤ JOURNAL/BLOG QUESTIONS

1.   Which goal in psychology is most important to you? What are your goals in taking this course? What part of your life or behavior would you like to describe, understand, or control better?

2.   Which area of specialization in psychology sounds the most interesting to you and why? Which area sounds the least interesting and why?

3.   Which topic of research sounds the most interesting to you? Why? Which topic sounds the least interesting? Why?

4.   What theories do you have about human behavior? Do you feel people are basically good or bad? Strong or weak? Controlled by genetics or molded by their childhood? Totally free to select their own lifestyle and behavior or controlled by unseen forces? What evidence can you cite to support your views?

5.   Your textbook makes the point that one can only draw causal inferences from controlled experiments. But not everything can be subjected to an experiment. One cannot, for example, randomly assign babies to either a "good diet" or "poor diet" condition and then measure intellectual development. Can the results still be considered "causal" for all intents and purposes? At what point can correlation be considered "causal"? What are the perils of making a "leap of faith"?

6.   How do you feel about psychologists studying people in a lab? Is it helpful or dehumanizing? Is it realistic or artificial? Is it ethical or manipulative?

➤ SUGGESTIONS FOR FURTHER READING

History:

Atkinson, R. C. (1977). Reflections of psychology's past and concerns about its future. *American Psychologist, 32*, 205-210.

Hergenhahn, B. R. (2009). *An introduction to the history of psychology* (6th ed.). Belmont, CA: Cengage Learning/Wadsworth.

Mueller, C. G. (1979). Some origins of psychology as a science. *Annual Review of Psychology, 30*, 9-29.

Definition:

Draguns, J. G., Gielen, U. P., & Fish, J. M. (2004). Approaches to culture, healing, and psychotherapy. In U.P. Gielen, J.M. Fish, & J.G. Draguns (Eds.), *Handbook of Culture, Therapy, and Healing* (pp. 1–9). Mahwah, NJ: Erlbaum.

Hebb, D. O. (1974). What psychology is about? *American Psychologist, 29,* 71-79.

Koch, S. (1981). The nature and limits of psychological knowledge: Lessons of a century qua 'science'. *American Psychologist,* I, 257-269.

Lilienfeld, S. O., Lynn, S. J., Ruscio, J., & Beyerstein, B. L. (2010). *50 great myths of popular psychology: Shattering widespread misconceptions about human behavior.* London: Wiley-Blackwell.

Wood, J. M., Nezworski, M. T., Lilienfeld, S. O., & Garb, H. N. (2003). The Rorschach Inkblot test, fortune tellers, and cold reading. *Skeptical Inquirer, 27*(4), 29–33.

Careers:

Hettich, P. I., & Helkowski, C. (2005). *Connect college to career: Student guide to work and life transition.* Belmont, CA: Cengage Learning/Wadsworth.

Sternberg, R. J. (2006). *Career paths in psychology: Where your degree can take you* (2nd ed.). Washington, DC: American Psychological Association.

Methods:

American Psychological Association. (2002). Ethical principles of psychologists and code of conduct. *American Psychologist, 57,* 1060–1073. Available from http://www.apa.org/ethics/code/index.aspx.

Browne, N., & Keeley, S. (2010). *Asking the right questions* (9th ed.). Englewood Cliffs, NJ: Prentice Hall.

Christensen, L. B., Johnson, R. B., & Turner, L. A. (2010). *Research methods, design, and analysis* 11th ed.). Boston: Allyn & Bacon.

Henrich, J., Heine, S. J., & Norenzayan, A, (2010). The weirdest people in the world? *Behavioral & Brain Sciences, 33,* 61–135.

Koocher, G. P & Keith-Spiegel, P. (2008). *Ethics in psychology: Professional standards and cases.* Oxford: Oxford University Press.

Shaughnessy, J. J., & Zechmeister, E. B. (2008) *Research methods in psychology* (8th ed.). New York: McGraw-Hill.

Slater, L. (2004). *Opening Skinner's box: Great psychological experiments of the twentieth century.* New York: Norton & Company.

Stanovich, K. E. (2010). *How to think straight about psychology* (9th ed.). Boston: Allyn & Bacon.

Yanchar, S. C., Slife, B. D., & Warne, R. (2008). Critical thinking as disciplinary practice. *Review of General Psychology, 12*(3), 265-281.

➤ VIDEO SUGGESTIONS

Educational Films and Videos

Career Encounters: Psychology, (1991), Insight Media, 28 min. Produced by the American Psychological Association, this video provides a more detailed examination of the field of psychology than the shorter version, *Careers in Psychology.* It examines various career opportunities in the field including private practice, science, public interest, and education.

Careers for the 21st Century, Psychology: Scientific Problem Solvers, American Psychological Association, 14 min. This APA video provides an introduction to careers in psychology and to the important subfields of the discipline.

Career Paths in Psychology I, Arizona State Films, 29 min.

Discovering Psychology: Past, Present, and Future, Annenberg, 30 min.

Do Scientists Cheat? (1988), NOVA, 58 min. This is an interesting and provocative Nova program exploring the possible motivations for dishonest research, professional reactions, and the methods of those who have exposed the issues. There is a brief simulation of a hoax early in the 20th century, followed by more recent cases of dishonest research, and the program concludes with a discussion of safeguards to reduce cheating. The "publish or perish" syndrome present in some academic environments also receives some attention.

Ethics in America: The Human Experiment, (1988), Columbia University, Annenberg/CPB, 58 min. Program 9 in series. Although this film does not deal directly with psychological experimentation, it does present the ethical considerations one needs to consider. It is primarily a medically-oriented film, presenting the views of four doctors: Vincent DeVita (National Cancer Institute), Arnold Relman (New England Journal of Medicine), Alexander Capron (professor of law and medicine, University of Southern California), and Frank Young (U.S. Food and Drug Administration). These professionals discuss the ethics of experimental testing, including the need for information versus the rights of the patients.

Issues in Psychology, (1990), Coast Community College District Telecourses, 30 min. Part of the *Psychology—The Study of Human Behavior Series*, this video presents a discussion with leading psychologists and teachers of important topics in psychology.

Landmarks in Psychology, (1990), Insight Media, 50 min. Recommended and acclaimed by several organizations, this still-image video highlights the principal contributions of Freud, Jung,

Adler, Pavlov, Sullivan, Horney, Maslow, Watson, and Skinner. Through historical narrative and case study dramatizations, the interpersonal, behavioral, humanistic, and existential approaches to psychology are explored.

Methodology—The Psychologist and the Experiment, 1975, McGrawHill/CRM, 31 min.

New Directions, (1990), Annenberg/CPB, 30 min. The last of the *Discovering Psychology* films, this video presents interviews with several prominent psychologists about their opinions of the future of psychology in the 21st century. The development of new theories is discussed, along with new directions for research and new applications of the discipline. Interviewed individuals include Howard Gardner, Jean Gleason, and B. F. Skinner. This is a well-produced film about the possible direction that psychology can take to improve the overall quality of life.

NOVA: Secrets of the Mind, WGBH Boston, 60 minutes.

Past, Present and Promise, (1990), Annenberg/CPB, 30 min. First in the *Discovering Psychology* series, hosted by Phillip Zimbardo of Stanford University, this program looks at all levels of psychologists' work. From studying the roles of various hormones, to overt behavioral studies such as simple stimulus reaction times, to therapeutic work, the program concludes with psychology's emergence as a science and some of the key early figures in that transformation. This is a good overview and wrap-up to the first lecture on the history of psychology, as well as a preview of psychology's methods. It also introduces students to one of the modern giants of psychology, Phillip Zimbardo.

Prisoners of Silence, (1995), PBS, 60 min. Excellent for showing how testimonials can be proven erroneous with good experimental design. Fascinating footage of how a technique called *facilitated communication* (supposedly used to allow autistic children to speak by having an attendant guide the hands of an autistic onto a keyboard) was shown to be false. Very good design elements and the logic behind them are demonstrated.

Research Methods for the Social Sciences, (1995), Insight Media, 33 min. Examines types of experimental design, describing when they would be most appropriate. It considers the use of control and experimental groups and dependent and independent variables, and discusses clinical, correlational, and field methods. It details the seven steps of the scientific method and explains how to gather and interpret data. It also considers ethical issues in experimentation.

Research Methods, (1990), Coast Community College District Telecourses, 30 min. Part of the *Psychology—The Study of Human Behavior Series*, this video shows footage of lobotomy, autism, and police investigators employing cognitive interview techniques.

Research Methods in Psychology (2001), Insight Media, 30 min. This program provides an overview of the processes of observational and descriptive research.

Scientific Method, (2000), Films for the Humanities & Sciences, 25 min. Recommended by *School Library Journal*, this program examines the basic elements of the scientific method: defining and researching the problem, forming a hypothesis, gathering information through experimentation and observation, analyzing the data, forming a conclusion, and communicating the results. Practical applications of the scientific method, such as testing new medicines and analyzing the performance of sporting goods, are included as well. A Cambridge Educational Production.

Statistics and Psychology, (2000), Films for the Humanities & Sciences, 25 min. A look at how to statistically test the relationship between experimental data and reported historical findings. This program uses data from the Applied Psychology Unit at Cambridge University, which studies the negative effects of certain patterns that can cause eyestrain, headaches, and epileptic fits. Clear illustrations are given of the use of the Pearson correlation coefficient, positive and negative correlations and what they mean, the difference between linear and nonlinear associations, the rationale behind the Spearman approach, and contingency table analysis.

The Search for the Mind: The Mind Series, (1988), PBS, 60 min. Part of *The Mind* series, this film provides a historical overview of the study of the human mind, ranging from ancient times through the mid-1900s. Aristotle, Darwin, and Sigmund Freud are but a few of the individuals that the film mentions. In addition, the film presents some interesting information on memory, especially the difference between episodic and procedural memory, and some information on split-brain findings.

Understanding Research, (1990), Annenberg/CPB, 30 min. Host Philip Zimbardo of Stanford University presents an overview of psychological research, the scientific method, and empirical thinking. The video explores various methodologies, data collection, and statistical analysis. Interpretation of findings is discussed as it relates to critical thinking skills. The program moves quickly without getting bogged down.

What Is Psychology? (1990), Insight Media, 30 min. In this video, leading psychologists discuss major approaches, subfields, and historical developments in the field of psychology. They describe how in their work they seek to understand the varieties of human behavior. These experts assert that psychology offers explanations that enable us to understand and, at times, to predict and control human behavior.

➤ COMPUTER AND INTERNET RESOURCES

PSYK.TREK 3.0
Unit 1: History & Methods
1a. "Psychology's Timeline"
1b. "The Experimental Method"
1c. "Statistics: Central Tendency and Variability"
1d. "Statistics: Correlation"
1e. "Searching for Research Articles in Psychology"

INFOTRAC®

Below you will find two journal articles obtained from INFOTRAC® that relate to information contained in this chapter. Instructors should encourage students to utilize this invaluable resource to improve their research skills. Have students locate and read the following articles and answer questions relevant to each article.

The Journal of Physical Education Recreation and Dance, October 1993 v64 n8 p43 (4) The evaluation of leisure programs: Applying qualitative methods.

1.   List the four qualitative information collection and analysis techniques used in this study.

   Answer: observation, interview, review of documents, and content analysis.

2.   What were the implications for professional practice?

   Answer: The evaluation process provides a means of factual decision making because information about enjoyment, meaning, and satisfaction is obtained from the participants themselves.

Australasian Business Intelligence, October 27, 2004. Personality profiles: Fact or fiction (a brief article).

1.   What two ways can personality tests become distorted?

   Answer: (a) by the commentary provided with the test scores, and (b) by individuals taking the test who fake their scores.

WEB LINKS

Knowledge Builder Web Links

1. The Science of Psychology
   Definition of "Psychology": http://www.sntp.net/psychology_definition.htm
   Self-Quiz on Psychology and Science: http://www.psywww.com/selfquiz/ch01mcq.htm
   What is Psychology?: http://psychology.about.com/od/psychology101/f/psychfaq.htm
   Psychology: An Overview:
      http://www.bbc.co.uk/science/humanbody/mind/articles/psychology/what_is_psychology.shtml

2. Critical Thinking and the Scientific Method in Psychology
   Critical Thinking in Everyday Life: 9 Strategies:
      http://www.criticalthinking.org/articles/sts-ct-everyday-life.cfm
   Logic in Everyday Life: http://www.princetonreview.com/podcasts/lsat.asp
   The Scientific Method:
      http://www.sciencebuddies.org/mentoring/project_scientific_method.shtml

3. History and Contemporary Perspectives

Today in the History of Psychology: http://www.cwu.edu/~warren/today.html

Classics in the History of Psychology: http://psychclassics.yorku.ca/

Women's Intellectual Contributions to the Field of Psychology:
http://womenshistory.about.com/od/psychology/Psychology_Women.htm

4. Psychologists and Their Specialties

Divisions of the American Psychological Association:
http://www.apa.org/about/division.html

Careers in Psychology: http://www.apa.org/careers/resources/guides/careers.aspx For
Students of Psychology: http://www.apa.org/students/

5. The Psychology Experiment

The Experimental Method: http://www.ppsis.cam.ac.uk/bartlett/ExpMethodinPsych.htm

The Simple Experiment:
http://psychology.about.com/od/researchmethods/a/simpexperiment.htm

Ethical Principles of Psychologists and Code of Conduct:
http://www.apa.org/ethics/code/index.aspx

6. Nonexperimental Research Methods

Psychological Research on the Net: http://psych.hanover.edu/Research/exponnet.html

The Jane Goodall Institute: http://www.janegoodall.org/

Research Methods and the Correlation:
http://psy1.clarion.edu/mm/General/Methods/Methods.html

7. The Science of Psychology

That's Infotainment!: http://www.csicop.org/

The Oregon UFO Wave That Wasn't: http://www.burlingtonnews.net/ufohoaxes.html

Psychology and the News Media: Reflections on a Ten Year Initiative:
www.apa.org/divisions/div46/articles/carll.pdf

Additional Web Links

Careers in Psychology
http://www.apa.org/careers/resources/guides/careers.aspx

APA Online
http://www.apa.org/

American Psychological Society
http://www.psychologicalscience.org/

The Difference Between a Theory and a Hypothesis (National Public Radio piece exploring how the term *theory* is used in science. Evolutionary theory is the example.)
http://www.npr.org/templates/story/story.php?storyId=4671318

Skeptics Society
http://www.skeptic.com/

Introduction to the Scientific Method
http://teacher.nsrl.rochester.edu/phy_labs/AppendixE/AppendixE.html

Psychology World Wide Web Virtual Library:
http://www.vl-site.org/index.html

Women's Intellectual Contributions to the Field of Psychology:
http://womenshistory.about.com/od/psychology

PSYCHOLOGY IN THE NEWS

Help4Teachers:
http//www.help4teachers.com/hottopics.htm
Read the latest topic in psychology including the latest research as they are released.

The New York Times: Health Times
http://www.nytimes.com/pages/health/index.html

Psych Central:
http://www.psychcentral.com/news
This link provides daily psychology news and head.

CHAPTER 2

Brain and Behavior

Survey Questions
Discussion Questions
Lecture Enhancements
My brain's confused!
An anencephalic baby
Applying my mind to understand my brain
Technology and the brain
It all works together
Brain-body interaction
What's it like to have a split brain?
The brain's map of the body
Making neurological models

Role-Playing Scenarios
Value-Clarification Statements
One-Minute Motivators
Brain weight
A model of a neuron
Analogies for a neuron
The function of neurotransmitters
Neurotransmitter imbalances
How fast is the brain?
Are men smarter?
The wrinkled cortex
Contrasting sequential vs. holistic processing
The tiny but powerful hypothalamus
How inconvenient!
How do I remember all this stuff?

Broadening Our Cultural Horizons
Religious beliefs about life and death
Two case studies
Cultural attitudes toward mental illness
Cultural valuing of brain lateralization
Don't touch that!

Supplemental Activities
Exercise 2.1: Lateral Eye Movement
Exercise 2.2: How Many Reflexes Can You Find?
Exercise 2.3: Our Attitudes Toward Our Brains
Exercise 2.4: Activity of the Brain
Exercise 2.5: Brain Function

Journal Questions
Suggestions for Further Reading
Video Suggestions
Computer and Internet Resources

41

➤ SURVEY QUESTIONS

Module 2.1 Neurons and the Nervous System

Survey Question: How do neurons operate and communicate?

Survey Question: What are the major parts of the nervous system?

Module 2.2 Brain Research

Survey Question: How are different parts of the brain identified?

Survey Question: What do the different parts of the brain do?

Module 2.3 Hemispheres and Lobes of the Cerebral Cortex

Survey Question: How do the left and right hemispheres differ?

Survey Question: What are the different functions of the lobes of the cerebral cortex?

Module 2.4 Subcortex and Endocrine System

Survey Question: What are the major parts of the subcortex?

Survey Question: Does the glandular system affect behavior?

Module 2.5 Psychology in Action: Handedness—Are You Dexterous or Sinister?

Survey Question: In what ways do right- and left-handed individuals differ?

➤ DISCUSSION QUESTIONS

1. If you could change the brain or nervous system in any way to improve them, how would you do it and why?

2. Your brain has three million miles of axons, but axons in the brain are very short (0.1 mm), while some axons in the body can be up to a meter in length. Why are axons in the brain so short? In what ways is brain function different than body function? i.e., Why would it be an advantage to have shorter axons in the brain?

3. What effect would you expect a drug to have if it raised the firing threshold for neurons? If it mimicked the effect of a neurotransmitter? If it stimulated the reticular formation? If it suppressed activity in the medulla?

4. What symptoms might you expect to see if there was a problem in the way that the sodium and potassium pumps worked? In other words, if the pump action were too slow, what effect might that have?

5. Neurons in the central nervous system do not have the capacity to regenerate. Develop your own hypothesis about why, based on your understanding of the structure and function of the neuron. Why do you think that neurons in the peripheral nervous system are able, at times, to repair damage to themselves?

6. People with Parkinson's disease don't have enough dopamine, while people with schizophrenia have too much. Is it possible to have Parkinson's disease and schizophrenia at the same time? Why or why not? (Answer – yes, it is possible to have too much in one part of the brain and not enough in another part.) What would be some of the challenges of trying to treat someone who had both disorders?

7. Have you known someone who had a stroke or other brain injury? What were the effects? How did the person cope with the injury?

8. A member of your family has been having outbursts of hostile and aggressive behavior. In the past year, they have become virtually uncontrollable. Brain surgery has been recommended as a way to alter the person's behavior. Would you condone its use?

9. Anabolic steroids are synthetic testosterone. In addition to increasing muscle mass, they can also cause personality changes and anger problems ("roid rage"). Why?

43

10. Is it possible for someone to die from voodoo? Why or why not? (extreme sympathetic nervous system arousal) Is it possible for someone to be scared to death? What might be the cause of death for someone who died after being cursed? Would this likely happen to any of you? Why or why not?

11. Have you ever touched a hot or sharp object and felt the touch a split second before you felt the pain? Why might that occur?

12. Do you think a sharp distinction between right and left hemisphere function is valid? For example, are there verbal skills involved in music, dance, or art?

13. Robert Ornstein has urged us to recognize that full use of human potential should take advantage of the specialized skills of both cerebral hemispheres. Roger Sperry has charged that "our educational system tends to neglect the nonverbal form of intellect. What it comes down to is that modern society discriminates against the right hemisphere." Do you agree? What changes would you make in educational systems if you do?

14. Many psychologists suggest that the split-brain person does not show deficits except in the lab because one hemisphere is able to learn from the other. How could this take place?

15. If a person were kept alive with only the spinal cord intact, what kinds of responses would be possible? What if both the spinal cord and medulla were functioning? The spinal cord, medulla, and cerebellum? The spinal cord, medulla, and subcortex? All brain areas except the association cortex?

16. A marathon runner completes a race but discovers that she has severely torn major ligaments in her calves. Why didn't she notice this during the race? Explain the series of events that you think probably took place.

17. Can the brain ever expect to understand itself completely? Or, is the brain studying the brain like trying to lift yourself up by your bootstraps?

18. If the parents of an average-sized child wanted to give the child growth hormone to make him or her taller, would you consider it ethical? Why or why not?

19. Brain transplants done on lab animals typically make use of fetal brain tissue. It is possible that cells for transplants will eventually be grown in laboratory dishes. If this does not prove possible, and fetal cells are the only source for transplants, would you consider transplants ethical? If so, under what conditions?

20.   You have taken your superb understanding of psychology and physiology to the corporate world. You have decided to reorganize your new company according to the general plan of the human brain. What corporate activities would be most similar to the function of the different lobes of the cerebral cortex? To the function of the thalamus, the hypothalamus, and the hindbrain?

21.   The neurological system is very specific: A specific pathway will trigger a specific behavioral response. The endocrine system is very global: A specific hormone will trigger very general changes throughout the body. Why do we possess both systems? What is the adaptive value of this combination?

22.   You are viewing a PET scan of the brain and the scan shows four "bright spots" in the left hemisphere, which are related to language. Discuss the different aspects of language as they are related to this increased brain activity.

23.   You suspect that a certain part of the brain is related to memory. What part is that? How could you use clinical studies, ablation, deep lesioning, and EBS to study the structure?

24.   Discuss how learning the functions of the brain lobes are like learning to read a map.

25.   If a left-handed person is forced to write with the right hand since childhood and continues to write with the right hand now, would that person be more accurately described as a "rightie" or a "leftie?" Why?

26.   If you wanted to increase the surface area of the cerebrum so that more cerebral cortex would fit within the skull, how would you do it?

27.   Subcortical structures in the human brain are quite similar to corresponding areas in animals. Why would your knowing this allow you to predict, in general terms, what functions are controlled by the subcortex?

45

© 2012 Cengage Learning. All Rights Reserved. May not be copied, scanned, or duplicated, in whole or in part, except for use as permitted in a license distributed with a certain product or service or otherwise on a password-protected website for classroom use.

➤ LECTURE ENHANCEMENTS

Students often describe this chapter as one of their favorites. The ideas are novel and exciting, yet the processes are potentially confusing and abstract. It is typically useful to spend class time clarifying processes and encouraging students to articulate the processes in their own words. It may help some students to think of this as a travel adventure into an intriguing foreign land. Transparencies can become their map and travel brochure.

Unless you have access to sophisticated lab equipment, only rudimentary demonstrations can be done to illustrate concepts from Chapter 2. In many cases the most effective recourse will be to obtain one of the films listed at the end of this section. If your department owns either of the videotapes "The Mind" or "The Brain," you will find many segments to enhance your presentations. Other visual aids can also be very helpful in clarifying difficult concepts. A model brain, which can be disassembled to show its components, is particularly effective. These can often be obtained from college or university biology or physiology departments.

1. **My brain's confused!** If you would like to try some simple class demonstrations, the following can be interesting:

    a) This demonstration is a surefire illustration of cortical localization and interference. Begin by asking the entire class to simultaneously move the right hand and right foot in a clockwise direction for a few seconds. This should be quite easy for everyone. Next, ask that the right hand and left foot be moved in a clockwise direction. This is also easy. Next, have students make circular movements in opposite directions with the right hand and the left foot. This is more difficult, but most students will master it. Finally, have students attempt to move the right hand and right foot in opposite directions. This is extremely difficult for most people. After making these observations, students should be challenged to explain them. If they need a hint, ask them to think in terms of probable activity in the motor areas of the cortex.

    b) Alternately, it is easy to demonstrate how the brain can be confused about which is the right hand and which is the left. Divide students into pairs and have them designate themselves "A" and "B." Taking turns, one person ("A") should perform the following task:
    a) Holding the arms out straight, cross the arms and then put the palms together.
    b) Clasp the fingers.
    c) Draw the arms downward and fold up to the chest.
    d) At this point, the fingers will be multiply crossed, like a human pretzel.

46

Once the hands have been crisscrossed, the other person ("B") <u>should point at but not touch</u> one of "A's" fingers, and "A" should try to move that finger. Most will find this difficult. Then, "B" should <u>point at and touch</u> a finger. This will be much easier (because the corpus callosum can coordinate right and left). When they have finished, they can switch places and repeat the process.

2.   **An anencephalic baby.** A national news service once reported the case of a child born without a brain. According to the doctors interviewed at the time, such cases occur about once a year. In this instance the defect was not discovered until the child was several months old. The baby, who appears outwardly normal and healthy, began to cry excessively, and tests were performed to determine the cause. These tests revealed that the child had no brain. Doctors speculate that a cyst formed during prenatal development at the stem where the brain should have been and prevented further growth. The child survived because that portion of the brainstem that controls vital functions had already developed before the cyst formed. After students have read Chapter 2, they should be able to predict the kinds of abilities one might expect from such a child. You could ask them to describe the likelihood of this child having a personality, motivation, awareness, intelligence, and so forth.

3.   **Applying my mind to understand my brain.** Students are usually very interested in addressing the subject of the relationship between the brain and the mind. You might begin a discussion of this topic by pointing out that many philosophical speculations regarding this issue have lost their relevance in light of new and innovative techniques (e.g., PET scans) for studying the human brain. The subject is, nevertheless, still very complex, and a lively class discussion can be generated by describing the following hypothetical experiment:

You are looking at a PET scan of a brain while the radiologist taking the scan is sitting with you. You are discussing the activity depicted on the screen. Assume that the PET scanner is slightly advanced over what is presently available and depicts glucose utilization immediately. (State-of-the-art scans require a 30- to 45-minute lead time.) As you are staring at the PET scan, the radiologist points out that the most active areas seen on the screen are in the left hemisphere, particularly the language area and the visual areas toward the back of the brain. At this moment you hear some music, and almost immediately the activity pattern of the scan changes. Now there is activity in the right hemisphere as well, and you call the radiologist's attention to that change. "That's in a region associated with the perception of music," she responds. Then a few minutes later she asks, "Do you have any comments on the PET scan?" "What do you mean?" you reply, and, at this point, you notice another change. The auditory areas, as well as the frontal lobes, light up. You look toward the radiologist and see that she is smiling, and you finally realize that the PET scan is depicting your own brain activity! It is showing a shift as you change from one thinking activity to another.

Now ask the students to consider the following questions: Is this an example of their minds studying their brains, or can they adequately explain it as the brain studying itself? For more speculation on this topic, see R. Restak's *The Brain,* Bantam Books, 1984.

3. **Technology and the Brain.** Watch the segment of "The Brain" series that shows a person walking with a computerized prosthesis. Clarify that Delgado's research has not been replicated (Who would want to?) but that the concept of controlling behavior through stimulating different parts of the brain is a mainstream part of the new technology.

4. **It all works together.** Demonstrate the inter-relatedness of the parts of the brain, the endocrine system, the autonomic nervous system and the body. To show the complexity of the whole system, ask students to brainstorm all of the physiological events that would happen if they were out for a walk and encountered a bear. (e.g., the sympathetic nervous system would increase heart rate and respiration, secrete adrenaline, dilate the pupils, and take digestion offline. The eyes would send a message to the occipital lobe, and the message would be passed on to the motor cortex, the amygdala, the reticular formation, and the frontal lobe, where a decision would be made about what to do. All of this would occur in just a few seconds.)

5. **Brain-body interaction.** A good way to demonstrate how the brain and the body influence each other is to discuss how the birth control pill works. In the case of estrogen pills, the woman is actually tricking her brain into thinking she is pregnant. During pregnancy, the woman's body secretes high levels of estrogen. This estrogen message travels through the blood stream to the brain and the brain/hypothalamus interprets this signal as "we're pregnant." In this case, the brain takes no action (mission accomplished already!) and no egg is released. If a woman is not pregnant, and is not on the pill, or if she misses a pill, the brain interprets the lower level of hormone as being "not pregnant." In this case, the brain acts to "correct" the problem by producing FSH (follicle stimulating hormone) and LH (luteinizing hormone). The FSH and LH travel through the bloodstream to the ovaries to stimulate egg maturation.

6. **What's it like to have a split brain?** It is possible to give a sense of what it would be like to have a split brain by dividing students into groups of four. One person serves as the split-brain subject, another serves as the experimenter, the other two as the two hemispheres. Ask each "hemisphere" to say something into the split-brain subject's ear at the same time. Prepare a script of questions for the experimenter to ask. If the experimenter says, "Tell me," the subject gives the answer the left hemisphere processed; if the experimenter says, "Point to the right answer," the subject gives the answer the right hemisphere processed. Students should have to pause at first to think carefully about which response to give. Quickly, they will learn the cues.

48

7.   **The brain's map of the body.** Demonstrate the sensitivity of body areas by using two pencils on the back and the cheek of a student who has his or her eyes closed. The student tells you whether there is one point or two. Gradually make the points closer and closer until they are perceived as one. The student will usually perceive one point even when there is about an inch of distance on the back between the two pencil points. On the face, the two pencils almost always seem like two points. Have the class "map" the body of their partner, making a sketch and indicating which areas are most and least sensitive. Compare this map to the sensory homunculus depicted in Chapter 2.

8.   **Making neurological models.** Give small groups of students a pile of wooden blocks in various shapes and colors. Have them put together a model of a neuron, the brain, or of the nervous system. Have them explain their model to the class. Is it a structural or a functional model of the brain?

➤ ROLE-PLAYING SCENARIOS

1.   **What would it be like to have facial agnosia?** What problems would you experience? What reaction do you think you would encounter from others? How would you feel? Enact this role as you attempt to interact with members of the class.

2.   **Try to behave as if you possessed only the abilities of the left hemisphere.** Then try to limit your behavior to that based on the specialized functions of the right hemisphere. (Other students can question the person enacting these roles. They should also note when behavior inappropriate to each role occurs.)

3.   **Try getting through an entire day while using your nondominant hand.** What kind of problems do you run into? What is the most frustrating problem? How would you feel if someone (say, a teacher) told you that you must use this hand from now on?

4.   **What's it like to be missing a hemisphere?** In rare cases, people have had one entire hemisphere removed because of an extreme medical condition. Since the right side of the brain controls the left side of the body, and vice versa, have students take turns trying to do simple tasks as if they were missing a hemisphere. The other group members should point out areas where the depiction is incorrect. For example, a person would not be able to talk properly, smile, pick things up, etc. Most students will underestimate how all-encompassing it would be to lose control of half their body!

➤ VALUE-CLARIFICATION STATEMENTS

1.   Brain surgery should be required for individuals convicted of serial murders.

2.   Personality is mostly a free choice, not a biological state.

3.   Parents should do everything possible to make sure that their child develops maximum intellectual abilities.

4.   Taking psychiatric medication for problems in the brain is no different than taking medication for any other organ that isn't functioning properly.

5:    People who are suffering from depression because of a serotonin deficit should be able to work through their problems without anti-depressants.

6.   People who carry the gene for genetically-related brain disorders, such as Parkinson's, should be discouraged from reproducing.

7.   If I knew I were carrying a gene for some form of mental illness (e.g., Parkinson's disease, schizophrenia, etc.) I would go for genetic testing.

8.   If people want to take brain-altering drugs (including party drugs and steroids) then so be it; it's nobody else's business what they do with their bodies.

9.   A parent has the right to decide whether medical treatment is given to his/her child, even if the child's life may be endangered by the decision.

10.   A person should be able to write a "living will" and prevent hospitals from using extreme measures to keep his or her body alive.

11.   Transplantation of brain tissue to cure human diseases and to reverse paralysis should be done even if fetal brains remain the only source of tissue.

12.   The moral issues surrounding stem cell research are too great, even where there is medical advancement.

13.   A person could be a better athlete if he/she were ambidextrous.

➢ ONE-MINUTE MOTIVATORS

1. **Brain weight.** Perhaps the model you have of the brain does in fact weigh about three pounds. If not, develop one with clay. Pass it around the class. Students can best appreciate the size of the brain if you could also find an object weighing about three pounds.

2. **A model of a neuron.** Tinkertoys® can be used to create a model of a neuron. These can be placed on the eraser-ledge of a chalkboard. A few nerve pathways could extend onto a desk. Use one color for the excitatory pathways and another color for inhibitory pathways.

3. **Analogies for a neuron.** In order to conceptualize the firing of the neuron, students often need analogies to concrete objects. Possible analogies include: a radio, a telephone, a text message, the process of sending mail, etc. The analogy must be developed carefully: It must clarify, not mystify or confuse. A cap pistol can be used to dramatize the all-or-none quality of the action potential. Since the text refers to a "domino effect" of sorts, set one up on a tabletop.

4. **The function of neurotransmitters.** The power of neurotransmitters can be demonstrated using a squirt gun filled with laundry bleach. Squirt a colorful fabric; then squirt a glass or porcelain plate. The point made is that neurotransmitters must adhere to appropriate receptor sites before an action potential can be triggered.

5. **Neurotransmitter imbalances**. Patients with schizophrenia have too much dopamine, while Parkinson's patients don't have enough. Ask students whether it is possible to have schizophrenia and Parkinson's disease at the same time. Most will say "no." Ask the people who say "yes" why they think that. Answer: It is possible to have "too much" dopamine in one part of the brain and "not enough" in a different part of the brain. Because both disorders affect only a small percentage of people, it is unlikely that any one person will develop both disorders, but it has happened. The problem in this case is that efforts to treat one disorder make the other one worse.

6. **How fast is the brain?** Neural impulses travel at about 200 m.p.h. In order to demonstrate how effective the brain is, ask students to form a circle, holding hands. You will "start" a neural impulse on its journey by squeezing the hand of the person on either your right or left. That person will then squeeze the next person's hand, and so on, and the signal will eventually return to you through your other hand. Track how long it takes by looking at the second hand of a clock. Repeat to see if things get faster with practice. You can do variations of this exercise by alternating right or left, allowing students to keep eyes open, or asking them to close their eyes. You can make the initial squeeze predictable (time, direction) or unpredictable. You will likely see a number of trends:

"dropping" the impulse, "false starts," etc. When the exercise is over, remind students that the impulse has to travel all the way up one arm and through the brain, enter the sensory cortex, be transferred to the motor cortex, and travel all the way back down the other arm. You can also try it with students tapping foot-to-foot to see if it takes longer.

7. **Are men smarter?** Compared to other species, humans have very large brains, particularly with regard to the cerebral cortex. Although the human brain weighs about three pounds on average, men's brains tend to be slightly larger than women's brains. Ask your students if this means that men are smarter. Once they answer, ask them to explain their answer. If they get stuck, tell them that an elephant's brain weighs about 10 pounds, and some whales' brains weigh about 16 pounds, the largest on the planet (http://en.wikipedia.org/wiki/Whales). A whale's brain is about .02 percent of its body size, while humans' brains are a full 2 percent of body size. But even here, there are exceptions: hummingbirds have an even higher brain-to-body ratio than humans. Hopefully, your students will realize two things: that bigger bodies typically have bigger brains, and that size is not as important as function. In addition, autopsies of the brains of geniuses often show enlargement of some area of the brain, but do not usually show a larger brain size overall.

8. **The wrinkled cortex.** To illustrate the enhanced surface area of the cortex, wad up a piece of foil or aluminum foil to create a convoluted brain surface.

9. **Contrasting sequential versus holistic processing.** To contrast sequential and holistic processing, play some music. Ask half of the class to tell you what mood it puts them in; ask the other half to learn the lyrics or the melody.

10. **The tiny but powerful hypothalamus.** Pass around a sugar cube, which is about the size of the hypothalamus in humans. Remind students that the very small hypothalamus monitors and triggers a myriad of very complex processes.

11. **How inconvenient!** Ask all students (with special help from left-handers) to make a list of all of the inconveniences of living in a right-handed world.

12. **How do I remember all this stuff?** Break students into groups of five to six people and have each group brainstorm ways to remember the location and function of different parts of the brain. Often what is corny works well. For example, memory is processed by the hippocampus, and a hippo is a lot like an elephant. And elephants supposedly never forget! Once the groups have come up with their various memory "tricks," mnemonics, acronyms, and so on, compile a list for the whole class.

➤ BROADENING OUR CULTURAL HORIZONS

1. **Religious beliefs about life and death.** Different religions have diverse attitudes concerning the rights of humans to intervene medically to save a life and concerning the disposition of a person's body after death. Compare and contrast the following views.

   a. Blood transfusions should not take place.
   b. The body should not be violated after death.
   c. Parts of the dead body should be immediately used for transplants.
   d. A person's body should be cremated at death.

2. **Two case studies**. Below are two case studies. Would the answers be different if each dying person's cultural background or religion were known?

   A 25-year-old woman is dying of cancer. She has asked that "no extreme procedures be used to prolong life." She is now comatose and can only be kept alive with machines. How would you decide whether her will should be respected?

   A 25-year-old man is dying of cancer. He has asked that "no extreme procedures be used to prolong life." He is now comatose and can only be kept alive with machines. How would you decide whether his will should be respected?

3. **Cultural attitudes toward mental illness**. Western culture tends to be individualistic, whereas Eastern cultures tend to be collectivist. Emphasis is placed on the wellbeing of the group and on not bringing shame on the family. Neurotransmitter imbalances cause or contribute to some types of mental illness. In North America, individuals often refuse to get help because they feel that they are giving up control to another person. There is also a perception that the individual should be able to "help him/herself." With a greater emphasis on collectiveness and helping others, would these types of illnesses be less likely to hold the same stigma in Eastern cultures? Or would bringing "shame" on the family be even more damaging in terms of people failing to get help? If you have a culturally diverse classroom, you can invite students to help each other understand their respective cultures. If your classroom is not diverse, you can turn this into an assignment (internet or other).

3. **Cultural valuing of brain lateralization.** In what ways might different cultures make greater or lesser use of the various strengths of the right and left cerebral hemispheres?

4. **Don't touch that!** In many Middle Eastern cultures, using the left hand for eating or touching another person is forbidden. What kind of difficulties might a naturally left-handed person encounter in such a culture? How might children be trained to be right-handed, and what effect might that have on the growing child?

> **SUPPLEMENTAL ACTIVITIES**

TO THE INSTRUCTOR:

Exercise 2.1: Lateral Eye Movement
An in-class activity that will demonstrate the functioning of the left and right hemispheres of the brain and that shows dominance of one hemisphere over the other involves observing lateral eye movement. A study by Schwartz, Davidson, and Maer serves as a model for this exercise. They were able to show that spontaneous lateral eye movement reflects activity in one or other of the hemispheres of the brain. Eye movement to the left seemed to indicate involvement of the right hemisphere, and movement to the right appeared to involve the left side. It has been observed that some people shift their eyes to the left more often than to the right. These are called left-movers. Others typically shift to the right and are called right-movers.

A conclusion drawn by researchers in this area is that left-movers have right hemisphere dominance and tend to be more artistic, creative, and intuitive thinkers. Right-movers have left hemisphere dominance and tend to be more logical, analytical, verbal, and numerical. These conclusions are considered to be general tendencies and therefore should be viewed with a skeptical eye. More study and research is needed to support these conclusions.

Lateral Eye Movement (or, Look Left and You'll Be Right)

1. Select five students to be the subjects of the demonstration. Ask them to leave the room while preparations are made. Distribute **Handout 2.1.**

2. Explain to the rest of the class that you will ask the subjects a list of questions. The students are to observe and record the eye movements of each subject when the questions are asked. Caution them that the eye movements may be slight and will be to the left or right. They will have to observe with care (and they will not have the benefit of slow motion or instant replays).

3. Provide each student with a copy of the record sheet that contains the questions and a space to record the subject's responses.

4. Admit the subjects, one at a time, and have each one stand in front of the class in full view of the students.

5. You should ask each question and give the subject time to respond. The students will record their observation for each question. You should accept whatever answer is given and move on.

6. After all subjects have been questioned, tally the number of observed left and right eye movements for each question and each subject.

54

7. An analysis of the results should attempt to see:
   a. which items tended to elicit a left eye shift, indicating right hemisphere activity, and which elicited a shift to the right, pointing to a left hemisphere involvement.
   b. if any subject had a tendency to shift more in one direction than the other, indicating a left or right hemisphere dominance

8. The record sheet has a series of questions that follow a pattern. All odd-numbered items should elicit left hemisphere activity (eye shift to the right), and even-numbered items should elicit right hemisphere activity (eye shift to the left).

Exercise 2.2: How Many Reflexes Can You Find?

Although reflexes are among the "simplest" behaviors, they can help students appreciate the extent to which much of their behavior traces back to the "wiring" of the nervous system. The following exercise will help students observe a number of reflexes beyond those with which they are already familiar. Distribute **Handout 2.2**. Students should work in pairs.

Exercise 2.3: Our Attitudes Toward Our Brains (exercise and mini-lecture)

The brain is an amazing organ, but like any organ, it can malfunction. Neurotransmitter imbalance is one such case. When the brain is "sick," though, people react to the problem much differently (and usually more negatively) than when other organs are "sick." Have students anonymously complete **Handout 2.3.** When they are finished, collect their answers for discussion. You will likely find a number of trends:
   a) A continued expectation that the problem can be fixed without drugs, even though the example said that other alternatives had been exhausted.
   b) A reluctance to seek help, for fear of looking weak.
   c) A belief that antidepressants are addictive, don't work, or make people worse.
   d) A belief that taking antidepressants is "artificial," "unnatural," or a "crutch."

When the students have completed their responses, you can comment on some of their beliefs. Below is a list of some of my favorite quips. It is <u>very</u> important, however, to deliver these sentiments in a way that does not make fun of students' beliefs, or sound at all sarcastic.

You can open the discussion with information about how SSRIs actually work. It is important to acknowledge that we are all uncomfortable with the possibility that the brain might malfunction. We would like to think that the brain is different from other organs. We certainly act as though it is different. But really, it's just an organ. And when it is sick, it needs to be treated. Sometimes therapy works, and sometimes therapy alone is not enough. The stigma attached to mental illness prevents people from seeking the help they need, and makes millions of people suffer needlessly. I am not suggesting that everyone should run out and get a prescription for antidepressants, nor am I "pushing Prozac." But it is important to recognize the biological reality that some people face.

   a) If you had chronic chest congestion that would not go away, would you continue to suffer with possible pneumonia, bronchitis, or other ailment, or would you go to the doctor?

b) If you had a broken leg, would you just "tough it out," or would you get a cast on it?

c) If your vision is poor, would you consider wearing glasses to be "artificial" or "unnatural"?

d) If a person had diabetes, would you tell him or her to just "will themselves" to get better, or would you encourage them to remain on their insulin?

e) If a person were on heart medication, and had taken it for a while, would you advise them to stop because they really didn't need it anymore?

f) People on Prozac don't feel the need for a "Prozac fix" if they forget to take a pill *(in response to the fear that antidepressants are addictive).*

g) Some people are allergic to penicillin. Does that make it a "bad" drug? No drug works for everyone. Some of you are probably allergic to penicillin, but penicillin has saved millions of lives *(in response to the inevitable example that "I know someone who took Prozac and they had so many problems with it…").*

Exercise 2.4: Activity of the Brain

In **Handout 2.4**, students will answer questions regarding the action of parts of the brain. This handout can be used for self-study, or to be handed in as a course requirement or extra credit.

Exercise 2.5: Brain Function

Students often have difficulty remembering which part of the brain performs which function. **Handout 2.5** is designed as an organizational chart. Give each student three copies of the chart. They should fill it in once while they are learning the material, once halfway through their studying (from memory), and once more as a final self-test before the exam.

Handout 2.1: LATERAL EYE MOVEMENT RECORD SHEET:

TO THE STUDENT:

Record your observations on this sheet. Mark an L for left and an R for right. Remember that you are recording the subject's eye movement to HIS or HER right, not to yours. Do not do anything to distract the subjects, or yourself, since the eye movement may be slight.

		SUBJECT				
		1	2	3	4	5
1.	How many weeks are there in a year?					
2.	On what coin is John F. Kennedy pictured?					
3.	What is the last line of "The Star-Spangled Banner"?					
4.	Without looking at me, what is the color of my shirt (tie, skirt)?					
5.	Define the term *psychology*.					
6.	On which side is the steering wheel of a car in England?					
7.	Why do people pay taxes?					
8.	Who is pictured on the front of a five-dollar bill?					
9.	What do the letters in "NASA" stand for?					
10.	About how far is it to the moon?					

Handout 2.2: HOW MANY REFLEXES CAN YOU FIND?

TO THE STUDENT:

Work with your partner to develop a list of reflexes that can be observed in humans. Expand your list with the following reflexes. Decide who will be the experimenter and who will be the subject. The experimenter will use the following instructions to try to demonstrate some additional reflexes.

1. Ask your partner to close his/her eyes. Cover the eyes with your hands. Then ask your partner to turn toward the brightest corner of the classroom and to open his/her eyes. What changes take place in the size of the pupils?

2. Ask your partner to open one eye and close the other. What changes take place in the size of the pupil of the open eye?

3. Ask your partner to gaze at a distant object in the room. Then ask him/her to look at a pencil that you hold six inches from the eye. What changes take place in the size of the pupil?

4. Suddenly clap your hands in front of the eyes of your partner. Record whether the blink is typical (T), partial (P), or if there is no blink (N). Clap for 20 trials, recording the type of blink each time. Then ask your partner to try to inhibit the blink for the next 20 trials. What pattern did you notice? Can reflexes be modified by conscious control? What else might explain any changes in the pattern of response?

5. Take your partner's pulse. Record the rate per minute three times to find an average. Ask your partner to close his or her eyes and use a hand to put moderate pressure on one eyeball. While this is done, measure the pulse rate again. Record that number. Then ask your partner to remove the pressure. How long does it take for the heart rate to return to normal? (This is the ocular-cardiac reflex.)

Share your reactions to this demonstration with the class.

Handout 2.3: DEPRESSION QUESTIONNAIRE

Please answer the following short answer questions. Do <u>NOT</u> put your name on the sheet.

Suppose that you have been suffering with serious depression. This refers to serious depression, not just a case of "the blues." It is debilitating and lasts weeks or months. You have been suffering from depressive episodes on and off for some time. Things improve, but the depression keeps coming back. You have had some success with psychotherapy/counseling, but the positive results are not enough to eliminate the problem.

1.   Would you consider taking an antidepressant?

2.   Why or why not? (List as many reasons as applicable.)

3.   Have you ever known someone who was seriously depressed?

4.   Have you ever known someone who has taken antidepressants? If so, what were the results?

5.   Do you understand how SSRIs (Prozac/ Fluoxetine, Paxil/ Paroxetine, etc) work?

Handout 2.4: ACTIVITY OF THE BRAIN

Answer the following short answer questions:

1. What part of the brain processes visual information?

2. What part of the brain processes what you hear?

3. What parts of the brain are involved when you hear something and look at it?

4. What parts of the brain will be "working" when you reach for something and pick it up?

5. What parts of the brain will be "working" when you hear someone ask you a question and you give the answer?

6. How could you informally evaluate someone's language skills?

Handout 2.5: ORGANIZATIONAL CHART

Filling in the chart below will help you learn the parts of the brain and their function.

Anatomy	Location	Function/Characteristics
Central nervous system		
Amygdala		
Wernicke's area		
Temporal lobe		
Reticular formation		
Hypothalamus		
Occipital lobe		

Handout 2.5: ORGANIZATIONAL CHART

Motor cortex		
Pons		
Parietal lobe		
Medulla		
Sensory cortex		
Neuron		
Thalamus		
Limbic system		

Handout 2.5: ORGANIZATIONAL CHART

Frontal lobe		
Hippocampus		
Action potential		
Pituitary		
Midbrain		
Corpus callosum		
Broca's area		
Hindbrain		

Handout 2.5: ORGANIZATIONAL CHART

Cerebral cortex		
Forebrain		
Brainstem		
Adrenal glands		
Sympathetic nervous system		
Endocrine system		
Dendrite		
Parasympathetic nervous system		

➤ JOURNAL QUESTIONS

1. Describe a time in your life when you were so involved in what you were doing that you didn't realize you were hungry, thirsty, or in pain.

2. Which hemisphere of your brain do you think you rely on most to process information? Under what conditions is such reliance most effective? When is it least effective?

3. Do you know anyone with an unusual neurological condition? Examples would include someone who is paralyzed, has a mental illness, or has a disease, such as dementia. Which types of disabilities do you fear most and why? Would you live your life differently if you knew that you were going to get some kind of neurological problem 20 years from now?

4. Do you remember a time when your sympathetic nervous system was "turned on" for a long period of time? What did that feel like? What behaviors did you use to try to decrease sympathetic nervous system over-arousal?

5. Describe your relationship to your brain: Do you think of your "self" as residing in your brain? Do you feel that you exist in some way that is apart from the brain? Do you make a distinction between your mind and your body? Do you regard your brain as part of your body? How can your brain be aware of its own existence?

➤ SUGGESTIONS FOR FURTHER READING

Barrett, D., Greenwood, J. G., & McCullagh, J. F. (2006). Kissing laterality and handedness. *Laterality: Asymmetries of Body, Brain & Cognition, 11*(6), 573–579.

Begley, S. (2006). *Train your mind, change your brain*. New York: Ballantine.

Bhushan, B., & Khan, S. M. (2006). Laterality and accident proneness: A study of locomotive drivers. *Laterality: Asymmetries of Body, Brain & Cognition, 11*(5), 395–404.

Brown, S. G., Roy, E., Rohr, L., & Bryden, P. (2006). Using hand performance measures to predict handedness. *Laterality: Asymmetries of Body, Brain & Cognition, 11*(1), 1–14.

Bryden, M. P. "Perhaps not so sinister." *Contemporary Psychology, 1999, 38*, 71-72.

Congdon, P. J (1994). *Lefty: a story of left-handedness*. London: Gifted Children's Information Centre Publications.

Damasio, A. R. (2001). *The Scientific American book of the brain*, Windsor, UK: Lyons Press.

Ida, Y., & Mandal, M. K. (2003). Cultural differences in side bias: Evidence from Japan and India. *Laterality: Asymmetries of Body, Brain & Cognition, 8*(2), 121–133.

Ramachandran, V. S. & Oberman, L. (2006). Broken mirrors: A theory of autism. *Scientific American,* October, 63–69.

Wang, S., & Aamodt, S. (2008). *Welcome to your brain: Why you lose your car keys but never forget how to drive and other puzzles of everyday life*. New York: Bloomsbury.

➤ VIDEO SUGGESTIONS

Feature Films

Awakenings (Robin Williams, Robert DeNiro), Drama. This movie is about a neurologist who works in a ward at a hospital who is very distraught at the sight of his patients. All of the patients had encephalitis lethargica as children, and were left with no ability to speak, comprehend, or even live. The doctor sees a seminar on L-Dopa and chooses one patient to administer the drug to in an experimental run to see if it would help. After a few doses, the patient wakes up and becomes "normal." They start giving everyone on the ward the medication after seeing his progress and they all have the same results. But after a while, the initial patient's progress starts to deteriorate until he eventually returns to his previous state, along with the rest of the patients.

Memento (Guy Pearce, Carrie-Anne Moss, Joe Pantoliano), Dramatic Thriller. This dramatic movie presents a protagonist, Leonard, who is unable to form new memories, suffering anterograde memory loss because of damage to his hippocampus. While able to develop skills and learn certain kinds of tasks, he is unable to hold new personal memories. He has developed a note-keeping system to help himself collect information and keep track of everyday functions such as hygiene.

Raging Bull (Robert DeNiro, Cathy Moriarty), Drama. This movie portrays the life of prizefighter LaMotta, a man who needs to find purpose and meaning in life outside of the ring. He has all kinds of problems in his life and it gets really bad when he has to remove the jewels from his World Middleweight Championship belt and sell them. He suffers from incredibly impaired judgment and has other problems associated with concussions.

Gattaca (Ethan Hawke, Uma Thurman), Drama. Genetic engineering is the main topic of the film. The official site of the picture contains cast and picture information, an interactive game, and trailers from the movie. http://www.gattaca.com

Regarding Henry (Harrison Ford, Annette Benning), Drama. Harrison Ford plays an attorney who experiences memory loss and personality change after an accident. He must relearn skills and choose a new way of life consistent with his new sense of self.

Educational Films and Videos

Discovering Psychology Series: The Behaving Brain, Annenberg 1990, 30 min. Hosted by Dr. Phillip Zimbardo, this video provides an excellent review of basic brain structure including: the functioning of the neurons, subcortical structures, and neurotransmitters.

The Mind, Sections #12, 16, Worth Publishers.

The Mind: Language Processing in the Brain, Worth, 6:19 min. This video shows the versatility of the PET scan as a research tool.

All in the Mind: Understanding the Complexity of the Brain (2000), BBC, 50 min. Cases drawn from the history of brain research—from the earliest and crudest studies of the effects of brain injury to the latest data derived from brain surgery on patients who are awake and alert—offer insights. Is it possible that humankind's deepest spiritual feelings are simply the result of complex electrical activity in the temporal lobe?

Alzheimer's Disease, from *The Mind Teaching Modules*, 2nd Edition, # 19 (2000), Worth, 7 min. This is a case study of Eleanor, who has Alzheimer's disease.

Anatomy of the Human Brain (2000), Films for the Humanities & Sciences, 35 min. Neuropathologist Dr. Marco Rossi dissects and examines a normal human brain. Using three methods of dissection—coronal plane, CT-MRI plane, and sagittal plane—Dr. Rossi separates the hindbrain from the midbrain, and removes a portion of the brain containing the substantia nigra. The anterior and posterior of the forebrain are dissected, and each section is examined, along with the left occipital lobe. After separating the brain stem from the cerebellum, both are sectioned and examined.

Biology and Psychology (2006), *Psychology Digital Video Library 3.0 Handbook,* from Thomson Higher Education, 19 min. A brief description of the brain and how it affects behavior.

Brain and Nervous System—on DVD (1997), Cambridge Educational Productions. This interactive DVD allows users to play the *Brain and Nervous System* video in its entirety or directly access specific segments to view the information of their choice. Using an analogy of computers and the Internet, this program explores the brain and nervous system. Supplemental teacher materials are included for use with Pioneer Educational DVD players equipped with a bar code reader.

Brain and Nervous System: Your Information Superhighway (1999), Cambridge Educational Production, 31 min. Using the analogy of computers and the Internet, this program explores the brain and nervous system. It includes segments on electrical impulses and how nerve messages travel; parts of the brain and their functions; protection of the brain and spinal cord; the senses; diseases and drugs, and their effects on the brain and nervous system. Part of the series *The Human Body: Systems at Work.*

Brain Anomaly and Plasticity: Hydrocephalus, from *The Brain Teaching Modules*, 2nd Edition #7 (1998), Annenberg/CPB, 7 min. This video emphasizes two points: First, brain injury that occurs early in life is different from brain injury experienced after maturity; second, hydrocephalic individuals, although their brains are distorted, have a cortex that is essential to normal human brain function.

Brain Attack (2000), Discovery Channel, 51 min. Filmed at St. Luke's Hospital in Kansas City and the UCLA Medical Center, this program uses case studies to explain the warning signs of strokes and demonstrate the techniques being used to save lives and minimize long-term post-stroke debilitation.

Brain Mechanisms of Pleasure and Addiction, from *The Mind Teaching Modules*, 2nd Edition #6 (2000), Worth, 6 min. This video focuses on biological motivation and addictive behavior. These studies provide an excellent backdrop for class discussion about the application of animal research to the human situation and the ethical implication of human brain stimulation.

Brain Story: New Frontiers in Brain Research (2000), BBC, 6-part series, 50 min. each. Enhanced by outstanding 3-D graphics and intimate case studies, this eye-opening six-part series explores the grand themes emerging from the latest brain research—research that, with the aid of modern technology, is producing a whole new model of brain function. In each program, neuroscientist Susan Greenfield, biologists, psychologists, linguists, and other experts investigate the physiological basis of why people think, feel, and act as they do.

Brain Transplants (1994), 4 Corners, 45 min. Investigates the doctors attempting to reverse brain damage in their patients by implanting brain cells from an aborted fetus.

Brain Transplants in Parkinson's Patients, from *The Mind Teaching Modules*, 2nd Edition, #31 (2000), Worth, 11 min. This video describes the surgical procedure of implanting human fetal brain tissues into the basal ganglia of Parkinson's patients. The results of the operation are dramatic.

Discovering Psychology: Updated Edition, episode 25, *Cognitive Neuroscience* (2001), WGBH Educational Foundation, 30 min. This program looks at scientists' attempts to understand how the brain functions in a variety of mental processes. It also examines empirical analysis of brain functioning when a person thinks, reasons, sees, encodes information, and solves problems. Several brain-imaging tools reveal how we measure the brain's response to different stimuli.

Discovering Psychology: Updated Edition, episode 3, *The Behaving Brain* (2001), WGBH Educational Foundation, 30 min. This program looks at the structure and composition of the human brain: how neurons function, how information is collected and transmitted, and how chemical reactions relate to thought and behavior.

Discovering Psychology: Updated Edition, episode 4, *The Responsive Brain* (2001), WGBH Educational Foundation, 30 min. This program explores how the brain alters its structure and functioning in response to social situations. You'll learn about the impact of different stimuli on human and animal brains, from the effect of human touch on premature babies to the effect of social status on the health of baboons.

Dopamine Seduction: The Limbic System (2000), Films for the Humanities and Sciences, 25 min. This program illustrates the function of the limbic system in a subject named Greg, following the activity of his brain as he staves off danger and hunger. Extraordinary 3-D computer animation such as the release of hormones into the bloodstream and brain cells transmitting nerve impulses.

Effect of Mental and Physical Activity on Brain/Mind, from *The Mind Teaching Modules*, 2nd Edition #18 (2000), Worth, 10 min. This video shows the effect of aging on both mental and physical decline.

Eric's Brain (1994), NBC News, 20 min. A news magazine style report showing brain surgery on a man having a tumor removed. Fascinating footage of the effects of surgery on behavior and thought.

Inside Information: The Brain and How it Works, (1992), Films for the Humanities and Sciences, 58 min. This award winning video focusing on the latest brain topics includes a discussion of pattern recognition, individual part functioning, and possible computer analogies. It is visually memorable and packed with information.

Language and Speech: Broca's and Wernicke's Areas, from *The Brain Teaching Modules*, 2nd Edition #6 (1998), Annenberg/CPB, 8 min. Both Broca's area and Wernicke's area are presented in terms of their importance in language comprehension.

Language Processing in the Brain, from *The Mind Teaching Modules*, 2nd Edition #8 (2000), Worth, 6 min. This video shows the versatility of the PET scan as a research tool.

Left Brain, Right Brain (1980), Filmmakers Library, 56 min. Dr. Norman Geschwind introduces this film on recent breakthroughs in brain research. As the film indicates, in most people the left hemisphere processes information with an analytic time-dependent sequential strategy, while the right hemisphere processes information with a holistic strategy that is independent of time and order. Researchers demonstrate a variety of tests that pinpoint the exact geography of brain functions. Highlights include a fascinating demonstration of split-brain research techniques.

Mysteries of the Mind, (1988), Films for the Humanities and Sciences, 58 min. This video examines the neurochemical and genetic components of various psychological disorders and some of the latest research into the mysteries of the brain. It may serve as a good advance organizer for other topics to come in the introductory psychology class.

Nerves (1992), Insight Media, 24 min. This BBC presentation uses animation to demonstrate the formation and propagation of action potentials and the transmission of an impulse across a synapse. It investigates the roles of transmitters, agonists, antagonists, and second messengers, and shows techniques used in studying brain slices and single neurons. It also considers such disorders of the nervous system as Alzheimer's disease, Parkinson's disease, depression, and anxiety.

Neurorehabilitation, from *The Brain Teaching Modules*, 2nd Edition #32 (1998), Annenberg/CPB, 12 min. The important message of this program is that people can recover significantly from brain damage. For rehabilitation to be most effective, remediation should be combined with teaching compensatory strategies.

The Biology of Behavior, from *Psychology: The Study of Human Behavior Series* (1990), Coast Community College District, 30 min. Focuses on the human nervous systems and neurotransmission.

The Brain Series, General Psychology Teaching Module 1 (1988), Annenberg/CPB, various times. *General Psychology Teaching Modules: The Brain Series* contains brief excerpts from *The Brain Series* originally co-produced by WNET/New York and Antenne 2 TV/France. The first module in the series contains 16, 4–10 minute segments covering key topics like: overview of brain organization, language and speech, Broca's and Wernicke's areas, split brain, brain tissue transplants in Parkinson's patients, and hormones and sexual development. This abbreviated video format lends itself well to use in an introductory course where you may not want to spend an entire class session showing a video on only one topic.

The Brain: Teaching Modules (1999), 35 modules, 5 to 15 minutes each. The modules present current findings on language processing, drug treatment and addictions, and cognitive development throughout the life span. The programs also cover mood and personality disorders, and pain and its treatment.

The Brain–Mind Connection (1990), Insight Media, 30 min. This video examines how the brain influences and is influenced by thought and the environment. It explores hemispheric lateralization and the effects of enriched environments.

The Enlightened Machine (1984), Annenberg/CPB, 58 min. This film from *The Brain, Mind, and Behavior* series uses microphotography and interviews with neuroscience experts to explain the functions of the brain. The research of Gaul, Florence, Broca, and Wernicke is discussed, and the viewer is introduced to modern recording techniques: CAT, PET, and EEG. This film also discusses several degenerative brain disorders that reveal information about the brain's function (stroke, Parkinson's disease, epilepsy, Huntington's disease, multiple sclerosis, hydrocephalus, and others). It is an excellent film concerning the relationship between CNS illness and behavior.

The Frontal Lobes and Behavior: The Story of Phineas Gage, from *The Brain Teaching Modules*, 2nd Edition #25, (1998), Annenberg/CPB, 12 min. This program is a reenactment of the tragic accident that destroyed Phineas Gage's capacity to function normally.

70

The Human Brain (1997), Insight Media, 25 min. *The Human Brain* takes a look at how brain function and development is influenced by environment.

The Nervous System (2002, from *Psychology—The Human Experience Telecourse,* Coast Community College Telecourses, 30 min.) This video looks at the components of the nervous system and the methods used for studying the brain through the story of a split-brain patient.

The Physiology of Behavior (1993), Films for the Humanities and Sciences, 60 min. This video includes segments covering recent work on addiction, development of the human brain, dreams, genetic testing, memory, the nervous system, and other topics. A videodisc version allows the instructor to play only those segments wanted in an easy, user-friendly way.

Through a Glass Darkly (1994), Films for the Humanities and Sciences, 58 min. This program demonstrates how we study the brain, while tracing the development of increasingly sophisticated and accurate windows into its functioning. The program looks at a number of different approaches to the subject to demonstrate how we can now almost literally see into the living brain at work.

➤ COMPUTER AND INTERNET RESOURCES

PsykTrek 3.0
Unit 2: Biological Bases of Behavior
2a. "The Neuron and the Neural Impulse"
2b. "Synaptic Transmission"
2c. "Looking Inside the Brain: Research Methods"
2d. "The Hindbrain and Midbrain"
2e. "The Forebrain: Subcortical Structures"
2f. "Cerebral Cortex"
2g. "Right Brain/Left Brain"
Simulation 2: "Hemispheric Specializations"

INFOTRAC®

Below you will find two journal articles obtained from INFOTRAC® that relate to information contained in this chapter. Instructors should encourage students to utilize this invaluable resource to improve their research skills. Have students locate and read the following articles and answer questions relevant to each article.

Science, November 2, 2001, v294 i5544 p102 (7), The neurobiology of slow synaptic transmission. (Review: Neuroscience).

1.   How do slow-acting neurotransmitters control the efficacy of fast synaptic transmission?

    Answer: By regulating the efficiency of neurotransmitter release from presynaptic terminals and by regulating the efficiency with which fast-acting neurotransmitters produce their effects on postsynaptic receptors.

2.   This article uses the analogy of computer hardware/software to explain how nerve cells communicate with each other. Which is the hardware and which is the software in understanding slow and fast synaptic transmission?

    Answer: The fast synaptic transmission is like the hardware of the brain, and slow synaptic transmission is the software that controls fast transmission.

The Lancet, Jan 6, 1996 v347 n8993 p31(6), Addiction: brain mechanisms and their treatment implications.

1.   Why are some substances addictive? What makes one substance more addictive than another?

    Answer: The processes of addiction involve alterations in brain function because misused drugs are neuroactive substances that alter brain transmitter function. For most drugs of misuse, the molecular sites of action are receptors or transporter sites; in general the faster the drug enters the brain the more reinforcing it is.

2.   Which three brain chemicals (neurotransmitters) are the most likely to be involved in addiction? What are some of the after effects of psychoactive drugs?

    Answer: Most drugs that produce elevations of mood or euphoria, including nicotine and alcohol, release **dopamine** in either the nucleus accumbens or the prefrontal cortex in animals. When the drug is stopped, dopamine release is decreased below normal; this explains the "crash" after stimulant discontinuation. Dopamine overactivity probably underlies alcoholic delirium tremens.
    Misused opioids, such as heroin, act at the same receptors as the natural opioid system **(endorphins)**. However, because they have much higher efficacy than the endogenous transmitter they "hijack" the natural system by producing a much exaggerated response. Endogenous opioids are thought to be involved in the actions of other misused drugs such as alcohol and stimulants.
    The activity of noradrenergic neurons **(noradrenaline)** is decreased by opioids. Some clinical data suggest that longer-term reduction in noradrenaline activity may predispose alcoholics to relapse.

Serotonin, amino acid receptors (**GABA**), and other neurotransmitters may also play a role in addiction, as well as certain receptors (e.g., nicotinergic receptors).

WEB LINKS

Knowledge Builder Web Links

1. Neurons and the Nervous System
   Neural Transmission:
      http://www.brainexplorer.org/neurological_control/Neurological_Neurotra
      nsmission.shtml
   Synaptic Transmission:
      http://intro.bio.umb.edu/111-
      112/112s99Lect/neuro_anims/s_t_anim/WW36.htm
   The Nervous System:
      http://www.usu.edu/psycho101/lectures/chp5nervous/nervous.htm

2. Brain Research
   The Whole Brain Atlas: http://www.med.harvard.edu/AANLIB/home.html
   The PET Scan: http://www.clevelandclinic.org/health/health-
      info/docs/3400/3462.asp?index=10123
   fMRI for Newbies: http://www.fmri.org/fmri.htm

3. Hemispheres and Lobes of the Cerebral Cortex
   Split Brain Consciousness:
      http://www.macalester.edu/psychology/whathap/UBNRP/Split_Brain/Spli
      t_Brain_Consciousness.html
   Probe the Brain: http://www.pbs.org/wgbh/aso/tryit/brain/
   Brain Maps: http://brainmaps.org/

4. Subcortex and Endocrine System
   The Patient's Journey: Living With Locked-In Syndrome:
      http://www.bmj.com/cgi/content/full/331/7508/94
   Endo 101: http://www.hormone.org/endo101/
   Anabolic Steroid Use: http://www.steroidabuse.org/

5. Psychology in Action: Handedness – Are You Dexterous or Sinister?
   What is "Handedness?": http://www.drspock.com/article/0,1510,5812,00.html
   The Sinister Hand: http://www.drspock.com/article/0,1510,5818,00.html
   Left Brain, Right Brain: http://www.funderstanding.com/right_left_brain.cfm

Additional Web Links

APA Online
http://www.apa.org/

Basic Neural Processes Tutorials
http://psych.hanover.edu/Krantz/neurotut.html

Brain Images on the Web
http://www.med.harvard.edu/AANLIB/home.html

Brain Images on the Web— species comparisons
http://thebrain.mcgill.ca/flash/i/i_05/i_05_cr/i_05_cr_her/i_05_cr_her.html
http://serendip.brynmawr.edu/bb/kinser/Int3.html

Scientific American: His Brain, Her Brain
http://faculty.washington.edu/chudler/heshe.html

Biology of Mental Illness
http://www.medicinenet.com/mental_illness/article.htm

Neurons
http://serendip.brynmawr.edu/bb/kinser/Nerve7.html

Neurology Related Web Sites:
http://www.neuroscience.com
http://www.neurology.org/

Society for Neuroscience:
http://www.sfn.org/

PSYCHOLOGY IN THE NEWS

DANA Brain Center:
http://www.dana.org/
This site is a gateway to brain information, resources, and research.

Psych Central:
http://www.psychcentral.com/news
This link provides daily psychology news and headlines.

Psych Port News:
http://www.apa.org/news/psycport/index.aspx
This site is a portal for psychology information created by the APA.

Medical News Today:
http://www.medicalnewstoday.com/sections/neurology/
Includes news on nervous system disorders and discoveries, research related to the brain, memory, how we perceive the environment, and much more.

Medscape:
http://www.medscape.com/neurology
This site contains news and resources.

Neurology News:
http://www.aan.com/
News on Neurology.

CHAPTER 3

Human Development

Survey Questions
Discussion Questions
Lecture Enhancements
        The observational method
        Show and tell
        Assumptions of heredity
        Imprinting
        Parenting 101
        When does an organism become a human?
        What's dying like?
        Alternative birthing practices
        Parental accountability
        Generational differences
        Speaker on aging
        Interviews across the lifespan
        Diversity in aging
        What do seniors want?
        Sowing seeds for old age
        Moral development
        Moral dilemmas
        Kohlberg and Piaget
        Rate your parents

Role-Playing Scenarios
Value-Clarification Statements
One-Minute Motivators
        Childhood pictures
        Sensitive periods
        Conservation of volume
        Monopoly and development
        Children and creativity
        Sibling rivalry
        Experiencing dyslexia
        Adolescent experiences
        Discipline
        Choosing daycare
        What's your attachment style?
        The social clock
        What do you want from life?
        Identity development
        You're showing your age
        The clock is ticking
        Ageism and language
        You have one month left

Broadening Our Cultural Horizons	Communal child rearing
	Perceptions of childhood
	Blended families
	Universality of facial expressions
	Adolescent rites of passage
	Culture and child rearing
	Gender and perceptions of cognitive development
	Child discipline across cultures
	Treatment of the elderly
Supplemental Activities	Exercise 3.1: Supplemental Lecture: Prenatal Development and Genetics
	Exercise 3.2: Conservation
	Exercise 3.3: It's in the Genes
	Exercise 3.4: Ages and Stages
	Exercise 3.5: Moral Reasoning
	Exercise 3.6: Aging
	Exercise 3.7: Interviewing the Elderly
Handouts	Handout 3.1: Genetics and Prenatal Development
	Handout 3.2: Conservation: Data Sheet
	Handout 3.3: Ages and Stages: Work Sheet
	Handout 3.4: Moral Reasoning
	Handout 3.5: Aging: Work Sheet
	Handout 3.6: Growing Older

Journal Questions
Suggestions for Further Reading
Video Suggestions
Computer and Internet Resources

Module 3.1 The Interplay of Heredity and Environment

Survey Question: How do heredity and environment affect development?

Module 3.2 The Neonate

Survey Question: What can newborn babies do?

Module 3.3 Social Development in Childhood

Survey Question: Of what significance is a child's emotional bond with adults?

Survey Question: How important are parenting styles?

Module 3.4 Language Development in Childhood

Survey Question: How do children acquire language?

Module 3.5 Cognitive Development in Childhood

Survey Question: How do children learn to think?

Module 3.6 Adolescence, Young Adulthood, and Moral Development

Survey Question: Why is the transition from adolescence to adulthood especially

challenging?

Survey Question: How do we develop morals and values?

Module 3.7 Challenges Across the Lifespan

Survey Question: What are the typical tasks and dilemmas through the lifespan?

Survey Question: What is involved in well-being during later adulthood?

Survey Question: How do people typically react to death?

Module 3.8 Psychology in Action: Effective Parenting—Raising Healthy Children

Survey Question: How do effective parents discipline and communicate with their

children?

➤ DISCUSSION QUESTIONS

1. A friend of yours has a child whose grasping reflex was absolutely phenomenal during the first year of life. Your friend was sure that her daughter would become an Olympic gymnast. Now the child is one year old and the power of the grasp seems to be waning. Why?

2. Why do babies seem to prefer complex visual patterns? Why would an infant progress from preferring familiar stimuli to a preference for the unfamiliar? What adaptive value is there in these tendencies?

3. How should a caregiver respond to a crying baby? Can't a baby become spoiled? Why or why not?

4. In talking to a two-year-old baby, should parents use "baby talk" or normal, complex sentences? What would be the advantages or disadvantages of each?

5. Should humans try to control their own heredity? Who would decide what characteristics should be developed? Who would get them? For what purpose? Would you endorse use of genetic engineering to delay or prevent aging?

6. What are your thoughts on the practical and ethical questions that follow? Should children conceived by donor artificial insemination or by donor egg be told about their parentage? Should records be kept that would allow them to find their donor fathers or mothers if some extraordinary need were to arise? What might be the psychological impact of knowing that you were conceived *in vitro*?

7. Traditionally, mothers and fathers played a different role in the development of the baby. What effect would these different styles have on sex role development? Many girls are now raised only by their father; many boys are now raised only by their mother. How could that affect their social and interpersonal development?

8. What kind of a national infant care leave policy do you think would be appropriate? What impact would such a policy have on the child's development? On the parents' ability to be responsive to the child's needs? On businesses? If you were a politician, would you support such legislation? Why or why not?

9. For those in the class who come from large families and are older siblings, ask for their insights into the issue of reciprocal influences in child rearing. Did their parents treat all of the younger children the same? Or did their parents use different parenting approaches for different children? If the approach used was the same, did some of the younger siblings respond to it better than others?

80

10.   You have asked your 5-year-old to select a birthday gift for his 12-year-old sister. What will he probably select? Why? What does this tell us about his cognitive development?

11.   What types of toys would you select for an infant or young child? Do you think simple toys or elaborate toys would be best? Why? Would your choice change for an older child? Why?

12.   What, if anything, can a parent do to increase the rate at which a child learns a language or a sport? Why would a parent want to do this? Would this be to the child's advantage or detriment?

13.   Describe an incident from your own childhood that you consider growth promoting. Describe an incident that set you back or had a negative effect on you. How do these incidents differ? How much of an impact has this incident had on your life, years or decades later?

14.   If you have students in the class who are also parents, ask them which abilities their babies had that surprised them, either positively or negatively.

15.   Some babies are ready to be toilet trained at age two, and others are not ready for several more months. What might be some of the negative consequences of trying to toilet train a child before he or she is ready? What signs might there be that the child is ready to learn toilet training?

16.   Why do children have temper tantrums, from a developmental perspective? What are some ways to help a child avoid having to resort to a tantrum? If a tantrum does occur, what is the best way to deal with it?

17.   Perhaps you remember being grouped in elementary school according to your skills in reading, writing, or math. Could such groupings (as well as competitive sports) contribute to feelings of inferiority? Why or why not?

18.   How might reading instead of watching TV help a child develop good language skills? Did your parents encourage reading? Were you interested in reading?

19.   What factors do you think would make adolescence especially turbulent for an individual? How is it that some teens seem to thrive in the terrible physical and emotional conditions?

20.   Many children are now part of "blended" step-families. How would this affect the development of a child's sense of identity?

21.   In what ways do parents add to the conflicts of young adults who are seeking independence?

22.   Which of Erikson's crises do you think is most difficult to deal with? Which is most enjoyable or trouble-free? Why?

23.   Think back to your adolescence. Which things were of great interest to you then that are of no interest now? Can you remember a time when your judgment was poor, and you did something that you would never do now? (It doesn't have to be something illegal or dangerous; it could be an interpersonal judgment issue.)

24.   Did you have a curfew when you were a teenager? Were you allowed to go out on school nights? What were the rules for going out with your friends? Discuss the issue with regard to out-of-control teenagers.

25.   How would using calculators instead of learning pencil-and-paper math skills affect cognitive development? Which of Piaget's stages would be most relevant to this issue?

26.   How did you answer Kohlberg's moral dilemma about the husband who stole a drug for his sick wife? Did you use Kohlberg's justice perspective or Gilligan's caring ethic in formulating your answer?

27.   Do you think the "draft dodgers," antiwar activists, or conscientious objectors of the 1960s were acting in self-interest or at higher levels of morality? What level of moral reasoning is most frequently displayed by the characters in TV dramas, comedies, or commercials? What level of moral reasoning would you say fits the actions of "Dr. Death", Jack Kevorkian, the doctor who publicly supported people's right to die?

28.   Anthropologist Margaret Mead once charged, "We have become a society of people who neglect our children, are afraid of our children." Do you agree? Why or why not?

29.   Do we need a "children's liberation movement" to establish the civil rights of children? (Keep in mind that few parents show their children the courtesy they show strangers.)

30.   From a developmental perspective, what reasons might there be for the shootings that have taken place in schools over the past few years, such as those at Columbine High School in Littleton, Colorado, on April 20, 1999? Are there any ways to prevent these shootings?

31.   What cultural factors do you think would affect the length of adolescence? The onset of puberty? The social effects of early and late maturation for males and females?

32.   How common do you think it is to experience a "midlife crisis"? Would you expect people of other cultures to experience a similar crisis? People born in various decades have very different life experiences. How much do you think this affects patterns of development and the likelihood of problems at midlife?

33. When and how would you prefer to die? If you had a terminal illness would you want to be told? Do you think sudden death or death with forewarning would be better?

34. Should passive euthanasia be allowed? Should active euthanasia be allowed? What are the arguments for and against each? Do you think a "living will" is a good idea? Why or why not?

35. If you could choose to remain a particular age, which would you choose? Why? What are your attitudes toward aging and death? Will these attitudes change as you age?

36. Mel Blanc's tombstone reads "that's all, folks." What do you want on your tombstone? How would you like to be remembered?

37. Why do you think dying individuals so often feel isolated? How could the emotional needs of dying persons be better served than they are now in hospitals and nursing homes?

➤ LECTURE ENHANCEMENTS

Since all of us were once children, students begin this chapter with considerable knowledge. We learn best about children by being with children.

1. **The observational method.** Given that Chapter 3 is concerned with development in childhood, observing children at various ages makes a good outside assignment. Children may be observed at home, in a college preschool or daycare center, or at private nursery schools. Students should write a detailed description of a half-hour sample of a child's behavior, giving special attention to cognitive skills such as those described by Piaget. Such observations provide many examples of chapter concepts for class discussion. Prior to the observation, discuss with the class appropriate guidelines for behavior during objective observation, as well as obtaining necessary permission to observe.

2. **Show and tell.** If you have willing parents in class, arrange for an infant and a pre-operational (four- or five-year-old) child to visit the class. With the infant you can demonstrate a lack of object permanence (or its presence, depending on the age of the child) by holding a toy in the child's view and then behind your back. Simple sensory-motor coordination and purposeful behavior will be apparent in the child's attempts to touch a desirable toy. Separation anxiety can be illustrated by having the parent briefly leave the room. Bring some props for the pre-operational child so that you can demonstrate a lack of conversation of length, volume, or area. Conversations with pre-operational children can be entertaining and instructive. Videotape the demonstration if possible. During the next class session, discuss not only the child's behavior but the reaction of your students to children of different ages.

3. **Assumptions of heredity.** Although few psychologists would deny the pervasive effects of heredity on development, the general public often tends to over-emphasize hereditary effects. To illustrate, you may want to approximate a technique originated by David Rosenhan of Stanford University. Professor Rosenhan shows a slide of his two children and encourages students to note the ways in which the children resemble each other and him. Once students are thoroughly drawn in, he tells the class that his children are adopted! To make the same point, you could show a slide of two unrelated persons and tell the class they are siblings; then, after discussion, reveal that they have no hereditary connection. Follow with a discussion of hereditary/environmental interactions.

4. **Imprinting.** (Internet exercise) Have students research imprinting on the Internet and compare it to human sensitive periods. How are these two concepts similar and different? Why do humans have sensitive periods instead of critical periods?

5. **Parenting 101.** While deciding whether or not to become a parent is one of the most important decisions anyone will ever make, it is surprising how little thought students have given to this subject. It is particularly surprising since the overwhelming majority of them will, in fact, one day become parents. As a way to explore their motives for producing children, you could have students fold a sheet of paper down the center, and on the left side list all the advantages of parenting and on the right side all the disadvantages. After they are finished, put some of their responses on the board and use them to generate a class discussion.

6. **When does an organism become a human?** Raise the question that is a burning issue today: When is the developing organism a human being? The abortion issue has focused intense debate on this question. At what point between conception and birth is the organism human? Opinions will vary from the point of conception to the time when the fetus is viable. You should not try to convince students about your personal opinion. Rather, try to keep the discussion focused on the issue using as much scientific data as possible. One way to get students to step back from their positions, which may be somewhat hardened, is to ask them what scientific evidence they would require to change their opinions. You might also ask them to list the criteria for being human and then provide exceptions. For example, if the criteria for being human is the ability to self-reflect, or to make moral decisions, then what about a baby that is born with no brain (anencephalic)? If having human chromosomes is the criteria, then what about people who are missing a chromosome (such as some cases of sex chromosome abnormalities)? Hopefully, this will encourage students to see how complex the question is, rather than just choosing a philosophical position.

7. **What's dying like?** How general are the emotional stages of death described by Kübler-Ross? Do they describe the reactions (before death) of people you know who have died?

8. **Alternative birthing practices.** Alternative birthing practices have generated recent interest and debate. Given that feelings are strong, a debate or panel discussion can be quite interesting. Try to involve students who have had experience with alternative birth procedures, who work in medical settings, or who have a strong interest in the topics (e.g., prospective parents). Ask each to do research and find evidence for his or her position before the discussion is held.

9. **Parental accountability.** To stir up a rousing discussion on parenthood, read these news excerpts in class:

BOULDER, COLO. (UPI) Tom Hansen doesn't like the way his life has turned out and says it's because he was reared improperly. Hansen, 25, has filed suit against his mother and father, seeking $350,000 in damages because they reared him improperly and he will need psychiatric care the remainder of his life.

85

BOULDER, COLO. (AP) A mother sued for "parental malpractice" by her son is going to court herself to sue her son's psychiatrist who encouraged her son to sue her "for therapeutic reasons."

What would the class consider evidence of "parental malpractice"? Should or could parents be held responsible for the way their children turn out? If placed in the position of the judge, would students hear the case? (It was thrown out of court.)

10. **Generational differences.** Have students help you make a list of interesting topics that bear on generational differences. Give students four forms. Ask them to describe their attitudes (positive to negative) on a five-point scale and the attitudes of a person who is two decades older or younger. Topics could include: *institutionalized religion, premarital sex, dual-career marriages, punk hair styles, rap music, donating money for the poor,* and so on. Then ask the student to give two forms to the person whose attitudes they rated. Ask that person to rate their own views as well as the views they think your student holds. Ask your student to sit down with this person and compare their views, acknowledging differences but focusing on areas of similarity. Students should be prepared to discuss their observations in class.

11. **Speaker on aging.** If your community has an Adopt-a-Grandparent program, Gray Panthers group, Council on Aging, or similar organization, invite a speaker to discuss the problems of the aged and misconceptions about aging.

12. **Interviews across the lifespan.** For an interesting outside assignment or project on aging and changes over a lifetime, ask students to interview one or more people from each of the following age brackets: 15–25, 35-55, 65 or up. Questions can deal with issues such as, "What is middle age?" "When does a person become old?" "Do you (or did you) look forward to retiring some day?" "Did you experience a midlife crisis?" and "What has been the best period of your life so far?"

13. **Diversity in aging.** Ask students to interview three people over 75 who live in different settings: a condominium, a senior citizen development, and a convalescent hospital. Either prepare questions for the entire class or have each student (or group) develop a set of questions. Hopefully, students will conclude that while health can impact aging, there is tremendous diversity in the way people experience being 75.

14. **What do seniors want?** While society may be insensitive to the needs of senior citizens, we occasionally assume their needs are different from the needs of all citizens. Develop (or have the class develop) a questionnaire asking what legislation citizens would want to pass. For example, "I would vote for legislation to:"
    a.   *Increase social security*
    b.   *Increase Medicare coverage*
    c.   *Decrease property taxes*
    d.   *Provide money for the homeless*

86

e. *Provide money for elementary education*
f. *Provide money for research on garbage disposing and recycling techniques*
g. *Increase police protection*

Distribute the questionnaire to people of many different ages. Tally the frequencies for each age group. Remind students that senior citizens are a powerful political force with both specific interests and interests similar to people of other ages.

15. **Sowing seeds for old age.** Have students fill out a behavioral contract that will contribute to the quality of their "young age" (for example, passing a weekend without smoking, overdrinking, overeating, overspending, under socializing, or under exercising). Remind students that the person they are now may in many ways predict the senior citizen they will become.

16. **Moral dilemmas.** Give students the Kohlberg and Gilligan hypothetical situations before they read this chapter. Ask them how they would resolve the described dilemmas. Save these individual explanations for discussion when the concept of moral development is presented in class.

17. **Kohlberg and Piaget.** Psychologist Lawrence Kohlberg (1981) held that we learn moral values through thinking and reasoning. To study moral development, Kohlberg posed dilemmas to children of different ages. The following is one of the moral dilemmas he used (Kohlberg, 1969, adapted).

    A woman was near death from cancer, and there was only one drug that might save her. It was discovered by a druggist who was charging 10 times what it cost to make the drug. The sick woman's husband could only pay $1,000, but the druggist wanted $2,000. He asked the druggist to sell it cheaper or to let him pay later. The druggist said no. So the husband became desperate and broke into the store to steal the drug for his wife. Should he have done that? Was it wrong or right? Why?

    Discuss the connection between Kohlberg's theory and Piaget's cognitive levels. Have students share their answers, and have them determine which Piagetian level they are indicative of: Pre-operations, Concrete Operations, or Formal Operations.

18. **Moral development.** All of us make decisions that reflect various levels of moral development. Ask students to complete the following inventory.

When you make a decision about the following issues, what kind of moral analysis do you usually engage in? To the right of the following decisions, write PRE, CON, or POST: Kohlberg's pre-conventional, conventional, and post-conventional levels.

Driving speed _____
Following parents' rules, directions, or wishes _____
Donating time or money to charities _____
Involvement in institutionalized religion _____
Eating behavior _____
Sexual behavior _____
Reasons for attending college _____
Use of alcohol and/or other drugs _____
Honesty on classroom tests _____
Action taken after finding lost money or valuables _____
Decision to vote or not to vote _____
How to spend a million-dollar lottery prize _____

After collecting the anonymous responses, ask students to role-play post conventional and caring explanations for choosing to engage in (or not engage in) various behaviors in the categories listed. Mention studies showing that our moral development is greatly influenced by modeling and the kinds of interaction we have with others.

19. **Rate your parents.** Ask students to rate their parents on the ratio of "I-statements" versus "me-statements" they used. Would their parents agree with their assessment? Ask students which one of their parents' discipline guidelines they would most like to repeat with their own children.

➤ ROLE-PLAYING SCENARIOS

1. **Ask students to respond on paper, in pairs, or in small groups to a series of hypothetical situations:**

   a. You are taking care of a three-month-old nephew. Suddenly he begins to cry hysterically. What should you do? Why? (Change the wording on part of the forms to "niece." Do students respond differently?)

   b. You are a physician working with a mother who cannot decide what kind of infant delivery would be best. What guidance would you give her? Under what conditions is natural childbirth most desirable?

88

c. You are a father who has been excluded from the delivery room and the birth of your child. How do you feel? How do you behave?

d. You are a father who does not want to become involved in your child's delivery because you are afraid. Explain your feelings and your behavior.

e. You are a mother whose husband has decided to become very involved in the delivery process. You are not pleased or grateful. What are you feeling and thinking? Why?

f. You are a husband whose wife is going through postpartum depression. What should you say? What should you do? What should you not do? Why?

g. You just inherited a child's toy manufacturing company. You want to extend the product line to include toys that would increase cognitive development. What toys would you manufacture for various age ranges?

h. You are a preschool teacher. What should you do to foster the cognitive development of your students?

i. You are a third-grade teacher and you want to create an enriched intellectual environment. What would you do? Why?

2. **While you were in the bathroom, your two-year-old climbed out of the playpen,** onto the kitchen counter, and in the process of grabbing a cookie, knocked the jar to the floor. What should you do?

3. **Your son is not a skilled athlete yet he says he wants to play** competitive team soccer. Should you encourage him? Why or why not?

4. **You are 40 years old.** You have been working for a supermarket chain for 20 years and have received every promotion possible. Now you manage a large store. But you have no college background and know this is the highest level you will be able to achieve. You are feeling bored and trapped. What else are you feeling? How are these feelings being translated into behavior? Is there anything you can do to change the feelings and/or the behaviors?

5. **Your child has horrible dreams and gets in bed with you each night.** The bed is too small and you usually sleep poorly. What is your child feeling? How are you feeling? What should you do?

6. **Your 10-year-old child is very negative and unpleasant to be around.** She has no real friends and clings to you constantly. You are becoming increasingly annoyed. How is she feeling? What should you do?

7. **You are the parent of a child with autism.** You feel frustrated, angry, and sad that your child is not "normal." Describe your feelings in detail. How do you try to cope with those feelings? What could you do to better cope?

8. **Your 30-year-old single son has moved back into the house.** He has completed his education and has a good job. While at first you enjoyed his presence, you now think that he is taking advantage of you. What is he feeling? What are you feeling? What should you do?

9. **You just received news of a death in the family.** What are you feeling? What should be said to you? What should not be said?

10. **Your mother has developed serious memory problems and can no longer live alone safely.** How do you discuss the possibility of changing her living arrangements? Should you take her into your home? Should you force her into an assisted living facility or nursing home? How does she feel about her loss of independence? How might you feel about having her live with you and your family? How will your spouse feel? Your children?

➤ VALUE-CLARIFICATION STATEMENTS

1. A mother convicted of abusing drugs during pregnancy should be required to prove abstinence for the entire first year of the child's life or give up the baby for foster care.

2. People who know that they are carrying serious genetic diseases, such as muscular dystrophy or cystic fibrosis, should adopt rather than risk passing the genes on.

3. All employers should be required to provide for (or pay for) preschool child care for the children of their employees.

4. Basic parenting skills should be taught in the public schools sometime before students reach childbearing age.

5. Infants should be allowed to cry themselves to sleep.

6. It is better for young children to have a stay-at-home mom (or dad) than to be in daycare.

7. Women are naturally better at caring for children.

8. Temper tantrums are an inevitable part of the "terrible twos."

9. It is normal for all children to run away from home at least once in their childhood.

90

10. Stimulants should be used to help control hyperactivity.

11. Teens should be able to make most of their own rules.

12. The disadvantages of marrying before age 25 outweigh the advantages.

13. Being an adult is harder than being a kid.

14. Movies now rated PG-13 should be rated PG-18.

15. Adults should not try to dress like teens.

16. Having a "midlife crisis" is a normal part of life.

17. It is the responsibility of people over 65 to disengage in order to allow younger people into professional and social roles.

18. A person should be convicted of murder if the person intentionally ends the life of another, regardless of the circumstances.

19. Providing assisted suicide for terminally ill people is morally wrong.

20. Government funds should be spent on providing more hospice facilities.

➤ ONE-MINUTE MOTIVATORS

1. **Childhood pictures.** Collect photographs of students taken during their childhood years. Ask students to try to guess which classmate matches which childhood picture.

2. **Sensitive periods.** Break students into groups and have them make a list of all the abilities they think are subject to "sensitive periods." Have them create another list of abilities that are simply the result of the biological clock. When they are finished, discuss their lists.

3. **Conservation of volume.** Conservation of volume can be easily demonstrated with two glasses of unequal size. Ask students how to handle the following situation: Your four-year-old wants the same amount of milk as your eight-year-old receives. You only have two glasses of different sizes. How could you resolve this situation to the satisfaction of both children?

4. **Monopoly and development.** Ask students to generalize the "Monopoly a la Piaget" example from the text to sports. How do children at the different stages play soccer or

91

baseball? What techniques should a coach of a team of 5-year-olds use to teach the game? What techniques should be used with a team of 10-year-olds?

5. **Children and creativity.** Bring a box of household items to class. Put them on the front desk. Divide the class quickly into groups. Give each group three minutes to devise ways that the objects in front could be transformed into exciting toys for preschool children.

6. **Sibling rivalry.** Ask students to think about whether there was sibling rivalry in their families when they grew up. Was it between same-sex siblings? Was it affected by closeness in age? Did it get better or worse as they grew up? Do they think that they are still affected by it even though they may no longer be living at home?

7. **Experiencing dyslexia.** Give students a paragraph written so that many of the letters are backward, as the dyslexic person might see them. Point out how difficult it would be to rapidly read chapters in a college text if one were afflicted by dyslexia.

8. **Adolescent experiences.** Early researchers, including Freud, proposed that adolescence was a time of turbulence and conflict. Later researchers have suggested that this view of adolescence was exaggerated and pessimistic. While it is true that some adolescents have conflicts with parents and peers, many do not have any particular difficulties. Ask your students how well they got along with their parents when they were 15. You can ask them to rate it on a scale of 1–5. Then ask them how well they get along with their parents now. Has there been a large change, or is the relationship fairly stable? Lastly, ask them whether they expect their relationships with their parents five years from now to be better, worse, or about the same.

9. **Discipline.** What do you think are the best ways to discipline children? How would your approach be classified? What are its advantages and disadvantages? Depending on your class, you might also wish to have students compare their personal histories of how they were disciplined. You should make it clear that participation is voluntary, to avoid embarrassing anyone. You can also ask if there was a gender difference in type or amount of discipline.

10. **Choosing daycare.** If your students have not yet read the chapter, ask them to generate a list of factors that determine whether a particular daycare is good quality. What should they look for in choosing a daycare? Also generate a list of the positives and negatives for both home care and day care.

11. **What's your attachment style?** Ask students to categorize their own attachment style. When they have finished, have them write down their style and hand it in anonymously. Discuss the results.

12. **What do you want from life?** In the 1960s, young people were likely to list happiness and a meaningful life as the most important goals. Over time, material concerns became

more highly valued. Researchers are now beginning to see some return to values rather than wealth, but wealth remains high on people's lists. Ask your students how important money is to them relative to other goals. If you wish, you can write 10 items on the blackboard and ask them to rank-order their values on paper.

13. **The social clock.** The social clock is a culturally determined calendar of events in a person's life. Historically, people got married and had children at very young ages, in part because life expectancy was much shorter. Today, the social clock for many events occurs much later and varies much more widely from one individual to the next. Make up a list of questions to ask students and do a quick in-class survey of their choices. Be sure to provide ranges. Examples include:

At what age would you prefer to get married (under 20, early 20s, mid 20s, late 20s etc., or not at all)?
At what age would you prefer to have your first child?
What is the latest you would want to have a child?
Would you want one partner to stay home with children, or do you expect that both partners will work?
At what age do you expect to buy a house?
At what age would you want to retire?

14. **Identity development.** Have a "T-shirt" day where everyone wears a shirt that has a specific message on it. Briefly ask students to explain why their message is important to them and how it helps to communicate their "identity" to others.

15. **You're showing your age.** If your hair is not yet gray, gradually add a bit of gray paint (washable) to your hair. During the week of the unit, begin walking slower, wear earplugs so you talk louder, and squint at the chalkboard. During this time, have one or two students watch the reactions of your other students to your rapid "aging." Probably they won't notice anything at first. Remind students that aging is a gradual process that affects all of us.

16. **The clock is ticking.** Make a sign that says, "You are getting older and older minute by minute." Place it near the classroom clock. A few times during the class ask students their age (to the minute). At the end of class, remind students that "None of us will ever get these minutes back. I hope you feel we invested them well."

17. **Ageism and language.** Ask a female colleague to visit class. When she arrives ask her, "How old are you?" Then say, "You are pretty for your age." (This could also be done with a middle-aged student, if you have one in your class.) Then ask students, "What if I had said, 'You are very pretty for your race.' Would you have been offended?" Students should realize that that would be a racist comment. Next, point out that your original compliment was an ageist comment, suggesting that people in their 40s are not as pretty as younger people. It would have been better to simply say "You are very pretty."

93

18. **You have one month left.** Ask students to imagine how they would react if they were told that they have only one month to live. Ask them to come back the next class and describe how they would spend their last month. Remind students that none of us know when death will occur. All we can do is to make the most of the moments we have.

➤ BROADENING OUR CULTURAL HORIZONS

1. **Communal child rearing. (Internet exercise)** Ask students to collect information on the Israeli kibbutz system of childrearing. What are the advantages and disadvantages of this system?

2. **Perceptions of childhood.** Different cultures "see" children in different ways. How do you view children? Circle the number that is closest to your views:

   I see children (ages 5 to 12) as:

big babies	1	2	3	4	5	*little adults*
helpless	1	2	3	4	5	*responsible*
dependent	1	2	3	4	5	*independent*
fragile	1	2	3	4	5	*sturdy*
not smart	1	2	3	4	5	*very smart*
self-centered	1	2	3	4	5	*other-directed*

   Share your views with others in class. In what ways are your views similar and different?

3. **Blended families.** Often stepfamilies blend two very different "cultures" in terms of rules and expectations of behavior. What would you suggest stepfamilies do to minimize the cultural shock as the families merge?

4. **Universality of facial expressions.** Research suggests that certain facial expressions are universally expressed, from infancy. What does this suggest about the possibility of effective international communication?

5. **Adolescent rites of passage.** Ask students to make a list of adolescent rites of passage in American (or Western) culture versus the rest of the world. In some parts of the world, rites are rigidly defined and easily identified. In Western culture, there are some culturally-recognized passages that occur to most individuals at the same time (e.g., learning to drive at age 16 or 17) and other rites that happen only to some individuals (e.g., debutante balls), or happen to most individuals, but at widely varying times (e.g., losing one's virginity). If using an Internet search, use the keywords: cultural rites of passage.

94

6. **Culture and child rearing.** If any of your students are visiting from other countries, or if they are recent immigrants, ask them to tell how child-rearing practices differ in their home culture. Also ask them which North American child-rearing customs they find most and least appealing.

7. **Gender and perceptions of cognitive development.** Read the following summary to students, derived from an article that appeared in the *New York Times*, July 23, 1990:
   A new study of right-to-die cases has found that the courts treat women very differently from men. According to the study, published in the current issue of *Law, Medicine and Health Care,* the courts are far less likely to give weight to a woman's wishes regarding life support than to a man's. In a study of 22 right-to-die decisions from appeals courts in 14 states, Dr. Steven Miles found that **women are consistently portrayed as less capable of rational decision-making than men.** The cases studied are the bulk of the appellate decisions involving patients who had been mentally competent, but left no written directives for their care. In such cases, judges may try to "construct" the patient's preference from evidence of his or her values.

   Women are referred to by their first names, and construed as emotional, immature, unreflective and vulnerable to medical neglect, while men are called by their last names and construed as rational, mature, decisive, and assaulted by medical technology, Dr. Miles said. Only women are described as curled in a fetal position, while men are described as having contractures, the medical term.

   While a 31-year-old woman's comments on life support were characterized as "offhand remarks made by a person when young," a 33-year-old man's comments are characterized as "deeply held," showing "solemn intelligent determination." The study found that in cases involving women, the courts said they could not deduce the patient's preferences regarding life support in 12 of 14 cases, while in cases involving men, the court refused to construe the patient's preferences in only 2 of 8 cases.

8. **What are the implications of this trend for individuals of various ethnic backgrounds?** How can a person be sure that her or his wishes concerning death are followed?

9. **Child discipline across cultures.** What are the different styles of discipline used in cultures other than the United States? Ask students who are willing to talk about the ethnic backgrounds of their families to interview their parents or grandparents about discipline styles in their countries of origin. Other students might find willing acquaintances of a different ethnic background to interview. Discuss these differences in class.

10. **Treatment of the elderly.** Ask students if they will volunteer information about how different cultures treat their elderly. They can either use information about people they know or information they've read. Compare and contrast the information for the class.

➢ SUPPLEMENTAL ACTIVITIES

TO THE INSTRUCTOR:

Exercise 3.1: Supplemental Lecture: Prenatal Development and Genetics

Handout 3.1 provides more in-depth information on prenatal development and genetics for those who wish to supplement the textbook.

Exercise 3.2: Conservation

These demonstrations of conservation are certain to impress upon the students the idea that there is a qualitative difference in the cognitive functioning of a preoperational and a concrete operational child. They will see, furthermore, that this change does, in fact, occur at about seven years of age, as Piaget theorized.

This exercise can be done individually by each student if she/he can find enough subjects of the right ages. However, it is often easier to import a group of children for the class period. Students will probably have enough brothers, sisters, cousins, or neighbors of the right ages to do the project. Ask members of the class to volunteer to bring a child. This will take some planning since students will have to get the child's consent, the agreement of the parents, and permission from their schools to be absent on that day.

I.   **Preparation**

A.   Get students to volunteer to bring the subjects. You will need 10 altogether, a boy and a girl at each of the following ages: five, six, seven, eight, and nine. Set up a day and a time for the children to be at the school. The student or parent should bring them.

B.   Prepare a set of materials ahead of time. You will need two short, fat beakers filled with colored liquid (use food coloring); one tall, thin beaker; two large balls of modeling clay; and 10 square cubes (these can be small toy blocks).

C.   On the day of the exercise, seat the students and the children in a way that will be non-threatening and make the children comfortable. Have the class and the children talk a bit, perhaps even mingle so they get used to each other. The students should have been prepared ahead of time to observe these children to see how they behave. Is their behavior consistent with the theories about what is appropriate for their ages?

D.   Select a student to be the experimenter ahead of time. Be sure she/he has run through the experiment a few times to be ready for whatever happens. You can play the child's role for the practice session.

96

II. Demonstration

A. Remove the children from the room and set up the three exercises. They will be presented to each child one at a time. The experimenter should be trained so that she/he knows what to expect. Provide each student with a data sheet. **(Handout 3.2)**

B. Bring the children in one at a time, starting with the youngest, and have them do each of the three exercises. The students in the class are observers, and they should be recording on the data sheet what they observe in an unobtrusive way so that they do not disturb the subject.

C. When all subjects have been tested, they should be assembled again, given a treat (the whole class should give themselves a treat), and sent on their way home. The students should look over their results and, on the next class day, discuss the observations.

III. The Three Demonstrations

A. Place the two short, fat beakers, filled almost full of liquid in front of the subject. Ask the subject, "Are they both the same, or does one have more than the other?" The child will reply that they are both the same. If she/he says one has more and one less, then pour a little from one to the other until the child says they are the same.

Now pour the liquid from one of the beakers into the tall, thin one. Ask the child, "Are they both the same, or does one have more than the other?" If the child says the tall one has more, do not argue or question the child further, but, instead, simply pour the liquid back into the short, fat beaker. Again ask if they are now the same. After an affirmative answer, pour the liquid into the tall, thin glass and ask the question again. See if you get the same response.

B. Place the two round balls of modeling clay in front of the subject. Ask the child, "Are the two balls of clay the same size, or is one bigger than the other?" When you have an affirmative answer, take one ball and, in full view of the subject, roll out one into a long, thin shape, like a sausage. Now ask the child, "Are they the same, or is one bigger than the other?" This one need not be repeated regardless of the answer.

C. Place the ten blocks in two rows of five each in front of the child. Ask the child, "Do the two rows have the same number of blocks, or does one have more than the other?" After you get an affirmative answer, spread out the blocks in one row so the five blocks make a row about twice as long as the other five-block row.

97

Now ask the child, "Do both rows have the same number of blocks, or does one have more than the other?" This one need not be repeated.

IV.   **Discussion**

   A.   All observations should have been recorded by the students on their data sheets. It should have been evident at what age the change took place on each of the three tasks. You can also see if there were any differences between the boys and the girls.

   B.   What can you conclude about conservation in children?

   C.   Would the results obtained here be the same for all children of the same ages?

Exercise 3.3: It's in the Genes

You can generate some interest in the genetic influences on behavior by a few simple classroom exercises. The purpose is to show the direct relationship between genes and behavior. Be sure to emphasize the point that practice does not improve one's ability to do any of the tasks. It's in the genes.

Try any or all of the following exercises:

1.   **Tasting:** This activity requires the use of paper soaked in phenylthiocarbamide (PTC). You can obtain this from the chemistry department.

   Ask the students to place the treated paper on their tongues and report the taste. Although a variety of tastes may be reported, a significant number in the class will report a bitter taste. Those who do are called "tasters" because they have a dominant gene for this trait. Those who experience anything else are non-tasters. They have a pair of recessive genes for this taste trait.

   It has been estimated that about 70-75 percent of a typical class will be tasters. See how your class compares with this standard.

2.   **Color blindness:** The Ishihara test for color blindness is commonly used to measure color blindness. Information about the test and several of the test plates used can be found at http://en.wikipedia.org/wiki/Ishihara_color_test.

   If the class is big enough, you will almost certainly find one or more students who are color-blind.
   Ask students who are color blind to talk about their experiences. How do they handle traffic signals, clothing styles, color coding on forms and documents, etc.? They can recount many more such circumstances that could be problems. Color blindness is recessive and sex-linked. This means that it appears more often in males than in females.

98

3.   **Tongue curling:** There are two ways a person can curl the tongue. The first is known as tongue rolling. The second is tongue folding. In **tongue rolling** the person sticks the tongue straight out and turns the sides of the tongue up to form a U shape. In **tongue folding** the person folds the tip of the tongue back to touch the back of the tongue.

Some can roll and fold their tongues; others cannot. Those who can have a dominant gene, and those who cannot have the double recessive gene.

(Based on a demonstration by Dr. William C. Titus, Arkansas Tech University.)

4.   **Attached earlobes:** A quick check of the students will verify the statement that not all earlobes are alike. They have various shapes and sizes, some being very small and others large. However, a few people have what are called "attached" earlobes. This means the lobes are nonexistent, and the bottom of the ear slopes gently down to meet the neck.

Determine the proportion of persons in the class with attached earlobes. The number will be small. It is a recessive trait so it will appear in about 20-25 percent of the population.

Students could trace one of these traits in their family. As an additional exercise, ask them to check among their relatives and try to draw up a family tree identifying those who had the trait. Tracing attached earlobes can be amusing and instructive.

(Based on a demonstration by Dr. William C. Titus, Arkansas Tech University)

Exercise 3.4: Ages and Stages
The first exercise is based on Erikson's psychosocial stages. Students are asked to evaluate people they know using Erikson's descriptions of the stages of development. Answers should be recorded on **Handout 3.3**. They need to be encouraged to look at the behavior of the person first, and then see what stage they fit into. The temptation may be to assume that the person is, in fact, at the stage that Erikson says is appropriate for his/her age. This may not be true. When the exercise is completed, it should be shared with class members. A good way to do this is to form groups of four. Ask the students to explain to each other what their subjects are like and why they chose to see them at the stages they did. See if the group members agree. If not, what changes would they make?

Exercise 3.5: Moral Reasoning
The challenge of moral dilemmas is that there is often no correct answer. Give students a copy of **Handout 3.4**. Ask them to complete the examples on their own first, and then break them into groups for discussion. Ideally, the group will present individuals with aspects of the dilemma that they had not previously considered. If you wish to, you can treat the groups like mock juries for some examples and require that they return a verdict. This could, however, be very time-consuming! Additional examples of moral dilemmas can be found at:
http://www.friesian.com/valley/dilemmas.htm
http://www.haverford.edu/psych/ddavis/p109g/kohlberg.dilemmas.html

The point of moral reasoning is to work through a moral process, rather than come up with a "correct" answer. Depending on whether you want your students to wrestle some more with moral ambiguity, or whether you wish to indulge their curiosity, the "answers" are below:

1. The jury tried to return a hung verdict, but the judge would not allow it. The jury therefore convicted the captain and recommended a light sentence. The captain served six months of hard labor.
2. Churchill allowed the bombing to occur. The city of Coventry was devastated. Hundreds of people were killed, and thousands were injured. Thousands of homes were destroyed; many thousands more were damaged. The core of the city was destroyed and 75 percent of the city's factories were damaged. (Some reports indicate that Churchill knew which city, exactly, was to be bombed, and other reports indicate that the exact location was not known, only the date and time that a raid would occur.)
3. In the book, Val Jean chose to reveal his true identity and save the innocent man. (Of course, in fine literary form, he signed ownership of the factory over to the workers and managed to escape, living out his life on what little money he could take with him.)

Exercise 3.6: Aging

The second exercise focuses attention on old age. There are many myths and stereotypes. People often see the elderly in those terms rather than as individuals who are all different, each living with and coping with a unique set of circumstances and problems. Most of all, students need to think of the elderly as persons, and of old age as part of development.

All of the statements listed in **Handout 3.5** are false. Do a tally of the responses. See how many marked true for each item. Then ask students to explain their reasons. This should serve as a vehicle for a fruitful discussion on aging and old age.

Exercise 3.7: Interviewing the Elderly

A straightforward, but often valuable, assignment involves having students interview an elderly person. The questions provided on **Handout 3.6** should ensure that the interview is informative and thought-provoking.

Handout 3.1: GENETICS AND PRENATAL DEVELOPMENT

A. Chromosomes

Humans have 23 pairs of chromosomes, for a total of 46. Twenty-two of these govern the development of body cells and are called autosomes. The 23rd pair is the sex chromosomes, which determine biological sex and carry instructions on biological differentiation. The 23rd pair also carries information on a variety of "sex-linked" traits, including color blindness, male pattern baldness, etc. (see "E" below). The sex chromosomes are referred to as "X" and "Y" because of their shape. Females are XX and males are XY. While it is obviously possible to survive without a Y (as females do), it is not possible to survive without an X. The reason for this is that there is very little genetic information on the Y. Since a woman is XX, she can only give her children an X. Therefore, it is the father who determines the baby's biological sex, by giving either an X chromosome (daughter) or a Y chromosome (son) to his offspring.

B. Chromosomal Abnormalities

Sometimes in the process of replication of the chromosomes, tearing, damage, or other anomalies occur. This type of damage is referred to as a trisomy. With two exceptions, trisomies are lethal and will either prevent the pregnancy from occurring, will cause a spontaneous abortion (miscarriage), will cause stillbirth, or will cause death soon after birth. For every 100 conceptions, only half will result in pregnancy, defined as the egg implanting in the woman's uterus. Of that half, many more will spontaneously abort, often before the woman is even aware that she is pregnant. In the end, only one in four conceptions will result in a live birth. The remaining three-fourths are often naturally terminated because of defects, including trisomies. One non-lethal trisomy is trisomy 21, also known as Down syndrome. The other non-lethal one is trisomy 23, known collectively as sex-chromosome abnormalities. There are a variety of such abnormalities, but they often have in common problems in reproduction and often cause mild retardation. A full discussion of these problems can be found at: http://biology.about.com/od/basicgenetics/a/aa110504a.htm

C. Genotype and Phenotype

A person's genetic code is called the genotype. The person's physical appearance is called the phenotype. Genes combine in many ways to produce various phenotypes. In some cases, genes are simply the combination of maternal and paternal contributions. In other cases, genes operate according to the dominant-recessive principle. A dominant gene will appear in the phenotype if it is present in the genotype. Examples include brown hair, brown eyes, and curly hair. A recessive gene will only appear in the phenotype if no dominant gene is present. Usually, this means that two recessive genes must be present. Examples include blond hair, blue eyes, and straight hair. In the 23rd pair of chromosomes, however, only one recessive gene is needed because the Y chromosome is "missing" the gene pair that is present on the X chromosome. These are called sex-linked traits, and include color-blindness and male pattern baldness. In addition, many genes, including eye color, are regulated by the polygenetic principle, where several genes work together to produce a particular phenotype. An example is eye colors other than brown and blue.

101

Handout 3.1: GENETICS AND PRENATAL DEVELOPMENT (cont.)

D. Six Levels of Sex Differentiation
   a. Chromosomal sex. Sperm and egg unite and carry X (egg) and X or Y (sperm) genetic material.
   b. Gonadal sex. Reproductive organs that are not yet sex-differentiated are called gonads. Gonads have equipotentiality—the ability to become either male or female. Hormones determine whether the gonads will evolve into male or female organs.
   c. Sex of the internal reproductive structures (eight weeks after conception). If the fetus is XX, ovaries, fallopian tubes, and a uterus will develop. If the fetus is male, testes and vas deferens develop.
   d. Sex of the external reproductive structures (complete by week 12). In the female, the outer two-thirds of the vagina, clitoris, and the labia minora and major (inner and outer vaginal lips) develop. In the male, dihydrotestosterone (DHT) creates the scrotum, genital folds, and the penis.
   e. Sex differentiation of the brain. In male fetuses, testosterone androgenizes the brain, creating a larger hypothalamus and more specialized hemispheric function. In the female, a thicker corpus callosum and less specialized hemispheric function result.
   f. Gender. Sociocultural forces interact with biological sex to create a self-concept of being either male or female. In most cases, biological sex and gender are the same. In some cases, however, mismatches can occur because of inconsistencies in hormonal, prenatal development.

E. How to "Make a Man"
   In humans and other mammals, the "default condition" is to be female. In other words, the organism will naturally become female unless something is specifically done to change that outcome. It is the role of the Y chromosome to provide the instructions on how to create maleness. A number of factors work together to create this result. The Y chromosome begins to create androgens, or male sex hormones. These cause male systems to be activated by stimulating the Wolffian ducts. At the same time, the testes also release Müllerian Inhibiting Substance (MIS), which causes the Müllerian ducts to shrink. Therefore, to create a man, male systems must be activated and female systems must be suppressed. Occasionally, this process is imperfect, which can create ambiguous sex organs.

102

Handout 3.2: CONSERVATION: DATA SHEET

TO THE STUDENT:

Record your observations on the chart. Indicate the responses for females (F) and males (M) separately for each age. Enter an S if the subject says the two are the same and a D if she/he says they are different.

AGE	LIQUID		CLAY		BLOCKS	
	M	**F**	**M**	**F**	**M**	**F**
5						
6						
7						
8						
9						

103

Handout 3.3: AGES AND STAGES: WORK SHEET

TO THE STUDENT:

This is an assignment to help you understand Erik Erikson's eight stages of psychosocial development. Review the descriptions of behaviors appropriate to each of the stages.

Select three people of different ages whom you know well. One of them should be you. Try to identify which of Erikson's stages best describes the person's overall behavior. Don't be influenced by the person's age. People don't always "act their age"! You need to explain your decision in each case.

Subject #1 Age_____ Stage_____

Behaviors:

Reasons:

Subject #2 Age_____ Stage_____

Behaviors:

Reasons:

Subject #3 Age_____ Stage_____

Behaviors:

Reasons:

Handout 3.4: MORAL REASONING

For each of the following, indicate the decision you would make and why.

A. In 1842, the ship William Brown struck an iceberg and sank. There were more than 30 survivors crowded into a seven-person lifeboat. The accident occurred in the frigid waters of the North Atlantic and, to make matters worse, a storm was moving in. The captain had to choose whether to allow everyone to remain in the boat (and likely die) or whether to sacrifice some but save others. In order to have any chance to be rescued, the boat would have to be rowed a substantial distance. After 24 hours adrift in a leaking, listing boat, the captain gave the order to "lighten the load" and sacrificed the weakest survivors. 24 hours later, he gave the order again and more people were thrown overboard. Miraculously, the boat was rescued on the third day. The captain was put on trial for manslaughter. **Assume you were a member of the jury. Would you have convicted him? Why or why not? What action would you have taken in the same position and why?**

B. During the Second World War, the Allies were losing and Britain was in danger of being invaded. The British intercepted intelligence that would allow them to break the German code and potentially win the war. One of the first coded messages broken referred to a Nazi plan to bomb a British city. Churchill could stop the attack, but then the Germans would realize that the code had been broken and would simply change the code. Alternately, Churchill could protect the secret that the code had been broken and could continue to use German intelligence without being detected. To do so, however, he would have to allow the bombing to proceed without advance action. In other words, only when German bombers were actually spotted, and it was too late to stop the raid, would British planes be launched for defense, not before. **If you had been Churchill, what would you have done, and why?**

C. In the book *Les Miserables,* by Victor Hugo, the lead character Jean Val Jean went to prison for stealing a loaf of bread to feed his family. At the historical time of the story, even minor transgressions resulted in severe prison sentences. Val Jean escaped from prison and avoided recapture. He disguised his identity, changed his name, and became Mayor and chief benefactor of a small town by inventing a new product. In an obsessive quest to recapture Val Jean, inspector Javert was constantly on the lookout for the escaped convict. Eventually, Javert arrived in the same town and saw a man whom he believed was Val Jean. The innocent man, a victim of mistaken identity, would be sent back to prison as the escaped convict, probably for the rest of his life. Val Jean was a very good and moral man and did not want an innocent man to go to jail for his crime. At the same time, if Val Jean saved the innocent man by divulging his true identity, and went back to prison, the factory would close and hundreds of workers would lose their jobs. Some would probably even starve. Putting aside your own self-interest (not wanting to go to jail), **which choice would you make—save an innocent man from a terrible fate caused by your deception, or abandon the workers of the town? On what basis would you make your choice?**

Handout 3.5: AGING: WORKSHEET

TO THE STUDENT:

Below are 10 statements about the elderly. Write TRUE or FALSE beside each one, indicating whether or not you agree.

_____ 1.   Workers should be required to retire at a set age, such as 65.

_____ 2.   Most people do not adapt well to aging.

_____ 3.   It is better for elderly persons not to wear bright colors.

_____ 4.   It is unwise for elderly persons to try to look younger by dying their hair or seeking cosmetic surgery.

_____ 5.   The elderly are not as well informed as younger persons.

_____ 6.   The lives of the elderly are generally less rewarding than the lives of younger persons.

_____ 7.   It is a greater tragedy for a young person to die than for an elderly person to die.

_____ 8.   A large percentage of the elderly are unhealthy or infirm.

_____ 9.   The elderly are less independent than younger persons.

_____ 10.   An elderly person cannot do most tasks as well as a younger person.

Handout 3.6: GROWING OLDER

Interview Questions

Select a person to interview who is at least 20 years older than you are. Take very brief notes, jotting down the key ideas. Try to focus all of your attention on the person you are interviewing. Add questions to this list if you would like.

1. When and where were you born? How many siblings did you have, if any? What was your order of birth? What do you remember about your early childhood?

2. Describe one of the happiest times of your childhood. What friends and relatives do you associate with happy times?

3. What role did animals play in your childhood? How important are animals to your adult life?

4. Describe a sad time of your childhood. Did something specific take place? How did your family suggest that pain or sadness be dealt with?

5. What was your favorite childhood toy? What was your favorite childhood book?

6. What was your best memory from high school or college?

7. What were your early career aspirations? Did you ever work in that field? What was your career?

8. What were the rules of "dating" when you were a teenager or young adult? Who was your best friend? What did you do for fun?

9. What world event had the greatest impact on your life? Why?

10. What athletic interests did you have as a teenager and young adult? Are these interests the same now?

11. Did you marry? Why or why not? Did you have children? Why or why not? Were you employed outside the home? Why or why not?

12. What did you worry about most when you were in your early 20s? Your 30s? Your 40s?

13. What was the most difficult obstacle that you had to try to overcome in your life? Were you successful? Why or why not?

14. In what ways are you similar now to the way you were when you were 20? In what ways are you different?

15. If you could give advice to others younger than you, what would it be? What is the most exciting thing happening in your life at the moment?

107

➢ JOURNAL QUESTIONS

1. What forms of deprivation and enrichment have you experienced in your life? What impact did these experiences have on you? When you have children, what kinds of perceptual and intellectual stimulation are you going to encourage?

2. Have you ever spent time with a crying baby? How did you react? How did you feel? What advice would you give to a new mother?

3. What were your parents like when you were a child? Did your father and mother nurture you in different ways?

4. What are your earliest memories about your mother? Your father? Your siblings? If yours was a "non-traditional" family, or if you were an only child, write about the other people in your life, such as grandparents or aunts and uncles. Are your early memories mostly positive or mostly negative? If mostly negative, what is your earliest positive memory?

5. Did you attend child care or take your child to a preschool or a babysitter? What feelings did you have?

6. Interview family members about the pregnancy that preceded your birth, your delivery, your neonatal temperament, and your behavior as an infant. How much touching did your receive as a child? What feelings have you developed as an adult about touch?

7. In which way(s) are you the same as and different from a year ago? Five years ago? What will you be like in 5 years? In 10 years?

8. Which crises of Erikson's have you found most difficult? Why? What resources would have helped you develop the skills to resolve the crisis in a positive direction?

9. Write your parent(s) or your child a letter describing three ways that person has helped you in your own development. Discuss the advantages and disadvantages of actually mailing the letter.

10. What kind of a relationship did you have with your parents? Why? How? What could you do (or have done) to make the relationship better? What could your parents have done? What could you now do to let go of past problems in this relationship and move on?

11.   What relationship did you have with your siblings before adolescence? Why? How did your parents deal with sibling rivalry? What kind of a relationship do you have now with your siblings? If you are an only child, do you wish you had siblings? Why or why not?

12.   What feelings did you have about the timing and form of your physical maturation? How did others respond? Could anything have been done to help you deal more effectively with these physical changes?

13.   How do you spend your leisure time? Is this how you want to spend your leisure time in your old age?

14.   What do you want people to say at your funeral? What form of a memorial service do you want to have? How do you want others to grieve? If you wanted friends to be reminded of one very funny thing that happened in your life, what would it be?

15.   What are the factors and events in your life that give you the greatest degree of happiness?

➤ SUGGESTIONS FOR FURTHER READING

American Humane Association & Brittain, C. R. (2006). Understanding the medical diagnosis of child maltreatment: A guide for nonmedical professionals. New York: Oxford University Press.

Arnett, J. J. (2004). *Emerging adulthood: The winding road from late teens through the twenties*. New York: Oxford University Press.

Bloom, P. (2000). How children learn the meanings of words. Cambridge, MA: MIT Press.

Bolton, F., Morris, L., & McEachron, A. E. (1989). *Males at risk: The other side of child sexual abuse*. Thousand Oaks, CA: Sage.

Caplan, P. (2000). *Don't blame mother: Mending the mother-daughter relationship* (2nd ed). London: Routledge.

Craig, L. (2006). Does father care mean fathers share?: A comparison of how mothers and fathers in intact families spend time with children. *Gender & Society, 20*(2), 259–281.

Doherty, M. J. (2009). *Theory of mind: How children understand others' thoughts and feelings*. New York: Psychology Press.

Elkind, D. (2006). *The hurried child* (3rd ed.). Boston: Da Capo Press.

Erikson, E. H. (1963). *Childhood and society.* New York: Norton.

Erikson, E. H. (Ed.) (1978) *Adulthood.* New York: Norton.

Gilligan, C. (1982). *In a different voice.* Cambridge, MA: Harvard University Press.

Ginott, H. G. (1965). *Between parent and child: New solutions to old problems.* New York: Macmillan.

Ginsberg, H., & S. Opper (1997). *Piaget's Theory of Intellectual Development,* 3rd ed. Saddle River, NJ: Prentice-Hall, 1997.

Golden, J. (2005). *Message in a bottle: The making of fetal alcohol syndrome.* Cambridge, MA: Harvard University Press.

Harlow, H. F., & Harlow, M. K. (1962). Social deprivation in monkeys. *Scientific American, 207,* 136–146.

Kail, R. V. & Cavanaugh, J.C. (2008). *Human Development: A Life-Span View,* 5th ed. Belmont, CA: Wadsworth.

Kohlberg, L. (1969). The cognitive-developmental approach to socialization. In A. Goslin (Ed.), *Handbook of socialization theory and research.* Chicago: Rand McNally.

Kohlberg, L. (1981). *Essays on moral development (Vol. I): The philosophy of moral development.* San Francisco: Harper.

Matcha, D. A. (2009). *The sociology of aging: A social problems perspective.* Boston: Allyn & Bacon.

Mercer, J. (2006). *Understanding attachment: Parenting, child care, and emotional development.* Westport, CT: Praeger.

Ramachandran, V. S. & Oberman, L. (2006). Broken mirrors: A theory of autism. *Scientific American,* October, 63–69.

Rothbart, M. K. (2007). Temperament, development, and personality. *Current Directions in Psychological Science, 16*(4), 207–212.

Schaie, K. W., & Willis, S. L. (2009). *Adult development and aging* (5th ed). Englewood Cliffs, NJ: Prentice Hall.

Vaillant, G. E. (2002). *Aging well.* Boston: Little, Brown.

➤ VIDEO SUGGESTIONS

Feature Films

A.I.: Artificial Intelligence (Haley Joel Osment, Jude Law, Frances O'Connor) Drama/Science Fiction. David (Osment) is a robot of the future who replaces Henry and Monica's comatose son. When the couple's natural child recovers, David is abandoned and sets out to become "a real boy." A science fiction film that can be used to illustrate a variety of developmental and technological issues.

Jack (Robin Williams, Diane Lane, Jennifer Lopez) Comedy / Drama. Jack (Williams) is introduced as a 10-year-old who looks like a 40-year-old man. In a flashback it is discovered that Jack was born only 10 weeks after his mother became pregnant, and has a disorder causing rapid aging. Home-schooled until now, Jack decides to go to public school where fellow fourth graders tease him. His classmates soon see an advantage to having him around and grow to love Jack. A good film to discuss various differences between child and adult development stages.

Look Who's Talking (John Travolta, Kirstie Alley, Olympia Dukakis) Comedy. Infant Mikey is a "talking baby" protagonist who is a sarcastic observer of his new world. Mikey's mother (Alley) is searching for a father for Mikey. The perfect daddy is right under her nose, cab driver (Travolta), who was on the scene when she went into labor on the sidewalk. While a preposterous premise, it nevertheless provides an illumination of adult life from a baby's perspective.

Dangerous Minds (Michelle Pfeiffer), Drama. A school teacher discovers that it takes more than ordinary teaching skills and knowledge to get through to a class of "rejects from hell." With the use of bribery and intimidation, Lou Anne Johnson (Pfeiffer), a nine-year veteran of the Marine Corps, reaches out to students who need her the most.

The Breakfast Club (Emilio Estevez, Judd Nelson, Molly Ringwald), Comedy Drama. Nine hours of school detention bond five students who, until this day, were strangers and on different levels of the high school caste system. Faced with a villainous principal, who makes their lives miserable, the group decides they have one thing in common—they do not like adult society. A sensitive look at adolescent development and issues during a cross section of a day in their lives.

American Pie (Jason Biggs, Shannon Elizabeth, Alyson Hannigan), Comedy. Jim (Biggs), a high school senior and his three friends make a pledge to have sex with a woman three weeks before the senior prom. Jim attempts to seduce a beautiful Czech exchange student but fails miserably and ends up going to the prom with an annoyingly chatty girl. Each of the other boys have prospects but none of them look too promising. While some scenes may push the envelope a bit, sometimes so does adolescent behavior.

Citizen Kane (Orson Welles, Joseph Cotton, Buddy Swan), Drama. Charles Foster Kane (Welles), a very wealthy and powerful man, dies after uttering his last word "Rosebud." Thompson, a reporter working on an obituary film, is told to find out what "Rosebud" means. Thompson's search leads him to five people in Kane's private life.

Magnolia (Jason Robards, Jr., Julianne Moore, Tom Cruise), Drama. Earl Partidge (Robards), a successful producer of television game shows, leaves his wife who is sick with cancer to marry a younger woman, Linda (Moore). After their marriage Earl discovers that he has cancer and his wife Linda takes care of him. Earl would like to reunite with his son but his son wants nothing to do with his father.

The Mirror Has Two Faces (Barbra Streisand, Jeff Bridges). Two cerebral Columbia professors commit to a perfectly sensible but passionless paper marriage based on their intellectual common ground. The earth moves, however, when the wife redesigns her look in order to invoke the hots in her spouse and bolster her sagging self-esteem.

Safe House (Patrick Stewart), Drama. Patrick Stewart plays a retired government agent coping with Alzheimer's. He experiences growing paranoia, leaving everyone, including the viewers, wondering where his growing dementia ends and lingering aspects of his old spywork begin.

Educational Films and Videos

Excellent films and videotapes are available from the following sources:
National Association of Anorexia Nervosa and Associated Disorders
Box 7 Highland Park, IL 60035

Parents Anonymous® Inc.
675 W. Foothill Blvd., Suite 220
Claremont, CA 91711

Child Development

Basic Parenting Skills, (2000), Films for the Humanities & Sciences, 50 min. This program presents an overview of basic parenting skills in a dramatic format. Practical techniques for dealing with tantrums and other undesirable behavior are included. Specific ideas for building a healthy parent-child relationship are examined.

Better Babies--Raising Intellectual "Superstars," (1991), Filmmakers Library, 28 min. Does prenatal and early childhood learning produce geniuses? This video documents several early-learning programs. We see parents talking to their unborn children in the belief that they will accelerate verbal skills, and other parents in courses on how to raise geniuses. We are shown the hectic schedule of a toddler whose mother teaches him art, music, computers, geography, and Japanese. One couple displays pride in having raised four genius daughters, yet the eldest daughter does not plan to repeat her parents' experiments on her own children. This could be a good discussion-starter for your class.

Body Doubles: The Twin Experience, (1997), Films for the Humanities and Sciences, 50 min. Recommended by MC Journal. The study of twins is vital to research in psychology. Twins separated at birth and later reunited are often quite similar. This similarity begs the notion that personality is formed by experience, and suggests that personality is genetically predetermined. This excellent HBO documentary contains powerful interviews with numerous twins, including those conjoined, and a history of twin research from Josef Mengele of the University of Minnesota Twin Research Center.

Broken Child: Case Studies of Child Abuse, (2000), Films for the Humanities and Sciences, 61min. This film examines the effects of child abuse on its victims, including adult survivors of child abuse.

Capabilities of the Newborn, from *The Mind Series Teaching Modules*, 2ⁿᵈ Edition #13. This video demonstrates the startling abilities that newborns have, as determined by modern technology.

Cells: Baby and Child, (1998), Films for the Humanities and Sciences, 20 min. Section one of this program makes extensive use of microscopic imaging to create an overview of cells in their role as the building blocks of life. Section two describes the newborn experience, from birth to breastfeeding. Also covered are the mechanics behind a baby's improvement of vision and rapid language acquisition. Childhood play, social interaction, and schooling are touched upon as well.

Child Development, (2000), Films for the Humanities & Sciences, 60 min. This program examines a range of the major subjects categorized under the rubric of child development. Includes a videodisc with still images.

Child Sex Abusers, (1995), Films for the Humanities and Sciences, 28 min. This is a specially adapted Phil Donahue show featuring mothers and daughters who have been molested by brothers, half-brothers, and neighborhood kids. An expert who deals with abusive children counsels what to look for and what to do with abusive kids, and counsels kids who are being abused.

Citizen 2000: A Series on Child Development, (1993), Filmmakers Library, various times. This new and unique documentary series follows the lives and development of a group of children over a period of 18 years, from their birth in 1982 until they become adults in the year 2000. The series is being produced in consultation with experts in the fields of developmental psychology, sociology, linguistics, and pediatrics. The children, all British but from a wide variety of social, economic, and ethnic backgrounds, are filmed at home, in school, at play, and at major events in their lives. Because of the close relationship between the filmmakers and the children, the portraits are completely spontaneous. The series provides a compelling picture of childhood at the end of the twentieth century. Titles available now include: *Matthew: Portrait of a One-Year-Old,* 25 min.; *Turning 2: Out of Babyhood,* 51 min.; *Turning 4: New Skills,* 51 min.; *Rachel—A Difficult Year, The Death of a Sibling,* 25 min.; and *Fathers,* 52 min. Parts of this series have already won some film awards. Videocassettes may be purchased or rented as a series or individually.

Cognitive Development, (1990), Insight Media, 30 min. This video offers an excellent review of the basics of Piaget's theory including the areas of: language, reasoning, and remembering.

Corporal Punishment: "Loving Smacks," (2000), Films for the Humanities and Sciences, 52 min. In this program, noted psychologists discuss the myths, justifications, and effects of corporal punishment and present alternatives to the use of violence to maintain discipline.

Development, (1998), PBS Video, 55 min. Part of *The Mind* series, this film discusses the development of the CNS in humans. The film presents graphic representations of neuronal changes from the single germ cell to the brain of a six-year-old. The effects of drugs, alcohol, and radiation on the developing brain are also examined in both human and animal models. The film contains excellent graphics depicting differentiation within the human brain.

Emotional Intelligence: The Key to Social Skills, (1997), Films for the Humanities and Sciences, 28 min. There was a time when parents were expected to teach their children social skills, such as how to listen, share, and be kind. Today that job and the nurturing of emotional intelligence necessary to learn those skills have been turned over to schools. This program from *The Doctor Is In* looks at innovative teaching techniques that are helping students to develop emotional intelligence and the social skills that will help them lead happier lives. Psychologist Daniel Goleman discusses the nature of emotional intelligence and how it develops; child psychologist Maurice Elias explains the concept of emotional literacy. A Dartmouth-Hitchcock Medical Center production.

Erik H. Erikson, (1992), Davidson Films, 38 min. Using archival materials, interviews, and new footage, this video discusses Erikson's theory that the interplay of genetics, cultural influences, and unique experiences produces unique individual variability. The program also contains commentary by Erikson's colleague Margaret Brenman-Gibson, offering a sense of relationship between the life experience of a theorist and the work that is produced.

Everybody Rides the Carousel, (1980), Pyramid Film & Video, 72 min. This video presents psychologist Erik Erikson's theory of personality development, using delightful animation. The eight stages of life are presented in three main parts: infancy to childhood, school age to young adulthood, and maturity to old age.

Gender: The Enduring Paradox, (1991), University Film and Video, 56 min. Part of the *Smithsonian World* series. This video explores the ever-changing role of gender in American society, from the formation of gender roles in early childhood to the socially constructed roles of masculinity and femininity experienced throughout life. Segments look at the women's movement, fathers who nurture their children, and cross-cultural differences between the sexes.

Infant Cognitive Development, from *The Mind Series Teaching Modules*, 2nd Edition #14, Worth, 7:34. This video looks at recent research into the subject and demonstrates some of the recently developed research techniques for exploring the intellectual development of young children. It also points out where current findings differ from those of Piaget.

Language Processing in the Brain, from *The Mind Series Teaching Modules*, 2nd Edition #8, (1999), Worth, 6:19. This video discusses Neil Bohannon's work on children's development of receptive language, the precursor to productive language, and has insight into how kernel language structures are initiated.

Louder Than Words, (1991), University Film and Video, 57 min. Part of the *Childhood Series*. Jerome Kagan, a professor of developmental psychology at Harvard, discusses the connection between shyness, sociability, and biology. Benjamin Spock is also featured offering advice for parents and teachers.

Miracle of Life, (1983), Swedish Television and WGBH, Boston, 60 min. This excellent film uses microphotography to show the complex sequence of events that lead to conception and to the birth of a human baby.

Music and Early Childhood, (1994), Filmmakers Library, 28 min. This video makes a strong case for beginning music education at an early age because of its importance as a precursor to language skills. It shows groups of very young children engaged in musical activity, as well as psychologist Howard Gardner discussing musical intelligence.

Physical and Cognitive Development, Discovering Psychology Teaching Module 10, (1990), Annenberg/CPB, various times. The Discovering Psychology Teaching Modules contain excerpts from the *Discovering Psychology Series*. The most important programs in this module include: footage of Piaget performing conservation experiments, a demonstration of object permanence in infants, the acquisition of symbolic understanding in children, a discussion of memory loss and aging, and educational training of the elderly.

Piaget's Developmental Theory: An Overview, (1989), University Film & Video, 28 min. Using both archival footage of Piaget and newly shot footage of David Elkind conducting interviews with children of varying ages, this video offers an overview of the scope and content of Piaget's theory.

Seasons of Life, (1990), WQED Pittsburgh / University of Michigan, 60 min. each. This unique series consists of five hour-long videos and a supplementary series of 26 half-hour audiotapes (either may be purchased separately). The videos cover infancy and early childhood, childhood and adolescence, early adulthood, middle adulthood, and late adulthood. Each program is hosted by David Hartman, who interviews experts from a variety of sciences to examine how biological, social, and psychological forces affect our lives.

Self-Esteem and the Child, (1990), Cox Entertainment, 45 min. This video-based skill-building workshop includes dramatic vignettes and interviews with children and two self-esteem professionals. The program emphasizes five elements that lead to self-esteem: a sense of security, and sense of identity or self-concept, a sense of belonging, a sense of purpose, and a sense of competence. This video may be of special assistance for those teaching parents or for students who want to be teachers and counselors.

Sex Roles: Charting the Complexity of Development, (1991), Insight Media, 60 min. This film looks at the cultural ramifications of sex roles and the myths associated with them. Three theories of socialization (Freudian, social-learning, cognitive-development) are analyzed regarding how each theory views the nature-nurture controversy. The negative impact of sex-role stereotyping is examined.

115

Simple Beginnings? Child Development from Birth to Age Five, (1994), Films for the Humanities and Sciences, 24 min. This program explores the period of child development from birth to four to five years of age, providing an overview of several key topics in developmental psychology. The program features three experiments that display early abilities of infants to recognize rules, faces, and biological motion. The experiments test short-term memory capacities of young babies, register a baby's reaction to the mother and to a stranger, and demonstrate how babies appear to discriminate at a young age between biodynamic and non-biodynamic motion. The program goes on to explore the parents' role in structuring infants' learning experiences in early language development.

Social Development in Infancy, from *The Mind Series Teaching Modules*, 2nd Edition #15, Worth, 6:44. This video clip emphasizes the importance of social interaction in infancy in contributing to attachment and personality development.

Socialization—Moral Development, (1980), Harper Collins, 22 min. This video explores theories of morality and moral development through the demonstration of classic experimental work in social and developmental psychology.

Teratogens and Their Effects on the Developing Brain and Mind, from *The Mind Series Teaching Modules*, 2nd Edition #12. Teratogens are substances that can cause malformations of the fetus in the first and second trimesters of pregnancy. The embryonic stage, when the major organ systems are developing, is an especially sensitive time for the developing prenatal child. This video looks at some of the more common hazards and effects of exposure to these harmful substances.

The Developing Child Series, (1991-93), Magna Systems, Inc. times vary between 20–30 min. The Developing Child series videos present information on most of the key areas of child and adolescent development. Some of the best of the videos include: Module #10 (Infancy: Beginnings in Cognition and Language); Module #14 (Child in the Family); Module #20 (Early Childhood: Behavior and Relationships); Module #22 (Language Development); Module #23 (Self Identity and Sex Role Development); Module #28 (Preadolescence); Module #30 (Adolescence: Search for Identity); and Module #31 (Adolescence: Relationships with Others).

The Developing Child, (1990), Annenberg/CPB, 30 min. Part of the *Discovering Psychology* series hosted by Philip Zimbardo, this film examines the impact of heredity and environment on the development of the child. The arguments of nature and nurture are discussed and supported with results from human and animal research. Ultimately the film concludes that, even though newborns are equipped to respond to their environment, biology alone is not destiny. Experience can alter the development of the child. This excellent examination of the nature versus nurture debate promotes active discussion among students.

The Effect of Hormones and the Environment on Brain Development, from *The Brain Teaching Modules*, 2nd Edition #17, (1998), Annenberg/CPB, 6:50. This video presents some rather startling and significant findings that address the important topic of gender differences. The *in utero* photography is stunning.

116

The Infant Mind, (1992), Insight Media, 30 min. This fascinating video presents traditional Piagetian perspectives of objective permanence during the sensorimotor period. Then it challenges some of Piaget's assumptions to demonstrate that infants have a perception of cause and effect, number and object permanence much earlier than formerly believed.

Physicians Who Have Successfully Treated Their Own Autistic Children: The Defeat Autism Now! (DAN!) Doctors (T-110). Presented at the July 2001 Conference of the Autism Society of America. Panel Chairman: Paul M. Hardy, M.D., of the Professional Advisory Board of ASA. Three parent-physicians (Jeff Bradstreet, M.D., Amy Holmes, M.D., and Miriam Jang, M.D.) explain how they found conventional medicine ineffective at helping their autistic children—in contrast to the remarkable improvement achieved on their own, for their own children and for hundreds of other autistic children, with the DAN! approach. Tape contains the full presentations by the four physician-presenters, plus questions and answers from the audience. Two hours and 36 minutes. VHS cassette

The Psychological Development of the Child, (2000), Films for the Humanities & Sciences, 21-26 min. each segment. This eight-part series covers the development of the child from the womb to the end of the first year, covering such topics as the birth process, prenatal development, attachment, breast-feeding across cultures, the family, psychological development and the discovery of the outside world.

Theories of Human Development, (2002), The Teaching Company, 2 parts, 24 lectures by Professor Malcolm Watson, Brandeis University, 30 min./lecture. This course provides answers to questions of human nature—how we learn, adapt, and mature into our individuality and uniqueness.

Time To Grow (2002) from *Psychology: The Study of Human Behavior Series*, Coast Community College Telecourse, 30 min. each This 26-part series covers the entire gamut of child development, from birth to adolescence, including physical, cognitive, and psychosocial growth and development.

Touchpoints: Pregnancy, (1992), Piper Films Inc., 50 min. each. A series based on the Brazelton Study. By watching 12 families, all in unique situations, we are shown how and why children develop the way they do. In part 1, *Birth and First Four Weeks of Life*, questions explored include: What kind of parent will I be? What will my baby be like? What will delivery be like? This part also covers birth to first few weeks, newborn assessment, the work of attachment, and issues in the first three months (crying and calming, the work of becoming a family). Part 2, *First Month Through First Year,* covers issues concerning communication and adjusting to being a parent, cognitive and motor development, feeding, sleep, negativism, tantrums, and teasing. Part 3, *One Year Through Toddlerhood,* covers sibling rivalry, discipline, and toilet training.

Toys, (1994), Filmmakers Library, 47 min. This video airs divergent views of educators, from those who feel that natural materials such as wood, stones, and acorns are the only proper toys to those who believe that a child's world should be full of complicated objects, as this reflects the real world. It features psychologists Howard Gardner, Jerome Kagan, and others. The program highlights the dramatic changes that have occurred in the kinds of toys available, from blocks and stuffed toys to battery-operated toys that simulate reality (some violently) to computer games.

Twinsburg, Ohio: Some Kind of Weird Twin Thing, (1992), Filmmakers Library, 23 min. This award-winning film is about two very different identical twins living 3,000 mile apart who agree to meet at Twins Days in Twinsburg, Ohio. This documentary chronicles the continuing struggle of balancing the intimacy of a shared childhood against the adult need for individuality.

Adolescence, Adulthood, and Aging

Adolescent Development, (2002), from *Psychology: The Study of Human Behavior Series*, Coast Community College Telecourse, 30 min. This video identifies the principal features of adolescent intellectual development. Experts define the field and discuss development in puberty.

Adolescent And Adult Development, (2002), from *Psychology: The Human Experience Series,* Coast Community College Telecourses, 30 min. Explains the significance of peer relationships and Kohlberg's moral development theory. Erikson's theory on human development and Kübler-Ross' five stages of dying and death complete the overview.

Aging, (2000), Films for the Humanities and Sciences, 26 min. This film covers the physical processes of aging and the various body systems to see how and why they change as they age. It is shown that not all of the changes in older people are inevitable and that some, in fact, can be slowed down or reversed.

Aging: Growing Old in a Youth-Centered Culture, (2002), Films for the Humanities and Sciences, two-part series, 30 min. each. This series addresses the social aspects of aging, considering the increased longevity of our aging population.

Aging Well, (2000), Films for the Humanities and Sciences, 16 min. This film discusses how people are living longer than their parents did and why they are staying healthier. The program covers medical advances that continue to boost our life expectancy rate, and the role that lifestyle changes play.

Brain Transplants in Parkinson's Patients, from *The Brain Teaching Modules*, 2nd Edition, #31, (1998), Annenberg/CPB, 11:09. This video begins with a brief description of Parkinson's disease. One of the most promising new approaches to treating the disease involves the implantation of fetal tissue into the basal ganglia of Parkinson's patients. Note that it takes about one and a half years for the transplanted tissue to produce its full complement of dopamine. Even then, it does not produce all the dopamine needed by the patients, and so they continue to take L-dopa after surgery.

Death: An Overview, (2000), Films for the Humanities and Sciences, 50 min. This step-by-step program takes the myth and mystery out of the process of dying and death itself, and presents both as biological and clinical realities.

Death of One's Own, (2000), Films for the Humanities and Sciences, 87 min. In this program, PBS journalist Bill Moyers unravels the complexities underlying the many choices at the end of life, including the bitter debate over physician-assisted suicide.

Drinking Apart: Families Under the Influence, (2004), Films for the Humanities and Sciences, 71 min.) This film examines the effect that addiction has on the lives of families and what can be done to break those addictions.

Effect of Mental and Physical Activity on Brain/Mind, from *The Mind Teaching Modules,* 2nd Edition #18, Worth, 9:27. This video shows the effect of aging on both mental and physical decline.

Facing Death: Conversations with Caregivers, (1993), University Film & Video, 26 min. This video offers advice and guidance for professional hospice workers to help them become more comfortable with death. Five hospice workers share their personal experiences as caregivers and relate perspectives acquired from years of working with dying patients. Although aimed at hospice workers, this video is also useful for members of a psychology class studying the other end of the life cycle.

Gender and Relationships, (1990), Insight Media, 30 min. This program emphasizes that even the most respected authorities are not in agreement about what factors influence peoples' feelings of love, affection, and sexual attraction toward others. The film addresses such questions as: What is love? What makes sexual behavior "normal" or "abnormal"? Why and in what ways do men and women differ in their sexual attitudes, behaviors, and motives?

Healing Your Spirit, (1992), Thinking Allowed Productions, 30 min. This series of four interviews conducted by Jeffrey Mishlove concerns spiritual peace. In the first program, Wayne Muller suggests we can learn to let go of blaming others for our pain or even trying to understand why we were victims of misfortune. In the second program, Gay Gaer Luce proposes that the aging process need not occur in the manner prescribed by cultural stereotypes. In the third program, Rachel N. Remen discusses the loneliness and pain of illness as well as the opportunity for spiritual deepening that it affords. In the fourth program, Dale Borglum suggests that healing is facilitated when one does not deny the possibility of death. This series may be of special interest to those teaching a class of older students and adults.

Inside Stories: Journey into Self-Esteem Series, (1992), Filmmakers Library, 30 min. This award-winning four-part series shows how building self-esteem improves the quality of life and helps people deal more effectively with their problems. The programs are: (1) *Self-Esteem Begins in the Family*—deals with parenting issues; (2) *Self-Esteem and How We Learn*—shows the important role of the teacher in developing a healthy self-image, especially during adolescence; (3) *A Family in Recovery*—follows a seemingly perfect family on the road back from alcoholism; and (4) *Seniors' Esteem Issues*—focuses on later life. In all four programs we learn that people who have healthy self-esteem become capable of dealing with life's challenges. Examples from life are intercut with commentary by authority H. Stephen Glenn.

Inside the Teenage Brain, (2002), PBS, 60 min. New research into why teenagers behave differently from children and adults is examined in this video.

Kids Out Of Control, (1990), Films for the Humanities and Sciences, 25 min. This film discusses drugs, depression, rape, and suicide. It includes a five-question quiz to help determine whether a child is experiencing healthy rebellion or is troubled and in need of help.

Letting Go: A Hospice Journey, Films for the Humanities and Sciences, 30 min.

Like Two Peas in a Pod, (1991), Filmmakers Library, 55 min. This award-winning film from Quebec focuses on three sets of identical adult twins of various ages. It explores each set of twins and their combined and individual struggles for identity.

Living With Dying, (2000), Films for the Humanities and Sciences, 87 min. In this program, PBS journalist Bill Moyers describes the search for new ways of thinking about dying.

Maturing and Aging, Discovering Psychology. Annenberg/CPB Project, 30 min. This program is particularly effective in challenging society's myths about the aging process. For example, it shows that development is life-long, as indicated by Erikson's theory. Similarly, it explains research demonstrating that when no physical illness is present, psychological deterioration is the exception rather than the rule. Problems such as depression, anxiety, and stress are no more common among the elderly than among other age groups. Training methods have been developed to enable the elderly to recover loss in inductive reasoning, spatial orientation, or attention. Differences in lifestyle, diet, and exercise, as well as in locus of control and level of optimism, influence response to the aging process. As noted, development of an education program that changes our cultural stereotypes about aging is only the first step in meeting the pressing needs of older adults. In addition, we need early intervention programs that provide therapy for those with problems, and a redesigned environment that makes our health care delivery system more accessible and accommodating to those with limitations.

The Merchants of Cool, (2001), PBS, 60 min. This video explores the effect that our culture has on teenagers and their identity development.

Relationships in Old Age, (1993), Annenberg/CPB, 60 min. each. Key segments: (8) *Family and Intergenerational Relationships,* (9) *Work, Retirement and Economic Status,* (10) *Illness and Disability,* (11) *Dying, Death, and Bereavement,* (12) *Societal and Political Aspects of Aging,* and (13) *The Future of Aging.* While in an introductory class, even a short series of these programs may be difficult to schedule, they are presented here because of special emphases an instructor may wish to cover.

Self-Esteem and How We Learn, (1992), Filmmakers Library, 30 min. This program could also be used in the Learning topic unit. It focuses on the critical school-age years, especially adolescence, when self image is tested in an environment outside the home. The teacher may play a pivotal role in helping the adolescent feel accepted and productive. We are shown a model school where students and teachers work and learn with mutual respect.

Sex Roles: Charting the Complexity of Development, (1991), Insight Media, 60 min. This film looks at the cultural ramifications of sex roles and the myths associated with them. Three theories of socialization (Freudian, social-learning, cognitive-development) are analyzed regarding how each theory views the nature-nurture controversy. The negative impact of sex-role stereotyping is examined.

Teenage Mind and Body, (1990), Insight Media, 30 min. This video explores the areas of adolescent cognitive and physical development. Two highlights include David Elkind's discussion of formal operations and adolescent egocentrism, and a review of Kohlberg's theory of moral development and moral reasoning.

Teens: What Makes Them Tick, (1999), ABC, 43 min. This ABC News special includes John Stossel talking to a variety of teens and their parents. He visits the Harvard Medical School's Brain Imaging Center to reveal some surprising physiological reasons for teen behavior. The adolescent years are not only a time of huge growth spurts, but also an age of irrepressible passion and enthusiasm. This program concludes that despite their rebellion, most teens want to please their parents.

The Effect of Aging on Cognitive Function: Nature/Nurture, from *The Mind Teaching Modules,* 2nd Edition #16, Worth, 10:09. This video opens with still pictures of identical twins of many ages and races. The narrator tells us how the study of identical twins can help us to determine how factors such as lifestyle, diet, and stress may contribute to individual differences in the aging process.

The Unknown Generation X, (1995), Films for the Humanities and Sciences, 28 min. (Recommended by Booklist). "Generation X" is called a myth by some, a reality by others. Whatever the case may be, the generation of young adults born between 1965 and 1980 faces challenges that no other generation has had to deal with. Unemployment, underemployment, a huge national debt, a depleting Social Security system, negative stereotyping, and endless bombardment from advertisers are just a few of the issues confronting this generation. This program examines some of the stereotypes and issues that society has created for "Generation X." Featured in this program are Wendy Kopp, founder of Teach for America; Neil Howe, author of *13th Gen;* and Richard Thau, president of Third Millennium.

To Live Until You Die. (1984) Time-Life Video, 57 min. In this video, Elizabeth Kübler-Ross presents an interesting discussion of her stage theory of dying. She also offers her opinions on issues like hospice care, working with the terminally ill, and the need for spiritual assistance as death approaches.

➤ COMPUTER AND INTERNET RESOURCES

PsykTrek 3.0
Unit 9: Human Development
9a. "Prenatal Development"
9b. "Erikson's Theory of Personality"
9c. "Piaget's Theory of Cognitive Development"
Unit 9: Human Development
9b. "Erikson's Theory"
9d. "Kohlberg's Theory"

INFOTRAC®

Below you will find four journal articles obtained from INFOTRAC® that relate to information in this chapter. Instructors should encourage students to utilize this invaluable resource to improve their research skills. Have students locate and read the following articles and answer questions relevant to each article.

Pediatrics, Nov 2004 v114 (7) **Is this a behavior problem or normal temperament?**

1. What four major areas define the scope of temperament?

    Answer: Temperament is the stable pattern of reactivity and responsiveness. It is the foundation of personality. Temperamental characteristics influence all aspects of development and behavior. Certain clusters of temperamental characteristics are associated with an increased likelihood of behavioral concerns, discipline problems, and adjustment difficulties at particular points in development. Lack of fit or a mismatch of temperamental characteristics is often the source of difficulties for a parent or other child care provider.

2. With adverse temperaments, what are the four steps clinicians must take in discriminating between behavior problems and normal temperament?

    Answer: (a) recognition of the temperament by the clinician, (b) reorganizing of the parental understanding and strategies, (c) relief for the caregivers, and (d) referral to a mental health specialist, which should seldom be necessary.

The Journal of Men's Studies, Fall 2004 v13 i1 p85 (21) **The stability and change in the social support networks of widowers following spousal bereavement.**

1. In the above study, does the common assumption that men seek to replace their wives in order to have some care for them supported?

    Answer: It is clear that the common assumption that men seek to replace their wives in order to have someone to care for them is a stereotype that fails to hold true for this group of older men.

2. Briefly describe the differences in social support patterns by sex found in this study.

122

Answer: In addition to changes over time, there are several areas of sex differences worthy of attention. Widowers report different patterns of support and hassles with children when compared to widows. Older widowers also report feeling less dependent on their adult children for such issues as emotional, instrumental, or financial assistance when compared to widows. Widowers report less feeling of mutual dependence and, in fact, feel under-benefited in these exchanges as evidenced by the group's negative mean value at all waves of measurement. Finally, dependence equity considers the degree of discrepancy between the reported exchanges between older parents and adult children. The results indicate that widowers feel lower levels of positive support from friends and relatives at all waves when compared to widows.

Daedalus, Spring 2004 v133 i2 p18 (8) **The psychology of subjective well-being.**

1.   What are some of the benefits of happiness listed in this article?

Answer: Studies show that people who are at least mildly happy most of the time have more self-confidence and better relationships, perform better at work, are rated more highly by their superiors, are better creative problem solvers, are more likely to volunteer or engage in altruistic behavior, and even make more money than their less happy counterparts. Some evidence even suggests that they are healthier and live longer.

2.   What does longitudinal research suggest about happiness according to this article?

Answer: Longitudinal research suggests that happiness may actually cause desirable characteristics, not just follow them; it is likely that there is a psychological loop that reinforces itself, with success in marriage, work, and other life domains leading to continued happiness that, in turn, leads to more successes.

Journal of Mental Health Counseling, July 2004 v26 i3 p244 (16) **The human-animal bond and loss: Providing support for grieving clients.**

1.   What was the purpose of the study on human-animal bond and loss?

Answer: The purpose of this article is to increase mental health counselors' awareness of the importance of pets in the lives of their clients and to provide a greater understanding of the grief process accompanying the death of a companion animal. A broad framework for assessing clients' attachments to their pets and conceptualizing grief as it relates to pet loss is presented.

2.   List five things that are related to the intensity of grief responses after the death of a pet.

Answer: The intensity of grief responses after the death of a pet has been associated with several factors including the level of attachment to the pet, type of death (e.g., sudden versus expected, traumatic versus non-traumatic), perceived understanding from others, other stressful events, means of death, and negative mood pertaining to one's own death.

3. The article listed certain populations of pet owners that may be at higher risk for a prolonged or intense grief response. List them.

    Answer: High levels of attachment, low social support, and accumulated stressful events were predictive of high levels of grief over the death of a pet. Furthermore, their findings suggest that pet owners who live by themselves, are female, or have no child in the household may be especially susceptible to a strong grief response and social isolation after the death of their companion animal.

WEB LINKS

Knowledge Builder Links

1. The Interplay of Heredity and Environment
    Heredity versus Environment:
        http://www.pbs.org/newshour/bb/health/july-dec98/naturenurture_10-20.html
    Diving into the Gene Pool:
        http://www.exploratorium.edu/genepool/genepool_home.html
    Human Genome Project:
        http://www.ornl.gov/sci/techresources/Human_Genome/home.shtml
2. The Neonate and Early Maturation
    The Parent's Page: http://www.moonlily.com/parents/
    Parenthood.com: http://www.parenthood.com/
3. Social Development in Childhood
    I'm Embarrassed! http://www.talaris.org/spotlight_embarrassed.htm
    Attachment Theory:
        http://psychology.about.com/od/loveandattraction/ss/attachmentstyle.htm
    How to Choose a Daycare That's Right for Your Child:
        http://childcare.about.com/cs/daycarecenters/ht/daycare.htm
4. Language Development in Children
    Language Development in Children:
        http://www.childdevelopmentinfo.com/development/language_development.shtml
    How Does Your Child Hear and Talk?
        http://www.asha.org/public/speech/development/chart.htm
    Speech & Language: Talk to Me: http://www.pediatricservices.com/parents/pc-32.htm
5. Cognitive Development in Childhood
    Jean Piaget Archives: Biography: http://www.piaget.org/aboutPiaget.html

124

Jean Piaget and Cognitive Development:
   http://webspace.ship.edu/cgboer/genpsypiaget.html
Scaffolding as a Teaching Strategy: http://condor.admin.ccny.cuny.edu/~group4/
6. Adolescence, Young Adulthood, and Moral Development
   A Positive Approach to Identity Formation of Biracial Children:
      http://ematusov.soe.udel.edu/final.paper.pub/_pwfsfp/00000085.htm
   Kohlberg Dilemmas:
      http://www.haverford.edu/psych/ddavis/p109g/kohlberg.dilemmas.html
7. Challenges Across the Lifespan
   Welcome to Middle Age: http://www.middleage.org/
   The AARP: http://www.aarp.org/
8. Effective Parenting
   Nine Steps to More Effective Parenting:
      http://www.kidshealth.org/parent/positive/family/nine_steps.html
   Discipline: Logical and Natural Consequences: http://parentingtoolbox.com
   Ten Reasons Not to Hit Your Kids:
      http://www.naturalchild.com/jan_hunt/tenreasons.html

Additional Web Links

APA Division 20: Adult Development and Aging
http://apadiv20.phhp.ufl.edu/

Attention Deficit Disorder
http://www.chadd.org/

Autism
http://www.ninds.nih.gov/disorders/autism/detail_autism.htm

Caregiver Survival
http://www.caregiver911.com/

Childhood Sexuality—an often overlooked developmental issue
http://www.answers.com/topic/child-sexuality
http://www.sexualityandu.ca/professionals/sexuality-child.aspx

Developmental Psychology
http://classweb.gmu.edu/classweb/awinsler/ordp/index.html

Domestic Violence
http://www.abanet.org/domviol/home.html

Menopause
http://www.mayoclinic.com/health/menopause/DS00119
http://www.menopause.org/default.htm
http://www.menopause-online.com/pmsormenopause.html

Moral Dilemmas
http://www.friesian.com/valley/dilemmas.htm
http://www.haverford.edu/psych/ddavis/p109g/kohlberg.dilemmas.html

Puberty
http://www.coolnurse.com/puberty.htm
http://www.puberty101.com/
http://familydoctor.org/445.xml

Piaget
http://www.piaget.org/
http://www.learningandteaching.info/learning/piaget.htm

Temperament
http://www.temperament.com/clinical.html

PSYCHOLOGY IN THE NEWS

b-di.com Understanding Behavioral Individuality
http://b-di.com/
This site covers the current issues in the news, resources, and temperament assessment
test.

Child and Family Web Guide
http://cfw.tufts.edu/
Search topics by age, research news sites, and special topics.

Early Childhood.com
http://earlychildhood.com
Connect to the latest in the news with featured articles and links.

Daily News from WebMD's Team of Award-Winning Journalists
http://webmd.com/webmd_today/newscenter/default.htm
This news center keeps you up to date on the latest issues in psychology. You are able to
search by topic or gain access to news archives.

Psychology Articles
http://www.nytimes.com/college
The *New York Times* is a valuable resource for students and faculty.

Psych Central: Daily Psychology News and Headlines
http://psychcentral.com/news/
Headline news on issues related to psychology. You can search by topic and access
archives.

126

CHAPTER 4
Sensation and Perception

Survey Questions
Discussion Questions
Lecture Enhancements

The Archimedes Spiral
The "blind walk"
Genetics and taste sensitivity
Selective attention
Perceiving temperature
Guest lecturer
Laser vision correction
The transparent finger and the finger sausage
The Müller-Lyer illusion
Necker's Cube
Eye witness accounts
Amateur magician
Do you have ESP?

Role-Playing Scenarios
Value-Clarification Statements
One-Minute Motivators

Sensation and memory
Analogies for senses
Sensory waves
Transduction
Perception and awareness
The human camera
Ishihara plates
Pupil dilation and constriction
Gating pain
Hearing in man/woman versus beast
Sensation and evolution
Sensory adaptation
Perceptual habituation
Sensory adaptation
Bringing order to perceptions
Figure-ground processes
Perception in the cortex
Optical illusions
Perceptual learning
Perceptions
Visual restriction
Sound localization
Monocular depth perception
Altered perceptions
Contrast and perception
Novelty and habituation
Telepathy versus coincidence
Eyewitness accuracy
A day in court
Perception in the cinema

127

➢ SURVEY QUESTIONS

Module 4.1 Sensory Processes

Survey Question: In general, how do sensory systems function?

Module 4.2 Vision

Survey Question: How does the visual system function?

Module 4.3 Hearing, the Chemical Senses, and the Somesthetic Senses

Survey Question: What are the mechanisms of hearing?

Survey Question: How do the chemical senses operate?

Survey Question: What are the somesthetic senses?

Module 4.4 Perceptual Processes

Survey Question: In general, how do we construct our perceptions?

Survey Question: Why are we more aware of some sensations than others?

Module 4.5 Depth Perception

Survey Question: How is it possible to see depth and judge distance?

Module 4.6 Perception and Objectivity

Survey Question: How is perception altered by expectations, motives, emotions, and learning?

Module 4.7 Extrasensory Perception

Survey Question: Is extrasensory perception possible?

Module 4.8 Psychology in Action: Becoming a Better Eyewitness to Life

Survey Question: How can I learn to perceive events more accurately?

➤ DISCUSSION QUESTIONS

1. Why do we take our senses for granted? What can we do to better appreciate all of our sensory equipment?

2. What features of the environment are people "wired" to detect? Why? Would it be adaptive for us to be sensitive to other features? What would they be?

3. Is your brain sitting on a laboratory table somewhere? It is theoretically possible that your brain was donated to science some time ago. Let's say that it was preserved and recently reactivated and that a sophisticated computer is artificially generating patterns of nerve activity in the cortex by mimicking normal sensory messages in the nerves. These messages duplicate the sights, sounds, odors, and sensations of sitting in a college classroom. If this were happening right now, could you tell? Would you be able to discover that you had no body? Defend your answer.

4. Let's say that you would like to design a system that uses touch to convey "images" to a blind person. How would you proceed? What would be the advantages and disadvantages of using various body areas (hands, back, forehead, and so on)?

5. In Zen Buddhism there is a familiar koan, or riddle, that says, "Last night I dreamt I was a butterfly. How do I know today that I am not a butterfly dreaming I am a man?" Can you relate this to the idea that we construct a version of reality out of the more basic world of physical energies surrounding us?

6. How would our world be different if the majority of people could not hear? If they could not see? If they could not taste or smell?

7. How did the straw break the camel's back? If a load is only a pound, adding another pound is very noticeable. But if the load is 200 pounds, adding one pound is not at all noticeable to our senses. Discuss the issue of the relative threshold.

8. Is it possible to talk to the person next to you and still understand what is going on in the lecture? Can we really attend to two auditory events at the same time, or does the "cocktail effect" automatically take over? (Point to a student who has not been paying attention and ask his/her opinion.)

9. Which of your senses do you think is the most dominant and why? (Answer: vision dominates, as illustrated by the term *visual capture*.)

10. The eye is ingeniously constructed. Why is the eye filled with fluid rather than blood vessels? Why are there more cones than rods near the fovea? Why do cones pick up fine details better than rods? Why do some species have only rods or cones in their eyes? How might evolution have favored the development of sensitivity to movement in peripheral vision?

130

11. You are planning a new airport. What form of lighting would you use to maximize safety for the landing of planes?

12. Air-force and navy pilots are required to have 20/20 vision at the time they get their pilot's license. People who have had laser correction and now have 20/20 vision are not allowed. Why? Do you think this is appropriate? Why or why not? Would those of you who wear glasses or contacts consider laser correction? Why or why not?

13. Have you ever walked into some place that has an unpleasant smell, such as a poorly-run pet shop? Why don't the owners seem to be bothered by the smell? (habituation) Would they be more likely to smell it as strongly after re-entering, or is there also long-term habituation?

14. Have you ever leaned against something hot and noticed the contact with the object before you actually felt the pain? (Answer: sensory neurons fire faster than pain neurons.) How might these dual sensory pathways have evolved?

15. The vestibular system controls our sense of balance and equilibrium. How many of you get car sick (or plane sick)? Does it make a difference whether you are in the front seat or the back seat? Why do you think there is a difference? Did any of you get carsick as children, but not now? What do you think made the difference?

16. Why is acupuncture effective in reducing pain? How do "gating" and the impact of endorphins affect the perception of pain?

17. You are a pediatrician and must immunize small children. What could you do to reduce the pain caused by these injections?

18. Which of the perceptual "constancies" or "organizational tendencies" would be most difficult to be without?

19. Do you think that perceiving depth is instinctive or learned? What experiences do you think could interfere with a child's development of depth perception? What experiences could enhance the development of this ability?

20. Driving a car relies heavily on binocular depth perception. But people who are blind in one eye can still drive. Which of the eight monocular cues listed on pp. 186–187 would be most relevant to driving? Why?

21. Why might the "earth illusion" be different from the moon illusion if you were viewing the Earth from the surface of the Moon? (Hint: Would the horizon on the Moon appear to be as distant as it is on Earth?)

22. How might the perceptual abilities of a person raised in a vertical rain forest differ from those of a person raised in a flat desert?

23. Bicyclists and motorcyclists often complain that automobile drivers act as if cyclists are invisible. What perceptual factors might cause drivers to "look right at" cyclists without seeing them?

131

24. A professional basketball player is at the free throw line for the last shot in a tied championship game. What depth cues are available to him? A professional golfer is making the last putt for a $10,000 prize. What depth cues is she using?

25. Describe a situation you have misperceived. What influenced your perceptions?

26. Why do cigarette manufacturers place the government required health warning in the corners of their ads? How is this placement explained by theories of perception?

27. What role might habituation play in industrial accidents (especially on production lines) and in driving on arrow straight superhighways? What changes would you make in work procedures or highway design to combat habituation?

28. Why is the nervous system structured for both adaptation and habituation? How do both of these processes contribute to our survival?

29. How dependable do you think eyewitness testimony is in a courtroom? What factors other than accuracy of original perceptions might contribute to inaccuracies in testimony?

30. If you believe that ESP occurs, what would it take to convince you that it does not? If you do not believe that ESP occurs, what would it take to convince you that it does?

31. How many of you believe that telepathy is possible? Clairvoyance? Precognition? Psychokinesis?

32. Why do you think it is that many people have difficulty rejecting the idea of ESP?

➤ LECTURE ENHANCEMENTS

Depending on the equipment available to you, there are many classroom demonstrations possible for this chapter. You can use models to show microscopic parts of sensory systems, devices that make sound waves visible, and psychophysics experiments demonstrating the sensitivity of visual, auditory, olfactory, gustatory, and kinesthetic receptors. Students are fascinated with the chance to "see" silent, invisible processes at work. The effectiveness of these demonstrations depends on your access to up-to-date equipment and expertise for using and explaining the equipment. There is usually an exciting contrast between the interpersonal and interactional nature of the developmental chapter and the machine orientation of this chapter. Students enjoy becoming more aware of their sensory world and you can help enhance that awareness.

1.   **The Archimedes Spiral.** The senses do not simply mirror external "reality"—they shape our experiences in a multitude of ways. The Archimedes spiral can produce a powerful distortion of sensory experience, and thus bring home the fact that what we take for "reality" is greatly affected by the functioning of sensory system. To construct an Archimedes spiral, obtain a phonograph turntable. (An alternative is a child's phonograph with the tone arm missing. One can sometimes be purchased from a thrift store for less than a dollar.) Cut a large circle of white poster board (roughly 12–15 inches in diameter). Make a hole in the middle of the poster board disk so that it can be placed on the turntable like a phonograph record. Leave the hole small so that the disk will remain attached to the turntable when the phonograph is laid on its side for the class to see. Use a black felt tip marker to draw a wide, bold spiral from the edge to the center of the disk. When the disk is turning, the spiral may appear to be collapsing in toward the center, or expanding outward, depending on how it is drawn. Either type of spiral will work, but the inward-moving spiral tends to produce a stronger effect. It would be interesting to make one of each to see how each works.

Set the turntable on its side on the edge of a desk or table so that the poster board disk can rotate freely and be seen by the class. Set the turntable at its lowest speed. Have students fixate on the center of the spiral for at least one minute. Then ask them to look immediately at some other object (a clock on the wall or your face, for example). If the collapsing spiral has been used, a figural after effect occurs in which the object viewed after fixation appears to be expanding.

After the "oohs" and "ahs" die down, point out that a traditional test of the reality of an event is its consensual validation. If several people have the same experience simultaneously, it is thought to be "real." If only one has the experience, it may be considered a hallucination. The question becomes, then, did the clock (or your face) actually change size, or did it not? In terms of subjective experience, an entire classroom full of people could swear in court that it did. Yet in reality it did not.

2. **The "blind walk."** The frequently used "blind walk" helps students experience the emotional impact of a loss of vision, and of sensory loss in general. Put students in pairs. Ask one student to close his/her eyes while being escorted around campus just outside of the classroom. After a designated period of time, switch roles. You could follow your students, listening for unusual auditory stimuli (the sound of a bird, a passerby commenting on the exercise) and quiz them on return to the classroom. Be sure to discuss how difficult it is for many people to relinquish control and totally depend on and trust their partner. Beginning the chapter with this exercise often introduces students effectively to the importance of tuning in to the many sensations that are around us.

3. **Genetics and taste sensitivity.** To demonstrate genetic differences in taste sensitivity, obtain strips of litmus paper treated with the chemical phenylthiocarbamide (PTC). Most chemical supply houses carry this item, or the college biology department may have some in stock. It is very inexpensive. Pass out one strip to each class member. Have everyone taste the strip and ask for a description of subjective experiences. About 70 percent will have taste sensations, and about 30 percent will be genetic non tasters. Subjectively, the chemical exists for some and is a non stimulus for others.

4. **Selective attention.** In almost every classroom there are weak background stimuli that can be used to demonstrate selective attention. The buzzing of neon lights, the hum of an air conditioner, and the drone of street noise—any of these can be used to show that a stimulus may be present but not consciously perceived until attention is shifted to it. Simply stop in mid sentence and call attention to one of these stimuli.

5. **Perceiving temperature.** There is an age-old demonstration that students can do easily to illustrate that there are separate receptors for hot and cold and that temperature sensations are relative. Prepare three containers of water: one cold, one warm, and the third lukewarm. None should be extreme, not too cold or too hot. Have students put one hand into the cold water and the other into the warm. They should observe that one hand will feel cold and the other warm and also notice that the cold or warm feeling occurs mostly at the water line, where air and water meet. This is the only place on the skin where a comparison of air and water temperature can be experienced. The relative difference is what is reported as cold or warm. After being held in the containers for a few minutes, both hands should be put in the container of lukewarm water. Students will notice that the hand that was in cold water will feel warm, and the hand in warm water will now feel cold. Once again, a comparison of the sensations before and after is what is noted by the brain.

6. **Guest lecturer.** Any of the following can serve as an interesting guest lecturer for this chapter: an optometrist, an ophthalmologist, a hearing specialist, a kinestheologist, an audiologist, a sports medicine physician, a dentist, a clinician from a pain clinic, anyone conducting S&P research, or a Lamaze/prepared childbirth specialist. Students could also be given the opportunity to interview patients on sensory impairments, pain tolerance, or feelings about the upcoming birth of a child.

7. **Laser vision correction. (Internet exercise)** Have students look up the procedure, advantages, and long-term implications of laser vision correction.

8.   **The transparent finger and the finger sausage.** For a simple illustration of convergence, have students fixate on a distant point and then bring a finger up into the line of sight. The finger will appear "transparent" because the line of sight is nearly parallel. If students then look directly at the finger, it will once again become "solid" (convergence). A variation on this (which also illustrates retinal disparity and fusion) involves again fixating on a distant point. This time the tips of the index fingers of both hands should be brought together in the line of sight, about 12 inches from the eyes. Students should see a small "sausage" forming and disappearing between their fingertips as the two retinal images overlap.

9.   **The Müller-Lyer illusion.** Students often underestimate the effect of the Müller-Lyer illusion because they are so familiar with it. To demonstrate it in class, on a sheet of paper draw a horizontal line several inches long and place an "arrowhead" on one end and a "V" on the other. Be sure not to center the line within the borders of the page. Duplicate this figure and distribute it to the class. Ask the students to mark the spot that they think is the center of the horizontal line (without trying to correct for the illusion). Now fold the page so the tips of the horizontal line are matched up (to do this they will have to hold the paper up to the light) and crease the paper at the fold. Now ask them to unfold the page and compare the crease with the mark they made. The majority of the students will have erred in their bisection due to the illusion. This is a good launching point for a discussion of illusions.

10.   **Necker's cube.** Divide students into pairs. One student serves as subject; the other serves as experimenter. The subject will stare at a photocopy of Necker's cube. Manipulate the frequency of figure reversals by giving half of the subjects written instructions that say, "Most college students are able to see many dozens of reversals per minute." The other half are given written instructions that say, "Reversals may take place, but they are very rare." The experimenter counts the number of reversals within a three-minute period. Collect the data. Calculate a mean for each group. Discuss why a difference between the two groups is discovered. To what extent do expectations alter perceptions? A copy of Necker's Cube can be found at: http://phosphenism.com/accueil.html

11.   **Eye witness accounts.** For a dramatic and time honored demonstration of the inaccuracies of eyewitness testimony, arrange for a confederate to "make a scene" in class. Ideally, the confederate should wear unusual or distinctive clothing (different colored socks, an outlandish hat, etc.). The confederate should charge into class, ask loudly if you are Professor (your name), "douse" you with a bucket full of paper clippings, and then run out. Immediately after, ask the class to write a description of your "attacker." Then compare details of the descriptions. For an interesting twist, tell students to be sure to include the color of the visitor's socks in their descriptions. In this variation, of course, the confederate wears no socks!

135

12. **Amateur magician.** People of all ages enjoy watching magicians. Invite an amateur magician to class. Your students may be willing to do the planning and the introductions. After a short performance, you can hold a panel discussion on how easily our senses can be fooled. What perceptual principles help explain the illusions created by the magician? Involve the magician in the discussion if he or she is willing.

13. **Do you have ESP?** Ask students if any of them believe that they have extrasensory abilities, or whether they know someone else who claims to have them. Using cards (anywhere from four aces to a full deck), test this ability empirically on the person claiming to have the ability. Set up a partition. The class should be able to see which items the tester is holding up, but the subject should not be able to see. The class can record the number of correct responses and compare that total to whatever the chance level would be (e.g., 25 percent). You can choose to give the subject feedback as the trial proceeds or not. In some cases, you will also want to show the same card twice in a row, especially if the subject is being given feedback. Alternately, students can do this as a take-home exercise. You should, however, be sure to instruct them on order effects (i.e., if giving feedback, be careful not to use all four cards in every four-card trial).

➤ ROLE-PLAYING SCENARIOS

1. **Imagine that you have lost one of your major senses.** Which sense would be most difficult to lose? Why? Describe this situation as if it had actually happened to you. Next, imagine that you have lost only the ability to feel heat, cold, or pressure. How would you act? How would you cope?

2. **Place yourself in each of the following scenarios:**

   a. You are 40 years old, a college professor, and have never been able to hear. You lip-read and know American Sign Language. Describe your life and the reactions others have had to you.
   b. You are 40 years old, a college professor, and recently lost your hearing due to an infection that destroyed the structures of the inner ear. Describe your life and the reactions others have had to you.

3. **You suddenly become able to hear sounds above 20 kilohertz and to see infrared and ultraviolet light.** Try to explain what you are experiencing to a person with normal sensory thresholds.

4. **Ask a student to run through class and grab an item off a desk in the front (your purse, your wallet, your notes, etc.).** Try to express anger and surprise. While the student remains outside the class, choose a witness to question. Appoint two other students as inquisitors. These questioners should try to find out what the witness knows about the crime and which of the details provided by the witness are most reliable. Conclude by bringing the culprit back into view and discuss any inaccuracies in the witnesses' testimony.

5. **Set up a debate of the proposition that "ESP is a confirmed sensory process and research in this area should receive federal financial support."** Select two students to serve as the advocates for the proposition; select two students to oppose this statement.

6.   **Ask a student to mime the role of a person who lacks depth perception and who sees the world as if it were a flat surface.**

➤ VALUE-CLARIFICATION STATEMENTS

1.   Signs for public facilities should be written in Braille and positioned low enough to touch.

2.   It should be up to students to decide whether they can listen to lecture and do other activities (like other homework) at the same time.

3.   People who have their vision surgically corrected are just being vain.

4.   All traffic signals should have geometric shapes in addition to colors, to help people who are color blind (e.g. square for green, diamond for yellow, and circle for red.)

5.   Deaf people who can regain hearing through the use of cochlear implants should do it.

6.   All presidential and political press conferences should be required to provide a signing interpreter.

7.   Rock musicians should be prohibited from playing music at damaging decibel levels.

8.   Portable MP3 players like iPods, with headphones should be taken off the market because of potential misuse by children and damage to the children's ears.

9.   A person with impaired depth perception should not be allowed to drive a car.

10.   When children fall and hurt themselves (not seriously) the best policy is to tell the child to ignore the pain.

11.   It is impossible for parents to really understand how their teenage children perceive the world.

12.   Eyewitness testimony alone should never be allowed to determine the outcome of a trial.

13.   All juries should be instructed about the limitations of eyewitness testimony.

14.   Eyewitness testimony doesn't have a big impact on the verdict if the physical evidence is not there.

15.   Apparent examples of ESP are really based on coincidence.

16.   "Psychics" and other paranormal services prey on the uninformed.

➤ ONE-MINUTE MOTIVATORS

1.   **Sensation and memory.** Before beginning this chapter, put a series of objects (fruit, pieces of material, something made of steel, etc.) in front of the class. Ask students to describe these objects, in writing. At the next class meeting, pass the objects around. Ask students to explore them in more depth. After they have touched and smelled each object, ask them to again describe the objects. At the next meeting again ask students to describe the objects. This time, their descriptions should be richer and more detailed. Discuss how much sensory information there is in a single flower, leaf, or other common object.

2.   **Analogies for Senses.** Have students develop a series of analogies for each of the senses: Which sense is most like a video? A CD? A TV? A computer? A battery-operated child's toy? A balloon? A musical instrument? A tea pot? In what important ways are the senses different in each case?

3.   **Sensory Waves.** Drop a pebble in a dish of water. Watch the compression and refraction of the waves. If you use a clear glass pie plate, this can be shown to larger classes with an overhead projector.

4.   **Transduction.** A child's battery-operated toy musical instrument can serve as an example of a transducer. Pressing a key converts mechanical energy into an electrical current that activates a mechanical device that makes a musical sound.

5.   **Perception and awareness.** To demonstrate the idea that information is continuously flowing into our sensory system, but that it is not always attended to, play a tape of a waterfall or surf during your lecture. Ask students whether they feel they need to pay attention to information for it to trigger some kind of sensory response.

6.   **The human camera.** If you know a camera buff or a dynamic photography instructor, ask to have a camera taken apart for the class. Point out the parts that function in a way similar to parts of the eye.

7.   **Ishihara plates.** Although the reproduction of the Ishihara plates in the text is not adequate for formal testing, it is sufficiently accurate to allow detection of color-blind or color-weak students in the class. Usually such students can provide amusing anecdotes about their discovery of, or life with, impaired color vision.

8.   **Pupil dilation and constriction.** Ask students in pairs to observe each other's pupils. Flip a coin to select the "subject." Darken the room for a few minutes. Suddenly turn on the lights and have students estimate how many seconds it takes their partner's pupils to return to their original degree of constriction.

9.   **Gating pain.** Ask students to raise their hands if they are currently having a headache or other body pain. Then, do an in-class demonstration, or have them pair up and tell their friends what they're doing over the weekend, or give them some other distracter. Then,

138

ask if they had forgotten about their pain. This shows the influence of the reminding system and ability to "gate" the pain.

10. **Hearing in man/woman versus beast.** Bring a dog whistle and a dog to class. First have the class observe the behavioral response of a fellow student to "a very soft whistle." You may have false positives, so also fake blowing the whistle. Then bring in the dog and show the canine response.

11. **Sensation and evolution.** Humans tend to see their own species as the "most advanced" evolutionarily. Certainly, we have the biggest cerebral cortex. But other animals are equally "advanced" to be who they are. The hearing center in a cat's brain is, for example, much larger than a human's auditory cortex. Their vestibular system is astonishingly well developed. In what other ways is a cat superior to us? A dog? Why do humans not have all of these interesting qualities? What qualities are we lacking, and how do we compensate for them?

12. **Sensory adaptation.** The smell of ammonia, rotten eggs, or kitty litter could (if you are somewhat sadistic) be brought to class. Students rate the smell at the start of class and every 10 minutes after. Students will experience olfactory adaptation very quickly.

13. **Perceptual habituation.** Throughout the room, place a series of rags, some with nothing on them, and some with a distinct (but not too obnoxious) smell on them. Bleach is a good example. When they first enter the room, they will notice the odor, but as the class continues, their perception of it will fade. Toward the end of the class, send half the class out for some "fresh air." The other half of the class should attempt to locate the particular rags as quickly as possible. When the other half of the class returns after a few minutes, they will probably be able to locate the "smelly" rags more quickly, because their habituation will be gone. You can emphasize the concept by discussing how hard it sometimes is to locate a smell, even though you are sniffing around a room for it. Carpets are notoriously difficult surfaces on which to find an exact location. Briefly covering your nose with your shirt sleeve, however, will subsequently improve their ability to locate the exact location of the smell.

14. **Sensory adaptation.** Ask students to explain why individuals are often so insensitive to their own body and breath odor. How does sensory adaptation contribute to this insensitivity? How have advertisers tried to capitalize on the situation?

15. **Bringing order to perceptions.** Quickly demonstrate the factors that bring order to perceptions by grouping people within the classroom. Ask three students to stand near each other and ask a fourth to stand farther away; ask students wearing similarly colored shirts to stand together; ask students to create a large circle (note the distance between students) and then a closed circle by holding hands.

16. **Figure-ground processes.** Develop a five-minute video of close-ups of common objects. Show each close up and have students guess what the object is. Then show the entire object. Discuss how perceptual hypotheses and figure-ground processes explain the way objects are normally perceived.

17. **Perception in the cortex.** Use examples from *The Man Who Mistook His Wife for a Hat* (a reference is given in Suggestions for Further Reading) to remind students that our perceptions are the result of activities in the cortex.

18. **Optical illusions.** Visit one of the many websites that demonstrate optical illusions and present the pictures to students either as a power point demonstration, or as printed-out pictures. For a list of websites, see the multimedia resources section in this chapter of the instructor's manual.

19. **Perceptual learning.** How has perceptual learning affected your ability to safely drive a car? For example, what do you pay attention to at intersections? Where do you habitually look as you are driving?

20. **Perceptions.** Because perceptions are reconstructions or models of external events, we should all engage in more frequent reality testing. Can you think of a recent event when a little reality testing would have saved you from misjudging a situation?

21. **Visual restriction.** Ask everyone to bring to class a pair or two of sunglasses. Bring enough foil to cover one or two lenses on each set of glasses. Conduct class as usual. At the end, discuss how students felt to only have peripheral vision, partial vision, or one eye. Discuss the effects of glaucoma, cataracts, and other visual defects.

22. **Sound localization.** Divide students into pairs. Ask one student to sit with eyes closed. The other student claps to the left, to the right, and above that student. The above clap should be very difficult to localize.

23. **Monocular depth perception.** Pictorial depth cues can be demonstrated with a series of slides or transparencies. Ask students to name each cue and explain how it contributes to perceived depth.

24. **Altered perceptions.** Ask students to use a mirror to write their name, copy a geometric design, etc. Ask an observing student to note the nature of the errors made as their partner adapts to this new perceptual world.

25. **Contrast and perception.** Send three students outside to serve as subjects. Put three others in front of the class. Invite one subject in and ask the person to estimate the height of the middle student. Ask the middle student to remain; ask two other students to come up to the front. Invite another subject inside. The guesses should change depending on the height of the other two students as well as the height of the subject.

26. **Novelty and habituation.** Throughout your lecture, make a small but novel gesture every few minutes. The gesture should be something that would draw little attention if done once. Do students become aware of the gesture as it is repeated? Or do they habituate to it? Discuss their perceptions near the end of the session.

27. **Telepathy versus coincidence.** Provide students with apparent examples of "mental telepathy." In groups, have them decide how the following occurrences could be mere coincidences.

a.   "I suddenly woke up and knew that something tragic had happened to my mother. That morning I received the call that she had died at that precise hour."

b.   "My sister and I live 3,000 miles apart. We have never visited each other's homes. I didn't know what to buy her for a holiday gift but somehow knew she would like a specific set of towels. I was not surprised to learn that she had already bought one of that brand and color for her bathroom, and she needed the towels I sent to complete the set."

28.   **Eyewitness accuracy.** In groups, ask students to review the 12 factors affecting the accuracy of eyewitness perception and to devise a way to run an experiment manipulating each of the factors.

29.   **A day in court.** Have students visit a trial where eyewitness testimony is playing a significant role. Ask students to report back to the class on their observations.

30.   **Perception in the cinema.** Find a play or film that ends tragically because two people have inaccurate perceptions of each other. Discuss or reenact the concluding scene, showing how people can try to clarify their communication. Drama or speech students may want to perform a short vignette for your class.

➢ BROADENING OUR CULTURAL HORIZONS

1.   **Cultural approaches to pain management.** Various cultures have different approaches to pain management. Some groups suggest that pain should be ignored; others acknowledge pain but suggest specific ways to deal with the pain. What did the "mini culture" of your family suggest? If you suddenly felt pain in your chest, what has your culture taught you to do? Are these behaviors adaptive or maladaptive?

2.   **Culture and sensation.** Do various cultures emphasize different sensory channels to a greater or lesser degree? For example, do some cultures place more emphasis on touch, taste, or smell than North Americans do? What does the American preoccupation with television tell us about our culture? The French reputation for cooking? The Italian tendency to touch a person when talking to her or him?

3.   **Guest speaker—visual or auditory impairment.** Invite a hearing impaired and/or vision impaired person to class. Discuss the person's sensory world with her or him, with an emphasis on the subculture that exists among hearing impaired and/or vision impaired persons.

4.   **What's it like to be blind?** People sometimes mistakenly think that they can understand what it would be like to be blind simply by blindfolding themselves and stumbling around the room. But the loss of a major sense has huge implications that go far beyond the obvious. Have students brainstorm what life is like for a blind person. When they are finished, add any examples from areas that they had not considered. Examples include: identifying who is at your door, disrupted sleep patterns, availability and type of employment, buying groceries, choice of friends, using transportation, etc.

5.   **Alternative methods of pain management.** Westerners tend to take medications to control pain (ASA, acetaminophen, etc.), but in many parts of the world pharmaceuticals

are not as readily available, and not as valued as they are here. What are some of the ways that other cultures deal with pain? Discuss how pain is managed through meditation, voodoo, hypnosis, etc. Your students might be surprised to learn that these techniques can actually create physical changes, such as using the brain to regulate endorphin levels. They might also be surprised to learn that voodoo is a cultural practice that is not just about curses and evil potions, but is a cultural phenomenon that encompasses a wide range of applications.

6. **Culture and taste preference.** Using a world map, try to characterize the traditional cuisine of various regions as hot and/or spicy versus bland. Do any patterns emerge? What hypotheses can be advanced to explain cultural preferences for spicy or blander tastes?

7. **Perception in additional dimensions.** Find a science fiction story that includes a fourth and fifth dimension (or have students write such a story). Discuss how our earthly existence constrains the way we perceive the world.

8. **Perception and familiarity.** Ask students skilled in languages other than English to share with the class the alphabet of the language and a few key words. Using Russian, Japanese, or Chinese characters is especially effective. Discuss how meaningless the characters or words may seem at first. Rewrite the letters each day on the chalkboard. By the end of the week(s), the words should become meaningful. Remind students that English appears just as meaningless at first to the non-English speaker as the characters or words appeared to the English speaker.

9. **Cultural perceptions of beauty.** Collect photographs of arts and crafts from several cultures. In what ways are the various styles perceptually similar? How are they different? How strongly does culture influence perceptions of beauty?

10. **Perceptual attributes in different cultures.** While some cultures may associate tallness with high status, other cultures value other attributes. Describe a hypothetical culture where shortness and age are highly valued. How would these differing values affect the social structure of these two cultures? How would they affect the way people are perceived in job interviews?

➤ SUPPLEMENTAL ACTIVITIES

TO THE INSTRUCTOR:

The following exercises are developed in this section to help students understand some of the concepts in this chapter. The author of the text discusses the notions of cutaneous threshold, auditory localization, and the taste sensations. These are three types of sensory experience that can be examined in the first three exercises, while the last three exercises focus on aspects of perception.

Exercise 4.1: Cutaneous Two Point Threshold

This is an exercise to demonstrate the threshold for pressure on the surface of the skin. To carry out this exercise you need a subject, an experimenter, and a device with two points. The two-

142

point instrument could be a divider from a geometry set or some similar item that has two points that can be set at varying distances apart with some way to measure that distance.

This exercise can be done as a demonstration with several students selected to be subjects or by dividing up the whole class into pairs with each one alternating as subject and experimenter. The latter would require a large number of two-point instruments. The procedure for this activity is as follows:

1.   Identify the subject and experimenter. If the class is paired, each couple can determine this. If it is a class demonstration, identify several subjects and an experimenter. You should direct the demonstration and not be either the subject or the experimenter.

2.   Blindfold the subject to be tested.

3.   Provide the experimenter, or the whole class, with the data sheet **(Handout 4.1)** that indicates the area of the skin surface to be tested and the type of test to make. The experimenter will touch the surface of the skin with one point or two, varying the distance between the points with each trial. The subject will respond with "one" or "two" when each contact is made.

4.   Record all responses until the subject can no longer distinguish between one and two points on successive trials.

5.   If this is a class demonstration, have students record the responses for each subject. If the students are working in pairs, the experimenter will record each trial. After completing the trials, the two will change places and repeat the procedure. Provide students with enough data sheets for all subjects to be tested.

6.   After all testing is completed, collect the data and work out the thresholds for each part of the skin surface tested.

7.   Students should note and discuss differences found among students and differences from one part of the body to the other.

8.   Ask students to explain why there is a threshold and why it differs depending on the area of the body involved.

Exercise 4.2: Auditory Localization

Locating the direction of sound involves the binaural cue of time difference. Auditory stimulation reaches each ear at a different time because sound travels relatively slowly through the air. This is called the interaural time difference. This exercise will demonstrate this phenomenon. The subject will attempt to locate a sound with only auditory cues. Students will see that sound location will be most accurate when the interaural time difference is the greatest and least accurate when the difference is smallest. In preparation for this demonstration, students should read the section on hearing in this chapter with particular attention to the discussion of auditory information processing.

The only materials needed are a blindfold, 12 noisemakers (such as a cricket clicker) that will give a clear crisp sound, and 13 chairs.

Procedure:

1. Set up 12 chairs in a circle to resemble the numbers on a clock. Put the 13th chair in the center facing six o'clock and away from the chalkboard.

2. Select as many subjects as you want to use and send them out of the room during the preparation time. You will need one, and might consider two, if time permits.

3. Select 12 subjects to occupy the 12 chairs in the circle, all facing the chalkboard, and provide each with a noisemaker. Each student will be assigned a number corresponding to the numbers on a clock dial, with the student farthest from the chalkboard number 6, and the student nearest the chalkboard number 12.

4. Ask the remaining students to be recorders. Each should be provided with a data sheet. **(Handout 4.2)**

5. Use a random procedure to determine the order of clicks. A good way would be to prepare 48 slips of paper with the numbers 1 to 12 (each number repeated four times). Draw these slips out of a hat. The order should then be put on the record sheets and on the chalkboard.

6. Admit the student subject, seat him/her in the center chair facing away from the chalkboard, and put on the blindfold. Instruct the subject to face straight ahead, listen for the sound, and indicate the location by naming a position on the clock, with 6 o'clock being directly in front and 12 o'clock behind.

7. The instructor or a student should act as experimenter and point to each location on the chalkboard, one at a time. The person seated at that location should make one clicking sound. Give time for the subject to respond and the recorders to note the location given.

8. After all 48 trials are completed, students should check for the subject's accuracy at each of the 12 locations, noting the size of the error for each.

9. If a second subject is to be used, the positions for the trials should be re-randomized.

10. On completion of the trials for all subjects, the class should determine the average size of the error at each of the 12 positions.

11. Some questions for discussion:

    a. Is there a pattern to the error size? Where is it greatest and where is it smallest?

    b. What is the explanation for the differences found?

    c. Would there be any value in moving one's head when the location of a sound is ambiguous?

144

d.   What would be the effect of deafness in one ear? Could the person locate a sound? Discuss reasons for a yes or no answer to this question.

(Based on a demonstration by Dr. William C. Titus, Arkansas Tech University.)

Exercise 4.3: Measuring Good Taste

"Measuring Good Taste" can be used as an exercise in sensory analysis. Students do need to be encouraged to think through the food they bring so that students do not taste 10 different brands of potato chips and so that student allergies are respected.

The student assignment sheet might look like this:

Your assignment is to work as a pair to find an unusual food to bring to class. Let me know ahead of time if you have any food allergies. Research the cultural origins of the food and the traditions associated with it. Be sure that you know the ingredients. Bring enough of the food so that 10 students can have a bite. Do not bring anything that needs to be refrigerated or that could spoil. Do not bring anything that is expensive for you to prepare or purchase. I will bring napkins and utensils. Bring to class a soda so that you can refresh your taste between food samples.

You will be using this form to rate each of the foods. As you begin to taste a food, smell it carefully. Taste it slowly. Focus on the taste, the texture, the temperature of the food. Rate the food. Then the provider of that food will tell us about the cultural origins of the food and its ingredients. Rate each food in the following way. Rate its saltiness, sweetness, and bitterness on a scale from 1 to 5: 1 = not very; 5 = very.

For example, if you feel it is quite salty, the rating would be a 4 or a 5. Copy the following list for each food and put your ratings in the spaces to the right of each taste quality. After the ratings are completed and the food is described, we will share our ratings. Is "good taste" fairly universal? Or learned and culturally relative? Or a little of both?

FOOD _____

SALTINESS _____

SWEETNESS _____

BITTERNESS _____

LIKING? _____

Exercise 4.4: Perception/Attention: The Stroop Effect

In 1935, J. R. Stroop developed an experiment, which now bears his name, on how we process conflicting sensory data. It is called the Stroop Effect. He found that conflicting sensory data slows down the process of perception and increases the chance of error. With a small amount of preparation, you can do the experiment in class.

This exercise may be done as a classroom demonstration or as an all-class project. If you choose the former, select several subjects (about five would be sufficient) and ask them to leave the room. You will then bring them back, one at a time, and test them in front of the class, who will be observers and recorders. The latter method, involving the whole class, would require a bit more work to prepare but should pay off in greater student interest. You would pair up the students, having one be the subject and the other the experimenter. The roles could be reversed to test the bidirectional effect.

Procedure:

1. **Prepare three word color sheets.** The words should be spaced equally on both the horizontal and vertical dimensions. The list and arrangement are found at the end of this exercise. Each of the sheets will be a list of four colors: yellow, blue, green, and red. They will be presented in identical order but in different ways.

    a. **List #1:** This list will be done in black or blue ink. All will be the same color.

    b. **List #2:** This list will not be words but color patches. Each patch will be the color of the word on the list. These patches can be done with crayons or markers and should be small rectangles of color with no words.

    c. **List #3:** The words on this sheet should be the same as on List #1, except that the words should be printed in color. The color used should always be different from the color named in the word.

2. **If this is to be a classroom demonstration, prepare your subjects, experimenters, and recorders.** Otherwise, pair up the students in the class and identify the subjects and experimenters, who will also act as recorders. Each experimenter will need a watch, which will measure seconds for timing the subject. The three sheets should be placed facedown in front of the subject in order of presentation. Reading each list will constitute a trial. In each case, the subject will be instructed to read the list from left to right from the top line down, as quickly as possible. When finished, the subject should say, "done." The experimenter will time the reading of each list and note it on the data sheet.

3. **Present List #1 and ask the subject to read the words in order.** When presenting List #2, ask the subject to name the color on the patches in the same order as before. For List #3, ask the subject to name the color of the ink in which each word is printed.

4. **Collect the data (Handout 4.3) for all subjects and work out a class average for each of the three lists.** If the Stroop Effect has occurred, you should find that the subjects took about the same amount of time to read lists 1 and 2 and longer for 3.

146

5.   **If you have time, reverse the roles of experimenter and subject and repeat the experiment.** The only difference would be in reading List #3. The new subject would be asked to read the words on the third list instead of identifying the color of the word. This may provide a different average time when compared with the average time for the first subjects.

6. **Some questions for discussion:**

    a. Was the Stroop Effect evident? Explain how it manifested itself.

    b. How can you account for the differences in average time?

    c. Did the change in the reading of List #3 produce a different average time? How great was the difference? How could it be explained?

(Based on a demonstration by William C. Titus, Arkansas Tech University.)

Exercise 4.5: Mental Telepathy, or It's in the Cards

You can easily demonstrate an ESP experiment looking for evidence of telepathy by using the Zener cards. The cards can be made if no real deck is available. The Zener cards are made up of five symbols, one of which is on each card. You should have 25 cards in the deck, 5 of each symbol. If you make your own, use heavy cardboard so the symbol cannot be seen through the back. Select five symbols that are easily distinguishable from each other. For example, you should not use a square and rectangle as two of the symbols because of possible confusion. The cards and symbols need to be small enough to be easily shuffled and large enough to be easily seen by the whole class when shown.

Duplicate Handout 4.4 so that each student in the class can participate as a subject. The sheet has a place for students to respond to each of five trial runs through the deck. The student can also tally the responses and work out the percentage of correct answers.

Procedure:

1.   Distribute a response sheet to each member of the class and explain how it is to be used.

2.   Shuffle the deck of cards thoroughly in full view of the class and place the deck face-down on the table.

3.   Pick up one card at a time, look at it carefully for about two seconds, and place it face-down on a new pile. Do not let students see the face of the card. While concentrating on the card, try to shut out any distracting thoughts. If you are preoccupied with running the demonstration, have a student, prepared beforehand, do the telecommunicating.

4.   Give the students time to write down on their data sheets the symbol that they think you saw on the card. Note the correct symbol on your own record sheet. Proceed through the deck in the same way.

147

5.   After completing a trial (one run through the deck), shuffle the cards thoroughly and go through the stack again. Repeat this until you have completed five trials, being sure to shuffle the cards before each one; keep an accurate record of each card for each trial run.

6.   After the fifth run through the deck, give the students the correct listing of cards so they can score their sheets.

7.   Ask the students to total the number of correct responses for each of the five trials. They can work out the percentage for each run by dividing the number right by 25 and multiplying by 100.

8.   Then ask them to total the number right for all five trials. Divide this total by 125 and multiply by 100 to get a percentage for the whole experiment.

Discussion: Ask the students to discuss their findings. They should first determine what they could expect to score by chance alone, i.e., by guessing. Then they can compare their scores with the chance score to see if they did as well, worse, or better. Do those who did better have ESP? In this case, do they have the power of telepathy?

Exercise 4.6: The Interaction of Taste and Smell

As the text points out, "flavor," as we experience it subjectively, is actually a combination of olfaction and gustation. This can be demonstrated relatively easily. Bring to class some apple, potato, and onion cut into tiny bits. Have a student volunteer taste bits of each while blindfolded. Discriminating between different foods should be simple in this condition. Next, test the blindfolded volunteer while he or she pinches the nostrils closed. With more olfactory cues reduced, correctly identifying the food bits should be more difficult (although not impossible). Even if they correctly identify the foods in the second test, subjects will usually report greater difficulty. Typically, they must rely more on texture than on "taste" when olfactory cues are reduced.

Exercise 4.7: Take the Pepsi™ Challenge!

How different do the major soft drinks taste? How good are people at telling them apart? This exercise invites students to find out for themselves and also allows them to see how much the sense of smell affects the sense of taste. You will be doing a taste-test on two groups of students: one group will be able to taste and smell and the others will be able to taste only.

Materials:
Disposable cups—four per student
One blindfold
Three bottles of soft drinks, either Cola or lemon-lime (Consider using two national brands, and one store-brand.)
A large bottle of water
Pre-lettered cards with the trade name of each soft drink
A small screen or barrier
Enough data sheets for each student in the class. Use **Handout 4.5**.

148

Procedure

1. Before the experiment begins, arrange cups in randomized order to prevent order effects and guessing (ABC, CAB, BCA, etc.).
2. As each student comes to the front of the room, he or she will be blindfolded.
3. Before each student takes a sip of each soft drink, he or she will take a sip of water, "swish," and swallow to cleanse the taste buds.
4. Each student who takes the taste test will have one taste of each of three soft drinks.
5. Group A students will take the taste test normally—water, cola, water, cola, water, cola. After each sip, the student will indicate what he or she believes the beverage to be.
6. Once the student has made his or her guess, you will hold up the card to the class that indicates the correct answer. Each student will record the result as correct or incorrect on **Handout 4.5**.
7. Once all of the "A" group students have done their taste test, move on to group "B." This second group will repeat the procedure, except that before each sip, the students will pinch their noses tightly so that they can't smell anything. Record the results as before.

Handout 4.1: CUTANEOUS TWO POINT THRESHOLD: DATA SHEET

TO THE EXPERIMENTER:

Some guidelines for doing this exercise:

1.   Be sure the subject is securely blindfolded.

2.   Apply even, firm, but not excessive pressure, with one point or two, as directed. You should avoid causing pain to (or breaking the skin of) the subject.

3.   Make exact measurements when setting the two points for each trial.

4.   Do not repeat any trials.

5.   Ask the subject for a response after each application of pressure.

6.   Do not give hints or clues to help the subject. Encourage the subject to make an immediate response.

7.   For each response made by the subject, put a 1 or 2 in the appropriate box.

© 2012 Cengage Learning. All Rights Reserved. May not be copied, scanned, or duplicated, in whole or in part, except for use as permitted in a license distributed with a certain product or service or otherwise on a password-protected website for classroom use.

Handout 4.1: DATA SHEET (cont.)

On the chart below, the distance (Dst.) between points and the number of points (Pts.) to be applied are indicated. Record the responses (Res.) of the subjects in the space provided.

lower back			palm			fingertip		
Dst.	Pts.	Res.	Dst.	Pts.	Res.	Dst.	Pts.	Res.
2"	1 2 2		1 1/2"	2 1 2		3/4"	2 1 2	
1 3/4"	2 1 2		1 1/4"	1 2 2		5/8"	1 2 2	
1 1/2"	1 1 2		1"	1 2 1		1/2"	1 2 1	
1 1/4"	1 2 1		3/4"	2 2 1		3/8"	1 1 2	
1"	2 1 2		1/2"	1 2 1		1/4"	2 1 2	
3/4"	2 2 1		1/4"	1 1 2		1/8"	2 2 1	
1/2"	1 2 1		1/8"	2 1 2		1/16"	1 2 1	
1/4"	1 2 1		1/16"	2 1 2				

Handout 4.2: AUDITORY LOCALIZATION DATA SHEET

TRIAL LOCATION RESPONSE   TRIAL LOCATION RESPONSE

1	____	____	25	____	____
2	____	____	26	____	____
3	____	____	27	____	____
4	____	____	28	____	____
5	____	____	29	____	____
6	____	____	30	____	____
7	____	____	31	____	____
8	____	____	32	____	____
9	____	____	33	____	____
10	____	____	34	____	____
11	____	____	35	____	____
12	____	____	36	____	____
13	____	____	37	____	____
14	____	____	38	____	____
15	____	____	39	____	____
16	____	____	40	____	____
17	____	____	41	____	____
18	____	____	42	____	____
19	____	____	43	____	____
20	____	____	44	____	____
21	____	____	45	____	____
22	____	____	46	____	____
23	____	____	47	____	____
24	____	____	48	____	____

Handout 4.3: THE STROOP EFFECT: WORD COLOR LIST

YELLOW	YELLOW	BLUE	YELLOW
GREEN	RED	YELLOW	GREEN
GREEN	BLUE	RED	YELLOW
RED	GREEN	BLUE	RED
GREEN	BLUE	GREEN	BLUE
BLUE	RED	RED	YELLOW

Handout 4.3: THE STROOP EFFECT: DATA SHEET

SUBJECT	TIME (in seconds)		
	LIST #1	LIST #2	LIST #3
1			
2			
3			
4			
5			
6			
7			
8			
9			
10			

Handout 4.4: TELEPATHY: DATA SHEET

TRIALS	1	2	3	4	5
1					
2					
3					
4					
5					
6					
7					
8					
9					
10					
11					
12					
13					

TRIALS	1	2	3	4	5
14					
15					
16					
17					
18					
19					
20					
21					
22					
23					
24					
25					

Handout 4.5: TAKE THE PEPSI™ CHALLENGE

DATA SHEET

Condition #1

Person #/ Name	Beverage A	Beverage B	Beverage C
1			
2			
3			
4			
5			
6			
7			
8			
9			
10			
Number Correct			

Condition #2

Person #/ Name	Beverage A	Beverage B	Beverage C
1			
2			
3			
4			
5			
6			
7			
8			
9			
10			
Number Correct			

➤ JOURNAL QUESTIONS

1. Blindness is a severe sensory disability. Other than true physical blindness, in what other ways may a person be "blind"? Do you think that you have any "blind spots" in your intellectual or emotional life?

2. What is the worst physical pain you have experienced? What were the circumstances? What could others have done to ease your pain? What could you have done?

3. What pleasant thoughts and memories do you associate with certain smells or tastes?

4. Have you ever experienced the equivalent of a "runner's high"? If so, under what conditions? If not, try to explain the interest (if not addiction) of some people to running. Do they run because it feels so good to run or because it feels so good when they stop?

5. Try to describe all of the sensations that you are aware of at this moment. What happens to your description as your attention shifts from sense to sense?

6. Describe a time you jumped to the wrong conclusion about a situation. Why did you or others "misperceive" the situation? What was the consequence of the misperception? What could have been done at the time to have prevented it from happening?

7. If you were to look through a department store catalog (such as a Sears catalog), what items would most gain your attention? What does this tell you about your interests and motives?

8. Describe a time you felt you experienced some form of ESP. What other explanations can you give for the events you have described?

9. Have you ever been a witness to a crime or accident? To what extent were you "coached" to remember the incident in a certain manner? Include informal coaching by others witnesses, those with something at stake in the accident, and so on.

➤ SUGGESTIONS FOR FURTHER READING

Alcock, J. E., Burns, J., & Freeman, A. (2003). *Psi wars: Getting to grips with the paranormal.* Exeter, UK: Imprint Academic Press.

Atchison, D. A., & Smith, G. (2000). *Optics of the human eye.* New York: Butterworth-Heinemann.

Boduroglu, A., Shah, P., & Nisbett, R. E. (2009). Cultural differences in allocation of attention in visual information processing. *Journal of Cross-Cultural Psychology, 40*(3), 349-360.

Boksa, P. (2009). On the neurobiology of hallucinations. *Journal of Psychiatry & Neuroscience, 34*(4), 260-262.

Bressan, P., & Pizzighello, S. (2008). The attentional cost of inattentional blindness. *Cognition, 106*(1), 370–383.

Cammaroto, S., D'Aleo, G., Smorto, C., & Bramanti, P. (2008). Charles Bonnet syndrome. *Functional Neurology, 23*(3), 123-127.

Dixon, M. J., Smilek, D., & Merikle, P. M. (2004). Not all synaesthetes are created equal: Projector versus associator synaesthetes. *Cognitive, Affective, & Behavioral Neuroscience, 4*(3), 335–343.

Escher, M. C. (2000). *The magic of M. C. Escher.* New York: Abrams.

Fields, R. D. (2007). The shark's electric sense. *Scientific American, 297*(8), 74–81.

Gegenfurtner, K. R., & Kiper, D. C. (2003). Color vision. *Annual Review of Neuroscience, 26,* 181–206.

Goldstein, E. B. (2010). *Sensation and perception* (8th ed.). Belmont, CA: Cengage Learning/Wadsworth.

Hollins, M. (2010). Somesthetic senses. *Annual Review of Psychology, 61,* 243-271.

Horgan, J. (1990). See Spot see blue; Curb that dogma! Canines are not colorblind. *Scientific American, 262,* 20.

Johnson, K. J., & Fredrickson, B. L. (2005). "We all look the same to me": Positive emotions eliminate the own-race bias in face recognition. *Psychological Science, 16*(11), 875–881.

Keller, H. (1991). *Story of my life.* Garden City, NY: Doubleday.

Robinson, J. O. (1999). *The psychology of visual illusion.* Mineola, NY: Dover Publications.

Sacks, O. (1990) *Seeing voices: A journey into the world of the deaf.* New York: Vintage Books.

Sacks, O. (1998) *The man who mistook his wife for a hat and other clinical tales.* Carmichael, CA: Touchstone Books.

Sekuler, R., & Blake, R. (2006). *Perception* (5th ed.). New York: McGraw-Hill.

Smith, Jeff. (1992). *The frugal gourmet: On our immigrant ancestors.* New York: Avon Books.

➤ VIDEO SUGGESTIONS

Feature Films

The English Patient (Ralph Fiennes, Kristin Scott Thomas). Drama. In the closing days of World War II, Count Alamay is returning from North Africa when his plane is shot down. He suffers burns all over his body. During the ride in a Red Cross convoy, Nurse Hannah realizes he is dying and that the trip over the rough terrain is too painful for him. Alone she takes him to a villa to die.

Senseless (Marlon Wayans, David Spade). Comedy. A college student (Wayans) earns some extra money by becoming a test subject for an experimental drug that heightens the senses by five times. He finds that his enhanced hearing helps him receive distant conversations, and his increased coordination boosts his hockey game. Comic situations occur when an overdose allows only four of his five senses to be operative at any given time. While a comedy, it provides some food for thought, reflection, and discussion about the senses. In discussing this film, it may be advisable to recall with the students the sensitivity necessary in dealing with those who are impaired in one or more senses. Nevertheless, even those with a sensory disability have provided humorous anecdotes as well.

Educational Films and Videos

An Introduction to Visual Illusions, (1970), Pennsylvania University, 12 min. In a brief time and with simple explanations, this film describes how the eye works and how the brain perceives distance, perspective, and movement. It illustrates over 20 visual illusions, including depth, direction, extent, afterimages, reverse relief, diversion, and perceived movement. It also illustrates size variance as related to vertical/horizontal positioning and gamma movement caused by variations in light intensity. The film is designed for introductory psychology and science classes, so no complex terminology is included. It provides some memorable visual examples.

Color, (2000), Films for the Humanities and Sciences, 23 min. The perception of colors, the relationship between psychological responses and physical phenomena, and how colors are used in inks and paints.

Controlling Pain, (1995), Films for the Humanities and Sciences, 23 min. In this video, the complex process of pain is described. Additionally, it discusses ongoing research to find ways to alleviate pain, including chemicals and electrical stimulation techniques.

ESP—The Human "X" Factor, Indiana University, 30 min. Illustrates extrasensory perception and interviews J. B. Rhine.

Experimental Parapsychology, (1977), CTV Television Network Ltd., 145 min. Looks at the problems and patterns of alleged cases of paranormal events. Program contains a series of five cassettes, 29 minutes each.

Hearing Conservation, International Film Bureau, 22 min. This film discusses the prevention of environmentally caused hearing loss.
Hearing Things, Filmmakers, 55 min.

Inverted Vision, from *The Brain Series Teaching Modules,* 2nd Edition #10, Annenberg, 5:04 This video clearly illustrates the difference between sensation and perception for the student. It shows a woman adjusting her normal daily activities to seeing things upside down through special lenses during the course of a week. At the end of a week, she removes the glasses and finds that she has to readjust to normal conditions, but this takes place in only a few hours as opposed to a week.

An Introduction to Visual Illusions, Pyramid, 17 min.

Managing Pain, (1995), Films for the Humanities and Sciences, 18 min.

Perception: the Theories, from *The Psychology of Learning: Part Seven,* (2000), Films for the Humanities and Sciences, 45 min. Can perception be explained in terms of sensation? In this program, the senses, including proprioception, are described; the Structuralist, Gestalt, Constructivist, and Direct Perception theories are critically analyzed, focusing on both their strengths and weaknesses; and perceptual models such as those of Ulric Neisser and David Marr are presented. Many examples of the perceptual theories are provided. In addition, the roles of Wundt, Wertheimer, Gregory, and Gibson are discussed, along with key perceptual concepts such as Weber's Law, the Principle of Pragnaz, and the laws of Proximity, Closure, and Continuity. An excellent overview of perception theory and various interpretations.

The Mind and Perception, Part Two, (1984), from *Using Your Creative Brain Series,* Educational Dimensions Group, 42 min. Discusses the psychology, biology, and sociology related to the perceptiveness of the brain.

Mystery of the Senses, PBS, 60 min.

Patterns of Pain, Filmmakers, 28 min.

Phantom Limb Pain, from *The Mind Teaching Modules,* 2nd Edition # 20 (2000) Worth, 4:29. This video is short and to the point. It presents a vivid example of phantom limb pain and raises important questions about the origin of the pain.

Secrets of the Psychics with James Randi, (1993), NOVA, 60 min. In this video, the Amazing Randi spends time debunking a number of parapsychological phenomena and demonstrating the P.T. Barnum effect. There is also a discussion about why humans want to believe in the supernatural. A thorough and fun presentation.

Seeing Beyond the Obvious: Understanding Perception in Everyday and Novel Environments, (1990), NASA/Ames Research Center, 45 min. Interesting and informative video focusing primarily on visual perception. The first half of the video is devoted to depth (both monocular and binocular cues). The second half of the video focuses on visual perception in novel situations (e.g., while flying a jet).

Sensation and Perception, Discovering Psychology Teaching Module 3, (1990), Annenberg/CPB, various times. The Discovering Psychology Teaching Modules contain excerpts from the *Discovering Psychology Series*. Module 3 in this series (sensation and perception) contains several interesting sections including: a discussion by Hubel and Weisel of visual processing, the rat versus man illusion, and an example of visual compensation. Students are fascinated by the Ames room, and in this program, the apparent size of host Philip Zimbardo increases and decreases as he walks the length of the room several times. The program emphasizes visual perception, demonstrates current experimental procedures in studying edge perception, and explains why it is important to our experiences of the world.

Sensation and Perception, Discovering Psychology Teaching Module 8, (1990), Annenberg/CPB, various times. The Discovering Psychology Teaching Modules contain excerpts from the *Discovering Psychology series*. Module 8 in this series (consciousness) contains several interesting sections including: training people to become lucid dreamers, the structure/function of sleep, and a demonstration of hypnosis.

Sensation and Perception, (2000), Insight Media, 30 min. This video illustrates how information about the world is gathered by sensory receptors and interpreted by the brain.

Sensation and Perception, (2000), from *Psychology- the Study of Human Behavior Series,* Coast Community College Telecourse, 30 min. Demonstrates construction of reality from senses, interpretation and organization into meaningful patterns by the brain.

Sensation and Perception, (2006), *Psychology Digital Video Library 3.0 Handbook,* from Thomson Higher Education, 19 min. A brief description of our sensory processes.

Sensory-Motor Integration, from *The Brain Teaching Modules*, 2nd Edition #11, (2000) Worth, 3:27. This video uses Olympic Gold Medalist Greg Louganis as a good example of sensory-motor learning and how natural talent, combined with expert coaching and untiring practice, work together to achieve perfection.

Smell, (1995), Films for the Humanities and Sciences, 23 min. This video tells students what is known about the complex sense of smell. The process of making scented products is also described.

Smell And Taste, (2000), Films for the Humanities and Sciences, 30 min. Life without smell and taste is almost unimaginable. Think of the important connections between smell and memory. Does a certain odor evoke fond remembrances? This program from The Doctor Is In travels into the nose and mouth to find out what causes these sometimes wonderful, sometimes dreadful sensations.

The Case of ESP, (1984), WGBH for Nova, 57 min. If you cover ESP as part of the unit on sensation and perception, this is an excellent video about formal research and business

161

enterprises dedicated to the study of ESP in the areas of archaeology, criminology, and warfare. It presents vivid replications of ESP studies, as well as rare footage of some Russian ESP experiments. Among the many topics for discussion it includes are precognition, psychokinesis, and clairvoyance.

The Doors of Perception, (1991), Insight Media, 58 min. This highly acclaimed video explores the means by which humans construct an internal representation of their external world. Includes discussions of consciousness and culture and uses the works of William Blake to illustrate important concepts.

The Man Who Mistook His Wife for a Hat, Films for the Humanities and Sciences, 75 min. This is a collection of case studies of patients suffering neurological damage. The film relates the case of Dr. P., a well-known tenor who has visual agnosia, a condition in which he can see but cannot make sense of what he sees.

The Mind's Eye, (2000), from the *Brain Story Series,* Films for the Humanities and Sciences, 50 min. Drawing on the experiences of people with rare forms of brain damage, this program featuring Dr. Susan Greenfield reveals the tricks and shortcuts used by the brain to construct its version or illusion of reality.

The Nature of Science, (1972), Coronet Films, 11 min. A look at some of the shortcomings of sensory experience as a primary source of information about the environment. Illusions are used to demonstrate situations where sensory experience is inadequate and to give examples of the ways in which scientific methods produce more reliable explanations.

The Senses: Eyes and Ears, (1985), Films for the Humanities and Sciences, 26 min. This film looks at the "distance senses"—eyes and ears. Viewers are shown a young reckless driver careening down a road, and are then taken into his eye where the image of the potential crash site is shown. Also seen are scenes inside an ear, showing how the linked bones vibrate to a sound, and a computer graphic shows how the eye focuses on an image.

The Senses and Perception: Links to the Outside World, (1975), Indiana University, 18 min. A look at the way in which sense receptors send information to the brain, which then interprets it based on the information itself as well as on past experience.

The Senses, (1978), Insight Media, 29 min. A basic treatment of sensation with primary focus on transduction.

The Senses: Skin Deep, (1985), Films for the Humanities and Sciences, 26 min. This film looks at those sense receptors that depend on contact with the immediate world: taste buds, touch sensors, and olfactory cells. These senses lie in the skin—the largest organ of the body—which also senses heat, pain, and pressure. The complex world beneath the skin is seen from the viewpoint of the root of these receptors.

The Sensory World, (1971), CRM, 33 min. This classic film does a nice job of summarizing the major sensory systems. There is, however, an emphasis on visual processing issues (e.g., color blindness, illusions).

Sight, Films for the Humanities and Sciences, 23 min.

Treating Chronic Pain, from *The Mind Teaching Modules*, 2nd Edition #21 (2000) Worth, 14:23. This video provides an excellent example of how psychologists and medical practitioners work together under a shared set of assumptions about cause and treatment of chronic pain.

Understanding the Senses, (1988), Films for the Humanities and Sciences, 56 min. In this program, renowned neurologist Dr. Oliver Sacks and other specialists reveal the beauty and complexity of visual, audial, chemosensory, and tactile perception. Sense-related phenomena such as proprioception and applications, like a device designed to sniff out dangerous chemical signatures, are examined along with sensory malfunctions including color blindness, phantom limb syndrome, and the inability to see motion.

Visual Information Processing: Elementary Concepts, from *The Brain Teaching Modules*, 2nd Edition #8, Annenberg, 9:11. This video reviews how the visual stimulus travels from the environment to the visual cortex. It will help both visual and auditory learners improve their understanding of the visual process.

Visual Information Processing: Perception, from *The Brain Teaching Modules*, 2nd Edition, Annenberg, 8:45. A good illustration of brain research on visual perception in animals. Especially informative is the confirmation of specialized feature detectors, such as lines moving in one direction but not another.

➤ COMPUTER AND INTERNET RESOURCES

PsykTrek 3.0
Unit 3: Sensation and Perception
Module 3a: Light and the Eye
Module 3b: The Retina
Module 3c: Vision and the Brain
Module 3d: Perception of Color
Module 3e: Gestalt Psychology
Module 3f: Depth Perception
Module 3g: Visual Illusions
Module 3h: The Sense of Hearing

INFOTRAC®

Below you will find two journal articles obtained from INFOTRAC® that relate to information contained in this chapter. Instructors should encourage students to utilize this invaluable resource to improve their research skills. Have students locate and read the following articles and answer questions relevant to each article.

Advanced Imaging, May 2007 v22 i5 p30(2) **Stereopsis: two eyes, one 3D image: precise depth perception can make a lifesaving difference in disease diagnosis and treatment.**

1.   What is stereopsis, what causes it, and what percent of the population has it?

   Answer: Stereopsis is the most powerful source of human depth perception; it is the response created in our visual systems comparing the views we get from our two eyes. Our eyes are separated by about 65 mm, giving each a slightly different view. The visual system determines the relative depth of different objects in the visual scene. About 95 percent of the population has stereoptic vision.

2.   How do machines create the same 3D image that our eyes create?

   Answer: Machines create 3D images in one of two ways. You can either put two cameras side-by-side and click the shutters at the same time, or you can render a second view by shifting the camera about three degrees so you create a left and right view.

3.   What are some of the medical applications of this technology, and how do they work?

   Answer: A stereoscopic digital scanner consists of two x-ray images of the organ acquired from slightly different points of view on a digital mammography unit. The x-ray source is rotated 10 degrees between the two exposures. Then the stereo pair of mammograms is viewed on a high-resolution stereo display. The doctor views the display wearing polarized glasses, enabling him or her to see in depth the internal structure. In surgery, a stereo view helps the surgeon's depth perception, making the operation even safer.

British Journal of Psychology, Nov 2002 v93 i4 p487 (13) **The Mind Machine: a mass participation experiment into the possible existence of extra-sensory perception.**

1.   Many forced-choice ESP studies have been criticized on both methodological and statistical grounds. Briefly describe/define the following problems critics have pointed out about ESP studies as mentioned in the above article.

   a. "Sensory cueing"

   b. "Optional stopping"

   c. "Stacking effect"

   Answer: (a) participants inadvertently detect and utilize subtle signals about the identity of targets; (b) researchers are able to conclude an experiment when the study outcome

164

conforms to a desired result; (c) a statistical artifact that can occur when guesses from many participants are all matched against the same target material.

2. The Mind Machine was built upon this previous research, and its methodology was developed for several reasons. According to this article, the Mind Machine was built to overcome five methodological problems. Briefly describe each.

    Answer: First, the study had the potential to collect a huge amount of data from thousands of participants and thus possesses the statistical power to reliably detect the small effect sizes reported in many previous forced-choice ESP studies.

    Second, it is widely acknowledged that carrying out large-scale forced-choice ESP experiments is usually problematic.

    Third, as noted above, many previous forced-choice ESP studies have been criticized on various methodological grounds, including sensory shielding, opportunities for participant cheating, and also having the target selection carried out by a pseudo-random number generator that had been fully tested prior to use minimized possible randomization problems.

    Fourth, again, as noted above, critics have correctly noted that some previous forced-choice ESP studies have suffered from potential statistical problems, including optional stopping and stacking effects. The Mind Machine was designed to overcome these artifacts by specifying the size of the final database in advance of the experiment and generating a new target sequence for each participant.

    Fifth, the Mind Machine methodology could incorporate many of the factors that have positively correlated with study outcome in meta-analyses of previous forced choice studies. Studies providing immediate, trial-by-trial, feedback to participants obtained significantly higher effect sizes than those giving delayed or no feedback. Also, experiments testing participants individually had significantly higher effect sizes than those employing group testing.

WEB LINKS

Knowledge Builder Links

1. Sensory Systems and Selective Attention
   Psychophysics: http://users.ipfw.edu/abbott/120/thresholds.html
   Units in Visual Cortex:
        http://www.science.smith.edu/departments/NeuroSci/courses/bio330/vision.html
   Selective Attention: http://www.alleydog.com/cognotes/attention.html

2. Vision
    Eye Anatomy and Information about Eye Conditions:
        http://www.tedmontgomery.com/the_eye/index.html
    Organization of the Retina and Visual System: http://webvision.med.utah.edu/intro.html
    The Joy of Visual Perception: http://www.yorku.ca/eye/thejoy.htm

3. Hearing, the Chemical Senses, and the Somesthetic Senses
    Virtual Tour of the Ear: http://www.audiologynet.com/anatomy-of-the-ear.html
    Taste and Smell Disorders:
        http://www.nlm.nih.gov/medlineplus/tasteandsmelldisorders.html
    American Pain Foundation: http://www.painfoundation.org/

4. Perceptual Constancies and Perceptual Grouping
    Size Constancy in a Photograph:
        http://psych.hanover.edu/Krantz/SizeConstancy/index.html
    Form and Contour: http://psych.la.psu.edu/clip/Perception.htm
    Figure/Ground in Graphic Design:
        http://www.usask.ca/education/coursework/skaalid/theory/gestalt/figround.htm

5. Depth Perception
    Gallery of Illusions: http://dragon.uml.edu/psych/illusion.html
    Illusions: http://kids.niehs.nih.gov/illusion/illusions.htm

6. Perception and Objectivity
    Context and Expectations:
        http://www.aber.ac.uk/media/Modules/MC10220/visper05.html
    Perceptual Learning: http://www.britannica.com/eb/article-9059188/perceptual-learning
    Ames Room: http://www.moillusions.com/2007/03/ames-room-video-illusion.html

7. Extrasensory Perception
    James Randi Education Foundation: http://www.randi.org/
    The Skeptic's Dictionary: ESP:
        http://www.hauntedengland.net/Parapsychology/ESP/Skeptic-s-Dictionary-ESP-
        extrasensory-perception-l340.html
    The Skeptic's Dictionary: Cold Reading: http://en.wikipedia.org/wiki/Cold_reading

8. Psychology in Action: Becoming a Better Eyewitness to Life
    What Jennifer Saw: http://www.pbs.org/wgbh/pages/frontline/shows/dna/
    The Innocence Project: http://www.innocenceproject.org/
    Avoiding Habituation:
        http://telephonyonline.com/mag/telecom_complexity_prevents_habituation/

166

Additional Web Links

Skeptics
http://www.skeptic.com/
http://www.randi.org/
http://www.csicop.org/webmaster/randi/

Seeing, Hearing, and Smelling the World
http://www.hhmi.org/senses

Sidewalk Illusions
http://www.moillusions.com/2006/03/more-sidewalk-chalk-illusions.html

Ishihara Test for Colorblindness
http://www.toledo-bend.com/colorblind/Ishihara.asp

Virtual Tour of the Ear
http://ctl.augie.edu/perry/ear/hearmech.htm

Optical (Visual) Illusions (see also sidewalk illusions)
http://www.michaelbach.de/ot/
http://www.colorcube.com/illusions/illusion.htm
http://www.exploratorium.edu/exhibits/f_exhibits.html
http://www.niehs.nih.gov/kids/illusion/illusions.htm
http://www.illusionworks.com/

Perception Online
http://www.perceptionweb.com/index.html

PSYCHOLOGY IN THE NEWS

Psych Central: Daily Psychology News and Headlines
http:/www.psychcentral.com/news/
Get daily updates and the latest in headline news.

Science Daily
http://www.sciencedaily.com/releases/2005/11/051106180409.htm
A source for the latest research news.

Alleydog.com
http://www.alleydog.com/links-sp/sandp.asp
A glossary of news and trends for psychology students.

CHAPTER 5
States of Consciousness

Survey Questions

Discussion Questions

Lecture Enhancements

Examining shift work

Circadian rhythms and evolution

Sleep deprivation

Circadian rhythms and study habits

What's in a dream?

Sleep disorders and sleep clinics

Sleep patterns and experiences

Guest speaker from a sleep clinic

Misconceptions about sleep

Stage hypnosis and trickery

The two chair trick and hypnosis

The Charcot pendulum

Hypnosis and crime fighting

Drugs and religion

Role-Playing Scenarios

Value-Clarification Statements

One-Minute Motivators

Stimulus overload

Thinking critically about sleep and dreaming

What's in a dream?

I'm missing my REM!

Introducing hypnosis

Hypnotic suggestibility

Meditative walking

What's it like to be an addict?

Debating party drugs

Why do you smoke? Drink?

Broadening Our Cultural Horizons

Are dreams valued?

Cultural pathways to consciousness

Is sleep valued?

Cultural sleeping arrangements

Accepting hypnosis

The value of meditation

Drugs and American culture

Drug use in different cultures

Supplemental Activities

Exercise 5.1: Time to Sleep

Exercise 5.2: Foods that Affect You

Exercise 5.3: Dreaming

Exercise 5.4: Relaxation

Exercise 5.5: Reducing Drug Abuse

Exercise 5.6: Experimenting with Drugs

Handouts

Handout 5.1: Dreaming: Data Sheet

Handout 5.2: Prevention of Drug Abuse

Handout 5.3: Drug Use Experiences

Journal Questions
Suggestions for Further Reading
Video Suggestions
Computer and Internet Resources

SURVEY QUESTIONS

Module 5.1 States of Consciousness and Sleep

Survey Question: What is consciousness?

Survey Question: What are the effects of sleep loss or changes in sleep patterns?

Survey Question: Why do we sleep?

Module 5.2 Sleep Disturbances and Dreaming

Survey Question: What are some sleep disorders and unusual sleep events?

Survey Question: Do dreams have meaning?

Module 5.3 Hypnosis, Meditation, and Sensory Deprivation

Survey Question: What is hypnosis?

Survey Question: Do meditation and sensory deprivation have any benefits?

Module 5.4 Psychoactive Drugs

Survey Question: What are the effects of the more commonly used psychoactive drugs?

Module 5.5 Psychology in Action: Exploring and Using Dreams

Survey Question: How can dreams be used to promote personal understanding?

170

➤ DISCUSSION QUESTIONS

1. What strategies do you prefer to alter your states of consciousness, e.g., music, meditation, daydreaming, resting, caffeinated beverages? Do you use alcohol to relax or get "revved up"?

2. How would your life change if you needed to sleep 15 hours per day? How would it change if you only needed 2 hours a day? Would you give up sleep if you could?

3. How do you feel about sleep? Is it something that you actively seek out, or do you resent the time required for sleep? Do you sleep-in when you have a chance to, such as on weekends? Do you enjoy afternoon naps? For each answer indicate why or why not.

4. Have you ever gone without sleep for an extended period? If so, what were your reactions? Your greatest difficulties?

5. If you have left your studying for a test until the last minute, are you better to stay up all night and cram, or are you better to get a good night's sleep? Why? Do you think that being underprepared or sleep-deprived will more negatively affect your performance on the exam?

6. Describe a recent dream you have had. How does it relate to your daytime experiences and feelings? What additional meanings can you find in it? Do you think that recording your dreams would be worthwhile?

7. Are you a "morning person" or a "night hawk"? Do environmental factors affect whether one is a "day" or a "night" person? Have you switched from one to the other at any time in your life? Are you more comfortable with one pattern or the other, regardless of environmental influences?

8. What is the longest you have ever gone without sleep? What symptoms did you experience?

9. Is the onset of sleep more like passively taking your foot off the accelerator? Or is it more like actively shifting into another gear (form of consciousness)? Explain.

10. Have you ever solved a problem in your dreams? How much control do you have over what you dream? Are you able to use "directed dreaming"?

11. Have you ever had the experience of remembering something and being unsure of whether it was a dream or whether it actually happened? How are we able to keep track of which things are dreams and which are reality? How do you know you're dreaming? What does it feel like?

171

12. Respond to the statement, "The REM state is not sleep at all; during REM we are paralyzed and hallucinating." Do you agree?

13. Compare and contrast the two theories of dreaming. In what specific ways and under what conditions could both theories be correct?

14. Why would amphetamines be helpful in treating narcolepsy? Why or why not?

15. What kinds of things are most likely to cause insomnia in you? What do you do when you are having trouble falling asleep or staying asleep?

16. If you have ever seen a stage hypnotist or participated in a hypnosis demonstration, how did your experience compare with Barber's analysis of stage hypnosis?

17. If students have not yet read the chapter, ask them: Do you think it is possible to hypnotize people to do things that they are not really willing to do? What factors (besides the actual hypnosis) would contribute to people doing strange or embarrassing things at the request of a stage hypnotist? Is it possible to hypnotize someone who doesn't want to be hypnotized? Can everyone be hypnotized?

18. Have you ever been in a situation that produced sensory deprivation (such as a commercial "flotation tank")? How did you react? Why do you think brief sensory deprivation is restful and longer periods are stressful?

19. Do you think that seeking altered states of consciousness is "natural"? What altered states does our culture accept? About which states is it ambivalent? What altered states does it clearly reject? How do you think such differences developed?

20. If a person is primarily interested in relaxation and quieting mental activity, what alternative forms of "meditation" might he or she find helpful?

21. What is the difference between "tolerance" and "addiction"? How would you test a drug abuser to see if either or both conditions are present?

22. For the students in the class who smoke, what is their motivation for smoking? Ask students: Which situations are most likely to make you want to "light up"? Do you want to quit smoking? Why or why not? How easy do you think it would be to give up cigarettes?

23. Do you agree or disagree with the idea that prohibition of drug use leads to adulteration, black markets, organized crime, unwillingness of abusers to seek help, and greater injury through imprisonment than is caused by the drugs themselves? What arguments can you give to support your position?

24. In the novel *Brave New World,* Aldous Huxley described an imaginary drug called soma that made people feel continuously happy and cooperative. If such a drug existed, what controls would you impose on its use? Why? If a drug that could enhance creativity were discovered, what use would you allow for it? What about a drug to improve memory?

25. A friend of yours suggests that the conclusions drawn about the long-term effects of marijuana are "correlational" and that other factors cause these effects. What other factors could play a significant role?

26. What would be the combined physical and psychological effect of cocaine, alcohol, and marijuana abuse? Why do some people engage in polydrug abuse?

27. How would you define the difference between drug use and drug abuse? Is it possible to simply "use" drugs like cocaine, heroin, or ecstasy, or is any level of use automatically abuse with drugs like these?

28. Suppose you are out for the evening and a friend offers you a "party drug" like ecstasy or GHB. Aside for the issue of not abusing drugs, are there dangers to party drugs? What are they? (e.g., ultimate source is unknown, composition is unknown, drug might be "cut" with impurities, interaction with alcohol is a risk, etc.)

29. Have you ever used over-the-counter stimulants, such as some energy drinks?

30. In view of their addictive qualities, should advertising be allowed for tobacco and alcohol? Should American tobacco companies be allowed to promote smoking in other countries where there is less public awareness of the health hazards of tobacco?

31. If you had a totally free hand, how would you handle this country's drug abuse problem?

32. Do you believe that Ecstasy (MDMA) is a dangerous drug? Why or why not?

33. Should marijuana be made legal for medicinal uses? Why or why not?

➤ LECTURE ENHANCEMENTS

1. **Examining shift work.** Invite the manager or foreperson of a local plant or military base, or a firefighter to class to speak about factors taken into account when scheduling employees for all-night or rotating work shifts.

2. **Circadian rhythms and evolution.** The premise of evolution and natural selection is that our circadian rhythms, sleep cycles, and duration of sleep have evolved because they were a good fit to the environment, and those with adaptive traits survived and reproduced, while those with less adaptive traits did not. Humans have a number of characteristics as a result of this process: we are diurnal (as opposed to nocturnal), we are medium-length sleepers, and we have a second, smaller sleep cycle in the afternoon. Explain to students that predators tend to be long sleepers, and prey animals tend to be short sleepers.

    Choose several species, including humans, and generate a list of characteristics that show evidence of natural selection. Generate a second list for the "opposite" members of the species that did not survive. Good examples are rats, lions, sheep, and humans. For example, "short sleeping" lions would burn too much energy and would be less efficient at catching prey in the daytime. "Long sleeping," nocturnal lions would rest during the heat of the day, be better able to sneak up on prey at night, have excellent night vision (probably also as a result of natural selection), and be able to hear better at night when things are quieter.

    Repeat this process for the other species, and then look at humans. Humans have poor night vision, and are not very fast or very strong. Therefore, it makes more sense to be active in the daytime to hunt and gather, and be less active at night to avoid accidents or avoid being eaten by lions! It's also colder at night, so it makes more sense to curl up with others. Humans are closer to the top of the food chain, so they don't have to go without sleep as prey animals do, and they can't afford to sleep all the time because they are not as efficient at hunting.

3. **Sleep deprivation.** Generate a summary table of how many hours of sleep your students typically get and/or need. If your students are typical, many of them are sleep-deprived and don't realize it. Many underestimate how much sleep they actually need. Ask students to brainstorm a list of signs of sleep deprivation. Examples include: falling asleep during boring meetings or lectures, needing a nap to get through the day, falling asleep while watching TV, feeling drowsy while driving, or falling asleep after meals or after consuming only a small amount of alcohol.

    Behavioral examples include needing an alarm clock to get up, repeatedly pushing the snooze button on the alarm, or struggling to get out of bed. Cognitive-emotional consequences of sleep deprivation include feeling stressed or irritable, having difficulty concentrating, or having difficulty remembering things.

Once you have your list, ask students to count how many of the signs apply to them. If your students are typical, most will say "yes" to three or more of the signs. Some will go as high as six, seven, or eight!

Once students become aware that they are actually sleep deprived, ask them to generate another list of things that they can do to get more sleep. Examples include spending less time on the internet, keeping a strict bedtime that will allow the right amount of sleep, etc.

4.   **Circadian rhythms and study habits.** Ask students to indicate when they do most of their studying. Divide the day into time intervals (e.g., morning, midday, afternoon, early evening, late evening). Tally the number of students who choose each timeframe. Depending on whether you have a lot of working students in your class, you can ask the question to determine actual study times or preferred study times. In other words, if students had no schedule limitations (e.g., on the weekends), what is their preferred study time?

After you have finished the summary, you can relate it back to daily cycles. For example, studying at night has the advantage of memory consolidation during sleep and dreaming, but it is also the time when people are beginning to tire. You can also discuss studying as it relates to consciousness. For example, failing to break up studying into small sections leads to distractions and daydreaming, some of which might be combated by drinking caffeinated beverages. The ability to focus one's attention might be influenced by things like music, household noises, and so on. Finally, students sometimes fall asleep while studying, especially if they lie on the couch to study.

5.   **What's in a dream?** In small groups, ask students to share recent dreams and the extent to which dreaming is related to physical exhaustion and psychological stress. Students can devise their own system for the categorization of dreams. They can then collect data from the entire class on dreaming patterns.

6.   **Sleep disorders and sleep clinics.** There are now hundreds of "sleep centers" around the country for the diagnosis and treatment of sleep disorders. If one is near you, you may be able to arrange a guest speaker or a field trip. For information on the nearest sleep center go to http://www.sleepcenters.org.

175

7. **Sleep patterns and experiences.** A very interesting class discussion can usually be generated from comparisons of individual differences in sleep patterns and unusual experiences associated with sleep. Look for people who:

   a. Sleep very little or much more than average
   b. Have been deprived of sleep for long periods
   c. Have done shift work or have maintained unusual sleep/working cycles
   d. Have a relative or acquaintance who has had sleep disturbances such as somnambulism, night terrors, narcolepsy, sleep apnea, or insomnia
   e. Have done problem-solving in dreams
   f. Have had lucid dreams
   g. Have kept a dream journal or attempted dream control

8. **Guest speaker from a sleep clinic.** Invite the director of a sleep clinic or a drug abuse clinic to describe his/her program. Ask a recovering alcoholic to share the nightmares he/she may have experienced after quitting drinking. Ask an AA member to explain why this program has been successful for many alcoholics. At some other time, you may want to discuss AA's limitations.

9. **Misconceptions about sleep.** While many students express great interest in the topic of sleep and dreams, it is a subject about which they have many misconceptions. J. Palladino and B. Carducci developed a Sleep and Dream Information Questionnaire, designed to assess student awareness of current findings in sleep and dream research. This questionnaire can provide an interesting and informative way to introduce students to this material. Student responses can also be used to tailor lectures to meet the needs of the class. Finally, after students take the questionnaire, the instructor can discuss the items in class, thus giving students immediate feedback. Copies of the questionnaire, an appendix entitled "Explanation of Items Comprising the Sleep and Dream Information Questionnaire," and reprints are available from Joseph Palladino, Department of Psychology, University of Southern Indiana. For more information see J. J. Palladino and B. J. Carducci, "Students Knowledge of Sleep and Dreams," *Teaching of Psychology,* (3), October 1984.

10. **Stage hypnosis and trickery.** For a simple but dramatic demonstration of the fakery involved in much stage hypnosis, try the following. Tell the class that one of the most reliable phenomena available with hypnosis is anesthesia or pain analgesia. Tell them that earlier you used self-hypnosis to make your hand totally insensitive to pain and that now you need only use a post-hypnotic cue to produce numbness.

   Stroke your hand as if you were putting on a glove and explain that this is the cue. Pinch your hand a few times as if testing to see if it has become numb. Ask the class to watch carefully as you strike a match (a paper match, not a wooden match) and hold the flame to the palm of your outstretched hand. The trick, of course, is to keep the match moving at all times. (You may want to practice this at home first!) It is quite possible to leave

176

very impressive "scorch" marks (actually soot) on your hand without experiencing any pain. Explain to the students what you have done and point out that many examples of stage hypnosis rely on similar deception and a lack of questioning by the audience.

11.   **The two chair trick and hypnosis.** The spectacular stage trick of suspending someone between two chairs (pictured in this chapter) is worth repeating in class. Have a volunteer recline as shown. Be sure the head and feet touch the backs of the end chairs. Ask the subject to lift and remove the middle chair. The subject should have no difficulty maintaining this position. Now place a book on the subject's upper abdomen (diaphragm area). With the volunteer's permission, lean on the book with both hands to show that the subject can support extra weight without hypnosis. Then note that the upper abdomen is the only place a hypnotist could actually stand or sit on the suspended subject. For obvious reasons the entertainer is not going to position himself/herself on the subject's knees, pelvis, or chest. The only workable position is just a few inches from the front edge of the chair—which is why subjects can so readily support the weight.

12.   **The Charcot Pendulum.** The Charcot pendulum makes a good demonstration of the core elements of hypnosis. Prepare three pendulums by tying a small weight to one end of three foot-long strings. A nut, pendant, washer, fishing sinker, or ring works well. In class ask for volunteers. Have them stand in front of the class. Each should hold a string (with attached weight). Proceed by giving suggestions similar to these:

> The Charcot pendulum has long been used as a prelude to hypnosis. Today I will not be hypnotizing you, so just relax. For the pendulum to work, you must be able to concentrate and focus your attention as I instruct you. Begin by holding the pendulum at arm's length and at eye level. Focus your attention on the pendulum. Notice its texture and the way the light reflects from its surface. Relax and take a deep breath. Watch the pendulum and focus on it intensely. Let everything else fade away until the pendulum is at the very center of your attention. Now I'd like you to begin to use your concentration to move the pendulum. Do not move your hand or body. Just apply the energy of your concentration to the pendulum. Try to push it away from you. Each time it moves away push again, with your eyes, with your attention. Push and release, push and release.

> Follow it with your eyes as it begins to move. Each time it swings out, push and release. It's as if a magnet were pushing and releasing, pushing and releasing. Relax and follow it with your eyes. Let it swing wider and wider. Push, release (and so forth).

With continued suggestions such as these, most subjects will respond by swinging the pendulum in a broad arc. When questioned they will deny that they consciously moved the hand. The major point here is that the pendulum seems to move of its own accord, aided only by the "concentration" of the subjects. In this respect the experience is similar to hypnosis. Suggestion brings about a temporary suspension of reality testing and conscious intention, a change essential to hypnosis.

13. **Hypnosis and crime fighting.** Ask students to search the Internet for articles on the use of hypnosis for the solving of crimes. Print and make copies of the articles. Ask students to critically evaluate whether the memories were actually recalled or reconstructed. Discuss the problems of using hypnosis in court.

14. **Drugs and religion.** Debate statement: "If a drug is a recognized part of a religious ceremony, its use should be protected by the Bill of Rights." Students can discuss the preceding debate statement in pairs or in small groups. Then they can be provided with the information on the Native American Church, after which the issue can be discussed further. This is also a good launching point for a discussion of cultural differences in patterns of drug use and attitudes toward drugs.

The Native American Church

The Native American Church (also called Peyotism or the Peyote religion) is a widespread religious movement among North American Indians. The name of the religion comes from the use of the Peyote cactus tops as one of the sacraments of the religious ceremony. The tops contain mescaline, a drug that has hallucinogenic effects.

Many Indian groups have actively practiced this religion from the mid-19th century through current times. The religion first developed among the Kiowa and Comanche of Oklahoma. After 1891, the religion spread rapidly as far as Canada, and it is now practiced among more than 50 tribes. In 1965, it is estimated that one-third of the Oklahoma Indians practiced this religion. The Native American Church reports to have over 225,000 members.

The Native American Church combines Indian and Christian beliefs. Members believe in one supreme God (the Great Spirit) who guides men through "spirits." For example, the traditional water bird or thunderbird is the spirit that carries prayers to God. Christians see Jesus as God's messenger; often peyote itself is viewed as the vehicle God created for communicating with mankind.

The process of eating peyote helps people commune with God and with the spirits of people who have died and to receive spiritual strength, help, and healing. The ritual usually takes place in a tepee, with tribe members gathered around a crescent-shaped, earthen altar mound and a sacred fire. At around 8:00 p.m. Saturday, the tribe Chief begins the ceremony of prayer, singing, the sacramental eating of peyote, a series of water rituals, and time for meditation. The ceremony continues through the night.

At midnight, special songs are sung and testimonials are expressed until dawn. The ceremony ends with a communion breakfast on Sunday morning. Church members are encouraged to follow "the Peyote Road." The life values include the importance of the family, of giving and supporting others, and of maintaining self-support through steady work and avoidance of alcohol.

178

This religion has been persecuted by the non-Indian culture since its inception. It was banned by government agents in 1888 and later by 15 states. In the 1960s, anthropologists and others confirmed that the use of peyote is central to the beliefs of this religion. The right of the Native American Church to express its religion has been upheld in several state supreme courts.

➢ ROLE-PLAYING SCENARIOS

1. **You own a travel agency, and you are planning a five-day business trip to New York City for one of your clients.** What factors would you take into account when scheduling the flights? What can your client do to minimize jet lag?

2. **Why should a student try to get a REM-filled night of sleep the evening before a major exam?** Tell a fellow student about the value of sleep and variations in sleep quality.

3. **Pretend your room-mate is experiencing insomnia.** Give that person advice on how to solve the problem.

4. **Imitate the snoring of family members.** In most households, somebody snores. Imitations of snoring patterns are useful for helping students recognize the difference between normal snoring and sleep apnea or obstructed airway snoring. Students will typically find this humorous, but encourage those with relatives with abnormal snoring patterns to get assessed for possible sleep apnea.

3. **What arguments would you present to a friend to convince her or him to stop smoking?**

4. **What arguments would you present to a friend to convince him or her to stop using a recreational drug like Ecstasy? Marijuana?**

5. **Once a person has succeeded in quitting smoking for a month, what would the person have to do to maintain this change in behavior?** Give your friend some suggestions.

6. **Act out the role of a person who is increasingly abusing alcohol but continues to ignore the warning signs.**

7. **Act out some of the social pressures to drink, smoke, or take drugs.** Have students break into threes or small groups. One person (or half the group) should be the persuader(s) and half should be the refuser(s). Different groups can be assigned to different substances for the sake of the exercise; i.e., some groups will be smoking, while others will be drinking, etc. One person should be the secretary and write down the dialogue. Ask the persuader(s) to try to get a person to drink (or drink to excess), smoke,

179

or take marijuana or party drugs. The others should do their best to articulate their refusal. Emphasize that "just saying no" leaves the door open to other persuasive attempts and is a weak strategy. In each case, the responses should be age specific; e.g., for smoking, it would be teenagers.

8.   **You are running an "alcoholism rehabilitation" clinic.** What factors would you take into account in planning the therapy for a specific client? Imagine talking to a prospective client.

9.   **How would you go about trying to convince an alcoholic friend or relative to get treatment?** What could you do before the person "hits bottom"?

➤ VALUE-CLARIFICATION STATEMENTS

1.   It is unrealistic to think that people will ever stop experimenting with ways to alter consciousness.

2.   Most people could reduce their sleep time to about six hours per night without a significant loss of alertness or productivity.

3.   It is less likely a marriage will last if one spouse is a "day" person and the other is a "night" person than if their circadian rhythms are similar.

4.   People who sleep more than eight hours are lazy or depressed, or they are probably using sleep to avoid some responsibility in their life.

5.   Dreams are simply random neurological activity and mean absolutely nothing.

6.   Trying to remember one's dreams is both futile and of no value.

7.   There is nothing wrong with stage-hypnotism; everyone has fun and nobody gets hurt or exploited.

8.   The use of cocaine should be decriminalized.

9.   Binge drinking is a normal part of college life; there's nothing wrong with it.

10. There's nothing wrong with getting "stoned" on the weekend with drugs or alcohol. It doesn't affect the rest of my life.

11. Random drug testing should be required at all places of employment.

12. A person should be able to do anything he/she wants to his or her own body, including using addictive drugs.

180

13. It is hypocritical of adults to say that moderate alcohol consumption is acceptable for them but not for teenagers.

14. Marijuana should be legalized and sold in the same way that nicotine and alcohol are sold.

➤ ONE-MINUTE MOTIVATORS

1. **Stimulus overload.** Spend five minutes overloading the class with a videotape, a musical tape, three students reading different news stories aloud, and a thinking task or puzzle. Contrast this with five minutes of the dreariest and monotonous lecture you have ever given. Have students discuss their reactions to these brief samples of too much and too little stimulation. Suggest that each of us attempts to find an "optimal level of arousal" that is appropriate to the task we are trying to do.

2. **Thinking critically about sleep and dreaming.** Students are typically very interested about things that they have heard about sleep and dreaming. One example is the idea that if you dream that you are falling, and you hit the bottom, you will die. Ask them why this is an example of lack of critical thinking. Answer—because if you are dead, how is it possible to report what you were dreaming about when you died? And are there people who "hit bottom" and survive? Another example is the belief in precognition—that dreams can foretell the future. Remind them of the phenomenon of positive instances—when a dream "comes true," we tend to remember it. But we have hundreds or even thousands of dreams each year, and we forget about the ones that "didn't come true." Statistically, if you have enough dreams, some are bound to "come true." You can explore other myths that students may have heard.

3. **What's in a dream?** Students are often very interested in comparing their dream experiences with other people's. You can conduct a series of quick comparisons by asking for a show of hands for such questions as: How many of you remember your dreams regularly? Do you dream in color? Do you regard sleep as an enjoyable activity, or a burden? Are you a long sleeper or a short sleeper? Students can then volunteer their own questions.

4. **I'm missing my REM!** Ask students to think about how well, or how poorly, they slept when they took antihistamines or cold pills. Ask them to recall what happened when they went off these medicines. They will probably say they slept very well when taking the medicines but after they stopped the meds, slept poorly and dreamt a lot. That is because there is evidence that these medications inhibit dreaming or, at least, affect the sleep pattern. After stopping, however, there is a rebound effect, and dreams return full-force. Some students state that they feel they were at an "all-night movie" and woke up exhausted.

5. **Introducing hypnosis.** Ask students to close their eyes while you say, "Your body is becoming heavy," etc. Ask students if they felt at all hypnotized. If not, was their consciousness changed in other ways?

6. **Hypnotic suggestibility.** Ask students to predict their hypnotic susceptibility before they read this chapter. Then bring several students to the front of the class and make some of the suggestions from the Stanford Hypnotic Susceptibility Scale. Identify students who responded to most of the suggestions as good hypnotic subjects.

7. **Meditative walking.** Take students on the following meditative walk and discuss any alterations in consciousness they experience.

   Try to get comfortable in your seat. Close your eyes and begin deep breathing. Inhale through your nose and then exhale through your mouth, sitting deeper and deeper in the chair with each breath. Continue deep breathing as I talk. If your mind wanders away from what I am saying, let your thoughts go for a moment then pull them back.

   Imagine that you are in a beautiful green meadow. You can feel the warm but shaded sun on your arms and your legs. Your feet are bare, and you are walking down a dirt path. Your right foot is on the warm, soft dirt; your left foot is on cool grass. Watch yourself walk. Look at the rhythm of your movement as you focus on your left foot, then your right, then your left, then your right. Continue walking until you get to the end of the meadow and begin hearing and smelling the ocean. Watch yourself come out into a very warm clearing where suddenly the beach is in front of you. You walk down four warm, wooden steps, first putting down your left foot, then your right, then your left, then your right.

   Once on the beach you pause and listen very carefully to the surf. Hear the waves build up, break, roll into shore, and pull back out. Begin walking into the surf. Watch yourself get closer and closer to the water. Now you are on crusty sand that was wet a few hours ago. Hear it crunch as you walk. Now you are on moist sand; feel the coolness. Now you have stepped into the cool, very pleasant water. Watch yourself walking farther into the water. Feel the water at your ankles, then at your mid calf, then at your knees, and finally at your mid thigh. Pause to listen to the surf, to hear the birds, to smell the sea.

Take from a pocket in your shorts a list of 10 worries that you have. Read that list very slowly: 1, 2, 3, 4, 5, 6, 7, 8, 9, 10. You realize that you haven't even thought about those worries since you began your walk in the meadow. You realize that there is nothing you can do now to deal with these issues. You take your list and you tear up the biodegradable paper and toss the shreds into the sea beside you. You watch your worries scatter, the ink fading, and you let go of all worries for the moment. Then you look up at the sun and feel the glorious warmth on your face and your arms. You turn and begin walking back to the shore, feeling the water at your thighs, then at your knees, then at your mid-calf, and then at your ankles. When you get to the shore, you see a very special person about 100 feet from you at the end of the beach. This is the person in your life who is most able to comfort, support, and inspire you. You watch yourself approach this person; you watch yourselves embrace; you hear yourself describe one problem that you did not think you could handle yourself, but you hear yourself resolve the issue.

8. **What's it like to be an addict?** Ask a student to role-play the feelings of the cocaine addict. Others in class could verbalize the feelings of the addict's spouse, children, parents, and employer.

10. **Debating party drugs.** Set up a debate on the topic of party drugs, e.g., MDMA (Ecstasy), with one side taking the position that MDMA is a harmful drug and the other side taking the position that it is no more harmful than alcohol.

11. **Why do you smoke? Drink?** When discussing drugs, students often think of "street drugs" and forget other drugs, including alcohol and tobacco. Depending on the mix of students in your class, you can either discuss or have them anonymously write down why they use these drugs. Some students will know their reasons for use, while others may never have thought about the reasons, and may answer with "I just do."

➤ BROADENING OUR CULTURAL HORIZONS

1. **Are dreams valued?** What meaning or importance does American culture give to dreams? Do you think that this applies to other cultures? Do you think that it is appropriate? Did you discuss dreams in your family?

2. **Cultural pathways to consciousness.** The members of many cultures seek altered states of consciousness as pathways to enlightenment and personal power. What are the predominant means of altering consciousness in our culture? Are any of them potential pathways for personal growth?

3. **Is sleep valued?** Biologically, humans are "preprogrammed" to have one major sleep cycle at night and another short one in mid afternoon. In some cultures, a *Siesta* is the norm, while in other cultures people are expected to remain awake all day. Other cultures may emphasize practices that lead to sleep deprivation, such as working long hours, socializing until late at night, and getting up early in the morning. What attitudes does your culture have toward sleep? If you have a culturally diverse class, you can ask students about their cultures' attitude toward sleep. If not, you can assign this as a mini research project. (Internet key words: cultural sleep attitudes)

4. **Cultural sleeping arrangements**. "Rules" about sleeping vary from one culture to another. In North America, children typically sleep in individual beds, in a different room from their parents. How do sleeping arrangements vary across cultures, and what effect does this have on sleep? (Internet key words: cultural sleep patterns)

5. **Accepting hypnosis.** Since hypnosis depends on suggestion, do you think that a person could be hypnotized if he or she grew up in a culture that did not recognize this state or have a name for it? How much are we prepared to be hypnotized by believing that hypnosis exists?

7. **The value of meditation**. In what ways is the "passive, alert" state sought in meditation at odds with mainstream values in North American culture?

8. **Drugs and American Culture**. What role do drugs play in American culture? In your life? To what extent is your use of drugs (including non-prescription drugs) an expression of cultural patterns and values?

9. **Drug use in different cultures.** What cultural values do you think would increase the likelihood of drug use or abuse? What similarities would you guess would exist among drug abusers in various cultures, regardless of their gender, race, or ethnic background?

➤ SUPPLEMENTAL ACTIVITIES

TO THE INSTRUCTOR:

This chapter in the text has a varied collection of topics. It is good to engage the students in looking at some experiences they have had that fall into one or another of these categories. Two types of altered states have been singled out for these exercises. You could select any others that appeal to you. The main objective is for students to become aware of their own experiences and begin to examine them more objectively. Understanding the dynamics of these experiences makes them more meaningful.

Exercise 5.1: Time to Sleep
Ask students to have someone sit near them as they go to sleep and time how long it takes them to fall asleep. Have the observer write down any unusual movements, e.g., hypnic jerks, eye movements (REM), etc. Have students use this information to discuss similarities and differences in class.

Exercise 5.2: Foods that Affect You
Ask students to keep a food diary for a week and write down what and when they have eaten throughout the day. Then, each morning, have them note how well they slept that night. Were they restless? Did they have nightmares? Did they sleep extra well, etc.? Let them check and see if there are any relationships between food eaten, the time the food was eaten, and quality of sleep.

Exercise 5.3: Dreaming
Everyone dreams, but few people remember their dreams, and those who do find that the memory of the dream seems to fade away soon after awakening. To analyze the dream, the student must record it as soon as possible after waking. Suggest that students purchase a book or use the forms provided for this exercise. Students should write down the substance of a dream each day for about a week. The following items should be recorded on **Handout 5.1** each time that dreaming has occurred:

1. The main actions and events in the dream, including persons known or unknown, who appear.

2. Events of the day (or days) prior to the dream that were significant to the student, even if they seem unrelated to the dream. Ask them to pay particular attention to major events and also to those thoughts or activities that preceded going to bed. After doing this for a couple of days, students should become adept at it.

3. After these items have been collected for a few days, ask students in class to form groups of three to discuss the dreams. Group discussion is best because individuals often do not see connections between their own dreams and past events, but others do because they

are not personally involved. Some of the more interesting findings should be shared with the whole class.

4.   Compare the findings in class with the discussion about dreams in the text. Do they support the author's ideas about dreams and their origins?

Exercise 5.4: Relaxation

Altered states such as hypnosis and meditation require the subject to relax. Relaxation is not always easy to achieve, and most people need to work at it to do it successfully. Biofeedback techniques can help people learn to relax and gain control of their bodies. Students can discover how easy it is to relax, even in the classroom, by a simple exercise. Having experienced the benefits of relaxation of the whole body, the students will want to do it again. They will find it easier to cope with stress and anxiety if they can gain control of their bodies through relaxation.

1.   **This exercise requires students to:**
       a.   Clear their minds of all thoughts.
       b.   Consciously relax their muscles.
       c.   Breathe deeply and regularly.
       d.   Concentrate on relaxing and breathing.

2.   **Procedure:**
       a.   Ask students to sit comfortably in their chairs and close their eyes.
       b.   Ask them to clear their minds of all thoughts, try not to think about anything, and listen to your voice.
       c.   Tell them to breathe deeply and slowly, in and out, in and out. You should set the pace very carefully so they hold each breath and exhale slowly.
       d.   Tell the students to continue to do this as they begin to relax their muscles. First relax the toes; feel the toes relaxing. Then move to the feet, thighs, back, fingers, arms, chest, etc., progressing to the top of the head.
       e.   Remind them periodically to keep breathing deeply in and out.
       f.   As the exercise proceeds, you can interject relaxing scenes such as a tree swaying in the breeze, blue water on a lake, waves lapping at a shore, etc.
       g.   This exercise should take only about five minutes. To terminate it, stop talking and let the students sit quietly for a minute or two. Gradually each one will return from the activity relaxed and refreshed.

3.   **Discussion:**
       a.   Ask students to comment on:
              1.   How they felt after the exercise
              2.   What they felt during the exercise
              3.   Their confidence (or lack of it) in the exercise before it started
              4.   Their feeling about the effectiveness of the exercise after it is over
       b.   Discuss the use of relaxation as a way to deal with stress in daily life.

186

Exercise 5.5: Reducing Drug Abuse

Many experts believe that prevention through education and early intervention—rather than tougher enforcement—is the answer to drug problems (MacCoun, 1993). Drug expert Robert Julien (1998) suggests that a rational approach to reducing drug abuse should include at least the following elements:

- Drug education to discourage experimentation with drugs
- A scientifically based legal system for classifying psychoactive drugs
- A definition of "responsible use" that takes into account risk factors such as the drug used, and the time and place it is used (for instance, we currently make a distinction between drinking at a party and drinking while driving)
- Limits on pro-drug advertising, including ads for tobacco and alcohol and sponsorship of sporting events
- Taxes to discourage the purchase of legal drugs and to pay for the damage they cause
- Adults willing to set an example by using drugs responsibly, or not at all

Have students break into small groups, and ask each group to pick a different suggestion and come to a conclusion as to the effectiveness of the suggestion they've been given to work on. **(Handout 5.2)**

Exercise 5.6: Experimenting With Drugs

This exercise should ONLY be attempted if you have a large class where students cannot be identified by their responses. In addition, you might wish to have students complete this at home so that others cannot see their responses in class. Students should return the survey to you folded over for privacy. It should be stressed that they should NOT put their names on their papers. Alternately, they can record their responses on a scantron for easy tabulation.

Handout 5.3 asks a number of questions about drug use. Once you receive responses back, you can tabulate the results and discuss them at the next class session. The discussion should be general in nature. Giving exact numbers of responses should be either avoided, or care should be taken not to give data that would likely identify any student.

187

Handout 5.1: DREAMING: DATA SHEET

TO THE STUDENT: Record on this sheet the answers to the following questions about your dreams. Write your responses as soon as you awake in the morning.

1.   What dream(s) did you have last night? What happened? What people or animals were present?

2.   What were you doing or thinking about immediately before going to bed?

3.   What significant experiences did you have yesterday or in the last few days?

4.   Are you anticipating any important events today or in the next few days? What are they?

Handout 5.2: PREVENTION OF DRUG ABUSE

Do you think the suggestion your group has been given is an effective one? If not, what could you suggest to improve the effectiveness?

Such efforts might be a reasonable start in any effort to curb drug abuse. What do you think should be done?

If you were given the authority and resources to solve the problem of drug abuse, what steps would you take?

Handout 5.3: DRUG USE EXPERIENCES

Please answer the following questions honestly. Your answers will NOT be discussed individually, only as part of a class total. Do NOT put your name on the paper.

1. Do you currently drink alcohol?
a) No, I never have.
b) I used to, but I don't anymore.
c) Yes, I drink.

2. When you are out with your friends for an evening, what is your usual alcohol consumption?
a) I don't drink.
b) One or two drinks.
c) Three or four drinks.
d) Five or more drinks.

3) Have you ever been drunk?
a) no, never
b) once or twice
c) three or four times
d) five or more times

4) Have you ever passed out from drinking?
a) no, never
b) yes, once
c) yes, twice
d) yes, more than twice

5) Do you smoke?
a) No, I never have.
b) No, I used to but I quit.
c) Yes.

6) Could you quit smoking if you wanted to?
a) I have never smoked.
b) Yes – I quit already.
c) Yes – I can quit whenever I want to.
d) No or unsure – quitting is really hard.

7) Have you ever tried marijuana?
a) no
b) yes, once
c) yes, a few times
d) more than a few times

8) Have you ever tried "party drugs" (e.g., ecstasy, GHB, "special K")?
a) no
b) yes, once
c) yes, a few times
d) more than a few times

9) Have you ever used solvents to get high?
a) no
b) yes, once
c) yes, a few times
d) more than a few times

10) Have you ever used prescription or "over the counter" drugs to get high?
a) no
b) yes, once
c) yes, a few times
d) more than a few times

11) Have you ever tried drugs such as cocaine or heroin?
a) no
b) yes

12) Have you ever tried "meth" (methamphetamine)?
a) no
b) yes

➤ JOURNAL QUESTIONS

1. Spend 24 hours keeping a consciousness journal or use a tape recorder for dictating brief notes about the content of your "stream of consciousness." What thought patterns do you notice?

2. Describe a time when you wanted to stay awake, but sleep finally won out. What was the situation? How did you feel about losing control over your own consciousness?

3. Spend five days monitoring what you perceive to be your circadian "high" point. Have you ever slept with, lived with, or traveled with a person with the opposite kind of circadian pattern? How well did you get along?

4. Have you ever tried meditation? What was that like? Would you be willing to try meditation? Why or why not?

5. Record your sleeping patterns for a week. Write down the key events of the day, the time you turn the lights off, how long you think it takes you to go to sleep, the number of times you awaken and how long you think you are awake, the quality of your sleep, and if dreams are present, the general theme. What patterns do you see by the end of the week?

6. Describe any experience you have had with consciousness-altering drugs. What was the drug? What was the setting? Were other people present? What expectations did you have? What were the short-term effects? What were the long-term effects?

7. Has anyone ever tried to get you to use drugs (including nicotine and alcohol) when you didn't want to? What kind of strategies did that person use to try to convince you? How difficult was it to refuse? Were the strategies effective in persuading you?

8. Most people engage in some moderately compulsive behavior that they feel they have little control over and where the consequences of the behavior are ignored. Describe your compulsion (or the compulsion of someone you know well). Does this give you any insight into the compulsive behavior of someone who abuses drugs?

9. Keep a dream journal. What do the patterns of your dreams seem to say to you about your behavior and emotional life?

➤ SUGGESTIONS FOR FURTHER READING

Chabas, D., Taheri, S., Renier, C., & Mignot, E. (2003). The genetics of narcolepsy. *Annual Review of Genomics & Human Genetics, 4*, 459–483.

Ellickson, P. L., Martino, S. C., & Collins, R. L. (2004). Marijuana use from adolescence to young adulthood. *Health Psychology, 23*(3), 299–307.

Freud, S. (1900). *The interpretation of dreams*. London: Hogarth.

Gackenbach, J., Bosveld, J. (1994). *Control your dreams*. New York: Harper Mass Market Paperbacks.

Hart, C. L., Ksir, C. J., & Ray, O. S. (2009). *Drugs, society, and human behavior* (13th ed.). New York: McGraw-Hill.

Hobson, J. A., Pace-Schott, E. F., & Stickgold, R. (2000). Dream science 2000. *Behavioral & Brain Sciences, 23*(6), 1019–1035; 1083–1121.

Huxley, A. (1932/2007). *Brave new world*. Toronto: Random House.

Huxley, A. (1954/2009). *The doors of perception and heaven and hell*. New York: Harper/Collins.

Julien, R. M. (2008). *A primer of drug action: A comprehensive guide to the actions, uses, and side effects* (11th ed.). New York: Worth.

Kuhn, C., Swartzwelder, S., & Wilson, W. (2008). *Buzzed: The straight facts about the most used and abused drugs from alcohol to ecstasy* (3rd ed.).   New York: Norton.

Laberge, S. (2009). *Lucid dreaming*. Boulder, Co: Sounds True, Inc.

Leonard, K. E. & Blane, H. T. (1999). *Psychological theories of drinking and alcoholism,* (2nd ed.). London: Guilford.

MacCoun, R. J. (1993). Drugs and the law: A psychological analysis of drug prohibition. *Psychological Bulletin, 113*(3), 497–512.

Rock, A. (2004). *The mind at night: The new science of how and why we dream*. New York: Basic Books.

Siegel, R. K. (2005). *Intoxication: The universal drive for mind-altering substances*. Rochester, VT: Park Street Press.

Van de Castle, R. L. (1995). *Our dreaming mind*. New York: Ballantine.

Yapko, M. (2003). *Trancework: An introduction to the practice of clinical hypnosis*. New York: Brunner-Routledge.

193

➤ VIDEO SUGGESTIONS

Addiction, (2002), Films for the Humanities and Sciences, 23 min. This program explains current research into why people become addicted, what puts them at risk, and what the best treatments may be.

Body Rhythms, (2002), from Psychology: The Study of Human Behavior, Coast Community College Telecourses, 30 min. Provides vivid examples of various biological rhythms and mental states and describes research on the stages of sleep.

Consciousness, (2002), from Psychology: The Human Experience, Coast Community College Telecourses, 30 min. Illustrates how our consciousness and awareness vary throughout a typical day, including a look at circadian rhythms.

Discovering Psychology: The Mind Awake and Asleep, Annenberg, 30 min. The nature of sleeping, dreaming, and altered states of consciousness are explored.

Sleep: Dream Voyage, Films for the Humanities and Sciences, 26 min. What happens to the body during sleep? This program explores the mystery of REM sleep, shows a computer display of the waves that sweep across the brain during sleep, and presents extraordinary footage of a cat "acting out" its dreams. The analogy of sleep to a ship on automatic pilot graphically illustrates how some functions must and do continue while the conscious brain is asleep.

Dreams: Theater of the Night, Films for the Humanities and Sciences, 27 min. Why do dreams occur? What do they mean? This provocative program looks at the facts and examines various theories of dreaming. The program visits sleep research labs to explain REM sleep and explore the dreaming brain through EEG technology. A patient's reports of recurring dreams are also examined.

Drugs: Uses And Abuses, (2002), eight-part series, Films for the Humanities and Sciences, 17-39 min. An in-depth look at various classifications of legal and illegal drugs, including the history, effects, and varieties of each drug.

REM Sleep and Dreaming, The Brain Series, Ch. 6, 8 min.

Sleep: A Prerequisite for Health, Films for the Humanities and Sciences, 18 min. We all think we can tough it out and get by without sleep. This program shows the enormous fallacy of this concept. Fatigue was a factor in the *Exxon Valdez* disaster, the *Challenger* disaster, the Three Mile Island incident, and the Bhopal chemical leak; it is likewise a factor in a large percentage of plane and car accidents; and medical personnel, too, are subject to the effects of fatigue. The program shows just how fatigue develops, how it affects reactions and reaction time, and details the value of "proper sleep hygiene."

Sleep Alert, PBS, 30 min.

Sleep Apnea, Films for the Humanities and Sciences, 20 min. Sleep apnea affects 1–4 percent of the population, most of which don't even know they have it; and 80–95 percent of cases go undiagnosed. This program explains what sleep apnea is and what causes it, how the diagnosis is made, and why it is so dangerous. Symptoms can include memory lapses, morning headaches, personality changes, and irritability. In a sleep lab, we learn about the C-PAP mask and how it helped one patient; another required surgery to trim his palate to stop it from blocking his airway. The program stresses the importance of diagnosing and treating sleep apnea.

Sleeping Well, Films for the Humanities and Sciences, 28 min. Forty million Americans suffer from insomnia. Another 56 million can't sleep because of pain. This program from *The Doctor Is In* provides specific information on how to get a good night's sleep. The topics of breathing disorders such as apnea are discussed, along with the conditions of narcolepsy and restless legs. Dr. Peter Hauri of the Mayo Clinic and Dr. Allan Pack of the University of Pennsylvania Center for Sleep Disorders offer tips on how to fall asleep and how to manage sleep when working night shifts or traveling across time zones. For parents, Dr. Richard Ferber explains ways to help infants and children fall asleep and stay asleep.

The Mind Hidden and Divided, (2001), from the Discovering Psychology Series, Annenberg/ CPB, 30 min. A look at how the events that take place below the level of consciousness alter our moods, bias our actions, and affect our health as demonstrated in repression, discovered and false memory syndrome, hypnosis, and split-brain cases.

The Sleep Famine: The Effects of Sleep Deprivation and Chronic Fatigue, Films for the Humanities and Sciences, 54 min. What are the consequences of living in a 24/7 world, where sleep is simply not a priority? In this program, researchers from the circadian, neuroendocrine, and sleep disorders section of Boston's Brigham and Women's Hospital as well as a broad cross-section of shift workers discuss sleep deprivation and chronic fatigue. Studies involving astronauts, truckers, and teenagers quantify the effects of light and dark on human physiology, long-term fatigue on life span, and tiredness on academic performance. The impact of fatigue on decision-making and the societal implications of time-shifting the circadian clock are also considered.

Understanding Sleep, A Discovery Channel Production, 51 min. Shot in part on the road with the often sleep-deprived White House press corps, this program illuminates the integral role rest plays in our daily lives.

Wake Up America: A Sleep Alert, Films for the Humanities and Sciences, 24 min. Sleep disorders are a national problem, affecting millions and resulting in untold accidents. This program covers: the functions of sleep and why some people need more sleep than others; circadian rhythm and events that can disrupt our sleep-wake cycles; the different kinds of sleep problems, including sleep apnea, insomnia, and narcolepsy; signs and symptoms of a sleep disorder and how stress, anxiety, and depression affect sleep patterns; the pros and cons of over-the-counter sleep medications; and the workings of a sleep lab.

COMPUTER AND INTERNET RESOURCES

PsykTrek 3.0
Unit 4: Consciousness
4a. "Biological Rhythms"
4b. "Sleep"
4c. "Abused Drugs and their Effects"
4d. "Drugs and Synaptic Transmission"

INFOTRAC®

Below you will find four articles obtained from INFOTRAC® that relate to information contained in this chapter. Instructors should encourage students to utilize this invaluable resource to improve their research skills. Have students locate and read the following articles and answer questions relevant to each article.

Family Practice News, January 1, 2005 v35 i1 p59 (1) About one-third of people with asthma report poor sleep quality.

1.   How did the researchers determine the asthma baseline for the participants of this study?

      Answer: At baseline, the patients had mild to moderate asthma based on measurements of forced expiratory volume in one second (FEV) and the Juniper Asthma Control Questionnaire score.

2.   What percentage of participants reported insomnia?

      Answer: Forty-five percent reported insomnia.

3.   Was there a significant difference in the groups at either baseline or after six months of therapy?

      Answer: No, there was not a significant difference; none of the drugs significantly improved or worsened the participant's sleep quality.

US Newswire, Oct 24, 2007 Mayo Clinic Physicians Report Findings from Research on Sleep Disorders.

1.   What are the health consequences associated with obstructive sleep apnea?

Answer: Daytime fatigue, sleepiness, and sleep-deprived bed partners are several symptoms commonly observed in patients with obstructive sleep apnea. More serious, however, are the cardiovascular problems associated with this sleep disorder. Obstructive sleep apnea may be associated with strokes, coronary artery disease, and metabolic problems such as diabetes.

2.   What are the suggested treatments for sleep apnea, and what are some of the challenges in delivering treatment options?

Answer: Immediate or near-immediate introduction of continuous positive airway pressure (CPAP) therapy is recommended for these patients, however treatment can be difficult to administer for up to 40 percent of these patients.

3.   Most people do not act out their dreams because our bodies prevent us from doing so and injuring ourselves or others. This is not true in some people, however. Why? What behavior is seen in these unusual people?

Answer: People with REM Behavior Disorder (RBD) might yell or move excessively during sleep. This condition is usually brought to physicians' attention when a bed partner reports being struck or physically harmed, or observes the patient harming himself or herself in the midst of a dream enactment.

Newsweek, September 27, 2004 p76 Altered states: Hypnosis can help with problems from anxiety to pain; how it works, and what it does in the brain.

1.   How does Dr. David Spiegel address the ironies about hypnosis taking away control of the subjects?

Answer: "It's actually a way of enhancing people's control, of teaching them how to control aspects of their body's function and sensation that they thought they couldn't."

2.   What state-of-the-art imaging technology was used in studies to document changes in the brain that occur when someone is in a hypnotic state?

Answer: Several studies using positron emission tomography (PET) have looked at what goes on in the brain during hypnosis.

3.   Give two examples of how PET scans have supported brain changes in hypnotized patients.

Answer: (a) Altered blood flow in pain-related parts of the brain, and (b) brains normally activated during color perception were activated in the hypnotized subjects.

Newsweek International, December 6, 2004 p38 The addict's brain: Scientists think they're close to finding a single drug that can dampen the yen to smoke, drink, and do drugs.

1.   List three examples of how topiramate has been effective in helping to control addictions.

       Answer: (a) Drinkers who took topiramate were six times more likely than those on a placebo to remain abstinent for three months, (b) half the treated patients lost weight, and (c) one in five quit smoking cigarettes even though no one was asked to.

2.   Are there any side effects to topiramate? List them.

       Answer: Drowsiness and difficulty calling up words

3.   Are there any other examples of drugs that may be beneficial for addictions? Describe.

       Answer: Baclofen, a muscle relaxant, was shown in a 2002 trial in Italy to reduce the yen for alcohol. That same year, researchers reported that giving Baclofen to rodents stopped them from "self-administering" cocaine, heroin, nicotine, and methamphetamines.

4.   What "tricks" are scientists faced with when trying to identify drugs that will inhibit or reduce addictions?

       Answer: The trick will be to find the one that most efficiently targets the essential brain systems, while leaving the rest of the brain free for happier pursuits.

WEB LINKS

Knowledge Builder Web Links

1. Altered States and Sleep
       Sleepless at Stanford: http://www.stanford.edu/~dement/sleepless.html
       Sleep Patterns:
              http://healthysleep.med.harvard.edu/healthy/science/what/sleep-patterns-rem-nrem
       Sleep Paralysis: http://watarts.uwaterloo.ca/~acheyne/S_P.html

2. Sleep Disturbances and Dreaming
       The National Sleep Foundation: http://www.sleepfoundation.org
       Sleep Apnea: http://www.sleepapnea.org/
       Sudden Infant Death and Other Infant Death:
              http://www11.georgetown.edu/research/gucchd/nccc/projects/sids/index.html

3. Hypnosis, Meditation, and Sensory Deprivation
       Hypnosis and Self-Hypnosis: http://science.howstuffworks.com/hypnosis.htm/printable
       Meditation for Stress Reduction:
              http://www.mayoclinic.com/health/meditation/HQ01070

4. Psychoactive Drugs
        Higher Education Center: http://www.higheredcenter.org/
        National Council on Alcoholism and Drug Dependence: http://www.ncadd.org/
        Drugs and Behavior Links: http://www.uwsp.edu/psych/mp/tdrugs.htm

5. Psychology in Action: Exploring and Using Dreams
        Dreams and Lucid Dreams: http://www.dreamviews.com/
        How to Keep a Diary of Dreams:
            http://www.ehow.com/how_2383589_keep-diary-dreams.html

Additional Web Links

APA Online
http://www.apa.org/

Alcohol and Drug Abuse
http://www.ncadd.org/index.html
http://www.nida.nih.gov/NIDAHome.html

Consciousness Studies
http://www.consciousness.arizona.edu/

Freud's Interpretation of Dreams
http://psychclassics.yorku.ca/Freud/Dreams/index.htm

Hypnosis in History
http://en.wikipedia.org/wiki/History_of_hypnosis

Hypnosis
http://www.mayoclinic.com/health/hypnosis/MY01020

Center for Narcolepsy
http://med.stanford.edu/school/Psychiatry/narcolepsy/

Sleep, Sleep Disorders, and Sleep Research
http://www.webmd.com/sleep-disorders/default.htm
http://www.sleepfoundation.org
http://www.npi.ucla.edu/sleepresearch/

PSYCHOLOGY IN THE NEWS

Google News
http://news.google.com/intl/en_us/about_google_news.html
You pick the item that interests you, then go directly to the site that published the account you wish to read. You can also search archives by topic.

WebMD news
http://www.webmd.com/sleep-disorders/news-features

NIH sleep disorder articles
http://www.nlm.nih.gov/medlineplus/sleepdisorders.html

CHAPTER 6
Conditioning and Learning

Supplemental Activities	Exercise 6.1: Classical Conditioning of the Eye Blink Response
	Exercise 6.2: Distinguishing Classical Conditioning from Operant Conditioning
	Exercise 6.3: Conditioning as a Personal Experience
	Exercise 6.4: The Learning Curve
	Exercise 6.5: Behavior Modification Contract
	Exercise 6.6: Practicing Operant Conditioning
Handouts	Handout 6.1: Classical Conditioning—Human Eye Blink: Data Sheet
	Handout 6.2: Distinguishing Classical Conditioning From Operant Conditioning
	Handout 6.3: Conditioning as a Personal Experience
	Handout 6.4: The Learning Curve: Handout
	Handout 6.5: Carrying Out a Behavior Modification Contract Handout
	Handout 6.6: Practicing Operant Conditioning

Journal Questions
Suggestions for Further Reading
Video Suggestions
Computer and Internet Resources

202

Module 6.1 Learning and Classical Conditioning

Survey Question: What is learning?

Survey Question: How does classical conditioning occur?

Survey Question: Does conditioning affect emotions?

Module 6.2 Operant Conditioning

Survey Question: How does operant conditioning occur?

Survey Question: Are there different kinds of operant reinforcement?

Module 6.3 Partial Reinforcement and Stimulus Control

Survey Question: How are we influenced by patterns of reward?

Module 6.4 Punishment

Survey Question: What does punishment do to behavior?

Module 6.5 Cognitive Learning and Imitation

Survey Question: What is cognitive learning?

Survey Question: Does learning occur by imitation?

Module 6.6 Psychology in Action: Behavioral Self-Management—A Rewarding Project

Survey Question: How does conditioning apply to everyday problems?

DISCUSSION QUESTIONS

1. Over the years, balloons have occasionally popped in your face when you were blowing them up. Now you squint and feel tense whenever you blow up a balloon. What kind of conditioning is this? What schedule of reinforcement has contributed to the conditioning? How could you extinguish the response?

2. People are often resistant to change. Why? What is reinforcing about maintaining current behavior (even when it is maladaptive) and what is punishing about trying new behaviors?

3. How hard would it be to "teach an old dog new tricks"? Does learning become more difficult as we get older? Or does existing learning interfere with new learning?

4.   Sometimes, rapists cannot get an erection during consensual sex, but do become sexually aroused during coercive or violent sex. Explain how this might happen from a classical conditioning perspective. (UCS = sexuality; CS = violence from TV movies and pornography; and UCR and CR = sexual arousal)

5.   You are in charge of a group of fifth-grade children that meets regularly for recreation. Other members of the group have excluded a younger girl and a very shy boy from activities. How could you use reinforcement principles to improve this situation? (Include techniques aimed at both the excluded children and the group.)

6.   Your textbook states that we are more likely to wear a hat – or some other clothes - more often if we get complimented and less likely if we are ridiculed. But in some cases, a negative reaction from others might actually increase the behavior. Were learning theorists wrong? Why would someone continue to wear clothing, makeup, etc. that was not rewarded by others? What is maintaining this behavior?

7.   Sometimes "generalized fears" are adaptive; other times they are maladaptive. Give an example of each type of phobia.

8.   Often siblings rejoice in the fun of trying to break the younger child of a fear of spiders or water by throwing the child in a pool or dangling a spider in the child's face. Would you expect these procedures to work? Why or why not?

9.   In what ways do advertisers attempt to use both classical and operant conditioning to get us to buy their products? Describe commercials that use each type of conditioning.

10.   For those who have a dog, does your dog bark when there is a doorbell sound on the TV? Or does your dog ignore it? Barking versus ignoring are each called what?

11.   What role has reinforcement had in your selection of a major? Friends? A job? The clothes you wore to school today? Your life goals? Your values?

12.   Identify the antecedents and consequences that allowed you to get from home to school without mishap. Write down as many as you can. (A few examples include responding to the alarm clock, showering, obeying traffic signals, and leaving early enough to find a parking spot.)

13.   You have a friend who checks the coin return slot every time he/she walks by a phone booth. Very rarely is a coin discovered. How do you explain this behavior?

14.   From an operant conditioning perspective, why is it important for parents to "catch kids being good" and praise them? Why is this so difficult to do? What are parents conditioned to respond to?

15. From your point of view, what would be the ideal way to be paid at a job? Should pay be weekly, hourly, daily? Should it be tied to work output? Should rewards other than money be offered? If you owned a business, what would you consider the ideal way to pay your employees?

16. What are the problems in using primary reinforcers to change behavior? What are the problems of using secondary reinforcers? If you wanted to teach your roommate, spouse, or child a new behavior, which would you use? Why?

17. You are trying to teach your dog to use a newly installed doggie door instead of scratching holes in your expensive screen door. How do you begin?

18. Teaching your dog to bark to get a treat is relatively easy, since dogs naturally bark. But how would you get a dog to learn to "roll over and play dead," since this behavior is unlikely to happen spontaneously.

19. Whether a person tries to lose weight, stop drinking, or stop smoking, more often than not the unwanted behavior returns. Why? What should clinics or support groups try to do to make the behavioral changes more long lasting?

20. A child in the grocery store has a temper tantrum. His/her embarrassed father scolds the child and then quiets the child by giving the child a candy bar. Is this punishment or reinforcement? What kind? What other options did Dad have to keep this behavior from happening again in the future? Who is conditioning whom in such circumstances, and what kind of reinforcement or punishment is each receiving?

21. How would you teach your cat to stay down off the counter? (Punish for being on the counter; reward - **don't** ignore - the cat with food or praise when he/she jumps down; reinforce the cat for being in the kitchen and *not* being on the counters; and give the cat an alternate perch to satisfy instinctual drift.)

22. Can you think of anything you do that is not affected in some way by learning?

23. How could you include more feedback or more immediate feedback in your study habits?

24. If you could change procedures to enhance learning in an elementary school classroom, what would you do? What changes would you make in a high school classroom?

25. What is the ideal timing of punishment? Why? Aren't most inappropriate behaviors discovered long after they have taken place? How should these behaviors be punished?

26. How were you punished as a child? Which punishments were examples of *response cost?*

27. Corporal punishment has been banned in many schools. In your opinion, what would be the pros and cons of banning corporal punishment in homes?

205

28. Describe a behavior you learned by observation. What were the advantages of learning in this way? What were the disadvantages? What changes would have made the model you observed more effective?

29. When service dogs are being trained (e.g., seeing eye dogs, police dogs, etc) they learn faster when they can watch more experienced dogs than if they have to be taught "from scratch." Why? If the older dog is not immediately rewarded – in front of the young dog – will learning still take place? Will it happen as quickly? Why or why not?

30. What kind of an experiment would you do to assess the effects of TV violence on infants and small children? What ethical questions would you need to answer to run this experiment?

31. Over the last few years, many musical, athletic, religious, and political "heroes" have admitted involvement in drugs, sex, or illegal activities. Explain "hero worship" in terms of cognitive, conditioning, and imitative processes. Who is your favorite hero? Why?

32. Choose a bad habit you would like to break. How could you apply the principles discussed in this chapter to breaking the habit? How could others help you?

33. What incompatible responses can you think of that could be performed in public to prevent the following behaviors: smoking, knuckle cracking, swearing, fingernail biting, hand wringing, and eyelash plucking?

34. In your opinion, should TV programs come with a violence rating scale or a rating system like that used for movies? What, if anything, would you suggest be done about the quality of TV programs and the amount of violence they contain?

➤ LECTURE ENHANCEMENTS

Short demonstrations of conditioning help students learn the processes and vocabulary. Students experience a great sense of satisfaction actually changing the behavior of others, especially their instructor. They usually have strong feelings about issues of punishment, child rearing, willpower, and violence on television. These feelings work well in debates or value clarification activities. These often heated debates are especially effective in courses with a diverse student population.

1. **Classical conditioning and habituation.** Demonstrate classical conditioning by bringing in a balloon bouquet. Ask students to notice the response of people in the front row to the balloons. Then pull out a long darning needle and wave it around the balloons. Hand it to a student in the front row. Ask for it back. Ask a student to describe the reaction to the needle. Then use it to pop the balloon. Wave it around the remaining balloons again and pop another balloon. Discuss student reactions in terms of classical conditioning. Test for a reaction at the next class meeting and discuss extinction.

2. **The Skinner box.** The best demonstration of operant conditioning is to bring a Skinner box and a rat or pigeon to class. In lieu of that, an entertaining (if somewhat artificial) illustration of shaping can be done with a human subject—you! Students provide reinforcement in this case by tapping their pens or pencils on their desks. Leave class for a few moments to allow the class to choose a response or a series of responses for you to perform. When you return, begin moving around the room. Students should tap each time you perform a response that approximates the final desired pattern. Your task, of course, is to keep the tapping as loud as possible (it's a little like playing "hot, warm, and cold"). The result can provide a hilarious interlude and a surprisingly instructive experience.

3. **Bomb-sniffing dogs.** Law enforcement agencies now use dogs to locate drugs and bombs. How might such dogs be trained in these skills? Would you use shaping? How might generalization and discrimination fit into this kind of training? Well-trained dogs can also distinguish between normal and large amount of money. How is a dog taught to distinguish between different amounts of the same item?

4. **A behaviorally engineered community.** B. F. Skinner published *Walden Two* in 1948. It was the story of a model community based on behavioral engineering. That is, he applied the "technology of behavior," which he developed, to a community situation to show how an ideal community could exist if operant conditioning principles were applied. Organize the class into groups of five or six students and ask them to try to visualize and plan such a community. They should specify how the behavioral principles would be used and what kind of behaviors could be expected from the participants. They should try to think in terms of the details of daily life in the community as well as the overall welfare and spirit of the group. What behavior would they want to reinforce? The groups should then come together and share their ideas as a class.

5. **The development of phobias.** The text discusses the way in which conditioned emotional responses can become phobias. Generally those who have a phobia cannot identify its origins. However, some can do so, and often family members will relate the phobias to some experience the person had in early childhood. Ask students to generate a list of fears that they or their friends or relatives have. Try to restrict the list to only those fears that are intense and irrational (phobias) rather than other more common fears shared to some degree by most people. Ask those who contribute these items to try to recall or find out how they were acquired. Did the fear come from some legitimate unpleasant or painful experience, or did it come about vicariously? Some fears are learned from experience with the feared object. Sometimes children take on fears of their parents or some other person by imitation. Many of the fears will have no evident explanation. Be sure to discuss classical and operant conditioning principles in connection with these learned fears.

6. **Shaping behavior.** Give students an assignment to shape a specific behavior of a friend or someone with whom they live. Students should record the baseline frequency of the behavior and choose a reinforcer (typically praise) for altering the behavior. During the shaping period students should continue to record the frequency of the behavior to document any changes. In class, students can report on their successes and failures and discuss the difficulties of using operant conditioning in the "real world."

7. **The token economy.** Break students into small groups and ask them to generate ideas for using token reinforcers in classrooms. Assign different groups to different grade levels. Students can draw upon their own experiences from school, but should also generate some novel ideas.

8. **Why won't that child behave?** Have students discuss examples of bad behavior by children in public places such as grocery stores. What are the parents doing to contribute to the continuation of this behavior? If scolding the child doesn't work, explain way and propose an alternate strategy.

9. **That barking dog problem.** Most people have at some point had bad neighbors who allow their dog to bark continuously. Eventually, the owner yells at the dog and the dog stops barking briefly, only to resume barking a short time later. Have students break into small groups and generate a solution to the barking dog problem. The groups should identify why the dog is barking, why yelling at the dog only works temporarily, and what can be done using appropriate (and humane) operant conditioning techniques to solve this problem. Groups should generate a step-by-step plan for dealing with the problem. (e.g., every single time the dog barks, the dog should be brought into the house *without delay*. In addition, the dog should be praised when it is not barking. Squirting with water might also be used.)

10. **The role of feedback in learning.** Feedback is essential for effective human learning to take place. To illustrate this and to introduce the concept of biofeedback, locate three class members who do not know how to wiggle their ears but think they might be able to

208

learn. Have all three come to the front and face the class so that their ears are visible. Have them try for about a minute to master this skill. If anyone succeeds too easily, replace him/her with a new subject. When you have three subjects who clearly cannot wiggle their ears with more than minimal success, give each a hand mirror. Ask them to hold the mirror so that they can see their ears. Most will succeed with the addition of the feedback provided by the mirror.

11. **Taking modeling for granted.** The role of modeling in learning often seems so self-evident to students that they may not fully appreciate its importance in learning theory. To bring home the idea that modeling has a powerful and pervasive impact on human learning, invite a student to the front of the class and ask him/her to tell you verbally how to tie your shoe. Untie one of your shoes (make sure you're wearing shoes with laces) and follow the subject's instructions explicitly. Be sure not to lead, interpret, or show any signs of previous shoe-tying skill. If you are very literal in your interpretation of the student's instructions, the point will be made: In many cases learning would be virtually impossible or incredibly inefficient was it not for observational learning.

12. **Where's my map?** One very good way to illustrate the existence of cognitive maps involves asking students to draw a map of the campus or the layout in general of the community in which they live. Selected maps can then be projected on a screen and compared to one another and/or to formal maps.

14. **Cognitive Maps and learning styles.** Ask students to describe how they would get to their favorite shopping center, store, friend's house, etc. They can describe or draw it any way they want to. After collecting the papers, ask them how many drew a map or used a primarily visual description and how many listed the directions as a series of steps, e.g., turn left on Elm, or right on Main. People who draw maps or use lots of visual descriptions are more visual-spatial learners, and those who list are more auditory/verbal learners.

15. **Those annoying habits.** The general approach of the "Psychology in Action" section in this chapter provides a good way to review learning principles. Have students submit anonymous examples of troublesome habits (their own or those of family and friends). Select from these the most interesting and, at the next class meeting, ask students to use chapter concepts to suggest ways to alter the troublesome behaviors.

16. **Reinforcement in the real world.** Ask students to apply reinforcement principles to a "real world" problem such as waste recycling. How would they engineer better paper recycling on a university campus? In a college dorm? In a selected neighborhood?

In actual experiments of this sort, several techniques have proven effective. These include "recycling contests" (in which groups compete for a small cash award financed by selling the recycled paper) and raffles in which each bag of paper submitted for recycling earns a raffle ticket and a chance to win a small weekly prize.

209

(E. S. Geller, J. L. Chaffee, and R. E. Ingram, "Promoting Paper Recycling on a University Campus," *Journal of Environmental Systems,* 1975, 5, 39-57.)

17. **This could change your life!** Depending on the size of your classes and your relationship with students, your involvement in behavioral change may be limited to study habits and academic goals, or it may involve more personal changes of a clinical nature. Whether the issue is study habits, parenting behaviors, exercise, drug consumption, or a similar topic, a contract can be written to commit the student to a change in behavior. Students can complete the contract for extra credit or a grade. Students can also be encouraged to work with a friend or relative, helping that person change a behavior. A typical contract can be written as follows:

Behavioral Contract

The behavior I am concerned about is

_____

The situation where I perform this behavior most often is

_____

The people I perform this behavior most often with are

_____

The mood I am in when I usually perform this behavior is

_____

The reason I think I perform this behavior is

_____

The feelings I usually have after performing this behavior are

_____

The reactions of other people to this behavior are

_____

The immediate disadvantages of this behavior pattern are

_____

The long-term negative consequences of continuing this pattern are

_____

Other behaviors I could engage in to satisfy the same need include

_____

I plan to reduce the frequency of the undesirable behavior by

_____

I plan to increase the frequency of the more desirable behavior by

_____

I plan to change this behavior within the following time frame

_____

I agree to try to change the above behavior in the way described. Because an attempt to change is the first step in a permanent change, I agree to be honest in sharing the results of my efforts.

Signed   _____

Witness   _____

211

➤ ROLE-PLAYING SCENARIOS

1. **Have students describe typical discipline problems they have encountered with children.** Choose an example and have a student enact an "unenlightened" punitive response to the child's behavior. Then have another student role-play a more constructive use of punishment. A third student can role-play a reinforcement-based strategy. Discuss the results.

2. **Show your animal instincts.** Break students into pairs and have them pretend that one is the pet dog or cat and the other is the owner. Remembering that animals cannot understand instructions, the exercise should be done without verbal communication of the idea. Have the "owner" decide which trick to teach the "animal" and then shape the behavior. The "animal" should behave the way an animal would. When they are done, have them trade places. Discuss the results.

3. **Demonstrate a superstitious behavior or ritual.** Students should take turns demonstrating the behavior and the thought process behind it. The other students should identify why the superstition exists, and suggest ways to remedy the superstition. They should be sure to include an action plan for what happens if the superstition is accidentally confirmed (e.g. if the first time a player doesn't wear his/her lucky socks, he/she loses.)

4. **Verbalize the thoughts of an employee who is being paid an hourly wage, a weekly salary, a monthly salary, a salary plus a production bonus, and a person paid on a piecework basis. Discuss these thoughts in class.**

5. **Role-play a person playing a slot machine programmed on a FR-5 schedule, an FR-10 schedule, a VR-1 minute schedule, and a completely random schedule.** Say aloud what you are thinking on each schedule.

6. **Describe a minor behavior problem that a friend, roommate, or relative has.** Explain to that person how he or she could use conditioning principles to alter the behavior.

➤ VALUE-CLARIFICATION STATEMENTS

1. A person can cease having an extreme fear if they just try.

2. Classical conditioning is fine for understanding animal behavior, but has limited applicability to humans.

3. Physical punishment should only be used to stop a behavior that is endangering a person's life.

4. It's almost impossible to raise a child without using some physical punishment.

212

5.   Skinner's ideas about operant conditioning are really just about controlling and manipulating people.

6.   Children should be able to learn how to behave just by being taught; rewarding children for behavior that they are supposed to be doing anyway just spoils them and never teaches them to internalize good habits.

7.   Practice makes perfect.

8.   Actions speak louder than words.

9.   Any behavior can be changed, as long as we are patient enough to change it slowly.

10. Spare the rod.

11. Rock videos that combine sex with violence should be taken off television.

12. Children's television programming should be screened for violence and aggression.

13. All this talk about the negative effects of violence on TV is an over-reaction; people know the difference between reality and fantasy.

14. Bad models exceed good models on primetime network television shows.

➤ ONE-MINUTE MOTIVATORS

1.   **What's for dinner?** Begin the unit by asking students about their favorite foods. Discuss briefly why they like these foods and whether they also eat these foods often. Use this as a preface to concepts of classically conditioned feelings and to the effect that reinforcers have on behavior.

2.   **Reflexes.** Demonstrate reflex pupil dilation with a flashlight, the patellar reflex with a small rubber mallet, and the blink reflex by using a turkey baster to direct a puff of air to the eye.

213

3. **Why it happens.** In pairs, have students answer these questions. Why does your:

    a. Dog drool when you open the can of food before the food is given to him?

    b. Friend flinch before you tickle her or him?

    c. Little sister tremble at the sound of a dentist's drill?

    d. Fellow student begin blushing before he/she is called on to give a speech?

4. **Superstitious behavior.** Ask students to describe superstitious behaviors they have observed in televised sports events. How are these behaviors maintained? What makes them superstitious?

5. **Understanding procrastination.** Many people procrastinate, especially on tasks they dislike. Despite the fact that procrastination produces a number of punishers (stress, anxiety, late penalties, rushed work) we continue to do it. Ask students to brainstorm and identify why procrastination is rewarding. In other words, what maintains the behavior? Once these factors have been identified, suggest ways to decrease the rewarding value of procrastination and increase the reinforcement value of not procrastinating.

6. **Study Time?** There is substantial variation in the amount of studying done by different students. Most students understand that increasing study time improves grades, but the difference in study times persists. Ask students to identify why studying is (or is not) reinforcing. Also ask them to list their reinforcers for other behaviors. Perhaps by gaining some insight into their response contingencies, students will be able to modify their own behavior.

7. **Let me out of here!** To demonstrate negative reinforcement and operant escape, give half of the class this assignment: "As soon as you have written the alphabet backward three times, raise your hand and then write it a fourth time." Give this assignment to the other half: "As soon as you have written the alphabet backward three times, go outside and wait for further instructions." You will find those escaping from the boredom writing much more quickly than those with no escape option.

8. **Hey! No fair!** Give students a five-minute quiz on the preceding chapter. Collect all of the quizzes and place them in the trash. When students protest, discuss how frustrating it is to not receive knowledge of results, whether in terms of class exams, feedback at work, praise from friends, or even a thank-you note when you send someone a gift.

9. **Rethinking video games.** An alarmingly high percentage of computer and video games have violent content where the player is reinforced (given feedback) for virtual transgressions against others. Ask students to list popular computer or video games that provide reinforcing feedback without violence. What is this feedback? You can also ask them to break into small groups and "design" a new video game that would be both non-violent and appealing to the target market.

10. **Successful conditioning.** Ask students to think about which reinforcement schedule works best for completing items on an assembly line, assuming workers are paid for each item assembled. Which schedule works best in a casino when someone plays the slot

214

machines? Which schedule works best when someone has to baby-sit a child for a certain number of hours?

11. **What am I doing?** Have students stand and face the back of the room. Have one student come to the front of the class and mime the motions needed to fry an egg (e.g., place pan on stove, turn on burner, add oil, pick up egg, crack egg open, add salt and pepper, turn with spatula). As the student does this, she should try to tell the rest of the class what motions to make, to do what she is doing, without making any reference to cooking or to any objects. Ask students to guess what they are learning to do. When one does, discuss the model's frustration with verbal instruction and have her repeat the demonstration for those students who didn't guess what they were learning to do. Can they guess now what they were learning to do?

12. **Great commercial!** Show a short sequence of commercials recorded from commercial television and discuss the kinds of role models that are being presented. What messages are being reinforced?

➤ BROADENING OUR CULTURAL HORIZONS

1. **The meaning of symbols.** Have students help you make a list of symbols that have emotional meaning for a specific group of people. For example, religious, political, or sexual symbols (words, objects, gestures) can provoke emotional responses. Explain these associations in terms of conditioning.

2. **Prejudice and discrimination.** What is the relationship between stimulus generalization and discrimination and gender, ethic, or racial stereotyping, prejudice, and discrimination? In what ways are these processes similar and different?

3. **What's culturally normal?** Do you think other cultures use operant conditioning principles on children more or less than North American culture? If some students in the class are from other cultures, ask them to give an example of something that is done in North America that would not typically be done in their home country, or vice versa.

4. **International differences in education.** What factors are responsible for greater academic achievement in many countries, especially in math and science? Is reinforcement at the root of the difference, or is something else? Does the high level of TV-watching by North American children really make a difference to achievement? Explain why or why not from a Skinnerian perspective.

5. **Reinforcing cultural norms.** Cultural norms develop because a specific behavior is reinforced. Can you identify some behaviors that are typically reinforced in the United States that are not reinforced in other cultures? (For example, Korean businesspersons rarely smile at customers, because people who smile in public are thought to look like fools.)

6. **Want to play a game?** Some cultures focus on and invest much time in game playing. Interview friends of yours about their attitudes toward game playing. What types of games did their parents play? Was the outcome of the game primarily the result of chance or skill? What reinforced this behavior? If a person "lost" the game, what would be the consequences?

7. **Rewards and punishments in different cultures.** Are rewards more effective than punishment in all parts of the world? Are there some cultures where punishment is more or less effective than it is in North America?

8. **Cultural work ethic.** Stereotypes have developed about the "work ethic" of different cultures. Does your ethnic group or culture focus more on immediate or delayed reinforcers? How do you think that has developed?

9. **Conditioned sexual behaviors in different cultures**. Sexual behavior varies widely from one culture to another. In the U.S., most students have sex before graduating from high school, and the average age for the onset of sexual activity is 16. In other cultures, sex before marriage is less frequent. What factors in the U.S. reinforce teenagers for having sex? The U.S. is not the only country where teenagers typically have sex, but the U.S. has among the highest rate of teen pregnancy. What factors discourage the use of contraceptives, thus increasing the rate of teen pregnancies?

10. **Were you spanked as a child?** What view did your parents, your extended family, and friends of your parents take toward physical punishment? What cultural factors explain why some parents spank and other parents talk?

11. **Punishment and the legal system.** Have students research various cultures for methods of punishing criminal behavior. Do some methods seem to be more effective than others?

➤ SUPPLEMENTAL ACTIVITIES

Exercise 6.1: Classical Conditioning of the Eye Blink Response

I. Introduction:

Students should have read the section in the text on classical conditioning and received classroom instruction to clarify the concepts involved. They should be clear on what is to happen in this demonstration. The purpose is to condition the eye blink response to the sound of a clicker. Some other noisemaker may be substituted such as a buzzer or bell.

II. Apparatus:

The apparatus for this exercise is easy to get together. A clicker or noisemaker is needed. One that makes a clear, sharp sound is best. The apparatus to deliver a puff of air to the eyes is a little more difficult. You need a piece of rigid plastic tubing attached to a stand. The stand can be made or clamp stands can be borrowed from the chemistry lab. Flexible plastic tubing (about three feet long) should be attached to the rigid tube at one end and to a squeeze bulb at the other. A kitchen baster will deliver a generous puff of air for this purpose. A student handout to accompany this exercise can be found in **Handout 6.1.**

III. Procedure:

A. Organize the class into teams of three. One will be the subject, one the experimenter, and the third will be the recorder. If time permits, the students can rotate these roles so each one has an opportunity to be the subject.

B. Seat the subject and set up the apparatus so that the tip of the rigid tube will be about two inches from his/her eyes. The experimenter should be behind the subject, holding the clicker and the squeeze bulb. The recorder should sit directly in front of the subject. Throughout the experiment the recorder will note whether or not the subject blinked at each trial.

C. Begin the experiment by presenting the subject with a puff of air and observe the eye blink response. This should be done at least twice to be sure that the puff of air (unconditioned stimulus) is producing the eye blink (unconditioned response). Space the trials at 15-second intervals. A watch with a large second hand should suffice as a timer.

217

D. The conditioning trials should be done as follows. Click the noisemaker and immediately after (not at the same time) present the puff of air. Wait about 15 seconds and repeat. Do this 15 times. This should be sufficient to establish the eye blink (now a conditioned response) to the sound of the noisemaker (the conditioned stimulus). The recorder will note the eye blink for each trial on the data sheet.

E. After the 15 conditioning trials, continue with 15 more, presenting only the noisemaker with no puff of air. The recorder will note the presence or absence of the eye blink at each trial. It should be possible to see when extinction has occurred.

F. At this point the experiment could be concluded, or some variations could be tried. Here are some possibilities:
   1. Give the subject a rest period and then resume trials with only the clicker and see if spontaneous recovery will occur.
   2. Present the puff of air only occasionally while continuing clicking trials and then stopping the US to see how long it takes for extinction to occur.
   3. See if more than 15 conditioning trials will result in slower extinction.

G. **Discussion questions:**
   1. What is the change in behavior in this exercise?
   2. Why did it occur?
   3. Why did extinction take place?
   4. Does this kind of "learning" have a real value in our lives?

Exercise 6.2: Distinguishing Classical Conditioning from Operant Conditioning
Handout 6.2 gives a number of cases and asks students whether each one is classical or operant conditioning, and asks them to indicate which component is being illustrated. Answers are below.

1. This is a classical response. Bullying (UCS) automatically evokes fear (UCR). Through association, Trevor (CS) also comes to evoke fear (CR). The name "Trevor" also elicits fear because of stimulus generalization.

2. This is an operant example. When Justin participates in his father's *attitude improvement course*, he is being punished by being given extra chores. He is also experiencing response cost because he is losing his freedom on Saturday morning.

3. This is an operant example. Mary's improved studying has resulted in better grades (positive reinforcement) and less anxiety (negative reinforcement).

4. This is an operant example. Playing the music is positively reinforcing for the father because it gets the children out of bed. Staying in bed is punishing for the children, who dislike the music. Getting out of bed is negatively reinforced for the children because the music stops.

218

5. This is a classical example. Mary loves her father (UCS) and feels good (CS) whenever she is with him. The music (CS) reminds her of her father and makes her smile (CR). This is an example of classical conditioning of emotions.

6. The answer to this question could be either classical or operant, depending on whether dogs barking to sounds are considered a reflex (classical) or a voluntary behavior (operant). In both cases, though, Fido is exhibiting generalization and Rover is showing discrimination.

7. Fido is exhibiting an operant response. He has learned that going to the kitchen results in being fed. Food is positively reinforcing. The reason this is operant rather than classical is that Fido's behavior is <u>voluntary</u>. If Fido isn't hungry, or if there is something else that interests him, he may choose to stay where he is. It is likely that Fido also starts to drool when he hears the can opener. If so, then the can opener is a conditioned stimulus that elicits drooling (reflex). This example shows that classical and operant conditioning often occur together.

8. This is an operant example. Giving the pacifier is negatively reinforcing for Janice, who no longer has to listen to the crying. The baby's crying behavior is positively reinforced because the baby gets something to suck on when it cries.

Exercise 6.3: Conditioning as a Personal Experience
Students should be asked to identify personal experiences in which they were either classically or operantly conditioned. It might require some speculation on their part as to how it came about. However, it is important for them to realize the extent to which this type of learning occurs in their lives. If students use the classical conditioning model, Figure 7-3, they can see how the change in behavior occurred. For the operant conditioning experiences, they need to pay attention to the concept of reinforcement, or consequence of a response, when producing examples.

The students should be instructed to identify the source of motivation for the behavioral change and what is being associated in each example.

Handout 6.3 can be duplicated and given to students to write their examples. Many of the examples will be wrong the first time. You can help them to understand these concepts by going over the examples, showing them what is wrong, and suggesting how they could be done better. Then ask the students who were unclear to write some new examples.

219

Exercise 6.4: The Learning Curve

I.   **Introduction**

The purpose of this exercise is to give students an opportunity to see how learning follows a typical learning curve. This can be done by charting the progress of a student learning to follow a maze, provided the maze is not too easy or too complex. Student handouts and a copy of the maze can be found in **Handout 6.4**

II.   **Procedure**

A.   Divide the class into groups of three for this exercise. Designate one to be the subject, another to be the timer, and the third to be the recorder. Rotate the students so that all three will have an opportunity to be the subject.

B.   Provide each group with 45 copies of the maze, three data sheets, and three of each of the two graphs. Be sure that each group has a watch with a second hand to time the trials.

C.   Discuss with the students the way to do the timing, how to score the maze (time and errors), and how to plot points on the graphs.

D.   Be sure students complete their trials and complete the data sheets while doing the exercise. It would be best to have them plot the graphs while in the classroom so they can help each other and seek your assistance, if needed. Once all three students have completed the exercise, each student should plot the data for all three subjects on the same graph. Different colors could be used to identify each.

III.   **Discussion**

A.   Did a learning curve occur? What was its shape?

B.   What conclusions can you draw about maze learning in general?

C.   Would similar curves appear in the learning of other types of material?

D.   Is what you have learned from this exercise of any value to you in your learning?

Bring the class together to go over the results. Try to find out what problems were encountered and what results appeared. Then ask students to discuss the questions above. You may have some of your own to add or substitute.

Exercise 6.5: Behavior Modification Contract

Students can set this up as an exercise for any particular time that you decide. Most often, it takes one week or more. Have students follow the steps and carry out the contract using **Handout 6.5.**

1. Choose a target behavior.
2. Record a baseline.
3. Establish goals.
4. Choose reinforcers.
5. Record your progress.
6. Reward successes.
7. Adjust your plan as you learn more about your behavior.

Exercise 6.6 Practicing Operant Conditioning

Handout 6.6 includes a number of examples where operant conditioning can be applied. Students could come up with a variety of answers to each example, but all examples should include:

a)   Identifying the contingencies that are reinforcing the behavior.

b)   Removing the reinforcers and/or extinguishing the behavior and/or punishing the behavior.

c)   Identifying the alternate positive behavior.

d)   Identifying the contingencies that will increase that behavior.

e)   Emphasis on positive reinforcement over punishment.

221

Handout 6.1: CLASSICAL CONDITIONING—HUMAN EYE BLINK: DATA SHEET

TO THE STUDENT:

Record accurately what you observe. In this exercise it will be the presence or absence of an eye blink when the stimuli are presented to the subject. You should be sure not to communicate your expectations to the subject. Simply record what you see.

ACQUISITION PHASE		EXTINCTION PHASE	
TRIAL	BLINK (Y OR N)	TRIAL	BLINK (Y OR N)
1		1	
2		2	
3		3	
4		4	
5		5	
6		6	
7		7	
8		8	
9		9	
10		10	
11		11	
12		12	
13		13	
14		14	
15		15	

Handout 6.2: DISTINGUISHING CLASSICAL CONDITIONING FROM OPERANT CONDITIONING

For each of the following, first decide whether the example is classical or operant conditioning, and then identify the components. You will use the following terms: UCS, CS, UCR, CR, extinction, spontaneous recovery, generalization, discrimination, positive reinforcement, negative reinforcement, punishment, or response cost.

1. When he was a child, Richard was the object of bullying by Trevor. Even as an adult, Richard still grimaces whenever he meets someone named Trevor.

2. George is annoyed at his son Justin, who consistently breaks curfew. George creates what he humorously calls an *attitude improvement course*. Justin is required to spend Saturday helping his father clean out the garage.

3. Mary used to be a poor student. Lately, she has found that she gets better grades when she studies. She is happy that her GPA has improved and she also feels less anxious during exams.

4. Sally's father enjoyed the sound of military bands. The children did not. When the children would not get out of bed on Saturday mornings, their father would turn up the sound of a marching band full volume until the children got out of bed.

5. Sally is now an adult with children of her own. Whenever she hears a military band, she smiles and thinks about her father.

6. Fido and Rover enjoy sitting with the family while the TV is on. Every time the sound of a doorbell rings on the TV, Fido starts barking but Rover ignores it. Both Fido and Rover do bark when someone rings the doorbell of their home.

7. Fido jumps up from his spot on the couch and runs to the kitchen whenever he hears the can opener.

8. Janice takes her baby out for a walk and when the baby cries, Janice gives the baby a pacifier. The baby stops crying.

Handout 6.3: CONDITIONING AS A PERSONAL EXPERIENCE: DATA SHEET

Instances of classical and operant conditioning occur in everyday life. Your assignment is to think of two personal examples of each type of conditioning that you have experienced and briefly describe each one. Do not use examples found in the text or presented by your instructor in class. In each example, identify where the association bond is and what the motivation is for the change in behavior.

CLASSICAL CONDITIONING

1.

2.

OPERANT CONDITIONING

1.

2.

Handout 6.4: THE LEARNING CURVE: DATA SHEET

Record the time for each trial and the number of errors made on each. Try to be as accurate as possible in timing the subject and recording errors. Before starting, number the maze sheets from 1 to 15 and have the subject use them in order. An error is made each time the subject raises the pencil, enters a blind alley, or crosses a line. Crossing a line and returning into the path constitutes one error (not two) since the line has to be re-crossed to enter the path.

TRIALS	1		2		3	
	SECS.	ERRORS	SECS.	ERRORS	SECS.	ERRORS
1						
2						
3						
4						
5						
6						
7						
8						
9						
10						
11						
12						
13						
14						
15						

Handout 6.4: THE LEARNING CURVE: GRAPH I LEARNING

TO THE STUDENT: Plot the times for each trial on the graph. Join the points to produce a learning curve. The horizontal axis represents the number of trials, and the vertical axis the number of seconds per trial.

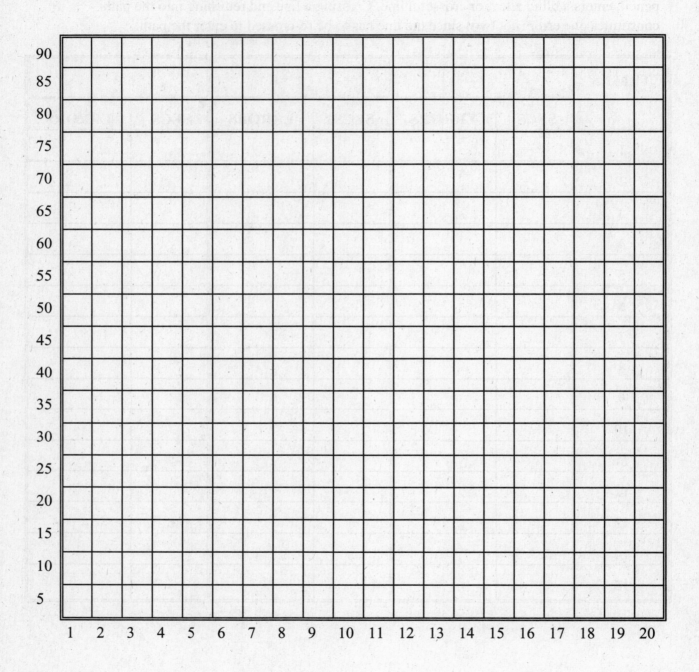

Handout 6.4: THE LEARNING CURVE: GRAPH II--ERRORS

TO THE STUDENT: An error is made each time the subject raises the pencil, enters a blind alley, or crosses a line. Crossing a line and returning into the path constitutes one error (not two) since the line has to be re-crossed to enter the path. Plot the number of errors made on each trial. Join the points to produce an error curve. The horizontal axis represents the number of trials, and the vertical axis the number of errors.

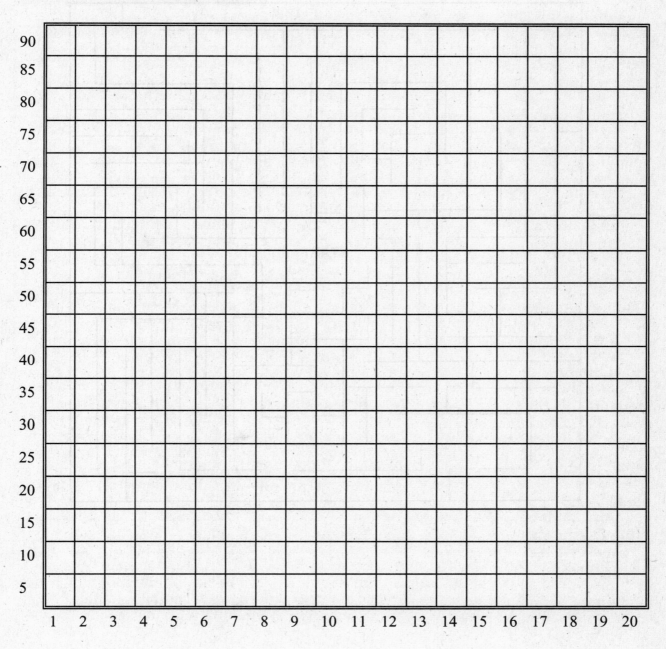

Handout 6.4: THE LEARNING CURVE: MAZE LEARNING

TO THE STUDENT: Follow the maze from the center to the exit. Do not raise your pencil from the paper once you begin. If you cross a line or go into a blind alley, return to the point where the error was made without lifting your pencil from the paper. Work quickly.

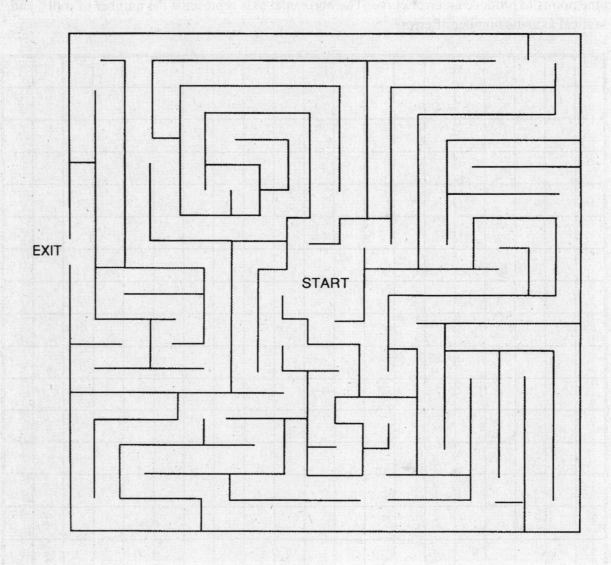

228

Handout 6.5: CARRYING OUT A BEHAVIOR MODIFICATION CONTRACT

The principles of operant conditioning can be adapted to manage your own behavior. Here's how:

1. **Choose a target behavior.** Identify the activity you want to change.
2. **Record a baseline.** Record how much time you currently spend performing the target activity, or count the number of desired or undesired responses you make each day.
3. **Establish goals.** Remember the principle of shaping, and set realistic goals for gradual improvement on each successive week. Also, set daily goals that add up to the weekly goal.
4. **Choose reinforcers.** If you meet your daily goal, what reward will you have earned? Daily rewards might be watching television, eating a candy bar, socializing with friends, playing a musical instrument, or whatever you enjoy. Also establish a weekly reward. If you reach your weekly goal, what reward will you earn? A movie? A dinner out? A weekend hike?
5. **Record your progress.** Keep accurate records of the amount of time spent each day on the desired activity or the number of times you make the desired response.
6. **Reward successes.** If you meet your daily goal, collect your reward. If you fall short, be honest with yourself and skip the reward. Do the same for your weekly goal.
7. **Adjust your plan as you learn more about your behavior.** Overall progress will reinforce your attempts at self-management.

Handout 6.6: PRACTICING OPERANT CONDITIONING

For each of the following, describe the best course of action using operant conditioning techniques.

1. Morgan is a 5th grade teacher. Johnny is in Morgan's class and is being disruptive. He talks out of turn and makes "smart" remarks. What should Morgan do?

2. Juanita is trying to discourage her cat from jumping up on the counter. What should Juanita do? Which things should she avoid doing?

3. Carl is 15 years old and has severe acne. Recently, he has started scratching at his sores and his face has become raw and sometimes bleeds. Carl's parents yell at him every time they see him scratching at the sores, but Carl won't stop. Why is yelling at Carl ineffective? What should his parents do instead?

4. A large city has problems with traffic congestion and smog from too many cars being on the roads. City officials realize that the problem cannot be solved overnight, but they also need some relief now. What short-term and long-term changes might city officials propose to bring this problem under control?

➤ JOURNAL QUESTIONS

1.   Describe what you consider to be a normal fear you have and describe a fear of yours that you think is a phobia. Where and how did each of these develop? How does each of these affect your life? What could you do to try to "extinguish" the fear? The phobia?

2.   Describe your favorite TV commercial or TV show. Why do you like it so? What conditioning process explains your feelings?

3.   What fears have you learned vicariously from family and friends? How do these fears affect your life? What could you do to extinguish this fear?

4.   Think about how your parents raised you. Which parts of classical or operant conditioning did they use to teach you things? Which ways of teaching you were the most and least effective? Did they tend to reward positive behavior, punish negative behavior, or do a combination of the two? Which strategies would you want to use in raising your own children? Which would you like to avoid?

5.   Think of a number of situations from your childhood where you felt rewards and punishments were not contingent upon specific behaviors. How did you feel when you did something desirable and you did not get recognition for that act? When you got punished in some way even when you did not do anything wrong?

6.   What ways were you disciplined at school? Did your teachers use more rewards or more punishments to get you to behave appropriately? Was there a big difference between teachers, or was the policy at your school pretty standard? Did the way teachers used rewards and punishments change much between elementary school and high school? Which one was more likely to rely on rewards to motivate students, and which was more likely to use punishments?

7.   Think of a time when you effectively managed the behavior of an animal or another person using some of the suggestions for effective punishment. Were you effective for the short term? For the long term? What could you have done to be more effective?

➤ SUGGESTIONS FOR FURTHER READING

Alberto, P. A., & Troutman, A. C. (2009). *Applied behavior analysis for teachers* (8th ed.). Englewood Cliffs, NJ: Prentice Hall.

Anderson, C. A. (2004). An update on the effects of violent video games. *Journal of Adolescence, 27,* 113–122.

Baumrind, D., Larzelere, R. E., & Cowan, P. A. (2002). Ordinary physical punishment: Is it harmful? *Psychological Bulletin, 128*(4), 580–589.

Chance, P. (2009). *Learning and behavior* (6th ed.). Belmont, CA: Cengage Learning/Wadsworth.

Domjan, M. (2010). *The principles of learning and behavior* (6th ed.). Belmont, CA: Cengage Learning/Wadsworth.

Evans, R. I. (1989). *Albert Bandura: The man and his ideas: A dialogue*. New York: Praeger.

Goodall, J. (2010). *Through a window: My thirty years with the chimpanzees of Gombe*. New York: First Mariner Books.

Hergenhahn, B. R., & Olson, M. (2009). *Introduction to the theories of learning* (8th ed.). Englewood Cliffs, NJ: Prentice Hall.

Leahey, T. H. & Harris, R. J. (2001) *Learning and cognition* (5th ed.). Saddle River, NJ: Prentice-Hall.

Lefrançois, G. R. (2006). *Theories of human learning: What the old woman said* (5th ed.). Belmont, CA: Cengage Learning/Wadsworth.

Martin, G., & Pear, J. (2007). *Behavior modification: What it is and how to do it* (8th ed.). Upper Saddle River, NJ: Prentice-Hall.

Pavlov, I. P. (1927). *Conditioned reflexes*. New York: Dover.

Pearce, J. M. (2008). *Animal learning and cognition* (3rd ed.). London: Psychology Press.

Robbins, S., Schwartz, B., & Wasserman, E. (2001). *Psychology of learning and behavior* (5th ed.) New York: Norton.

Schwartz, M. S., & Andrasik, F. (Eds.). (2003). *Biofeedback: A practitioner's guide* (3rd ed.). New York: Guilford.

Skinner, B. F. (1938). *The behavior of organisms: An experimental analysis*. New York: Appleton-Century-Crofts.

Skinner, B. F. (1948). *Walden Two*. New York: Macmillan.

➤ VIDEO SUGGESTIONS

Feature Films

An Officer and a Gentleman (1982) (Richard Gere, Louis Gossett, Jr., and Debra Winger) Drama. Two misfits seek directions in their lives, one by becoming a naval officer and the other by getting a husband. Gossett won the Best Supporting Actor Academy Award for his performance as a drill sergeant.

Liar, Liar (Jim Carrey) Comedy. An unscrupulous attorney who is a compulsive liar finds himself unable to lie for a day. He struggles to find ways to win a court case, prove himself to his son, and reconcile with his ex-wife while telling only the truth.

Mighty Joe Young (Charlize Theron) Comedy. In this 1998 remake of the 1949 classic, a young woman has been raised in the jungle alongside an oversized gorilla. To protect him from poachers, she accompanies him to an animal habitat in America, but no one else understands Joe the giant gorilla the way she does. A criminal pursuing Joe leads to an escape, a rampage, and a heroic rescue.

Educational Films and Videos

A Conversation with B. F. Skinner, (1971), Filmmakers Library, 23 min. This interview with B. F. Skinner centers on the meanings and implications of Beyond Freedom and Dignity. Skinner discusses the concept of behavior modification and the problems associated with implementing the technology in open and closed societies. The film specifically addresses the use and misuse of rewards and punishment to modify behavior on a cultural level. It is a thought-provoking introduction to applied psychology.

A Demonstration of Behavioral Processes by B. F. Skinner, (1971), Prentice-Hall, 28 min. In this documentary, B. F. Skinner offers an introduction to operant conditioning. In a classroom setting, Skinner reviews the history of operant conditioning and explains the experimental apparatus. He demonstrates differential reinforcement and "shaping" techniques used on a pigeon while showing how pigeons shape their own behavior. Finally, Skinner applies principles of operant conditioning to human behavior.

A Good Night's Sleep, (1990), ABC 20/20, 17 min. This segment features Dr. Richard Ferber, a children's sleep expert, demonstrating his behavior modification technique for getting children to sleep through the night. This film follows one family's successful effort with Dr. Ferber. This 20/20 segment is really liked by general psychology classes.

Albert Bandura, Volumes 1 and II, (1988), Insight Video, Vol. 1: 29 minutes, Vol. 2: 28 min. Part of the Notable Contributors series. In part 1, Bandura reviews his influences in theoretical and research development and discusses cognitive and social behavior modification, social learning, modeling, and aggression. In part 2, he recalls his classic Bobo doll experiment and discusses the effects of aggression and violence in the media, morality and moral disengagement, self-efficacy, reactions to criticisms, and plans for the future.

Animals: How Smart Are They? (1988) Films for the Humanities and Sciences, 26 min. This film compares the learning abilities of chimps, the famed gorilla Koko, and dolphins at the University of Hawaii. Research is asking whether language is defined by grammar, syntax, or creativity and whether humans are fundamentally different in terms of learning processes. The value and ethics of animal research are discussed.

Ape Language—From Conditioned Response to Symbol, (1986), Aims Media, Inc., 23 min. This video illustrates and documents research into the nature of language acquisition through the study of symbolic and syntactical skills in chimpanzees.

B. F. Skinner: A Fresh Appraisal, (1999), Davidson Films, 41 min. Other than Freud, no psychologist has been so discussed, critiqued, and at times maligned as B. F. Skinner. Using both archival and new footage, this video takes a new look at who the man was and what he really said in his 20 books. Like other thinkers who broke new ground, Skinner had to invent his own vocabulary to describe the phenomena he was studying. In this video, his terms are introduced in context so the student understands how they were intended to be used and the research that produced them. The video lays to rest some myths and credits Skinner with contributions not often attributed to him. Understanding the complex man behind his work enables students to better evaluate the importance and relevance of the work he inspired.

B. F. Skinner Keynote Address: Lifetime Scientific Contribution Remarks (2002) APA, 18 min. Behavioral psychologist Skinner presented this keynote address at the 1990 APA Annual Convention. In Dr. Skinner's last public appearance, he expresses his belief that the proper role for psychological science is the analysis of behavior. He speaks about the path psychology has followed over the years, from early introspection methods to three kinds of variation and selection, including natural selection, the evolution of operant conditioning, and the evolution of culture. VHS format.

Behavior Theory in Practice: Parts I-IV, (1966), Prentice-Hall, each part is 20 min. Basic and informative, these films present behavioral principles in considerable detail. Included in Part I are respondent versus operant behavior, selection of a response for basic research, the cumulative record, and operant conditioning and extinction. Part II covers schedules of reinforcement, shaping various operants, and programmed instruction. Part III features generalization, discrimination, motivation, reinforcement, punishment, avoidance, and intracranial reinforcement. Part IV describes sequences of behavior, homogeneous and heterogeneous chains, alternative responses, and multiple stimulus control.

Behavioral Treatment of Autistic Children, (1988), Pennsylvania State University, 44 min. This film presents a detailed explanation and demonstration of Ivar Lovaas' intensive behavioral treatment project for autistic children and illustrates various outcomes from the project, including normal functioning in half the children. It provides follow-up data from autistic children treated in the 1960s, seen 25 years later as adults. This is a new follow-up to the original film, Teaching Language to Autistic children, listed below. This is an excellent and powerful work.

Classical and Operant Conditioning, (2000), Films for the Humanities & Sciences, 56 min. This program explains the nature of behaviorism, so central to the study of human behavior, and its important applications in clinical therapy, education, and childrearing. It clearly explains, discusses, and illustrates the complex Classical and Operant conditioning theories of Pavlov and Skinner, and features archival footage of laboratory work with dogs and present-day research using rats in Skinner boxes as well as numerous examples of conditioning in everyday life.

Cognition and Learning (2005) 14 part series, Psychology Digital Video Library 3.0 Handbook, from Thomson Higher Education, approximately 30 min. total running time. This digital video unit contains brief segments on classical conditioning and operant conditioning. It also contains segments on neural networks in learning as will as a brief segment on Alzheimer's disease.

Further Approaches to Learning, (1998), Films for the Humanities and Sciences, 57 min. Explores alternative approaches and explanations of learning, including latent learning, learning sets, insight learning, ethology, social learning, and neuroscience. It emphasizes the recent move toward a cognitive theory of learning and examines the current research in this area. The program includes archival film featuring B.F. Skinner and Robert Epstein, who demonstrated apparent insight learning in pigeons using behaviorist techniques. Skinner, speaking just before his death, claims that reinforcement rather than higher mental processes is at work in learning.

Ivan Pavlov, (1981), Insight Media, 30 min. Edward de Bono conducts an interview with "Pavlov." This simulated interview helps the viewer to understand the revolutionary nature of Pavlov's work and the impact he had on the study of behavior.

Learning, (1990), from Psychology—The Study of Human Behavior Series, Coast District Telecourses, 30 min. This film focuses on classical conditioning, operant conditioning and real-world applications to behavioral psychology.

Learning, Discovering Psychology Series episode 8, (1990), Annenberg/CPB, 30 min. In this video from the Discovering Psychology series, Dr. Philip Zimbardo discusses the major players in traditional learning theory (e.g., Pavlov, Watson and Skinner) and the impact of these theories on modern life. For example, it describes how reinforcement is used to train dogs to assist in the care of disabled persons and how clinicians use behavior therapy to treat learned helplessness and agoraphobia. The behavioral perspective is highlighted throughout, but observational learning is not covered.

Learning (2002) from Discovering Psychology Series, Annenberg/CPB, 30 min.
The basic principles of classical and operant conditioning. Includes discussion of how Pavlov, Thorndike, Watson, and Skinner have influenced today's thinking.

Learning: Classical And Operant Conditioning (2002) from Psychology: The Human Experience Series, Coast Community College Telecourses, 30 min. This video discusses Pavlov's experiment and how it demonstrates the process of learning by an association or relationship.

Learning: Observational and Cognitive Approaches (2002) from Psychology - The Human Experience Series, Coast District Telecourses, 30 min. This video covers the topics of observational learning and cognitive processes in learning.

Nine Days of Hell--Japan's Toughest School, (1993), Filmmakers Library, 18 min. During holiday time, Japan's most ambitious parents send their children to a very intensive school to prepare them for the tremendous pressures of the Japanese school system. Up before dawn, drilled before eating, constantly quizzed, prodded, and harassed to learn by rote, the children are on constant alert except for a few hours of sleep at night. Each student must pass an oral examination, grilled by a stern panel of academicians, who goad and mock them and exhort them to present their ideas more fiercely. While many Japanese approve of this privately run program, some question whether it stifles creativity and independent thought.

Pain of Shyness, (1984), ABC 20/20, 17 min. This segment features Philip Zimbardo, author of The Shy Child, discussing just how disabling severe shyness can be. He also explains some of the techniques that have been used to overcome their shyness, including a demonstration of systematic desensitization.

Patient Like the Chipmunks: The Story of Animal Behavior Enterprises, (1996), Eclectic Science Productions, 45 min. This film tells the story of Animal Behavior Enterprises, the life's work of the Brelands and the Baileys. Keller and Marian Breland, authors of the classic "The Misbehavior of Organisms," were the first two graduate students ever to work with B.F. Skinner. They went on to apply behaviorist principles working with the military, the developmentally disabled, animal shows, advertising, and much more.

Think Like an Animal: Cognition Studies, (1988), Films for the Humanities and Sciences, 51 min. This intriguing program uses behavioral and communication research to open a window into the animal mind, as psychologists present their findings on innate animal intelligence gathered from the Ohio State University's Primate Cognition Project, the Smithsonian's Orangutan Language Project, and studies involving pigeons, parrots, and even octopuses. This research adds weight to the growing body of evidence that indicates animals do go beyond hardwired reflexes and responses to gather, organize, use, and retain information to solve problems.

Token Economy: Behaviorism Applied, (Insight, 23 min.)

➤ COMPUTER AND INTERNET RESOURCES

PsykTrek 3.0
Unit 5: Learning
5a. "Overview of Classical Conditioning"
5b. "Basic Processes in Classical Conditioning"
5c. "Overview of Operant Conditioning"
5d. "Schedules of Reinforcement"
5e. "Reinforcement and Punishment"
5f. "Avoidance and Escape Learning"

INFOTRAC®

Below you will find three journal articles obtained from INFOTRAC® that relate to information contained in this chapter. Instructors should encourage students to utilize this invaluable resource to improve their research skills. Have students locate and read the following articles and answer questions relevant to each article.

The Journal of General Psychology, October 2002 v129 i4 p364 (37). **Common processes may contribute to extinction and habituation.**

1.   List the 12 similarities between extinction and habituation.

      Answer: Characteristic 1: Spontaneous recovery
                  Characteristic 2: Dishabituation
                  Characteristic 3: Stimulus specificity
                  Characteristic 4: Stimulus exposure
                  Characteristic 5: Habituation without responding
                  Characteristic 6: Rate of stimulus presentation
                  Characteristic 7: Long-term habituation
                  Characteristic 8: Repeated extinctions
                  Characteristic 9: Generality
                  Characteristic 10: Sensitization by early stimulus present
                  Characteristic 11: Sensitization by stimuli from another modality
                  Characteristic 12: A negative exponential function

2.   According to the article, what is habituation and how do the researchers believe that habituation plays a role in extinction?

      Answer: Habituation is a decrease in responsiveness to a stimulus when that stimulus is presented repeatedly or for a prolonged time. Conditioned responding declines in extinction partly because habituation occurs to stimuli that support that responding.

3.   List six findings in this study that were not predicted by habituation.

        Answer: Findings that are not predicted by habituation:
        Problem 1: Representation-mediated extinction
        Problem 2: Conditions during acquisition alter extinction
        Problem 3: Other behavior during extinction
        Problem 4: Reacquisition may be faster than acquisition
        Problem 5: Behavioral variability may increase
        Problem 6: Specificity of extinction

Western Journal of Communication, Fall 2003 v67 i4 p357 (25) Sustaining the desire to learn: Dimensions of perceived instructional face-work related to student involvement and motivation to learn.

1.   This study sought to expand the working teacher's interpersonal communication repertoire by investigating relationships between what two mechanisms?

        Answer: (a) students' perceptions of instructional face-support in teachers' evaluations of student work and (b) students' intrinsic motivations to learn, interaction involvement, and task-mastery orientation.

2.   What is Goffman's (1967) definition of "face-work"?

        Answer: The desired self-image that individuals seek to both present and maintain in interaction with others. As an interactional accomplishment, face cannot be claimed for oneself but must be supported by others in the interaction.

3.   According to Brown and Levinson's (1987) politeness theory, what is positive face and negative face?

        Answer: According to Brown and Levinson's (1987) politeness theory, face includes two separate desires: the need to feel included, approved of, and appreciated by certain others (positive face) and the need to remain autonomous and unimpeded by others (negative face).

Education & Treatment of Children, Feb 2001 v24 i1 p99. The Effects of a Token Economy Employing Instructional Consequences for a Third-Grade Student with Learning Disabilities: A Data-Based Case Study.

1.   Who and what were the subject of this investigation?

Answer: The participant in this study was a 10-year-old, third-grade male. According to teacher reports, the participant exhibited high rates of multiple disruptive behaviors including out-of-seat behavior, talking-out, and poor seat posture. The participant had normal intelligence but was below grade level in the basic skills of reading and written language. The purpose of this investigation was to determine if a token reinforcement program could decrease three inappropriate behaviors (out of seat, talking out, and poor posture) of an elementary student with learning disabilities. Data were also gathered to assess the brief maintenance effects of the token program.

2.   What were the "tokens" in the token economy, and what could they being used to buy?

Answer: During the token economy, the participating student immediately earned a checkmark, if at the end of each minute, appropriate behavior occurred instead of the specific targeted behaviors. By the end of the case study, three checkmarks could be earned per period for the absence of all three target behaviors. The tokens could be exchanged for back-up rewards such as math worksheets, computer time, reading instruction, leisure reading, and playing academic games.

3.   Were there any limits or drawbacks to this approach?

Answer: A possible limitation of the present intervention data-based case study was that, while the results were very commendable, it may take too much time for the teacher to implement a token program and monitor student performance. In the present research, the teacher felt that implementing the token program, with its subsequent monitoring requirements, could reduce some other aspects of her teaching activities.

WEB LINKS

Knowledge Builder Web Links

1) Learning and Classical Conditioning
     Ivan Pavlov: http://www.ivanpavlov.com/
     Classical Conditioning Experiment: http://www.psylab.com/html/default_classic2.htm
     Conditioned Emotional Responses: http://psychclassics.yorku.ca/Watson/emotion.htm

2) Operant Conditioning
     B.F. Skinner:
          http://www.bfskinner.org/BFSkinner/Home.html
     Clicker Training for Animals: http://www.wagntrain.com/OC/
     Hardwired for Happiness: http://www.dana.org/news/cerebrum/detail.aspx?id=5514

3) Partial Reinforcement and Stimulus Control
Schedules of Reinforcement:
http://psychology.about.com/od/behavioralpsychology/a/schedules.htm
Stimuli: http://www.psychology.uiowa.edu/Faculty/wasserman/Glossary/stimuli.html
Positive and Negative Discriminative Stimuli in Animal Training:
http://www.clickertraining.com/node/164

4) Punishment
Ten Reasons Not to Hit Your Kids:
http://www.naturalchild.com/jan_hunt/tenreasons.html
Guidelines for Using Timeouts with Children and Preteens:
http://www.childdevelopmentinfo.com/parenting/timeout.shtml

5) Cognitive Learning and Imitation
Social Learning Theory and Criminality:
http://www.apsu.edu/oconnort/crim/crimtheory12.htm
Mirror Neurons and Imitation Learning:
http://www.edge.org/3rd_culture/ramachandran/ramachandran_p1.html
Media Violence: http://www.mediafamily.org/facts/facts_vlent.shtml

6) Behavioral Self-Management – A Rewarding Project
Psychological Self-Tools:
http://www.mentalhelp.net/poc/center_index.php?id=353&cn=353
Self-Management: http://www.slc.sevier.org/selfmgt.htm
Behavior Contract:
http://k6educators.about.com/cs/classroommanageme3/a/createcontract.htm

Additional Web Links

APA Online
http://www.apa.org/

Animal Training at SeaWorld
http://www.seaworld.org/infobooks/Training/home.html

Classical Conditioning
http://www.ryerson.ca/~glassman/behavior.html

Conditioning and Reinforcement
http://www.mcli.dist.maricopa.edu/proj/nru/

Understanding Learning
http://www.funderstanding.com/observational_learning.cfm

Training Your Pet
http://www.dogtrainingbasics.com/
http://www.perfectpaws.com/cpv.html
http://www.catsinternational.org/articles/training/walking_your_cat.html

240

Behavior Modification Techniques
http://www.webmd.com/add-adhd/guide/adhd-behavioral-techniques

Cognitive Learning Theory
http://teachnet.edb.utexas.edu/~lynda_abbott/Cognitive.html

PSYCHOLOGY IN THE NEWS

DistanceLearning.com
http://www.distance-educator.com
This site provides articles and daily news issues in distance learning.

Plebius Press Psychology Resource Center
http://psychology.plebius.org/news.php
News articles on a variety of subjects including psychology in the news; search by topic.

Psych Central: Daily Psychology News and Headlines
http:/www.psychcentral.com/news/
Get daily updates and the latest in headline news.

CHAPTER 7
Memory

➤ SURVEY QUESTIONS

Module 7.1 Memory Systems

Survey Question: How does memory work?

Module 7.2 STM and LTM

Survey Question: What are the features of short-term memory?

Survey Question: What are the features of long-term memory?

Module 7.3 Measuring Memory

Survey Question: How is memory measured?

Module 7.4 Forgetting

Survey Question: Why do we forget?

Survey Question: How does the brain form and store memories?

Module 7.5 Exceptional Memory and Improving Memory

Survey Question: What are "photographic" memories?

Survey Question: How can I improve my memory?

Module 7.6 Psychology in Action: Mnemonics—Memory Magic

Survey Question: Are there any tricks to help me with my memory?

➤ DISCUSSION QUESTIONS

1. Has anyone ever told you that you have a bad memory? Was it really a case of poor memory, or were you just not remembering the things the other person thought were a priority? Is your memory better for some things than others? How many of you "can't remember" names? Is that just a matter of motivation, or does memory really have strengths and weaknesses?

2. Have you ever asked someone to repeat something, but before they have a chance to answer you suddenly "hear" it? What part of memory is that? Have you ever experienced a similar phenomenon with vision?

3. Have you ever gone through an intersection, gotten to the other side, and suddenly thought "Was that light *green*?" Why do you think that happens? Is this phenomenon functional or not?

4. What kind of learner are you? Do you prefer learning by reading, writing, listening, or doing? Does the preference vary with the type of task to be learned? How might you improve your skills in your non-dominant areas?

5. Your text states that eyewitness testimony in court is notoriously unpredictable. Do you think most jurors know this? How important do you think it is to have an eyewitness, or is physical evidence enough? Should juries be told about eyewitness unreliability research? Why or why not?

6. If you were forced to give up either STM or LTM, which would you choose? Think carefully about your answer.

7. What do you think is the most important strategy for maximizing short-term memory? Explain why you think this.

8. Describe the types of long-term memory. Give an example of something you know that fits into each category.

9. What type of classroom testing do you prefer? Why? What would you consider an ideal way to be tested? ("Never" does not count as an answer!)

10. How do you prepare for tests? Which of your strategies are typical of recall, and which are typical of recognition? Do you study differently for essay tests versus multiple choice tests? What are the differences? Why might learning material using recall strategies be beneficial even during a recognition test, such as a multiple choice test?

11. Why do people forget? Compare and contrast the various theories of forgetting. Which process makes the most sense to you? Why?

12.   What is the relationship between cue-dependent forgetting and memory networks?

13.   We have seen that there are several reasons for forgetting. Which does the use of mnemonics most directly combat? How would you minimize the other major causes of forgetting?

14.   Would you like to have a memory like the man studied by A. R. Luria? What would be the advantages and disadvantages of such a memory? Mr. S. could not recognize faces. Can you explain why? If, as an adult, you retained eidetic memory, how would you go about using it?

15.   What role could adrenaline play in state-dependent learning?

16.   In 1989, a woman was raped and beaten in a notorious case of "wilding" that took place in New York City's Central Park. After she recovered, she couldn't remember events just prior to or during the attack, and she could not identify her assailants. Why?

17.   If scientists perfect a drug that improves memory, do you think it should be widely available? Would you want to try it? If a drug were perfected that could cause selective forgetting of memories, would you support its use for victims of rape, assault, disaster, or a horrifying accident?

18.   A person has a tumor in the hippocampus; what changes in that person's memory would you anticipate?

19.   What mnemonic strategies have you used in studying? Which have been most helpful? How could a person with limited mental imagery use mnemonics?

20.   The text provides a list of ways to improve your memory. Which do you think would be most helpful to college students and why? Now, choose one from the list that you do not already use. Would you consider it to be useful? Why or why not?

21.   What have you done to cope with remembering longer zip codes and telephone numbers?

22.   Describe a case of mistaken identity you have seen in the news. What aspect of memory contributed to the mistake?

23. In view of the text's discussion, do you think memories that occur during hypnosis should be allowed as evidence in court? One expert has suggested videotaping sessions during which witnesses or victims are questioned under hypnosis. If such tapes were available to juries, do you think testimony based on hypnosis would be more trustworthy? Why or why not?

24. How is redintegration related to cognitive hierarchies or networks? In what ways could redintegration explain the different types of long-term memory?

25. You are writing a book called *Three Steps to a Terrific Memory*. What will you use as the three key processes? What specific recommendations would you make for improving memory?

➤ LECTURE ENHANCEMENTS

1. **STM and random digits.** To illustrate the limited capacity of short-term memory, read a series of random digits to the class. Instruct the students to listen to the numbers and, after you stop, to write down as many as they can remember. Begin by reading a series five digits long: 5 1 9 2 3

   Next, try increasing the number of digits:

six:	9 1 9 2 5 8
seven:	9 8 2 2 9 3 1
eight:	3 8 5 4 9 6 5 7
nine:	3 8 0 4 7 1 3 6 9
ten:	5 3 2 1 9 6 1 2 1 6

   Reread the digits so the students can check their accuracy. The seven (plus or minus two) bit capacity of short-term memory should become quite apparent to the students.

2. **Encoding failure and forgetting**. Ask students go out on campus, select five people at random, and test their memories for these "familiar" facts. Return to class with the results.

   Questions:
   1) Who is on the penny, and which way is he facing? (Lincoln, right)
   2) How many states have the word "north," "south," "east," or "west" in their names? (Five: N. Dakota, S. Dakota, W. Virginia, N. Carolina, S. Carolina)
   3) Which U.S. state is the furthest west? (Hawaii)
   4) Who is the current mayor of your city?
   5) What is the license plate of your closest relative's car?

3. **Organizing memories.** At the end of this chapter, give students the assignment of creating an organizational or hierarchical diagram for either this class or some other class. You might even give this as an extra-credit assignment. The chart should be sufficiently

247

detailed to indicate various levels of the subject material. Collect all the charts and reproduce a "good," "moderate," and "poor" example of hierarchical organization. (Remove names, of course.) You can also point out that the very act of writing out the organization will, in itself, build stronger memories of the material.

4. **Interference and forgetting.** To demonstrate forgetting, the limited memory storage of short-term memory, and interference, read 10-15 digits from the list below. Before you begin, tell students that when you say "begin" they are to say the alphabet aloud until you say "stop." Immediately after you say "stop," they are to write, in reverse order, as many of the digits as they can remember. Try this after interference periods of 1, 3, 5, 7, 10, and 15 seconds. By the time you reach a 15-second delay, very few class members will be able to remember even the final digit.

```
5 1 9 2 3 2 2 7 2 9 8 2 3 9 6 4 0 4 5 8 1 2 1 5 6 5 4 5 6
9 1 9 2 5 8 4 6 2 5 7 8 1 9 6 5 3 2 8 7 7 7 5 1 2 4 6 2 1
2 1 4 5 4 8 4 7 4 9 6 5 4 7 2 5 4 1 8 7 6 5 4 2 3 1 5 9 8
1 2 5 4 3 2 6 5 1 4 8 7 9 5 6 2 3 1 5 4 7 8 2 5 1 3 4 5 7
```

5. **Do you remember an event, or were you told?** Does it match too closely? Has a relative ever told the student about the event? How confident are students that they really remember the event and they didn't just hear about it later? Discuss the difficulties of knowing if a memory is accurate or not.

6. **This is nonsense!** The lists below offer a simple illustration of the effects of meaningfulness on the organization and retention of information. The nonsense syllables in List A are rated as having 40 percent association value. List B is made up of meaningful, but unrelated words. In addition to being meaningful, the words in List C can be organized into a sentence. Divide the class into thirds. Give a different list to each person. Give everyone the same amount of time to learn the list. Then ask students to turn the paper over and to write down as many of the syllables as they can remember.

LIST A	LIST B	LIST C
JEK	DEN	THE
VEH	MIX	BOY
XIB	WON	AND
YAP	BUY	HIS
BIV	GET	DOG
MUP	HOW	MET
GEW	RUN	OLD
HIX	POD	MAN
WEG	CAP	WHO
CIH	FIT	HAD

248

7. **Which strategies are best?** Pass out copies of the list below and ask students to rank-order which memory strategies they think are the most effective. An elaboration of the terms can be found on in the text. Collect the papers and compile the results either item by item, or in terms of the most popular item. For the most popular item, the easiest thing to do is to simply ask for a show of hands of who picked each item.

Memory Strategies List:
1. ____Knowledge of results
2. ____Rehearsal
3. ____Selection
4. ____Organization
5. ____Whole versus part learning
6. ____Serial position
7. ____Cues
8. ____Overlearning
9. ____Spaced practice
10. ____Review

8. Chunking . Chunking can greatly extend the capacity of short-term memory. This can be shown by instructing half the class to use a chunking strategy while allowing the other half to memorize more haphazardly. Hand out to half the class an instruction sheet that reads:

A long list of words will be read to you. Try to memorize the entire list using "raw" memory ability. You should listen to the list and try to remember as much as you can, but do not attempt to apply any system or special technique in memorizing the list.

The second half of the class should receive a sheet that reads:

A long list of words will be read to you. Try to memorize the entire list. Your task will be easier if you memorize the words in groups of three. Try to form a mental image that includes the first three items as read and then try to form a new image for each following set of three. For example, if the first three words were, "skate, bone, and piano," you might picture a roller skate with a bone in it on top of a piano.

After students have read their respective instructions, read the list below from left to right. Read loudly and clearly, allowing a relatively long pause between words:

CAR	TREE	TOOTH	PENCIL	WATCH	CHAIR
VIOLIN	FLOWER	HOUSE	BICYCLE	RECORD	PIZZA
BOOK	DISH	NAIL	TOWEL	APPLE	MATCH
FISH	SKY	SHOE			

Wait a moment after completing the list and ask students to write as many items as they can remember.

Notice that there are 21 items on the list. Students who use the chunking strategy will have only seven chunks to contend with, which should be a manageable number for most. To determine if chunking improved retention, compute the mean number of items recalled by each group.

9.   **Clustering and free-recall.** One of the simplest and most obvious indications of organizational structure in memory is clustering (the tendency for related words to appear together in a free-recall situation). To demonstrate clustering, ask students to memorize the list below. You will likely find that students will naturally "chunk" groups of words together. In addition, check to see how many students falsely remembered a word that was not on the list but is a member of one of the categories. You should still see a serial position effect, even with opportunities for chunking.

apple	purple	green	pen	orange
book	ruler	melon	grapefruit	bear
red	banana	jaguar	yellow	desk
lion	buffalo	pencil	wolf	elephant

10.   **The serial position effect.** To demonstrate the serial position effect, the following word list should be read aloud fairly quickly (to avoid the use of mnemonic devices by the students). After one reading, ask the students to write down as many of the items as they can remember. Then present the list to the students using an overhead projector, and check by a show of hands how many remembered each item. More students will recall the first and last portions of the list than the middle, showing the serial position effect.

a.   Use the following *shorter* list of words:

desk	phone	moon	tree	dog
computer	bear	flower	picture	car

250

b. Use the following *longer* list of words:

house	cheese	star	pen	dish
book	highway	melon	horse	uncle
class	ocean	doorway	model	mustache
creature	cloud	prairie	train	plastic

11. **Mnemonic Strategies.** A discussion of mnemonic strategies and examples can provide skills of lasting value to students. You can begin by asking for examples of terms or information students have had difficulty learning in other classes. With the help of the class you can then devise mnemonic strategies. Names also make good examples. For interest, use names from the class roster, making transformations such as these:

Aaron = hair on; Carifiol = care if I oil; Chomentowski = show men to ski; Sellentin = sellin' tin; and so forth.

The mnemonic device of loci, or places, was developed by Simonides. In this approach, each item to be remembered is pictured in association with familiar locations—around the home, along a street, on campus, or on parts of the body.

To show how powerful mnemonic strategies can be, have the class call out a list of 30 objects. As each object is added, encourage students to imagine it placed on, or associated with, a part of the body. For example, if the first item is "pencil," students might imagine a pencil stuck between their toes; if the second is "bird," a bird might be imagined in place of the foot, and so forth. The following loci work well: toes, foot, heel, ankle, calf, knee, thigh, hip, waist, navel, ribs, chest, fingers, palm, wrist, forearm, ear, forehead, hair. This provides 29 loci, so the last item must be remembered by rote. After the list has been practiced once through, ask the class to recall it by trying to picture the object associated with each body part. Nearly all the items will be remembered by most class members—a unique experience for many of them.

12. **Your earliest memories.** *Psychology Today* has surveyed its readers regarding their earliest memories. Ninety-six percent of the respondents reported having memories prior to the age of six, with 68 percent reporting recall for events occurring when they were two or three. Further, a surprising 7 percent said they had memories prior to age one, and a few even claimed to have prenatal recollections as well as memories of their own birth! While some of the early memories were of traumatic experiences (such as the birth of a sibling, being injured, or the death of relatives or pets), the majority of recollections were of more mundane things (like being given a bath, having a picture taken, or being pushed in a swing). Interestingly, most of the memories involved images rather than events. People remembered things like curtains blowing in the breeze, a light shining on someone's face, and a mobile hanging in the air. This is probably because small children generally lack the language skills necessary to encode a complicated series of events. Many psychologists, in fact, believe that it is rare for people to remember things that occurred before they were able to talk.

251

Since students are usually fascinated by their own early lives, **you** can generate a high amount of interest in this topic by asking them to write the answer to the same question *Psychology Today* asked its readers: "What is your earliest memory and how old were you?" Before starting, your students need to be cautioned to try to make sure that it is a real memory and not something they've been told about or seen in photograph albums, etc. After they've finished, you should have them read some of the responses for the class. For more details see E. Stark, "Thanks for the Memories," *Psychology Today,* November 1984.

13.   **Meaningfulness and memory.** The following exercise provides another demonstration of the effect of meaningfulness on memory. Prepare three handouts as shown below. Ask students to attempt to memorize the words listed on **Handout A.** Then give them **Handout B** and have them practice the words again, this time with some meaningful context. Finally, give them **Handout C** and have them try to consolidate their learning. By the time they get to the third presentation, they should know the lists well, and they should have some insight into the organizational value of meaningfulness.

Handout A: Read the following list of words carefully. Try to remember as many words as you can.

Gather	End
Separate	Ball
Spray	Tie
Push	Walk
Wait	Run
Pull	Hold
Fasten	Jerk
Pile	Unravel
Corners	

Handout B: Read the following paragraphs carefully. Try to remember the words that are underlined.

Gather everything and carry it to one room. Separate. Spray. Check the temperature. Add the powder. Push the button. Wait for 30 minutes. Open the lid. Pull everything out and place in a basket. Walk outside and find the rope. Fasten each piece, overlapping corners just slightly. About two hours later, unpin everything, put it back in the basket, and fold and put it in piles. Carry one pile back to each room.

Find the end from the ball. Tie it to the corners of the wood. Walk to the top of a hill. As you run down the hill, hold onto the ball, gradually letting the long end go. Jerk the ball up if the corners of the wood swoop down. Continue to unravel the ball.

252

Handout C:

The following paragraph describes the process of doing laundry. Read the paragraph carefully. Try to remember the words that are printed in bold type.

Gather everything and carry it to one room. **Separate. Spray**. Check the temperature. Add the powder. **Push** the button. **Wait** for 30 minutes. Open the lid. **Pull** everything out and place in a basket. **Walk** outside and find the rope. **Fasten** each piece, overlapping **corners** just slightly. About two hours later, unpin everything, put it back in the basket, and fold and put it in piles. Carry one **pile** back to each room.

The following paragraph describes the process of flying a kite.

Find the **end** from the **ball. Tie** it to the **corners** of the wood. **Walk** to the top of a hill. As you **run** down the hill, **hold** onto the **ball,** gradually letting the long **end** go. **Jerk** the **ball** up if the **corners** of the wood swoop down. Continue to **unravel** the **ball.**

➤ ROLE-PLAYING SCENARIOS

1. **Your classmates are going to ask you questions about yourself.** Answer as if you lacked short-term memory. How do you feel about your memory deficit?

2. **You have just awakened from a coma and have no memory of the past month, or of what caused your coma.** How do you feel? What do you want to know?

3. **You are an attorney questioning a witness whose memory you want to challenge.** What questions can you ask the witness to demonstrate the unreliability of memory?

4. **You are a professor advising an older student who has returned to college.** The student is having trouble preparing for exams. What advice can you give the student for improving memory?

5. **Have a conversation with a "dementia patient."** Break students into small groups and tell them to have a pretend conversation with a person who has dementia. There will probably be students in the class who actually have relatives with dementia. They should be distributed among the groups to act as observers. One student should be the interviewer, and another should be the "patient." Imitate the behavior of a person suffering from a memory disorder, such as Alzheimer's disease. Ask the observers how close it was to the "real thing."

253

➤ VALUE-CLARIFICATION STATEMENTS

1.   Some people's memories are just naturally better than other people's.

2.   Working on improving one's memory is more trouble than it's worth.

3.   Testimony obtained with hypnosis should be used in court.

4.   When a person can't remember information for a class, it is usually because the information was not really learned in the first place.

5.   Students could remember course information better if instructors would help them visualize the ideas more often.

6.   Being able to forget embarrassing incidents is a good thing.

7.   A person should never stay up all night studying for a morning exam.

8.   The study strategies outlined in the book are not effective for most students.

9.   People who say they have a "photographic memory" are really people just like us who have learned memory strategies.

10.   Even if a "memory pill" could be manufactured, that pill should be illegal.

11.   Memory loss is just an inevitable part of aging

➤ ONE-MINUTE MOTIVATORS

1.   **I didn't know!** During the last five minutes of class before beginning this chapter, weave into your lecture/discussion an announcement of a quiz for the next class session (or write the announcement in some obscure corner of the chalkboard). Only one or two people should notice. Begin class by asking students to take out a piece of paper for the quiz. When students protest, begin a discussion of why we often fail to remember, including inattention and failure to record the information in the first place.

2.   **Sensory memory.** Use a tachistoscope (T-scope) to flash images quickly to demonstrate sensory memory. Read a series of words to the class to be remembered. Ask them to think about their initial processing of the words. Are they aware of an echo? Do they silently rehearse the words? Do they attempt to chunk them in some way? Do they try to link them to knowledge in long-term storage?

3.   **Keeping track of information.** Ask each student to state his or her favorite musical group and favorite food. Have students try to remember each classmate's favorites.

254

Discuss to what extent students used visual cues, the order of the information, and chunking to remember the information. What mnemonic strategies would make this task easier?

4. **The automatic nature of memory**. Ask students to write down which groceries they need to buy the next time they go grocery shopping. Ask them how they knew that they needed those items? In some cases, there was effortful encoding (I must remember to buy item "x"), but in most cases the memories were formed automatically.

5. **Eyewitness testimony. (internet exercise)** Have students research some cases involving eyewitness testimony and bring their findings back to class. In order to avoid too much duplication, and to generate a more diverse search, it is recommended that each student use two keyword phrases: "eyewitness" and another phrase of their choice. Examples include: murder, research, your state, prosecution, robbery, government, and so on.

6. **Serial position effect.** In a variation of the exercise above, ask a student to tell what her or his hobby is (or favorite movie, food, sport, color, etc.). The next student repeats what the first student said and adds his or her own information. Continue in this way until 10 students have spoken. Students will find that they remember what was said by the first few students and the person just before their turn. Discuss the serial position effect.

7. **Redintegrative memory.** To demonstrate redintegrative memory, ask students to try to remember the activities, demonstrations, and discussions that took place at an earlier class session. Then show them a photograph you took in class that day (if you did take any earlier) or tell them what major national and local news events took place that day. As one memory leads to another, discuss how important memory cues are.

8. **But I knew the material!** Students are often confused and frustrated when they get a disappointing grade on a test even though they "knew the material."

   You can help them understand that their knowledge wasn't as great as they thought it was by giving them a quick quiz in class the day the test is given back (as a demonstration only). Ask them to write down answers to 10 questions. When forced to write down the answers, as opposed to just recognizing them, many students will come to the realization that they didn't really know the material as well as they thought they did.

   You can start a discussion about ways to determine—before the test—if their knowledge base is as firm as they think. You might remind them that recognition is more superficial than recall. A good rule of thumb with regard to facts and definitions is that if you can't write it out, you don't know it. Students' ability to recognize the correct answer in a low-stress situation provides them with a false sense of confidence that often evaporates under actual test-taking conditions.

   Another suggestion is to review the material "cold." i.e., when students attempt study guide questions, they often do so immediately after learning the material. Then, they get questions correct because the memories are fresh. If, instead, they wait 24 hours and then attempt practice questions, they will be in a better position to know whether the memories have actually consolidated over night.

9. **Recall versus recognition.** Give students two comparable lists of terms. Ask students to recall one list and give them a recognition test for terms from the other list. (Embed the terms in a longer list and have students circle those that they learned.) Compare their memory scores.

10. **Test preferences.** Ask the students who prefers multiple-choice tests and who prefers essay tests. Then, ask them why. This is a good opportunity to illustrate the difference between recognition and recall. Some students prefer essay tests because they have used elaborative rehearsal and hierarchical organization. Other students prefer multiple choice tests because they rely primarily on recognition.

11. **What was different?** Add a few posters to the classroom. Do not draw attention to them. Take them down and ask the class about them. Discuss how difficult it is to remember if we never encoded the information in the first place. Share strategies for selective listening and note-taking.

12. **Examining flashbulb memories.** Ask students to report a "flashbulb" memory that is especially vivid for them. What role did emotion play in the formation of the memory? Have they rehearsed and retold the memory unusually frequently? How can flashbulb memories be explained? Many of your students will cite the events around 9/11 as a flashbulb memory. Even there, however, not all memories of the event will be the same, and students might disagree about details. Even flashbulb memories are subject to deterioration over time.

➤ BROADENING OUR CULTURAL HORIZONS

1. **Cultural priorities and memory.** Members of cultures that trade beads can recall the color patterns of long strands of beads; those who herd cattle can remember and recognize dozens of individual animals. Can you name some types of information that is easily remembered in our culture but that might be difficult for a member of another culture to encode (for example, the year and make of a number of automobiles)? In what ways does cultural experience prepare us to remember some things easily and other things with difficulty?

2. **Memory and meaning.** Why might a person who speaks English and Spanish equally well prefer to read or study physics in English and to learn poetry in Spanish?

3. **Culture, perception, and memory.** You are visiting a foreign country. You speak the language, but you are very unfamiliar with the culture. You stop a passerby on the street and ask for directions. Why might you find it difficult to remember the directions, and why might your helper have trouble giving them?

4. **Mnemonics in other cultures.** Talk to people in your class or on campus who were born in another country. Ask them how they remember the number of days in each month, for example, or any other information you remember with a mnemonic device. What device do they use? Is it very different from the device you were taught?

5. **Memory, culture, and organization.** Why is it often difficult for new immigrants to learn a country's monetary system? (Consider perceptual effects, such as a dime being smaller than a nickel, as well as memory.)

6. **Alzheimer's disease treatments in other countries.** If there are students from other cultures in your classroom, ask them how people with Alzheimer's disease are viewed and treated in that culture.

7. **Educational strategies in different cultures.** If your class is diverse, and includes students whose primary and/or secondary education took place in a different country, ask them what kinds of learning strategies were used. Then, compare them with the responses from the U.S. school system. Which countries are more likely to focus on rote learning, rehearsal, elaboration, critical thinking, student participation, small groups, etc.? Which strategies are most likely to be associated with retention? Are there any confounding factors that affect the quality of education, such as longer school hours?

➤ SUPPLEMENTAL ACTIVITIES

Exercise 7.1: Organize for Meaning

I. Introduction

This exercise is intended to show that when information is organized in a meaningful way it is learned, retained, and recalled more easily. You should be sure to relate this exercise, and the discussion before and after it, to the study habits of the students. They may not see the value of what they learn here unless it is pointed out. It is even better if they can be led to conclude this for themselves.

Two handouts are provided for this exercise. They should be distributed in such a way that half of the class gets one version of **Handout 7.1** and the other half gets the alternate version of Handout 7.1. A good way to do this would be to stack the handouts ahead of time alternating #1 and #2 in the pile.

List #1 contains a set of terms that are organized in a logical, meaningful way. List #2 has no particular logic, meaning, or order to the presentation. Only the form and raw content are the same as #1.

II. Procedure

A. Explain to the class that they will be given a brief learning task. Ask them to do their best on it, so they can see a learning principle at work.

B. Distribute the handout sheets, alternately stacked, to the students facedown, then give each student a data sheet for responding, also facedown.

C. Ask the students to turn the list over and study it for 45 seconds.

D. At the end of the time period, instruct the students to turn the list facedown and write as many words as they can remember on the data sheet. Give them about two minutes to do this.

E. Ask the students to check their work to see how many they got right.

F. Total the number right for those who had lists #1 and #2 separately and find the mean for each group. Those who studied list #1, which was organized in a meaningful way, should receive a higher mean score than those who did list #2.

III. Discussion

A. What is the difference between the two lists? You should show the two lists together on an overhead projector so the students can compare them.

B. Why is there a difference in performance on the two lists?

C. Some students who had the second list, the one lacking organization, will still do as well as or better than those in the other group. Identify those persons and try to find out what they did to recall so much. This could lead to some interesting discussion of memory techniques.

C. Can what has been found in this exercise apply to the study habits of the students? Discuss ways to make it work for them.

258

Exercise 7.2: Meaning and Memory.

In this exercise, students become the experimenters. Each student is instructed to test participants with three different word lists. Full instructions for the students, as well as data recording forms, can be found in **Handout 7.2**.

Exercise 7.3: Factors Affecting Memory

For this exercise, you will need to give each student one copy of **Handout 7.3A** and one copy of **Handout 7.3B**. After you have completed the chapter, ask students to list all their teachers from kindergarten to the end of high school. Generally, we are able to remember more recent events better than earlier events, and we also often have difficulty remembering childhood events in particular, because children's brains are not as fully developed. What is interesting, however, is that students may be able to remember primary school teachers better than high school teachers. They might also remember, for example, their first grade teacher but not their third grade teacher.

Handout 7.3A asks students to make the list and then speculate on why some teachers are more memorable than others. Generally, teachers from grades 7 and 8 will be remembered better than grade 9 teachers, partly because more time is spent with a single teacher (rather than multiple teachers), and partly because students' attitudes toward school and teachers might also undergo changes in motivation.

When students have completed the exercise themselves, have them take home Handout 7.3B and ask the parent to fill out the same sheet. Parents in families with several children might have some difficulty with the exercise because of interference.

The parents' sheet also asks the parent and student to compare each others' responses. In some cases, there will be disagreements about whose answer was correct. In those cases, explain to students that memory is not exact. Even when we feel that a memory is accurate, it might not be, because memories are not stored intact, but rather are reconstructed as needed.

Exercise 7.4. What is Dementia? (internet exercise)

One of the most widespread and devastating causes of memory loss are the various dementias that often affect the elderly. Examples include Alzheimer's disease, vascular dementia (multi-infarct dementia), and Parkinson's disease. There are more than 70 diseases or situations that can cause dementia. Multiple causes of dementia can also occur in any given person simultaneously.

Ask students to research Alzheimer's facts and myths and bring their findings to class. Each student should report on at least one finding that he or she found surprising, and why. After they have done their own research, for comparison purposes, **Handout 7.4** contains myths and facts about Alzheimer's disease, multi-infarct dementia (vascular dementia) and Parkinson's disease.

Links:
http://www.alz.org
http://www.ninds.nih.gov/disorders/multi_infarct_dementia/multi_infarct_dementia.htm
http://www.ninds.nih.gov/disorders/parkinsons_disease/parkinsons_disease.htm
http://www.michaeljfox.org

Handout 7.1: ORGANIZE FOR MEANING: LIST #1

FOOD

Meat		Vegetables		Fruit	
beef	pork	green	yellow	small	large
ground	chops	beans	carrots	grapes	apples
steak	ribs	peas	squash	berries	oranges
roast	loin	broccoli	rutabaga	cherries	melons

Handout 7.1: ORGANIZE FOR MEANING: LIST #2

FOOD

ribs   squash   oranges

peas   berries   chops   grapes   steak   carrots

large   apples   beef   melons   cherries   rutabaga

yellow   meat   beans   green   roast   pork

ground   vegetables   loin   small   fruit   broccoli

262

Handout 7.1: ORGANIZE FOR MEANING: DATA SHEET

TO THE STUDENT:

Write as many words from the list you have studied as you can, in any order. If you are not sure, you can guess.

1._____

2._____

3._____

4._____

5._____

6._____

7._____

8._____

9._____

10._____

11._____

12._____

13._____

14._____

15._____

16._____

17._____

18._____

19._____

20._____

21._____

22._____

23._____

24._____

25._____

26._____

27._____

28._____

Handout 7.2: MEANING AND MEMORY

TO THE STUDENT:

A. **Background and Purpose**

Psychologists have found that meaningful information is easier to remember than that which is not. This is because it is associated with information that is already in memory. The purpose of this project is to show that material that is higher in association value is easier to store in memory and recall.

B. **You will be testing subjects with three word lists.** One list has high association value, the second has medium value, and the third has low association value. Each subject will be given all three lists; however, they should be given one at a time, at separate times, with some time interval between the administration of each list. The subjects will be asked to write down as many words as they can remember after hearing the list once.

C. **Directions**

1. Select three subjects for this study. They should be over 10 years of age.

2. You need to meet with each subject three times to administer each of the three word lists.

3. Provide the subject with a pencil and sheet of paper.

4. Give each subject the high association word list first, then the medium list, and finally the low. Each should be given separately with a time interval in between.

5. Read the word list to the subject. Read the words in order, slowly, about one word per second.

6. The subject should listen carefully. After you finish reading the list, have the subject write down as many as (s)he can remember. Do the same for each list.

7. Record the results for each subject on each word list. Find the average number of words recalled correctly for each type of list.

8. Answer the questions about your results, discussing what you found and relating it to the material on memory in the text.

264

Handout 7.2: MEANING AND MEMORY (cont.)

WORD LISTS

High	Medium	Low
the	bee	yad
dog	nor	cif
ate	can	mul
two	but	bix
and	fee	pog
did	lob	zel
not	sit	riv
eat	old	mib
for	doe	daf
you	run	hib

RESULTS

SUBJECT	SCORES (number of correct words)		
	HIGH	**MEDIUM**	**LOW**
1.			
2.			
3.			
AVERAGE SCORE			

265

Handout 7.2: MEANING AND MEMORY (cont.)

D.   Discussion

1.   Based on the data you gathered, to what extent does association play a part in memory? Give reasons for your answer based on what you have learned about remembering and forgetting.

2.   What are the implications of an associationistic theory of memory for student learning?

3.   Give some examples of how a student might organize his/her study to take advantage of the association value inherent in the material.

Handout 7.3A: FACTORS AFFECTING MEMORY

WHO WERE YOUR TEACHERS?

Directions: List each of your teachers from kindergarten through 12th grade. For high school, be sure to list as many teachers as you remember for each grade level. If you cannot remember a particular teacher, leave the line blank. In each case, indicate what it was about that teacher that made him or her memorable.

Kindergarten

Grade 1

Grade 2

Grade 3

Grade 4

Grade 5

Grade 6

Grade 7

Grade 8

Grade 9

Grade 10

Grade 11

Grade 12

267

Handout 7.3B: FACTORS AFFECTING MEMORY

WHO WERE YOUR CHILD'S TEACHERS?

Directions: List each of your child's teachers from kindergarten through 12th grade. For high school, be sure to list as many teachers as you remember for each grade level. If you cannot remember a particular teacher, leave the line blank. In each case, indicate what it was about that teacher that made him or her memorable. When you are finished, compare your memories with your child's memories. Did either of you make any errors? If so, why?

Kindergarten

Grade 1

Grade 2

Grade 3

Grade 4

Grade 5

Grade 6

Grade 7

Grade 8

Grade 9

Grade 10

Grade 11

Grade 12

Handout 7.4: DEMENTIA FACTS

Introduction

A. Common myths about aging and dementia.
 1. *Senility is a natural consequence of aging.* Truth: "Senility" refers to a specific disease or group of diseases known as dementias.
 2. *If parents get dementia, this also means that their children will get dementia.* Truth: Some dementias have a clear or suspected genetic link. Even so, if a parent has a degenerative neurological disease, a child has only a 50 percent chance of developing the disease, since the parent has two sets of genes in each chromosomal pair. Secondly, many dementias (e.g., Alzheimer's disease) have an "early onset" form of the disease and a late onset form. Early-onset Alzheimer's in the parent may put the child at an elevated risk, but late onset is not considered to be genetic.
 3. *There is nothing you can do to prevent the onset of dementias; if it's your destiny, it will happen.* Truth: Remaining active and learning new and cognitively challenging tasks can greatly reduce the onset of many types of dementia. Genetic factors may play a role, but genes are not a guarantee that a person will get or avoid the disease. People whose relatives have the disease may be two to five times more vulnerable than people whose relatives do not have the disease.
 4. *Dementias are only a disease of the elderly.* Truth: Different dementias typically occur at different points in the lifespan. But even within each disease, age of onset can vary widely. The "average" age of onset for Parkinson's disease is 50 to 70 years of age.
 5. *There is a cure for dementia.* Truth: there is no cure for dementia. There are a number of treatments available that may slow the progression of the disease in some patients, but there are no cures. The best strategy is to engage in healthy behaviors that may reduce or delay the incidence of the disease, where possible. Examples include keeping cognitively active (Alzheimer's) and keeping blood pressure and cholesterol at healthy levels (vascular dementia).
 6. *Memory loss means that Alzheimer's disease or other dementias are occurring.* Truth: Some memory loss is a normal part of aging.
 7. *Aluminum causes Alzheimer's disease.* Truth: there is no definitive proof that aluminum is a cause of Alzheimer's, although research is ongoing. In the case of many types of dementias, their development is most likely a combination of many risk factors working together.
 8. *Vitamin supplements and memory boosters can prevent dementia.* Truth: research into the effects of various vitamins as well as ginkgo biloba is ongoing. At present, there is no clear evidence to support these claims.
 9. *All people with dementia are violent and aggressive.* Truth: Many dementias produce no personality changes. Amongst Alzheimer's patients, in specific, only some undergo dramatic personality changes and/or develop violent tendencies. In those cases, violent incidents can sometimes be prevented by reducing frustration, being patient, and being compassionate. In some people with Alzheimer's disease, aggression can, however, be a problem.
 10. *People with dementias cannot understand what is going on around them.* Truth: awareness varies with the stage of the disease. For most of the duration of the disease, however, people are aware but may be unable to communicate their needs or reactions. Care should be taken to avoid embarrassing or humiliating the person by assuming that he or she is unaware.

269

Alzheimer's Disease

1. Quick facts:
   a. Typical age of onset: after age 60 (rare cases as early as 30–40 yrs)
   b. Percent of people over 65 with the disease: 10 percent (over 85: 50 percent)
   c. Average duration: eight years from onset of symptoms until death. Range is 3–20 years.
   d. Estimated number of Americans with the disease: 4.5 million
   e. Estimate of future cases (2050): 11–16 million
   f. Family ties: 1 in 10 Americans have a family member with Alzheimer's.
   g. Seven out of 10 people with Alzheimer's disease live at home.
   h. Accounts for over 55 percent of all cases of dementia. (Estimates range as high as 80 percent.)

2. Biology:
   a. Cerebral shrinkage. The brain shrinks as a result of the degeneration of neurons and brain atrophy. The ventricular areas, however, become enlarged. The disease can only be diagnosed with certainty after death, although diagnostic techniques can shed some light on the possible cause of symptoms.
   b. Neurofibrillary tangles (microscopic). Filaments in the nerve cells become twisted and tangled.
   c. Dendritic plaque (microscopic). As the protein threads within the nerve cells become tangled, proteins build up on the outside of the cell, forming plaque.

3. Symptoms:
   Keep in mind that most of these symptoms are considered signs of Alzheimer's disease if they are frequent and pervasive. Everyone experiences times when they forget things, misplace things, or have a lapse in good judgment. In normal people, however, these incidents are isolated, or temporary— e.g., due to stress, fatigue, or preoccupation.
   a. Memory loss.
   b. Difficulty performing familiar tasks.
   c. Problems with language.
   d. Disorientation to time and place.
   e. Poor or decreased judgment.
   f. Problems with abstract thinking.
   g. Misplacing things or putting things in the wrong place.
   h. Changes in mood or behavior.
   i. Changes in personality, especially if dramatic or irrational.
   j. Loss of initiative, or development of passivity.

Handout 7.4: DEMENTIA FACTS (cont.)

Vascular Dementia (Multi-Infarct Dementia)

1. Quick facts:
   a. Typical age of onset: after age 65
   b. Strokes in general can be *hemorrhagic* (bleeding into the brain) or *ischemic* (blocking of blood vessels in the brain). Ischemic strokes are also called *infarcts*. 80 percent of strokes are ischemic.
   c. Unlike Alzheimer's disease, vascular dementia progresses in steps, rather than being a gradual decline.
   d. Personality is less likely to change than in Alzheimer's disease.
   e. Neural plaques and tangles are not evident in the "pure" form of the disease, but many patients suffer from both vascular dementia and Alzheimer's disease at the same time.
   f. In the end stage, symptoms are indistinguishable from Alzheimer's disease.
   g. Affects men more often than women.
   h. Accounts for 15–25 percent of all cases of dementia.

2. Biology:
   a. A series of small strokes (infarcts) block blood flow to the brain and create progressive decline in memory and other abilities. These strokes may not even be noticed individually; damage is cumulative.
   b. Patients may have periods of stability between strokes, as the brain attempts to compensate, but additional strokes collectively increase decline in function.
   c. Patients often experience transient ischemic attacks (TIAs). These are short-lived episodes (symptoms lasting about five minutes), causing temporary impairment to the brain from a loss of blood supply. Unlike major strokes, TIAs usually resolve within 24 hours, but still cause damage.
   d. Death occurs from stroke, heart disease, infection, or pneumonia.
   e. Treatment to lower blood pressure or thin the blood may slow the rate of additional attacks, but will not reverse brain damage.

3. Symptoms:
   a. Confusion or problems with short-term memory.
   b. Wandering, or getting lost in familiar places.
   c. Walking with rapid, shuffling steps.
   d. Losing bladder or bowel control.
   e. Laughing or crying inappropriately.
   f. Having difficulty following instructions.
   g. Having problems counting money and making monetary transactions.

Handout 7.4: DEMENTIA FACTS (cont.)

Parkinson's Disease

1. Quick facts:
   a. Typical onset after age 50. Early onset possible under age 40 (8 percent of those diagnosed).
   b. Rate of disease progression varies widely from person to person.
   c. Affects 1.5 million Americans.
   d. Affects 1 in every 100,000 people.
   e. Affects men and women equally.
   f. About 40 percent of Parkinson's patients develop dementia in the later stages.
   g. Accounts for about 8 percent of all cases of dementia.

2. Biology:
   a. The disorder is caused by the loss of dopamine-producing cells in the *substantia nigra* area of the brain.
   b. The cause of the disorder is believed to be a combination of genetic and environmental factors.
   c. The drug L-Dopa can be used to lessen symptoms, but there is no cure. L-Dopa also has debilitating side effects for some patients, including dyskinesia (involuntary movements and tics) and hallucinations. Other drugs are also available; many of them have serious side effects.
   d. Dementia begins when destruction of neurons and impaired neural transmissions reach threshold level.

3. Symptoms:
   a. Tremor or trembling in hands, face, or extremities.
   b. Slowness of movement (Bradykinesia).
   c. Postural instability.
   d. Impaired balance and coordination.
   e. Progression of disease causes impaired motor control.
   f. Late-stage disease causes dementia in some patients.

➤ JOURNAL QUESTIONS

1. What is your earliest happy memory? How old were you? Where were you? What were you doing? What is your earliest unhappy memory? Does this memory predate or follow your earliest happy memory?

2. What were you doing on September 11, 2001, the day Desert Storm began, the day John Lennon was killed, of the day the space shuttle exploded? Can you remember your first day of school or your first date? Describe the details. Are you able to recall days in your psychology class with the same vividness? Why not?

3. With the help of a parent or other family member, begin with a memory of something that happened during your childhood. If you don't remember the incident, ask the person to choose a different one. Write down that memory. Next, begin free associating in order to create redintegrative memories. Talk to your family member for a half an hour and write down all of the associated memories that come up in conversation. Indicate which ones you "knew" you had remembered, and which ones were recovered through this process.

4. How much do you remember of what you were taught in psychology class this week? Write down as many things about the material as you can remember. Write down anything your instructor said in class, or any jokes that were made. Now, compare what you have written to your notes. How much did you miss? Do your notes contain more information than you remembered? If not, you might consider getting help on how to take complete notes.

5. Have you ever been in an accident and lost some memories? What happened? What did you forget? How long did it take before some memories started to return? Which memories came back first?

6. If you have ever been to a high school reunion, were you able to remember names? If so, how were you able to remember?

7. What do you do to try to remember information in short-term memory? What specific strategies do you employ? Under what conditions are these strategies most successful?

8. What do you do to remember information in long-term memory? Under what conditions are you most successful?

9. Describe one of the most embarrassing moments for you when your memory system malfunctioned. What was the situation? Why weren't you able to remember?

10. What mnemonics did you learn as a child? Were they helpful? Do you use mnemonic devices now in your classes? Are there times they interfere rather than help?

➤ SUGGESTIONS FOR FURTHER READING

Anderson, J. R. (2010). *Cognitive psychology and its implications* (7th ed.). New York: Worth.

Atkinson, R. C., & Schiffrin, R. M. (1968). Human memory: A proposed system and its control processes. In K. W. Spence & J. T. Spence (Eds.), *The psychology of learning and motivation* (Vol. 2). London: Academic Press.

Blair, K. S., Richell, R. A., Mitchell, D. G. V., et al. (2006). They know the words, but not the music: Affective and semantic priming in individuals with psychopathy. *Biological Psychology, 73*(2), 114–123.

Bower, G. H. (1981). Mood and memory. *American Psychologist, 36,* 129–148.

Braun, K. A., Ellis, R., & Loftus, E. F. (2002). Make my memory: How advertising can change memories of the past. *Psychology & Marketing, 19,* 1–23.

Eichenbaum, H. (2008). *Learning & memory.* New York: Norton.

Loftus, E. F. (1980). *Memory: Surprising new insights into how we remember and why we forget* Boston: Addison-Wesley.

Loftus, E. F., & Ketcham, K. (1994). *The myth of repressed memory: False memories and allegations of abuse.* New York: St. Martin's Press.Luria, A. R. (1968). *The mind of a mnemonist.* New York: Basic Books.

McGaugh, J. L. (1983). Preserving the presence of the past: Hormonal influences on memory storage. *American Psychologist,* 1983, 161-174.

Miller, G. A. (1956). The magical number seven, plus or minus two: Some limits on our capacity for information processing. *Psychological Review, 48,* 337–442.

Neath, I., & Surprenant, A. (2003). *Human memory* (2nd ed.). Belmont, CA: Cengage Learning/Wadsworth.

Neisser, U., & Hyman, I. E. (1999). *Memory observed: Remembering in natural contexts.* New York: Worth.

Roediger, H L. (1990). Implicit memory: Retention without remembering. *American Psychologist, 45*(9), 1043-1056.

Schacter, D. L. (2001). *The seven sins of memory*. Boston: Houghton Mifflin.

Tulving, E. (2002). Episodic memory. *Annual Review of Psychology, 53,* 1–25.

Wells, G. L., Memon, A., & Penrod, S. D. (2006). Eyewitness evidence: Improving its probative value. *Psychological Science in the Public Interest, 7*(2), 45–75.

Willander, J., & Larsson, M. (2006). Smell your way back to childhood: Autobiographical odor memory. *Psychonomic Bulletin & Review, 13*(2), 240–244.

➤ VIDEO SUGGESTIONS

Feature Films

Memento (Guy Pearce, Carrie-Anne Moss) Mystery. Leonard (Pearce) is a man who struggles to put his life back together after the brutal rape and murder of his wife. Leonard was severely beaten by the same man who killed his wife, and the after-effects include a complete loss of short-term memory. He cannot retain any new information, so resorts to note-taking and Polaroid photos to keep track of each day's events. He retains long-term memory, including the murder of his wife. He becomes obsessed with finding and taking revenge on the man who ruined his life. This mystery brings many concepts of memory to the discussion table, including long-term and short-term memory, as well as memory devices to improve retention.

Sommersby (Richard Gere, Jodie Foster) Drama. Gere plays Jack Sommersby, a wealthy landowner who returns to his small Tennessee town three years after the Civil War's end. The soldier is ready to resume his life with his wife Laurel (Foster), except that Laurel, thinking her husband was dead, has become engaged to another man. She cancels the engagement. We learn that the war experience has made a dramatic change in Sommersby. He is no longer the cruel, callous, feared pre-war Sommersby. He is now sensitive, charming, and very caring for his community and the people in it. Some think he is an imposter pretending to be Sommersby. He is arrested and charged with a murder he committed years before, and the courtroom uncovers even more information about the past. This drama can surface much conversation regarding memory, memory disorders (amnesia, fugue state, post-traumatic stress disorder, etc.), as well as other memory-related topics.

Fire in the Sky (D.B. Sweeney, James Garner) Sci-Fi/Fantasy. A man claims to be have been kidnapped by aliens, but no one believes him. Reputedly based on a true story.

Overboard (Goldie Hawn, Kurt Russell). Hawn stars as Joanna Stayton, a snooty heiress who summons carpenter Dean Proffitt (Russell) to her lavish yacht, where she wants an expanded closet constructed that will house her valuable wardrobe. When Dean fails to build the closet out of cedar, Joanna haughtily dismisses him without payment. Later, Joanna falls overboard and is struck by another boat, causing amnesia. Seeing her story on the news, Dean constructs an elaborate scheme to pretend that Joanna is his wife, Annie. Soon, the former rich snob is cleaning Dean's home and babysitting his four rambunctious boys. Although at first she's a disaster, "Annie" grows into her role and begins to love being a mom and middle-class wife. When her real husband Grant (Edward Herrmann) comes looking for her, however, her memory is jogged, and she must decide between a life of privileged ease and a life of happy housework.
Total Recall, (1990), (Arnold Schwarzenegger) Action drama. The action in this film takes place

in a futuristic world. We are traveling in space and have colonized Mars and Saturn. Advanced technology is apparent in all the scenes. Doug wakes up from a dream about Mars in which he is in danger. He wakes up from his nightmare and is comforted by his wife, who tries to get him to forget about Mars. She tells him he did not like it when he was there. While traveling to work on the metro, Doug sees an advertisement by Recall Inc., a firm selling memories of pleasant vacations. In this technologically advanced world, dreams and memories of events can be purchased and implanted in your brain. Doug stops by Recall Inc. on his way home from work. Bob McCane, sales representative for Recall, greets him and tries to sell him a memory of a glorious vacation. He will store the memory in Doug's brain.

While You Were Sleeping (Sandra Bullock, Peter Gallagher, Bill Pullman) Comedy. Sandra Bullock plays Lucy, a lonely fare collector on the Chicago elevated railway who has a crush on a handsome commuter, Peter (Peter Gallagher), who never even notices here. Fate intervenes and Lucy saves Peter's life. While he is in a coma, she is mistaken for his fiancée after visiting him in the hospital. Peter wakes up and does not remember Lucy at all, but everyone assumes he has amnesia. And in the meantime Lucy has fallen in love with the right man: the sleeping man's brother, Jack (Bill Pullman).

Educational Films and Videos

A Super-Memorist Advises on Study Strategies, from *The Brain Teaching Modules*, 2nd Edition #20, (1998), Annenberg/CPB, 9:57. This video shows Rajan Mahadevan's memory for numbers is impressive. He can recite from memory the first 100,000 digits of pi. This video demonstrates the awesome potential of the brain.

Exploring Your Brain: Memory, (2000), Films for the Humanities & Sciences, 56 min. Part of a three-part series, this program investigates issues related to data storage and retrieval, including discussions of Alzheimer's, the effect of aging on memory, and steps to improve memory.

False Memories, (2000), Films for the Humanities & Sciences, 51 min. Drawing on scientific research into the workings of the brain as well as startling case studies of recall gone awry, this program exposes the frightening malleability of human memory. Dr Elizabeth Loftus discusses retrieval and the subtle power of suggestion.

Learning and Memory, (1984), PBS Video, 55 min. An introduction to one of the more interesting of the brain's functions, this film highlights some of the brain research on the formation, storage, and retrieval of memory. It presents chemical and physical theories of memory creation and storage and discusses the specialized functions of several brain structures, such as the hippocampus and amygdala. This media presentation is well produced and will greatly enhance the text's discussion of memory.

276

Life Without Memory: The Case of Clive Wearing, from *The Mind Series Teaching Modules*, 2nd Edition #10 (Annenberg 12:35) and *Clive Wearing, Part 2: Living Without Memory*. (32:35.) Describes the case of Clive Wearing, an English singer, conductor, and composer who was also an expert on the 17th century composer Lassas. The first video depicts Clive's general amnesia, preventing him from recalling most of his past and from learning new experiences as well. Reviews how Clive's hippocampus was destroyed by a bout of viral encephalitis and the subsequent loss of episodic memory and a good deal of semantic memory. However, Clive's procedural memory remains intact, as revealed by his ability to continue to compose, conduct, and sing. Students will get a clear impression of the difference between explicit and implicit memory. Part 2 expands on how Clive deals with his memory loss from day to day.

Living With Amnesia: The Hippocampus and Memory, from *The Brain Series Teaching Modules*, 2nd Edition #18, (Annenberg, 8:00.) Depicts the role of the hippocampus in creating new memories and how amnesia develops from injury to this vital organ in the brain.

Locus of Learning and Memory, from *The Brain Series Teaching Modules*, 2nd Edition #16, Annenberg, 6:49. This program explores the track of memory formation in the brain, and the role of various structures in creating memories.

Memory, from the Discovering Psychology series, Annenberg, 30 min.

Memory, (1980), CRM/McGraw-Hill, 30 min. This fast-paced examination of information-processing theory includes a discussion of sensory, short-term, and long-term memory. The film concentrates mainly on the improvement of long-term memory through the use of mnemonic devices, and viewers are provided with several methods for improving their own memories. The film also discusses what interference is and how to overcome it through conscious effort and practice. The applied aspects of this film make it a practical adjunct to the discussion of memory in the classroom.

Memory, (1990), Coast Community College District Telecourses, 30 min. Explains research in the nature and workings of memory; defines amnesia and Alzheimer's disease.

Memory, (1998), Films for the Humanities and Sciences, 56 min. Memories provide a sense of personal continuity and, to a large extent, define one's identity. This program investigates issues related to the brain's fundamental processes of data storage and retrieval, such as why people remember some things and forget others; how Alzheimer's disease affects the brain and what treatments are being developed to treat it; how aging affects memory; and what steps can be taken to preserve and improve retention. Panelists include experts from Harvard Medical School and the Howard Hughes Medical Institute, and the author of the book *Searching for Memory*.

Memory, (2001), Insight Media, 30 min. This program examines how memories are formed, stored, and recalled.

Memory, (2005), *Psychology Digital Video Library 3.0 Handbook,* from Thomson Higher Education, 20 min. A brief description of our memory processes.

Memory: Fabric of the Mind, (1988), Films for the Humanities and Sciences, 28 min. This film visits several internationally known memory research labs in an attempt to answer questions concerning memory. Brain chemistry is examined and the location of memory is sought. Ways to improve memory are also discussed, along with various reasons why we forget. This is a very good video on modern research into human memory.

Memory Fixing, (1985), The Program Source, 67 min. This film features an interview with Kenneth Cooper in which he explains the various levels of human memory. He discusses the type of information that is encoded and sorted in our memories and explains how people can "program" their subconscious memory to solve problems and inform their consciousness at a later time. The film is interactive and demonstrates several mnemonic devices for organizing thoughts: placing them in logical order, grouping them according to similarity, and linking them with language. This presentation of our ability to remember is an interesting blend of psychoanalytic and information-processing theory, and should be a valuable adjunct to a lecture on memory.

Memory Skills, (1992), Insight Media, 30 min. This video provides basic instruction on how one can improve his or her memory. It examines how elaborative processing can enhance memory for a wide variety of materials.

Memory—The Past Imperfect, (1994), Filmmakers Library, 46 min. Part of the *Nature of Things* series. This new video explores long- and short-term memory, hypnosis as a method of recalling the past, the phenomenon of amnesia, the memories of very young children, and the variability of eyewitness testimony. Several experts share their findings on these topics. This video was produced by the Canadian Broadcasting Company.

Persistence of Memory, (1980), PBS Video, 58 min. This is one of the films in the *Cosmos* series, narrated by Carl Sagan. He discusses the evolution, function, and physiology of the human brain, especially as it pertains to the storage of information. Cognition is discussed in relation to genetics and the brain's memory function. The film concludes with a discussion of the development of external information storage as a logical extension of human memory.

Remembering and Forgetting: Discovering Psychology Series, (1990), Annenberg/CPB, 30 min. Program 9 in the series. This film examines the complex processes involved in the creation of memory. Philip Zimbardo, the host, discusses how environmental stimuli are translated into neural codes that our brain can process, understand, and store. Several explanations of why we forget are mentioned, and the film concludes by demonstrating common retrieval aids that we can use to improve our memories. This half-hour film presents a clear overview of the process of memory with excellent graphics and commentary.

Sensation and Perception, Discovering Psychology Teaching Module 5, (1990), Annenberg/CPB, various times. The Discovering Psychology Teaching Modules contain excerpts from the *Discovering Psychology Series.* Module 5 in this series (memory) contains several interesting sections including: the anatomy of the brain and a memory demonstration with Dr. Philip Zimbardo.

Studying the Effects of Subliminal Stimulation on the Mind, from *The Mind Teaching Modules,* 2nd Edition #9, (2000), Worth, 4:46. This video presents an example of how researchers study a construct like the unconscious with state-of-the-art technology. This video is a good example of the impact that Freud has had on psychology.

The Nature of Memory, (1991), Films for the Humanities and Sciences, 26 min. This video examines the definition of memory in relation to its function. How does it work? Is it reality or a creation of our subconscious? And can it be manipulated by dreams or hypnosis? These are but a few of the questions answered by this film. Computer demonstrations provide insight into the processes of memory, and human amnesiac studies are discussed in relation to the encoding, storage, and retrieval of memories. The film also provides some information about how emotions affect memories and how they can be altered.

The Study of Memory. Films for the Humanities and Sciences, 74 min.

Thinking, (1988), PBS Video, 30 min. This film, part of *The Mind* series, examines the background and history of memory research. It focuses largely on prefrontal and frontal lobe studies and identifies these areas as the place where memory and other cognitions occur. The segments on prefrontal lobotomies are interesting, as are the examinations of stroke victims' memories.

Understanding the Mysteries of Memory, (1998), Films for the Humanities and Sciences, 53 min. This compelling program explores the extraordinary nature of memory through the stories of people who yearn to remember or long to forget. Case studies and interviews with experts, supported by computer graphics, throw light on the mechanics of implicit and explicit memory, savant syndrome, traumatic memory, flashbacks, "Flashbulb memories" such as the space shuttle Challenger explosion, mistaken identification, and memories twisted or even totally invented through suggestion. The effects of short-term memory damage, trauma-induced amnesia, and Alzheimer's disease are investigated as well.

➤ COMPUTER AND INTERNET RESOURCES

PsykTrek 3.0
Unit 6: Memory and Thought
6a. "Memory Encoding"
6b. "Memory Storage"
6c. "Physiology of Memory"

INFOTRAC®

Below you will find two journal articles obtained from INFOTRAC® that relate to information contained in this chapter. Instructors should encourage students to utilize this invaluable resource to improve their research skills. Have students locate and read the following articles and answer questions relevant to each article.

The Psychological Record, Spring 2001 v51 i2 p207 **Directed Forgetting in Explicit and Implicit Memory: The role of encoding and retrieval mechanisms.**

1.   In the above study, the researchers sought to study two things. What were they?

      Answer: (a) to determine whether directed forgetting influences tests of implicit (lexical decision) and explicit (recognition) memory, and (b) to examine the relative contributions of the encoding and retrieval mechanisms thought to mediate directed forgetting by having participants perform an external interference task (e.g., sequential finger tapping) at either encoding or retrieval.

2.   Contrast implicit and explicit memory.

      Answer: Implicit tests assess long-term memory that does not necessarily require intentional recollection or awareness of previously studied information. In contrast, explicit tests assess long-term memory that necessarily requires intentional recollection and awareness of previously studied information.

3.   According to the study, a distinction between implicit and explicit memory effects is based on the type of test administered at the conclusion of the directed-forgetting study list. What did the researchers find in this regard?

      Answer: Directed forgetting may be more accurately viewed as an ability that relies on distinct processing mechanisms in different memory systems, at least when considering the tests employed herein. Previous accounts of directed forgetting in implicit memory based on selective encoding may stem from the use of implicit tasks that can be performed by an explicit retrieval strategy. However, true tests of implicit memory that cannot be completed by explicit retrieval, such as speeded repetition priming in lexical decision, may be dependent on differential retrieval.

Science, August 21, 1998 v281 n5380 p1188 (4) **Building Memories: Remembering and forgetting of verbal experiences as predicted by brain activity.**

1.   What is encoding and what two unanswered questions are there regarding this process?

     Answer: Memory encoding refers to the processes by which an experience is transformed into an enduring memory trace. The first answered question is that the precise functional neuroanatomic encoding differences that predict whether a particular verbal experience will be remembered or forgotten are currently unknown. A second unanswered question concerns the exact roles of medial temporal structures in memory encoding.

2.   How did this study address the above concerns?

     Answer: To address these issues, the neural correlates of incidental word encoding were examined in two whole-brain functional magnetic resonance imaging (MRI) studies.

3.   What did the results of this study indicate?

     Answer: The current study together with previous results suggest that what makes a verbal experience memorable partially depends on the extent to which left prefrontal and medial temporal regions are engaged during the experience.

WEB LINKS

Knowledge Builder Links

1. Memory Systems
     Playing Games with Memory:
         http://www.exploratorium.edu/memory/dont_forget/index.html
     The Atkinson-Shiffrin Model: http://users.ipfw.edu/abbott/120/AtkinsonShifrin.html
     Working Memory, Language, and Reading: http://brainconnection.positscience.com/

2. STM and LTM
     The Magic Number Seven: http://psychclassics.yorku.ca/Miller/
     Q & A about Memories of Childhood Abuse: http://www.apa.org/topics/memories.html
     False Memory Syndrome Foundation: http://www.fmsonline.org/

3. Measuring Memory
     What is Déjà Vu?:
         http://science.howstuffworks.com/question657.htm
     Free Recall Test:
         http://psych.hanover.edu/JavaTest/CLE/Cognition/Cognition/freerecall_instructions.html

Memory: A Contribution to Experimental Psychology:
  http://psychclassics.yorku.ca/Ebbinghaus/index.htm
About Education: Fundamental Concepts of Forgetting and Learning:
  http://frank.itlab.us/~cfs/forgetting/index.html
Memory Loss and the Brain: http://www.memorylossonline.com/

4. Exceptional Memory and Improving Memory
  Does No One Have a Photographic Memory? http://www.slate.com/id/2140685/
  Famous Mnemonists: http://www.memoryelixir.com/history2.html
  Memory Strategies: http://www.studygs.net/memory/

5. Psychology in Action: Mnemonics—Memory Magic
  Memory Techniques and Mnemonics: http://www.mindtools.com/memory.html
  Memory Training Technique:
      http://www.bbc.co.uk/science/humanbody/mind/interactives/intelligenceandmem
      ory/memorytest/index.shtml
  Online Memory Improvement: http://memory.uva.nl/memimprovement/eng

Additional Web Links

Alzheimer's
http://www.pbs.org/theforgetting/
http://www.alz.org
http://www.ninds.nih.gov/disorders/multi_infarct_dementia/multi_infarct_dementia.htm
http://www.ninds.nih.gov/disorders/parkinsons_disease/parkinsons_disease.htm
http://www.michaeljfox.org

Amnesia
http://www.healthatoz.com/healthatoz/Atoz/common/standard/transform.jsp?requestURI=/health
atoz/Atoz/ency/amnesia.jsp

APA Online
http://www.apa.org/

Exploring Memory
http://www.exploratorium.edu/memory/

Learning and Memory
http://www.learnmem.org/

Memory and Aging
http://memory.ucsf.edu/Education/Disease/mci.html
http://www.med.nyu.edu/adc/forpatients/memory.htmlMemory Games
http://faculty.washington.edu/chudler/chmemory.html

Recovered Memories Debate
http://www.apa.org/topics/memories.html
http://mentalhealth.about.com/cs/dissociative/a/dabaterec.htm
http://www.kspope.com/memory/olio1.php
http://www.jimhopper.com/memory

Study Skills
http://www.how-to-study.com/
http://www.infoplease.com/homework/studyskills1.html

Test-Taking Strategies
http://www.d.umn.edu/kmc/student/loon/acad/strat/test_take.html
http://www.bucks.edu/~specpop/tests.htm

PSYCHOLOGY IN THE NEWS

About Memory:
http://www.memory-key.com
About Memory provides information about learning, memory impairment, memory improvement, and the effects of sleep on memory and learning.

Help4Teachers:
http://www.iecc.edu/occ/lrc/psych.htm
Read the latest topic in psychology including the latest research as they are released.

LookSmart Find Articles:
http://www.findarticles.com
A good link to the latest news articles in Psychology Today Online.

Psych Central:
http://www.psychcentral.com/news
This link provides daily psychology news and headlines.

Science News:
http://www.sciencenews.org/view/interest/id/2357/topic/Body_%2B_Brain
Interesting site regarding "body and brain."

CHAPTER 8

Intelligence, Cognition, Language, and Creativity

Survey Questions
Discussion Questions
Lecture Enhancements

Operational definitions of intelligence
Thought-provoking ideas
Objective versus subjective questions
Stereotypes of geniuses
Assessing intelligence
Poor test performance
Race, IQ scores, and confounding variables
Is it really language?
The subtlety of language
Remote Associates Test (RAT)
Is brainstorming better?
Functional fixedness
Cognitive understanding of the world
Eureka!
It's new!

Role-Playing Scenarios
Value-Clarification Statements
One-Minute Motivators

Flunk your prof!
Who's smart?
Which type of intelligence is important?
Gifted people
What can you do?
Are IQ tests valid and reliable?
What are you thinking?
What's the answer?
What is it?
How do you get there?
Categorizing concepts
Prototypes
Oxymorons
Body language
Language in pets
Speaking a second language
Solving problems
Functional fixedness
What's your talent?
Brainstorming
Brain versus computer

➤ SURVEY QUESTIONS

Module 8.1 Imagery, Concepts, and Language

Survey Question: What is the nature of thought?

Survey Question: In what ways are images related to thinking?

Survey Question: What are concepts?

Survey Question: What is the role of language in thinking?

Module 8.2 Problem Solving

Survey Question: What do we know about problem solving?

Module 8.3 Creative Thinking and Intuition

Survey Question: What is creative thinking?

Survey Question: How accurate is intuition?

Module 8.4 Intelligence

Survey Question: How is human intelligence defined and measured?

Survey Question: How much does intelligence vary from person to person?

Survey Question: What are some controversies in the study of intelligence?

Module 8.5 Psychology in Action: Enhancing Creativity—Brainstorms

Survey Question: What can be done to improve thinking and promote creativity?

➤ DISCUSSION QUESTIONS

1. In what ways is an artificial intelligence program similar to and different from a word processor, the computerized engine control of an automobile, and a robot that builds cars?

2. To what degree is intelligence culturally specific? Can an intelligent person from one culture learn the "rules" for surviving in another culture, or does that knowledge have to be developed at a young age? If a very intelligent person from our culture were to land in the middle of the Amazon, how "intelligent" would that person be, and how long would it take to "become" intelligent again?

3. To what kinds of tasks do you think artificial intelligence should be applied? Would you be comfortable with computerized medical diagnosis, for instance? What about the launch of a nuclear attack?

4. In what ways do you think our society encourages the development of different intellectual skills in males and females?

5. Should IQ tests be used on children? State both the advantages and disadvantages of administering IQ tests to children. Would there be any special advantages or disadvantages to using IQ tests on children with learning disabilities?

6. The WAIS test assesses different abilities —verbal and performance. Usually, a person scores in the same range on both halves. If a person had substantially different scores on the two halves, what might that indicate? Make a list of the possibilities.

7. What advantages or disadvantages would you expect to be associated with knowing your own IQ? With having a teacher who knows your IQ? With having your parents know your IQ?

8. How might public education be restructured to encourage full intellectual development for all children? How might grading be changed to reflect broader definitions of intelligence?

9. How would you define "gifted"? Why are definitions important? What are the negative consequences of defining intelligence and giftedness at all?

10. How would you feel about the application of eugenics to human reproduction? Are there circumstances under which you would or would not consider it acceptable?

11. The debate over the relative importance of heredity and environment in determining intelligence has raged for decades. Why do you think the debate has lasted so long and attracted so much interest? If the heritability of IQ could be known with certainty, what difference would it make?

288

12. An organization called the Repository for Germinal Choice in Escondido, California, served as a sperm bank for Nobel Prize winners and others possessing high IQs. Dozens of babies reportedly were produced by artificial insemination from the sperm bank. Do you regard this as wise or unwise, ethical or unethical, foolish or inspired?

13. According to the Flynn Effect, Western nations have shown average IQ gains of 15 points during the last 30 years. Do you think IQ scores will continue to improve? Why or why not?

14. If you suddenly lost your ability to mentally represent external problems, what changes would you have to make in your behavior?

15. Can animals reason and problem solve, or do they just learn from trial and error and reinforcement? How would you measure that ability in an animal (since they can't tell you)? If your pet dog or cat encounters a new problem, is your pet able to solve it without trial and error?

16. How do you read a road map? Can you look at the map right side up and mentally rotate the grid to match the direction you are traveling? Or do you physically turn the map so that it is pointing the same direction you are traveling? Does it make a difference whether you are finding a street in an area you know versus finding directions in a place you've never been before?

17. How good are you at giving directions to people? Do people think you give good directions, or do they prefer to ask someone else? When you are giving directions, do you give a lot of compass points (go north on…) or do you rely more on landmarks? Which kind of directions do you prefer when getting directions from others?

18. Kinesthetic imagery is a physical way of "thinking" about things. Example: you can't remember someone's phone number, but if someone gives you a phone, you can dial it correctly. Make a list of the times when you use kinesthetic imagery.

19. Many students taking introductory psychology have difficulty integrating all the new concepts in the course. But if your instructor reads about a new psychological finding, he or she is able to integrate the concept easily. Why? What concepts do you integrate quickly, maybe even more quickly than your instructor!?

20. Have you ever met someone whose concepts are objectively faulty? In other words, not simply someone with a different opinion, but someone who holds a concept that is factually inaccurate. How does that person respond when "corrected"? What concepts or counterarguments are used when a person refuses to accept the truth? What is that person's thought process? Think of someone you know who has refused to accept the truth. What was the issue about? Why do you think the person refused to adjust his or her concept?

21. In what ways does a large vocabulary make a person a more effective thinker?

22. In your opinion, are chimps that are trained to use hand signs really using language? Why or why not?

23. Describe a time when you have used imagery to solve a problem. What are the advantages and disadvantages of imagery in comparison to other modes of thought?

24. How do differences in connotative meaning contribute to arguments and misunderstandings? Do you think connotative meaning could or should be standardized?

25. The text implies that animals communicate but do not use language in the human sense. Do you agree? Can you give an example of animal communication that qualifies as a language?

26. What perceptual habits could contribute to barriers in problem solving?

27. Why do you think some people are better at solving problems than others? Is it a learned skill, or are some people just more gifted in this area? If you wanted to create a really good "problem solver" in a child, what things would you do? How can you improve your own problem solving abilities now that you are an adult?

28. Think of the most creative person you know. What is that person like? How does he or she differ from your less creative acquaintances?

29. In which areas of your life are you most creative? What types of creative pursuits do you enjoy and why? Which types do you dislike? Why?

30. In what ways is creativity different from intelligence?

31. In your opinion, should measures of divergent or creative thinking be used to select students for college admission? Why or why not?

32. You are the president of an advertising company. You want to hire a new account executive that is extremely creative. How would you go about identifying this person?

33. Can you provide a real-life example of each of Tversky and Kahneman's concepts (representativeness, base rates, and framing)?

34. What characteristics make a person wise, rather than just intelligent? Do you know anyone who is only average in intelligence, but is very wise? Why do you consider that person to be wise? Do you know anyone who is very intelligent and/or knowledgeable, but not wise? Why do you not consider that person to be wise?

➤ LECTURE ENHANCEMENTS

We all make assumptions about our own intelligence and the intelligence of others. Group activities can give students a chance to work together in a cooperative, non-threatening environment to solve thinking and creativity problems. Students should leave this chapter with specific strategies and skills for solving problems, and they should feel more competent for having studied these concepts. They should also be encouraged to examine the assumptions they make about the intelligence of others. Students can be reminded that each culture defines intelligence and creativity uniquely and that it is very difficult to develop culture-free measures of thinking.

1. **Operational definitions of intelligence**. To impress upon students the arbitrary nature of operational definitions of intelligence, have them write a list of skills or capacities they believe an intelligence test should measure (e.g., memory, computation, verbal ability, etc.) Ask a student to read his or her list, and no matter how long it is ask, "Is that all that's meant by intelligence?" Then call on others to add to the list. When the class has exhausted all its additions, point out that the definition is still vague, limited, and arbitrary. Also ask students to imagine how all these abilities might be tested by one or several tests. It might also be interesting to note the degrees to which student definitions of intelligence have been shaped by their many years of exposure to schooling.

2. **Thought-provoking ideas.** The quotations and notes that follow are almost sure to stir up worthwhile class discussion:
    a. "One thing I know. The IQ test does not truly measure intelligence. Our tests focus on such narrow things, the ability to acquire knowledge. What of human feelings? Are not these also important?" (Samuel C. Kohs, who helped develop the Stanford-Binet while a student of Lewis Terman)

    b. From a psychologist testifying for the defense in the Larry P. case (a lawsuit concerning the placement of an African American child into a class for mentally retarded students on the basis of a culturally biased IQ test alone): "…the surest and most effective action the Negro community could take by itself to achieve equality and education and jobs would be to limit dramatically the birthrate in those families providing the least effective environment for intellectual development."

    c. "I don't see any use for IQ tests during public school, except when a child has difficulty in learning. In that case, they are a valuable diagnostic tool. They can indicate a person lacks some ability to understand the world around them." (Arthur Jensen speaking in 1980)

    d. "Absolutely wrong" and "biological nonsense" were but a few denouncements by Nobel Prize winners when they learned of the Repository for Germinal Choice set up by a U.S. businessman as a bank for sperm contributed by Nobel laureates.

e. "The evidence about college entrance tests as predictors of academic success is no longer a subject of legitimate dispute... Most educators are quite familiar with the fact that the scores work in more cases than not, popular belief to the contrary notwithstanding." (William W. Turnbull, President of ETS in a 1974 speech) According to figures ETS presented in 1977, the average accuracy of ETS aptitude tests in predicting first-year grades is seldom better than random predictions.

Percentage of Predictions in Which Random Predictions with a Pair of Dice Is as Accurate as an ETS Test:

SAT (college)	88%
LSAT (law school)	87%
GRE (graduate school)	89%
GMAT (business school)	92%

The compilation of ETS validity studies found that high school grades alone are about twice as good as the SAT in predicting college grades. (Quote and table from "The Reign of the ETS" by Allan Nairn and Associates, *The Ralph Nader Report on the Educational Testing Service*)

f. Warner Slack and Douglas Porter of Harvard Medical School reported in the May 1980 *Harvard Educational Review* that coaching substantially improves scores on the SAT. ETS denies that coaching affects test results. Slack and Porter hold that the SAT tests measure "little-used vocabulary and tricky math" and that tutoring can raise scores enough to make the difference between acceptance and rejection to college.

3. **Objective versus subjective questions.** Ask students to write a series of questions that would test what they think is "intelligence." Then, have them rate them as being objective (one possible answer) or subjective (several possible answers).

4. **Stereotypes of geniuses.** Have students make a list of behavioral and physical characteristics that they think typify "geniuses." Ask them to think about movies, television shows, books, etc. where "geniuses" have been portrayed and describe them in these terms. After there is a total list with numerous stereotypic characteristics, bring in Terman's research on the gifted and compare stereotypic versus realistic characteristics.

5. **Assessing intelligence.** To help students appreciate the difficulty in understanding what intelligence is, propose the following as measures of intelligence. Ask the students to decide which would be best:
a. A standardized IQ test
b. A person's college GPA
c. Giving the person $100 to invest and seeing how much (s)he has after 12 months
d. Leaving the person out in the wilderness for three days with only an ax and a box of matches
e. Giving an extensive exam of general knowledge
f. How much information on a particular topic the person can find on the Internet
g. A person's grade in his/her course in psychology

There will likely be a good deal of disagreement about which would be best. Most students will know someone whom they consider very bright but who has done poorly in college or high school. Ask them how they know the person is bright in the first place. What are their criteria? Challenge the class to propose a better way to measure intelligence.

6. **Poor test performance.** To help students understand that intelligence is different than abilities, ask them to generate a list of situations where an intelligent person might do poorly on an IQ test. Possibilities include learning disabilities, brain damage, test anxiety, cultural differences, gender or racial bias on IQ tests, vision problems, and so on. When they have compiled their list, ask them to generate ideas for overcoming these various obstacles for testing, and determine how intelligent a person actually is.

7. **Race, IQ scores, and confounding variables.** (exercise and mini-lecture)
Before you begin, make a number of points clear:
   a. Most reputable scientists agree that "race" is a meaningless biological category. There is no trait (blood type, skin color, lactose intolerance, etc.) that reliably distinguishes one race from another. Rather, race is a social construct.
   b. Knowing the averages from IQ tests for different groups gives NO information about how well an individual will perform on an IQ test, or in class. Individual differences are much greater than group differences.
   c. It is impossible to separate "race" from socioeconomic status and cultural differences when examining group differences in IQ scores.
   d. The traditional 15 point average difference in IQ scores between Black and White Americans is closing—fast. Average gains of between four and seven IQ points have occurred in just the past 20 years.
   e. IQ scores measure all members of the group collectively. Black Americans who grew up during segregation, and who never finished school, form part of the average for African Americans.

Once you have laid out the above parameters, ask students WHY the groups differ in IQ scores. Many students will point to bias in the tests. Although it is difficult to make a completely culture-free (or at least culture-fair) test, most of the obviously biased items have been removed. Most of the difference, therefore, lies not in test bias, but in differences in life experience.

Ask students how the lives of Black Americans (on average) differ from the lives of White Americans (on average). Initially, they might have difficulty specifying the differences, but once they get rolling, the list should grow. Here are some (but not all!) of the possibilities:
   a. School systems. Schools in poor neighborhoods typically have older books, fewer facilities, fewer after-school clubs and extra-curricular activities, higher student to teacher ratios, and less money to hire the best teachers.

293

b. Poverty affects nutrition (prenatally and for children), availability of food (e.g., going to school without breakfast), restricted access to health care, inferior pregnancy and well-baby care, etc.

c. Compared to suburbs, urban neighborhoods typically have more crowding, more pollution, more crime, fewer community resources, and generally more stress.

d. Poor parents are less likely to have achieved an education themselves, and may be unable to help children with homework. They might also work more hours, be more likely to be a single-parent, and place less value on education than middle-class parents. If a child is having trouble, there is less money for enrichment or tutors.

e. Environmental toxins, such as lead in the paint in old buildings, continue to be a source of intellectual damage in children.

When you have completed the brainstorming session, ask one more question that really emphasizes the point that IQ scores aren't about race, but about differences in environments. The question is simple: If you compare White students from New York and California with White students from poorer states—especially rural areas—will you see a difference in average IQ scores? Will students from Beverly Hills outperform students from a Virginia coal-mining community, on average?

8. **Is it really language?** The research team of Sue Savage-Rumbaugh, Duane Rumbaugh, and Sarah Boysen has advanced a cogent argument against the notion that true language usage has been achieved by apes trained in ASL or computer language systems. For a critical and thought-provoking appraisal of primate language programs, see their article, "Do Apes Use Language?" in *American Scientist,* Jan.-Feb. 1980, 49 or the more recent *"Language and Apes"* in *Psychology Teacher Network,* 1994, 9.

9. **The subtlety of language.** The semantic differential provides an interesting look at the subtleties and similarities of the connotative meanings of words. To illustrate, duplicate the semantic differential scales shown in the text and give copies to the class. Then have them rate words such as: MOTHER, FATHER, MONEY, SEX, LOVE, STUDENT, PROFESSOR, COLLEGE, POLITICS, LIBERAL, etc. To what degree are connotations shared? Do individual differences in connotative meanings match students' perceptions of themselves, their interests, and values?

10. **Remote Associates Test.** Mednic's Remote Associates Test (RAT) is a good example of a creativity test that combines divergent and convergent thinking. The RAT consists of groupings of three words. The words in each group have a single word in common associated with them. The object is to find that word. For example, if the words were "shake, cow, and carton," the common element is "milk" (milkshake, milk cow, and milk carton). The items below are similar to the RAT. They may be used in class to raise the question of what distinguishes creative thought from other types of problem solving. The class may also want to discuss whether or not the RAT actually tests creativity.

1. ball home naval
2. stream goose town
3. dance ladder door
4. dog pepper rod
5. sand mouse door

6. ball shake lotion
7. puff whipped ice
8. bowling cushion hair
9. sun bulb sky
10. wrench stove line

Answers for the preceding items are: 1. base 2. down 3. step 4. hot 5. trap 6. hand 7. cream 8. pin 9. light 10. pipe.

11. **Is brainstorming better?** Is "brainstorming" really superior to individual problem solving for producing creative solutions? A small in-class experiment may shed some light on this issue for students. Begin by dividing the class in half. Form four-person groups out of one-half of the class. If possible, separate the groups from the remaining individuals. Beforehand, prepare a brief summary of brainstorming from the discussion in the text and give it to the four-person groups to read. Tell the students their task is to imagine as many possible uses for a brick as they can. Groups are to work according to the rules for brainstorming. Individuals are to work by themselves. At the end of a five-minute period, collect the lists of uses and arbitrarily group the solutions of individuals by fours. Then compare the number of uses generated by the brainstorming groups to the number produced by groups of four individuals working independently. In addition to determining if the cross-stimulation produced more ideas, the originality of group and individual solutions can be compared. After discussing brainstorming, you may wish to use this exercise to illustrate the value of breaking sets. Write the following attributes on the board: weight, color, rectangularity (sharp edges, flat surfaces), porosity, strength, roughness, storage and conduction of heat, electrical insulation, hardness. Then ask students to try adding to their lists of uses by considering each of the listed attributes. Does this increase the number, flexibility, and originality of their answers (Adams, 2001)?

12. **Functional fixedness**. The One-Minuter Motivator listed later on can also be expanded to form a good lecture enhancement.

13. **Cognitive understanding of the world.** Charles Croll has interviewed children of different ages, asking them, "Is Santa Claus real? Why? Why not?" Students can ask children the same question regarding Santa, the Tooth Fairy, the Easter Bunny, magic, cartoon characters, animals, germs, and so forth. The percentage of children who respond correctly shows a nice progression through ages four through seven. This is an easy way for students to get a glimpse into the cognitive world of younger children.

14. **Eureka!** Ask each student to write down a situation where they had sudden insight (a Eureka! moment). Asking them to write it down will force every student to participate. Check to make sure that each one has written something down, to discourage the "I don't know" response. When they are done, ask them to share. To get them started, you might remind them that moments of insight often occur after they have "slept on it."

295

15. **It's new!** It is always an interesting exercise for students to form groups and to brainstorm a new product. Students should describe the size, type, function, cost, potential market, and so forth.

➤ ROLE-PLAYING SCENARIOS

1. **You are the Director of a "Gifted and Talented" Program.** Explain to a group of parents how you select elementary students to be a part of your program.

2. **You are a psychologist who has just tested a child and found that his IQ is 95.** Tell his parents what to expect and how they should view their child's score.

3. **You are a parent who has just found out that your child has a mild intellectual disability.** What kind of questions do you have for the professional who has just informed you of this fact? What kind of concerns do you have for your child's future? For your future?

4. **You are the parent of a 10-minute-old healthy infant.** Explain to a nurse what you plan to do from this moment on to encourage the intellectual development and creativity of your child.

5. **You are the 12-year-old child of a pair of pushy, yuppie parents.** You understand that they are supposed to encourage your intellectual development, but you feel that being grounded for your first "B" is a little extreme. Tell them your feelings.

6. **You want your child to develop his or her creativity.** Explain to your friend what steps you are going to take to make this happen.

7. **Pretend that you are a researcher who is teaching chimpanzees how to use sign language.** Make your case for the value of this research in understanding human language.

➤ VALUE-CLARIFICATION STATEMENTS

1. People who know that they are carrying genes that might result in children with intellectual disabilities should either not reproduce, or should be encouraged to adopt instead.

2. Amniocentesis shows that the fetus will never develop into an adult with an IQ over 50. This fetus should be aborted.

3. People with mild forms of Down syndrome should not be put in normal schools; it will only frustrate them and make them feel "stupid."

296

4. Children should be pushed to learn; otherwise, they will never be able to compete well in the adult world.

5. Improving a child's intellectual potential should be a priority for all parents.

6. Having children learn things that machines can do is a waste of intellectual development.

7. Most IQ tests are a waste of time.

8. Humans' ability to form concepts makes them superior to other animals.

9. When people fall victim to functional fixedness, it's because they never learned how to think creatively.

10. It is cruel to take chimps from their natural environment to teach them sign language.

11. In the "real world," creativity is more important than intelligence.

➤ ONE-MINUTE MOTIVATORS

1. **Flunk your prof!** Ask students to write a short IQ test that their instructor will flunk.

2. **Who's smart?** Describe the smartest person you have known. Do you think that person would score high on an IQ test? Or did they possess other kinds of intelligence?

3. **Which type of intelligence is important?** Which of Gardner's eight types of intelligence are valued in this culture? Make a list of successful professions that use types of intelligence that are not valued in the school system. Should schools be doing more to foster career opportunities for non-academic intelligences?

4. **Gifted people.** Tell the class about someone you know who has an intellectual "gift" in one area, but seems lacking in other areas. Is the person really lacking in that area, or does he or she simply prioritize some abilities over others?

5. **What can you do?** Most college-age students have experienced people being surprised or frustrated that they do not know certain skills that other generations can perform easily. Make a list of these "missing" abilities (examples include: 1. not knowing long division, relationships between numbers, etc., from over-reliance on calculators, 2. lack of spelling and grammar skills, because of computer spell-check programs, or 3. not knowing certain "basic" historical facts). Make a list of things that today's students "don't know" and a list of things that older generations don't know. Should everyone be proficient in the "three Rs" or have computers made these skills redundant? Why or why not?

6.   **Are IQ tests valid and reliable?** First, define validity and reliability to students. Then, ask them to tell you whether IQ tests have problems with validity, reliability, or both. Ask them to back up their answers with reasons. Typically, their responses will make it clear that reliability and validity are difficult for students to distinguish. Secondly, you will likely find that students will argue that the tests lack reliability because they don't produce the "same" score every time. This will give you an opportunity to explain that the IQ range is more important (and accurate) than a specific number.

7.   **What are you thinking?** Ask students to spend a few moments summarizing the contents of their thoughts just before class begins. What elements of thinking were present?

8.   **What's the answer?** Ask students to process these numbers: 15 times 2 times 7 divided by 3 minus 20 (the answer is 50); to think of all the words they can make from the letters THINK; to say (without looking) how many circles there are on the back of $1.00; to say what dogs, cats, parakeets, and goldfish have in common. Do students use different elements of thought to answer these questions?

9.   **What is it?** Bring an unusual object to class. Keep the object covered. Allow students to ask questions about the object until they can identify it. How much did they rely on language? Concepts? Imagery?

10.   **How do you get there?** Ask students to answers questions such as: how to get to the nearest theater, how to run a special football formation, what he/she did yesterday, and about a recent holiday. Ask a few students to watch the degree to which hand movements took place.

11.   **Categorizing concepts.** Categorize these concepts as conjunctive, disjunctive, or relative: "yellow fruit," "American state capitals," "female vocalists," "all-star athletes," "under," "spouse," "student," "west."

12.   **Prototypes.** Flash a series of slides that show atypical chairs, vases, trees, animals. Discuss prototypes.

13.   **Oxymorons.** Ask students to develop a list of oxymorons (e.g., "government intelligence," "jumbo shrimp"). Discuss semantic problems.

14.   **Body language**. Give students a list of emotional states and ask them to specify the body language (paralanguage) that goes with each state. What do people do with their hands, arms, eyes, posture, etc.? Many experts believe that paralanguage is more consistent and harder to alter than spoken language.
      Examples: How do you know if a person is lying? What is the body language of someone who is happy? Sad? Angry? Etc.

298

15. **Language in pets**. Ask students to think of examples where they believe their pets understand what they are saying. Some students may insist that not only do their pets understand, but they try to imitate simple words.

16. **Speaking a second language.** Ask students if they speak any other languages. Which aspects of the language (grammar, syntax, connotation, pronunciation) were the hardest to learn? In what ways was the other language most different from English? For those students in the class who speak English as a second language, what aspects of English are the most difficult for them?

17. **Solving problems.** Ask students to describe the specific problem-solving strategies that they used to select this course and that they would use to select a job, a book, or a movie.

18. **Functional fixedness.** There are many ways by which fixation in problem solving can be illustrated. A typical problem you may wish to pose to students is this: How could you put your left hand completely in your right hand pants pocket and your right hand completely in your left hand pants pocket at the same time while you are wearing the pants? The answer is to put the pants on backward, whereupon the task becomes quite easy. Students often miss this solution due to conventions about the "right" way to wear a pair of pants.

    A large number of problems similar to the preceding are offered by Eugene Raudsepp in a Psychology Today article. (July 1980 issue of *Psychology Today*: 71–75, 88–90.)

19. **What's your talent?** All of us have talents to share. What is yours?

20. **Brainstorming.** Brainstorm unusual uses for a brick, ways to conserve water, and uses for discarded "pop-top" tabs. Analyze potential solutions in terms of fluency, flexibility, and originality.

21. **Brain versus computer.** Ask students to think about the advantages and disadvantages of the human brain over a computer. Answers can be grouped by speed, capacity, searching abilities, creativity, work while "shut off," etc.

➢ BROADENING OUR CULTURAL HORIZONS

1. **Care of the people with intellectual disabilities in different cultures**. Have students do some online research into other countries' approaches to educating and housing individuals in their society who are classified as being "retarded." Compare those findings, which they bring into class, with our approach in this country. Ask students to think about what it would be like to have a sibling who has an intellectual disability (some may) and how the extra care and support affects the family structure. They may want to discuss the concept and reality of institutionalization or special homes.

2. **Cultural differences in education of the gifted**. Ask students to investigate programs for the gifted in this country as well as a sample of other countries, Western and non-Western. What are the major differences?

3. **Culture, prototypes, and categories.** To what extent does cultural or ethnic background affect the kinds of prototypes we use to categorize objects and events? Would these prototypes affect the way we think?

4. **Culture and connotation**. Discuss the ways in which connotations can be culture-specific. Ask students for examples of misunderstandings they have encountered that can be traced to differences in connotative meanings.

5. **The Whorfian hypothesis in action**. According to Benjamin Whorf, not only does thought influence language, but language determines (or at least influences) thought. Ask students to examine how men and women are treated in language, and whether that alters the way we see each gender. For example, most adult males would object to being called a boy because it connotes immaturity and lack of power. But adult females are often called "girl." Does this mean that we regard adult females differently than we regard adult males? Why do we use the term *girl* instead of *woman*? Does someone who uses sexist language (chick, babe, honey, dear) do so because of their views of women, or does the language determine the attitude? Do people who grow up with sexist versus non-sexist language view women the same way?
Alternately, you can examine the language of racism, ageism, homophobia, etc.

6. **American Sign Language.** Invite a person to class who is fluent in American Sign Language. Would a non-hearing person "perceive" the world differently than a hearing person because of using a different language structure? Teach students to sign the words to a current popular song.

7. **Deaf culture**. Sometimes people who are deaf and who have deaf children refuse to allow cochlear implants (where possible) to be put in either themselves or their child, on the basis that being able to hear would make them lose their cultural connection to the deaf world. Is hearing really about culture, or is it just a physical characteristic? Which parts of deaf culture make it unique and valued? What would it be like being deaf? How is deaf culture different from hearing culture?

8. **Culture and functional fixedness.** What cultural "rules" or values could contribute to functional fixedness? Why are some cultures regarded as more inventive than others?

9. **Is there a culture-free test?** Discuss with students if it is possible to develop a "culture-free" test. If a test cannot be culture free, can it be "culture fair"?

➤ SUPPLEMENTAL ACTIVITIES

TO THE INSTRUCTOR:

Solving problems may become difficult or impossible because of a predisposition, or set, to see the problem in a particular way or to try to solve it by a predetermined method. Students should readily see that they have fallen into this trap when they do the first two exercises. The first exercise involves a story problem that is sure to baffle the listeners because of the obvious (but faulty) solution. The second exercise establishes a mental set in the first five problems. Because of the set that is now established, the students will have a harder time doing the next three.

Exercise 8.1: It Pays to Tip

This is a classroom exercise that demonstrates the effect of set on thinking and problem solving. Students should be asked to read the section on mental set in the text prior to this exercise. You should have a stopwatch or some other timing mechanism to inform students of the time it takes them to solve the problem. The value of this exercise lies in the discussion of the students' attempts at problem solving and the evident mental set that made the problem difficult or impossible to solve.

I.   **Procedure**

A.   Ask students to have a piece of paper and pencil or pen handy for problem-solving purposes. Advise them that you are going to read a story and ask a question. They are to solve the problem and note the time, in seconds, that it took them to find the solution.

B.   After reading the story, watch the time and note the elapsed time in 10-second intervals on the chalkboard as the students work on the solution.

C.   Stop the exercise after five minutes regardless of how many are finished.

D.   The following story should be read slowly and clearly while the students listen:

Three friends went to a restaurant to have a leisurely drink and lunch. They finished their meal and paid their bill while lingering over coffee and conversation. The bill came to $30.00, so each paid $10.00 to the waiter, who went off to pay the bill. The bartender, who handled the cash register, noticed that the waiter had charged full price for the drinks, which were on a two-for-one special. The actual bill should have been $25.00, so he gave the waiter $5.00 and told him to return the money to the customers. On the way back to the table the waiter decided that since the diners did not know they had been overcharged, he would return $1.00 to each and keep $2.00 for himself. That is exactly what he did. Now each of the diners had paid $9.00 for the food and drinks, and the waiter kept $2.00. Three times nine equals 27 plus 2 equals 29. Where is the other dollar? (There is no "other dollar." Twenty dollars went to the restaurant, three to the diners, and two to the waiter. Alternately, the diners paid a total of $27—25 of which went to the restaurant, and two of which went to the waiter.)

301

II.   **Discussion**

    A.   Find out how many solved the problem.

    B.   Ask students to discuss how they tried to find a solution. See how many ways were tried.

    C.   Discuss what factors made it difficult to solve this problem.

    D.   See if students can see how mental set can be a factor in their day-to-day experiences.

Exercise 8.2: Measure for Measure

Beginning with an apology to Shakespeare for that title, we can also give thanks to Luchins for his classic experiment with the water jars. The subject is given a set of three jars of varying sizes and a goal to achieve. The person is to fill and empty the three jars until the goal of a specified number of pints of water is attained. Since the goal is never identical to the capacity of any of the three jars, some strategy needs to be developed to end up with the exact amount specified. Suppose, for example, the subject were given a 20-pint jar, a 4-pint jar, and a 3-pint jar and had to end up with exactly 10 pints of water. The solution requires the subject to fill the 20-pint jar and then pour out 3 pints twice and 4 once, leaving 10 pints. It could be written as 20 minus 3 minus 3 minus 4 equals 10.

I.   **Procedure**

    A.   Explain the exercise to the class, indicating the type of problem being presented. Students should be given the demonstration item above and shown how to record their answer on the data sheet.

    B.   Distribute **Handout 8.1** to each student.

    C.   Write the problems given below on the chalkboard, one at a time, asking the students to record their solution after each one.

    D.   After all eight are completed, discuss items one through five. Two elements are needed for a correct solution to each of these items. The correct amount of water remaining is essential. Also, the way it was arrived at is important because it will demonstrate mental set. In each case, manipulation of the jars of water was needed to arrive at the exact amount.

    E.   Now go on to items six through eight. These can be solved directly without manipulation of the amounts of water. However, after solving one through six, students will probably try manipulation first and may never see the direct method. (Note that for item six, 7 plus 8 equals 15.)

302

| PROBLEM | WATER JAR SIZE | | | GOAL |
	A	B	C	
1	20	31	2	7
2	20	57	3	31
3	5	48	8	27
4	20	100	11	58
5	3	84	7	67
6	7	38	8	15
7	4	17	3	7
8	9	29	6	15

(From A. S. Luchins, "Mechanization in Problem-Solving: The Effect of "Einstellung.'"
Psychological Monographs, 1942, 54.

II.   **Discussion**

A.   Discuss the trial-and-error method needed to learn the best way to solve the problem when starting out.

B.   Have students identify the mental set that was established by the first five items.

C.   How many made the shift to the easy way to solve items six through eight? Now, how many stuck to the "old-fashioned way," which was learned while doing items one through five?

D.   Discuss the extent to which mental set plays a part in our everyday lives.

Exercise 8.3: Analogies

This exercise can serve at least two purposes. One is to arouse interest in the topic of intelligence. The second is to illustrate the use of analogies as a measure of this ability. Most tests of mental ability use some items of this kind, acknowledging that this is a measure of intelligence. The Miller Analogies Test, used as an entrance examination into some graduate programs, is a series of 100 analogies. Charles Spearman's theory of intelligence describes operations of general intelligence (g), which can be measured by analogies. Simply stated, an analogy requires the subject to see a relationship in the first half of a statement and to apply it in the second half. Spearman referred to these operations as education of relations and education of correlates. This test is timed. Spearman believed that speed of response is a factor in intelligence. On this test, students get four minutes with the understanding that most will not finish. This should make the test more discriminating at the top levels.

I.   **Procedure**

      A.   **Giving the test**

            1.   Make enough copies of **Handout 8.2** so that each student will have one.

            2.   Without discussion, distribute the tests, placing them facedown on the students' desks. Ask them not to look at the test until told to do so.

            3.   When everyone is ready, ask them to turn over the test and read the directions as you read them aloud.

            4.   After the directions have been read, do the examples with the students. Point out the correct answer in the first example. Ask a student to give the answer to the second example. Clear up any questions before continuing.

            5.   Tell the students to begin. After four minutes ask them to stop and put their pencils down. DO NOT ALLOW STUDENTS TO CONTINUE IF NOT FINISHED.

            6.   Ask the students to put their names on the test papers and collect them. Do not leave the test with the students if you plan to use it again.

      B.   **Scoring the test**

            1.   Check the items and find the number of correct responses for each student. The scoring key follows.

304

2.   Work out the mean and standard deviation for the class. If you have given it to several classes, include all scores. Larger scores represent more meaningful results. You can develop a set of percentiles for the group that will tell each student how (s)he did in relation to all those who have taken the test.

3.   You can convert the mean and standard deviation into T-scores with a mean of 100, and you will have a deviation IQ score.

4.   Report the results to the students in a way that maintains the confidentiality of their scores, but do not return the tests.

II.   Discussion

A.   You can discuss the test items for validity.

B.   You can discuss the results obtained and what they mean.

C.   The simple statistics used can also be explained to show how data are assembled and interpreted by psychologists.

III.   Analogies Scoring Key

1.	kitten	11.	deaf	21.	betray
2.	herd	12.	sap	22.	rim
3.	shoe	13.	finished	23.	client
4.	light	14.	81	24.	vice
5.	door	15.	author	25.	L
6.	quart	16.	cuff	26.	Wednesday
7.	fruit	17.	seed	27.	laziness
8.	floor	18.	sparrow	28.	create
9.	trees	19.	chairperson	29.	surface
10.	dust	20.	48	30.	run

(Based on the Laycock Mental Abilities Test, S. R. Laycock, University of Saskatchewan, Canada.)

Exercise 8.4: Is It a Good Test?

Distribute **Handout 8.3** to each student. Their task is to go to the internet and find two online "intelligence" tests. When they have found the tests, have them complete their handout for either class discussion, class assignment, or extra credit.

Handout 8.1: MEASURE FOR MEASURE: DATA SHEET

TO THE STUDENT:

In the space provided, show any calculating that you need to do to arrive at a solution. You will have two minutes to do each problem. Your instructor will demonstrate how the problems are to be done and how your answer should be written.

ITEM	SOLUTION	CALCULATIONS
1		
2		
3		
4		
5		
6		
7		
8		

Handout 8.2: ANALOGIES

TO THE STUDENT:

Read each item, then find and circle the word that best completes the statement. First, do the sample items. If you do not understand what to do, ask your instructor. You will have four minutes to complete the test.

SAMPLES:

1. Day is to night as yes is to—perhaps, no, maybe, if.

2. Ship is to ocean as car is to—land, desert, forest, lake.

DO ALL OF THE FOLLOWING LIKE THE SAMPLES

1. Dog is to puppy as cat is to—mouse, dog, rat, kitten.

2. Sheep are to flock as cattle are to—herd, pack, bunch, group.

3. Head is to hat as foot is to—toe, hair, shoe, knee.

4. Dry is to wet as heavy is to—light, hard, soft, firm.

5. Handle is to hammer as knob is to—lock, key, door, brass.

6. Sugar is to pound as milk is to—cream, quart, sweet, barrel.

7. Table is to furniture as apple is to—fruit, cherry, seed, leaf.

8. Wash is to face as sweep is to—broom, nail, floor, straw.

9. Book is to pages as forest is to—wood, trees, leaves, deer.

10. Chat is to flat as must is to—how, cow, shop, dust.

11. Eye is to blind as ear is to—hear, deaf, wax, hearing.

12. Man is to blood as trees are to—leaves, branches, sap, water.

13. Die is to dead as finish is to—finishing, finishes, will finish, finished.

14. 8 is to 64 as 9 is to—54, 81, 90, 45.

15. Picture is to painter as book is to—author, artist, school, and library.

16. Neck is to collar as wrist is to—hand, cuff, coat, and elbow.

17. Peach is to pit as apple is to—peel, red, tree, seed.

18. Fish is to trout as bird is to—sing, nest, sparrow, tree.

19. Trial is to judge as meeting is to—rules, speakers, chairperson, hall.

20. 3 is to 12 as 12 is to—24, 36, 48, 60.

21. Promise is to break as secret is to—betray, keep, guess, trust.

22. Lake is to shore as plate is to—horizon, beach, rim, ford.

23. Doctor is to patient as lawyer is to—judge, trial, prisoner, client.

24. Honesty is to virtue as stealing is to—vice, lying, criminal, trial.

25. H is to C as Q is to—P, M, L, N.

26. Monday is to Saturday as Friday is to—Tuesday, Sunday, Wednesday, Thursday.

27. Success is to ambition as failure is to—loss, defeat, energy, laziness.

28. Discover is to invent as exist is to—find, create, know, remove.

29. Point is to line as line is to—surface, curve, dot, solid.

30. Evolution is to revolution as crawl is to—baby, stand, run, creep.

Handout 8.3: INTERNET INTELLIGENCE TESTS

To complete this exercise, you should go to the internet and locate two different "intelligence tests." Don't just choose the first two that are displayed; look around for two that seem interesting. When you have completed the test, answer the following questions:

1.   What are the internet addresses of the two tests?

2.   Which test did you prefer, and why?

3.   What were the strengths and weaknesses of each test?

4.   Did the tests measure a variety of intellectual skills, or were the questions mostly of one or two types?

5.   Was your score on the test what you expected? If it was different, what do you think that means?

309

➤ JOURNAL QUESTIONS

1. The "average" IQ is 100. What do you think your IQ is? Why? Is this number representative of your intelligence? What experiences have you had over your life that make you think of yourself as a very smart or a not-so-smart person?

2. Do you know friends who were part of the "gifted" program in elementary or high school? If you were a part of this program, how did you feel? If you were not a part of it, how did you feel?

3. Consider the concept of multiple intelligences proposed by Gardner. Rate yourself on the various categories. How does that make you feel about yourself? Do you think that the categories where your strengths lie would be useful for the things you want to do in life? How do you feel about the areas that are not as strong for you? Are there any that interfere with what you want to do in life? Is there a way to compensate for your weaker areas? Is there any way to make them stronger?

4. How much emphasis did your parents put on your intellectual development? Did they push you to excel, or did they let you find your own degree of comfort in academic pursuits? If your parents were well educated, did they push you to become well educated too, or was that your own choice? If your parents did not have a lot of formal education, did they push you to develop your intellectual potential, or did they let you make your own choices?

5. Examine your own study skills with respect to developing concepts. How do you get a concept "into" your brain? What strategies do you use to strengthen the concept? Why would writing out notes or creating charts or diagrams give a person an advantage in concept acquisition that is superior to simply reading the book? If you only read the book, why are you resistant to adopting new ways of learning concepts?

6. What strategies are you most likely to use when attempting to solve problems (e.g., heuristics, understanding, mechanical solutions, or insight)? What is it about your preferred method of solving problems that appeals to you? Why do the other choices not appeal to you?

7. Were you raised in a "stimulating" or a "boring" environment? Did your childhood environment add to or take away from your intellectual development?

8. How creative do you think you are? Why? What experiences have made you feel you are or are not creative?

9. Describe a time when intuitive thinking served you well. Describe a time when it got you in trouble or let you down.

10. Do you believe intelligence is mostly inherited or mostly learned? Support your position.

11. Which of the elements of thought do you rely on the most? Do you make much use of images? Or do you tend to think more in language, symbols, or concepts? Do you have any awareness of muscular imagery in your thinking?

12. What feelings and images do you associate with the words "exam," "mother," "sex," "flag," "cross," and "blood"? How do your feelings compare with the denotative meanings of these words?

13. Do you have a pet? To what extent do you think your animal (or the pet of a close friend) has the capacity to "think"?

14. Give an example of a time you solved a problem through "trial and error." What other strategies do you use? How could you have solved this problem more effectively? What heuristics might have helped?

15. Who is the most "insightful" person you have ever known? In what situations do you behave most "insightfully"?

➤ SUGGESTIONS FOR FURTHER READING

Adams, J. (2001). *Conceptual blockbusting* (4th ed.). New York: Basic Books.

Anderson, J. R. (2010). *Cognitive psychology and its implications* (7th ed.). New York: Worth.

Bransford, J. D., & Stein, B. S. (1993). *The ideal problem solver: A guide to improving thinking.* New York: Freeman.

Carroll, D. W. (2008). *Psychology of language* (5th ed.). Belmont, CA: Cengage Learning/Wadsworth.

DeBono, E. (1990). *Lateral thinking: Creativity step-by-step.* New York: HarperCollins.

Distin, K. (2006). *Gifted children: A guide for parents and professionals.* London: Jessica Kingsley Publishers.

Eugene Raudsepp, E. (1980). More creative growth games. *Psychology Today, July,* 71-75, 88-90.

Flynn, J. R. (2007). *What is intelligence? Beyond the Flynn Effect.* New York: Cambridge.

Gardner, H. (2004). *Frames of mind* (10th anniversary ed.). New York: Basic.

Johnson, L, G., & Hatch, J. A. (1990). A descriptive study of the creative and social behavior of four highly original young children. *Journal of Creative Behavior, 24* (3) 205.

Montagu, A. (2002). *Race and IQ*. Oxford: Oxford University Press.

Premack, D. (1983). Animal cognition." *Annual Review of Psychology, 34* 351-362.

Reed, S. K. (2010). *Cognition: Theory and applications* (8th ed.). Belmont, CA: Cengage Learning/Wadsworth.

Rosenthal, R., & Jacobson, L. (2003). *Pygmalion in the classroom: Teacher expectation and pupils' intellectual development*. Norwalk, CT: Crown House.

Segerdahl, P., Fields, W., & Savage-Rumbaugh, S. (2005). *Kanzi's primal language: The cultural initiation of primates into language*. New York: Palgrave.

Urbina, S. (2004). *Essentials of psychological testing*. New York: Wiley.

White, J. (2006). *Intelligence, destiny and education: The ideological roots of intelligence testing*. New York: Brunner-Routledge.

➢ VIDEO SUGGESTIONS

Feature Films

Charly (Cliff Roberson, Claire Bloom) Drama. Based on *Flowers for Algernon* by David Keyes, a sympathetic caseworker becomes attached to a mentally retarded man as a scientific experiment turns him into a supergenius. The story takes a poignant turn when he discovers that the process is reversing and he is losing his enhanced intelligence.

Dr. Dolittle (Eddie Murphy, Ossie Davis) Comedy. Dr. John Dolittle (Murphy) discovers he has a gift for holding conversations with animals. While others show concern, Dolittle happily takes on animal clients who teach him many things about being human. Technically an excellent weaving of real animals, Henson animatronics, and computer graphics. A whimsical comedy, it nevertheless allows for discussions about the other scientists, namely those who have studied ape and whale languages, as well as those who have taught sign language to primates.

Finding Forrester (Sean Connery, Rob Brown, F. Murray Abraham) Drama. An aging reclusive novelist (Connery) who hasn't written anything since winning a Pulitzer Prize decades earlier, is apprehensive about mentoring a 16-year-old with a desire to write. Each begins to encourage the other's writing, and they become unlikely friends despite their ages and backgrounds. A study in intellect and the intellectual relationship between two writers of very different generations.

Good Will Hunting (1997) (Matt Damon and Ben Affleck) Drama. The location for the film is Massachusetts Institute of Technology (MIT), a prestigious university in the United States. The noted professor of mathematics challenges his class in advanced studies. He places a difficult problem on the blackboard in the main hall and challenges the students to solve it before the end of the semester. The student who solves the problem will get special recognition. The problem was solved overnight, yet no student has claimed the prize. The professor is puzzled. The professor places another problem on the blackboard in the main hall. The next evening, the professor sees someone writing on the blackboard, trying to solve the problem. The person is a janitor named Will who secretly solved the first problem.

I Am Sam (Sean Penn, Michelle Pfeiffer) Drama. Penn stars as a developmentally disabled adult who has been working in a coffee shop and raising his daughter Lucy for seven years. He receives help in parenting from a circle of disabled friends (including two real-life developmentally challenged actors). While he provides a loving and structured environment for Lucy, she begins to surpass him in mental ability. When Lucy begins to intentionally stunt her own mental growth so as not to hurt her father, a social worker removes her from her home and places her in a foster home. Penn seeks the help of a lawyer (Pfeiffer) to take his case to court. During the case, Pfeiffer's character comes to care for her client and his daughter, and considers the limitations of her own abilities as a parent.

Nell (Jodi Foster, Liam Neeson) Drama. Jodie Foster plays a backwoods innocent who barely speaks English yet still teaches valuable lessons to snooty scientists.

Rain Main (Dustin Hoffman, Tom Cruise) Drama. Cruise plays Charlie, a young man who discovers he has an older brother, Raymond, who has autistic disorder. At first Charlie is interested only in his brother's share of their inheritance, but he comes to appreciate Raymond as an individual human being. Along the way, Raymond displays some impressive skills, like memorizing a phone book or performing complicated multiplication in his head—abilities that would label Raymond an "autistic savant."

Real Genius (Val Kilmer, William Atherton) Comedy/Drama. Idealistic whiz kid is recruited into a college think tank working on a laser project. The students are appalled to discover that they have been working on a military project without being told that their achievements would be used in weapons research.

Educational Films and Videos

A Home of Our Own—Independent Living for the Mentally Challenged Films for the Humanities and Sciences, 24 min.

Animal Einsteins—How Smart Are They? PBS, 50 min.

Animal Language, from The Mind Series Teaching Modules, 2nd Edition #27, Annenberg. Discussion of nonhuman communication systems and research with chimpanzees, elephants, and giraffes in language acquisition is reviewed.

Animals—How Smart Are They? Films for the Humanities and Sciences, 26 min.

Aspects of Individual Mental Testing, (1960), Pennsylvania State University Audio Visual Service, 33 min. This black and white film presents a review of the items contained on the 1937 version of the Stanford-Binet Intelligence Test. While some material is dated, the film offers an up-close and personal view of the construction and administration of a classic measure of intelligence.

Better Babies: Raising Intellectual "Superstars," (1991), Filmmakers Library, 28 min. Does prenatal and early childhood learning produce geniuses? This video documents several early-learning programs. We see parents talking to their unborn children in the belief that they will accelerate verbal skills, and other parents in courses on how to raise geniuses. We are shown the hectic schedule of a toddler whose mother teaches him art, music, computers, geography, and Japanese. One couple displays pride in having raised four genius daughters, yet the eldest daughter does not plan to repeat her parents' experiments on her own children. This could be a good discussion-starter for your class.

Brain Traps: Problem-Solving Skills, (1997), Insight Media, 15 min. This short video uses a series of interesting problems to illustrate how normal patterns of thinking can lead us into "brain traps." This video is intended to help students become better problem solvers.

Chimp Talk, (1998), Films for the Humanities and Sciences, 14 min. Paul Hoffman, editor of Discover magazine, explores the controversial issue of language use by apes with primatologist Dr. Sue Savage-Rumbaugh. Dr. Sue Savage-Rumbaugh's 20-year study with chimpanzees reveals that they can use language with the astounding accuracy of a two-year-old human, which includes a rudimentary syntactical ability. However, Petitto's research indicates that humans have a cognitive predisposition for language lacking in chimps, which leads to the conclusion that although apes communicate by associating symbols with objects and actions, they do not have language abilities in the way that humans do. If the scientific community should eventually accept language use by apes, will the last scientific distinction between humans and animals be lost?

Cognitive Processes, Discovering Psychology Series, Annenberg/CPB Project, 30 min. Psychologist Donald Broadbent viewed the mind as a computer, and today's cognitive psychologists use this type of information-processing model to describe the thought process. Discussion of mental groupings called concepts. Complex concepts, or schemas, are ways of looking at the world that organize our past experiences and provide a framework for understanding our future experiences. This program also explores the physiological basis for thinking, showing how psychologist Michael Posner studies the electrical and chemical changes that occur in the brain as a person solves problems.

Decision-Making and Problem Solving, (1990), Coast Community College District Telecourses, 30 min. Part of the Psychology—The Study of Human Behavior Series, this video explains rational and irrational influence on human thought.

Dyslexia: Diagnosis and Therapy, (1995), Films for the Humanities and Sciences, 52 min. This program features eight children and adults of different ages who have had their lives severely affected by dyslexia. The video stresses the importance of early recognition and alerts students to the signs of dyslexia and possibilities for therapy.

Faces of Culture: Language and Communication, (1983), Coast Community College, 30 min. Program 6 in the series. This video discusses the structure of language and its relationship to thought. It examines the influence of culture on language, explores body language as a form of communication, and studies speech as a reflection of culture. Comments from linguists Keith and Claudia Kernan are included.

Faces of Culture: Language and Communication, (1993), Coast Community College, 30 min. One of the few videos to explore the relationship between thought and language, this excellent video's main focus is on the cultural influence on language and how speech reflects one's culture.

Human Consciousness and Computers, (2000), Films for the Humanities & Sciences, 28 min. In this program two major experts, Roger Penrose of Oxford University and Stuart Hammeroff of Arizona University, discuss the nature of human consciousness and whether computers can ever be taught to think. Excellent animation illustrates many of the concepts presented.

Human Language: Signed and Spoken, from The Mind Teaching Modules, 2nd Edition #25 (2000) Worth, 6:08. The module opens with a scene of a young deaf child communicating with her family through sign language. Next the viewer sees Dr. Ursula Bellugi, who studies the basic elements of signing in an effort to sift out the properties of language that are due to the mode in which language is transmitted—either by signing or speaking. This video also provides an opportunity to enrich the discussion of language by including other subjects such as hemispheric specialization, language acquisition, the nature of language formation, and methodology. This video may also be referred back to in the module on good emotion, specifically on the topic of differentiating between facial expression and body language.

Infant Speech Sound Discrimination, from The Mind Teaching Modules, 2nd Edition #23, (2000), Worth, 4:03. This video has to do with infant speech development. It demonstrates how young infants are able to discriminate between very subtle sound differences.

Intelligence from Psychology: The Study of Human Behavior Telecourse, (2002) Coast Community College Telecourses, 30 min. This program graphically demonstrates differences between the intellectually gifted and the developmentally disabled.

Intelligence and Culture, from The Brain Series Teaching Modules, 2nd Edition #4, Annenberg, 4:02. This video tries to explain how culture can influence traditional measures of intelligence. For many cultures, the cognitive skills necessary for scoring highly on the standardized test are not emphasized because they are not adaptive in the particular culture. Students are given examples of cultures in which this is true and should develop a new perspective of the intelligence of people of color.

Intelligence Tests on Trial—Larry P. and P.A.S.E., (1982), San Diego State College, 46 min. This video focuses on the major issues involved in two federal court cases dealing with the cultural bias of individually administered intelligence tests and the use of the tests in placement of black children in EMR/EMH classes.

Intelligence, (1990), Insight Media, 30 min. This video offers an excellent description of variations in intelligence (from retardation to giftedness). One of the main focuses of this video is the concern over the effectiveness of IQ tests as measures of aptitude (versus achievement).

Intelligence: A Complex Concept, CRM, 28 min.

Intelligence and Creativity (2001) Insight Media, 30 min. This video investigates the effects of nature and nurture on intelligence and probes the history and criticisms of intelligence testing.

Intelligence and Creativity (2002) from *Psychology: The Human Experience,* Coast Community College Telecourses, 30 min. This program explores what intelligence means in different environments and cultures and discusses nature versus nurture and biases of intelligence testing.

Intelligence, Creativity, and Thinking Styles, (2000), Films for the Humanities & Sciences, 29 min. This film explores multiple intelligences, traditional IQ scores, the role of the teacher and the family in shaping student intelligence, and presents Sternberg's triarchic theory of intelligence.

Intelligence: A New Definition for the Information Age, (1997), Films for the Humanities and Sciences, 77 min. Success in the Internet era seems to rely more and more on that intangible quality called intelligence. This thought-provoking program critically examines intelligence and technology in today's world, skewering outdated assumptions and arguing for an all-encompassing perspective that incorporates the full range of human capabilities. Encounters that run the gamut from school children to computer hackers and from behaviorists to brain specialists offer a new perspective on humanity's most mysterious capacity and how it is defined.

Judgment and Decision Making, Discovering Psychology Series, Annenberg/CPB Project, 30 min. In general, the program seeks to explain the error and irrationality occurring in much of the human decision-making process. Amos Tversky and Daniel Kahneman are interviewed and discuss their research into decision-making heuristics such as availability, representativeness, framing, and anchoring and adjustment. The value of this video is in the different examples and in hearing the explanations from the researchers themselves.

Language, (1988), PBS Videos, 60 min. Program 7 in The Mind series. This is an excellent video on the evolution of language and the phenomenon of speech. Many examples are illustrated during the hour. It identifies an innate drive in humans to communicate and the linguistic ability that exists even without speech and hearing. The program provides much information and fuel for discussion.

Language, (1990), Coast Community College District Telecourses, 30 min. Part of the Psychology—The Study of Human Behavior Series, this video describes how language is the product of learning, environmental influences, and human genetic endowments.

Language, (1995), Insight Media, 23 min. This video explores the relationship of language abilities and specific areas of the brain. This program examines, from an evolutionary perspective, both human and nonhuman animal language development.

Language and Culture, from The Mind Series Teaching Modules, 2nd Edition #28, (1988), Annenberg, 4:42. This short program relates to possible cultural differences in language and cognition in connection with the linguistic-relativity hypothesis of Benjamin Whorf. It looks at specific language differences as a product of culture rather than reflecting cognitive inferiority. The program's value lies in reaffirming the fact that most cultural differences are due to people in different environments adapting to those environments, not to racial or ethnic inherent inferiority.

Language and Thinking, (1992), Insight Media, 30 min. This video explores the issue of phonetic and grammatical acquisition during childhood. In addition, it offers a brief discussion of the relationship between language and cognition.

Language Development, (1990), Annenberg/CPB, 28 min. This interesting video, hosted by Philip Zimbardo, describes language acquisition from the earliest coos and babbles. Concepts covered include nature/nurture interaction, cerebral maturation, and physiological development.

Examples of several languages and cultures are presented, and similarities are demonstrated with an electronic voiceprint. In addition, the complexities of language in social communication are studied.

Language Predisposition, from The Mind Teaching Modules, 2nd Edition #24, (2000), Worth, 3:44. This video deals with language, development, and research methodology. It is a good demonstration of our remarkable sound recognition abilities.

Language and Cognition (2002) from *Psychology: The Human Experience,* Coast Community College Telecourses, 30 min. This program explores the fact that most animals have the ability to communicate, but only humans have language, symbols for objects, actions, ideas, and feelings.

Language Development (2001) from *Discovering Psychology Series,* Annenberg/CPB, 30 min. The development of language and the study of how children use language in social communication.

Maturity and Creativity, (1982), Karol Media, 30 min. In this film, Rollo May discusses his views on maturity and his own work on the process of creativity. In this interview, he also evaluates his contributions to psychology, reacts to his critics, and discusses his future plans.

May's Miracle, (1983), Filmmakers Library, 28 min. This is a fascinating presentation of the abilities of a musical idiot savant. The film consists of an interview with his parents who describe the evolution of his remarkable ability, and he is shown through photographs as he slowly developed his talent.

Out of the Mouths of Babes: The Acquisition of Language, (1984), Filmmakers Library, 28 min. This award-winning film offers an excellent opportunity to see and hear the chronology of language acquisition during the first six years of life. We see the gradual progression that occurs from random babbling, to jargon and one-word sentences, to the use of complicated structures and linguistic concepts. This film provides a clear, informative description of linguistic development. Also interesting are the carefully structured games and tests that researchers have devised. This video was produced by the Canadian Broadcasting Company.

Secrets of the SAT, (1999), PBS Video, 60 min. This Frontline program, aired on October 4, 1999, examines the many controversies that surround the SAT's merits. Noting the test's critical role in the college admissions process, the video shows how test preparation has become a multimillion-dollar business, with students investing hundreds of hours in an effort to obtain higher scores. The history of the SAT's development, the debate over its predictive validity, and its impact on colleges' racial diversity are all explored. Both supporters and critics of the SAT are interviewed.

Signs of the Apes, Songs of the Whales, (1983), Nova Series, 57 min. If your students are already familiar with The First Signs of Washoe, here is the sequel: Washoe revisited almost 10 years later. In this excellent program, language experiments with chimps, gorillas, dolphins, and sea

318

lions are demonstrated. In addition, the complex signals that whales use to communicate among themselves are explored. This film is excellent fuel for class discussions.

Talk to the Animals, (1987), CBS—60 Minutes video, 14 minute segment. This brief journalistic-type video is significant in two ways: First, it illustrates research in communication with chimpanzees through both sign language and an original syntax designed to be used with a computer. Second, it illustrates the potential of teaching language skills to retarded children. Overall, it is a rather good cross-section of current theory, research, and application in the field, especially if you face time constraints.

Teaching Computers to Think, Scientific American Frontiers Series, 10:05 min.

Testing and Intelligence: Discovering Psychology Series, (1990), Annenberg/CPB, 30 min. In this video from the Discovering Psychology series, Dr. Philip Zimbardo explores the nature of psychological assessment and intelligence. This superior production offers an excellent review of the history of intelligence testing (from Galton to modern times) and the methods used to construct an intelligence test. In addition, the use of a single score as a measure of the complex topic of human intelligence is questioned. The program examines the debate over whether intelligence is a general ability or several specific abilities. Howard Gardner's theory of multiple intelligences receives special attention. The program concludes with a look at research efforts linking intelligence with information-processing speed.

The Bilingual Brain, from The Mind Series Teaching Modules, 2nd Edition #26 Annenberg, 7:29. This short program reviews research into the functioning of the brains of bilingual people. It explores how they might operate or be organized somewhat differently than the brains of monolingual individuals.

The Creative Spirit, (1991), Ambrose Video, 59 min. Each of these four programs blends animation, humor, original music, and on-location action to capture the emerging spirit of innovation and creativity. Through observations of creative people and places, we discover that creative solutions to problems begin with basic human qualities: passion, persistence, vision, caring, and trust in oneself and others.

The Elementary Mind, (1992), Pennsylvania State University / PCR, 28 min. Part 17 of the Time to Grow series. This video examines the fundamental changes that occur in intellectual abilities during middle childhood and how cognitive abilities increase during this period, becoming effective tools for further learning and development. Researchers offer views on intelligence and the problems with IQ tests.

The First Signs of Washoe, (1974), Nova Series, 58 min. This classic film is widely known and still used. It provides an interesting and amusing glimpse of field research by the Gardners with the chimp Washoe during a five-year language-acquisition study using American Sign Language. The film also chronicles the work of Rumbaugh and von Glasersfeld at the Yerkes Primate Institute with the chimp Lana, who communicates through a specially constructed language used

319

with a computer. Fouts' research, which is also explored, attempts to teach groups of chimps to sign among themselves.

The Ideas of Chomsky, (1995), Films for the Humanities and Sciences, 47 min. Linguist and political activist Noam Chomsky of the Massachusetts Institute of Technology transformed the nature of linguistics before he was 40. In this program with world-renowned author and professor Bryan Magee, the outspoken Chomsky challenges accepted notions of the way language is learned, examines the relationship of language to experience, and discusses the philosophical nature of knowledge. A BBC Production.
The IQ Myth (CBS, 50 min.)

The Unbiased Mind: Obstacles to Clear Thinking (1994) Insight Media, 23 min. This video demonstrates how we are sometimes victims of flawed thinking. It has a particularly good section on the confirmational bias.

Thinking, (1988), PBS Videos, 60 min. Program 8 in The Mind series. This video combines the topics of brain physiology and thinking and is a good review of both. The initial focus is on the frontal lobes and the prefrontal cortex, where memory, emotion, and intelligence come together to produce conscious activity. The program explores current research attempts to pinpoint where thoughts originate and how they are stored.

Unlocking Language, (1998), Films for the Humanities and Sciences, 29 min. Approximately 70,000 years ago, humankind began talking, and hasn't stopped since. In this fascinating program, a diverse group of experts—an evolutionary linguist, a neurologist, a geneticist, a neuropsychologist, a developmental cognitive neuroscientist, and an oxford professor of communication—discuss the birth, development, and transmission of the mysterious phenomenon called language. Topics explored include the ability of language to express abstractions; the role of evolution in the development of languages; language as an innately guided behavior in unborn babies, infants, and toddlers; the parts of the brain involved in language; the relationship between genes and language disorders; and the isolation of the Speech 1 gene.

You Must Have Been a Bilingual Baby, (1992), Filmmakers Library, 46 min. This new and interesting video explores how babies become bilingual, how school children fare in language immersion classes, and how adults cope with learning foreign languages. It shows a bilingual class in Virginia where Spanish- and English-speaking children learn together while developing a sense of pride in their respective cultures. This video also shows a program where adults have the satisfaction of attaining fluency in a second language.

➤ COMPUTER AND INTERNET RESOURCES

PsykTrek 3.0
Unit 7: Cognition & Intelligence
7a: Types of Psychological Tests
7b: Key Concepts in Testing
7c: Understanding IQ Scores
7d: Heredity, Environment, and Intelligence
7e: Problem Solving
7f: Decision Making

INFOTRAC®

Below you will find three journal articles obtained from INFOTRAC® that relate to information contained in this chapter. Instructors should encourage students to utilize this invaluable resource to improve their research skills. Have students locate and read the following articles and answer questions relevant to each article.

Roeper Review, April 2001 v23 i3 p151 **Understanding intelligence, giftedness and creativity using the PASS theory.**

1.   What does "PASS" stand for and what is its theory?

    Answer: The PASS (Planning, Attention, Simultaneous, and Successive) theory is a cognitive processing approach to children's abilities that is based on the neuropsychological, information processing, and cognitive psychological research of A. R. Luria (1966, 1973, 1980, and 1982).

2.   According to this article, the basic cognitive processes of attention were associated with different areas of the brain by a number of researchers that Luria (1972) recognized. The three functional units of attention are associated with what areas of the brain?

    Answer: The first functional unit of attention is associated with the brain stem, diencephalon, and medial regions of the hemispheres; the second with the occipital, parietal, and temporal lobes posterior to the central sulcus; and the third regulated by the frontal lobes, especially the prefrontal region.

3. What are the two main weaknesses of traditional IQ testing which are especially relevant to the question of identification of gifted children?

Answer: The two main weaknesses that are especially relevant to the question of identification of gifted children are: first, the age of traditional IQ tests has not permitted integration of current understandings of intelligence that have emerged from research conducted over the past 50 years; second, traditional IQ tests are based on a weak theoretical foundation of general ability with vaguely defined constructs and tests that are clearly achievement-laden.

4. The cognitive revolution has impacted the way intelligence is conceptualized and measured. The cognitive revolution provided important foundational research for redefining intelligence as a cognitive process that has resulted in alternatives to traditional IQ tests. Name two of these new tests.

Answer: This new breed of tests includes the Kaufman Adolescent and Adult Intelligence Test (K-ABC) and Cognitive Assessment System (CAS).

5. According to this article, in what ways are creativity and planning related? Briefly explain each.

Answer: There is a particular connection between planning and creativity. The important role of planning in creativity is found in both empirical studies and in philosophical theory. Guastello, Shissler, Driscoll, and Hyde (1998) studied eight cognitive styles and found that the planner was significantly positively correlated with creative productivity. Baker-Sennett (1995) argued that both planning and improvisation were positively related to creativity. Redmund, Mumford, and Teach (1993) found that more time spent planning and re-planning a project resulted in more productivity and higher creativity. In Finke, Ward, and Smith's (1992) theory of creative cognition, they propose a Geneplore model. This model features two central cognitive processes that contribute to creativity. One process is generative, in which an idea is initially created; the other process is exploratory, in which this idea is then examined and interpreted in different ways. Both of these processes require significant planning for successful execution. Indeed, the exploratory phase of creative cognition in which the generated ideas are explored is a good example of the regulation phase of planning.

Amabile (1983, 1996) presents a componential theory of creativity, which also shows the influence of planning. Her three components are domain-relevant skills (i.e., knowledge, technical skills), task motivation, and creativity-relevant skills.

Another link between creativity and planning ability is metacognition. Metacognition, the act of thinking of one's own cognitive processes (Feldhusen, 1995), is a key aspect of planning.

The Journal of General Psychology, January 2005 v132 i1 p67 (14) **Effect of trait anger on cognitive processing of emotional stimuli.**

1.   What theory does the trait-congruency hypothesis posit?

Answer: The trait-congruency hypothesis posits that affective traits are also linked to the heightened activation of congruent emotion networks (Rusting, 1998). Thus, for instance, an individual who possesses an "anxious personality" may bias attention toward anxiety-related information, more accurately recall anxiety-related information, or process anxiety-related cues more rapidly. As such, these trait-related cognitive biases purportedly increase the likelihood that a particular emotion (e.g., anxiety) will be experienced.

2.   How do the authors of this study define "trait anger"?

Answer: Trait anger is conceptualized as an enduring disposition to experience anger more frequently, more intensely, and for a longer period of time.

3.   What were the results of the current study with regard to trait anger?

Answer: Results indicated that individuals who reported high levels of trait anger displayed facilitative biases in the processing of semantic anger-related stimuli. This predisposition to more readily processed anger-related information may underlie their propensity to experience intense feelings of anger when provoked.

4.   What were the general conclusions of this study with regard to "trait anger"?

Answer: Although the interaction of trait and state anger seem to facilitate cognitive processing for anger-related stimuli, research findings concerning the independent impact of an anger-related trait on cognitive processing remain equivocal. This is an important distinction because confirmation of independent trait-related biases would suggest that some individuals (i.e., those with high trait anger) are more likely to possess cognitive biases toward anger-related stimuli without becoming angered.

Human Ecology Forum, Wntr 1998 v26 n1 p24(1) **Gaps in test scores between race and class groups have narrowed.**

1.   Is the IQ gap between black and white Americans increasing or decreasing, and how is that being measured?

       Answer: Racial differences in intelligence narrowed by about half between 1970 and 1988 and have since remained fairly constant.

       Socioeconomic class differences between the upper and lower thirds have continued to decline gradually since 1932. IQ scores between these two groups have, in fact, converged about 25 percent in the past 50 years or so.

       PSATs (Preliminary Scholastic Assessment Tests), which are given to representative samples of high school juniors (as opposed to the self-selected high school seniors who take the SATs) reflect relatively stable score differences between the top and bottom quarters since 1961.

       The arguments that Americans are getting "dumber" because low-IQ parents are outbreeding high-IQ parents is not supported.

2.   What factors are believed to be responsible for the changes?

       Answer: The most dramatic convergence of scores, however, has been in racial differences in IQ during the 1970s and 1980s, which we think were due to nongenetic factors. During this period, our country spent substantially more for education targeted at minorities, and at the same time, the educational attainment of minority parents increased enormously and their families grew smaller.

       The closing of the racial gap was due to gains in test scores by black students, not reductions in white students' scores.

WEB LINKS

Knowledge Builder Web Links

1. Intelligence
       American Mensa: http://www.us.mensa.org
       Intellectual Disabilities: http://www.aaidd.org/
       Multiple Intelligences in Education:
            http://www.education-world.com/a_curr/curr054.shtml

2. Imagery, Concepts, and Language
       Amoeba Web Psychology Resources: Cognitive Psychology:
            http://www.vanguard.edu/faculty/ddegelman/amoebaweb/
       International Dyslexia Association: http://www.interdys.org/
       Koko.org: http://www.koko.org/index.php

3. Problem Solving
How Experts Differ from Novices: http://www.uidaho.edu/psyc325/lessons/10/
Functional Fixedness:
http://www.eruptingmind.com/mental-sets-functional-fixedness/

4. Creative Thinking and Intuition
Creativity Web: http://www.csus.edu/indiv/k/kiddv/CreativeSolutions/pages/links.htm
Creative Thinking Techniques: http://www.virtualsalt.com/crebook2.htm
Thin Slicing: http://www.gladwell.com/blink/

5. Culture, Race, IQ, and You
Be Careful of How You Define Intelligence:
http://www.psych.utoronto.ca/users/reingold/courses/intelligence/cache/define.html
The Knowns and Unknowns of Intelligence: http://webspace.ship.edu/cgboer/iku.html
The Bell Curve: http://www.indiana.edu/~intell/bellcurve.shtml

Additional Web Links

APA Online
http://www.apa.org/

Autistic Savants
http://www.autism.com/fam_autistic_savants.asp

Chimpanzee language (Washoe)
http://www.cwu.edu/~cwuchci/
http://www.friendsofwashoe.org/visit_the_chimpcam.shtml

Concepts and Cognition
http://www.cogsci.indiana.edu/

Cognition and Brain Sciences
http://www.mrc-cbu.cam.ac.uk/

Edward de Bono's Official Website (creative thinking)
http://www.edwdebono.com/

Intelligence Tests
http://www.iqtest.com
http://www.psychtests.com
http://psychology.about.com/library/bl/bleq_measure.htm

Mental Retardation
http://www.cdc.gov/ncbddd/dd/ddmr.htm
http://adam.about.com/encyclopedia/001523.htm?terms=mental+retardation
http://www.hmc.psu.edu/childrens/healthinfo/m/mentalretardation.htm

Neural Basis of Cognition
http://www.cnbc.cmu.edu/

Sign Language
http://www.masterstech-home.com/ASLDict.html
http://deafness.about.com/od/signlanguage/Sign_Language.htm
http://www.nidcd.nih.gov/health/hearing/asl.asp

Mensa
www.us.mensa.org
www.mensa.org/workout2.php (Mensa fun test)

Amoeba Web Psychology Resources: Cognitive Psychology
http://www.vanguard.edu/faculty/ddegelman/amoebaweb

International Dyslexia Association
http://interdys.org/

National Aphasia Association
http://www.aphasia.org/

The American Association of Artificial Intelligence
http://www.aaai.org/

PSYCHOLOGY IN THE NEWS

Action, Brain, and Cognition
http://psy.otago.ac.nz/research/actionbraincognition/
The latest news in neuroscience and cognitive techniques to examine the neural and cognitive
underpinnings of complex action, with a focus on bimanual actions, speech and conceptual
processes, and memory processes.

AI in the News

http://www.aaai.org/

This site provides the latest in news, frequently asked questions, and news archives regarding artificial intelligence.

Center for the Brain Basis of Cognition

http://cbbc.georgetown.edu/news.html

News and updates from Georgetown University on the brain basis of cognition.

Plebius Press Psychology Resource Center

http://psychology.plebius.org/news.php?new_topic=16

News articles on language, thought, and cognition.

CHAPTER 9

Motivation and Emotion

Survey Questions
Discussion Questions
Lecture Enhancements

What's it worth?

Hunger, satiety, and activities

Attitudes toward eating

Is this a good diet?

What's your BMI?

Take the sensation-seeking scale

Projecting the need for achievement

Basic needs

Applying Maslow's theory to everyday problems

What motivates you in a job?

What is "willpower"?

Gotcha!

The sympathetic nervous system and GSR

Measuring sympathetic nervous system response

Lie detection and you

Emotional intelligence

Value-Clarification Statements
One-Minute Motivators

Homeostasis and thermostats

Intracellular thirst

But I'm curious!

Optimal arousal

Need for achievement

Why are you here?

Medications for pain and sex drive

Increasing stress and arousal

Do you understand?

Smile!

Can facial expressions change our emotions?

Fight or flight response

Measuring emotional intelligence

Broadening Our Cultural Horizons

Cultural food preferences

Sample this!

Cultural priorities and weight

Culture and eating disorders

A brave new world

What's the sexual message?

Who's "sexy"?

Sensation seeking and cultural bias

Society, behavior, and reinforcement

Family orientation toward achievement

Motivating a culturally diverse group

Are Maslow's motives universal?

Diversity and goal attainment

Supplemental Activities

Handouts

Journal Questions
Suggestions for Further Reading
Video Suggestions
Computer and Internet Resources

➤ SURVEY QUESTIONS

Module 9.1 Overview of Motivation

Survey Questions: What is motivation? Are there different types of motives?

Module 9.2 Hunger, Thirst, Pain, and Sex

Survey Question: What causes hunger? Overeating? Eating disorders?

Survey Questions: Is there more than one type of thirst? In what ways are pain avoidance and the sex drive unusual?

Module 9.3 Arousal, Achievement, and Growth Needs

Survey Question: How does arousal relate to motivation?

Survey Questions: What are learned motives? Social motives? Why are they important?

Survey Question: Are some motives more basic than others?

Module 9.4 Emotion and Physiological Arousal

Survey Question: What happens during emotion?

Survey Questions: What physiological changes underlie emotion? Can "lie detectors" really detect lies?

Module 9.5 Emotional Expression and Theories of Emotion

Survey Question: How accurately are emotions expressed by the face and "body language"?

Survey Question: How do psychologists explain emotions?

Module 9.6 Psychology in Action: Emotional Intelligence—The Fine Art of Self-Control

Survey Question: What does it mean to have "emotional intelligence"?

➤ DISCUSSION QUESTIONS

1. Which of the primary drives do you consider the strongest? Why? Which occupies the greatest amount of your time and energy? How could the strength of the primary drives be determined for animals?

2. How could you apply the concept of incentives to improve your motivation to study?

3. For those of you who have worked shift work, which shift (mornings, afternoons, or "midnights") is most difficult? Why? For those who have worked "midnights," do you ever become completely used to it? Do you ever notice things that suggest that your body is programmed to be asleep during this time?

4. Some species are active at night (nocturnal) while others are active during the daytime (diurnal). What would be the evolutionary advantage for humans to be diurnal? What would be the disadvantages for us to be nocturnal? (Note: Remind students that evolutionary trends were formed long before there were cities, artificial lighting, and modern conveniences.)

5. If you were an airline pilot, what steps would you take to minimize the constant disruption to your circadian rhythms?

6. Discuss some of the factors that contribute to overeating at Thanksgiving or during a similar feast.

7. You have just finished a large dinner in a restaurant and you are "stuffed." Then, the dessert cart goes by and you see the most delicious-looking desserts. Do you indulge? What goes through your mind when you see the goodies but you are already full? How hard is it for you to resist?

8. Have you ever developed a taste aversion? What was the food and what were the circumstances? Have you since been able to eat that food? Are there any cases where you subsequently overcame a previous food aversion? How did you do that?

9. What are some strategies for reducing the "damage" caused by fast foods? In other words, if you want fast food, what are some of the strategies you can use to minimize the negative effects while still satisfying your "junk food" craving?

10. What would be some of the disadvantages of trying to control eating by burning out (ablating) the lateral hypothalamus?

11. It is noon in July in the desert. You have been sweating in the sun and enjoying the warmth. You are suddenly thirsty. Why? What should you do about it?

12. The sex drive is not essential for individual survival, and it can be easily interrupted by any of the other primary drives. Why do you think so much energy is directed toward sexuality in our culture?

13. Why do most menopausal women report no significant reductions in sexual arousal and activity?

14. In what ways have you observed the stimulus motives at work in human behavior? Does learning contribute to curiosity or needs for stimulation?

15. You are the manager of a professional football team. How do you motivate the team? What do you say? Explain your responses in terms of the ideas from this chapter.

16. Does the American emphasis on competition (in your opinion) encourage achievement or discourage it? (Consider the effects, for example, when only one person can be considered the "winner" in many situations.)

17. In *Lady Windermere's Fan,* playwright Oscar Wilde said, "In this world there are only two tragedies. One is not getting what one wants, and the other is getting it. The last is the real tragedy." What do you think Wilde meant? Where does your motivation come from?

18. If you had a guaranteed income, would you "work"? What do you think you would spend your time doing? For how long? What, if anything, does this reveal about sources of intrinsic motivation?

19. Is it possible for someone to die from "voodoo" or being "cursed"? Why or why not? Which concepts from your text might explain cases of voodoo death?

20. If you were accused of something that you didn't do, would you take a lie-detector test to demonstrate your innocence? Why or why not? If you were accused of something that you DID do, would you take a lie-detector test to convince people that you were innocent? Why or why not? Did your response to the possibility of taking a lie detector test vary depending on whether you were innocent or guilty? If so, why?

21. In your opinion, what limits, if any, should be placed on the use of lie detection devices by businesses? By the military? By the government?

22. Do you consider yourself more emotional or less emotional than average? What role has learning played in the development of your emotional life? (Consider the influence of family, friends, and culture.)

23. In what ways have emotions contributed to your enjoyment of life? In what ways have they caused problems for you?

24. Imagine a time when you have "faked" a smile. Does it feel different than a real smile? How so? Can you tell the difference between a fake smile and a real smile in someone else? How?

25. Imagine that you are in traffic and someone "cuts you off." How do you feel? How do you react? (i.e., do you just continue on, or do you become emotional?) Now imagine that you are in a traffic jam and no one is moving. How do you respond? Do you get upset, or do you take it philosophically? Make a list of the ways people deal with "road rage" (or at least road "irritation").

26. There is an element of truth to each of the theories of emotion. What parts of each seem to apply best to your own emotions?

27. What would be the advantages and disadvantages of being emotionless? (You might use Mr. Spock from the *Star Trek* movies, Mr. Data from *Star Trek: The Next Generation,* or Mr. Tuvok from *Star Trek: Voyager* as a model for answering this question.)

28. Did you learn "body language" from your parents? How similar are your facial and hand gestures to theirs?

29. An atmosphere of competition and evaluation pervades many schools. How might this contribute to test anxiety? Do you think that the amount of testing done in schools should be increased or decreased? What alternatives would you propose if testing decreased?

➤ LECTURE ENHANCEMENTS

1. **What's it worth?** To explore the idea of incentive value, give students play money. Write various goals on the chalkboard, such as: "How much would you pay to lose 10 pounds? To have a regular sex partner? To get an A in this class? To get a well-paying job? To improve a personal relationship? To live to the age of 100?" Then conduct an auction. Ask students to explain why they bid as they did.

2. **Hunger, satiety, and activities.** Have students brainstorm a list of activities that are best on an empty or full stomach, and why. (For example, it is best to eat BEFORE going grocery shopping!)

Attitudes toward eating. The "Attitudes Toward Eating" survey that follows can be completed individually by students. The purpose is not to formally score the scale, but rather to alert students to the types of behaviors associated with eating disorders. However, students who agree with many of the items may realize that they may have an eating disorder, so be prepared to refer them to a campus clinic or eating disorder program if either is available.

This questionnaire is based on ideas that have been used successfully to predict the likelihood a client will develop anorexia nervosa and/or bulimia nervosa. (For more information see Garner & Garfinkel, 1997.) Also ask your students if they have ever seen a website devoted to celebrating anorexia ("Ana") or bulimia ("Mia").

DIRECTIONS: Select the number that describes how frequently you behave this way or have these feelings about your behavior. Write that number to the left of each statement.

1 = never 2 = rarely 3 = sometimes 4 = usually 5 = always

_____ 1. I feel terrified about being overweight.
_____ 2. I don't eat even when I am feeling physically hungry.
_____ 3. I am preoccupied with thoughts about food.
_____ 4. I experience eating binges and find it difficult to stop eating.
_____ 5. I cut my food into a specific number of small pieces.
_____ 6. I am aware of the calorie content of the foods I eat.
_____ 7. I eat foods rich in grain carbohydrates but low in fat, e.g., bread, rice, potatoes.
_____ 8. I feel that others would prefer if I ate a greater quantity of food.
_____ 9. I vomit after I have eaten.
_____ 10. I feel extremely guilty after eating.
_____ 11. I often think about wanting to be thinner.
_____ 12. I am aware of the number of calories I burn up when I exercise.
_____ 13. Other people think I am too thin.
_____ 14. I am upset when I discover fat on my body.
_____ 15. I eat very slowly in comparison to others.
_____ 16. I avoid foods that contain sugar.
_____ 17. I eat foods manufactured for dieters.
_____ 18. Food seems to control most of my life.
_____ 19. I demonstrate great self-control when around food.
_____ 20. Others seem to pressure me to eat.
_____ 21. I think too often about food.
_____ 22. I feel uncomfortable after eating sweets.
_____ 23. I am always trying to cut down on the amount of food I eat.
_____ 24. I enjoy the feeling of having an empty stomach.
_____ 25. I enjoy tasting new foods, even if the food is high in calories or fat.

4. **Is this a good diet?** Ask students to bring to class their favorite diet. Make a few copies of the best and worst examples. Give the diets to small groups of students for discussion. Ask them to predict the short-term and long-term effectiveness of each diet. What makes a diet effective?

5.   **What's your BMI? (Internet exercise)** On a piece of paper, have student write down their current weight and their ideal weight. Then, either provide the chart for the Body Mass Index (BMI) or have students go online and read about it. Have them write down the BMI for their current and ideal weights and compare it to their BMI. Also have them record the weight associated with their optimal BMI. Have students indicate whether or not they were surprised, and what they think about the BMI. You can also collect the responses anonymously and review them. A copy of the BMI can be found at: http://www.nhlbisupport.com/bmi/bmicalc.htm

6.   **Take the sensation-seeking scale. (Internet exercise)**
        An abbreviated version of the sensation-seeking scale can be found at: http://www.rta.nsw.gov.au/licensing/tests/driverqualificationtest/sensationseekingscale/ If you prefer to use Zuckerman's full scale, go to literature review sources and type in "Zuckerman" and "Sensation Seeking" to locate books and articles.

7.   **Projecting the need for achievement.** An exercise can be developed around the results of a projective approach to assessing nAch (need for achievement). Find a somewhat ambiguous photo in a magazine and ask students to write a short story telling what led up to the situation portrayed, what is happening now (including the feelings of the characters), and what will happen next. Stories can be scored (rather loosely) for the number of references to achievement themes and imagery (references to striving, trying, goals, excellence, success, planning, achievement, and so forth). Interview students with unusually high nAch as a basis for discussion and illustration. Other themes that can be interesting to look for are power, affiliation, and fear of success.

8.   **Applying Maslow's theory to everyday problems.** Try to show how Maslow's theory helps us understand everyday problems. How could an owner of a business use the hierarchy of needs to understand her employees, and how could she change conditions to improve morale and increase productivity? How could the theory apply to your own classroom, to problems between parent and child, boyfriend and girlfriend, etc.?

9.   **Gotcha!** A good way to clarify the cognitive view of emotion is to seek examples from the class in which they were "fooled" by an emotional situation, so that an initial reaction of fear or apprehension gave way to relief or laughter. Point out that the foundation of physiological arousal remained—only the perception or interpretation changed.

10.   **Basic needs.** Have the class rate the importance of each of the following clusters of needs on a 10-point scale (1 = of little importance to me; 10 = extremely important to me). Which cluster gets the highest rating? Where does this place the individual on Maslow's hierarchy of motives? Does this placement correspond to his or her self-perception? In what way does one's culture affect the area of emphasis on the hierarchy? Do students agree with Maslow's ordering of needs?
        a.   A safe and secure house, dependable income, good health, predictable future, general sense of security

336

b. Respect from colleagues or coworkers, valued by others in the community, self-respect, and self-esteem

c. Perfection, justice, beauty, truth, autonomy, meaningfulness, simplicity

d. A close circle of family or friends, loved and cared for by others, loved by a special person, accepted in the community

e. Good food, drink, sex, physical comfort, rest and vigorous activity, good night's sleep, life's physical pleasures

It is fairly obvious that the items represent (in this order): 1) safety and security; 2) esteem and self-esteem; 3) self-actualization (meta-needs); 4) love and belonging; and 5) physiological needs. The items are likely to be transparent even for a naive subject. Therefore, to get the most out of this exercise, it should probably be given before students have studied the material in Chapter 10 but discussed when the chapter has been read.

11. **What motivates you in a job?** Distribute the following list to students and ask them to rank their priorities from one to ten. Either by a show of hands or by collecting the responses, determine the top answers and/or the mean of the responses for each item.

What is most important to you in a job? Please rank each of the following from one to ten, with *one* being the most important.

1. ____ Being able to be creative
2. ____ Being able to influence people
3. ____ Making a lot of money
4. ____ Being happy in my job
5. ____ Having a challenging job
6. ____ Having opportunities for advancement
7. ____ Believing in what I do
8. ____ Having a job that is interesting
9. ____ Having a lot of social interaction
10. ____ Having a good work schedule

12. **What is "willpower"?** Discuss the notion of willpower with students. This is a problem for many people. Most of us have "too little" of it, whatever it is. Have the students examine this concept in light of the theories they have been studying. Behaviorists would say there is no such thing; our actions are simply the result of association and reinforcement. The notion of motivation as a force to generate behavior would be unacceptable to a behaviorist. Willpower, from a cognitive point of view, is an internal force that moves a person in some direction. Behavior is powered by strong needs, or guilt, or anxiety. How would humanistic psychologists view this concept? Using this kind of discussion, you should be able to get students to see how these theories explain behavior more clearly. Instead of willpower, you could use conscience as the concept to be discussed.

337

13. **The sympathetic nervous system and GSR.** If you can obtain a galvanic skin response instrument, you can show the sympathetic nervous system in action. Attach the sensors to the fingers of a volunteer and have the class ask some provocative questions. (You may need to screen them ahead of time to avoid being provoked or embarrassed yourself.) Even without a verbal response from the subject, the GSR will show an increase in the level of moisture on the skin (perspiration) due to sympathetic nervous system arousal.

14. **Measuring sympathetic nervous system response.** At the beginning of the period, create an excuse to have students measure their pulse. You can tell them that everyone has a different metabolism and that you want to demonstrate the variety of resting heart rates in the class. Then, about halfway through the class, hand out a "pop quiz." Most of them will object to being unfairly surprised. After maximum response has occurred, have them take their pulse again. Debrief them on the deception. Ten minutes later, have the students take their pulse a third time.

15. **Lie detection and you.** You have discussed the polygraph and how it works. Students are aware of its usefulness and its limitations. Raise some questions with the class about its use and abuse. Ask them to respond to the following questions:

   a.   How would you react if your employer demanded regular polygraph tests of all employees?

   b.   Should the polygraph be used to check up on government officials?

   c.   What do you think about "lie detecting" in the future? How will it be different?

16. **Emotional intelligence.** Have students rank the five characteristics of emotional intelligence according to: a) which ones they think are more and less important, and b) which ones they think they are strongest and weakest in personality.

ROLE-PLAYING SCENARIOS

1. **You are a person who finds it impossible to gain weight.** You are very tired of people asking you if you are anorexic and treating you as if you are emotionally unstable.

2. **You just lost 50 pounds.** You are receiving positive feedback about your appearance, but you don't seem to be any happier than you were before.

3. **You are the first person from your family to graduate from high school, and now you are starting college.** You know you can succeed, but there is a part of you that is afraid of the responsibilities that success in college can bring. Tell your best friend about these feelings.

338

4. **You have just taken a polygraph exam at your place of employment.** The polygraph operator says that you failed and that you are suspected of stealing. You know that you are innocent. Defend yourself.

➤ VALUE-CLARIFICATION STATEMENTS

1. Changing our circadian rhythms is just a matter of willpower.

2. If a person consistently exercises, he or she can lose weight.

3. People who are overweight just eat too much.

4. If people are really motivated to lose weight, they will.

5. Bulimia nervosa is a symptom of a larger problem—an inability to delay gratification.

6. Women are too concerned with how they look.

7. People who engage in high risk activities (like skydiving) are just being reckless.

8. Children should not be paid for getting good grades.

9. The best measure of success in life is material wealth.

10. Success is 1 percent inspiration and 99 percent perspiration.

11. The results of polygraphs should be admissible in court.

12. New employees should not be required to take a lie detector test before starting a new job.

13. It would be better if humans never felt emotion.

14. It's a sign of weakness to display too much emotion.

15. Being able to display emotions is a sign of mental health.

16. Subliminal stimuli in advertising should be banned.

➤ ONE-MINUTE MOTIVATORS

1. **Homeostasis and thermostats.** Depending on the season and your classroom, you can demonstrate homeostasis by turning the thermostat in your room up or down and waiting until a student complains and asks you to alter the temperature.

339

2. **Intracellular thirst.** Provide students with many baskets of chips and salty peanuts. Be sure that no one has any liquid in class to drink. Wait until one student asks to run outside for a drink of water. Discuss intracellular thirst.

3. **But I'm curious!** Give students the first five minutes of class to complete a large wooden or jigsaw puzzle. Stop students before the puzzle is complete and return to lecture/discussion. Be sure the puzzles are within touching distance of many students. Ask a student before class to count the number of times students reach out to complete the puzzles. Discuss human curiosity and manipulation needs. You may also want to discuss the motivational properties of frustration that result from interrupted goal seeking.

4. **Optimal arousal.** Arrange students in pairs. Ask half of the pairs to engage in five minutes of aerobic exercise. Ask the other half to meditate. Then give each pair some pickup sticks. Each pair should decide who the observer is and who the subject is. Count the number of sticks that can be carefully picked up. Discuss optimal arousal.

5. **Need for achievement.** Play a quick series of games with points. Ask trivia questions, guess numbers, or the like. Keep track of each student's points. Ask students to share feelings about winning and losing with a person sitting near them. What does this say about each person's need to achieve?

6. **Why are you here?** Students have many different reasons for attending college. Some are there because they actually want to learn. Others want a better job. Some are there primarily because their parents expect them to be. Ask students what motivates them to be in college. Does the reason for attending make a difference in their willingness to study? At what point does it become more about intrinsic interests and less about external rewards? Have any of them experienced that change from internal to external? What did that feel like?

7. **Medications for pain and sex drive.** With medications such as Viagra and hormone replacement therapy, ask students how they feel about using them when they need to. Do they believe they shouldn't "fool mother nature," or is it that "all's fair in love and war"?

8. **Increasing stress and arousal.** Have students brainstorm a list of activities that they engage in to intentionally increase their arousal (e.g., roller coasters).

9. **Do you understand?** Ask students working in pairs to conduct an entire conversation using only facial expressions and gestures. How much was understood? Why?

10. **Smile!** Ask students to spend one day intentionally smiling. Ask them to jot down their feelings and the reactions of others to them. Ask them to share their feelings the next day of class.

11. **Can facial expressions change our emotions?** Ask half the class to put a pencil crosswise between their teeth for five minutes while you lecture (inducing a smile). Ask the other half to put a pencil between their lips (inducing a frown). At the end of five minutes, show them a cartoon and ask them to rate how funny it is on a five-point scale. Discuss the facial feedback hypothesis.

12. **Fight or flight response.** Call on people for impromptu speeches. Break a balloon or turn on a buzzer just prior to pulling out a name. Discuss the role of anxiety and arousal as they relate to the fight or flight reaction. Remind students that these are normal reactions and that the challenge is to channel such responses into adaptive behaviors.

13. **Measuring emotional intelligence. (Internet exercise)** There are some brief and fairly well-designed quizzes on the Internet to measure emotional intelligence. One of these sites is at http://quiz.ivillage.co.uk/uk_work/tests/eqtest.htm
Assign this quiz to students and reassure them that their results are confidential. Ask them to examine the results and determine if they agree with the assessment. What can be done to increase the validity of this assessment?

BROADENING OUR CULTURAL HORIZONS

1. **Cultural food preferences.** Some cultures encourage people to eat a sweet, fat, high-variety diet. Other cultures encourage more savory, low-fat, and less varied foods. Ask students to study the eating habits of different cultures. Is the Far Eastern diet becoming westernized? Or is the Western diet becoming Easternized?

2. **Sample this!** Ask students to bring to class the most unusual ethnic foods they can find. Ask students to taste the food. Then have the provider describe the food and its cultural background.

3. **Cultural priorities and weight.** How has our culture contributed to eating problems such as obesity, anorexia nervosa, and bulimia? In some cultures, a degree of fatness is considered desirable as a hedge against starvation. Do we label people "fat" when they are perfectly healthy?

4. **Culture and eating disorders.** What cultures would you expect to have the least frequency of anorexia? Why are most people with eating disorders female? As traditional gender roles continued to be "blurred," will this gender difference change? How? Why or why not?

5. **A brave new world.** Imagine a society without ads for food. People can only eat what they raise. Money can be used to buy tangible objects or services, but it cannot be used to buy food. What kinds of eating disorders would occur?

6. **What's the sexual message?** Cultures vary widely in how they view sex. In some cultures, sexuality is accepted as part of normal life. In other cultures, it is strictly regulated and is potentially regarded as something shameful. Ask students to do some research on sex in other cultures and report their findings to the rest of the class. Alternately, ask them to critique the sexual messages in this culture. On the one hand, sex is glorified in movies, on TV, and in advertising. On the other hand, it is shrouded in secrecy and shame; parents often don't want to talk about the "birds and the bees," but they also don't want sex education in school. You can brainstorm positive and negative cultural messages with your students.

7. **Who's "sexy"?** North American culture places a great deal of emphasis on a woman's weight in its appraisal of whether she is considered physically attractive. Some other cultures have a clear preference for more "roundness" in women's bodies. What cultural reasons might account for these differences? On what basis are men considered "sexy" in this and other cultures?

8. **Sensation seeking and cultural bias.** What cultural biases may exist in the Zuckerman Sensation-Seeking Scale? What assumptions does this scale make about human behavior?

9. **Society, behavior, and reinforcement.** Make a list of all the ways a culture could reinforce social behaviors. What social behaviors do you perform? How are these reinforced? Do different ethnic groups and subcultures encourage different social behaviors?

10. **Family orientation toward achievement.** Look at your own family culture. What forms of success are you encouraged to work toward? Do you think that other cultures share the same goals or define "success" in the same way?

11. **Motivating a culturally diverse group.** What characteristics define "success" and "achievement" in Western culture? How might a collectivist culture define these concepts? What are the advantages and disadvantages with the way that Western culture defines success? Do these concepts affect happiness? Why or why not?

12. **Are Maslow's motives universal?** Imagine a culture where social needs were more important than self-actualization needs. How would you test the universality of self-actualization? Are there many different ways self-actualization can be expressed?

13. **Diversity and goal attainment.** Most colleges have an increasingly diverse student population. Imagine that you are one of five student government leaders wanting to put together a recycling campaign. One student is a 40-year-old Indian man; another is a 25-year-old single woman; another is a 32-year-old white single father; another is an 18-year-old man; and finally another is a 22-year-old married Japanese woman. How would you go about motivating this diverse group of people?

➤ SUPPLEMENTAL ACTIVITIES

TO THE INSTRUCTOR:

The exercises that follow are designed to give students an opportunity to evaluate motivation in an objective manner. They should be able to see how a psychologist tries to assess motivation. At the same time, they should become aware of the difficulty of doing it scientifically and getting hard data to work with.

Exercise 9.1: nAch(oo!)

Pardon the pun! But just as the sneeze may be a precursor of a cold, so some behaviors indicate the existence of a need and the intensity of the drive to satisfy it.

I.   **Introduction**

The items in this exercise describe some behaviors that are related to achievement motivation. People do not experience them all to the same degree, but put together they can be an indicator of the strength of the need for achievement. Have the students respond to the scale, total the points on all items, and report their scores. The highest possible score is 50 points; the lowest would be 10. On the scale, achievement motivation could be evaluated as follows:

High: 40 to 50   Medium: 20 to 40   Low: 10 to 20

This could leave some people on the borderline with scores of 20 or 40. Other factors may need to be taken into account to determine in which group the student belongs. Students should be put at ease about this exercise. Be sure they understand that the results will not affect their standing in the class nor will it be a basis for personal judgments.

II.   **Procedure**

A.   Distribute the scale to the students **(Handout 9.1)**. Ask them to read the directions and follow them. They should be given as much time as needed—about 10 minutes.

B.   Ask students to total their ratings to arrive at a score for the scale. They should note their own scores for future reference.

C.   Collect the scales for further analysis.

343

D. Prior to the next class develop the following data:

    1. Find a mean score for the class.
    2. Identify the high and low achievers.
    3. Pick out the items that distinguish most clearly between high and low achievers. You do this by identifying those items that all or most low achievers scored lowest on and high achievers scored highest on.

III. **Discussion**

A. Make copies for the students of the items identified as common to high and low achievers. Discuss achievement motivation using these items as a starting point. Begin by asking students why they responded as they did.

B. Ask students if they felt this scale adequately sampled their achievement motivation. Could it be improved? How? (For this discussion you could put a copy of the scale on an overhead projector or into a PowerPoint slide.)

Exercise 9.2: Needs: A Hierarchy

I. **Introduction:** This is an exercise that should help students better understand Maslow's hierarchy of needs. The goal is to have students examine their own experiences and find ways they satisfy needs at each of the five levels. They should use everyday examples such as the following:

A. **Physiological needs**

    1. The need to get a sweater when the classroom is cold
    2. The need to get a cup of coffee after a "long, hard class"

B. **Safety needs**

    1. Carrying a safety alarm when walking alone at night
    2. Putting a double lock on the front door

C. **Love and belonging needs**

    1. Joining the French Club at college
    2. Checking on your best friend when she or he is sick

D. **Esteem needs**

    1. Working hard to get good grades
    2. Helping mother with dishes after supper

E.   **Need for self-actualization**

      1.   Taking dancing lessons to be better at it

      2.   Volunteering to work with handicapped children at the park district pool

II.   **Procedure**

A.   Pass out the worksheets **(Handout 9.2)** to students to use for this exercise.

B.   Group the students in threes so they can discuss their experiences and select those that fit each level more easily.

C.   Ask students to produce their own list after sharing and discussing their ideas. Each student should produce his/her own list.

D.   Allow about 10 minutes for this part of the exercise, then ask them to return to their own places.

E.   Now ask the students to evaluate these levels and try to see where they are at the present time. Each student should try to determine the level at which (s)he has the most difficulty and why. They should be asked to explain this in the space provided at the end of the worksheet.

F.   Have students turn in the worksheet for your review. You should not grade the sheet but read it and make supportive comments on what is said. You will learn a good deal about your students from this exercise.

Exercise 9.3: Personal Fears

I.   **Introduction**

This exercise is intended to get students to think about their own fears. Fears can be a serious problem if they affect the quality of life of an individual. Often people don't face up to their fears but instead develop a lifestyle that avoids confronting situations that might cause feelings of fear to occur.

In doing this exercise students can, in a non-threatening way, assess their fears and try to evaluate the effect they have on their lives. If they are willing to share some of these with the class, they will have an opportunity to think them over and perhaps do something to change.

345

II. Procedure

A. Hand out to students a copy of the fear intensity scale **(Handout 9.3)** that follows this exercise.

B. Ask students to record on the scale fearsome things, events, or situations that they can think of. They should place these items on the scale where they think they should fall. Each item should be clearly stated.

C. Students should then be asked to think about ways to reduce the fears. Begin with the top item and work down.

III. Discussion

A. It would be good to start off some discussion in class by asking students to volunteer to give their top-rated fear. If a cooperative environment exists, students will try to help each other with suggestions.

B. Be sure to bring in some psychological principles. You could have them explore the possibility of using techniques for extinction of unwanted behavior, and reinforcement and shaping of new behaviors.

C. Either individually or in groups, students should think of ways to change this behavior. Ask them to write down ideas for changing their fear behaviors.

Exercise 9.4: Words and Emotion

I. Introduction

Words and numbers, as symbols, have no special significance themselves besides their designated meaning. However, they take on added meaning and/or value as they are used in a culture. A number sequence such as 38-22-36 may have no special significance in itself, but when the number sequence is attributed to anatomical measurements, it takes on additional meaning. Word association techniques are used for diagnostic purposes because words are both motivational and emotional. Freud used word association in his psychoanalytic approach to behavior problems. Free association is initiated by words that have emotional content for the patient.

Some psychologists have found significance in not only the word or words used but also in the length of time taken to respond and the behavior of the subject while responding. This exercise is designed to determine whether words that are emotional in content produce a different behavior than neutral words. For this study, the variable under observation will be the length of time between the stimulus word and the response.

346

II. **Procedure**

    A.   Make copies of the word list and data sheet **(Handout 9.4)** for the students in the class.

    B.   Divide the class into groups of three. Ask each group to identify a subject, who is immediately sent out of the room. The other two in each group should divide up the work to be done; one will be the experimenter and the other the timer.

    C.   Distribute a copy of the word list to each experimenter. Ask the experimenters to read over the directions while you read them aloud. Be sure both experimenters and timers know what they are to do. Review the role of each as follows:

        1.   Experimenter: presents one word at a time, waiting after each for a response from the subject.

        2.   Timer: uses a watch with a large second hand or a stopwatch. Note the period of time between the stimulus word and the reaction time. Do not stop timing until the subject has given a complete word. Utterances such as, "uh," laughter, remarks like, "That's a tough one," are not responses.

    D.   Instruct the students to work out the average response time for the neutral words and the emotion-laden words.

III. **Discussion**

Some questions that can be raised with students should include the following:

    A.   Was there any difference in response time between the neutral and emotional words? If a difference occurred, how do you account for it?

    B.   Were there any differences between response times for the neutral words? Were reaction times any different to neutral words given after an emotional word than to those after a neutral word? If so, can you explain why?

    C.   Does the level of association value make a difference in response time?

    D.   If no significant differences occurred between the two means, does that mean that emotional connotations do not affect reaction time?

Handout 9.1: MOTIVATION NEED FOR ACHIEVEMENT (nAch)

TO THE STUDENT:

This is a five-point rating scale. Your responses should be based on how you feel about each item at the present time. This is not an evaluation of your work in this course, and your responses will be anonymous. Try to respond as accurately as you can. Rate each item as follows:

Not characteristic of me	1
Seldom characteristic of me	2
Sometimes characteristic of me	3
Usually characteristic of me	4
Very characteristic of me	5

1. I tend to be competitive and strive to excel in most activities I undertake. _____

2. I often go out of my way to take on outside responsibilities in the college _____ and community.

3. When thinking about the future, I emphasize long-term goals more than _____ short-term goals.

4. I get bored easily by routine. _____

5. I tend to get upset if I cannot immediately learn whether I have done well _____ or poorly in any situation.

6. I am generally not a gambler; I prefer calculated risks. _____

7. In choosing a career, I would be more interested in the challenge of the _____ job than in the pay.

8. When I cannot reach a goal I have set for myself, I strive even harder to _____ reach it.

9. If given the choice, I would prefer a highly successful stranger as a _____ coworker to a friend as a coworker.

10. I believe people should take personal responsibility for their actions. _____

TOTAL FOR THIS SCALE _____

Handout 9.2: HIERARCHY OF NEEDS: A WORKSHEET

TO THE STUDENT:

In the space provided, try to identify and record some things that you do that are intended to satisfy needs at each level. Provide several examples of each. You can discuss this with your group members, but put down your own behavior, not theirs.

1. Physiological needs

2. Safety needs

3. Love and belonging needs

4. Esteem needs

5. Need for self-actualization

Indicate the level of needs that you feel takes up most of your time and energy at the present time. At what level do you find yourself functioning most of the time? Explain what you do at that level and why it is keeping you occupied at present.

Handout 9.3: PERSONAL FEARS: INTENSITY SCALE

INTENSE

STRONG

MILD

WEAK

100-
95-
90-
85-
80-
75-
70-
65-
60-
55-
50-
45-
40-
35-
30-
25-
20-
15-
10-
5-

TO THE STUDENT: Indicate on the scale the intensity of some of your fears. Below, write some of the reasons for the more intense fears and some ideas you have for changing them.

350

Handout 9.4: WORDS AND EMOTION: WORD LIST

TO THE EXPERIMENTER:

Read the following list of words to the subject, one at a time. Pause after each word to give the person time to respond. Give the recorder time to write the response and time. Emotion-laden words are designated by an asterisk (*).

Say to the subject:
I am going to give you a list of words, one at a time. After I read each word say the first word that comes into your mind. My partner will write down what you say. Here is the first word.

1. cloud

2. abuse*

3. leaves

4. chair

5. brother

6. failure*

7. flower

8. communism*

9. dog

10. abortion*

11. holiday

12. paper

13. table

14. chocolate*

15. groceries

351

Handout 9.4: WORDS AND EMOTION: WORD LIST

TO THE RECORDER:

Be sure to note the *exact time* (number of seconds) between the stimulus word given by the experimenter and the response of the subject. Also, make a note of the response in the appropriate place. Emotion-laden words are designated by an asterisk (*).

STIMULUS WORD	RESPONSE	RESPONSE TIME
1. cloud		
2. abuse*		
3. leaves		
4. chair		
5. brother		
6. failure*		
7. flower		
8. communism*		
9. dog		
10. abortion*		
11. holiday		
12. paper		
13. table		
14. chocolate*		
15. groceries		

MEAN response time for: NEUTRAL WORDS   _____

                                         EMOTIONAL WORDS   _____

➤ JOURNAL QUESTIONS

1. Make a list of your five key "needs." What drives the responses you take to reach a specific goal?

2. How long can you recline without doing anything? If you haven't tried this recently, give yourself a few hours to recline (no sleeping allowed). How does it feel? What kinds of thoughts did you have?

3. Can a person get too much of a "good thing"? Or could receiving a large quantity of "something" alter a person's perception and definition of a good thing?

4. Keep a "hunger pang journal." For three days try to avoid eating at habitual times and in response to external cues. Instead, delay eating until your body says that you are hungry. What do you find?

5. Record your calories. For one week, record all the calories you eat or drink outside of your regular meals, i.e., snacks. Don't forget to include coffee and soft drinks or juice. Most prepared snacks list the calorie content on the package. Also, remember that "one" drink or snack often includes two or more servings. Be sure to add in the extra servings. At the end of the week, total your list. How many calories per week do you consume outside of meals?

6. What emotional states predict when you will overeat or undereat?

7. What influences your sex drive? Aside from obvious sexual images, what psychological states make you more or less interested in sex? For example, when some people are stressed, they lose interest in sex, while others use sex as a release for stress. List 10 non-sexual physical or psychological states that make you more interested in sex, and 10 states that make your sexual interest wane.

8. Do you perceive yourself to be an under-achiever, over-achiever, or at-ability achiever? For which specific abilities? Why?

9. Which level of needs in Maslow's hierarchy do you spend the greatest time satisfying? Keep a "motives" log as you move through the day from one level to another.

10. Make a list of those things you do daily that you would stop doing if it weren't for extrinsic reward. What activities are most intrinsically rewarding for you?

11. How moody are you? What cues do you give others to let them know "now" is not a good time to ask for a favor? Do you feel that you handle emotion well?

➤ SUGGESTIONS FOR FURTHER READING

Berlyne, D. E. (1960). *Conflict, arousal, and curiosity.* New York: McGraw-Hill.

Buckworth, J., Lee, R. E., Regan, G., et al. (2007). Decomposing intrinsic and extrinsic motivation for exercise: Application to stages of motivational readiness. *Psychology of Sport & Exercise, 8*(4), 441–461.

Darwin, C. (1872/2009). *The expression of emotions in man and animals.* New York: Penguin Classics.

Leming, M. R. and Dickinson, G. E. (2011). Understanding *Dying, death, and bereavement* (7th ed.). Belmont, CA: Cengage Learning/Wadsworth.

Franken, R. E. (2007). *Human motivation.* (6th ed.). Belmont, CA: Cengage Learning/Wadsworth.

Goleman, G. (2006). *Emotional intelligence: 10th anniversary edition; Why it can matter more than IQ.* New York: Bantam Dell.

Reiss, S., & Havercamp, S. M. (2005). Motivation in developmental context: A new method for studying self-actualization. *Journal of Humanistic Psychology, 45*(1), 41–53.

Kübler-Ross, E. (1975). *Death: The final stage of growth.* Englewood Cliffs, NJ: Prentice-Hall.

Fredrickson, B. L. (2003). The value of positive emotions. *American Scientist, 91,* 330–335.

Deckers, L. (2010). *Motivation: Biological, psychological, and environmental* (3rd ed.). Boston: Pearson/Allyn and Bacon.

McGee, M. G., & Snyder, M. (1975). Attribution and behavior: Two field studies. *Journal of Personality & Social Psychology, 32,* 185-190.

Orbach, S. (1994). *Fat is a feminist issue.* Berkeley, CA: Berkeley Publishing Group.

Plutchik, R. (2003). *Emotions and life: Perspectives from psychology, biology, and evolution.* Washington, DC: American Psychological Association.

Garner, D. M., & Garfinkel, P. E. (Eds.) (1997). *Handbook of treatment for eating disorders* (2nd ed.). New York: Guilford.

Seligman, M. E. P. (1994). *What you can change and what you can't.* New York: Knopf.

➢ VIDEO SUGGESTIONS

Feature Films

Meet the Parents (Ben Stiller, Robert DeNiro), Comedy. Ben Stiller plays a young man meeting his girlfriend's parents for the first time. Her father, a retired CIA officer, talks Ben into submitting to a polygraph test. Other mishaps ensue as they strive to find common grounds and understanding.

Boys Don't Cry (Hilary Swank), Drama. The true story of Brandon Teena, who seduced young women in a small, rural community in Nebraska and was later discovered to be a woman posing as a man. Local authorities are unresponsive when Brandon is raped. Shortly after that, Brandon is brutally murdered.

Lean on Me (Morgan Freeman, Robert Guillaume, Beverly Todd), Drama. Joe Clark (Freeman) is a high school principal who in 1987 is given the task of reforming an inner city Eastside High School in Paterson, NJ. The school is considered the worst school in New Jersey and is in danger of being taken over by the state. If Clark is able to turn the school around he may keep his job. His hard line policies and uncompromising campaign helps him achieve his goals and also fame.

Remember the Titans (Denzel Washington, Will Patton, Donald Faison), Drama. In 1971, a court order forces three high schools in Alexandra, Virginia, to integrate their student bodies and faculties. Coach Bill Yoast (Patton) is replaced by Herman Boone (Washington) who becomes the school's first black faculty member. Neither students nor staff welcome Boone, and the team members have no respect or trust for one another. Against long odds, Boone helps his team become a force to be reckoned with and wins their respect and trust.

Alive (Ethan Hawke, Vincent Spano, Josh Hamilton, John Haymes Newton, David Kriegel, Bruce Ramsay), Drama. The true-life adventure of a Uruguayan team of rugby players who survive a plane crash in the desolate Andes Mountains in 1972. For 10 weeks they struggled against impossible odds and freezing temperatures to stay alive.

Billy Elliott (Julie Walters, Jamie Bell, Jamie Driven, Gary Lewis), Drama. The young son of a poor English coal miner dreams of being a ballet dancer. The film takes place during a 1984 miners' strike in Durham county where Tony (Driven) and his dad (Lewis) are protestors. Billy (Bell), who's father talks him into taking boxing lessons, meets Mrs. Wilkinson (Walters), a ballet teacher, while working out at the gym. Billy has natural talent and is encouraged by Mrs. Wilkinson to try out for the Royal Ballet School. Billy's father does not approve but slowly comes around to the idea of Billy going into ballet as a way to escape the dangerous life of a miner. An excellent study in motivation, achievement, and relationships.

355

Good Will Hunting (Matt Damon, Robin Williams, Ben Affleck), Drama. A rebellious 20-year-old MIT janitor Will Hunting (Damon), gifted with a photographic memory, anonymously leaves the correct solution to a problem that professor Lambeau has on the hallway blackboard for his students. Lambeau tracks down Hunting, who is having problems with the police, and offers an out for him. Hunting must visit a therapist and attend weekly math sessions. Sean McGuire (Williams), the therapist, helps the uncooperative Hunting deal with his past and his future.

Instinct (Anthony Hopkins, Cuba Gooding, Jr.), Drama. After living among the Rwandan gorillas he has been studying, a primatologist has become an aggressive individual more interested in animals than humans. An ambitious psychiatric resident seeks to determine if the man is insane and whether or not he murdered some park rangers.

Oh Brother, Where Art Thou? (George Clooney, John Turturro, Tim Blake), Comedy. Ulysses McGi (Clooney), Delmar, (Nelson) and Pete (Turturro) are serving time on a prison gang in the South during the depression. Everette knows where $1.2 million is hidden, and the three manage to escape to seek their fortune. However, a stranger says that they may find their fortune but not the sort they are looking for. As they take to the road they meet a variety of people and even make a hit record.

Raising Arizona (Nicolas Cage, Holly Hunter, Trey Wilson), Comedy. H.I. McDonnough (Cage) is a career criminal who has been arrested so many times that he gets to know the officer who takes his mug shots, Ed (Hunter). H.I. and Ed marry after H.I. promises to give up his career as a criminal. They move to Arizona and are blissfully happy until they discover that Ed cannot have children. The couple decides to kidnap a baby from a couple who just had quintuplets, figuring that they'll have a baby and the other couple will have less of a burden with one less child.

Educational Films and Videos

AIDS: No Nonsense Answers, (1995), Films for the Humanities and Sciences, 10 min. This brief and extremely informative video demonstrates and motivates prevention behaviors and lifestyle changes while presenting the basic facts about AIDS and HIV. Many questions that your students have will be answered in this film including, "If one in a group of children is positive, are the others at-risk?"

Childhood Sexual Abuse, Films for the Humanities & Sciences, 26 min. This program looks at the ways adult women learn to work out the problems caused by sexually abusive fathers. Includes input from psychiatrists, social workers, and law enforcement officials.

Dying to be Thin, (1995), Films for the Humanities and Sciences, 28 min. This video profiles a young woman obsessed with the desire to be thin. It has taken one woman four hospitalizations and years of outpatient therapy to overcome her problem. Additionally, the characteristics of anorexia and bulimia are explored.

Eating Disorders, (2002), Films for the Humanities and Sciences, 26 min. This film describes the personality profile of an individual more likely than others to develop anorexia, the symptoms of the disease, and the treatments available.

Emotion, (1990), Coast Community College District Telecourses, 30 min. Part of the *Psychology—The Study of Human Behavior Series*, this video illustrates the universality of certain human emotions.

Emotion, (1990), Insight Media, 30 min. This video discusses both theoretical and applied issues in emotions. Theoretical highlights include a discussion by Paul Ekman of his theory concerning his hypothesis involving the possible connection between facial expressions and emotions. On the applied side, the program offers a brief discussion of the topic of sports psychology.

Emotional Intelligence with Daniel Coleman, PBS, 62 min.

Emotional Intelligence, Insight Media, 28 min. This video addresses the relationship between coping and health, using the concept of emotional intelligence.

Emotional Intelligence—A New Vision for Educators, Insight Media, 40 min.

Exploring Your Brain: Men, Women, and the Brain, Films for the Humanities & Sciences, 56 min. Part of the three-part series, Exploring Your Brain, this video explores a number of the intriguing and sometimes puzzling differences between the brains of men and women.

Finding Out: Incest and Family Sexual Abuse, Kinetic Films, 25 min. This film concentrates on the role of the victim's mother in dealing with family sexual abuse. Viewers are shown Robin, a victim since age nine, who talks about the devastating emotional effects of sexual abuse. Her mother tells how she dealt with the disclosure and the subsequent breakup of her marriage.

Gender and Relationships, Coast Community College District Telecourses, 30 min. Part of the *Psychology—The Study of Human Behavior Series*, this video explores the complexities of emotional interactions and attachments.

Gender and the Interpretation of Emotion, (2002), Films for the Humanities and Sciences, 25 min. A report on an extensive investigation on the differences between men and women in the thoughts and feelings they ascribe to others.

Homosexuality: What Science Understands, (1987), Insight Media, 54 min. This video traces research on homosexual behavior from the original Kinsey studies in 1954 through the late 1980s. Highlights of the video include a discussion of the decision to remove homosexuality from the DSR III and the issues of homophobia and AIDS.

Incest: The Family Secret, Filmmakers Library, 57 min. As this film indicates, incest is a widespread problem that occurs in all kinds of families. Most commonly, it takes the form of sexual child abuse inflicted by the father on a non-consenting daughter while she is still a child. In this very frank program, adult women talk about the childhood experiences that so traumatized their later lives.

Konrad Lorenz's Discussion with Richard Evans: Motivation, (1975), Association Sterling films, 30 min. Lorenz discusses his notions of the role of social approval, Harlow's rhesus deprivation research, and instinctual versus learned behavior. The film presents Lorenz's controversial theory that social motives are hereditary rather than learned.

Motivation, (1990), Coast Community College District Telecourses, 30 min. Part of the *Psychology—The Study of Human Behavior Series*, this video describes what motivates people to think, behave, and make choices.

Motivation and Emotion, Discovering Psychology Series, (1990), Annenberg/CPB 28 min. In this video, which is part of the *Discovering Psychology* Series, Dr. Philip Zimbardo reviews research on several key aspects of motivation including: 1) Freud's approach to motivation; 2) Maslow's hierarchy of needs; 3) Seligman's views of the role of cognitive factors in motivation and emotion, and the role of socialization in the motivation process. Also, regarding emotion, the program indicates that the components include physical arousal, thoughts, feelings, and behavior. Robert Plutchik's theory of eight basic emotions is highlighted. His theory proposes that these basic emotions can be combined in different ways to produce a variety of emotional experiences. The video also reviews Paul Ekman's cross-cultural research indicating that facial expressions of certain emotions are identifiable cross-culturally.

Motivation and Self-Actualization, (1969), Psychological Films, 60 min. This film discusses Maslow's hierarchy of needs and variables related to the attainment of self-actualization.

Motivation, (1990), Insight Media, 30 min. This video offers a great overall review of the major issue involved in human motivation. Using dramatic examples, this video explores why people think, behave, and make the choices the way they do. Motivational factors are explored including curiosity, need for achievement, and intrinsic and extrinsic rewards. The video provides examples of PET scanning used to discover the brain's role in motivation. Maslow's hierarchy of needs is also presented. In another section the topic of risk-taking behavior is addressed.

Motivation: It's Not Just the Money, (1981), Document Associates, 26 min. Through interviews with employees, managers, and behavioral scientists, the factors that contribute to satisfaction and productivity on the job are examined. As the film shows, it is becoming increasingly evident that while wages and benefits are important, a range of non-material needs must also be met by modern organizations. The film features a look at the Volvo plant in Sweden, where an innovative approach to manufacturing was established that better met the needs of employees.

Obesity: Pain and Prejudice, (2002), Films for the Humanities and Sciences, 40 min. The problem of obesity is discussed against the backdrop of the recent trial of a San Francisco mother convicted of child abuse after her seriously overweight daughter died as a result of obesity.

Pleasure Power, (1998), Films for the Humanities and Sciences, 53 min. The scientific quest to fully understand and harness the mysterious power of pleasure has revealed some exciting possibilities. Enhanced by computer imaging and 3-D animations, this program interviews Mihaly Czikszentmihalyi—author of the best-selling *Flow: The Psychology of Optimal Experience*—and a battery of psychologists, physiologists, and neuroscientists. Together with several recovering addicts, they explore the intriguing nature and effects of pleasure, including biological underpinnings, its role in boosting physical and mental wellbeing, and if taken too far, its ability to destroy a person's life.

Productivity and the Self-Fulfilling Prophecy: The Pygmalion Effect, (1987), CRM/McGraw-Hill, 30 min. This program, part of the *Behavior in Business* series, may be useful if you are applying the topic of motivation to the business community. It explores ways that managers (and teachers) can affect employee morale and performance, often without conscious knowledge of doing so. It illustrates the research of Robert Rosenthal, Rensis Likert, and Douglas MacGregor. The Pygmalion effect occurs whether or not we are aware of it and can influence both negatively and positively. This film explores how we can use it positively to its fullest potential.

Scare Me, (1990), Films for the Humanities and Sciences, 53 min. Under certain conditions, fear can actually trigger a feeling of euphoria, promote group bonding, and stimulate personal growth. In this program, psychologists and other medical professionals—along with a video game designer and a movie director—explore the subject of fear in exacting detail, discussing topics such as the physiological mechanics behind it; factors that enhance and suppress it; the use of extreme sports, horror movies, computer technology, and thrill rides to deliberately induce it; and proven ways to master it.

Stress and Emotion: The Brain Series, (1984), PBS, 60 min. This video is designed to introduce students to the relationship between stress and emotions. Of particular interest is information concerning some of the major theories of emotional acquisition.

The Brain: The Sexual Brain, Films for the Humanities & Sciences, 28 min. Part of the six-part series, The Brain, this video shows some startling effects of hormone injections on brain structure and raises provocative questions about the sexual and reproductive roots of structural differences between males and females.

The Differences Between Men and Women, (1995), Films for the Humanities and Sciences, 23 min. The old question "Are the differences between men and women conditioned by biology or by family and social environment?" is answered with recent research, which claims that the male and female brains are far from identical. The video also looks at cultural influences on gender-related behaviors.

The Mystery of Happiness, ABC, 55 min. This ABC Special narrated by John Stossel details the research on happiness by Dr. David Meyers. Stossel reviews the various research strategies psychologists use to assess people's feelings of wellbeing as well as the results of their work.

The Opposite Sex, Insight Media, 55 min. Human beliefs about differences between the sexes inform social organization, law, religion, literature, and humor. This video considers men's and women's bodies, brains, emotions, and public and private behavior. Using a combination of science, observation, and opinion, it links biological and psychological studies to generate a composite interpretation of gender difference.

The Silent Hunger: Anorexia and Bulimia, (2002), Films for the Humanities & Sciences, 46 min. This program specifically examines anorexia nervosa, bulimia nervosa, and binge-eating syndrome. Interviews with seven females who have all suffered from eating disorders, the father of a woman who died as a result of her disorder, and health professionals are included.

What Is Motivation? Insight Media, 30 min. This video, with a business theme, looks at the classic theories of Taylor, Maslow, and MacGregor.

The Will to Win, (1993), Films for the Humanities and Sciences, 28 min. This video covers the individual's determination to succeed—in early childhood, on the playing field, in business, and in the way the body responds to illness.

Understanding Sex, (2000), Films for the Humanities & Sciences, 51 min. Narrated by Candice Bergen, this program explores the biology, genetics, and psychological components of sex, including sexual orientation and assisted conception.

➤ COMPUTER AND INTERNET RESOURCES

PsykTrek 3.0
Unit 8: Motivation & Emotion
8a. Hunger
8b. Achievement Motivation
8c. Elements of Emotion
8d. Theories of Emotion

INFOTRAC®

Below you will find two journal articles obtained from INFOTRAC® that relate to information contained in this chapter. Instructors should encourage students to utilize this invaluable resource to improve their research skills. Have students locate and read the following articles and answer questions relevant to each article.

The Review of Metaphysics, December 2004 v58 i2 p279 (26) Emotions and biology: Remarks on the contemporary trend.

1.   According to the above article, how did William James define emotion?

       Answer: William James defined emotion as feeling: "Emotion is nothing but the feeling of the reflex bodily effects of what we call its object."

2.   What are the four basic themes over which emotion theory struggles today?

       Answer: (a) Emotion is feeling; (b) What emotion feels is the body; (c) The bodily symptoms felt in emotion are common to all (or at least to many) emotions; (d) Emotion is to be studied strictly as a function of the nervous system.

3.   How did Walter Cannon deal James' theory a fatal blow?

       Answer: Cannon surgically detached his laboratory animals from their viscera and found that they still reacted emotionally.

4.   Recent work in brain imaging has revealed patterns of neural activity that differ for each of which emotional experiences?

       Answer: Happiness, sadness, fear, and anger.

360

Science, May 15, 1998 v280 n5366 p1005 (3) Probing the biology of emotion.

1.   According to this article, how does current research support the concept of "temperament"?

Answer: Increasingly, researchers are finding that intense emotions, particularly at key times in early life, can trigger not only behavioral changes but long-lasting physical changes in the brain. These persist long after the emotions themselves have passed and shape emotional responses later in life. This inside-out approach is also lending new insight into another favored Victorian notion—that of emotional temperaments. Individuals who are fearful or resilient not only have characteristic behaviors, they have distinct patterns of brain activity, too.

2.   What is one of the most important emotional sites in the brain?

Answer: One of the most important emotional sites, as shown over the last 15 years by New York University neuroscientist Joseph LeDoux and others, is the amygdala—an almond-shaped structure in the center of the brain that is a key station in the processing of fear.

3.   Describe the asymmetry of brain activity found by Davidson.

Answer: People who are negative or depressed according to standardized psychological tests tend to show more baseline prefrontal activity on the right, he says. And the happy-go-lucky folks who are more likely to bounce back when life throws a curve ball tend to show more activity in the left prefrontal cortex.

4.   Davidson speculates that what part of the cortex modulates the emotional activity of the amygdala? How?

Answer: He speculates that the prefrontal cortex modulates the emotional activity of the amygdala. People with more left prefrontal cortex activity can shut off the response to negative stimuli more quickly, he says. "Being able to shut off negative emotion once it's turned on is a skill that goes with left activation." He adds that it's not yet known whether such temperaments are inborn or a product of very early life experiences.

361

WEB LINKS

Knowledge Builder Links

1. Overview of Emotion
   Theories of Motivation:
   http://changingminds.org/explanations/theories/a_motivation.htm
   Sleeplessness and Circadian Rhythm:
   http://www.emedicinehealth.com/sleeplessness_and_circadian_rhythm_disorder/article_em.htm
   Drive Reduction Theory and Incentives in the Regulation of Food Intake:
   http://www.flyfishingdevon.co.uk/salmon/year3/psy337eating/PSY337foodintake.htm

2. Hunger, Thirst, Pain, and Sex
   Eating Disorders Website: http://www.nationaleatingdisorders.org
   Healthy Dieting: http://www.livestrong.com/article/12503-dieting
   The Facts about Aphrodisiacs: http://www.fda.gov/fdac/features/196_love.html

3. Arousal, Achievement, and Growth Needs
   Sensation-Seeking Scale:
   http://www.rta.nsw.gov.au/licensing/tests/driverqualificationtest/sensationseekingscale/
   The Yerkes-Dodson Law: http://en.wikipedia.org/wiki/Yerkes-Dodson_law
   Achievement Motivation in Business: http://www.accel-team.com/human_relations/hrels_06_mcclelland.html

4. Emotion and Physiological Arousal
   An Overview of the Affective System:
   http://www.edpsycinteractive.org/topics/affsys/affsys.html
   Learn the Truth about Lie Detectors:
   http://www.usatoday.com/news/nation/2002-09-09-lie_x.htm

5. Emotional Expression and Theories of Emotion
   The Expression of the Emotions in Man and Animals: http://www.human-nature.com/darwin/emotion/contents.htm
   What's in a Face? http://www.apa.org/monitor/jan00/sc1.html
   Controlling Anger: http://www.apa.org/topics/anger/control.aspx

6. Emotional Intelligence – The Fine Art of Self-Control
    Emotional IQ Test:
        http://www.queendom.com/tests/access_page/index.htm?idRegTest=1121
    Emotional Intelligence: http://www.eqi.org/eitoc.htm
    Emotional Intelligence Links: http://en.wikipedia.org/wiki/Emotional_Intelligence

Additional Web Links

APA Online
http://www.apa.org/

The Brain and Emotion
http://www.edpsycinteractive.org/topics/affsys/affsys.html

Controlling Anger
http://www.apa.org/pubinfo/anger.html

Eating Disorders
http://familydoctor.org/063.xml
http://www.nlm.nih.gov/medlineplus/eatingdisorders.html
http://www.nationaleatingdisorders.org
http://www.mayoclinic.com/health/eating-disorders/DS00294

Emotional Intelligence
http://changingminds.org/explanations/emotions/emotional_intelligence.htm

Facial Expressions
http://en.wikipedia.org/wiki/Facial_expression
http://www.cs.cmu.edu/afs/cs.cmu.edu/user/ytw/www/facial.html
http://www.apa.org/monitor/jan00/sc1.html

Physiology of Hunger
http://www.csun.edu/~vcpsy00h/students/hunger.htm
http://en.wikipedia.org/wiki/Hunger

Polygraphs ("Lie Detectors")
http://skepdic.com/polygrap.html
http://people.howstuffworks.com/lie-detector.htm

Sexual Disorders
http://www.athealth.com/Consumer/disorders/Sexual.html
http://en.wikipedia.org/wiki/Sexual_disorder
http://www.mental-health-matters.com/disorders/dis_category.php?catID=36

Sexual Response Cycle
http://en.wikipedia.org/wiki/Human sexual_response_cycle
http://www.engenderhealth.org/res/onc/sexuality/response/pg2.html
http://sexuality.about.com/od/anatomyresponse/a/sexualresponse.htm

Theories of Motivation
http://www.westmont.edu/_academics/pages/departments/psychology/pages/smith/general/lectur
eoutlines/11motivation/theoriesmotivation.html

PSYCHOLOGY IN THE NEWS

Psychology in the News
http://www.psycport.com/
This site provides the latest in press releases and up-to-date news in the field of psychology.

Management News
http://www.swlearning.com/management/management_news/mgmt_news_motivation.html
This site provides summaries of the latest management news stories. Review the brief summaries
and for stories of interest.

UC Davis News and Information
http://www.news.ucdavis.edu/search/news_detail.lasso?id=6887
Explores the book *The Psychology of Gratitude* (Oxford: Oxford University Press).

University of Michigan News Service
http://www.umich.edu/news/?Releases/2005/Feb05/r020105
This site provides news releases, search archives, and updated research findings on a variety of
topics in psychology including emotions and motivation.

Yahoo News
http://health.yahoo.com/news/54272
Yahoo News allows you to search by topic on health-related topics such as your emotions and
health.

CHAPTER 10

Sex, Gender and Sexuality

Survey Questions
Discussion Questions
Lecture Enhancements

What do you think about it?
How big are gender differences?
Safe sex
Pass the hat—What do you want to know about sex?
Internet questionnaires
Androgyny
Who's the best fit?
Where did you learn about the birds and the bees?
Gay rights speaker
Gender, roles, and perceptions

Role-Playing Scenarios
Value-Clarification Statements
One-Minute Motivators

What if I were the "opposite" sex?
Who told you that?
Gender and feelings
Clothes with gender links
The rules for dating
What are teenagers doing? And is anyone helping them?
Myths and facts about homosexuality
What's a heterosexual?
What's it like to be straight?
Sterilization as birth control

Broadening Our Cultural Horizons

What if?
Rites of passage
Attitudes toward homosexuality
Gender and competence ratings
What's the sexual message?
What's normal?
Are North Americans sexually repressed, or sexually permissive?
Public versus private
International rates of rape
Frequency of anorexia across gender and culture

Supplemental Activities

Exercise 10.1: The Sexual Information Survey
Exercise 10.2: Who Does What?

Handouts

Handout 10.1: Sexual Information Survey
Handout 10.2: Who Does What?

Journal Questions
Suggestions for Further Reading
Video Suggestions
Computer and Internet Resources

➤ SURVEY QUESTIONS

Module 10.1 Sexual Development and Sexual Orientation

Survey Question: What are the basic dimensions of sex?

Survey Question: What is sexual orientation?

Module 10.2 Gender Development, Androgyny, and Gender Variance

Survey Question: How does one's sense of maleness or femaleness develop?

Survey Question: What is psychological androgyny (and is it contagious)?

Survey Question: What is gender variance?

Module 10.3 Sexual Behavior, Response, and Attitudes

Survey Question: What are the most typical patterns of human sexual behavior?

Survey Question: To what extent do females and males differ in sexual response?

Survey Question: What are the most common sexual disorders?

Survey Question: Have recent changes in attitudes affected sexual behavior?

Survey Question: What impacts have sexually transmitted diseases had on sexual behavior?

Module 10.4 Psychology in Action: Sexual Problems—When Pleasure Fades

Survey Questions: How can couples keep their relationship more sexually satisfying? What are

the most common sexual adjustment problems?

➤ DISCUSSION QUESTIONS

1. Suppose a woman has an over-active adrenal gland that is producing excess androgens. How would this affect the appearance of her body?

2. Consider that an unusual event occurred during conception: An egg containing an X chromosome is fertilized by a sperm that had only 22 chromosomes and no sex chromosome (normally there are 23). What effect would this probably have on the child's internal and external sexual organs?

3. A mother took a drug that increased her fetus' prenatal exposure to androgens. What effect could this have on her baby girl?

4. Imagine that you were born as a member of the opposite sex. In what ways would your life so far have been different? (Consider relationships, self-image, clothing, recreation, interests, career plans, and so forth.)

5. In your opinion, what are the advantages and disadvantages of distinctly different male/female sex roles?

6. Is biological sex the same as sexual identity? Do you identify yourself as male or female simply because you are in that body? What if aliens had switched your body at birth to an opposite-sex body? Would you still feel "male" (if you are male) or "female" (if you are female)? Or would you now "feel" like the other sex?

7. In some Native American cultures, there are four genders rather than two. The berdache is a biological male who has traditionally "female" psychological characteristics, and there is also a female who is traditionally male. Is the Western idea of being strictly "male" or "female" the best way to look at things? Why or why not? If our culture allowed for more flexible definitions of gender, would that be more liberating for some people, or more confusing?

8. Can you name any public personalities (entertainers, politicians, athletes, artists, musicians) who seem to be androgynous? Are any of your friends or acquaintances androgynous? Do you agree or disagree with Bem's assertion that these people are more adaptable?

9. How would you go about collecting data to confirm or not confirm the existence of androgyny?

10. Mentally change your male friends to females and your female friends to males. Can you separate the "human being" or "core person" from your friends' normal gender identities and sex roles? What effect does this have on your perception of others?

11. What social learning factors explain why many women report negative reactions to sexually explicit pictures?

12. How would you react if you found out that your child's teacher was gay? Would it make a difference whether the teacher was male or female?

13. Some adults in their 30s and 40s report infrequent sexual activity. What factors could explain this pattern?

14. In some countries it is considered "abnormal" for a woman not to achieve orgasm during sex. In other countries, female orgasm is considered deviant. In North America, it is not unusual for a woman to not achieve orgasm during sex. Why do you think North American women don't experience the same universal expectation (and experience) of orgasm as they do in some countries?

15. Kaplan and Singer have suggested that a "desire" stage precedes the excitement stage described by Masters and Johnson. Do you agree or disagree? Why?

16. In what ways does sexual contact differ from non-sexual touching? Do you feel that people should touch more? Why or why not?

17. In recent years there has been an increase in child molestation trials involving daycare workers. Some teachers and childcare workers complain that they are now afraid to touch or hug children. Is this new reticence to touch an overdue correction or a saddening loss?

18. Female sexual behavior appears to be changing more rapidly than male behavior. To what do you attribute the different rate of change?

19. Sadism and masochism are listed in your textbook as paraphilias. Have S&M concepts filtered into mainstream culture and advertising? List some examples. Is this an acceptable trend, or does it encourage abnormal sexual behavior? Why or why not?

20. Recall your own education about sex. In what ways and at what age would you recommend that children learn about sex?

21. The American teen pregnancy rate is alarmingly high. What do you think is the cause? What should be done to change this trend?

22. How should a couple go about deciding whether they are ready for a sexual relationship? What can be done to reduce the frequency of STDs?

23. Sex therapists sometimes suggest that couples experiencing "dysfunction" often "get something" out of the problem. What do you think would be the "rewards" of sexual problems?

24. What effect would arousal of the sympathetic nervous system have on sexual arousal? If a man found it difficult to become erect, would relaxation exercises help? Or would this make his sexual dysfunction more severe?

25. There is no doubt that sexual abuse of children is widespread. How do you think our society should approach the problem of protecting children?

26. Which do you think is a bigger problem, unreported child molestation or misidentification of perpetrators after the child grows up?

27. Why would alcohol increase sexual dysfunction when it seems to function as an aphrodisiac?

28. How could vaginismus be the result of classical conditioning? How is the treatment similar to systematic desensitization?

29. You work in the critical care unit of a hospital and are assigned to work with a patient with AIDS. Should you be worried about contracting the disease? Why or why not?

➤ LECTURE ENHANCEMENTS

Our perceptions of sex and the norms guiding sexual behaviors are changing. Perhaps no other chapter in the text is more important in terms of clarifying values. The value statements should provoke dialogue, if not dramatic disagreement. If value clarification is used earlier in the semester, students will know that this classroom is a safe place for honest discussion. Many people used to speak of the other gender as the "opposite" sex, opposite in interests, biology, and abilities. Now we speak of the "other" sex, still different in some ways but eventually to be valued equally.

1. **What do you think about it?** A high-interest class exercise involves having students in small groups discuss their attitudes toward various sexual topics. Before class, write 10 to 15 of the terms in the chapter on 3 x 5 cards (e.g., masturbation, oral sex, premarital sex, etc.). Make a separate set of cards for each group. In class, assemble the students in groups of four or five and place a set of cards in front of one member of each group. That person is instructed to randomly draw a card, announce the topic, and then express his or her own attitudes and feelings about the subject. After each person in the group has expressed his/her opinions on the topic, the person next to the one who started the discussion draws a second card, which again goes around the group with each person expressing his/her opinions. The exercise continues with each person taking a turn at initiating the discussion. After all the groups have finished, it is useful to conduct a general class discussion on reactions to the exercise.

2. **How big are gender differences?** (Internet exercise) Have students search the Internet for information about the degree of difference between males and females on various abilities such as: speech, spatial abilities, math, nurturance, and so on. Each student should choose one psychological characteristic and report their findings to the class. Alternately, a summary of overall differences can be located using the key words "gender differences" and "meta-analysis." Alternately, these findings are discussed in most textbooks on gender or psychology of women.

3. **Safe sex.** (Internet exercise) Have students do some research from reputable Internet sources, such as the Centers for Disease Control, or the Kinsey Institute on ways to promote safe sex in order to protect themselves against pregnancy and sexually-transmitted diseases.

4. **Pass the hat—What do you want to know about sex?** Students are often curious about sex, but are afraid to ask. Give each student an identical piece of paper and ask them to write down any questions they have about sex. To avoid anyone becoming embarrassed about writing while his/her classmates are not writing, tell students that you want everyone to write something down, so that no one feels self-conscious. If they truly have no questions about sex, they can write down something unrelated. Go around the room and let students drop their questions into the hat (or bag). Read the submitted questions and answer them for the whole class.

5. **Internet questionnaires.** The Internet provides access to a wide variety of questionnaires. Some are more scientific than others. Certainly, you should remind your students that any information taken from the Internet should be interpreted with caution, particularly if the website proposes to in any way rate or diagnose a person without knowing the individual. They should also be aware of the limitations of web-based "studies."

    If, however, you want to tap into your students' opinions, Internet questionnaires can provide the catalyst for increasing classroom discussions. These questionnaires can also be accessed by the students on their computer at home.

370

http://www4.semo.edu/snell/scales/MSQ.htm (sexuality)
http://www4.semo.edu/snell/testing.htm (gender, romance, sexuality, AIDS)
http://www.something-fishy.org/isf/questionnaire.php (eating disorders)

6. **Androgyny.** A good way to introduce the topic of androgyny is to select a number of adjectives that describes people's behavior towards others. Write them on the board and ask students to indicate by a show of hands whether men (then women) tend to rank high or low in the quality named by the adjective. Plot two profiles to compare ratings of males and females. This should define some clear-cut "masculine" traits, "feminine" traits, and "neutral" traits, at least as they exist in the minds of many. Alternately, you should be able to locate Bem's Androgyny Scale in any textbook on gender or sexuality or online at **fp.arizona.edu**/humansexuality/**Bem Androgyny** Test.doc.

7. **Who's the best fit?** Give students five descriptions of applicants for the position of manager of a small corporation: a male with stereotypical male qualities, a male with androgynous qualities, a female with stereotypical female qualities, a female with male qualities, and a female with androgynous qualities. Ask them to rank the five candidates. Who should be selected for this job? Why?

8. **Where did you learn about the birds and the bees?** A topic that usually generates lively discussion is the question of where and how students gained their knowledge of and developed their attitudes toward sexuality. Studies have indicated that parents are often uncomfortable discussing sex with their children and leave them to gain their information from other sources.

9. **Gay rights speaker.** Invite a representative of a gay/lesbian/transgender rights organization to speak to the class. If possible, invite a professional to discuss some aspect of his or her area of expertise. After students have accepted the person as an expert ask, "Has being gay (or lesbian) affected your acceptance as a (name of profession)?" Discuss with students the effects of homophobia and the prejudices homosexual persons have faced. How has sexuality affected acceptance in society, with regard to family, employment, etc.?

10. **Gender, roles, and perceptions.** Give half the class a form where the story describes "Linda;" give the other half the version that describes "Ted."

Linda is a very attractive 25-year-old who enjoys wearing the current style of clothes, who is warm, friendly, and uses touch and direct eye contact in meeting others. One night Linda is at a bar and orders a margarita for the first time. Unaccustomed to drinking, Linda becomes mildly intoxicated and begins dancing very affectionately with a stranger. Getting a bit dizzy, Linda holds the stranger very closely for support and accepts a ride home. The stranger walks Linda to the apartment and asks to use the phone. Once inside the apartment, the stranger begins to make sexual advances, clothes are ripped off, and because of the drinking, Linda is not able to fight off the advances.

Ted is a very attractive 25-year-old who enjoys wearing the current style of clothes, who is warm, friendly, and uses touch and direct eye contact in meeting others. One night Ted is at a bar and orders a margarita for the first time. Unaccustomed to drinking, Ted becomes mildly intoxicated and begins dancing very affectionately with a stranger. Getting a bit dizzy, Ted holds the stranger very closely for support and accepts a ride home. The stranger walks Ted to the apartment and asks to use the phone. Once inside the apartment, the stranger begins to make sexual advances, clothes are ripped off, and because of the drinking, Ted is not able to fight off the advances.

➤ ROLE-PLAYING SCENARIOS

1. **Explain to your partner why you think he or she should be primarily responsible for cooking.** How convinced are you by your own arguments?

2. **Summarize your mental script for a first date.**

3. **You are a sex therapist giving ideas to a couple having trouble coordinating their lovemaking.** What do you suspect is the problem? What would you suggest they do to develop a more satisfying sexual relationship?

4. **Eloise was raised in her early years by an affectionate but weak mother and a cold but hard-working father.** Her father suddenly vanished when Eloise was 12 and has not been heard from since. Now Eloise has trouble relating sexually to her husband. Why? What can be done to help Eloise and her husband?

5. **Elmer feels he and his wife make love too often; Erica feels they don't make love enough.** Give them advice about how to resolve this conflict.

6. **Norma likes to make love quickly and go to sleep; Norman prefers to make love slowly and cuddle and chat afterward.** How should they resolve this difficulty?

7. **Veronica has dated many men and has experienced many sexual relationships.**
Vincent has never been with anyone but Veronica. Veronica is tired of the missionary position; Vincent has never tried anything else. Help them talk about this issue.

➤ VALUE-CLARIFICATION STATEMENTS

1. Fewer women have received the Nobel Prize than men. This confirms that on the average men are smarter than women.

2. Women are born talkers.

3. People are clearly either male or female, with nothing in between.

4. Women are better at raising children than men are.

5. Gender differences in achievement in math or language are primarily the result of biological differences between the sexes.

6. All children, regardless of gender, should learn how to cook and clean, and how to fix things and do yard work.

7. In countries where men are required to be trained for and used in direct combat in the armed services and police departments, women should also be trained.

8. People should either not have sex before marriage, or should only have one or two partners.

9. People who are attracted to the same sex should seek treatment for it.

10. Even a single experience of sexual molestation will affect the typical person for the rest of his or her life.

11. Convicted pedophiles should be required to undergo drug therapy before release from prison.

12. A person convicted of rape should be sentenced to life imprisonment.

13. Convicted male sexual molesters should be required to be castrated.

14. If a person has a one-night sexual contact that they know will never be repeated, they still should disclose this to their spouse.

➤ ONE-MINUTE MOTIVATORS

1. **What if I were the "opposite" sex?** Ask students to do the following: List five traits of your personality, five interests, and five behaviors you usually engage in. Then close your eyes and imagine yourself as the other gender. Picture yourself doing and feeling these same things. If you had been born the other gender, in what ways would your identity be similar or different?

2. **Who told you that?** Ask students to write down answers to the following questions. They can either be handed in anonymously or, depending on the comfort level of your students, can be discussed orally.

    Who told you the names of your sexual organs?
    Where did you find out about the "birds and bees"?
    Were you prepared for puberty or not? (e.g., nocturnal emissions in boys or menarche in girls)
    For those who were not told ahead of time, what was that experience like for you? How did you react?

3. **Gender and feelings. Ask students to complete the following:**
    I feel nurtured when . . .
    I feel angry when . . .
    I feel most attractive when . . .
    I feel most vulnerable when . . .
    Do male and female students have different responses to these questions? Are the male students resistant to answering questions #1 and 4?

4. **Clothes with gender links.** Carry a purse or wear an earring, man's necktie, man's hat, or some other cross-gender cue to class. Ask students how their perceptions are affected. How do such objects come to have such powerful gender-linked meanings?

5. **The rules for dating.** Most students have learned the rules for dating intuitively. On the board, draw one column for "male" rules and one column for "female" rules and ask students to quantify the rules. Put an asterisk beside those that show a high degree of agreement.

6. **What are teenagers doing? And is anyone helping them?** Ask students how the issue of sex education was handled at their school. Was it an "abstinence-only" approach, basic biology, or comprehensive sex ed. (e.g., including interpersonal issues, assertiveness, etc.)? You can also ask them how teens at their school viewed sex. Is there still a double standard? Is it seen as part of a committed relationship, or just a recreational activity? Is virginity valued or disparaged? What qualifies as "sex"? Does oral sex "count" in terms of whether or not a person has "had sex.") Are resources available (e.g., counseling, contraception, etc.)?

374

7. **Myths and facts about homosexuality.** Break students into small groups and ask them to generate stereotypes about homosexuality. Once they have completed their lists, ask them to share with the rest of the class. Encourage discussion and discuss facts that refute these stereotypes.

8. **What's a heterosexual?** Students often confuse sexual orientation with sexual behavior, or see them as identical. If a man has sex with another man, is he "gay"? (Most will say yes.) What about a person who is married, and has always had heterosexual sex, but subsequently comes "out of the closet"? Was that person always gay? Or did he become gay? Is a person who is engaging in heterosexual behavior therefore "straight"?

9. **What's it like to be straight?** Gay people are frequently asked what it's like to be gay. An amusing and instructive exercise is to turn the issue around. Turn to individual students and ask them what it's like to be straight. The questions seem ridiculous to students when the sexual orientation is changed. Sample questions include:
   1. Does your family know you're straight?
   2. What's it like to kiss someone of the opposite sex?
   3. Do you tell your friends that you're straight?
   4. Have you always been straight?
   5. How do you know you're straight?
   6. Have you ever dated someone of the same sex? Maybe you're not really straight after all.
   7. How old were you before you knew you were a heterosexual?

10. **Sterilization as birth control.** Ask students to think about different types of birth control and consider whether they would want to have either a tubal ligation or vasectomy to be free from using other types of control and not have to worry about getting pregnant or causing pregnancy. Also ask them if they think the man or the woman should have the operation done when a couple decides not to have any more children. Ask them to support their answer.

➢ BROADENING OUR CULTURAL HORIZONS

1. **What if?** Imagine a society where one gender is domineering, shrewd, and responsible for the home. The other gender is team-oriented, cooperative, and the breadwinner. What would the rest of the society be like? What would be the role of the family? Of competition?

2. **Rites of passage.** Many cultures have special rites of passage into puberty. A few have circumcision rites for both males and females. What are the rites of passage into puberty for your culture?

3. **Attitudes toward homosexuality.** (Internet exercise) Have students choose a country and research attitudes and/or laws concerning homosexuality in that country. Ask students to bring their findings to class.

4. **Gender and competence ratings.** Students can be asked to evaluate a written essay, a work of art, or an accomplishment. With half of the class, the author can be a female name; with the other half, a male name can be used. Quickly collect the data and see if the ratings differ because of the supposed gender of the author. Would such differences in judgments occur if the work was attributed to a person from a culture very different from ours?

5. **What's the sexual message?** (Internet exercise) Cultures vary widely in how they view sex. In some, sexuality is accepted as part of normal life. In others, it is strictly regulated, and is regarded as potentially shameful. Ask students to do some research on sex in other cultures and report their findings to the rest of the class. Alternately, ask them to critique the sexual messages in this culture. On the one hand, sex is glorified in movies, on TV, and in advertising. On the other hand, it is shrouded in secrecy and shame; parents often don't want to talk about the "birds and the bees," but they also don't want sex education in school. You can brainstorm positive and negative cultural messages with students.

6. **What's normal?** Try to imagine a culture where one of the sexual "deviations" listed in the text is accepted as a normal behavior. How would our society be different if this deviation was accepted as normal?

7. **Are North Americans sexually repressed, or sexually permissive?** If you have students from other cultures in your class, ask them what differences they notice in sexual attitudes and behaviors in North America compared to their own countries. For those who believe that North Americans are more open about sex, what do they think about that? Is it a positive or a negative?

8. **Public versus private.** All cultures differ in not only what they actually do in private but what they talk in public about doing in private. Which sexual deviation do you feel is most loudly denounced in public? Which one is most often performed in private?

9. **International rates of rape. (Internet exercise)** Have students choose a country and search for their rate of rapes (per capita). Discuss their findings. You will probably also want to discuss the distinction between rates of rape and rates of reported rape. In some countries, woman rarely report rape because that are blamed for the rape.

10. **Frequency of anorexia across gender and culture.** What cultures do students guess would have the least frequency of anorexia? Why are most people with eating disorders female? As women play a more prominent role in business, will this gender difference change? How? Why or why not?

➤ SUPPLEMENTAL ACTIVITIES

Exercise 10.1: The Sexual Information Survey

Since students may feel inhibited about sharing their views and knowledge, the Sexual Information Survey can get them into the proper mindset. It also becomes easier to talk about something that has become somewhat impersonal by first responding on paper. The Survey contains a sampling of facts that are often misunderstood. Students sometimes feel very sophisticated but have a good deal of misinformation about sex. You may want to add to the list given in **Handout 10.1**. If so, simply type a second page and add it to the questionnaire.

Have the students score their own papers. If the surveys are not signed, you could collect them at the end of the period and report on the next class day, giving students an idea of how informed and misinformed they are as a group. If you use this survey in several classes, you could also get overall statistics for each item to report to the class. However, keep in mind that the survey is intended to be a discussion starter and a means of letting the students know that they have more to learn about the topic. Its purpose is not simply to show them how uninformed they are.

The correct answers to the items:

1. T	5. F	9. F	13. T	17. T
2. F	6. T	10. F	14. T	18. T
3. T	7. F	11. F	15. F	19. F
4. T	8. T	12. F	16. F	20. T

Exercise 10.2: Who does what?
Ask students to write down all the tasks their mothers do, and those their fathers do. For those students with only one parent, have them ask an aunt and uncle, or some other relative. Once students hand in their lists, tally the characteristics for the class as a whole. Which chores are the most gender-specialized, and which are the least? **Handout 10.2** contains a list of typical household chores.

Handout 10.1: SEXUAL INFORMATION SURVEY

This survey is intended to evaluate how much information you have about some topics that will be discussed in the section on human sexuality. You should not sign the survey so your responses will remain anonymous.

Mark each item either true (T) or false (F).

_____ 1.   Sex education in school is favored by most parents.

_____ 2.   There is clear evidence that the incidence of sex crimes is directly related to the availability of pornographic materials.

_____ 3.   Highly educated males are more likely to masturbate than males who have very little education.

_____ 4.   American culture is more restrictive regarding sexual activity than most other cultures.

_____ 5.   Sexual intercourse is considered proper only in marriage in nearly all cultures.

_____ 6.   Impotence in men and frigidity in women usually have no physical cause but are learned behaviors.

_____ 7.   Homosexuality is caused by unsatisfactory sexual experiences in the childhood or teen years, according to most recent studies.

_____ 8.   Most transsexuals and transvestites are male.

_____ 9.   The sex of a child is determined at conception by the genes in the ovum of the female.

_____ 10.   It is predicted by most social scientists that marriage will eventually disappear in this country.

_____ 11.   A person can expect serious physical and emotional harm from excessive masturbation.

_____ 12.   Venereal diseases are usually spread by prostitutes.

_____ 13.   Incest taboos are found in some form in all societies.

_____ 14.   Sexual arousal can occur without direct stimulation of the erogenous zones.

_____ 15.   A person with a small penis is unable to stimulate the most sensitive areas of the vagina.

_____ 16.   A vasectomy causes a reduction in sexual desire because male hormones are no longer produced or available.

_____ 17.   Sexual desire and response are not affected by a hysterectomy.

_____ 18.   A survey of women indicates that about two-thirds of those entering marriage for the first time have had an orgasm.

_____ 19.   Frequency of sexual intercourse between married couples increases up to about age 35 and then gradually decreases to near zero by about age 60.

_____ 20.   Homosexual women have far fewer sexual partners than do homosexual men.

Handout 10.2: WHO DOES WHAT?

For each of the following chores, indicate which of your parents does which chore. If you have only one parent, use an aunt and uncle or some other friend or relative for comparison. If your parents live in an apartment, indicate who would do the chore if you were in a house. There are also three additional spaces, for chores not on the list.

Chore	Usually Mom	Usually Dad	Shared
Cooking			
Dishes			
Dealing with landlord/neighbors			
Cleaning basement/garage			
Vacuuming			
Dusting			
Washing the floors			
Taking kids to activities			
Paying the bills/banking			
Fixing things			
Grocery shopping			
Caring for pets			
Putting the kids to bed			
Running errands			
Cutting the lawn			
Weeding/gardening			

Please also answer the following questions:

1. Do both parents work the same amount outside the home? If not, who is home more often?

2. What is the division of chores in your current relationship? How did this division begin?

3. Should boys and girls each learn to do all of these chores? Or is the traditional model sufficient?

4. What is your gender?

➤ JOURNAL QUESTIONS

1. When did you first notice the development of secondary sexual characteristics? How did you feel about these changes? Did you tell anyone about the changes? If so, what did they say to you?

2. Have you ever taken the SAT? How did you perform on the verbal and the math portions? Is this the result of your genetics or your social environment? Explain.

3. What is the earliest age you remember? What were you doing? Can you even imagine yourself as anything but your own gender? Explain.

4. How aggressive are you? Are males and females different in their "inherent" aggressiveness or are they simply socialized to express aggression in different ways?

5. Make a list of all the characteristics that you believe are essential for an American president to have. Now, make a list of all the characteristics you think would make someone unsuitable to be president. When you have finished, indicate whether you think a woman is just as able to satisfy these requirements as a man. If not, why not? Would you vote for a qualified woman for president (assuming that you agreed with her political position)?

6. If you have brothers or sisters, how did your parents treat you in comparison with your siblings? What kinds of "jobs" were you assigned as a child? Were decisions based on your unique skills, on age, or on gender?

7. In what ways did your parents "teach you" to be either male or female? Were there some behaviors that were encouraged? Were there other behaviors that were forbidden? What activities and toys did they give you? Were you ever given "lessons" on how to "be a man" or "be a lady"?

8. Some writers suggest that women are the "more sexual gender." Why?

9. Have you ever known a person who engaged in an extramarital affair? If so, how do you explain that person's behavior? What effect did the affair have on the person's marriage?

10. What is your opinion of premarital sex? How did this opinion develop?

11. Have most of the cohabiting couples you know eventually married? If so, do you think they have a better or worse chance than noncohabitators to stay married? Explain.

12. What messages did your parents send you about sexuality? If you have a religious background, what messages were you given about sexuality from your religion? How have these themes affected your behavior?

380

➢ SUGGESTIONS FOR FURTHER READING

American Psychological Association. (2007). *Report of the APA Task Force on the sexualization of girls*. Washington, DC: American Psychological Association. Retrieved March 21, 2010, from http://www.apa.org/pi/women/programs/girls/report.aspx.

American Psychological Association. (2010). *Sexual orientation and homosexuality*. Washington, DC: American Psychological Association. Retrieved March 21, 2010, from http://www.apa.org/helpcenter/sexual-orientation.aspx.

Bem, S. L. (1974). The measurement of psychological androgyny. *Journal of Consulting & Clinical Psychology, 42*(2), 155–162.

Best, D. (2002). Cross-cultural gender roles. In J. Worell (Ed.), *Encyclopedia of women and gender*. New York: Oxford.

Bockting, W. O., & Ehrbar, R. D. (2005). Commentary: Gender variance, dissonance, or identity disorder? *Journal of Psychology & Human Sexuality, 17*(3-4), 125-134.

Carroll, J. L. (2010). *Sexuality now: Embracing diversity* (3rd ed.). Belmont, CA: Cengage Learning/Wadsworth.

Centers for Disease Control. (2009). *Understanding sexual violence: Fact sheet*. Atlanta: National Center for Injury Prevention and Control. Retrieved March 23, 2010, from http://www.cdc.gov/violenceprevention/pdf/SV_factsheet-a.pdf.

Crooks, R., & Baur, K. (2011). *Our sexuality* (11th ed.). Belmont, CA: Cengage Learning/Wadsworth.

Diamond, M. (2009). Human intersexuality: Difference or disorder? *Archives of Sexual Behavior, 38*(2), 172.

Ellis, A. (1974). *The sensuous person*. New York: Signet.

Hall, C. M. (1989). *Women & identity: Value choices in a changing world*. New York: Hemisphere Publishing.

Hendrick, S. (2004). *Close relationships*. Boston: Pearson/Allyn and Bacon.
Hyde, J. S., & DeLamater, J. D. (2011). *Understanding human sexuality* (11th ed.). New York: McGraw-Hill.

Janus, S. S., & Janus, C. L. (1994). *The Janus report on sexual behavior*. New York: Wiley.

Mosher, W. D., Chandra, C., & Jones, J. (2005). *Sexual behavior and selected health measures: Men and women 15–44 years of age, United States, 2002.* Atlanta: Centers for Disease Control and Prevention. Retrieved March 28, 2010, from http://www.cdc.gov/nchs/data/ad/ad362.pdf.

Ore, T. (2008). *The social construction of difference and inequality: Race, class, gender and sexuality* (4th ed.). New York: McGraw-Hill.

➤ VIDEO SUGGESTIONS

Feature Films

Meet the Parents (Ben Stiller, Robert DeNiro), Comedy. Ben Stiller plays a young man meeting his girlfriend's parents for the first time. Her father, a retired CIA officer, talks Ben into submitting to a polygraph test. Other mishaps ensue as they strive to find common grounds and understanding.

Boys Don't Cry (Hilary Swank), Drama. The true story of Brandon Teena, who seduced young women in a small, rural community in Nebraska and was later discovered to be a woman posing as a man. Local authorities are unresponsive when Brandon is raped. Shortly after that, Brandon is brutally murdered.

Educational Films and Videos

AIDS: No Nonsense Answers, (1995), Films for the Humanities and Sciences, 10 min. This brief and extremely informative video demonstrates and motivates prevention behaviors and lifestyle changes while presenting the basic facts about AIDS and HIV. Many questions that your students have will be answered in this film including, "If one in a group of children is positive, are the others at risk?"

AIDS, The Family, and The Community, (2002), Films for the Humanities and Sciences, 26 min. This film describes how AIDS is transmitted and ways AIDS is already affecting all of us in some way.

Childhood Sexual Abuse, Films for the Humanities & Sciences, 26 min. This program looks at the ways adult women learn to work out the problems caused by sexually abusive fathers. Includes input from psychiatrists, social workers, and law enforcement officials.

Child Sex Abusers, (2002), Films for the Humanities and Sciences, 28 min. The typical sex abuse cycle—abused as a child, abuser as adult—is being replaced by an even more frightening scenario: more of today's abusers appear to be children. This specially adapted Phil Donahue program features mothers and their daughters who have been sexually abused by brothers, half-brothers, and neighborhood kids—one of the molesters was 13, and his victim was 3. The program also features an expert who deals with abusive children, who counsels on what signs to look for and what to do when it comes to abusive kids, and who counsels kids who are being abused.

Finding Out: Incest and Family Sexual Abuse, Kinetic Films, 25 min. This film concentrates on the role of the victim's mother in dealing with family sexual abuse. Viewers are shown Robin, a victim since age nine, who talks about the devastating emotional effects of sexual abuse. Her mother tells how she dealt with the disclosure and the subsequent breakup of her marriage.

Gender and Relationships, Coast Community College District Telecourses, 30 min. Part of the *Psychology—The Study of Human Behavior Series,* this video explores the complexities of emotional interactions and attachments.

Gender and Reproduction: A Natural History, (2002), Films for the Humanities and Sciences, 19–28 min. each. Throughout the realms of living beings—in bananas and humans, in jungles and zoos, in test tubes and ocean depths—survival depends on adaptation, and adaptation on variation. And variation is the product of sexual reproduction. Through 12 half-hour films of fascinating photography, the viewer observes the many ways beings of all kinds reproduce: how male and female find one another, attract one another, couple, and produce one or more of a new generation that is alike but not identical; and how anatomical, behavioral, and social characteristics of a species are linked to the genetic goal of reproduction.

Homosexuality: What Science Understands, (1987), Insight Media, 54 min. This video traces research on homosexual behavior from the original Kinsey studies in 1954 through the late 1980s. Highlights of the video include a discussion of the decision to remove homosexuality from the DSR III and the issues of homophobia and AIDS.

Incest: The Family Secret, Filmmakers Library, 57 min. As this film indicates, incest is a widespread problem that occurs in all kinds of families. Most commonly, it takes the form of sexual child abuse inflicted by the father on a non-consenting daughter while she is still a child. In this very frank program, adult women talk about the childhood experiences that so traumatized their later lives.

Love and Sex, (2002), Films for the Humanities and Sciences, 52 min. This film describes the discrepancies between male and female behavior, between biological sexual needs and social constraints, and between the ideal of a long-term relationship and divorce statistics. The problem of teen pregnancy is raised, and the distinction between a love and a sexual relationship is discussed.

Men, Women, and The Sex Difference: Boys And Girls Are Different, (2002), Films for the Humanities and Sciences, 43 min. In this ABC News special, ABC News correspondent John Stossel raises questions about the nature/nurture debate and seeks to discover if many parents' gut instincts—and the findings of many researchers and psychologists—about differences between little girls and boys have been right all along. The program speaks with parents who have tried to foster gender-neutral behavior in their children and specialists who illustrate differences in male-female brain functions and hormones. The program also features feminists Gloria Steinem, the late Bella Abzug, and Gloria Allred, who question whether the issue of gender differences should even be raised.

Rape: an Act of Hate, (2002), Films for the Humanities and Sciences, 30 min. Hosted by Veronica Hamel of *Hill Street Blues,* the film describes why people rape and what potential victims (who are all of us) can do to protect ourselves. Winner of an Emmy and an American Women in Radio and Television Award.

Sex and Gender, (2001), from the *Discovering Psychology Series,* Annenberg/CPG, 30 min. This video explores the ways in which males and females are similar and different and how sex roles reflect social values and psychological knowledge.

Sex Roles: Charting the Complexity Of Development, (1991), Insight Media, 60 min. Looking at the cultural ramifications of sex roles and the myths associated with them, this video examines three theories of socialization: Freudian, cognitive-developmental, and social learning. It analyzes how each theory views the nature-versus-nurture controversy. It also explores the impact of sex role stereotypes on the developing child, looking at the differences these stereotypes create in scholastic achievement, interaction with peers, and expectations for the future.

The Brain: The Sexual Brain, Films for the Humanities & Sciences, 28 min. Part of the six-part series, The Brain, this video shows some startling effects of hormone injections on brain structure and raises provocative questions about the sexual and reproductive roots of structural differences between males and females.

The Differences Between Men and Women, (1995), Films for the Humanities and Sciences, 23 min. The old question "Are the differences between men and women conditioned by biology or by family and social environment?" is answered with recent research, which claims that male and female brains are far from identical. The video also looks at cultural influences on gender-related behaviors.

The Opposite Sex, Insight Media, 55 min. Human beliefs about differences between the sexes inform social organization, law, religion, literature, and humor. This video considers men's and women's bodies, brains, emotions, and public and private behavior. Using a combination of science, observation, and opinion, it links biological and psychological studies to generate a composite interpretation of gender difference.

Understanding Sex, (2000), Films for the Humanities & Sciences, 51 min. Narrated by Candice Bergen, this program explores the biology, genetics, and psychological components of sex, including sexual orientation and assisted conception.

➤ COMPUTER AND INTERNET RESOURCES

INFOTRAC®

Below you will find two journal articles obtained from INFOTRAC® that relate to information contained in this chapter. Instructors should encourage students to utilize this invaluable resource to improve their research skills. Have students locate and read the following articles and answer questions relevant to each article.

Newsweek International, March 28, 2005 p42 The truth about gender: The rift between the sexes just got a whole lot bigger. A new study has found that women and men differ genetically almost as much as humans differ from chimpanzees.

1.   According to this article, what was one of the most intriguing findings concerning genetic differences between men and women?

       Answer: One of the most intriguing findings concerns the genetic differences between men and women. A study published in the journal *Nature* puts this difference at about 1 percent. Considering that the genetic makeup of chimpanzees and humans differs by only 1.5 percent, this is significant.

2.   Compare/contrast the influence of hormones and genetic influences on brain development.

       Answer: Scientists have found that while hormones wreak havoc on just about every part of adolescent physiology, they have almost no effect on brain development. Genetic variations, on the other hand, have a huge impact on the brain.

3. After reviewing this article, how, then, do female brains differ from male brains? Briefly describe.

Answer: Men tend to think spatially; brain scans of men and women engaged in rhyming words show that they use different brain circuits to perform the same task. Women also have 15 to 20 percent more gray matter (ordinary neurons) than men. And their white matter (long neurons that help the brain distribute its processing tasks) is concentrated at the juncture between the brain's left and right hemispheres and may help women use both sides of their brain for language-related tasks.

Sex Roles: A Journal of Research, July 2004 v51 Do boys and girls act differently in the classroom: A content analysis of student characters in educational psychology textbooks.

1. What was the hypothesis of this research study? What were the researchers studying?

Answer: The focus of the present study was to examine the presence of gender stereotypes in educational psychology textbooks.

2. In general, what has research on gender stereotyping in higher education textbooks demonstrated?

Answer: In summary, research on gender stereotyping in higher education textbooks has clearly shown that although gender-stereotyped representations of men and women have improved over time, instances of bias in the way men and women are portrayed still exist.

3. To be included in the study, textbooks were surveyed using three different coding criteria. What were they?

Answer: Textbooks were surveyed for examples of student characters. To be included for analysis, an example either had to present a student character in a classroom situation or interacting with another student or teacher outside of class. Second, to examine if authors portrayed student characters in a gender biased manner, characters were coded for evidence of stereotypically masculine and feminine personality traits. And, finally, characters were also coded for their involvement in stereotypically masculine and feminine activities.

4.   What were the results of this study? What did the study reveal?

        Answer: Results revealed that male characters were depicted with negative masculine traits, such as aggression, significantly more often than were female characters. However, no differences were found for positive masculine traits or for feminine traits. Male characters were also portrayed as engaging in stereotypically masculine activities significantly more often than female characters, although no difference was found in science activity as a function of gender.

WEB LINKS

Knowledge Builder Links

1. Sex, Gender, and Androgyny
        Human Sexual Reproduction:
                http://www.biology.iupui.edu/biocourses/N100/2k4ch39repronotes.html
        Sex and Gender:
                http://www.hawaii.edu/PCSS/online_artcls/intersex/sexual_I_G_web.html
        My Life as an Intersexual: http://www.pbs.org/wgbh/nova/gender/beck.html

2. Sexual Behavior and Sexual Orientation
        Sexual Scripts: http://www.kff.org/mediapartnerships/Seventeen_surveys.cfm
        Facts about Sexual Orientation: http://psychology.ucdavis.edu/rainbow/html/facts.html

3. Sexual Response, Attitudes, and Behavior
        Sexual Response: http://sexuality.about.com/od/anatomyresponse/a/malesexualrespo.htm
        Paraphilias and Sexual Disorders: http://allpsych.com/disorders/paraphilias/index.html
        Child Molestation: http://www.stopcsa.org/

4. Sexual Problems: When Pleasure Fades
        Sexual Arousal Disorder: http://www.merck.com/mmhe/sec22/ch250/ch250f.html
        Premature Ejaculation: http://www.mayoclinic.com/health/premature-
                ejaculation/DS00578
        Sexuality and Intimacy: http://cas.umkc.edu/casww/sa/Sex.htm

Additional Web Links

Companion Site
http://www.thomsonedu.com/psychology/coon

APA Online
http://www.apa.org/

Gender Studies
http://www.radford.edu/~gstudies/

HIV/AIDS
http://www.cdc.gov/hiv/topics/surveillance/basic.htm
http://www.cdc.gov/hiv/resources/factsheets/index.htm
http://www.avert.org/aids-statistics.htm

Sexual Assault
http://www.rainn.org/statistics/
http://www.uww.edu/sart/statistics.htm
http://en.wikipedia.org/wiki/Sexual_assault

Sexual Disorders
http://www.athealth.com/Consumer/disorders/Sexual.html
http://en.wikipedia.org/wiki/Sexual_disorder
http://sexuality.about.com/cs/sexualdisorders/

Sexual Response Cycle
http://en.wikipedia.org/wiki/Human_sexual_response_cycle
http://www.engenderhealth.org/res/onc/sexuality/response/pg2.html
http://sexuality.about.com/od/anatomyresponse/a/sexualresponse.htm

PSYCHOLOGY IN THE NEWS

ABC News
http://abcnews.go.com/Technology/story?id=98013&page=1
Explores the issue that, despite changes, boys still choose instruments by gender.

Ezine Articles
http://ezinearticles.com/?Sex-or-Gender&id=19585
This site provides the latest articles and news about the issues of sex and gender.

Gender Studies News
http://www.indiana.edu/~libsalc/molsmith/gender/newsletter_gender.html
This site provides useful information on gender studies, which includes new web resources, recommended reading, and numerous other links and resources.

388

Internet Resources for Instructor
http://college.hmco.com/psychology/resources/instructors/news/news_20020504.html
This site provides an interesting article on *Single Sex Schools: Back to the Future*, which addresses the learning differences between the sexes as it relates to education.

University of Virginia News

http://www.virginia.edu/topnews/releases2001/gender-aug-30-2001.html

CHAPTER 11
Personality

Survey Questions
Discussion Questions
Lecture Enhancements
                                         Personality testing
TV personalities
Situational determinants of behavior
Fidgeting—a personality trait
Make your own inkblots
Watch out for pop psychology!
Pop psychology—2
Birth order and personality
Free association exercise
What would the ego say?
What influences you?
Make your own TAT test

Role-Playing Scenarios
Value-Clarification Statements
One-Minute Motivators
                                         Do we see me the same way?
What are your five central traits?
Trait theory meets reinforcement theory
Interview a set of identical twins
Was Freud right?
The effect of early experiences on personality
Your earliest memory
I did a good job!
What's in a joke?
Influence of reinforcement on personality
Are you shy?
Personality dynamics
Self-reinforcement
Gender expectations and personality

Broadening Our Cultural Horizons
                                         Who are your heroes?
Culture, traits, and rewards
Cultural priorities
Individualism versus collectivism
Cultural traits in childrearing
Horoscopes and zodiac symbols
How universal are Freud's concepts?
Influence of popular media on personality development
Shyness around the world

Supplemental Activities
                                         Exercise 11.1: Personality Traits
Exercise 11.2: State versus Trait
Exercise 11.3: Personality Types
Exercise 11.4: "To Dream the Impossible Dream"
Exercise 11.5: Who Am I?

Handouts

Handout 11.1: Personality Traits: Instructions
Handout 11.2: State versus Trait
Handout 11.3: Introverted? Extroverted? Which are you?
Handout 11.4: To Dream the Impossible Dream: Rating Scale
Handout 11.5: Who Am I ? Response Sheet

Journal Questions
Suggestions for Further Reading
Video Suggestions
Computer and Internet Resources

➤ SURVEY QUESTIONS

Module 11.1 Overview of Personality
Survey Questions: How do psychologists use the term *personality?*

Module 11.2 Trait Theories
Survey Question: Are some personality traits more basic or important than others?

Module 11.3 Psychoanalytic Theory
Survey Question: How do psychodynamic theories explain personality?

Module 11.4 Humanistic Theories
Survey Question: What are humanistic theories of personality?

Module 11.5 Behavioral and Social Learning Theories
Survey Question: What do behaviorists and social learning theorists emphasize in their approach to personality?

Survey Question: How do traits and situations affect personality?

Module 11.6 Personality Assessment
Survey Question: How do psychologists measure personality?

Module 11.7 Psychology in Action
Survey Questions: What causes shyness? What can be done about it?

➤ DISCUSSION QUESTIONS

1. If you could select only three personality traits, which three would you consider most basic? Discuss why you feel this way.

2. If you were selecting candidates for an extended space flight, how would you make your choices? What could you do to improve the accuracy of your judgments of candidates' personalities?

3. Do you think that there is such a thing as "national character"? That is, do all Germans, all French, all Americans, all Canadians, and so forth have some traits that are common to their national group? How likely is it that these perceived traits, if any, are actually stereotypes?

4. *For those who have not yet read the text:* What percent of personality do you think is the result of temperament (inherited, biological aspects) and what percent is the result of learning/environment? (Answer: estimates of temperament in personality development range from 25–50 percent.)

5. Do you think that animals have personalities? Defend your answer.

6. How could the personality of a child affect and shape the child's environment? How might different personalities affect the way parents interact with the child? How might expectations about twins affect the way the twins develop?

7. Why do you think media coverage of reunited twins (those separated soon after birth and reunited as adults) has exaggerated the role of genetics in human behavior and personality?

8. The textbook states that personality is only 25–50 percent biologically determined, and that personality traits are not "wired" for life. How hard is it to change one's personality? Can people in middle or old age change their personalities? Why do many people resist changing their personalities, even when they are unhappy?

9. Can you describe an action you performed recently that seems to represent operation of the id, ego, or superego? How would a behaviorist or a humanist interpret the same event?

10. Have you ever "caught yourself" giving into an id impulse when you shouldn't have? Have you ever stopped yourself from acting on id impulses? Why do you think you gave in or stopped? Was it your conscience, or was it the situation (reality)?

11. Can you cite a behavior or an experience that seems to support the existence of the unconscious or of unconscious motivation?

12. Can you cite observations that support Freud's scheme of psychosexual stages? Can you cite observations that contradict it?

13. As a child, with whom did you identify? What effect did this have on your personality? How does imitation differ from identification?

14. In his time, Freud was heavily criticized for his assertion that children had sexual instincts. What behaviors do children exhibit that Freud believed that children do, in fact, have sexuality?

15. Freud thought that adolescent males who clash with adult male authority figures (teachers, ministers, policemen, and so forth) are experiencing a carryover of the Oedipus conflict. What do you think?

16. Freud believed that adolescence was a time when one could go back and re-work earlier psychic conflicts and potentially undo fixations. Examine the behavior of teenagers. What are some teen behaviors that suggest they are working through oral, anal, and phallic stage issues?

17. Which parts of Freud's theory do you think have the most and least merit, and why?

18. Recent studies show that teachers continue to treat boys and girls differently. Why is it so difficult to change these behaviors?

19. What experiences have you had that have contributed to personal growth? What experiences set you back or were otherwise negative in their effects? Which personality theory best explains the differences between these experiences?

20. Do you think Maslow's concept of self-actualization is admirable? Achievable?

21. Presently, what are the most prominent "possible selves" you visualize? How have these self-images influenced your behavior?

22. Which theory of personality seems to best explain your personality?

23. How would Freud explain the value of projective tests?

24. Have you ever been interviewed or given a personality test? How accurate did you consider the resulting assessment of personality?

25. How easy do you think it would be to "fake good" or "fake bad" on the MMPI? Under what circumstances would people want to "fake good"? Under what circumstances would people want to "fake bad"?

26. Under what circumstances would you consider a personality test an invasion of privacy? Do you think it is acceptable for personality tests to be used to select job applicants?

27. Which methods of assessing personality would be most appropriate for each major view of personality?

28. How would Freud explain the shy personality? How would Skinner, Rogers, and Maslow explain shyness?

➤ LECTURE ENHANCEMENTS

1. **Personality testing.** For an ambitious exercise, administer a complete personality inventory to class members. Appropriate tests are the Guilford-Zimmerman Temperament Survey and the Sixteen Personality Factor Questionnaire. These tests can be attained from Pearson Education, Inc. http://psychcorp.pearsonassessments.com/pai/ca/cahome.htm

   An excellent alternate source of psychological tests is a classic trade book by Rita Aero and Elliot Weiner, titled *The Mind Test* (New York: William Morrow, 1981). This book includes a variety of scales and questionnaires appropriate for class administration. Some of the areas covered are personality, stress, fear, anxiety, depression, marriage, vocation, and interpersonal relationships. Most of the scales presented were drawn from journal articles and are of good quality.

   The following listings are particularly suitable for classroom use: Locus of Control Scale, Self-Consciousness Scale, Death Concern Scale, Marital Adjustment Test, Beck Depression Inventory, Interest Check List, Social Interest Scale, and the Assertion Questionnaire.

   Many personality tests are available on the Internet, if one is careful about the selection. The Keirsey Temperament Sorter can be found at http://www.keirsey.com, and the Big Five Personality Test can be found at http://www.outofservice.com/bigfive/

   As an alternative to in-class testing, plot the personality profiles of one or two individuals (real or hypothetical) on the rating forms for one of the tests mentioned above. Duplicate the profiles for class distribution or present them with an overhead projector. Discuss the meaning of the various scales and the picture that emerges of the individual's personality based on their scores.

2. **TV personalities.** Students love to play "amateur psychologist" and are often inclined toward analyzing people in their lives. In reality, most personalities are very complex, and any attempts at analysis by untrained observers either focus only on one aspect of a person, or create family fights! A safer and perhaps less complex analysis of personality types can be performed using TV characters as "subjects." Today's TV characters are arguably much more complex than characters of the past. Nevertheless, most are not

395

presented as being as complex as a real person, largely because of time and format limitations. In addition, most TV characters are seen only in one or two different situations, e.g., work.

Ask students to analyze three characters from their favorite shows with respect to Freudian theory (or, if you prefer, some other personality theory). Ask them to identify the characters' motivations, fixations, defense mechanisms, and personality structure. Have them bring their descriptions back to class for discussion. In order to encourage the completion of this exercise, you might consider making it either part of their grade or an opportunity for extra credit.

3. **Situational determinants of behavior.** To illustrate the importance of situational determinants of behavior, you might find it interesting to share this bit of information with students: L. R. Kahle of the University of Michigan has reported that nearly half of the male students he tested cheated when they were deliberately given a chance to change test answers. Kahle used hidden pieces of pressure-sensitive paper to find out which students did or did not change answers on the test. You may want to discuss this finding in conjunction with the concepts of the psychological situation, expectancy, and reinforcement value.

4. **Fidgeting—a personality trait.** Fidgeting is described as engaging in actions that are peripheral to ongoing tasks or activities. The cited article offers a 40-item fidgeting questionnaire along with scoring instructions. High scores on the questionnaire are related to tendencies to engage in extraneous activities (consuming alcoholic drinks, cigarette smoking, eating, daydreaming, restlessness, insomnia). High scores are also correlated with binge eating, physical activity, anxiety, and hostility. This is an interesting individual difference that students can easily relate to. Fidgeting can be viewed in state or trait terms, and the topic offers a chance to discuss correlations among related behaviors and the disposition-situation debate (Mehrabian & Friedman, 1986).

5. **Make your own inkblots.** Students can simulate a Rorschach test by making their own inkblots. The instructor should bring a large bottle of a dark-colored liquid and an eyedropper. Ask students to fold a sheet of paper in half then open it up. Put a few drops of the liquid into the fold and close it, pressing it flat. More than one application of drops may be needed to create a blot that is symmetrical and large. Students can then compare blots and discuss what they each see.

An additional exercise might be to ask students to show their blots to several persons not in their class and record their responses. They should ask their subjects to respond to both the overall image and to particular parts of it.

Student discussion of the results should center on similarities and variations in responses with some speculation on reasons for this.

NOTE: you should be sure to emphasize that the Rorschach is **not** just a random set of inkblots. The blots that were retained were those that differentiated between normal and abnormal personalities.

6. **Watch out for pop psychology! (Internet exercise)** It might be wise in connection with this chapter to remind students of the problems associated with easy acceptance of overly generalized and self-contradictory personality descriptions. These are frequently found in magazine articles, popular psychology books, and online. A recent example is an online test (available at http://www.colorquiz.com/) purporting to analyze personality on the basis of one's color preferences, loosely based on some early work by psychologists studying the impact of color. As with many such "tests," the descriptions given are fairly general and could apply to anyone. Here's a sample of a similar test result to share with your class:

> If your choice is red, you are an aggressive, extroverted person with strong desires and a craving for action. You are energetic, impulsive, and have a tremendous drive for success. You are quick to take sides and make judgments. However, you are not unreasonably stubborn and, in fact, may sometimes be too easily swayed in your feelings and attitudes. You dislike monotony in any form, and your search for activity may sometimes make you appear fickle. You tend to lack perseverance but may reach success through sheer energy and force of personality.

7. **Pop psychology—2.** For an even more entertaining demonstration of the personality test for colors mentioned above, you can do this exercise in class, in reverse. Pre-print the personality descriptions for each color and ask students to choose the one that best describes them. **After** they have made their choices, ask them write down their favorite color. Lastly, reveal which color matches which description. Ask for a show of hands for how many students had a match. Be sure to remind them that, on a probability basis, some matches would be right, but most will be wrong.

8. **Free association exercise.** To convey the flavor of the Freudian view of unconscious thought patterns, meanings, and associations, try having students follow a chain of associations to see where it leads. Begin by asking the class to write the first word or thought that occurs to them when they hear one of these words: mother, father, death, birth, money, love, failure, breast, gun, rival. (Choose words you consider most interesting or likely to produce interesting responses.) After the first association has been written, ask students to write their first association to that word or idea. Continue through a series of 8 or 10 associations and then select a few papers for discussion. The linkages and endpoints can be fascinating.

Birth order and personality. (Internet exercise) Interest in environmental influences on personality traits can be heightened through the effects of birth order. An exercise that dramatizes the differences in ordinal position consists of arranging students in small groups by birth order. Have students get into groups of only children, first-borns, middle, and youngest children. Have each group select a recorder and give them about 15 minutes to list what the group members consider to have been the advantages and disadvantages of their birth positions. After they are finished, have the recorder read the list aloud to the rest of the class. This exercise usually generates a great deal of interest and a lively discussion.

After student have recorded their observations, they can look up Adler's original list of personality traits related to birth order at: http://en.wikipedia.org/wiki/Birth_order

9. **What would the ego say?** For a further investigation into Freudian dynamics, have students complete the statements that follow. Can the resulting statements be categorized as id, ego, or superego responses?

1.	I want to...	6.	One should never...
2.	If I could do anything, I would...	7.	I won't ever...
3.	Why do I...?	8.	Realistically, I...
4.	My plan is to...	9.	I can't seem to...
5.	I think a responsible person...	10.	Ideally I...

10. **What influences you?** Another good way to illustrate situational determinants and the behavioral view is as follows: Instruct students to keep a careful record for a day of each person they talked with. Students should include a brief description of the circumstances, setting, nature of the interaction, and apparent reinforcement (information, approval, needed goods, etc.) provided by interacting with others. When the records are brought to class, ask students to discuss the external variables influencing how "sociable" their personalities appeared on the day in question.

11. **Make your own TAT test.** You can give the students a chance to experience a projective test by preparing a TAT-like card. Find a picture that is ambiguous and that can be copied. Magazines and newspapers are good sources. The picture should fit on an 8½ x 11" sheet of paper. Make copies so that each student can have one. Ask the students to write a story about the card. What is going on in the scene? What led up to the action? What will happen next? When they are finished, ask the students to look over their responses. Look for themes and motives, such as aggression, achievement, love, and anger. Students should be asked to share some of their stories with others. Ask other students to look for themes and motives in the reader's story. **NOTE:** you should be sure to emphasize that the TAT is **not** just a random set of pictures.

➢ ROLE-PLAYING SCENARIOS

1. **You are interviewing for a job.** What nonverbal cues usually accompany the following thoughts? Pose for these thoughts: "I really care about this job." "I have the skills to do this very well." "I don't think this job pays enough." "I have been fired from other jobs; I hope they don't find out." "I don't want this job at all—just the experience of interviewing."

398

2. **You are a psychologist seeing a client who gets extremely anxious whenever he is near a woman who has red hair, like his mother's.** Explain his feelings to him as a Freudian psychologist might. Next, explain his feelings from a social learning perspective.

3. **What would the id, ego, and superego say in each of these situations?** What would you do in these situations?
    a. You can't decide whether or not to eat a huge, very fattening hot fudge sundae after an already filling dinner.
    b. You have been invited to a party the night before your psychology final exam.
    c. You just found a wallet with $20 in it on campus. There is no identification in the wallet.
    d. Your family is having a party on the same day when your friends are getting together.

4. **Your usually quiet and reserved 12-year-old daughter is suddenly getting into fist-fights at school.** Her sudden explosions of rage worry you. What should you say to her?

5. **Myrtle is trying to stop smoking.** But all it takes is the sight of matches and the craving returns. Speaking as a behaviorist, give her some hints about things she could do to make quitting easier. How did her craving begin?

6. **You are majoring in medicine because your parents have always pressured you into becoming a doctor.** You aren't really happy in this field and have begun to have some health problems and a lot of anxiety. How would you explain your feelings using Carl Rogers' humanistic theory?

7. **A child has just brought home a disappointing report card.** Demonstrate how a parent would respond if he or she were showing unconditional positive regard. Now, imitate a parent who is imposing conditions of worth.

➤ VALUE-CLARIFICATION STATEMENTS

1. A person's personality does not change greatly from one situation to another.

2. It is a bad idea to dress identical twins identically.

3. Our real personality is primarily unconscious and something we may never really know.

4. Freud's concepts of the anal-retentive and anal-expulsive personalities make absolutely no sense at all.

5. Freud's theory has no value in psychology today.

6. Most people put themselves down too often.

7. Children should be pushed to be toilet trained by the age of two.

8. Skinner's theory is too mechanistic to explain the complexity of human personality.

9. People are basically good.

10. Most of the humanistic principles are too optimistic for the real world.

11. Personality assessment is not much better than an educated guess.

12. When all is said and done, people choose their own personality traits.

13. Shyness is really just a case of poor social skills.

➤ ONE-MINUTE MOTIVATORS

1. **Do we see me the same way?** Ask students to check items on the Adjective Checklist in the text that they believe describe their personality. Before the next class session, students should ask their best friend to check items describing the student on a duplicate list. Ask students to discuss the ways in which their choices differed from those made by their friend. This can be related to personality traits, testing, or self-concept.

2. **What are your five central traits?** Ask students to write down and hand in the five traits from the Adjective checklist that they think best describe them. Discuss the issue of cardinal traits (which few people have) and central traits.

3. **Trait theory meets reinforcement theory.** How does our society reinforce the traits students used to describe themselves?

400

4. **Which traits are the "best"?** Ask students to write down their five central traits (in any order). Summarize the responses on the board. Why were these traits chosen? What's "wrong" with the least popular ones? Which traits are endorsed by a majority of students?

5. **Interview a set of identical twins.** Talk to each twin separately (with one waiting outside class). In what ways do they feel they are similar and different? Then bring them together for a joint discussion.

6. **Was Freud right?** After you have completed your lecture on Freud's theory, ask students which parts of the theory they most and least agree with. You can also ask them to brainstorm and generate a list of areas where Freud's influence has found its way into contemporary society. Examples include: referring to uptight people as "anal," using phrases like "orally fixated", or acknowledging the Freudian slip. You can also ask them to examine the lyrics of popular music for themes that might have been influenced by Freudian concepts, including the ideas of "mama's boy" and "daddy's girl."

7. **The effect of early experiences on personality**. According to both Freud and Skinner, personal history plays a role in the development of who we are. Freud in particular was more likely to stress the role of childhood experiences in personality development, while Skinner focuses on reinforcement history. Ask students if they remember a particular incident from childhood that they believe had a lasting effect on them. It could be an event, or something that someone said to them. This should, of course, be on a volunteer basis. You can also discuss with them the "butterfly effect," or the idea that even a small thing can produce a domino or ripple effect that ultimately influences much more than its original scope.

8. **Your earliest memory.** To demonstrate the preconscious, ask students to recall their earliest memory of a family holiday celebration.

9. **I did a good job!** Give each student a 3 x 5" card. Ask students to write three statements of self-praise for some behavior done frequently during the week. Pass these around the class so everyone can read each other's statements. Read a few of the statements in class. Then ask students to take their own card home and to place it in a visible location for a week. A week later discuss whether students noticed the card and whether they think it had any impact on their view of themselves.

10. **What's in a joke?** Ask students to write a joke on a 3 x 5" card. Ask for a group of volunteers to read through the cards and quantify the number of jokes that they perceive to be "hostile" versus "not hostile." Is it difficult to think of un-hostile humor? Are jokes perpetuated because they express unconscious hostility? Because of the rewarding effects of tension-release? Because of the social reinforcement of making others laugh? Because they express or enhance one's self-image?

11. **Influence of reinforcement on personality.** Think about people you know and the way they show emotions, e.g., joy and sadness. If you know members of their family, think

about what might happen if the individuals behaved differently. For example, in families where members are mostly stoic, what happens if the individual acts more flamboyant? Or vice versa?

12. **Are you shy?** Ask each student to engage another student in a five-minute conversation. Repeat the same procedure with three other people. Ask students how they felt about the dialogue? Did they feel shy? Did they act shy? What did they do effectively in the conversation? What could they have done more effectively?

13. **Personality dynamics.** According to your text, the ego is the executive of the personality. What kind of behavior would you expect to see if the id were in charge? Or the superego? What would happen if the ego refused to listen to the needs of either the id or the superego?

14. **Self-reinforcement.** Photocopy the list of statements of self-reinforcement in the text and distribute it to students. Ask them to check off as many as apply and turn their list in anonymously. Tally the distribution to allow students to see how they compare. Point out that those who scored lower might consider what changes they could make in their lives to increase their level of self-reinforcement.

15. **Gender expectations and personality.** Sophie Tucker once said, "From birth to 18, a girl needs good parents, from 18-35 good looks, from 35-55, a good personality, and from 55 on CASH." Type this four ways: using "girl," "boy," "woman," "man." Distribute the forms randomly to the class and discuss whether the statement is true. Interestingly, many men in the class will find the term "boy" offensive but "girl" appropriate. Discuss gender-based differences in personality and expectations.

➤ BROADENING OUR CULTURAL HORIZONS

1. **Who are your heroes?** Who do you identify with? How has this affected your self-concept? How has your culture helped define your heroes and models? Would other cultures make heroes of the same people we do?

2. **Culture, traits, and rewards.** Imagine a society where people are rewarded when they give to the poor, live humbly, and stay physically fit. What common traits would you expect to find in such a society? What do you think are the common traits of American society?

3. **Cultural priorities. (classroom or Internet)** If you have students from other countries, ask them if they notice a difference in which traits are most valued in their country of origin. Alternately, have students pick a country and do an Internet search on personality traits that are valued in that country.

4. **Individualism versus collectivism.** Examine the concept of "self actualization." How does the American emphasis on individual rights and personal achievement relate to self-actualization? Is it a coincidence that the humanistic school of psychology is largely associated with American theorists Maslow and Rogers? How do European societies and psychologists view the self-actualizing tendencies of Americans? How might the concept of self-actualization actually create interpersonal difficulties in collectivist (largely Eastern) cultures? Is self-actualization a goal we should aspire to, or is it a type of selfishness? What problems does the concept of self-actualization present for American culture?

5. **Cultural traits in childrearing.** Cultures vary widely in their views of toilet training and breast-feeding. What patterns are considered normal and desirable in mainstream American culture? What variations are you aware of in cultural or ethnic groups with which you are familiar?

6. **Horoscopes and zodiac symbols.** Ask students whether they believe their horoscope and/or their astrological sign have any (even a little) merit in the development of their personality. Count how many students agree that the "stars" have an influence. Then, ask them whether they believe that their year of birth (Chinese or Japanese zodiac) affects personality. Count that number. It is likely that more of them will believe in Western astrology/horoscopes than in Eastern concepts. Ask them why their astrological sign is "better" than their Chinese Zodiac sign. Hopefully, a number of them will recognize that the two "systems" are culturally equivalent expressions of superstitious behavior. You can also debunk the validity of astrology by explaining that the descriptions are typically vague and self-flattering. A discussion of Asian zodiacs can be found at:

    http://www.c-c-c.org/chineseculture/zodiac/zodiac.html (Chinese)
    http://japanese.about.com/library/weekly/aa011302a.htm (Japanese)

    Alternately, you can present students with the descriptions of the Chinese or Japanese zodiac without the year or animal listed, as some students will know their "animal" sign. Ask them to choose the description that they believe is most like them. Then, tell each student which year/animal the description belongs to, and record the number of correct matches.

7. **How universal are Freud's concepts?** Would the strength and the role of each of Freud's structures of personality differ in various cultures? For instance, aren't some cultures more pleasure-oriented than others? Don't some acknowledge more libidinal energy than others? Could a boy develop a conscience if he never felt any rivalry with his father?

8. Influence **of popular media on personality development.** People of almost every generation have commented on how the next generation differs from their own. The comparison is often prefaced by the (sometimes pejorative) statement *"Kids these days…"* or *"When I was a boy/girl…"*

    Ask students whether they think their generation's basic personalities are different from their parents' generation, and if so, how. Also ask them if they see differences in the generation younger than themselves. Once you have gathered these descriptions, ask them how much they think the media has contributed to shaping the character of each generation. Do shows like *Leave it to Beaver* versus *Alien* or *CSI* change the way people view themselves and model their behavior? Or are the shows on TV a reflection of the world around them?

9. **Shyness around the world.** Researchers traveling in China claim that they have never encountered a shy Chinese child. What kinds of cultural differences do you think would account for this observation? How would you change our culture to reduce the incidence of shyness?

➤ SUPPLEMENTAL ACTIVITIES

Exercise 11.1: Personality Traits

The purpose of this exercise is twofold. The first is to focus students on their traits and determine which are important. The second is to give each student a chance to see that his/her view of the self may not be the same as what others see or think is important.

This exercise is complete with instructions, a rating sheet, and a summary sheet to collect all the ratings. The student is given directions and some questions to stimulate thought. You may wish to add to these.

You will need to duplicate sufficient copies of the rating sheet so that each student will be able to rate him/herself and have three or four raters. Each student will need one copy of the directions and the summary sheet. See **Handout 11.1**

Exercise 11.2: State versus Trait

Trait theorists often take the position that many behaviors that appear to be "state" are actually "trait." First, explain to students the difference between state and trait. Then, use the example below to illustrate the trait theorists' position that underlying traits are often the motive for behavior, even when the situation appears to be the cause of the behavior. Of course, Mischel and others favor the explanation that behavior is a complex interaction of traits and situations working together to produce an interactive effect. But for a pure trait theorist, the emphasis is on the trait itself.

Example: Johnny is agreeable, helpful, and cooperative at home, but at school, he is disruptive and uncooperative. Is Johnny's behavior an example of the power of the situation, or does Johnny have an underlying trait that motivates both behaviors?

Answer: Johnny has a high need for attention, which is achieved by being cooperative at home, but which takes the form of negative attention-seeking at school.

Possible answers for **Handout 11.2**:
1. High in emotionality
2. High in competitiveness
3. Social anxiety/introversion
4. Traditional views about men's gender roles
5. Perfectionism
6. High need for acceptance

Exercise 11.3: Personality Types

This introversion-extroversion scale can be administered to students in class or as a take-home project. It should generate interest in personality types and illustrate a typical self-report instrument. **See Handout 11.3.**

Once the scores are obtained, you should give students an opportunity to discuss the results. They will have some immediate reactions to the validity of the scale based on their scores and their perceptions of themselves.

Another interesting classroom activity would be to plot all the scores on a single scale to see what kind of distribution is found in the whole class. A graph could be constructed that would give the students an idea of the variability that exists.

Exercise 11.4: "To Dream the Impossible Dream"

This exercise should help students see the difference between the way they are (or think they are) and the way they would like to be. Often people don't realize there is a real difference, even though they know that they fall short of what they think they ought to be. This should make the concepts clearer and more understandable.

405

Procedure:

1. Discuss self-concept and self-ideal so students know what they are and how to determine the level of each.

2. Explain the purpose of the rating sheet and provide one for each student. (**Handout 11.4**)

3. Read the directions to the students as they read them. Clear up any questions about what to do.

4. Once students have completed both ratings, ask them to subtract the lowest rating from the highest and note the difference in the space at the right of each scale. The difference will be either zero, if both evaluations are the same, or they will be one or more units apart. Do not be concerned about which is higher or lower. (There should be no negative difference.)

5. Ask students to respond, in writing, to the discussion sheet. It is important for each one to think out the meaning of the scores for him- or herself. If the discussion is oral, only some will respond, and many will tend not to examine their scores or the concepts critically.

6. Once the scales are done, and the responses turned in, some general discussion is useful to give students a chance to express their feelings and questions.

Exercise 11.5: Who Am I?

I. **Introduction**

This exercise on self-concept is built around Louis Zurcher's (1977) Twenty-Statement Test (TST). The students are asked to complete the statement, "I am..." 20 times. Then they are asked to categorize the statements into the four categories as outlined on the Interpretation Sheet. Zurcher found that the TST statements of an individual often fall into one category more than the others. He labeled the four categories as follows:

Category 1: the physical self
Category 2: the social self
Category 3: the reflective self
Category 4: the oceanic self (selfhood independent of the preceding three categories)

406

II.   **Procedure**
    A.   Distribute **Handout 11.5** to the students. Ask them to follow the directions and complete the forms.

    B.   When they have finished, pass out the **interpretation sheet** and ask them to follow the directions. Circulate and help those who are uncertain about how to categorize a statement.

    C.   Ask them to indicate in which category their answers predominate.

III.   **Discussion**
    A.   How do most students see themselves? Is there a majority in any one category?

    B.   Speculate on why the results came out as they did.

    C.   Zurcher says that a balance among all four components would be best for a person. Ask students if they agree and why.

Handout 11.1: PERSONALITY TRAITS: INSTRUCTIONS

TO THE STUDENT:

Attached is a list of terms that describe personality traits that are commonly found in the population. You can probably think of many others, but stick with these for this exercise.

The purpose of this exercise is to compare your own self-ratings with the ratings of others. Do others see you in the same way that you see yourself? Follow the directions to discover this.

1. Make several copies of the list of terms. Ask three people to each separately rate you on the list of traits. You should also rate yourself. Select a variety of people to do the rating, such as a family member, friend, coworker, neighbor, teacher, spouse, etc.

2. You and each of your raters should select and check off 20 traits that describe you best. It may be hard to stick to 20, but force yourself (and your raters) to do so.

3. On the summary rating sheet, check off your choices and the choices of each of the raters.

4. Now you can compare how you see yourself with the way others see you. You can also compare the responses of the different raters. They may not all agree with you or with each other!

408

Handout 11.1: PERSONALITY TRAITS: RATING SHEET

Rater's I.D._____ (Rater may wish to be anonymous.)

Identification of personality traits of _____

Instructions: Check the 20 traits from this list that best describe the person named above. Your evaluation should be based on behavior that you have observed.

__boastful	__generous	__optimistic	__shy
__candid	__good-natured	__orderly	__sincere
__clumsy	__gracious	__outgoing	__skeptical
__compulsive	__grouchy	__patient	__sloppy
__considerate	__headstrong	__perceptive	__sly
__cooperative	__honest	__persistent	__smart
__cordial	__idealistic	__persuasive	__sociable
__courageous	__imaginative	__pessimistic	__studious
__courteous	__kind	__prejudiced	__suspicious
__crafty	__logical	__prideful	__tactful
__daring	__loyal	__punctual	__tense
__dependable	__mature	__reasonable	__truthful
__diligent	__methodical	__rebellious	__understanding
__efficient	__modest	__reliable	__unselfish
__energetic	__naive	__respectful	__vain
__ethical	__neat	__sarcastic	__versatile
__forgetful	__nervous	__sexy	__warm
__friendly	__open-minded	__short-tempered	__wholesome

Handout 11.1: PERSONALITY TRAITS: SUMMARY SHEET

In order to compare your own rating of yourself with the ratings of others, put your own 20 checks on this chart first. Then put each rater's checks in the boxes provided.

	RATERS			
	ME	1	2	3
boastful				
candid				
clumsy				
compulsive				
considerate				
cooperative				
cordial				
courageous				
courteous				
crafty				
daring				
dependable				
diligent				
efficient				
energetic				
ethical				
forgetful				
friendly				
generous				

	RATERS			
	ME	1	2	3
good-natured				
gracious				
grouchy				
headstrong				
honest				
idealistic				
imaginative				
kind				
logical				
loyal				
mature				
methodical				
modest				
naive				
neat				
nervous				
open-minded				
optimistic				
orderly				

Handout 11.1: PERSONALITY TRAITS: SUMMARY SHEET (cont.)

	RATERS			
	ME	1	2	3
outgoing				
patient				
perceptive				
persistent				
persuasive				
pessimistic				
prejudiced				
prideful				
punctual				
reasonable				
rebellious				
reliable				
respectful				
sarcastic				
sexy				
short-tempered				
shy				

	RATERS			
	ME	1	2	3
sincere				
skeptical				
sloppy				
sly				
smart				
sociable				
studious				
suspicious				
tactful				
tense				
truthful				
understanding				
unselfish				
vain				
versatile				
warm				
wholesome				

411

Handout 11.1: PERSONALITY TRAITS: EVALUATION

Now you need to evaluate the results. The following questions should help you.

1.   Overall, does your selection of traits present a favorable or unfavorable picture of your personality?

2.   Do the traits identified by your raters present a favorable or unfavorable picture?

3.   How different are the traits selected by your raters from your own selections? In what ways do they differ?

4.   How do you explain the difference?

5.   Which of your traits appear to be most positive based on all ratings?

6.   Which of your traits appear to be most negative based on all ratings?

7.   What do you think about this type of evaluation of personality? Explain what you mean.

Handout 11.2: STATE VERSUS TRAIT

For each of the following descriptions, identify a possible underlying personality trait.

1. Jenny is described by her coworkers as overly sensitive, critical, and impatient. Her family describes her as warm and supportive.

2. Matthew is described by his coworkers as cold and insensitive, but his friends see him as a great friend and teammate who is always ready for activities with "the guys."

3. Sarah's neighbors notice that her house and garden are always immaculate and that she is a "homebody." Her coworkers think that she is a disorganized scatterbrain.

4. George is one of the most popular coworkers in his office. But when George goes home, he frequently argues with his wife about child-care issues.

5. Mary is valued by her employer for her high level of quality work and her excellent behavior as an employee. Recently, Mary has been volunteering at her local animal shelter and frequently becomes argumentative and critical with the other volunteers.

6. Joe likes to "party" with his friends and is always willing to try something new. At work, though, Joe is a "yes man" who hangs on his boss's every instruction and rarely deviates from company policy.

413

Handout 11.3: INTROVERTED? EXTROVERTED? WHICH ARE YOU?

TO THE STUDENT: To find out, mark true (T) or false (F) next to each of the statements below and then follow the scoring instructions.

_____ 1.   I tend to keep in the background at social events.

_____ 2.   I prefer to work with others rather than alone.

_____ 3.   I get embarrassed easily.

_____ 4.   I generally tell others how I feel regardless of how they may take it.

_____ 5.   I really try to avoid situations in which I must speak to a group.

_____ 6.   I am strongly motivated by the approval or interest of others.

_____ 7.   I often daydream.

_____ 8.   I find it easy to start conversations with strangers.

_____ 9.   I find it difficult to make friends with the opposite sex.

_____ 10.   I particularly enjoy meeting people who know their way around the social scene.

_____ 11.   I would rather read a good book or watch television than go out to a movie.

_____ 12.   I would rather work as a salesperson than as a librarian.

_____ 13.   I spend a lot of time philosophizing and thinking about my ideas.

_____ 14.   I prefer action to thought and reflection.

_____ 15.   I am often uncomfortable in conversations with strangers.

_____ 16.   I am mainly interested in activities and ideas that are practical.

_____ 17.   I would prefer visiting an art gallery over attending a sporting event.

_____ 18.   I enjoy open competition in sports, games, and school.

_____ 19.   I make my decisions by reason more than by impulse or emotion.

414

___ 20.   I have to admit that I enjoy talking about myself to others.

___ 21.   I like to lose myself in my work.

___ 22.   I sometimes get into arguments with people I do not know well.

___ 23.   I am very selective about who my friends are.

___ 24.   I make decisions quickly and stick to them.

SCORING:

1.   Go through the odd-numbered items and add the number of true and false responses. Put the numbers in the appropriate boxes.

2.   Go through the even-numbered items, adding the true and false responses. Enter the numbers in the proper boxes.

3.   Add only the ODD-false items to the EVEN-true items.

4.   The total thus obtained should be marked on the introversion-extroversion scale.

ODD ITEMS	True	False			
		True	False	EVEN ITEMS	
TOTAL					

INTROVERT			EXTROVERT	
0	6	12	18	24

Handout 11.4: TO DREAM THE IMPOSSIBLE DREAM: RATING SCALE

TO THE STUDENT:

I. **Rating Scale**

On a separate sheet you will be given a personal profile to complete. On it, there are 15 rating scales, each measuring a personality trait. Each trait is on a nine-point scale with opposing aspects of the trait indicated at each end. You should do four things in the following order:

A. Circle the number on each scale that best describes where you believe you are at present regarding the trait indicated. Do all 15 in this way.

B. Then do all 15 again. This time mark an X over the number that best describes where you would like to be or hope to be some day in regard to each trait.

C. Indicate the size of the difference between the two marks for each trait in the space on the right.

D. Work out the average of the differences. To do this, add up all 15 differences as indicated in the spaces on the right. Divide that number by 15. That will give you the average.

II. **Discussion**

After completing the rating scales and the calculations as directed above, write a brief response to each of the following:

A. As you look over all 15 scales, do the differences between your present status and your ideal vary greatly?

B. Which traits had the largest differences and which had the smallest?
largest: smallest:

C.   How do you feel about those traits where larger gaps exist between how you see yourself (your self-image) and where you would like to be (your self-ideal)?

D.   Do any of the larger differences exist because someone else has imposed the ideal on you? Or have you accepted someone else's idea of what you should be rather than deciding for yourself?

E.   Indicate those traits that you would like to change and feel could be changed to narrow the difference. What would you do differently?

F.   What do you think of the overall picture of yourself that you have identified? Do you see problems because of the size of the difference?

(Based on an exercise by Wayne Weiten, University of Nevada, Las Vegas.)

Handout 11.4: SELF-CONCEPT VERSUS SELF-IDEAL: RATING SCALES

1. Decisive | Indecisive | _____
    9   8   7   6   5   4   3   2   1

2. Tense | Relaxed | _____
    9   8   7   6   5   4   3   2   1

3. Easily Influenced | Independent Thinker | _____
    9   8   7   6   5   4   3   2   1

4. Very Intelligent | Not Very Intelligent | _____
    9   8   7   6   5   4   3   2   1

5. In Good Physical Shape | In Poor Phys. Shape | _____
    9   8   7   6   5   4   3   2   1

6. Undependable | Dependable | _____
    9   8   7   6   5   4   3   2   1

7. Deceitful | Honest | _____
    9   8   7   6   5   4   3   2   1

8. A Leader | A Follower | _____
    9   8   7   6   5   4   3   2   1

9. Unambitious | Ambitious | _____
    9   8   7   6   5   4   3   2   1

10. Self-confident | Insecure | _____
    9   8   7   6   5   4   3   2   1

11. Timid | Adventurous | _____
    9   8   7   6   5   4   3   2   1

12. Extroverted | Introverted | _____
    9   8   7   6   5   4   3   2   1

13. Physically Attractive | Phys. Unattractive | _____
    9   8   7   6   5   4   3   2   1

14. Lazy | Hardworking | _____
    9   8   7   6   5   4   3   2   1

15. Good Sense of Humor | Poor Sense of Humor | _____
    9   8   7   6   5   4   3   2   1

Handout 11.5: WHO AM I? RESPONSE SHEET

TO THE STUDENT:

Complete each of the 20 "I am" statements below. Complete each sentence saying something about yourself. Do not be too concerned about exactness. Say whatever you think of as it occurs to you.

1. I am_____
   _____

2. I am_____
   _____

3. I am_____
   _____

4. I am_____
   _____

5. I am_____
   _____

6. I am_____
   _____

7. I am_____
   _____

8. I am_____
   _____

9. I am_____
   _____

10. I am_____
    _____

11. I am_____
    _____

12. I am_____
    _____

13. I am_____
    _____

14. I am_____
    _____

15. I am_____
    _____

16. I am_____
    _____

17. I am_____
    _____

18. I am_____
    _____

19. I am_____
    _____

20. I am_____
    _____

419

Handout 11.5: WHO AM I? INTERPRETATION SHEET

TO THE STUDENT:

You now have a difficult job to do. You need to classify each of your statements into one of four categories below. Read over all four categories. Be sure you understand what they are. Ask your instructor if you need clarification. Put each of the item numbers under the heading that seems most appropriate based on the descriptions below:

Category 1: Physical or traditional identification—includes one's sex, age, address, religion, etc. For example, "I am a woman," "I am from New York."

Category 2: Social relationships—family, occupation, membership, etc. For example, "I am a student," "I am a middle child."

Category 3: Situation-free behavior—likes, dislikes, attitudes, etc. For example, "I am a lover of music," "I am for nuclear disarmament."

Category 4: Identity—this is how you describe yourself. You say who you are. For example, "I am a citizen of the world," "I am a living individual," "I am a person."

Place the number for each of the 20 statements in the columns below as you make your decision about which category is best.

Category 1	Category 2	Category 3	Category 4
_____	_____	_____	_____
_____	_____	_____	_____
_____	_____	_____	_____
_____	_____	_____	_____
_____	_____	_____	_____
_____	_____	_____	_____
_____	_____	_____	_____

➤ JOURNAL QUESTIONS

1. If you could divide the people of the world into three categories, what would your categories be?

2. In what ways would our society deem you to be a "good" person? What unique qualities do you have that are not recognized by our society?

3. Where do you study? What could this say about your personality?

4. What traits do you have? How are these behaviors affected by your current life situation?

5. What childhood experiences were key in the development of your personality?

6. Check off the traits (from the adjective checklist in the text) that apply to your personality. Which of these traits did you have as a child? Of the traits that have changed (strengthened or weakened) what is the reason for the change? When you are finished, ask your parent(s) to rate your current traits and your childhood traits.

7. Which part of your personality is most dominant—the id, the ego, or the superego? When? What kind of anxiety do you experience according to Freud? How would Freud categorize your personality?

8. How did your parents handle your toilet training? If you don't remember, ask one of your parents or a sibling.

9. What did your parents do to shape your personality? What did your friends do?

10. Your textbook states that, according to behaviorists, characteristics such as kindness, generosity, and honesty can be learned in the same way as other habits. Think back to your childhood and adolescence. What did your parents do to reinforce these behaviors? How did they react when you were unkind, selfish, or dishonest?

11. Think of a habit you have that you are proud of. How did it develop? How would Dollard and Miller explain this behavior?

12. Think of a habit you are not proud of. What cues could you try to pay attention to as a way to change this behavior?

13. Think of someone from your childhood who provided you with inconsistent affection or responsiveness. How did that affect the person's "reinforcement value" and your behavior?

14. What "conditions of worth" were applied to you as a child?

15.   What are you willing to change in your life? What are you not willing to change, at least not now?

16.   How self-actualized do you feel you are? Using a one- through seven-point scale, rate the degree to which the 10 characteristics of self-actualizers seem to apply to you.

17.   To what extent do you consider yourself shy? How has this part of your personality developed? Under what circumstances do you feel more or less shy? Are you more publicly or privately self-conscious?

➤ SUGGESTIONS FOR FURTHER READING

Adler, A. (1929). *The science of living*. Garden City, NY: Doubleday.

Allport, G. W. (1961). *Pattern and growth in personality*. New York: Holt.

Ashcraft, D. (2009). *Personality theories workbook* (4th ed.). Belmont, CA: Wadsworth.

Ashton, M. C. (2007). *Individual differences and personality*. San Diego: Elsevier.

Bandura, A. (2001). Social cognitive theory: An agentic perspective. *Annual Review of Psychology, 52,* 1–26.

Bauer, J. J., McAdams, D. P., & Pals, J. L. (2008). Narrative identity and eudaimonic well-being. *Journal of Happiness Studies, 9*(1), 81–104.

Canfield, J. W. (1990). *The looking-glass self: An examination of self-awareness*. New York: Praeger.

Cattell, R. B. (1965/2009). *The scientific analysis of personality*. Piscataway, NJ: Aldine Transaction, 2009.

Corey, G. & Corey, M. S. (2010). *I never knew I had a choice: Explorations in personal growth* (9th ed.). Belmont, CA: Cengage Learning/Wadsworth.

Engler, B. (2009). *Personality theories* (5th ed.). Belmont, CA: Cengage Learning/Wadsworth.

Freud, S. (1949/2003). *An outline of psychoanalysis*. New York: Penguin Classics, 2003.

Jacobs, M. (2003). *Sigmund Freud*. Thousand Oaks, CA: Sage.

Kagan, J. (1989). Temperamental contributions to social behavior. *American Psychologist, 44*. 668-674.

Kammrath, L. K., Mendoza-Denton, R., & Mischel, W. (2005). Incorporating I f...Then...personality signatures in person perception: Beyond the person-situation dichotomy. *Journal of Personality & Social Psychology*, 88(4), 605-618.

Maddi, S. R. (2001). *Personality theories: A comparative analysis* (6th ed.). Belmont, CA: Brooks/Cole.

Mehrabian, A., & Friedman, S. (1986). An analysis of fidgeting and associated individual differences. *Journal of Personality*, *54*(2), 407-429.

Olds, L. E. (1981). *Fully human*. Englewood Cliffs, NJ: Prentice-Hall.

Pervin, L. A., Cervone, D., & John, O. P. (2005). *Personality: Theory and research* (9th ed.). Hoboken, NJ: Wiley.

Schultz, D. P., & Schultz, S. E. (2009). *Theories of personality* (9th ed.). Belmont, CA: Cengage Learning/Wadsworth.

Triandis, H. C., & Suh, E. M. (2002). Cultural influences on personality. *Annual Review of Psychology, 53,* 133–160.

Urbina, S. (2004). *Essentials of psychological testing*. New York: Wiley.

Zimbardo, P. G. (1990). *Shyness: what it is, what to do about it*. New York: Perseus Press.

Zurcher, L. A. (1977). *The mutable self,* Thousand Oaks, CA: Sage.

➤ VIDEO SUGGESTIONS

Feature Films

Proof of Life (Meg Ryan, Russell Crowe, David Morse), Drama. Alice (Ryan), whose marriage is in trouble, finds herself falling for a new man as Peter (Morse), her husband's, life is in danger. Terry (Crowe) is hired to rescue Peter from the radical Marxist faction gearing up for a revolution in Tecala. Alice and Terry work closely together to rescue her husband but at the same time Alice is having new feelings for Terry. A film that raises many issues related to personality and social relationships.

Schindler's List (Liam Neeson, Ralph Fiennes), Drama. Liam Neeson plays a shrewd German businessman who startles everyone—including himself—when he begins trying to save Jews during WWII.

Twins (Danny DeVito, Arnold Schwarzenegger), Comedy. Twin brothers, hardly identical, are separated at birth. One is raised on an island with the perfect environment; the other is left in New York to survive. When each discovers the other exists, they reunite and set off on a comic adventure in search of their mother.

Freud (Montgomery Clift), Biographical Drama. Biography of the early days of Freud starring Montgomery Clift as Sigmund Freud. Some good background information here, and certainly much material for discussion and analysis.

Educational Films and Videos

Albert Bandura, (1988), Insight Media, 28 min. In this interview with social learning theorist Albert Bandura, he compares his approach to the study of personality with other significant approaches. In Part I, he describes what influenced the development of his theories and research. He also discusses behavior modification, social learning, modeling, and aggression. In Part II, he discusses his classic Bobo doll experiment, as well as morality and moral disengagement and the effects of aggression and violence in the media.

Being Abraham Maslow, (1972), Filmmakers Library, 30 min. This older film presents a sensitive interview with Maslow by Warren Bennis of the University of Cincinnati. Maslow discusses his humanistic theory and the factors that shaped his life and ideas. He also provides reasons for rejecting Freud's view of our need to repress instincts and rejects the behaviorists' position that our actions are simply responses to environmental stimuli. He describes his goal of trying to develop a more humanistic attitude in psychology.

Birth Order and Its Effects, (1997), Films for the Humanities and Sciences, 18 min. Heredity, environment, intelligence, and family birth order all help shape the personality throughout the formative years and into adulthood. Each position in a family can influence how a child interacts with other family members and friends. This program examines the only child, the firstborn, the middle child, and the youngest child, giving insight into behaviors and attitudes that seem to be shaped by birth order.

Body Doubles: The Twin Experience, (1997), Films for the Humanities and Sciences, 51 min. The study of twins is vital to research in biology and psychology. Twins separated at birth and later reunited are often quite similar. This similarity begs the notion that personality is formed by experience and suggests that personality is genetically predetermined. This brilliant HBO documentary—with powerful interviews with numerous twins, including those conjoined, and a history of twin research from Josef Mengele to the University of Minnesota Twin Research Center—offers vehement arguments for and against this idea.

Carl Rogers Interviews Phillip, (1981), Insight Media, 45 min. This video features a session in which Carl Rogers interviews a client, Phillip, who wants to get in touch with his feelings and blames his lack of maturity for his anxieties.

Conscience of a Child, Indiana University, 30 min.

Discussion with Dr. Carl Jung, (1968), Pennsylvania State University, 36 min. In this film Jung talks about his theories of personality and discusses his differences with Freud and Freudian psychoanalysis.

Freud Under Analysis, (1987), WGBH/NOVA, 58 min. This video, which was produced by WGBH for the *NOVA series*, provides a superior review of the psychodynamic theory of Sigmund Freud. In addition to describing the major tenants of Freud's approach (e.g., the id, ego, super ego, psychosexual stages, and defense mechanisms), the video has actual footage of Freud in his famous office.

Freud: The Hidden Nature of Man, University of Illinois, 29 min.

Maslow and Self-Actualization (Parts I and II) Psychological Films, 30 min. each. Maslow discusses themes of honesty and awareness in Part I and of freedom and trust in Part II.

Outstanding Contributors to the Psychology of Personality Series. Pennsylvania State University, 50 min. each. Interviews with well-known personality theorists. Films appropriate for this chapter cover Gordon Allport and Raymond Cattell.

Personality, CRM/McGraw-Hill, 30 min.

Personality, (2002), from *Psychology: The Study of Human Behavior*, Coast Community College Telecourses, 30. min. This video introduces major theories of personality.

Personality, (1990), Insight Media, 30 min. Psychoanalytic, humanistic, behavioral, and social-learning approaches to personality are presented in this video. Also addressed are the "big five" factors of personality.

Personality Theories, (2002), from *Psychology: The Human Experience Series,* Coast Community College District, 30. min. This video explores the three major theories of personality: Freudian, humanistic, and social-cognitive perspective—by examining the life of the former president of South Africa, Nelson Mandela.

Personality Traits and Assessment, (2002), from *Psychology: The Human Experience Series,* Coast Community College Telecourses, 30. min. This video looks at the ways we can evaluate and assess the many parts of our individual personalities.

Reactions to Psychoanalytic Concepts, (1982), Karol Media, 30 min. In this film Rollo May discusses his reactions to the ideas of Sigmund Freud, Otto Rank, Harry Stack Sullivan, Alfred Adler, and Alan Watts.

Reflections: Carl Rogers, American Association for Counseling and Development, 59 min.

Sigmund Freud, (1995), Insight Media, 50 min. This video examines the life and work of Sigmund Freud, from his boyhood to his medical training to the development of his theories. It discusses his studies of hypnosis with Jean Charcot and his collaboration with Joseph Breuer on the case of Anna O. The program examines Freud's development of the concept of transference, and explains how through self-analysis he discovered the value of dream analysis and free association. It also explores his collaboration and conflict with C.G. Jung and his theories of drives and the Oedipus complex.

Sigmund Freud: His Offices and Home, Vienna, 1938, (1974), Filmmakers Library, 17 min. This film presents a behind-the-scenes look at the private world of Sigmund Freud. Through the use of rare photographs taken by Edmund Engleman in 1938, we are introduced to the man and the therapist. Eli Wallach narrates. By examining his home, office, and antiquities, students of psychology can gain insight into the famous Dr. Freud. This film is well worth the time.

The Humanistic Revolution: Pioneers in Perspective, Psychological Films, 32 min.

The Interpretation of Dreams, (1996), Films for the Humanities and Sciences, 52 min. Few figures have had so decisive an influence on modern cultural history as Sigmund Freud, psychology's grand theorist—yet few figures have also inspired such sustained controversy and intense debate. In this program, Freud historian Peter Swales; Freudian psychoanalyst Barbara Jones; Peter Kramer, author of *Listening to Prozac;* and others analyze *The Interpretation of Dreams,* the concepts it contains, and the growing movement to reject them. Biographical details, dramatizations of Freud at work, and archival footage and photos add a personal dimension. A Discovery Channel production.

The Psychology of Jung, (1991), Films for the Humanities and Sciences, 60 min. each, #5 is 90 min. This five-part series provides a thorough examination of the life and work of Carl Jung, including the sources and themes of Jungian psychology. Evocative dream recreations provide an additional avenue of access to Jung's work. Programs include: (1) *Passions of the Soul,* (2) *Carl Gustav Jung: An Introduction,* (3) *Mind and Matter,* (4) *Symbols and Symbolism,* and (5) *Self-Knowledge.*

The Self, Discovering Psychology episode 15, (1990), Annenberg/CPB, 28 min. Phillip Zimbardo examines how perspectives on the self have varied throughout the history of psychology, beginning with William James' view of three aspects of self and Sigmund Freud's id, ego, and superego, followed by Rogers, Bandura, Snyder, Adler, and more.

The Story of Carl Gustav Jung, (2000), Films for the Humanities & Sciences, 93 min. This three-part series from the BBC archives explores the life and work of Carl Jung. Part One, *In Search of the Soul,* explores how Jung developed his pagan vision of reality, and how he attempted to reconcile science and religion. Part Two is *67,000 Dreams,* in which his search for the root of his conflict with Freud and his development of the concept of the collective unconscious are outlined. Part Three, *Mystery That Heals,* has a psychiatrist talking about how Jung's ideas are used in therapy.

426

The World Within, (1990), Insight Media, 60 min. This video offers a tour-de-force of the philosophy and life of Carl Jung. Some of the more memorable moments include Jung's discussion of his ideas concerning dreams, archetypes, and memory.

Theories of Personality, (1994), Insight Media, 20 min. Interviewing clinical and research psychologists, this video examines five theories of personality, and is an excellent adjunct to any coverage of personality. The subjects: psychoanalytic (Freud, Jung, Erikson, Adler), humanistic (Maslow, May, Rogers), social-learning (Pavlov, Thorndike, Bandura, Skinner), cognitive (Kelly), and trait (Allport, Cattell, Eysenck). It explores relative emphases and considers whether or not personality is stable over time.

Young Dr. Freud, (1980), Films for the Humanities and Sciences, 99 min. This docudrama is an introduction to Freud's work and explores the influences that made Freud what he was: the effects of alienation, of medical studies, which he neither enjoyed nor mastered, and of his discovery of a subject area in which he could make a unique contribution. Also discussed are the men who shaped his ideas: Breuer, Charcot, Janet, and Fliess as well as some of the famous cases, such as that of Anna O.

➢ COMPUTER AND INTERNET RESOURCES

PsykTrek 3.0
Unit 11: Personality Theory
11a. "Freudian Theory"
11b. "Behavioral Theory"
11c. "Humanistic Theory"
11d. "Biological Theory"

INFOTRAC®

Below you will find two journal articles obtained from INFOTRAC® that relate to information contained in this chapter. Instructors should encourage students to utilize this invaluable resource to improve their research skills. Have students locate and read the following articles and answer questions relevant to each article.

Personality & Social Psychology Bulletin, July 1998 v24 n7 p750 (9) **Diamonds in the rough: Implicit personality theories and views of partner and self.**

1. Dweck and Leggett (1988) identify two main types of implicit personality theories that individuals hold. What are they?

    Answer: Entity theorists are those who believe that people's attributes are relatively fixed and unchangeable. Incremental theorists, on the other hand, believe that attributes are malleable and can be improved. These implicit theories affect individuals' goal orientations in various situations. For example, entity theorists may see social or performance situations as an avenue for evaluating their abilities, whereas incremental theorists may see performance situations as opportunities for improving their abilities.

427

2. The current study extends current implicit theory research in what new direction?

Answer: The current study suggests that implicit personality theories will also have implications for the extent to which individuals' views of themselves and their close relationship partners predict their overall well-being and satisfaction with their relationships. Instead of categorizing people as incremental theorists or entity theorists, the researchers in this study assess where individuals' beliefs fall along a continuum ranging from high malleability beliefs (analogous to an incremental theory) to low malleability beliefs (analogous to an entity theory).

3. What were the two primary hypotheses of this study?

Answer: The **first** hypothesis is that the stronger the individuals' malleability beliefs are, the weaker the relationship between views of the partner and relationship well-being will be; in other words, if the individual thinks that the partner's characteristics may change, negative characteristics may not be as distressing, and positive characteristics may not be as beneficial as if the individual thinks that they are permanent. The **second** hypothesis is that the stronger the individuals' incremental beliefs are, the weaker the relationship between views of self and general well-being will be.

4. This study found that implicit personality theories moderated two important associations. What two associations or relationships do the researchers discuss?

Answer: The **first relationship** was the one between perceptions of partner and relationship quality. Implicit theories moderated this relationship; the relationship between perceptions of partner and relationship quality was weaker for those with strong beliefs about the malleability of traits (those who could be labeled incremental theorists) than for those with low malleability beliefs (those who could be labeled entity theorists). Even if the partner is perceived as having negative characteristics, these characteristics may not bother the individual as much if the individual believes that the partner's characteristics may change. If the partner is seen in a positive light, this may not be as satisfying to the individual if he or she thinks that the partner might change. **Second,** implicit personality theories also moderated the association between perceptions of oneself and overall well-being. In this study, the stronger the individual's malleability beliefs were, the weaker was the relationship between self-perceptions and overall well-being.

5. Were there also main effects in this study?

Answer: Yes, there were main effects of views of self or partner on both relationship quality and general well-being. In other words, at average levels of malleability beliefs, the more negatively people viewed their partners or themselves, the lower their relationship quality or general well-being was.

428

Sex Roles: A Journal of Research, December 2001 p767 (18) **Sexual harassment in the workplace: Exploring the effects of attractiveness on perception of harassment.**

1.   What was the above study designed to explore?

   Answer: This study was designed to explore the effect of attractiveness on perceptions of sexual harassment.

2.   According to this study, what two ways might attractiveness influence the interpretation of a behavior as sexual harassment?

   Answer: One way is that a potential harasser's attractiveness could lead to the inference that this person has positive qualities, leading to the assumption that this person is not likely to engage in a socially undesirable behavior. A second way attractiveness might influence the interpretation of the behavior is through a more direct effect of the attractiveness stereotype.

3.   What were the results of the study? Explain.

   Answer: The results of this study were quite clear in documenting an effect of appearance cues on perceptions of sexual harassment. Ambiguous behaviors were more likely to be perceived as instances of sexual harassment when the potential female victim was more attractive and when the potential male harasser was less attractive. The effect of the attractiveness of the female target of harassment was particularly strong, influencing ratings more than the attractiveness of the male harasser. The interaction between an attractive male and an unattractive female was least likely to be perceived as sexual harassment. This was true for both male and female raters. Overall, females were more likely than males to rate a behavior as sexual harassment.

WEB LINKS

Knowledge Builder Links

1. Overview of Personality
   Personality Theories: http://www.ship.edu/~cgboeree/perscontents.html
   The Personality Project: http://www.personality-project.org/
   Personality: Theory & Perspectives:
        http://www.wilderdom.com/personality/personality.html

2. Trait Theories
   Raymond Cattell: http://www.indiana.edu/~intell/rcattell.shtml
   Internet Personality Inventory: http://test.personality-project.org/
   The Big Five Dimensions: http://www.outofservice.com/bigfive/

3. Psychoanalytic Theory

The Freud Archives: http://users.rcn.com/brill/freudarc.html

Freud and Women: http://psychology.about.com/od/sigmundfreud/p/freud_women.htm

Psychodynamic and Neo-Freudian Theories:
http://allpsych.com/personalitysynopsis/psychodynamic.html

4. Behavioral and Social Learning Theories

Julian Rotter: http://psych.fullerton.edu/jmearns/rotter.htm

Information on Self-Efficacy: http://www.des.emory.edu/mfp/BanEncy.html

Controlling Your Own Study Behavior:
http://www.coun.uvic.ca/learning/motivation/self-reinforcement.html

5. Humanistic Theories

About Humanistic Psychology: http://www.ahpweb.org/aboutahp/whatis.html

Maslow's Hierarchy of Needs: http://chiron.valdosta.edu/whuitt/col/regsys/maslow.html

Some Observations on the Organization of Personality:
http://psychclassics.yorku.ca/Rogers/personality.htm

6. Personality Assessment

Personality and IQ tests: http://www.2h.com/

The MMPI: http://www.pearsonassessments.com/tests/mmpi_2.htm

The Classic Rorschach: http://www.rorschach.org/

7. Psychology in Action

The Shyness Homepage: http://www.shyness.com/

Shake Your Shyness: http://www.shyness.com/

Additional Web Links

APA Online
http://www.apa.org/

Freud—Personal History and Works
http://en.wikipedia.org/wiki/Sigmund_Freud
http://www.freudfile.org/
http://www.richardwebster.net/freudandcharcot.html
http://en.wikipedia.org/wiki/Anna_Freud
http://users.rcn.com/brill/freudarc.html

MMPI
http://psychology.about.com/od/psychologicaltesting/a/mmpi.htm
http://en.wikipedia.org/wiki/Minnesota_Multiphasic_Personality_Inventory

Personality
http://keirsey.com/
http://www.personality-project.org/
http://www.personalityresearch.org/

Personality Tests (For fun only!)
http://www.2h.com/personality-tests.html

Research, Books, and Journals
http://www.questia.com/Index.jsp?CRID=personality_disorders&OFFID=se1&KEY=personality
_disorders

Projective Testing
http://psychology.about.com/od/psychologicaltesting/a/mmpi.htm
http://images.search.yahoo.com/search/images?_adv_prop=images&imgsz=all&imgc=&vf=all&
va=thematic+apperception+test&fr=yfp-t-405&ei=UTF-8

PSYCHOLOGY IN THE NEWS

ABC NEWS: Personality, Not Values Make the Marriage
http://abcnews.go.com/Health/
Search ABC News for related articles.

BBC News
http://news.bbc.co.uk/2/hi/science/nature/1348871.stm
You can search BBC News online for articles related to personality and other issues.

Dr.'s Grohol's Psych Central
http://psychcentral.com/resources/Psychology/Newsgroups/
This site provides reliable and free mental health, support, and psychology information and
newsgroups where you can search by topic.

Plebius Press Psychology Resource Center
http://psychology.plebius.org/
Plebius Press Psychology Resource Center allows you to search by topic and locate interesting
links and articles related to personality.

New Scientist Breaking News
http://www.newscientist.com/article.ns?id=dn3713
This free e-zine brings you the hottest stories from NewScientist.com; you can also receive free
NewScientist.com newsflashes to alert you to breaking news stories.

CHAPTER 12

Health, Stress, and Coping

Journal Questions
Suggestions for Further Reading
Video Suggestions
Computer and Internet Resources

➤ SURVEY QUESTIONS

Module 12.1 Health Psychology

Survey Questions: What is health psychology? How does behavior affect health?

Module 12.2 Stress, Frustration, and Conflict

Survey Questions: What is stress? What factors determine its severity?

Survey Question: What causes frustration and what are typical reactions to it?

Survey Questions: Are there different types of conflict? How do people react to conflict?

Module 12.3 Defenses, Helplessness, and Depression

Survey Question: What are defense mechanisms?

Survey Question: What do we know about coping with feelings of helplessness and depression?

Module 12.4 Stress and Health

Survey Question: How is stress related to health and disease?

Module 12.5 Psychology in Action

Survey Question: What are the best strategies for managing stress?

➢ DISCUSSION QUESTIONS

1. Which of your current unhealthy behaviors do you think are going to most negatively impact your health as you grow older? At what age do you think your bad habits will "catch up with you"?

2. Why do you think people engage in behaviors that they know are unhealthy? What are the things that reinforce the undesirable behaviors? How might we as a society better reinforce alternative positive behaviors?

3. How could you reduce conflict or avoid an unfortunate decision in the following situations: choosing a school to attend, choosing a major, deciding about marriage, choosing a job, buying a car?

4. What do you consider the most prominent sources of stress in our society? What do you think should or could be done to combat these stresses?

5. What would it be like to have no stress in your life? Imagine switching places with a well-fed, pampered house cat. Would that appeal to you? What distinguished eustress from negative stress? What are some of the things you do that intentionally bring stress into your life?

6. Over a decade ago, journalist Alvin Toffler predicted that large numbers of people would become victims of "future shock." According to Toffler, future shock is a condition of shattering stress and disorientation brought on by overly rapid social change. In your view, is there any truth to the idea that we are "future-shocked" or that we may be in the near future?

7. When you are confronted with a stressor, do you most typically respond to it as a threat or as a challenge? Name a recent stressor that you viewed as a threat and re-examine it as a challenge instead. How difficult was that to do? How did it make you feel?

8. How would you integrate the concept of problem-focused coping and emotion-focused coping into the process of making a decision? What should you do first, second, and third to cope with stress?

9. What do you do when you feel frustrated?

10. How should you go about deciding which stressors you can and cannot control?

11. Explain why you agree or disagree with the following statement (attributed to the famous Professor P. T. Barnum, of Barnum and Bailey Circus): "Television is the opiate of the people. If all the TV tubes in the United States suddenly went blank, the mental health of the nation would crumble because people could no longer escape their problems by watching television."

12. How could you best deal with the following sources of frustration: delays, losses, lack of resources, failure, and rejection?

13. Many people report becoming extremely frustrated as they learn to use a computer or learn a foreign language. Why? In what way can this frustration be explained by the concepts of stress?

14. Which type of conflict do you encounter most in your daily life (i.e., approach-approach, approach-avoidance, or avoidance-avoidance)? Which type of conflict is the most stressful and why? What are some of the behaviors that people engage in when they are faced with avoidance-avoidance behavior?

15. Acts of racial and religious prejudice have increased in frequency over the last few years. Why?

16. The defense mechanisms listed in this chapter were described in psychodynamic terms, that is, in terms of the balance of forces within the personality. Can you advance a learning theory explanation for any of the defenses? (Hint: Think in terms of avoidance learning and the rewards connected with defensive responses.)

17. What are the advantages and disadvantages of using defense mechanisms? Do you think it would be possible for a person to be completely free of defense mechanisms?

18. In what ways do schools, parents, and the government encourage feelings of helplessness? In what ways do they (or could they) add to feelings of confidence, competence, or "hope"?

19. Calculate your life change score using the Social Readjustment Rating Scale (SRRS). (http://chipts.ucla.edu/assessment/Assessment_Instruments/Assessment_files_new/assess _srrs.htm). If your score is elevated, what could you do to reduce the chances of illness? If it is low, what could you do to put more excitement in your life? Can you see any relationship between periods of illness you have had and the number of life changes or hassles that preceded them?

20. Some state lottery winners have reported that their life is more stressful after winning the money. Why? How?

21. What is the SRRS? What does it measure? In what ways has this instrument been criticized? In what way is the instrument biased? How would you go about developing a more "accurate" predictor of illness?

436

22. Describe the principles of biofeedback. How effective is biofeedback? Why? For what kind of problems would biofeedback be most effective?

23. What are the advantages and disadvantages of being a Type A person? What is a Type B person like? How are these two personalities similar to and different from the "hardy" personality?

24. In view of the relationship between smoking and health, should the government continue to give a large yearly subsidy to tobacco growers? Why or why not?

25. Why do you think the relationship between behavioral risk factors and health is so widely ignored? How important is health to you? How do your acquaintances rationalize their unhealthy behaviors? How do you?

26. Why do support groups help people deal with the elements of burnout? How do support groups help people reduce stress?

27. How might stress be related to the recent increase in murders committed by students and employees in schools and offices?

➤ LECTURE ENHANCEMENTS

1. **Design an anti-smoking campaign**. Design an anti-smoking campaign for teenagers. Break students into small groups and have them list the ways a school could help prevent the onset of smoking. Teams should specify the age group that is targeted and design the message to appeal to that age group. The campaign should address multiple aspects of students' lives (e.g., cognitive, behavioral, and emotional) and should also take into account all sources of influence.

2. **Stress and disease**. (Internet exercise) Have students choose a disease and research its relationship to stress. They should be able to find a wealth of information by entering the keywords "stress" and "their specific disease." They should choose reputable websites, and should report back to the class any interesting findings. Encourage them to research diseases that are not immediately obvious. A good starting point might be to use a disease that is affecting a family member or friend.

3. **Rank your job stress**. Ask students to decide which of the top 10 work stressors described in the text most affects them. Ask for a show of hands for each item and record the results on the board. When you are finished, ask them to estimate what the biggest stressor is for their parent(s) or caregiver. Does the ranking of the stress change as we move through our careers?

437

4. **This is frustrating!** Although everyone has plenty of experience with frustration and can provide numerous examples, creating a little frustration in class can dramatize the subject and encourage discussion. The music department on your campus may own a device called an Echoplex (or a similar device). Internally it has a continuous tape loop that allows auditory input to be delayed for short time intervals for replay. You will also need a microphone, a small amplifier, and a speaker. Connect and adjust the equipment so that a word spoken into the microphone is heard from the speaker with a delay of about one-half second. The resultant delayed auditory feedback makes it virtually impossible to speak into the microphone without tremendous interference and frustration. (This effect is similar to the interference caused by the echo of a poor public-address system in a large auditorium.) Invite a student to the front of the class and ask him/her to tell the class some things about him/herself (college major, interests, what he or she has been doing for the last few days, etc.). The speaker should speak into the microphone, and the speaker volume should be as loud as, or slightly louder than, his/her voice. Under these conditions, the speaker will stutter, stammer, and become thoroughly frustrated. Allow the tension to build and then interview the student about the frustration experience.

5. **The "Hassles and Uplifts Scale."** The scale shown here can be completed by students individually. Either a class discussion can take place or students can be encouraged to share the details of their hassles and uplifts in small groups. (Note: The questionnaire is similar to the ideas of Delongis, Folman, and Lazarus, published in the *Journal of Personality and Social Psychology,* 1988, Vol. 34(3), 486-495.

Hassles and Uplifts Scale

Hassles are things that annoy or bother a person. **Uplifts** are events that are pleasurable or satisfying. Sometimes an event is only a hassle OR only an uplift; sometimes the event can be both a hassle AND an uplift. Complete this questionnaire at the end of the day just before bed. Think of the extent to which each event of the day was a hassle AND/OR an uplift. Write the number to the left to describe the degree to which it was a hassle; write the number to the right to describe to what extent the event was an uplift.

For both scales: 0 = not at all 1 = somewhat 2 = quite a bit 3 = to a great extent

HASSLE   UPLIFT

_____   1. Your child/children

_____   2. Other relatives

_____   3. Your spouse or significant other

_____   4. Sexual expression

_____   5. Your friends

_____   6. Your fellow workers or your work

_____   7. Enough money for necessities

_____   8. Enough money for recreation

_____   9. Your smoking or drinking habits

_____   10. Your health or physical appearance

_____   11. The air quality or noise of your environment

_____   12. Political or social issues

_____   13. Housework and/or yardwork

_____   14. Debts or investments

_____   15. Taxes and legal matters

                                            TOTAL

Add up the points in the "hassle" column. Add up the points in the "uplift" column. Subtract the hassle total from the uplift total. Compare your answer to the answer of others in your class. What does this score tell you about the quantity of stress in your life? What does it tell you about the specific source of most of your stress? What can you do to reduce the hassles in your life? What if you don't have many hassles but you don't have many uplifts either? What, if anything, should you do?

6.   **Those darned carnival games!** Obtain a large narrow-mouthed jar. You will also need two metal rods about three-sixteenths of an inch in diameter and 18 inches long. (These may be obtained at most hardware stores; welding rods also will work well.) Place a marble or ball-bearing in the bottom of the jar. In class, ask if someone would like to play a game. Tell the volunteer that he/she has one minute to use the metal rods to lift the ball out of the jar. The jar may not be picked up or touched; the lifting must be done directly with the rods. To make things more interesting you might offer to add five points to the student's last test score for succeeding within the time limit. Be sure to test the task first before using it in class. If the dimensions are right, it hovers right on the edge of possibility—and is devilishly frustrating. Discussion can clarify conditions under which frustration is likely to occur.

7.   **Approach-avoidance and your grades.** To introduce the topic of conflict, it might again be valuable to create a little conflict in class. Ask if someone would like to play a "game of chance" with you. Tell the volunteer that you are going to flip a coin. If it comes up heads, three extra points will be added to the student's last test score. If it is tails, five points will be

subtracted from the last test score. Give the student a few moments to decide if he/she still wants to play. Then discuss the approach-avoidance conflict that has been created.

If the student declines or wins, ask if anyone else wants to play. Tell this volunteer that he/she must guess if heads or tails will appear when you flip the coin. If he/she guesses wrong, five points will be deducted from his or her last test score; if he/she guesses right, three points will be deducted. When the student says he/she does not want to play, tell him/her that choosing not to play will result in 10 points being subtracted from his or her last test score. This should produce a good spontaneous display of emotion. Force the choice and discuss the conflict created (avoidance-avoidance). After demonstrations such as these, it is probably best to announce that three points will be added to each volunteer's grade for class participation and that the supposed effects of their decisions will be ignored.

8. **Life Change Scale for students.** One of the limits of the Social Readjustment Rating Scale (http://chipts.ucla.edu/assessment/Assessment_Instruments/Assessment_files_new/assess _srrs.htm) is that many of the changes listed (such are death of spouse or divorce) are unlikely to affect college students. Ask students to complete the College Life Stress Inventory in the text and submit their totals anonymously. List the totals on the board. Then, have students share some of the strategies they use to deal with school-related stress.

Alternately, distribute copies of the College Life Stress Inventory and have students hand in their completed survey anonymously. Tabulate the five most frequent stressors and then brainstorm a list of ways to deal with those stressors.

9. **Type A, type B, and goals.** Type A personality characteristics can be illustrated in this way: Give each student three pages completely covered with random digits. (These can be duplicated from a table of random numbers.) Tell students that their task is to cross out as many single, odd digits as they can after you say, "Begin." Start students and let them work for 30 seconds. Have students count the number of digits crossed out. Announce that students will get a second try at the task, and have each student write down his or her goal for the second trial. Give the class 30 seconds to work. Students should again record their scores and set a goal for the third test. This completes the demonstration, since it is not necessary to conduct the third test; the point of this exercise is the goal-setting.

On the board make a distribution of the number of digits students set as a goal for the third test. Research has shown that on similar tasks Type As and Type Bs do not differ on average performance. However, Type As consistently set higher goals than Type Bs. This pattern of goal-setting seems to reflect the Type As preference for a rapid pace of activity. Students whose announced goals were at the top of the distribution are presumably Type As; those at the bottom, Type Bs. (Based on B. R. Snow. "Level of Aspiration in Coronary Prone and Non-Coronary Prone Adults." *Personality and Social Psychology Bulletin.* 1978, 4, 416-419.

440

➤ ROLE-PLAYING SCENARIOS

1. **Attitude inoculation.** One strategy that is used to prevent teens from falling victim to peer pressure is attitude inoculation. Teens are given a chance to practice refusal techniques so that they can subsequently withstand pressure to smoke, drink, use drugs, have unsafe sex, or engage in dangerous behaviors. Break students into groups of three or four and let them practice refusal techniques on four different issues. Students can alternate being the refuser or being a member of the peer group. Have students assess their attitudes before and after this exercise.

2. **Act out a scene of emotion-focused coping.** Contrast it with an "instant replay" done using problem-focused coping. Issues to be enacted could include: spousal disagreement over money or children, dealing with spending too much money, caught in a traffic jam, preparing to give a speech.

3. **Ask each student to describe a conflict he/she is dealing with at the moment.** Ask two others to play the two forces that are literally pushing and pulling the person in two different directions. As a trio, ask students to discuss the feelings that result from conflicts.

4. **Role-play being hassled by a teacher, a student, a parent, a child, and a boss.** What strategies should a person use for dealing with hassles?

5. **Have students try the following:**

    a. Role-play being a person who is homeless, who rents an apartment, who owns a condo, who owns a home, and who is an affluent public figure. How do each of these people feel "caught" by their economic circumstances?

    b. In what ways do the following people feel "caught" by their social circumstances: a person in a marriage of 10 years, a person who is single (with no children), a single parent, a divorcee (with no children), and a divorcee with two children and a joint custody agreement?

    c. In what ways do the following people feel "caught" by their physical circumstances: very tall person, a very small person, a person with a physical impairment, a person lacking intellectual skills, and a person lacking emotional stability?

6. **Role-play a Type A talking to a Type A, a Type A to a Type B, a Type A to a hardy personality, and a Type B to a hardy personality.** Which conversation was the most frustrating? Why?

7. **Ask students to write a list of difficult situations to deal with (cheating, stealing, tax evasion, participating in gossip, and so forth).** Ask students to role-play "refusal" behaviors.

8. **You are a student government leader who wants to develop a campus-wide health campaign.** What specific behaviors do you want to change? How would you go about doing it?

➤ VALUE-CLARIFICATION STATEMENTS

1. Our society is no more stressful than society was a hundred years ago.

2. I would avoid entering an occupation that has a high rate of burn-out.

3. There's not a lot you can do to escape the stresses of urban life.

4. I either get sick or don't get sick as a matter of chance; it doesn't make much difference whether I practice healthy behaviors or not.

5. When a person is frustrated, he/she should act on the anger in a constructive way.

6. If I just had more money, my life would be less stressful.

7. When people feel depressed, they need to just "shake it off."

8. People who repress their anger eventually explode.

9. Public elementary schools tend to encourage feelings of helplessness in many students.

10. Most of the stress of college life can be avoided with good study habits and time-management techniques.

11. It is difficult to succeed in today's society unless one becomes a Type A personality.

12. In terms of achieving goals, it's everyone for themselves.

13. Cigarettes should be illegal.

14. The drinking age should be raised to 25.

442

➢ ONE-MINUTE MOTIVATORS

1. **Your bad habits**. Ask students to rank their top five bad habits using the chart in the text, with #1 being their biggest issue. Beside each behavior, ask students to indicate how much they are motivated to change that behavior, with zero being "not at all" and five being "very much." Discuss the results either orally or after tallying the results on paper.

2. **Unpredictability and stress.** Suddenly give students a pop quiz or lecture very rapidly. They will quickly tell you that the quiz isn't fair or to speak more slowly. Begin talking about stress.

3. **Poverty and helplessness.** Poverty is the norm in many cultures, and it is a continuing problem in the U.S. Discuss the helplessness that occurs with poverty. How do the poor feel? What can be done to help each of us feel less helpless in dealing with poverty?

4. **Stress and perception.** Ask students how many would be excited to receive a "C" in this class, to weigh 140 pounds, to receive $20,000 as a full-time salary, and so forth. Some would be excited and pleased; others will be disappointed. Discuss primary appraisal.

5. **Primary appraisal.** Ask students to interview each other, making a list of activities found to be "boring," "relaxing," "fun," and "stressful." Most likely many activities will be listed in different categories by different people. Discuss perceptual differences in primary appraisal.

6. **Reacting to frustration.** Create a list of typical stressful or frustrating situations and ask students—either aloud or on paper— how they react. For each reaction, ask them if there is an alternative way to handle the situation that might be less likely to increase the stress they already feel. Examples include: being stuck in slow-moving traffic, losing a parking spot in the student lot, getting into a disagreement with friends or family, being "broke," doing poorly on an exam, or losing a job. Some students will respond to these stressors by taking direct action to correct the problem or compensate for it. Others will sulk, become aggressive or manipulative, or engage in unhealthy or impulsive behaviors. Others will "sublimate" their stress into exercise, or will use distraction. Discuss the pros and cons of these various approaches.

7. **Acting out frustration.** Put students in groups of six. One person stands in the middle. The other five put their arms around the waists of the people on either side. The person in the center has one minute to break out of the circle. Count backward for the final 10 seconds. Usually you will see students increase the vigor of their attempts during the last few seconds. Caution students against expressing their frustration aggressively.

8. **Displaced aggression.** Use a pillow to be the recipient of displaced aggression. Ask students to think of someone they're angry at while briefly pounding the pillow. Do they feel better? Why or why not? Discuss Freud's concept of catharsis. Research does not support this theory. Why not?

9. **Reducing stress.** Have students brainstorm a list of the positive ways they cope with the stress of school and exams, and the negative ways they cope. Encourage them to include both direct and indirect behavior, and also to look at their social context.

10. **Coping with "the blues."** Everyone experiences "the blues" from time to time, often in response to environmental stressors. How we respond influences how long we will feel "down" and might even influence whether or not full-blown clinical depression will develop. Ask students to indicate, either one-by-one or in rank order, their most likely responses to feeling blue. Possibilities include: eating *healthy* comfort foods, eating *unhealthy* comfort foods, exercising, "vegging," sleeping, crying, sulking, analyzing, talking, seeking out others, avoiding others, engaging in comfort behaviors (e.g., a hot bath), meditating, or taking it out on objects or other people (verbally or behaviorally).

11. **I meant to, but…** Have students help you make a list of humorous rationalizations for not having done their homework. Discuss the value and costs of rationalization and other defenses.

12. **Using alcohol and cigarettes to combat stress.** Ask students to make an honest estimate of the amount they spend on alcohol and tobacco for one week. Collect the amounts and total them; then multiply by 52.

13. **Stress busters?** Ask students whether they have heard or seen commercials for "stress busting" products, including herbs, supplements, drinks, etc. Make a list of all the products on the blackboard. Ask them how effective they think these products are. You can also use this exercise as an opportunity to discuss the fact that these products are often not scientifically evaluated for effectiveness, not regulated as drugs by the FDA, and not always tested for harmful effects or consistency. Lack of regulation can lead to products that are either inconsistent, unsafe, or completely ineffective (placebos). You can also discuss the fact that some even have the possibility of negatively interacting with medications. For example, ginseng has implications for diabetics, and for blood pressure and blood clotting. St John's Wort can create dangerous interactions when mixed with anti-depressants and can interfere with the effectiveness of the birth control pill and HIV or other anti-viral drugs. Before taking any herbal supplements, consult your doctor to determine possible safety and side effects.

    Discussions of the hazards of some of these products can be found at:
    http://www.herbalsafety.utep.edu/factsheet.asp
    http://nccam.nih.gov/health/supplement-safety/

➤ BROADENING OUR CULTURAL HORIZONS

1. **Which countries are the healthiest?** (Internet exercise) Have students pick a country and research the rates of heart disease, smoking, ulcers, obesity, stress, life span, or other health related issues. For ease of comparison, choose countries that are affluent by world standards. Which countries are the "healthiest"? Why?

2. **Life stressors of the poor.** Poverty is the norm in many cultures, and it is a continuing problem for many in the United States. Discuss the helplessness that occurs with poverty. How do the poor feel? What can be done to help each of us feel less helpless in dealing with poverty?

3. **Gender differences in depression.** Depression is much more common among women than men. Why? What social and environmental factors contribute to depression? Could men be just as depressed as women but select different behaviors for dealing with this emotion?

4. **Depression and stress.** North America has one of the highest rates of depression in the world. Depression can be seen as both a cause and a result of stress. Ask students to brainstorm which factors cause higher levels of these two conditions in North America. If you have a culturally diverse class, ask for the insights of students from other cultures. Alternately, ask students to speculate about how other cultures do things differently and therefore reduce stress. Examples include differences in lifestyle, diet, family constellations, attitudes toward work and material success, and different priorities.

5. **Frustration and violence.** In recent years, there has been an epidemic of kids killing kids. In what ways might frustration have led to many of these acts of violence? How might children be taught to manage their frustration in ways other than lashing out violently (and often fatally) at their peers?

6. **Does the LCU apply well to poor people?** Rewrite the "Life Change Units" scale in terms of the principal stressors of the poor. Would the stressors be the same? Would the rankings be the same?

7. **Cultural influences on personality type.** What cultural values would encourage Type A behavior? Type B behavior? More hardy personalities? Why?

8. **Is stoicism cultural?** Some cultures, especially those marked by poverty and privation, place a high value on stoicism and quiet tolerance of suffering. How does this compare with the hardy personality? How might it be adaptive? How is it maladaptive?

9. **Stress and anti-social behavior.** How might the actions of the terrorists in the Middle East be related to stress? In blaming the United States for their social ills, what defense mechanism(s) might be in effect?

445

➤ SUPPLEMENTAL ACTIVITIES

Exercise 12.1: Stress in Your Life

The exercise that follows should provide students with a good deal of thought-provoking material. It is based on the idea that stress in a person's life can lead to a crisis, to illness, and/or accidents. Changes in one's life, whether positive or negative, can be stressors. Because we live through these events one by one, we may not put them together or see how much stress we are under at any particular time. This questionnaire forces the student to look back over the past year to see what stressful events occurred. The Social Readjustment Rating Scale is available at http://chipts.ucla.edu/assessment/Assessment_Instruments/Assessment_files_new/assess_srrs.htm. Students are asked to take from that list any events they have experienced over the last 12 months. The total score can then be interpreted by the values given on the interpretation sheet.

TO THE INSTRUCTOR:

Procedure

A. Provide all students with a **data** sheet, an **interpretation and reaction** sheet, a **health problems** sheet, and a **discussion** sheet. (all **Handouts 12.1**)

B. Ask students to review the Social Readjustment Rating Scale (SRRS). They should pick out those events that apply to them and record them on the data sheet.

C. Instruct students to get a total of the LCUs and proceed with the **interpretation and reaction** sheet.

D. Finally, ask the students to check off and total the health problems from the list.

E. Ask students to complete the **Discussion** sheet and submit it with the figures for their total LCUs and their total health problems. This can be done anonymously.

F. Select the 25 percent of the LCU scores that were the highest and the 25 percent that were the lowest. Find the average of LCUs from the high group and the low group. Find the average number of health problems for the high and low groups. See what differences there are and let the class discuss these.

Exercise 12.2: Lifestyle Choices

If you have a fairly large class—one where students' responses will be relatively anonymous—you can distribute a survey of some of the risky behaviors that students sometimes take. It should be clear that participation is voluntary. Care should be taken to ensure that responses remain private. Alternately, if you use internet-assisted teaching, you can set up an online poll where students can anonymously respond to the survey. Obviously, once you have tallied the responses, you should reveal only totals or percentages, and never raw data. **Handout 12.2** lists some risky

446

behaviors. Risky behaviors are related to stress in several ways: a) the possibility of negative outcomes, b) worry about negative outcomes (getting caught, pregnancy scares, etc.), and c) wear and tear or disease on body systems.

Exercise 12.3: Defense Mechanisms Worksheet

In order to give students additional practice at understanding defense mechanisms, distribute **Handout 12.3**. Answers are below.

1. Reaction formation	2. Rationalization
3. Compensation	4. Repression
5. Reaction formation, sublimation	6. Regression
7. Sublimation, displacement	8. Displacement
9. Rationalization	10. Reaction formation

For other examples of defense mechanisms, see the following quizzes:

http://psychology.about.com/library/quiz/bl_defense_quiz.htm
http://www.cord.edu/faculty/covey/defense.html

Exercise 12.4: Approach-Avoidance (and supplemental lecture)

Handout 12.4 provides an opportunity for students to better understand approach-avoidance theory and apply it to their own lives.

A. Begin this lecture by explaining the basics of approach-avoidance to them. Reproduce the middle chart of **Handout 12.4** on the blackboard. The following assumptions are true with regard to approach-avoidance theory:
   i.   The gradient (slope) of avoidance is always steeper than the gradient of approach.
   ii. The point where the two lines cross is called the point of vacillation.
   iii. The gradients of either approach or avoidance can change their angle and/or their strength, as long as avoidance remains steeper than approach.

B. Begin with the example of a hungry animal. The animal wants food, but it is also fearful because you are standing near the food. The further it is away from the goal, the stronger will be the approach, since it is relatively safe (approach is higher than avoidance).

   As the animal approaches the goal (food), it will reach the point of vacillation where it will be in conflict about whether to approach the food or flee from the threat. If it continues toward the food, avoidance will become stronger, and the animal will typically flee back to a safe distance. At that point, approach will again be stronger than avoidance, and the animal will once again approach the goal and then stop at the point of vacillation. As time goes on, the animal will become hungrier and might also become less afraid of you. Move the lines for approach and/or avoidance up or down to show that changes in the strength of the two gradients will change the point of vacillation.

   If you make a sudden move toward the animal, you might raise the avoidance gradient so high that approach and avoidance will no longer intersect, and the animal will simply disappear. By contrast, a domestic animal typically has little fear of people, and approach will be much stronger than avoidance.

447

C. Now, you are ready to give **Handout 12.4** to your students. The example here deals with the issue of studying (avoidance) versus the desire for good grades (approach). The conflict arises because students want good grades, but they don't want to study.

   i. The first of three charts shows a student who really dislikes studying and doesn't place much emphasis on grades. In this case, the point of vacillation occurs very early, and the student simply gives up and doesn't study.

   ii. The second chart shows a student who places about the same values on grades as on avoiding studying. This student will study some, until he or she gets bored, frustrated, or decides that his/her level of knowledge is "good enough" to get adequate (if not stellar) results.

   iii. The third chart shows a student who is either very motivated to get good grades, or who doesn't mind studying— or both.

D. After students have had an opportunity to go through these three examples, you can have a discussion about where their priorities are, since it is their priorities that determine the strength of the two gradients. You might wish to acknowledge that most people don't regard studying as a favorite activity, but some regard it more negatively than others, for various reasons. It is possible that if students can understand their own motives, they can alter their approach-avoidance conflict.

E. Lastly, you will want to bring up the issue of multiple approach-avoidance. Studying for an exam isn't just about avoiding studying versus getting good grades. There are also other activities that impact a student's decision of whether or not to study, such as going out with friends, being tired, liking or disliking the subject area, or going to work. In the case of going out with friends, even a dedicated student might experience a conflict between losing study time and losing an opportunity to socialize. The other factor is the passage of time—usually, even the most reluctant student will increase the strength of his or her approach as the exam gets closer!

Handout 12.1: STRESS IN YOUR LIFE: DATA SHEET

TO THE STUDENT:

This data sheet consists of two parts. The first is an inventory of significant life events that you have experienced in the last 12 months. The Social Readjustment Rating Scale (SRRS) lists 43 life events that could add stress to your life. No doubt you could think of others. For this exercise, restrict yourself to those listed in the table. You will see that each event has a value, stated in Life Change Units (LCUs). Go through the list and pick out those events that you have experienced over the past year (12 months). List them below with their corresponding units. Then total the LCU scores and compare yours with the standards given on the interpretation sheet.

SIGNIFICANT LIFE EVENT	LCU
--------------------	-----
--------------------	-----
--------------------	-----
--------------------	-----
--------------------	-----
--------------------	-----
--------------------	-----
--------------------	-----
--------------------	-----
--------------------	-----
--------------------	-----

Total: _____

449

Handout 12.1: STRESS IN YOUR LIFE: INTERPRETATION

Interpretation of the LCU score is based on samples of subjects who have been given the Social Readjustment Rating Scale. See if you fit the description of those who had scores similar to yours.

SCORE	DESCRIPTION
0 - 150	Persons scoring in this range should be suffering very little stress. Their chances of suffering illness or crisis are small.
150 - 199	Scores in this range indicate that you are experiencing MILD stress with a possibility of crisis or illness being fairly low—about 33 percent.
200 - 299	Scores in this range indicate a MODERATE stress situation. This could result in a greater possibility of accident, illness, or some other crisis—about 50 percent.
300 or more	Those scoring in this range are experiencing high levels of stress and therefore run a much higher risk of crisis or illness. This is considered a major risk area, about 80 percent chance of experiencing some problems.

My LCU score _____

REACTION: Indicate how you feel about the significance of your score. Are you surprised? Did you expect it to be higher? Or lower? Has this been a typical year for you?

450

Handout 12.1: STRESS IN YOUR LIFE: HEALTH PROBLEMS

Below is a list of health problems that are common in the population. You will recognize many. Try to think back over the past 12 months and see if you can recall having had some of these. Check off all of those that you can remember.

___ allergies	___ diarrhea	___ minor accident
___ appendicitis	___ earache	___ muscle strains
___ asthma	___ eye problems	___ nausea
___ athlete's foot	___ flu	___ nerves (anxiety)
___ backache	___ hay fever	___ sexual problems
___ blisters	___ headaches	___ shortness of breath
___ bloody nose	___ hearing loss	___ sinus problems
___ boils	___ hernia	___ skin disease
___ bruises	___ high blood pressure	___ skin rash
___ chest pains	___ hives	___ sleep problems
___ colds	___ indigestion	___ sore throat
___ constipation	___ injury to joints	___ stomach problems
___ cough	___ insomnia	___ tonsillitis
___ cuts	___ kidney problems	___ ulcers
___ dental problems	___ major accident	___ urinary problems
___ depression	___ menstrual problems	___ vomiting

TOTAL HEALTH PROBLEMS _____

Handout 12.1: STRESS IN YOUR LIFE: DISCUSSION

TO THE STUDENT:

Enter your LCU score and your total number of health problems in the space provided. Then write brief comments on the discussion questions.

       LCU score   _____

       Health problems   _____

1. In which of the four LCU categories did you find yourself? Does this seem to fit in with your idea about your stress level and possibility of crisis or illness?

2. How does your level of health problems compare with your LCU score? Do you see any relationship between the two?

3. Are you taking any significant steps to reduce the stress level in your life? Do you see any need to do so?

Handout 12.2: LIFESTYLE CHOICES

Please answer each of the following. Do **NOT** put your name on the paper. For each item, make your best estimate for the **past YEAR.**

1.   How often do you drive more than 10 mph over the speed limit in the city?
     ___ never
     ___ rarely
     ___ sometimes
     ___ often
     ___ usually

2.   How often do you drive more than 20 mph over the speed limit in the city?
     ___ never
     ___ rarely
     ___ sometimes
     ___ often
     ___ usually

3.   How often do you wear your seatbelt?
     ___ never
     ___ rarely
     ___ sometimes
     ___ often
     ___ usually

4.   How often do you participate in "binge drinking" (more than four drinks at a time)?
     ___ never
     ___ rarely
     ___ sometimes
     ___ often
     ___ usually

5.   Have you ever missed a test, appointment, or work because of alcohol or drug use?
     ___ never
     ___ once
     ___ twice
     ___ more than twice

6.   How often do you smoke?
     ___ never
     ___ rarely
     ___ sometimes (once a week or more)
     ___ often (several times a week)
     ___ usually (daily)

453

7.   How often do you eat "fast food"?
___ never or rarely
___ once or twice a month
___ once a week
___ twice a week
___ more than twice a week

8.   Have you ever tried "hard drugs" (cocaine, ecstasy, uppers, downers, etc.)?
___ never
___ once
___ twice
___ more than twice

9.   How often do you smoke marijuana?
___ never
___ rarely
___ sometimes
___ often

10.   Have you had a "one night stand"?
___ never
___ once
___ twice
___ more than twice

11.   Have you ever had unprotected sex with someone you didn't know very well?
___ never
___ once
___ twice
___ more than twice

12.   Have you/your partner had a "pregnancy scare"?
___ never
___ once
___ twice
___ more than twice

13.   How often do you get into arguments with family, friends, or roommates?
___ never
___ rarely
___ sometimes
___ often

14.   Have you ever been in a physical fight?
___ never
___ once
___ twice
___ more than twice

15.   Have you ever been disciplined at work or school?
___ never
___ once
___ twice
___ more than twice

Handout 12.3: DEFENSE MECHANISMS WORKSHEET

For each of the following situations, choose the defense mechanism that best fits the explanation. Choices: repression, reaction formation, regression, displacement, sublimation, denial, rationalization, or compensation.

1. Sally is 18 years old and unexpectedly pregnant. She had big plans to go to college, but now tells everyone how much she is looking forward to being a mother.

2. Juan recently broke up with his fiancée. Now he is telling all of his friends that he was bored with the relationship.

3. Frankie is always trying to keep up with his older brother when playing sports, but he can't. He takes great delight in bringing home a good report card instead.

4. LaVonne was broken hearted when her dream date stood her up for the prom. Now, one year later, she is having trouble remembering what his last name was.

5. Harry and his sister Louise are twins who do everything together. They capture bugs and do nasty experiments on them, sometimes resulting in the bugs dying. When they grow up, Harry goes to work for an animal rights organization, and Louise becomes a veterinarian. Which defense mechanism is each one using?

6. Ali is six years old. After the new baby arrives, he becomes jealous and clings to his parents for attention.

7. Tess hates her new boss. One night, her racquetball partner notices that Tess' game has become much more competitive lately. She also notices that she is hitting the ball much harder than she used to.

8. Sarah's children know that whenever Sarah has a fight with her husband, the kids get assigned more chores.

9. Morgan just lost a promotion at work and now wonders whether he will be able to advance in the company at all. He starts going to bars and drinking with his friends more often than he used to. He tells people that he has decided that there is more to life than just money.

10. Jeremy was caught by his mother trying to peek into the girls' locker room. Now that Jeremy has grown up, he has become active in anti-pornography political activities.

Handout 12.4: UNDERSTANDING APPROACH-AVOIDANCE

Example #1 – Student does not study

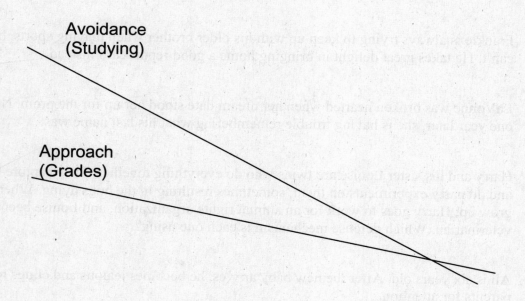

Avoidance
(Studying)

Approach
(Grades)

The goal (good grades) is on the far left.

On the right hand side of the diagram, you can see that the desire to study is slightly stronger (higher) than the dislike of studying.

The point of vacillation is where the two lines cross. This is where the conflict creates the greatest anxiety.

To the left of the point of vacillation, the dislike of studying is stronger (higher) than the desire for good grades.

Handout 12.4: UNDERSTANDING APPROACH-AVOIDANCE

Example #2 – Student studies some

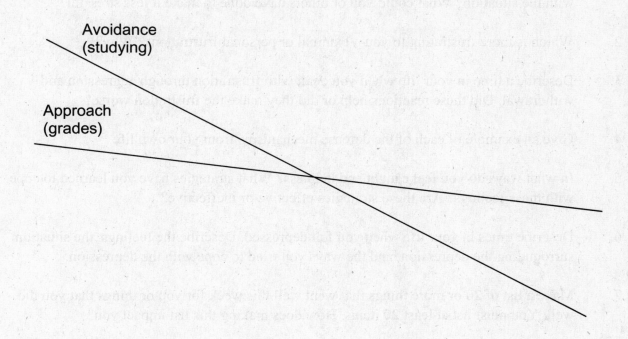

Avoidance
(studying)

Approach
(grades)

Example #3 – Student studies a lot

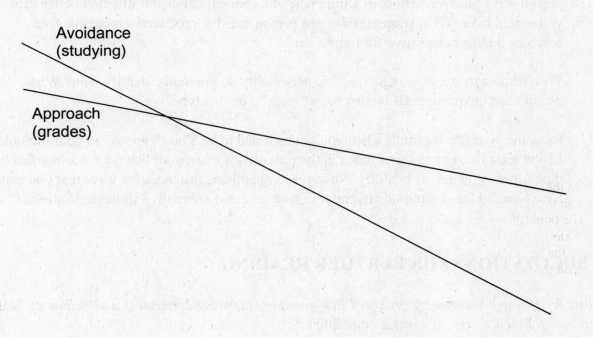

Avoidance
(studying)

Approach
(grades)

➢ JOURNAL QUESTIONS

1. Describe your most stressful life experience. Why was it stressful? How did you deal with the situation? What could you or others have done to make it less stressful?

2. Which is more frustrating to you—external or personal frustrations? Why?

3. Describe a time in your life when you dealt with frustration through aggression and withdrawal. Did these reactions help or did they make the frustration worse?

4. Give an example of each of the defense mechanisms from your own life.

5. In what ways do you feel caught and helpless? What strategies have you learned to cope with these feelings? Are these strategies effective or ineffective?

6. Describe times in your life when you felt depressed. Describe the feelings, the situation surrounding the depression, and the ways you tried to cope with the depression.

7. Make a list of 20 or more things that went well this week for you or things that you did well. You must list at least 20 items. How does making this list impact you?

8. Think about the most positive person you know. How are some of the ways that this person stays positive? Think of a time when this person handled a situation better than you would have. What strategies did that person use that produced a more positive outcome and/or perspective for him or her?

9. With respect to stress, which "type" of personality do you most identify with? What genetic and environmental factors have "made" you this type?

10. Examine your life for times when you are included to be a bit "Type A" in your outlook. List at least five examples of times in the past month when your behavior was marked by time urgency, anger, or hostility. Now, reexamine those instances for ways that you could have handled the situation differently. List at least two alternative strategies for each incident.

➢ SUGGESTIONS FOR FURTHER READING

Andre, R. *Positive Solitude: A Practical Program for Mastering Loneliness and Achieving Self-Fulfillment. Lincoln, NE:* iUniverse.com, 2000.

Biracree, T. and Biracree, N. *Over Fifty: The Resource Book for the Better Half of your Life.* New York: HarperCollins, 1991.

Cherey, L. "The Man Who First Names Stress." *Psychology Today,* March 1978, 64.

Davis, M., Eshleman, E. R., McKay, M., and Fanning, P. *The Relaxation and Stress Reduction Workbook,* 6th ed. Oakland, CA: New Harbiner, 2008.

Dienstfrey, H. *Where the Mind Meets the Body.* New York: HarperCollins, 1992.

Dollard, J. *Frustration and Aggression.* Westport, CT: Greenwood, 1980.

Dreher, D. *The Tao of Inner Peace.* Copake Falls, NY: Plume, 2000.

Dyer, W. W. *No More Holiday Blues.* New York: HarperCollins, 1993.

Dyer, W. W. *Ten Secrets for Success and Inner Peace.* Carlsbad, CA: Hay House, 2002.

Feinstein, D., and Mayo, P. E. *Rituals for Living and Dying.* New York: HarperCollins, 1990.

Freedman, A. and DeWolf, R. *Woulda, Coulda, Shoulda: Overcoming Regrets, Mistakes, and Missed Opportunities.* New York: HarperCollins, 1990.

Hojat, M., and Crandall, R. (Eds.). *Loneliness: Theory, Research, and Applications.* Thousand Oaks, CA: Sage, 1990.

Kasl, C. D. *Women, Sex, and Addiction.* New York: HarperCollins, 1990.

Lazarus, R. S. "Little Hassles Can Be Hazardous to Health." *Psychology Today,* July 1981.

Levi, L. *Society, Stress, and Disease: Working Life.* Oxford: Oxford University Press, 1982.

Levi, L. *Society, Stress, and Disease: Old Age.* Oxford: Oxford University Press, 1988.

Mandler, G. *Mind and Body: Psychology of Emotion and Stress.* New York: W. Norton, 1984.

Meichenbaum, D. "Stress-Inoculation Training." In *Cognitive Behavior Modification.* New York: Plenum, 1977.

Saltzman, A. *Downshifting: Reinventing Success on a Slower Track.* New York: HarperCollins, 1991.

Schafer, W. *Stress Management for Wellness.* Belmont, CA: Thomson Wadsworth, 1999.

Selye, H. *The Stress of Life,* 2nd ed. New York: McGraw-Hill, 1978.

Smith, J.C. *Stress Scripting: A Guide to Stress Management.* New York: Praeger, 1991.

Spodnik, J. and Cogan, D. P.. *The 35-Plus Good Health Guide for Women.* New York: HarperCollins, 1991.

VIDEO SUGGESTIONS

Feature Films

Leaving Las Vegas (Nicholas Cage, Elisabeth Shue), Drama. Nicholas Cage goes to Las Vegas to drink himself to death in the company of a prostitute played by Elizabeth Shue.

Analyze This (Robert DeNiro, Billy Crystal, Lisa Kudrow), Comedy. Dr. Ben Sobel (Crystal) is a New York psychiatrist whose client is Mafia kingpin Paul Viti (DeNiro). Viti is having panic attacks brought on by stress and guilt over his father's assassination. Just as Sobel and Viti are having a breakthrough the FBI attempts to persuade Sobel that Viti is going to have him murdered. Comical situations, but still illustrates a variety of stress-related topics.

Falling Down (Michael Douglas, Robert Duvall, Barbara Hershey), Drama. William Foster (Douglas), after being laid off from his defense job, gets stuck in a major traffic jam. Abandoning his car, Foster begins walking and slowly unravels mentally. He finally snaps at a fast-food restaurant. It is up to Prendergas (Duvall), a cop on the eve of his retirement, to bring Foster and his arsenal of weapons to a halt.

Ferris Bueller's Day Off (Matthew Broderick, Alan Ruck, Mia Sara), Comedy. Teenaged Ferris Bueller (Broderick) is notorious for cutting classes and getting away with it. Just before graduation Ferris decides to make one last grand cut from classes with the principal on his trail. {After first trying to foil his plans,} Ferris' sister eventually joins in the fun and helps her brother. Can be used to discuss stress, coping, and especially adolescent responses.

The Horse Whisperer (Robert Redford, Kristin Scott Thomas), Drama. The film based on the best-selling story features Robert Redford as the cowboy who knows just what to say to the unruly horse and its comely owner.

The Program (James Caan, Halle Berry, Omar Epps), Drama. Easter State University Coach Winters (Caan) is under considerable pressure to bring in a winning season since the college is not doing well. Coach Winters does just about anything to recruit some promising young players out of high school. He and the college overlook almost any obnoxious behavior of the boys.

Sleepers (Kevin Bacon, Robert DeNiro, Dustin Hoffman), Drama. Four childhood pals from Hell's Kitchen are sent to reform school after accidentally killing a man during a cruel prank. The boys are raped and beaten by several guards at the reform school. After the boys' release, two of the boys, now grown men, kill one of the guards at a restaurant in cold blood. They stand trial and their other friends and Father Bobby (DeNiro) pledge to free their friends and get even with the guards.

Terms of Endearment (Debra Winger, Shirley MacLaine, Jack Nicholson), Drama. Widow Aurora Greenaway (MacLaine) and her daughter Emma (Winger) are at odds when Emma marries a wishy-washy college teacher, Flap (Daniels). Emma and Flap have three children before Flap has an affair with a student. Aurora is pursued by next-door neighbor Garret Breedlove (Nicholson). The mood of the film changes when Emma discovers she has terminal cancer.

Educational Films and Videos

Addiction: The Family in Crisis, (1995), Films for the Humanities and Sciences, 28 min. This program tells the story of one man's addiction to alcohol. It explains the process of addiction in the brain and the role of the family in "enabling" the drinking behavior. The program follows the alcoholic through a treatment program as he learns the causes of his addiction and how to keep his alcoholism under control— abstinence.

Alcohol Addiction: Hereditary Factors, from *The Mind Teaching Modules*, 2nd Edition #29, (2000), Worth, 11:40. This video deals with alcoholism, addiction, biological evidence for hereditary traits and how science progresses through replication and the development of new technologies.

Alcohol and Human Psychology, (1985) Aims Media, 23 min. Describes psychological aspects of alcohol consumption.

Alcoholism: Life Under the Influence, (1984), Ambrose Video, 57 min. This Nova series film discusses the most common and least admitted disease. Alcoholism is related to 90 percent of all physical assaults, 50 percent of all homicides, and 25 percent of all suicides in America. In the film, an interdisciplinary panel of experts discusses the disease and its implications. In addition, therapists, researchers, and alcoholics are interviewed in order to gain a better understanding of the problem.

Biology, Brain, and Behavior: Seasonal Affective Disorder, (1992), Pennsylvania State University, 25 min. This video concludes that for victims of seasonal affective disorder, an illness that grips them during the short days and long nights of winter, only half-hour doses of bright light during the darkness can alleviate their suffering. The program turns to the world of biology to gain insights into this strange illness, investigating such things as circadian rhythms and secretion of the hormone melatonin.

Can't Slow Down, (1995), Films for the Humanities and Sciences, 28 min. This program examines American's increasingly hurried lifestyle, working 160 hours a year more than they did in 1970. Because of the urge to acquire, the pressure to achieve or be fired, the need to achieve outside the home, and longer commutes to work, couples are too busy to talk to one another. The program asks how we are spending our time and how the constant rush is affecting our relationships and our health.

Coping with Stress, (2000), Films for the Humanities & Sciences, 23 min. This program explains that stress is a biological response of an organism to its environment, and indispensable to survival. When stress becomes chronic it can lead to illness or even death.

Coping with Stress: Locus of Control and Predictability, from *The Brain Series Teaching Module*, 2nd Edition #22, Worth, 2:49. This video illustrates the importance of animal research as a means of promoting human well-being. This program can be used to lead into a lively discussion with students by having them identify stress-related factors in their lives and examines the elements they can control and predict that could reduce stress for them. Different types of stress are demonstrated in experiments, and their implications are discussed.

Emotions, Stress, and Health, from *The Brain Series Teaching Modules*, 2nd Edition, Worth, 10:59. This module goes into detail regarding the interaction of emotions, stress, and health. Students will be able to see and hear from patients dealing with life-threatening illness, and how they manage their emotions.

Getting a Handle on Stress, (1988), Films for the Humanities and Sciences, 26 min. This film focuses on identifying stress factors, determining the effects of stress, and finding intervention strategies to handle stress. The film host, Jim Hartz, undergoes a battery of physical, psychological, and stress tests at Denver's Institute of Health Management and Stress Medicine to determine his susceptibility. The film explains what stress is and how it can be effectively managed by interviewing experts who demonstrate stress-reducing techniques to the viewer. This program is well produced and contains practical advice that all students will find interesting and useful.

Handling Stress: Today and Tomorrow, (2000), Films for the Humanities & Sciences, 30 min. This program helps students identify circumstances that can be stressful, and provides ways to manage the pressure. It also explains how to handle tension by channeling the energy to positive feelings and how individuals can accomplish goals rather than waste time worrying about failures.

Healing and the Mind, Volumes 1-5, (1993), Insight Media, 330 min., total time. In this series, reporter Bill Moyer discusses numerous aspects of health psychology and behavioral medicine. Some of the highlights include: 1) a discussion and demonstration of biofeedback; 2) Eastern approaches to medicine (including meditation); and 3) changes in U.S. medical practices as a result of the incorporation of psychological issues in medicine.

Health, Mind, and Behavior: Discovering Psychology Series, (1990), Annenberg/CPB, 30 min. This video from the *Discovering Psychology Series* presents an interesting review of how the new biopsychosocial model (which emphasizes the role of psychological processes in medical problems) is replacing the traditional biomedical approach. Included among health psychology's concerns are the social and environmental factors that put us at risk for physical and psychological disorders. Hans Selye's general adaptation syndrome describes the body's typical reaction to stressful events. Richard Lazarus' concept of cognitive appraisal suggests that our perception and interpretation of an event are as crucial as the event itself in understanding the cause of stress. Health psychologists develop strategies for coping with stress and teaching behaviors that promote wellness. Their important contribution to the understanding and treatment of illness is reflected in Thomas Coates's recent work on the AIDS epidemic. Highlights also include a discussion of the utility of traditional Native American medical techniques in modern medicine and the use of biofeedback in stress management.

Health, Stress, and Coping, (1990), Insight Media 30 min. This video explores a variety of topics including stressors, physiological reactions to stress, and strategies for coping with stress.

Learning to Live with Stress: Program Min. The Body for Health, (1979), Document Associates, 19 min. This film contains interviews with two authorities in the study of stress and its effects on the human brain and body: Dr. Hans Selye, who introduced stress into the medical vocabulary, and cardiologist Dr. Herman Benson of Harvard. Both describe stress as a force causing heart problems, hypertension, and a multitude of other known and unknown threats to health.

Male Stress Syndrome, (1987), Films for the Humanities and Sciences, 28 min. This film, presented by talk show host Phil Donahue, looks at the effects of stress on men. The etiology of the disease is discussed, along with the differences between male and female stress. Donahue is joined by Georgia Witkin-Laniol, who is an authority on stress in males, and sports figure Arthur Ashe. This presentation is an interesting examination of a gender-specific type of stress.

Managing Stress, (1989), CRM, 34 min. This color film does an excellent job of describing the impact of stress in the work place. Students are introduced to numerous issues including: 1) sources of stress, 2) Type A and B personalities, and 3) stress reduction techniques (e.g., biofeedback, relaxation training).

Managing Stress, (2000), Films for the Humanities & Sciences, 19 min. This brief program discusses the difference between negative and positive stress. The body can become stronger while under the influence of positive stress and weaker through the effects of negative stress. The film depicts the result of these two stresses on the individual and presents several ways to reduce their effects. Although an elementary introduction to the topic of stress, it should be considered when classroom time is limited.

No More Shame: Addiction, (2000), Films for the Humanities & Sciences, 23 min. This program explains current research into why people become addicted, what puts them at risk, and what the best treatments may be. The program profiles a recovering alcoholic.

One Nation Under Stress, (1988) Films for the Humanities and Sciences, 52 min. Stress is everywhere and it is being increasingly implicated in immune system dysfunction, cancer, hypertension, heart disease, ulcers, and a host of other illnesses. This program seeks to help viewers understand what causes stress, explain its consequences, and demonstrate ways stress can be turned into a positive force. Hosted by Merlin Olsen, the program emphasizes that stress is a different variable for everyone and shows different ways people are coping with it.

Psychology—The Study of Human Behavior Series. This video presents a discussion of Hans Selye's General Adaption Syndrome (GAS), stress and physical illness, and psychological stress.

Post-Traumatic Stress Disorder, Films for the Humanities and Sciences, 28 min. Host Jamie Guth interviews a Vietnam vet and a woman who is an incest survivor, both of whom have PTSD. Treatment techniques are discussed.

Psychobiology of Stress, (1988), Insight Media, 10 min. This video provides a nice, brief presentation of the body's stress response.

Relationships and Stress, (1980), Time-Life Video, 30 min. This film from the *Coping with Serious Illness* series discusses ways of handling changing relationships between a terminally ill person and family, friends, and medical personnel. Several experts explain how a serious illness can change existing relationships and how a person can cope with the stress that inevitably follows a terminal diagnosis. This film is strongly recommended for its open portrayal of a serious topic.

Running Out of Time: Time Pressure, Overtime, and Overwork, (1994), Films for the Humanities and Sciences, 57 min. This program explores the impact of time pressure and overwork on American society, how much activity people fit into their busy lives, how much responsibility they increasingly assume, and how little leisure time actually remains. The program contrasts expectations about saving time with the reality that there are more time-savers but less time to use them, and compares conditions in other countries and at other times.

Stress and Emotion, (1984), PBS Video, 58 min. This film from *The Brain* series explains what is known about the chemical and physical changes that occur in the brain as a result of prolonged stress. The film focuses particularly on the stresses of pain and anxiety on the individual's behavior and contains a dramatization of the accidental frontal lobotomy of Phineas T. Gage in 1848. A segment on the stressful life of an air traffic controller is also included to further clarify the concept of stress and its effects on a person's wellbeing.

Stress and Hypertension, (1986), Encyclopedia Britannica Educational Corporation, 19 min. This video's main focus is the effect of stress on blood pressure. Stress is defined as an unwanted byproduct of an overly demanding lifestyle, the principal sources being one's family and work relationships. High stress can result in dangerously high blood pressure (hypertension), which can be life-threatening. The film discusses several methods of coping with stress that are beneficial to one's health, especially dieting, reducing salt intake, and meditating.

Stress in the Later Years, (1983), Churchill Films, 24 min. From the *Be Well* series. This film examines the special forms of stress that the elderly are likely to encounter, such as loss of a loved one, loneliness, retirement, failing health, and more. It explains the stress and health correlation and offers a variety of helpful suggestions for coping with life events and their consequences. Some examples are mental relaxation, physical exercise, hobbies, new relationships, and finding support groups. This should be of interest to viewers with elderly parents or grandparents.

Stress Management: Coping With Stress, (1986), Insight Media, 30 min. A variety of stress management techniques are presented in this video. They include cognitive reappraisal, imagery, deep breathing, and other relaxation techniques.

Stress, (1995), Films for the Humanities and Sciences, 23 min. This program explains that stress is a biological response of an organism to its environment and is necessary to survival. However, when stress becomes chronic it can lead to sickness and even death.

Stress and Health (2005) *Psychology Digital Video Library 3.0 Handbook,* from Thomson Higher Education. A brief description of the effects of stress on our health.

Stress, Health, and Coping (2002) from *Psychology: The Human Experience,* Coast Community College Telecourses, 30 min. This video chronicles a breast cancer survivor who employs successful coping strategies to aid in maintaining good health in stressful situations.

Stress, Health and You. (1980), Time-Life Video, 18 min. From the *Stress, Health and You* series. The subject is the effect of stress on our physical and psychological health. Noted researcher Hans Selye explains how stress can be both beneficial and detrimental to our health. This film also has Richard Rahe, co-developer of the Life Change Scale, illustrating how changes in our life can affect our wellbeing. This is an important film that will allow your students to analyze the stress that affects their health.

Stress: A Disease of our Time, Time-Life, 35 min.

Stress: Keeping Your Cool, (1994), Films for the Humanities and Sciences, 36 min. This program looks at the impact that stress has on our society and describes positive and negative stress, stress control, and ways to simplify a hectic lifestyle. Experts identify what causes stress, why women are experiencing such high levels of stress in their lives, and how teenagers are particularly prone to stress. The program explores the relationship between stress levels and health and the growing recognition in medical circles that physical ailments are often linked to, if not caused by, mental and emotional stress and anxieties.

Stress: The Body and the Mind, (1986), University of Illinois Film Center, 60 min. Examines physiological manifestations of stress.

The Addicted Brain, (1987), Films for the Humanities and Sciences, 26 min. This documentary takes viewers on a tour of the world's most prolific manufacturer and user of drugs—the human brain. The biochemistry of the brain is responsible for joggers' highs, for the compulsion of some people to seek thrills, for certain kinds of obsessive-compulsive behavior, even for the drive to achieve power and dominance. The program explores developments in the biochemistry of addiction and addictive behavior.

The Mind-Body Connection, (1993), Ambrose Video, 58 min. Bill Moyers talks with scientists and doctors who are on the frontier of mind-body research. Through careful studies to understand how our thoughts, emotions, and even our personalities can affect our physical health, they are gaining new insights into how the mind and body work together. This program distinguishes between positive stress and negative stress, and shows the effects of different types of stress and how an individual can reduce stress. This program explains that stress is a biological response of an organism to its environment, and indispensable to survival. When stress becomes chronic it can lead to illness or even death. This program helps students identify circumstances that can be stressful and provides ways to manage the pressure. It also explains how to handle tension by channeling the energy to positive feelings and how individuals can accomplish goals rather than waste time worrying about failures.

The Science of Stress (2002) Films for the Humanities and Sciences, 50 min. This program explores the link between stress and illness by staging a day in the life of a lawyer. Various professionals in the health field comment on his stress factors and the way he handles them. Type A and Type B personalities are discussed.

Women and Stress, (1987), Films for the Humanities and Sciences, 28 min. Women are not shielded from stress and experience it just as men do, but they tend to conceal their stress reactions more than men. Host Phil Donahue is joined by Georgia Witkin-Laniol, author of the book *The Female Stress Syndrome.* Together with a panel of women, they discuss stress and offer suggestions for coping with overwhelming events. This film offers a variety of practical suggestions for handling stress and should be considered an adjunct to the *Male Stress Syndrome* film.

Wounded Healers, (1993), Ambrose Video, 58 min. Bill Moyers visits Commonwealth, a retreat for people with cancer, and follows a group of people over the course of a week as they learn to navigate the life passage called cancer. The program addresses the afflictions that have wounded their minds and spirits.

➤ COMPUTER AND INTERNET RESOURCES

PsykTrek 3.0
Unit 12: Abnormal Behavior & Therapy
12f. "Types of Stress"
12g. "Responding to Stress"

INFOTRAC®
Below you will find two journal articles obtained from INFOTRAC® that relate to information contained in this chapter. Instructors should encourage students to utilize this invaluable resource to improve their research skills. Have students locate and read the following articles and answer questions relevant to each article.

Black Enterprise, August 1992 v23 n1 p86(3) **Coping with on-the-job stress.**

1.   Everyone experiences stress at work. What additional stressors are there for African American workers?

    Answer: Everyone is required to meet rigorous performance standards; however, white executives are often permitted a wider range of behavioral styles to achieve them. There may also be a conflict in work style and your company's management style; sometimes this is attributed to race instead of style differences.

2.   What professional challenges contribute to the frustration for black Americans?

    Answer: According to the U.S. Department of Labor, while gains have been steady, they have also been slow. In 1983, there were 482,000 African Americans, or 4.5 percent, in executive, administrative and managerial ranks. At the end of 1991, there were 858,000, or 5.7 percent, who held those positions. Over a period of eight years, the net gain was a dismal 1.2 percent. This is a source of frustrations for black Americans, who must often work twice as hard to reach the same levels as their white counterparts.

3.   What other areas of stress and frustration are particularly relevant to black professionals?

    Answer: Black Americans are often excluded from informal channels of communication ("the grapevine"), where information is often shared. Feelings of isolation and frustration can develop from not being "in the loop."

4.   What are some of the suggested coping mechanisms for combating this frustration?

    Answer: Suggestions include: understand the unwritten rules, know oneself, get career counseling, select an environment that would be most conducive to success, strike a balance between work and personal life, relax and exercise regularly, and be happy and understanding of one's motivations.

Natural Health, March 2005 v35 i3 p72 (6) **The healing power of animals: People with pets have reduced levels of stress, depression, and heart risk.** Find happiness and well-being through this primal connection.

1. Briefly describe the function of the Dolphin Research Center in Grassy Key, FL.

    Answer: The program is designed to enrich the lives of children and adults with special needs by working on increasing motor skills, lessening stress, and focusing attention.

2. In Celtic tradition, horses are known as what?

    Answer: Horses are known as aman cara—soul friends.

3. According to this article, can a dog motivate someone to lose weight? If so, how?

    Answer: The answer, according to a recent study, is a resounding yes, says researcher Robert Kushner, M.D., medical director of the Wellness Institute at Northwestern Memorial Hospital in Chicago. Study participants were asked to do 30 minutes of moderate-intensity activity at least three times a week. Because dogs change their behavior once they start exercising, people reported they'd come home tired in the evening, but their dog would greet them at the door ready to go. "This really made a difference," says Kushner, who now routinely asks all his overweight patients if they have a dog.

4. Does a certified therapy dog have the same legal rights as a professionally trained service dog?

    Answer: A therapy dog—even a certified one—doesn't have the same legal rights as a professionally trained service dog. Under the Americans with Disabilities Act, professionally trained service dogs are allowed access to any public place their human charge can go.

WEB LINKS
Knowledge Builder Links

1. Health Psychology
   APA Division 38: http://www.apa.org/about/division/div38.html
   Careers in Health Psychology:
       http://www.wcupa.edu/_ACADEMICS/sch_cas.psy/Career_Paths/Health/Career0
       2.htm
   The Longevity Game:
       http://www.northwesternmutual.com/learning-center/the-longevity-game.aspx

2. Stress, Frustration, and Conflict
   The Discovery of Stress:
       http://brainconnection.positscience.com/
   Psychoneuroimmunology: http://en.wikipedia.org/wiki/Psychoneuroimmunology
   Burnout: http://www.helpguide.org/mental/burnout_signs_symptoms.htm

3. Defenses, Helplessness, and Depression

    Defense Mechanisms:

        http://www.planetpsych.com/zPsychology_101/defense_mechanisms.htm

    Learned Helplessness: http://www.answers.com/topic/learned-helplessness?cat=health

    Depression and Control:

        http://www.clinicaldepression.co.uk/Understanding_Depression/control.htm

4. Stress and Health

    Social Readjustment Rating Scale:

        http://chipts.ucla.edu/assessment/Assessment_Instruments/Assessment_files_new/
assess_srrs.htm

    Stress, Anxiety, Fears, and Psychosomatic Disorders:

        http://www.psychologicalselfhelp.org/Chapter5/

    Type A behavior:

        http://www.psychtests.com/tests/personality/type_a_personality_access.html

5. Psychology in Action

    Self-growth.com: http://www.selfgrowth.com/

    Preventative Health Center: http://www.md-phc.com/

    Stress Management Resources: http://www.mindtools.com/smpage.html

468

Additional Web Links

APA Online
http://www.apa.org/

Biofeedback
http://www.aapb.org/

Defense Mechanism Quizzes
http://psychology.about.com/library/quiz/bl_defense_quiz.htm
http://www.cord.edu/faculty/covey/defense.html

Herbal Supplements Information and Risks
http://www.herbalsafety.utep.edu/factsheet.asp
http://nccam.nih.gov/health/supplement-safety/

Meditation
http://www.how-to-meditate.org/
http://www.learningmeditation.com/

Self-Growth
http://www.allaboutlifechallenges.org/self-worth.htm

Stress—Symptoms, Causes, Remedies
http://www.stress.org/
http://www.cultural-connections.org/programs/meeting_notes/stress_busters.pdf

Stress Management
http://mentalhealth.about.com/od/stress/Stress_Management.htm
http://www.mindtools.com/smpage.html
http://www.mayoclinic.com/health/stress/SR99999

Stress and Personality
http://www.tellmemytype.com

Test Stress Levels
http://www.StressDiagnosis.com

Type A Personality
http://stress.about.com/od/understandingstress/a/type_a_person.htm
http://stress.about.com/library/Type_A_quiz/bl_Type_A_quiz.htm
http://www.stressdoctors.com/st-typea.html

PSYCHOLOGY IN THE NEWS

Counseling Resources Online
http://counsellingresource.com/sitenews/index.shtml
This site features a daily mental health news page that allows you to search by topic.

Keep Media
http://www.keepmedia.com
Check out the featured news every day; search by topic.

National Public Radio
http://www.npr.org/
Search health and science news and archives; this site allows you to listen to news broadcasts.

New York Times
http://health.nytimes.com/pages/health/research/index.html
Search the mental and behavior section for the latest in news from the *New York Times*.

PsychCentral
http://psychcentral.com/newsletter/news_update.htm
Provides mental health and psychology news updates.

Topix.net Psychology News
http://www.topix.net/science/psychology
Psychology News, continually updated from thousands of sources around the net, provides many links to news resources in psychology. Search by topic.

CHAPTER 13
Psychological Disorders

Survey Questions	
Discussion Questions	
Lecture Enhancements	Attributes of psychologically healthy individuals
	Did you see that?
	Who's crazy?
	Judging mental illness
	Depression versus "the blues"
	Suicide statistics
	Bipolar interview
	Guest speaker on mental health
	Impact of labeling
	Schizophrenia case study – quadruplets
	Tour of a mental hospital
	Statistics on suicide
Role-Playing Scenarios	
Value-Clarification Statements	
One-Minute Motivators	What's normal?
	The "victim" mindset
	Name that disorder!
	Why do mentally ill people scare us?
	What are you doing?
	Social needs and narcissism
	What worries you?
	Nervous breakdown
	Who's a sociopath?
	Compulsive partying
	What's your phobia?
	New phobias
	Mental illness and stigma
	Anxiety and depression
	How many people have been affected by depression?
Broadening Our Cultural Horizons	What's normal where you live?
	Definitions of normalcy across groups and cultures
	Culture-bound syndromes
	Gender and depression
	Culture and mental illness
	Rates of depression in North America
	Cultural frequency of suicide
	Cultural definitions of mental illness
	What's normal here?
	Are terrorists mentally ill?
Supplemental Activities	Exercise 13.1: What Is Normal?
	Exercise 13.2: The Deviant Among Us
	Exercise 13.3: Psychiatric Labeling
	Exercise 13.4: Identifying Irrational Thoughts
Handouts	Handout 13.1: What Is Normal?
	Handout 13.2: The Deviant Among Us:
	Handout 13.3: Identifying Irrational Thoughts

Journal Questions
Suggestions for Further Reading
Video Suggestions
Computer and Internet Resources

➢ SURVEY QUESTIONS

Module 13.1 Normality and Psychopathology

Survey Question: How is abnormality defined?

Survey Question: What are the major psychological disorders?

Survey Question: Can psychiatric labeling be misused?

Module 13.2 Psychosis, Delusional Disorders, and Schizophrenia

Survey Question: What are the general characteristics of psychotic disorders?

Survey Question: What is the nature of a delusional disorder?

Survey Questions: What forms does schizophrenia take? What causes it?

Module 13.3 Mood Disorders

Survey Questions: What are mood disorders? What causes them?

Module 13.4 Anxiety-Based Disorders and Personality Disorders

Survey Question: What problems result when a person suffers high levels of anxiety?

Survey Question: How do psychologists explain anxiety-based disorders?

Survey Question: What is a personality disorder?

Module 13.5 Psychology in Action: Suicide—Lives on the Brink

Survey Questions: Why do people commit suicide? Can suicide be prevented?

➤ DISCUSSION QUESTIONS

1. Can you think of a behavior that would be considered "abnormal" under any possible set of circumstances? What cultural factors affect what is considered "abnormal"?

2. Your textbook states that one in four American adults suffers from a diagnosable mental disorder in any given year. Does this statistic surprise you? Why or why not? If it surprises you, what factor(s) might account for the difference between your perception and the book's statistic? Do you think this statistic is overblown, or overly-inclusive?

3. What are the advantages and disadvantages of having discrete categories for defining psychological problems? Is there another method of classification that would be more advantageous?

4. Women experience a higher rate of generalized anxiety disorder than men. Why? List as many factors as possible.

5. In some cases, women may be at higher risk for being **incorrectly** labeled with anxiety or other disorders than men, and more likely to be prescribed anti-anxiety drugs—minor tranquillizers. (Women are less likely to be checked for medical problems, more likely to be labeled as "overreacting," etc. Disorders such as endometriosis and autoimmune disorders—which affect women more than men— are also sometimes mislabeled hysteria or hypochondriasis.)

6. How might your perception of a person change if you knew he or she were an "ex-mental patient"?

7. To what extent does "maladjusted" or "sick" mean "different from me"?

8. Has anyone ever told you that he or she had a psychiatric disorder and, if so, how did you react? If you had one of the disorders listed in the text, such as anxiety disorders or depression, would you tell people? If so, which people and under what circumstances?

9. In the 1950s, a book called the *Age of Anxiety* was published. Using the categories of abnormal behavior, how would you label our current decade? What would need to take place for it to be a decade of "mental health"?

10. Are standards of "normality" in our society broad enough to accommodate varying life-styles?

11. We all have habits. How do normal habits differ from obsessive compulsive habits? Most of you probably brush your teeth either before or after you shower and you probably do it in the same order every day. You probably go through your shower routine the same way, too. What is the difference between a routine and a ritual? How would you react if your normal shower routine were disrupted? How would a person with OCD react? Why? (See the Arts & Television series *Hoarders* and *Obsessed* for interesting examples.)

473

12. Children tend to have a high number of obsessive-compulsive habits (e.g., you must chew your food 20 times). In most cases, they grow out of them. Generate a list of childhood compulsive behaviors.

13. Critics of Dissociative Identity Disorder argue that the disorder is over-diagnosed and easy to fake. What kind of person would either intentionally or unintentionally show evidence of multiple personalities? Why?

14. In what ways might our ultracompetitive society contribute to the development of a sociopathic personality?

15. Suppose a person who is experiencing grief walks into a room and momentarily "sees" the recently departed loved one sitting in his or her favorite chair. Does this hallucination mean that the person is psychotic? Why or why not? How does a grieving person react to a hallucination? How does a schizophrenic react to a hallucination?

16. Briefly summarize the features of psychosis. Are "normal" behaviors completely without these qualities? Compare these to the qualities of normal functioning. Are psychotic behaviors different from normal behaviors in terms of kind or degree?

17. If reality were the same as TV, in what percent of cases would the insanity defense be used? How often do you think it is used in real life? How often do you think it is successful? (Answer: In reality, it is used *less than* 1 percent of the time—in some jurisdictions, it is as little as $1/100^{th}$ of 1 percent. When it is used, it is successful in securing an acquittal only one-quarter of the time.)

18. Some psychologists suggest that the majority of American families are dysfunctional. Can we expect that the incidence of schizophrenia will increase? Why or why not?

19. The most common psychotic disorders are the dementias (e.g., Alzheimer's disease and other dementias). Is there anything you can do to reduce the chance that you will develop Alzheimer's? What kind of activities do you intend to engage in once you retire?

20. The majority of families with a member who exhibits schizophrenic behaviors do not have other members with a history of schizophrenia episodes. Why?

21. Under what circumstances would you consider it reasonable for a stranger to be involuntarily committed? A friend? A close relative? Yourself?

22. In your opinion, how could a person experiencing a severe "problem in living" be most effectively helped?

23. Should a mental patient have the right to refuse medication? To demand legal counsel and alternative medical opinions? To refuse to work in a mental hospital or to choose the work that will be done? To communicate by phone, letter, or in person with anyone at any time? To keep personal property (including drugs, matches, pocketknives, and other potentially harmful materials)? To request an alternative to legal commitment to a mental hospital? To be represented by an independent "advocate" who is not on the hospital staff?

474

24. In view of what you know about the causes of psychosis, how valid do you consider the medical model of mental illness? What are the advantages and disadvantages of such a model? What are the advantages and disadvantages of a psychological model?

25. If the genetic component is large in major problems such as schizophrenia and mood disorders, should we try genetically to identify individuals at risk when no sure treatments are available? Should people who are close relatives of affected persons receive special counseling? What would the advantages and disadvantages of this be?

26. If you suffered from major depression, would you consider taking anti-depression medication? Why or why not? If you were diabetic or had heart or liver problems, would you take those medications? Why do we react differently when the brain (an organ) is not functioning properly, as compared to how we react to other organs' dysfunction?

27. The parents of John Hinkley (who attempted to assassinate President Reagan) have complained, "The comedian Robin Williams has great fun making sick jokes about 'crazies' like our son John, but does he joke about muscular dystrophy or cancer? Of course not." Do you agree or disagree with the point they are making?

28. How do you feel about forcing mentally ill homeless people into an institutional setting and treating them for their "own good," even if they refuse the treatment?

29. Discuss your feelings about the "death penalty" for convicted offenders who have been found to be legally sane but mentally ill.

30 A person is diagnosed as a pedophile, is convicted of child sexual abuse, is sentenced to 10 years in prison, and serves his/her prison term. After the individual's 10-year sentence has been completed, he/she is then court-ordered to remain "institutionalized" for mental health treatment for his/her pedophilia. The person may refuse treatment but can remain institutionalized indefinitely if they refuse the treatment. In essence, the person is being held for something they "might" do again instead of for something they have already served time for. How do you feel about this issue?

31. Why do you think men are more "successful" at suicide than women? What social factors may play a role?

➢ LECTURE ENHANCEMENTS

Films are often most effective when they are short, dramatic, and introduced as a way to activate the student rather than to induce drowsiness. To prevent students from distancing themselves from the concerns, issues, and plight of the mentally ill, the films can be stopped and students can be asked for their opinions or feelings. For example, after watching a film, students can be asked to view the depicted behavior from the perspective of family members.

If you do not have a clinical background, consider inviting a clinical or counseling psychologist to class. Because the chapter includes vocabulary that many students are not familiar with, it is important to help students rehearse and review terms as well as address issues and controversies.

1. **Attributes of psychologically healthy individuals.** Although the emphasis in this chapter is psychopathology and perspectives on abnormality, it should be useful to devote some class time to the concept of mental health. Earlier discussion of Maslow's research on self-actualization advances one view of mental health. What does the class perceive as the basic attributes of a psychologically healthy individual? Can psychopathology be defined in the absence of some notion of health? As a starting point for discussion, you may want to present Jahoda's list of attributes:

    a.   accurate self-concept, self-awareness, self-acceptance
    b.   self-actualization, full use of potential
    c.   autonomy
    d.   integration, a coherent outlook on life
    e.   accurate perceptions of reality, social sensitivity
    f.   competence and mastery of the environment

    (The preceding list is from Jahoda, 1980.)

2. **Did you see that?** A good way to illustrate the relativity of most definitions of abnormality is to ask the class to describe examples of odd or unusual behavior they have observed in public. After getting several examples, return to each and ask if there is any set of circumstances under which the behavior observed might be considered normal. (For example, the person observed had lost a bet, was undergoing an initiation, was practicing a part for a play, was part of a psychology experiment, etc.) The point is that the behavior may have been truly eccentric, and perhaps pathological, but that few behaviors are universally normal or abnormal.

3. **Who's crazy?** Ask students to give examples of someone whom they think is "mentally ill" or "crazy." Be sure that the example is NOT the student him/herself, to avoid subsequent embarrassment. Also, no names should be used. After two or three students have described the person, have them differentiate the behavior according to the criteria in the textbook: statistical abnormality, social non-conformity, subjective discomfort, and maladaptive. Do the people in the case studies fit all the criteria, or just some of them?

4. **Judging mental illness.** "Craziness" is not only cultural; it varies in time and space. Choose a classical story and adapt it to reflect a modern theme. (Bible stories are great for this, and the Old Testament is common to Judaism, Christianity, and Islam, so it is inclusive to most of your students) Make up a case study based on the relevant parts of the story. Possible examples include: Abraham following God's instructions to kill his son, King Solomon ordering two women in a custody battle to tug the baby between them, etc. Relate the modern story and ask your students to comment on the person in the case study. With sufficient imagination, your description will have them making all kinds of diagnostic statements! Once they have analyzed your scenario, inform them that it is not real and that you made it up based on a bible story. Ask them if anyone knows which one. (Usually someone will.) Ask them to retell the original story. Compare the original story with yours. Why are they considered different? Why is the person in your case study mentally ill, but bible characters are not? Did they consider the mental health of the characters, which many of them heard about as children? Be careful to be respectful of students' religious beliefs and make it clear that religion is not on "trial." Alternately, if you are a history buff, you can do the same thing, basing the case on some historical figure.

476

Here is an example story: *A man arrived home to find his two terrified children hiding in the closet. Their mother was sitting in the kitchen with a knife. The children said that their mother had chased them around the house, trying to kill them because a voice told her to. She had stopped because the voice had told her to stop. The man called 911 and his wife was admitted for psychiatric observation. She said that she loved her children and had no desire to harm them, but felt compelled to follow the directions of the voice.*

5. **Depression versus "the blues."** Students often misunderstand major depression as being just a more extreme case of "the blues." In order to help them understand that depression is also qualitatively different than "the blues," have some volunteers be blindfolded for a few minutes and try to navigate the classroom. Then, ask them if they now understand what a blind person's life is like. Make a list of all the ways that a blind person's life differs from simply being blindfolded (examples: work and home life, relationships, entertainment, mobility, etc.)

6. **Bipolar interview.** The Audio-Visual Center at Indiana University has produced a fascinating videotape that consists of interviews with four individuals suffering from a bipolar affective disorder. In the first sequence a therapist interviews a young woman while she is in the depressive phase of this disorder. This same young woman is then shown being interviewed during a manic episode. The change is so dramatic that students have great difficulty believing it is the same person. The tape then shows interviews with three different young men, each of whom is experiencing a hypomanic episode. Students find these interviews extremely interesting, and they produce a great deal of class discussion. The half-hour videotape can be obtained by writing to Indiana University Audi-Visual Center, Bloomington, IN 47401 and requesting Bipolar Affective Disorders, tape No. EVH 2198.

7. **Guest speaker on mental health.** If there is a chapter of the National Association for Mental Health in your area, volunteer speakers can often be arranged through this organization. Also, interested students may themselves participate as volunteers in outpatient programs or other mental health services.

8. **Impact of labeling.** For some reason, a simple description of the dangers of psychiatric labeling fails to impress many students with the profound impact such labeling can have. The dramatization described here must be handled with great care and sensitivity, but if it is done well, it may be one of the more memorable sessions of the course. Here is what you can say and do:

"Today we have a very special opportunity. After our last meeting a student from this class approached me and said that he had been hospitalized for schizophrenia several years ago. This student has volunteered to share with us his experiences while hospitalized. I told him I thought it was an excellent idea and added a twist of my own. One of the secondary problems often associated with mental hospitalization is the stigma that follows a person afterward. Many people believe that if a person becomes psychotic, that person will be 'crazy' for life. To illustrate how complete recovery from schizophrenia is, I'm going to call three people up to the front of the class. One is the student we will be talking to, and the other two don't know I'm going to call on them."

477

Select three students from the class and call them to the front. (It is best to select three students you know to be stable and adaptable. To avoid gender complications, select all male or all female students. In this example, male students are used.)

"In a few moments we're going to do an interesting thing. I want to prove that it is impossible to correctly identify a 'former mental patient.' To give you something to go on, I'm going to ask each of these people to tell us a little about themselves, their major in school, or their interests."

Have each student give his or her name and speak for one or two minutes. Then ask the class to decide which person they think was hospitalized at one point in his life. Tell them to write their choice. Just as they begin, tell them to stop and cross out anything they have written. Reveal to the class what you have done and emphasize that you selected the students because of their maturity and that you know nothing about their backgrounds. Begin discussion by interviewing the subjects. Given that each knew that he was not the former patient, his perceptions of the other two subjects are usually radically affected. Also note that what subjects choose to say about themselves under these circumstances is usually very safe and very normal. Next, interview the rest of the class and discuss how labeling affected their immediate perceptions and their interpretation of the past behavior of each subject. Be sure to point out that, while many were hesitant to choose one of the subjects, most did choose because of the labeling. Finally, be sure to thank the students who participated and ask the class to show their appreciation to them.

9. **Schizophrenia case study—quadruplets**. There is a case on record of four identical quadruplets all of whom developed schizophrenia. The odds against this happening are truly staggering. Identical quadruplets occur only once in every 16 million births, and less than half of them survive to adulthood; only one in a hundred of these is schizophrenic, and the odds against all of them being schizophrenic seem overwhelming. This case, then, could seem to provide evidence for the heritability of schizophrenia. However, you should point out to your students that the quadruplets shared many other things besides their genes. For example, they all shared their mother's uterus where they could have contracted a viral infection or been exposed to some chemical substance. They all had the possibly brain-damaging liability of being born with very low weights. All of them were placed in incubators and spent the first six weeks of their lives in a hospital. They all grew up with constant publicity surrounding their daily activities. Finally, they all shared a father who was known for eccentric and erratic behavior and who remained extremely close to them even into adulthood.

10. **Tour of a mental hospital.** If there is a mental hospital in your area, arrange to take your students on a tour of the facility. There will be an office for volunteers in the hospital. They will set it up or direct you to someone who will. Some of the students may wish to become volunteers once they know of the opportunity. You should give a thorough briefing, preparing the students for the observation. Discussion, films, or a visit by a volunteer would also help prepare the students so they get the most out of the trip. Otherwise, the students will not know what to look for, and the experience will become a matter of simply feeding their curiosity.

478

11. **Statistics on suicide.** As a take-home Internet assignment, have students research suicide rates in other countries or regions. Each student should choose one country with a higher suicide rate, and one with a lower suicide rate and list 3–5 sociocultural reasons for the difference in rates.

12. **Suicide statistics.** Look up some recent statistics you may want to discuss with your classes (The NIMH is good for this; see e.g. http://www.nimh.nih.gov/health/publications/suicide-in-the-us-statistics-and-prevention/index.shtml; see also http://www.teensuicide.us/): Suicide is the third leading cause of death among the young. And about 25 adolescents attempt suicide for every one who succeeds. Only accidents and homicide kill more young people. In general, male adolescents are about 4 times more likely to die from suicide while more female adolescents actually attempt it.

➤ ROLE-PLAYING SCENARIOS

1. You are a defense attorney interviewing a psychologist who has testified that your client was sane when he committed a crime. What questions will you ask the psychologist about how she reached her conclusion?

2. You're a psychiatrist. A woman comes to you complaining that her mother seems frightened and refuses to leave the house. Explain what the mother's problem is and help the daughter understand it.

3. Choose a phobia (fear of heights, spiders, etc.) and act-out the behaviors, thoughts, and emotions of a person who has a strong phobia. Role-play some of the treatment exercises.

4. Your friend Larry is showing paranoid symptoms. Suggest to Larry that he see a psychologist. What difficulty do you face in making this suggestion?

5. Imitate a person who is talking to a hallucination. Now contrast that with someone who is "thinking out loud" and talking to themselves. How would you know which is which?

6. You are a physician. Your patient has suddenly lost his ability to smell. There is no damage to his nose. You want to know whether your patient has a brain tumor. Explain to your patient why you want to use a CT scan rather than a PET scan.

7. Tanya feels her life is meaningless and hopeless. She has trouble functioning at work and at school. She continues to withdraw into herself more each day. How would you label her behavior? Why? What would you suggest that she do to break this pattern?

8. Because of a terrible mix-up you have been involuntarily committed to a mental hospital. Convince the ward psychologist that you are not psychotic and that a mistake has been made.

479

➤ VALUE-CLARIFICATION STATEMENTS

1. Psychotic people are not responsible for their behavior and should not be prosecuted for injuring others.

2. A person could easily fake symptoms and fool others into thinking they are psychotic.

3. It is better to occasionally err by providing government assistance to people who don't need it than to withhold help from those who do.

4. People are either mentally healthy or mentally unhealthy, with not a lot in between.

5. I would oppose a halfway house for mentally ill people in my neighborhood.

6. A person showing a pattern of schizophrenic behaviors should not be allowed to hold a full-time job that is even somewhat stressful.

7. A person with schizophrenia should not have children.

8. All a person needs to do to stop being depressed is to think of happy events.

9. Psychiatric drugs for anxiety and depression are just a "crutch" for a lot of people.

10. A person who admits to having attempted suicide or who has been treated for depression should be prohibited from running for president or vice president of the United States.

11. People who attempt suicide are just cowards.

12. A person convicted of manslaughter due to uncontrolled aggression should be required to receive psychosurgery.

13. Nothing can be done to stop a person who wants to commit suicide.

➤ ONE-MINUTE MOTIVATORS

1. **What's normal?** Prepare a list of unusual behaviors and ask students if they are normal or abnormal for: A man? A woman? A person? A culture emphasizing passivity? A culture emphasizing aggression?

2. **The "victim" mindset.** During the late 1980s, support groups developed to assist people who were victims of abuse, neglect, alcoholism, rape, family violence, etc. What are the advantages and the disadvantages of a "victim mind-set"?

3. **Name that disorder!** Read definitions of major DSM-IV categories and see if students can name the defined disorder. Remind students that the diagnosis of disorders may change over time and that a new edition of the DSM (DSM-V; see http://www.dsm5.org/Pages/Default.aspx) is due to be published in 2012.

480

4. **Why do mentally ill people scare us?** Ask students why the stereotype of the mentally ill as dangerous is so widespread. Statistically, most mentally ill people are not dangerous, and most dangerous people (murderers, rapists, thieves, burglars, drug dealers, etc.) are not mentally ill according to DSM categorization. Their answers will provide a good example to discuss the issues of baseline rates of various behaviors in the general population, as compared with the mentally ill population. You can also point out that whenever a mentally ill person is involved in a crime, their mental status is almost always part of the report, whereas it is not when other people commit crimes. Ask students if they have ever seen a headline like "person with no history of mental illness kills three coworkers." To them, the headline seems absurd, since they assume that mentally healthy people don't do things like that, whereas mentally ill people are "predictably" problematic.

5. **What are you doing?** Lecture while standing on a table, in the corner, or while walking from desktop to desktop. Or, make a repeated "fly catching" movement with your hand as you speak. Discuss the role of social norms in defining abnormal behavior. Also discuss how minor and undramatic a behavior may be and still raise questions about a person's normality.

6. **Social needs and narcissism.** We all have social needs, many of which depend on drawing other peoples' attention to ourselves. We all try to make ourselves look better (social desirability), and most of us see ourselves and our actions through rose-colored glasses (self-serving bias). However, some believe that celebrities are more likely to display traits of narcissism than other people. Where is the "line" between favorable self-presentation and narcissism? Is narcissism a cause or an effect of celebrity status? Name some celebrities you think do and don't have narcissistic qualities.

7. **What worries you?** Pass a transparency around the class. Ask students to list "worries." Share the transparency with the class as a prelude to discussing anxiety.

8. **Nervous breakdown**. A nervous breakdown is often mentioned when discussing mental illness. Ask students what has broken down. What "nerves" are affected and where are they? It should lead to a discussion of identifying disorders by symptoms instead of labels.

9. **Who's a sociopath?** When most students think of sociopaths, they think of serial killers or other high-saliency descriptions. Ask students to give examples of sociopathic characters. (One example might include unethical business people who steal from pension funds.) Evaluate these "ordinary" people according to the criteria for antisocial personality disorder.

10. **Compulsive partying.** Have students estimate the number of parties they attended during the preceding month. Make a frequency distribution on the chalkboard. Challenge the class to help you draw a line that defines "compulsive partying." As an alternative, collect data on the number of hours of television watched per week and define "TV addiction" by establishing a cut-off point.

481

11. **What's your phobia?** Asking students to self disclose is always tricky, as some unintentionally embarrass themselves or later feel self-conscious. But phobias are so widespread and unlikely to result in social stigma that it is usually interesting to students to discuss their own fears. Ask for a quick show of hands for those who are afraid of, for example, bugs, heights, flying, dogs, cats, or snakes. Ask if there are any additional phobias that you missed. Get a volunteer who is afraid of bugs to describe what he or she would do, think, or feel if there was a spider within 10 ft. or in the same room. Also ask student which phobias they had as children that they no longer have, since children typically have a high rate of phobias.

12. **New phobias.** Ask students to help you name some humorous new phobias, such as Muzakophobia (fear of being trapped in an elevator with insipid piped-in music playing in the background), or cellulitophobia (fear that one's thighs are turning to cottage cheese).

13. **Mental illness and stigma.** How would you react if you found out that a friend or neighbor was a "formal mental patient"? Make a list of all the things that you have done in the past when you heard that someone was a psychiatric patient (current or past).

14. **Anxiety and depression.** Students should be asked to recall times they felt sad or anxious. Have them write a few sentences describing their mood and behavior. What events precipitated these feelings? What helped them feel better? At what time during experiencing these feelings, is it appropriate to seek our professional help?

15. **How many people have been affected by depression?** Ask students by a quick show of hands how many of them know someone (family, friend, coworker) who has suffered from major depressive episode. How many of them know more than one person? Be sure to warn students about self-disclosure in the classroom environment, which is not confidential or private, and perhaps limit this discussion due to these concerns.

➤ BROADENING OUR CULTURAL HORIZONS

1. **What's normal where you live?** What effect might living in different parts of town, membership in a different ethnic group, or growing up in a different culture have on perceptions of "normality"?

2. **Definitions of normalcy across groups and cultures.** Prepare a list of unusual behaviors and ask students if they are normal or abnormal for: A man? A woman? A person? A culture emphasizing passivity? A culture emphasizing aggression?

3. **Culture-bound syndromes.** Your textbook discusses a number of culture bound syndromes—uniquely cultural disorders—such as *amok*, *susto*, or *Koro*. Do you think there are any disorders that are unique to Western culture? (Possible answers include higher rates of eating disorders and depression, and a number of sexual disorders, such as female anorgasmia, which are virtually unheard of in some cultures.) What factors in Western culture contribute to these disorders?

482

4.   **Gender and depression.** Depression is much more frequent among females than among males. Why? (e.g., dual role stress, stay-at-home moms and homemakers, different ways of coping, hormonal changes, poor self esteem, lower earning potential, etc.) What disorders are more common among males? (e.g., substance abuse) Why? Females tend to internalize problems, whereas males tend to externalize them. Sociopathy and hysteria tend to run together in families, with sociopaths being primarily male and hysterics being primarily female. Children who witness physical abuse in the home have an elevated risk of becoming abusers (males) or battering victims (females.) Children who are victims of sexual abuse have an elevated risk of becoming either sexual predators (rapists and pedophiles – males) or becoming promiscuous (females – many prostitutes have histories of sexual abuse).

5.   **Culture and mental illness.** Read about a culture very different from your own. What category of mental illness would you guess would be most frequent? Why?

6.   **Rates of depression in North America**. North Americans have one of the highest rates of depression in the world. Why? We also have more depression than our culture had 100 years ago. Why? How has our culture changed? Is the rate really higher, or is it just diagnosed more accurately today?

7.   **Cultural frequency of suicide.** Challenge students to compare the frequency of suicide in our culture to the frequency in another culture. How would they explain the difference?

8.   **Cultural definitions of mental illness.** Collect a few clips from *National Geographic* episodes and ask the class whether the behaviors shown would be perceived as "episodes of mental illness" within another culture.

9.   **What's normal here?** In many European countries, men's restrooms are tended by women. Discuss the implications this has for any attempt to create a culture-free definition of abnormal behavior.

10.   **Are terrorists mentally ill?** Recently, a number of Middle Eastern young persons have committed suicide by blowing themselves up, usually taking many innocent lives with them. Is this a form of mental illness? If so, into what category would this behavior fall?

➤ SUPPLEMENTAL ACTIVITIES

Abnormality has many different meanings. Certainly students come to this course with misconceptions and fixed ideas. To get students thinking along the same lines, you can use one or all of these exercises. By the time they are finished with the exercises and your class discussion of what they produced, they should be open to a more realistic appraisal of what is "normal" and what is not.

Exercise 13.1: What Is Normal?

In this exercise students will be asked to distinguish between what is normal behavior and what is abnormal. There are a number of ways to do this:

1. Statistically—this approach says that the mean is the norm, and any deviation from the mean is abnormal. The further one's behavior is from the mean, the less normal the person is, or, conversely, the more abnormal. Those furthest from the mean are the most abnormal. Notice that from this viewpoint, both positive and negative deviations are equally abnormal.

2. Clinically—people are judged as abnormal only if they display behaviors that deviate negatively from the norm. The greater the deviation, the greater the abnormality.

3. Humanistically—well-adjusted people are somewhat rare, and they occupy the top of the distribution: They are self-actualizers. All others are maladjusted to some degree. Those who are further down the scale are more maladjusted than those higher up.

Procedure

A. Discuss the three approaches to normality/abnormality outlined above.

B. Distribute the **Handout 13.1** for their responses.

C. Organize the class into small groups of three or four students so they can discuss the questions and record their conclusions on their worksheets.

D. After the students have completed the discussion, you should ask them to report their conclusions. As each group reports, the whole class can comment. This should generate a good deal of interest in the topic of behavior disorders.

E. Collect the students' work. Be sure that each student has written something. This is the best way to get students to think about the concepts being discussed.

Exercise 13.2: The Deviant Among Us

This exercise, if carefully planned and executed, can be very beneficial to students. The main objective is to provide an opportunity for them to observe people's reactions to deviant behavior. They will, moreover, get to try out some observation techniques and will need to look more closely at behavior than they are accustomed to doing.

The students will observe people's responses to deviant behavior. It will be their own deviant behavior! Organize the students into groups of three for this exercise. One will be the deviant behavior, and the other two will be the observers. If time and opportunity permit, they could rotate and each takes a turn at being deviant.

Students should form groups and plan a deviant behavior to perform and one or more locations in which to perform it. You should monitor this closely so that the behavior is inoffensive, and the locations are appropriate. Any mistakes here could be embarrassing and/or costly!

Suggest that the "deviant" student might join a table of two or three who are eating lunch in the cafeteria. He/she could then be unresponsive to any gestures of friendship and/or mumble to him/herself while eating. The observers should be at a nearby table appearing to eat lunch but unobtrusively noting the behavior of those at the table. Other possibilities might be talking loudly (to no one) while walking down a crowded hall or sobbing uncontrollably in a busy lounge. Other ideas will come up. Be sure the students clear their plans with you before proceeding. Students should use **Handout 13.2** for this assignment.

When the students return to class after completing the assignment, you should have a great discussion, including:

1. Reactions of the unsuspecting subjects to the "deviant"

2. The negative sanctions applied by the subjects

3. The feelings of your students before, during, and after the assignment was carried out

4. Their thoughts about what it means to be normal or abnormal

Have their ideas on that changed with this exercise?

It would be good to ask the students to write-up this project as an assignment for credit. They should describe the deviant behavior, the location, the reactions of the subjects, and their own reactions. This is a good way to give the students a chance to deal with their feelings about this assignment.

Exercise 13.3: Psychiatric Labeling

This is an exercise that should help students appreciate the problems created by using labels to identify the problem behaviors that people have. The persons become identified with the label, and our stereotypes take over. It is difficult for someone who has been labeled with a psychological problem to shake the image no matter how (s)he behaves.

PROCEDURE

1. Invite a person unknown to your students to come to class to describe their experience as a patient in a psychiatric hospital. The person needs to be a convincing actor who will feel comfortable in front of the class, but also one who will not embellish certain stereotypical behaviors of people who have been hospitalized. It is best to choose someone who has familiarity with a mental hospital—possibly someone who has worked or volunteered in one.

2. Prepare your class for the visit. Tell them that this person was diagnosed as paranoid schizophrenic and has spent a couple of brief periods of therapy in a mental hospital. Students should be asked to review the appropriate material in the text and to prepare questions about hospital life. Ask them to be sensitive to the feelings of the "patient."

485

3. After the speaker has departed, ask the students to discuss his/her behavior. They should look at it from a variety of points of view. Ask them to respond to questions such as those following. You may have others.

    a.   What was their impression of this person's behavior?
    b.   Did the person show any symptoms of the disorder for which she/he was hospitalized?
    c.   Does she/he appear to be "cured" of this disorder?
    d.   Did his/her thinking appear to be normal?
    e.   Were his/her emotions flat or inappropriate?
    f.   Did the students notice any side effects of medication?
    g.   Were there any peculiar or unusual behaviors?

DISCUSSION

After the discussion questions above are completed, tell the students what you did. Now discuss their reactions to this revelation. Also discuss their responses to the above questions. Did labeling influence their reactions and observations?

Exercise 13.4: Identifying Irrational Thoughts

According to Aaron Beck and Albert Ellis, one of the most significant aspects of depression is irrational thoughts. Although people with depression have disproportionately high numbers of irrational thoughts, everyone has some. This exercise can be tied in to the supplemental lecture "How Depressives Think" or can be a more abbreviated version.

Ask students to examine their thoughts and identify the irrational ones. Once they have done this, they should rewrite a more rational thought. So, for example, someone might express thoughts such as: "I'll never get through this course," or "I broke up with the only person I will ever really love," or "I missed my bus. I can't do anything right!"

You can accomplish this exercise one of two ways:
    a) Ask them to generate their own list of thoughts and identify why they are irrational (either general or with respect to Ellis's definitions).
    b) Distribute **Handout 13.3**—"Irrational Thoughts" and ask the students to identify recent thoughts they have had that fit each category.

486

Handout 13.1: WHAT IS NORMAL? WORKSHEET

TO THE STUDENT: In the space provided, report your group's decisions about each of the questions below. If you disagree with the rest of your group, indicate your disagreement and reasons. You will be asked to turn in this sheet after the discussion.

A. List five behaviors that would be considered abnormal according to all three approaches to the question of maladjustment explained by your instructor: statistical, clinical, or humanistic:

1.

2.

3.

4.

5.

B. List five behaviors that would be considered statistically abnormal but not from the other two points of view:

1.

2.

3.

4.

5.

C. List three behaviors that would be considered mentally healthy from the humanistic point of view:

1.

2.

3.

Handout 13.2: THE DEVIANT AMONG US: WORKSHEET

1. "Deviant" student_____

2. Observer students_____

3. Location_____

4. Description of deviant behavior:

5. Description of subjects (number, sex, approx. age, etc.):

6. Reactions of subjects:

488

Handout 13.3: <u>IDENTIFYING IRRATIONAL THOUGHTS</u>

For each of the following categories, <u>identify a recent thought</u> that you have had that is typical of this concept. <u>Then, rewrite the irrational thought</u> and replace it with a more rational, more positive, or less pessimistic thought. In other words, consider that your negative thought might be inaccurate or exaggerated.

1.   All-or-nothing thinking. This type of thinking is black-and-white, e.g., either you are a success or a failure, with nothing in between.

2.   Overgeneralization. You see a single negative event as evidence of an overall negative pattern.

3.   Mental filter. You dwell on a single negative event or remark until it takes over.

4.   Disqualifying the positive. You reject positive events or interpretations. You categorize positive events as exceptions to the rule.

5.   Jumping to conclusions. You immediately assume the worst, or make a negative conclusion about something.

6.   Magnification/catastrophizing. You exaggerate the severity of the negative outcome, or exaggerate your imperfections.

7.   Emotional reasoning. You assume that negative emotions are consistent with reality.

8.   "Should" statements. You are intolerant of anything that falls short of your standards for yourself or others. You punish yourself or others for being imperfect.

9.   Personalization. You see yourself as more responsible for a negative outcome than you really were.

10.   Labeling and mislabeling. You assume your error is evidence of some negative trait (self or other). e.g., I failed a test, therefore I'm a failure.

489

➤ JOURNAL QUESTIONS

1. Has anyone ever called you or someone you love "crazy" or "insane"? How did it make you feel?

2. Think of a behavior that you would label "abnormal." Which definition are you using for this labeling process?

3. Imagine that you heard from others in class that someone in your class was "psychotic." How would you feel? How would this information probably affect your behavior?

4. What phobias do you have? Write down all of your phobias and indicate why you think there is something to fear. Where do you think this phobia came from? How did you learn to be afraid of this? Did you used to have any phobias that you no longer have? Why did you have those phobias? Why don't you have them anymore? Could you get rid of your current phobias too? Why or why not?

5. Have you ever known someone who abused or became dependent on drugs? How did the drugs affect their ability to function at home or at work? Were they able to eventually stop using the drugs? If so, how?

6. Do you ever feel depressed? What situations seem to make the depression worse? What do you do to try to stop feeling depressed?

7. Describe one of your irrational fears. When and how did the fear develop? How does it affect your behavior? What could be done to reduce the fear?

➤ SUGGESTIONS FOR FURTHER READING

Achenback, T., & Edelbrock, C. (1984). Psychopathology of childhood. *Annual Review of Psychology, 34*, 227-256.

Alvarez, A. (1990). *The savage god: A study of suicide.* New York: Norton.

American Psychiatric Association (2000). *Diagnostic and statistical manual of mental disorders DSM-IV-TR* (4th ed., Text Revision). Washington, DC: American Psychiatric Association.

Durand, V. M., & Barlow, D. H. (2010). *Essentials of abnormal psychology* (5th ed.). Belmont, CA: Cengage Learning/Wadsworth.

Green, H. (1964). *I never promised you a rose garden.* New York: Penguin.

Hansell, J. H. (2007). *Abnormal psychology: The enduring issues* (2nd ed.). New York: Wiley.

Hare, R. D. (2006). Psychopathy: A clinical and forensic overview. *Psychiatric Clinics of North America, 29*(3), 709–724.

Hayward, L. C., & Coles, M. E. (2009). Elucidating the relation of hoarding to obsessive compulsive disorder and impulse control disorders. *Journal of Psychopathology & Behavioral Assessment, 31*(3), 220-227.

Heinrichs, R. W. (2001). *In search of madness*. New York: Oxford.

Jahoda, M. (1980). *Current concepts of positive mental health*. Manchester, NH: Ayer Company Publishers, 1980.

Kesey, K. (1962/2002). *One flew over the cuckoo's nest*. Tonbridge, Kent, UK: Viking Press.

Laing, R. D. (1983). *The politics of experience*. New York: Random House.

Levy, D. L., Coleman, M. J., Sung, H., et al. (2010). The genetic basis of thought disorder and language and communication disturbances in schizophrenia. *Journal of Neurolinguistics, 23*(3), 176-192.

López, S. R., & Guarnaccia, P. J. (2000). Cultural psychopathology: Uncovering the social world of mental illness. *Annual Review of Psychology, 51,* 571–598.

Meyer, R., Chapman, L. K., & Weaver, C. M. (2008). *Case studies in abnormal behavior* (8th ed.). Boston: Allyn & Bacon.

Nasar, S. (2001). *A beautiful mind: The life of mathematical genius and Nobel Laureate John Nash*. Carmichael, CA: Touchstone Books.

North, C. S. (1987). *Welcome, Silence*. New York: Simon & Schuster.

Rosenhan, D. L. (1973). On being sane in insane places. *Science, 179,* 250–258.

Ross, C. A. (2000). *Bluebird: Deliberate creation of multiple personality by psychiatrists*. Richardson, TX: Manitou Communications.

Schreiber, F. R. (1973/2009). *Sybil*. New York: Warner Books.

Stoppard, J. M., & McMullen, L. M. (Eds.). (2003). *Situating sadness: Women and depression in social context*. New York: New York University Press.

Styron, W. (2007). *Darkness visible: A memoir of madness*. New York: Random House.

Szasz, T. (1984). *The myth of mental illness*. New York: HarperCollins.

Torrey, E. F. (2006). *Surviving schizophrenia: A manual for families, patients, and providers*. New York: Harper Collins.

Winstead, B. A., & Sanchez, J. (2005). Gender and psychopathology. In J. E. Maddux & B. A.

Winstead (Eds.), *Psychopathology: Foundations for a contemporary understanding*. Mahwah, NJ: Erlbaum.

Young, S. M., & Pinsky, D. (2006). Narcissism and celebrity. *Journal of Research in Personality, 40*(5), 463–471.

➢ VIDEO SUGGESTIONS

Feature Films

A Beautiful Mind (Russell Crowe, Jennifer Connelly, Ed Harris), Drama. The film is based on the true story of prominent mathematician John Forbes Nash, Jr. who is played by Crowe. Nash is a brilliant professor with a bright future and a beautiful wife, Alicia (Connelly). Everything begins to fall apart as his paranoid schizophrenic activities are revealed. Nash learns to live with his illness and wins the Nobel Prize for his work. An award-winning film.

Agnes of God (1985). Jane Fonda stars in a film depicting a confrontation between religion and psychiatry.

Alligator Shoes (1982). A family deals with the problems that arise when a mentally ill aunt moves in.

As Good As It Gets (Jack Nicholson, Helen Hunt). In this film, Nicholson displays behavior showcasing obsessive-compulsive disorder.

At Close Range (1986) Sean Penn stars in a film that depicts the effects that a psychopathic father has on his sons.

Beaches (Bette Midler). Midler, who plays a famous musician with an ailing friend, displays histrionic personality disorder in this film about life-long friendship.

A Bronx Tale (Robert De Niro, Chazz Palminteri, Lillo Brancato), Drama. Calogero, (Capra) is witness to a murder committed by Sonny. Sonny befriends him and introduces the young man to the mob. Calogero idolizes Sonny but loves and respects his honest father, Lorenzo Anello (DeNiro). It takes a major tragedy for the 17-year-old boy to decide his true course in life.

Copycat (Sigourney Weaver). Weaver plays a psychologist specializing in serial killer behavior that becomes agoraphobic after a near-death experience with a serial killer. Weaver becomes involved in a police investigation when a serial killer begins copying famous serial killers' signature murders.

Deep Red (Michael Biehn, Joanna Pacula, Jack Andreozzi), Drama/Science Fiction. Gracie (Haun), a young person whose bloodstream is infected by a strange, extraterrestrial element known as "Deep Red," is possibly immortal. Thomas Newmeyer, a researcher, wants to drain all of the blood from her body, but hero Joy Keys (Biehn) stops Newmeyer and in the process patches up his relationship with his wife.

The Deer Hunter (1978). DeNiro stars in a powerful film that deals with the psychological consequences of war.

The Dream Team (1989). The character played by Michael Keaton leads three other psychiatric patients on an adventure through the streets of New York.

Fatal Attraction (Michael Douglas, Glenn Close). Woman with signs of borderline personality disorder stalks a philandering husband.

First Blood (Sylvester Stallone). A Vietnam veteran experiences post-traumatic stress disorder.

Frances (1982). Jessica Lange portrays a woman who suffers as a result of her nonconformity.

Girl, Interrupted (Winona Ryder, Angelina Jolie), Drama. Winona Ryder gets diagnosed with borderline personality disorder and loses herself in an Oz-like netherworld, but more insane and dangerous.

Jackknife (1989). A Robert DeNiro film that deals with post-traumatic stress disorder.

K-PAX (Kevin Spacey, Jeff Bridges, Mary McCormack), Drama, Science Fiction. Prot (Spacey) claims that he is an alien from the Planet K-PAX. After an incident at New York's Grand Central Station, Prot is placed in a mental hospital under the care of Dr. Mark Powell (Bridges). Powell becomes involved with his patient and wonders if his patient's story of being from another planet is true. Prot claims that he must leave Earth and the pressure is on for a psychiatric breakthrough before the departure date.

Nuts (1987). The concept of legal sanity is debated in a courtroom drama starring Barbara Streisand.

One Flew Over the Cuckoo's Nest (1975). A classic film starring Jack Nicholson that raises the question of what is in the best interest of the institutionalized patient.

Prince of Tides (Nick Nolte, Barbra Streisand, Blythe Danner), Drama. Tom Wingo (Nolte) is stuck in a hopeless marriage and feels trapped in his life, and is suddenly awakened when his sister tries to kill herself. He goes to his sister's side in New York where he meets Susan Lowenstein (Streisand), his sister's psychiatrist. Susan and Tom begin a relationship as Tom learns to deal with the feelings he has for his mother and his wife.

Requiem for a Dream (Ellen Burstyn, Jared Leto, Jennifer Connelly), Drama. Four people are trapped by their addictions. Harry (Leto) and his best friend Tyron (Wayans) are heroin addicts living in Coney Island, NY. Harry's girlfriend Marion (Connelly) is also an addict who is trying to distance herself from her wealthy father. Harry's mother, Sara, becomes addicted to amphetamines when she goes to a doctor to loose weight for a game show she is appearing on. *Silence of the Lambs* (Jodie Foster, Anthony Hopkins, Scott Glenn), Thriller. Clarice Starling (Foster) is a student with the FBI's training academy who is sent to interview Dr. Hannibal Lecter (Hopkins), who is behind bars for murder and cannibalism. Through the interview Clarice hopes to gain insight into a vicious murderer named Buffalo Bill. Lecter is willing to give her advice but it has a price. In exchange he wants to speak with Clarice about her past.

The Three Faces of Eve (Joanne Woodward, David Wayne, Lee Cobb), Drama. A young Georgia housewife, Eve (Woodward), suffers from multiple personalities. Eve's husband (Wayne) seeks help from a psychiatrist (Cobb). With the use of hypnosis the doctor is able to find out that each

493

of Eve's personalities is aware of the other's existence. After months of therapy, Eve is cured. Joanne Woodward stars as "Eve"—classic case study of Chris Sizemore, which first brought dissociative identity (multiple personality) disorder to the public's attention.

Educational Films and Videos

Abnormal Psychology, (2000), Films for the Humanities & Sciences, (various times). This reference is an entire 18-page catalog of films and videos in abnormal psychology. The catalog is available from the following address: P.O. Box 2053, Princeton, New Jersey, 08543-2053, or you can access their website at http://www.films.com.

ADHD: What Can We Do? (1992), University Film & Video, 35 min. This video focuses on ways to manage attention-deficit hyperactivity disorder (ADHD). It details parent training methods and demonstrates effective strategies for situations at home, at school, and in public places. It also provides examples of techniques teachers can use, and describes medications for managing ADHD.

ADHD: What Do We Know? (1992), University Film & Video, 37 min. This video outlines the history, etiology, and prevalence of attention-deficit hyperactivity disorder and discusses long-term outcomes for those affected. It documents the impact of this disorder on young people and their families, as well as the special problems presented at school.

Aggression, Violence, and the Brain, from *The Brain Teaching Modules*, 2nd Edition #24 (1998) Annenberg/CPB, (7:17). The topic of aggression and violence is discussed.

Anxiety-Related Disorders: The Worried Well (2002) Films for the Humanities and Sciences, 15 min. each. Each of the six programs in this series addresses a different condition. During powerful and moving interviews, two patients with each condition share their distressing stories of how the disorders have wreaked havoc on their lives and how they've learned to cope. Several people have achieved a semblance of normality in their lives in spite of their dysfunctions. Leading experts in each field provide brief explanations of the condition.

Autism: A Strange, Silent World, (1991), Filmmakers Library, 57 min. This award-winning video takes a sensitive and comprehensive view of autism by focusing on three children of different ages, each with very different behavior patterns. It also introduces us to parents, teachers, and therapists who strive to maximize the potential of these children.

Behind Closed Doors, (1993), Filmmakers Library, 46 min. This award-winning documentary portrays domestic violence from a very personal perspective. It focuses on two people, an abuser and, in a different case, a victim. Both discuss their difficult childhoods, their low self-esteem, their feelings of shame, and their determination to break the patterns of violence that have governed their lives.

Behind the Curtain: A Search for Solutions to Autism, (1993), Filmmakers Library, 28 min. This brief but information-packed video explores the possible origins of autism and the therapies developed for treatment. It introduces us to a broad spectrum of professionals who have differing views on this disorder. The documentary shows four principal therapies for autistic children.

Borderline Syndrome: A Personality Disorder of Our Time, (1989), Filmmakers Library, 74 min. Patients diagnosed with borderline personality disorder are a growing population in mental health facilities. Rare footage in this award-winning video shows in-depth conversations with patients and hospital staff members.

Bulimia, (1987), Films for the Humanities and Sciences, 28 min. If you cover the topic of eating disorders, which are becoming increasingly common in our society, you might want to use this video. It deals with the topic from the perspectives of both patients and therapists. Hosted by Phil Donahue, the program explores the pressure to be thin and how it may lead to the self-destructive eating disorder of bulimia. Low self-esteem, depression, and anger are both its causes and effects. This cycle is usually reversible through psychotherapy. Experts include Craig Johnson of the Psychosomatic-Psychiatric Center in Chicago and Susan Wooley of the Clinic for Eating Disorders in Cincinnati. Bulimic patients also discuss the illness from a first-person perspective.

Case Study of Multiple Personality, (1973), CRM/McGraw-Hill, 30 min. This is an assemblage of scenes from the film *Three Faces of Eve*; it depicts multiple personality and includes actual interviews.

Childhood's End, (1982), Filmmakers Library, 57 min. This is a documentary portrait of three suicidal youngsters, one of whom succeeded in killing himself. The film does not try to simplify a complicated phenomenon and leaves a strong impression of the tragedy and waste of this irreversible action.

Dealing with Alzheimer's Disease, (1990), Terra Nova films, 21 min. This video deals especially with communication techniques, both verbal and nonverbal, for Alzheimer's patients. It was produced with the Alzheimer's Treatment and Research Center, and Ramsey Foundation.

Depression and Manic Depression, (2002), Films for the Humanities and Sciences, 28 min. This program from *The Doctor Is In* explains the disease through the experiences of several people, including *60 Minutes* host Mike Wallace; Kay Redfield Jamison, psychiatrist and author of a book on her life with manic-depressive illness; artist Lama Dejani; and State Department official Robert Boorstin. The program also provides an overview of medications and therapy being used.

Depression: Beating the Blues, (1985), Filmmakers Library, 28 min. As this film indicates, unlike normal feelings of being blue, which may last for hours or days, true clinical depression can last for weeks and months. The film investigates the latest research on the causes of depression and explores the variety of treatments available. Among the treatments highlighted are chemotherapy, electroconvulsive therapy, and psychotherapy. This film has historical value.

Depression: Beyond the Darkness, (1991), Insight Media, 58 min. This video presents a nice discussion of the various psychological theories concerning the origins of depression (e.g., cognitive, biological). It also explores the nature of treatment through a review of intervention techniques, including cognitive therapy, drug treatments, and electroconvulsive therapy.

Dyslexia: A Different Kind of Mind, (1997), Films for the Humanities and Sciences, 29 min. (Finalist, AMA International Health & Medical Film Competition) Dyslexia, a learning disability that affects oral and written language, often masks the presence of a gifted mind. People with dyslexia learn differently. This program from *The Doctor Is In* explores that cognitive difference by examining how dyslexic students learn, and how new teaching techniques are helping them succeed in school. These teaching approaches are explored at the Washington Lab School—a pioneer in the implementation of innovative teaching methods. Thomas West, author of *In the Mind's Eye,* discusses our society's need for the visual talents possessed by many people with dyslexia. (May also be used with Ch. 6.) A Dartmouth-Hitchcock Medical Center production.
Full of Sound and Fury: A Film About Schizophrenia, (1985), Filmmakers Library, 54 min. What is it like to suffer from schizophrenia? This film explores the lives of three individuals who have been profoundly affected by this elusive mental disorder. For the families of those suffering from schizophrenia, the experience is tragic, and the film presents an interview with the mother of a young man whose torment ultimately drove him to suicide.

Getting Anxious, (1984), Insight Media, 30 min. This video presents the common symptoms found in a variety of anxiety disorders including phobias, obsessive-compulsive disorders, and panic attacks. It also reviews the effectiveness of various therapies employed to treat anxiety disorders.

I'm Still Here: The Truth About Schizophrenia, (1996), Insight Media, 67 min. This video debunks a number of myths about schizophrenia. Illustrates how patients afflicted with the illness are still able to live extraordinarily productive lives.

John's Not Mad: Tourette Syndrome, (1993), Filmmakers Library, 28 min. This powerful documentary portrays an adolescent who suffers from a severe case of Tourette's, which causes him to make involuntary sounds, including a constant stream of profanity. He feels that these words and sounds are forced out of him beyond his control. It should be noted to your classes that most people with Tourette syndrome are not as severely affected as the patient in this video, who represents the extreme end of the spectrum.

Leonard's Travels, (1994), Filmmakers Library, 20 min. Although brief, this video offers a human face to mental illness. Leonard is a seven-foot-tall bearded giant who has spent the first 20 years of his adult life in and out of mental institutions. We see a peer counseling session and hear the client's candid comments about an antiquated mental health system. It's worthwhile for any instructor wanting to present a brief case study of a sensitive person wanting to help others.

Leslie: A Portrait of Schizophrenia, (1990), Filmmakers Library, 57 min. This award-winning video is about a young black man suffering from paranoid schizophrenia. Hearing voices and hallucinating as a child, abandoned by his parents in his teens, 21-year-old Leslie obeyed voices telling him to jump from a fifth-floor apartment window. This is an especially interesting video

496

in that Leslie himself conceived and developed the outline for the program, including drawing the artwork and graphics and composing the original music. This allows your students to see a contributing side to schizophrenia.

Living with Tourette's, (1992), Encyclopedia Britannica Educational Corporation, 25 min. This program examines the personal, emotional, and communication difficulties involving a person with Tourette's syndrome. The short duration of this video may make it appropriate for classroom use, even though you may not emphasize Tourette's syndrome in classroom content.

Madness, (1992), Brook Productions, 58 min. Produced for BBC television and KCET/Los Angeles, this series has five parts: (1) *To Define True Madness*—explores past and present myths about mental illness and how our current-day perceptions and fears compare with earlier superstitions; (2) *Out of Sight*—looks at the history of institutionalized treatment for mental patients; (3) *Brain Waves*—discusses the history of medical discoveries about the structure and functioning of the brain; (4) *The Talking Cure*—looks at Sigmund Freud and some modern variations on his work; and (5) *In Two Minds*—discusses schizophrenia, the most baffling of mental diseases.

Masks Of Madness (1998) Insight Media, 49 min. Featuring the personal stories of recovered mental illness patients, this video explains how help comes first in the form of a label—like schizophrenia, manic depression, or personality disorder—and then as medication. It reveals the problematic side effects of many medications and highlights the increasing success of strategies that involve vitamin therapy and nutrition.

Mental Illness, (1990), Films for the Humanities and Sciences, 23 min. Everyone is exposed to some form of mental illness, observing, if not undergoing, what can range from a minor annoyance to a serious affliction. This program describes the most common mental illnesses: phobias, anxiety attacks, and nervous breakdowns, as well as schizophrenia, the most insidious and complex of mental afflictions. Although there is much we have yet to learn about them, mental illnesses are increasingly being deciphered by scientific and medical research.

Mood Disorders: Hereditary Factors, from *The Mind Teaching Modules,* 2nd Edition, #32 (2000) Worth, 6:11. This video discusses bipolar disorders. A 10-year study involving 12,000 volunteers from an Amish community is discussed.

Mood Disorders: Mania and Depression, from *The Mind Teaching Modules,* 2nd Edition #31 (2000) Worth, 7:34. This video presents vivid examples of the mood fluctuations of patients who suffer from periodic affective episodes.

Mood Disorders (2002) Films for the Humanities and Sciences, 39 min. Mood disorders, or affective disorders, are discussed in this program together with their symptoms and differential diagnoses. The two main classifications of mood disorders—manic and depressive—are clearly defined and differentiated according to symptoms. The persistent mood disorders cyclothymia and dysthymia are discussed, along with medical causes of mood disorders.

Multiple Personality Disorder (1999) Insight Media, 50 min. Multiple personality disorder, now termed dissociative identity disorder, remains one of the most misunderstood mental disorders today. Although it is usually triggered by abuse or trauma, there are many cases with no apparent cause behind the onset of the affliction. This program enters the minds of several people who have battled multiple personality disorder, offering an intimate look at what life is like for those who live with strangers in their own minds. It takes an in-depth look at the Sybil case.

Multiple Personality Disorder: In The Shadows (2002) Films for the Humanities and Sciences, 24 min. Multiple personality disorder (MPD), now known as dissociative identity disorder, is a completely preventable medical condition. Studies show that the average MPD patient spends seven years and receives three incorrect diagnoses before receiving an accurate diagnosis and appropriate treatment. It is now recognized that MPD is the result of severe childhood trauma, usually sexual and physical abuse—and it develops as a coping mechanism in young children, who develop other personalities to deal with pain, fear, and danger. As the child grows older, this dissociation ceases to be a coping mechanism and becomes a block to normal functioning. This program shows how therapy can integrate the multiple personalities and make a patient "whole" again. Following two MPD patients and health care professionals, the program traces the struggles and triumphs in treating this disorder.

Multiple Personalities, (1994), Insight Media, 30 min. This video does a good job of presenting dissociative identity disorder by depicting three individuals diagnosed with the disorder. It explores the roots of the disorder to be found in childhood abuse.

Multiple Personality, from *The Brain Teaching Modules*, 2nd Edition #23, (1998), Annenberg/CPB, 9:09. The program begins by defining dissociative identity disorders. DID starts in childhood, triggered by the need to flee psychologically from real physical or sexual abuse. DID elicits great interest among students due to the number of movies and TV epics that dramatize the disorder.

Mysteries of the Mind, (1988), Films for the Humanities and Sciences, 58 min. This program explores manic-depression, obsessive-compulsive, alcoholism, and other mood disorders whose victims show a lack of control over their behavior and their life. It examines the neurochemical and genetic components of these disorders, as well as physiological, neurological, and biomedical research into the mysteries of the brain; the program also shows the nature of these mood disorders and the pain they cause patients and their families.

Neurotic, Stress-Related, and Somatoform Disorders, (2002), Films for the Humanities and Sciences, 45 min. This program discusses the following disorders and their differential diagnoses: phobic anxiety, anxiety, obsessive-compulsive disorder, stress reactions and adjustment, and dissociative disorders. Several sub-disorders, such as Korsakov's syndrome and post-traumatic stress disorder, are also discussed.

Panic, (2002), Films for the Humanities and Sciences, 26 min. This film explains anxiety disorders, including panic attacks and phobias. People with phobias are interviewed, and the treatment procedures are explained. The biological factors contributing to anxiety disorders are described.

Panic Attack: Causes and Treatments, (1991), Films for the Humanities and Sciences, 29 min. You are in a cold, clammy sweat and pervaded by fear. These are two symptoms of a panic attack, a debilitating mental disorder that affects thousands of people worldwide. This program explores the possible causes of the condition and examines treatments, particularly cognitive therapy. Three patients talk about their lives lived under the pall of panic attacks. One patient, whose first occurrence was on a train trip, takes a short train journey as part of her liberating therapy. A BBC Production. Color.

Personality Disorders, (2002), Films for the Humanities and Sciences, 26 min. This program looks at the most common personality disorders—paranoid, schizoid, antisocial, and emotionally unstable.

Psychopathology, (1990), Annenberg/CPB, 30 min. This program from Zimbardo's *Discovering Psychology* series is excellent because it presents the text from a historical and a contemporary perspective. Symptoms and causes are the specific content areas covered. A cultural case study shows the impact of our society on the Native American population.

Psychotic Disorders, (1990), Coast Community College District Telecourses, 30 min. Part of the *Psychology—The Study of Human Behavior Series*, this video discusses schizophrenia, its treatment and possible causes.

Schizophrenia: Etiology, from *The Brain Teaching Modules*, 2nd Edition #27 (1998) Annenberg/CPB, 14:45. This video shows the impact of both organic and environmental factors on schizophrenia.

Schizophrenia: Symptoms, from *The Brain Teaching Modules*, 2nd Edition #26 (1998) Annenberg/CPB, 5:39. This video focuses on schizophrenia as a disease. This is a realistic view of what the disease involves and how disabling it can be.

Schizophrenia and Delusional Disorders (2002) Films for the Humanities and Sciences, 46 min. Schizophrenia, acute and transient psychoses, persistent delusional disorders, and schizoaffective disorders are examined in this program. Specific symptoms of each disorder are discussed.

Seasonal Affective Disorder, (1993), Encyclopedia Britannica Films, 25 min. This video examines biological rhythms and their influence on the behavior of animals and humans. It illustrates the influence of light and the hormone melatonin, using a variety of natural activities including sleep, mating, and emotional experiences.

Suicide: The Parents' Perspective, (2002), Films for the Humanities and Sciences, 26 min. This film helps parents listen more sensitively for signs of potential suicide.

Suicide: The Teenager's Perspective, (2002), Films for the Humanities and Sciences, 26 min. This film suggests that peer groups can be successfully trained to notice signs and to give friends support. Jim Wells, a nationally recognized expert on suicide, suggests that teens don't want to die and they do want help.

Sybil, (1976), a made-for-TV movie. A classic film in which Sally Field portrays a young woman who supposedly had 17 personalities.

The Addicted Brain, (1987*),* Films for the Humanities and Sciences, 26 min. This documentary takes viewers on a tour of the world's most prolific manufacturer and user of drugs—the human brain. The biochemistry of the brain is responsible for joggers' highs, for the compulsion of some people to seek thrills, for certain kinds of obsessive-compulsive behavior, even for the

© 2012 Cengage Learning. All Rights Reserved. May not be copied, scanned, or duplicated, in whole or in part, except for use as permitted in a license distributed with a certain product or service or otherwise on a password-protected website for classroom use.

drive to achieve power and dominance. The program explores developments in the biochemistry of addiction and addictive behavior.

The Compulsive Mind, (1995), Films for the Humanities and Sciences, 28 min. This program focuses on a woman with obsessive-compulsive disorder (OCD) who has a fear of contamination. This woman describes her cleaning routine, which includes 200 hand washings a day. This video illustrates the role of medication and behavior modification in the treatment of OCD. This program observes the client as she works with her therapist.

The Diagnosis and Treatment of Attention Deficit Disorder in Children, (1995), Films for the Humanities and Sciences, 27 min. This program from *The Doctor Is In* shows how a diagnosis of Attention Deficit Disorder (ADD) is made and what treatments are working. The program follows children at home and school, both on and off medication. An innovative private school specializing in alternative education for children with ADD is profiled, and the program explains how best to structure school and home environments. Psychiatrists John Ratey and Ned Hallowell, experts in this field, provide background and perspective. A Dartmouth-Hitchcock Medical Center production.

The Many Faces of Marsha, (1991), Insight Media (48 min.). The fascinating case of Marsha is presented in this video from CBS's *48 Hours*. The video does a good job of presenting the mysteries of dissociative identity disorder as it explores many of Marsha's 200 personalities.

The Politics of Addiction, (1998), Films for the Humanities and Sciences, 57 min. The story of how our society meets the challenge of translating what scientists, doctors, counselors, and recovering addicts have learned into rational public policy is complex and sometimes contradictory. This program looks at Arizona's recent struggle to find an alternative to current policies. Proposition 200 proposed a reassessment of the status of nonviolent drug addicts now serving time, and emphasized treatment over incarceration. The movement was supported by an alliance from across the political spectrum. On the Washington scene, members of Congress, doctors, and policy activists have joined in a movement with recovering people that is pushing for new public policy.

The Silent Epidemic: Alzheimer's Disease, (1982), Filmmakers Library, 25 min. This film describes Alzheimer's disease and shows the problems raised by its ever-increasing incidence. The film notes that although the disease can be diagnosed, there is still no cure for its degenerative and ultimately fatal course. Also discussed is the issue of whether Alzheimer's patients should be cared for in their homes or in other facilities.

The Spiral Cage, (1991), University Film and Video, 28 min. This video documents the life of Al Davison, a middle-aged English novelist born with spina bifida. Through interviews and illustrations, it captures the stigma and fear Al experienced as a taunted schoolboy. Al discusses the continuation of verbal and physical abuse into adulthood and his growing self-acceptance and determination to live a full life. This sensitive film should increase the acceptance level of your class.

The Touching Tree, (1993), Awareness Films, 38 min. This short but sensitive drama portrays a young boy with obsessive-compulsive disorder: how he faces his fears and begins the slow process of recovery with professional help and the attention of an understanding teacher. You may want to show this if you have future teachers or counselors in your class.

Understanding Borderline Personality Disorder, (1995), Insight Media, 35 min. This video presents clinically relevant features of borderline personality disorder (BPD) based on DSM-IV criteria. Marsha Linehan describes the underlying causes of the disorder, emphasizing biosocial factors, and traces the development of her treatment approach, dialectical behavior therapy. Viewers see segments of actual case sessions.

Understanding Psychological Disorders, Parts I & II, (2002), Coast Community College Telecourses, 30 min. each. Part of the *Psychology: The Human Experience Series,* these videos present research on both obsessive-compulsive disorders and schizophrenia, including a look at the daily lives of such patients and the prognosis for the future.

The Violent Mind, (1998), PBS Video, 60 min. Program 9 in *The Mind* series. This research-oriented program deals with the anatomy and biochemistry of the brain and the changes that may cause violent behavior. Some conclusions suggest that even the violent acts of serial killers may have a biological or genetic origin. The program also discusses the ethical issues and legal complications of those conclusions. If you like to encourage spirited discussions with your class after media programs, this program provides much to discuss.

The World of Abnormal Psychology, Volumes 1–13, (1992), Annenberg/CPB, 60 min. each. This highly acclaimed series from Annenberg covers a wide variety of topics including anxiety disorders, personality disorders, sexual disorders, mood disorders, schizophrenia, and disorders of childhood. Each of the disorders is vividly illustrated by the use of people actually diagnosed with the disorder. Causes, cures, and prevention are all discussed.

Through Madness, (1993), Filmmakers Library, 30 min. Winner of numerous awards, this powerful documentary demystifies mental illnesses and humanizes those who suffer from them. We hear about psychological disorders from three people who describe them from the inside out: a schizophrenic, a paranoid schizophrenic, and a manic-depressive. Each of these individuals presents an engrossing tale of despair and hope, and teaches us about the fragile boundary between sanity and insanity.

Twins: A Case Study, (1990), Filmmakers Library, 52 min. This award-winning video provides a remarkable portrait of 45-year-old Yorkshire twins who dress alike, speak in unison, share everything, and are inseparable. Trusting no one but each other, they have fixated on one man as a love object. Among questions addressed is whether they are both psychotic, or whether one is just imitating the other.

What Is Normal? (1990), Insight Media, 30 min. This video discusses the distinctions between normal and abnormal behavior. Experts in the field explain at what point people need help, describe treatment strategies, and show how professionals classify disorders.

➢ COMPUTER AND INTERNET RESOURCES

PsykTrek 3.0
Unit 13: Abnormal Behavior and Therapy
13a. "Anxiety Disorders"
13b. "Mood Disorders"
13c. "Schizophrenic Disorders"

INFOTRAC®

Below you will find three journal articles obtained from INFOTRAC® that relate to information contained in this chapter. Instructors should encourage students to utilize this invaluable resource to improve their research skills. Have students locate and read the following articles and answer questions relevant to each article.

Internet Wire, March 7, 2005 **Common schizophrenia symptoms often overlooked by physicians, according to expert panel, these untreated symptoms are roadblocks to patient recovery.**

1.   Historically medications to treat schizophrenia have focused on "positive symptoms." What are positive symptoms?

 Answer: Positive symptoms include hallucinations, delusions, and disorganization of thinking.

2.   Newer medications introduced in the early 1990s known as atypical antipsychotics are designed to treat what type of symptoms in schizophrenia?

 Answer: To control the often overlooked symptoms of depression, suicidal thoughts, and problems remembering or concentrating (affective and cognitive symptoms).

3.   What percentage of schizophrenic patients believed their doctors placed a great deal of importance on cognitive symptoms? What percentage of schizophrenics on antipsychotics said their medication does not adequately help their ability to focus and concentrate, or does not adequately control depression?

 Answer: 37 percent; 77 percent; 74 percent

Family Practice News, Oct 15, 2004 v34 i20 p38 (1) **More than half of patients with major depression have chronic pain.**

1.   How does the International Association for the Study of Pain define chronic pain?

 Answer: The International Association for the Study of Pain conservative definition of chronic pain—pain lasting six months or longer and diagnosed by a physician.

2.   The strongest association between pain and depression is found in what age group?

 Answer: The strongest association between pain and depression was found in those age 25–45 years.

3.   Briefly describe the relationship between pain/depression and measures of aggressiveness.

Answer: Other data from the survey provide hints about the association between pain and depression. MDD patients with chronic pain score significantly higher on several measures of aggressiveness—notably anger, suicidal ideation, and suicidal attempts. Dr. Ohayon hypothesized a "vicious circle" in which pain leads to psychomotor agitation, which leads to irritability, which leads to aggressiveness, which leads to depression and more pain.

Clinical Psychiatry News, Sept 2006 v34 i9 p18(1) **Treating antisocial personality disorder.** (FINK! STILL AT LARGE) *Paul J. Fink.*

1.   How common is this disorder for various groups of people?

Answer: Epidemiologic surveys show that the prevalence of antisocial personality disorder is 2–3 percent among community samples and can climb to 60 percent among male prisoners.

2.   What is the difference between a sociopath and a psychopath, and how does this affect treatment?

Answer: The individuals who have antisocial qualities but lack psychopathic features are the patients who have at least a chance to get better. The subset of antisocial patients with psychopathy have characteristics that may include highly narcissistic qualities, glib speech, grandiosity, lack of remorse and empathy, manipulativeness, deceitfulness, ruthless behavior, and refusal to accept responsibility when confronted with what they did. That combination of qualities is not just hard to treat, it's impossible to treat. Psychopaths who score high on the psychopathy checklist devised by Robert Hare, Ph.D., and his colleagues have a very poor likelihood of staying clean once they are released from prison or a forensic hospital.

3.   What "myths" about antisocial personality disorder does the author dispute?

Answer: The author dismisses the following ideas: a) APD does not exist, b) APD is an excuse for bad behavior, c) People with APD are evil, d) Antisocial is another term for criminal, e) People with APD never improve, and f) The outlook for APD is hopeless because there are no effective treatments.

4.   What is at the root of antisocial behavior?

Answer: Participation in antisocial activities can be seen as a primitive coping mechanism for people who have little self-esteem and whose major way of dealing with the world is to externalize. For most people with APD, the crimes or acts fall outside of social norms. These actions are taken mostly to gain the satisfaction of the moment.

WEBSITES

Knowledge Builder Links

1) Normality and Psychopathology
   Against All Odds: http://record.wustl.edu/news/page/normal/2425.html
   The Insanity Defense: http://en.wikipedia.org/wiki/Insanity_defense
   Psychiatric Disorders: http://psychcentral.com/disorders/

2) Personality Disorders and Anxiety-Based Disorders
   Personality Disorders: http://www.mayoclinic.com/health/personality-disorders/DS00562
   Anxiety Disorders: http://www.adaa.org/
   Famous People with Phobias:
         http://www.phobias-help.com/Famous_People_With_Phobias.html

3) Psychosis, Delusional Disorders and Schizophrenia
   Psychotic Disorders: http://www.nlm.nih.gov/medlineplus/psychoticdisorders.html
   William Utermohlens Self-Portraits:
         http://www.37signals.com/svn/posts/81-william-utermohlens-self-portraits
   Schizophrenia: http://www.schizophrenia.com/

4) Mood Disorders
   Depression Test: http://depression.about.com/cs/diagnosis/l/bldepscreenquiz.htm
   Bipolar Disorder: http://bipolar.about.com/
   Seasonal Affective Disorder:
         http://www.mayoclinic.com/health/seasonal-affective-disorder/DS00195

5) Suicide and Suicide Prevention
   Suicide: http://www.suicide.org/
   American Foundation for Suicide Prevention: http://www.afsp.org/
   Are You Worried About a Friend or Loved One?:
         http://www.stopasuicide.org/downloads/Sites/Docs/StopASuicide_SuicideRiskQu
   estionnaire_Military.pdf

Additional Web Links

Disorder-Specific Websites
http://www.schizophrenia.com/
http://www.psycom.net/depression.central.html
http://www.depressionalliance.org
http://www.depression-screening.org/
http://www.healthline.com/galecontent/dissociative-identity-disorder
http://www.nimh.nih.gov/healthinformation/anxietymenu.cfm
http://www.algy.com/anxiety/
http://bipolar.about.com/
http://www.phobialist.com/
http://www.mayoclinic.com/health/personality-disorders/DS00562
http://www.nlm.nih.gov/medlineplus/obsessivecompulsivedisorder.html

504

Psychological Disorders
http://www.mental-health-matters.com/disorders/list_alpha.php
http://www.mentalhealth.com

Psychological Disorders in Children
http://www.psychologyinfo.com/problems/children.html

Psych Web
http://www.fidnet.com/~weid/disorders.htm

Films on Psychopathology for Students
http://www.psychfilms.com

PSYCHOLOGY IN THE NEWS

Bipolar Disorder Daily News

http://www.healthline.com/news/bipolar-disorder
This website provides articles and news releases on new updates and research on bipolar disorder.

Depression Alliance News

http://www.depressionalliance.org/docs/news/news.html
Provides the latest news, access archives, and press releases on mood disorders.

QualityCounts.com

http://qualitycounts.com/fpschizophrenia.html
This site provides the latest news on medication to treat schizophrenia as well as other news articles featuring the latest updates in research.

CHAPTER 14

Therapies

Survey Questions
Discussion Questions
Lecture Enhancements

Guest speaker – clinical psychology
Dream analysis and free association
Sensitivity techniques
How does it work?
Fine-tuning therapeutic approaches
Electroconvulsive shock therapy
Systematic desensitization and relaxation
Constructing a fear hierarchy
Dueling therapists!
Active listening
Aversion therapy and smoking cessation
Recognizing and changing irrational thoughts
Patient rights
Who needs therapy?

Role-Playing Scenarios
Value-Clarification Statements
One-Minute Motivators

What's a therapist?
Freud at a different time and place
What do you think of Freud?
Dream and daydream journal
Importance of reflection
Expressing your feelings
Freud versus Rogers
Unconditional positive regard
Things left unsaid
Stop that!
What's wrong with therapy?
Effects of sadness on cognition
I'm OK!
Listening carefully to each other
Controlling behaviors
Modifying bad habits or phobias
Teaching behaviors to pets
What makes a good therapist?
What's important in therapy?

Broadening Our Cultural Horizons	Cultural methods of change
	Psychotherapy in other cultures
	What would they think?
	Behaviors that need to change in different cultures
	How therapy is viewed in other cultures
	Reinforcing culture-specific disorders
	Culturally-sensitive therapy
	Reinforcements and aversive stimuli in other cultures
	My job is making me crazy!
Supplemental Activities	Exercise 14.1: Locating Professional Help
	Exercise 14.2: Behavior Self-Modification
	Exercise 14.3: Behavior Modification and Study Habits
	Exercise 14.4: Our Attitudes Toward Our Brains
Handouts	Handout 14.1: A Friend In Need: Worksheet
	Handout 14.2: Behavior Self-Modification: Worksheet
	Handout 14.3: Behavioral Modification of Your Study Skills

Journal Questions
Suggestions for Further Reading
Video Suggestions
Computer and Internet Resources

➢ SURVEY QUESTIONS

Module 14.1 Treating Psychological Distress

Survey Question: How did psychotherapy originate?

Survey Question: Is Freudian psychoanalysis still used?

Survey Question: How do therapies differ?

Module 14.2 Humanistic and Cognitive Therapies

Survey Question: What are the major humanistic therapies?

Survey Question: How does cognitive therapy change thoughts and emotions?

Module 14.3 Behavior Therapies

Survey Question: What is behavior therapy?

Survey Question: What role do operant principles play in behavior therapy?

Module 14.4 Medical Therapies

Survey Question: How do psychiatrists treat psychological disorders?

Module 14.5 Contemporary Issues in Therapy

Survey Question: What do various therapies have in common?

Survey Question: What will therapy be like in the future?

Module 14.6 Psychology in Action: Self-Management and Seeking Professional Help

Survey Question: How are behavioral principles applied to everyday problems?

Survey Question: How could a person find professional help?

➤ DISCUSSION QUESTIONS

1. What preconceptions did you have about psychotherapy? Has your understanding of therapy changed? Has your attitude changed? Why?

2. This chapter defines psychotherapy as "any psychological technique used to facilitate positive changes in a person's personality, behavior, or adjustment." Give three examples of dialogues about problems that are not a form of psychotherapy.

3. At what point should people seek help? Should they wait and see if the problem gets better on its own? Should they "nip it in the bud"? Should they only go if the problem disrupts their lives?

4. Discuss the role that the passage of time plays in a person's improvement during and after psychotherapy.

5. In psychoanalysis, the term *resistance* refers to a blockage in the flow of ideas. Sometimes, people resist not only specific ideas, but also resist getting help. Why would a person who is in psychological pain resist going for help?

6. Existential therapist Rollo May said that there has been a loss of individual freedom, faith, and meaning in today's society? Do you agree? Why or why not?

7. Which form of psychotherapy do you find the most appealing? Why? For what type of problems?

8. What similarities would Carl Rogers see in the job of being a "good therapist" and the job of being a "good parent"?

9. Much has been written about media psychologists such as Dr Phil. Do media psychologists have value? What are the potential drawbacks? Is it just entertainment, or does it help people? Do the changes resulting from a few minutes of insight from Dr. Phil contribute to lasting changes? Is it ethical to expose people's vulnerabilities on TV for the purpose of entertainment?

10. What psychological services are available in your area? Would you know how to find or make use of them? What factors would affect your decision to seek help?

11. Describe a time when you helped someone resolve a personal problem. Describe a time when you were unsuccessful in helping. What factors seemed to make the difference?

12. Do you think it would be right for a therapist to allow a person to make suicide an "existential choice" or an expression of "free will"?

13. Which style of therapy would you expect a computer program to most closely duplicate? If a computer were programmed to provide help for a limited problem, such as test anxiety, would you find computer therapy more acceptable?

14. In your opinion, are radio psychologists engaged in education or therapy? Is talk-show psychology ethical? What value is there for listeners and callers in talking with a radio psychologist? With an online therapist over the Internet?

15. Psychotherapy is based on trust and confidentiality. Do you think that therapists should be legally required to report dangerous thoughts or fantasies revealed by clients? If a therapist misjudges the seriousness of a client's intent to do harm, should the therapist be held legally responsible? Why or why not?

16. Under what conditions would you condone the use of behavior modification? When would you oppose it?

17. Based on what you have learned about behavioral techniques, would you work with a therapist who wanted to use behavior therapy? Are there some techniques you find acceptable and others not?

18. Select a bad habit you would like to break or a positive behavior you would like to encourage and explain how you might use a behavioral or cognitive behavioral technique to alter your behavior.

19. Some critics have charged that the use of tokens in the classroom encourages students to expect artificial rewards. Behavior theorists reply that explicit rewards are better than inconsistent rewards such as praise and attention. What are the advantages and drawbacks represented by each position?

20. How do you feel about the use of behavior modification in prisons and psychiatric hospitals? Is behavior therapy any different from the involuntary administration of tranquilizers or other drugs? Why or why not?

21. Some states have tried at times to ban the use of aversive therapy techniques for severely disturbed people. Do you think that such treatment decisions should or should not be limited by law?

22. Many people develop stronger (not weaker) fears of water when pushed into the pool. Why? Under what conditions could this form of "therapy" (often called "implosive therapy") work?

23. For what kind of person and for what problems would Ellis' REBT be most effective?

24. If you were going to become a therapist, would you become a psychologist or a psychiatrist? Why?

25. Should people take therapeutic drugs for non-psychotic problems such as anxiety or depression? Why or why not? Should a person with a headache take a painkiller? Why or why not? Are these the same? Are they both cases of taking something to relieve pain? If they are different, why are they different?

26. What positive and negative roles do mental institutions play? Are they needed? Should they be publicly or privately run?

27. How effective do you think self-management techniques would be for you? Do you think most people have the self-discipline to see the changes through? Which of the self-management techniques discussed in the text would be the easiest to do? The hardest? (covert sensitization, thought stopping, covert reinforcement, or self-directed desensitization)

28. How effective are self-help books? What makes the difference between a good self-help book and a poor one? Why have so many been published?

29. Students have the opportunity to rate their professors. Should patients/clients be able to rate their therapists? What problems might there be if therapists' ratings were available to people?

➢ LECTURE ENHANCEMENTS

This chapter offers many opportunities to use role playing to demonstrate therapeutic principles. Students can be invited to come to the front of a large lecture hall to demonstrate the procedures. Students can be asked to share some of the worries, anxieties, and fears they are dealing with at this time in the semester. Students can be provided with literature on peer counseling, and the definitive differences between peer support and formal counseling can be discussed. Be prepared for an increase in requests from students for referrals.

1. **Guest speaker– clinical psychology.** Students will undoubtedly find a visit by a clinician interesting in conjunction with the readings in this chapter. If possible, invite a clinical colleague or clinician in private practice to class. Even if you yourself are a clinician, the inclusion of a person with different viewpoints and experiences will enrich discussion.

2.   **Dream analysis and free association.** It is not too difficult in the classroom to simulate some basic approaches to psychotherapy. Ask for a volunteer and begin by asking the student to recount a recent dream. Select an interesting element from the dream and ask the student to free-associate to it. Follow a few of the interesting thoughts through further free association and make note of any apparent resistances. Point out that you are using psychoanalytic techniques, and then ask the student what he or she would like to talk about next. Shift into a nondirective style and simulate a Rogerian approach. As soon as this approach has been illustrated, begin watching for an irrational assumption in what the student is saying. When you find one, shift to the more confrontative and didactic tone of REBT. Again point out what you have done. Finally, return to some topic that has already surfaced and demonstrate the theatrical "here and now" approach of Gestalt therapy. For example, ask the student to say something to an empty chair representing a parent, roommate, lover, etc. Next ask the student to sit in the chair and answer as that person, and then to stand up and reply to the imagined person, and so forth. Conclude by reviewing and discussing all the techniques that have been illustrated.

3.   **Sensitivity techniques.** A brief illustration of one or two sensitivity techniques can be interesting. A trust walk is a good choice. Randomly pair students and instruct them to walk to some point on campus. On the way to the chosen point, one student should be blindfolded while being guided by the second. On the way back, they should reverse roles. For a more dramatic demonstration, have a student stand with several students arranged behind him or her. The student must close his/her eyes and fall backward to be caught by the group. This takes real trust!

4.   **How does it work?** (Internet exercise) The textbook briefly describes aversion therapy for drinking. Have students go online and search for information about specific programs (key words: aversion therapy, Antabuse, treatment for alcoholism, or shock therapy alcohol). How well do these programs work? What is the rate of relapse for alcoholics who have gone through these therapies, as compared to other treatment approaches? Do alcoholics simply avoid taking Antabuse when they wish to drink, knowing that it will have no aversive effects?

5.   **Fine-tuning therapeutic approaches.** As various therapies are tried, modified, and developed, the possibility of controlling maladaptive behavior increases. It is possible to foresee a time when such techniques will be perfected to the point where behavioral change, and therefore behavioral control, will be much easier to accomplish and more certain. Ask the students to consider some questions about this because it would be possible, then, to control not only maladaptive behavior but any behavior. Is it a good idea to go that far? Can we keep the knowledge for good purposes and keep it out of the hands of manipulators who want to exploit others? Who should decide when and how a therapeutic technique should be used? Who will protect the interests of the mentally ill who could be exploited?

6. **Electroconvulsive shock therapy.** Invite an experienced psychiatrist who has successfully used electroconvulsive shock therapy to class to discuss its use, value, and consequences. Students should be prepared ahead of time with good questions; otherwise, they tend, on first hearing the specifics of the procedure, to be bothered by what they imagine to be an unpleasant and painful experience since any reference to electric shock has negative connotations. Good preparation can make for a productive class discussion.

7. **Systematic desensitization and relaxation.** To give students experience with the basic elements of systematic desensitization, it can be interesting to guide them through the steps of deep muscle relaxation. When they are thoroughly relaxed, announce that one of the reasons you wanted them to be relaxed is that in a moment you are going to give a surprise test on behavior modification. At that point, ask students if they were able to notice an increase in tension or anxiety when you announced the test. If they could, tell them they did not pass the item, "surprise quiz announced in class," on a hierarchy of test anxiety and that they will have to repeat the relaxation exercises! This will allow them to see what actually occurs in systematic desensitization.

8. **Constructing a fear hierarchy.** Students' understanding of systematic desensitization is enhanced when they have an opportunity to experience it. Another way to provide this experience is to combine Jacobson's traditional relaxation exercise with the construction of a class anxiety hierarchy. Most students seem to have an aversion to tarantulas, which can provide a suitable topic for the generation of an imaginary hierarchy. Have class members combine relaxation techniques with visualization of scenes from the hierarchy. If all goes well, some students can be brought to the point of imagining, without obvious discomfort, dozens of tarantulas crawling all over them. (Jacobson's relaxation technique is described in Goldfried & Davidson, 1976)

9. **Dueling therapists!** For an interesting discussion starter, have two teams of students prepare a debate reflecting the opposing viewpoints of insight therapists and behavior therapists. Another good topic for debate is the question of whether or not, or under what circumstances, behavior modification techniques should be used in schools, the military, prisons, programs for the mentally retarded, mental hospitals, and other institutional settings.

10. **Active listening.** (Internet assignment) Have students locate an example of active listening and bring it to class. What is the difference between active/reflective listening and simply repeating what the other person has said? Why does active listening work? How can the features of active listening be incorporated into everyday life? Would they work well outside the therapist's office? What are some of the reasons that interfere with people's ability to listen actively?

11. **Aversion therapy and smoking cessation.** If it is possible to find someone who has undergone aversion conditioning at one of the many commercial stop-smoking services, invite him/her to be a guest speaker. Interview him/her with respect to the effectiveness of the technique, the degree of discomfort experienced, how long the effects lasted, how

he or she now feels about the issue of behavior control, etc. A point worth exploring is the cost of the treatment. It could be argued that expensive and aversive procedures simply produce strong commitment to a nonsmoking regimen by creating a powerful cognitive dissonance effect rather than actually conditioning aversions.

12. **Recognizing and changing irrational thoughts.** Review a list of cognitive distortions. (http://en.wikipedia.org/wiki/Cognitive_distortion). Help students understand how these exist in everyday thought and how they may accompany thoughts a person with depression might have.

13. **Patient rights.** A number of issues relating to diagnosis, pharmacotherapy, hospitalization, and patient rights can be addressed by asking the class to consider this hypothetical situation:

John has spent much of the last month curled up in a fetal position under the dining room table in his apartment. A worried neighbor called the local county mental health unit. John has been hospitalized on a 72-hour hold for observation.

There are several questions for discussion:
Who should decide if he should be further hospitalized?
Should he be given drugs, with or without his consent?
When should he be released?
Who should decide: his parents, a psychiatrist, a judge, John alone?

14. **Who needs therapy?** Prepare copies of the following three hypothetical situations. Give everyone in class one of the three cards. Students are given one week to decide whether the person needs psychotherapy, and if so, the specific person in their community who could help. Encourage students to research how much the therapy would cost and how many weeks of contact would be expected. A letter can be sent to resource people in the community "advising" them they could be receiving a barrage of calls. If your class is large, appoint only a few researchers to do this investigation who can report their findings to the class.

Xavier has trouble sleeping. He is worrying about problems at his job and feels tired at work. He is on edge most of the time and is having trouble tolerating the behavior of an abrasive coworker. His personal relationships are not affected by the problems at work.

Jan experiences intense highs and lows. For weeks her "blues" deepen to thoughts of suicide; then she will feel her body come out of the depression and for a few weeks she will feel on top of the world. During her energetic periods, she sometimes makes poor decisions. Last week she was so certain she was going to get a job advertised in the newspaper that she spent $2,000 of her savings on new work clothes. She didn't even get an interview.

514

Nestor has trouble concentrating in class. Often he will find himself thinking about aviation disasters and he will hysterically laugh. He feels "evil" as if surrounded by a poisonous cloud that will contaminate anyone nearby. He'll answer questions in class, but he gets distracted and ends up talking about unrelated ideas. His classmates give him looks of confusion and seem to avoid him on campus. Yesterday he was certain he smelled smoke in the classroom. When he began shouting, "Fire!" his professor removed him from class and reprimanded him saying, "Your joke wasn't funny."

➤ ROLE-PLAYING SCENARIOS

1. Ask students to work in pairs to act out a psychoanalytic therapy session. One partner begins by free-associating, saying anything that comes to mind for about 10 minutes. The other jots down the topics mentioned. At the end of the 10 minutes, the "patient" is asked to elaborate about either a personal topic not mentioned or the topic mentioned least often. Switch roles. Discuss as a pair, or as a class, defenses, resistance, and transference.

2. Ask students to work in pairs. Give one partner (the "client") a file card on which is printed a behavior that would usually trigger shock or disapproval. Make sure the behavior is realistic and appropriate. The other partner (the "therapist") is to respond to this issue, showing unconditional positive regard, empathy, and authenticity. Students enjoy developing the shocking examples.

3. Break students into pairs and have them practice active listening. Offer them topics that are fairly generic and not too personal—such as their feelings about getting through school, an annoying co-worker, etc. Have one student be the "client" and discuss the problem. Have the other student use active listening. That person cannot agree or disagree, give advice, or otherwise give direction. How long did the conversation last? How hard was it to do? Since most students will run out of steam quickly, how do Rogerian therapists maintain the discussion?

4. In pairs, share decisions you have made this semester. How did you make these choices? What were the consequences of these choices for you? What could be done to help you make wiser decisions and accept the responsibility for the decisions that you make?

5. Form small "self-help groups." Spend 30 minutes talking as:
   a. Parents concerned about their teen's driving habits
   b. Parents concerned about their teen's drinking behavior
   c. Teens concerned about their parent's drinking behavior
   d. Students upset about favoritism and racism in one of their classes
   e. Employees angry about low wages
   f. Husbands confused about their domestic role in an era of women's liberation

6.   Role-play a family meeting. Assign parent and sibling roles. One of the children is chairing this meeting. Ask each person to bring an issue to the family "agenda"; have the family work together to decide which issue to discuss and what to do on that particular issue. Highlight the difficulty in running such a meeting and the need for years of professional training and supervision that is needed to do so.

7.   Psychodrama often includes the use of role-reversal. Break students into small groups and have students role-play a discussion that their parents might have with a friend. The topic of conversation is—the student! Students should try to sincerely act out the role from the parent's perspective, without using sarcasm or ridicule. Afterwards, students can discuss whether they were able to "step into" the parent's shoes, or whether they were only able to see things from their own perspective.

8.   You have a friend who smokes. You have decided that you can no longer tolerate this behavior in your presence. What would you say or do to change this behavior without destroying your friendship?

9.   A very physically fit truck driver and his highly religious wife have come to you for sex therapy. They have been married 10 years and have stopped making love. What would you ask them? What would you tell them? Which therapeutic approach would you use? Why?

10.   You have been asked to direct an experimental electronic prison. Electronic devices monitor the behavior of inmates, open and close doors, and prevent inmates from having contact with guards and with each other. Describe to your staff the challenges you expect as the new director.

11.   You are a psychiatrist treating a patient who is exhibiting schizophrenic episodes. Explain to the patient's relatives why you would (or would not) use pharmacotherapy.

12.   You are the director of a halfway house for psychiatric residents. A woman is arriving this afternoon that was able to learn to take the medicine for her mild schizophrenic episodes and to reduce stress through a token economy system in the hospital. What can you do to help her improvement in therapy generalize to the situation within your halfway house?

516

➤ VALUE-CLARIFICATION STATEMENTS

1. Dreams are simply random thoughts and have no meaning whatsoever.

2. Freud's approach to therapy is the only way to get at the real causes of human unhappiness and maladjustment.

3. Freud's form of therapy has outlived its usefulness.

4. Most people are not willing to accept responsibility for their own behavior.

5. Humanistic therapists' assumption that the client is capable of directing his or her own therapy is naïve.

6. It's not important to understand the problem existentially; just correct the problem behaviors.

7. Media psychology (talk radio, television, and online therapy) is harmful and should be banned from radio stations, television, and the Internet.

8. Sensitivity and encounter groups are social, not therapeutic, events.

9. Token economies and other forms of behavioral therapy are too mechanistic.

10. Aversion conditioning is an inhumane way to treat people.

11. Irrational thoughts are the cause of depression, not the result.

12. Psychotherapy should be made available freely to all taxpayers.

13. Nobody needs to spend more than six months in therapy.

14. The problem of therapists having sex with their clients has been blown out of proportion by the media.

15. Anything shared in a psychotherapy session is confidential and cannot be revealed to anyone under any circumstances.

16. Electroconvulsive shock therapy (ECT) is too dangerous to use and should be banned.

17. If a therapist truly falls in love with his or her client, it is acceptable for a romantic relationship to develop, even while the therapist is still providing the client with therapy.

18. Tranquilizers and energizers should only be prescribed as a last resort.

517

19.   Antipsychotic drugs should be prescribed as the first form of intervention so that psychotherapy can be most effective.

➤ ONE-MINUTE MOTIVATORS

1.   **What's a therapist?** Ask students to help clarify what the difference is between a friend, religious leader, and psychotherapist.

2.   **Freud at a different time and place.** Briefly describe the historical, economic, political, and sociological times of Freud. If Freud were beginning his career now, how would his theory and therapy be different?

3.   **What do you think of Freud?** Most of your students will have an opinion of the father of psychotherapy—some positive, some negative. List Freud's main therapeutic points on the board along with two columns and ask students by a show of hands which they think are effective or ineffective. This will only work if you get everyone to respond (some don't like to participate!). The major concepts are: free association, dream analysis, resistance, and analysis of transference. If you wish, you can include other terms such as unconscious motivation, psychic determinism, defense mechanisms, sexual and aggressive instincts, and stages of development. When you have tallied the results, ask them why they think "x" was valuable and "y" was not.

4.   **Dream and daydream journal.** Ask students to keep a "daydream journal" by jotting in the margin of their notes the topic of any daydreams they have. At the end of a week, ask students to evaluate their daydreams. What are the themes? How frequently do the daydreams occur? What do the dreams say about the student's feelings toward this course or other events in their life? Do they reveal unconscious desires as postulated by Freud?

5.   **Importance of reflection.** Ask students to reflect on your lecture presentation. At the end of a few sentences, call on a volunteer to restate what you said. Invite a student who heard your ideas differently to provide his/her view. After three or four attempts to rephrase satisfactorily, it should be clear how important "reflecting" is for really understanding what we are saying to each other.

6.   **Expressing your feelings.** To focus on the "here and now," suddenly ask a student what he/she is feeling at the moment. Continue with the lecture. Ask another student. If students have trouble expressing their feelings, use Gestalt techniques to clarify their immediate experience.

7.   **Freud versus Rogers.** Calvin Hobbes believed that society was necessary to impose appropriate behavior on people, while Jean Jacques Rousseau believed that society corrupted the "noble savage" in us. To some degree, this is similar to the debate between Freudian and Rogerian concepts. Which belief holds more merit? Were they both right? Were they both wrong? What is the nature of the human character? Is it driven by dark impulses, or does it strive toward self-actualization?

518

8. **Unconditional positive regard**. Carl Rogers believed that unconditional positive regard was a cornerstone to healthy development. Ask students why they are in school. Is it because their parents expect them to be, or is it for other reasons? How would their parents react if they dropped out of school? How many would continue to show unconditional positive regard for the person, even if disappointed in the decision? How many students would lose their parents' unconditional positive regard? How does that make the students feel (sad, angry, hurt, confused, frustrated, resentful, etc.)?

9. **Things left unsaid.** Ask students to turn to the person next to them and to share "things left unsaid" to someone they care about. If they could talk to anyone in the world to add closure to the relationship, who would they call? What would they say?

10. **Stop that!** Ask students to think of something that they are currently doing that they wish they would not do. Then pass out a rubber band to each student. Encourage them to zing themselves with the rubber band every time they think about doing that disgusting behavior. Discuss the pros and cons of aversive techniques.

11. **What's wrong with therapy?** A number of people who will readily seek treatment for physical disorders will refuse to seek treatment for mental/emotional disorders. Why? What's "wrong" with going for therapy?

12. **Effects of sadness on cognition**. Encourage students to think of five good things that happened today. If they have been feeling depressed, is this difficult to do? Is it helpful?

13. **I'm OK!**. Ask the class to repeat in unison, "I am a valued, competent person." What are the limits of the "positive thinking" inherent in much cognitive therapy?

14. **Listening carefully to each other.** Ask students to practice active listening, clarifying, and focusing on feelings. Students can share the activities of the previous weekend or their feelings about friends, relatives, work, or this class. Students should find that active listening is time-consuming, exhausting, and tremendously important. Most of us have not really been trained to listen to each other.

15. **Controlling behaviors.** As various therapies are tried, modified, and developed, the possibility of controlling maladaptive behavior increases. It is possible to foresee a time when such techniques will be perfected to the point where behavioral change, and therefore behavioral control, will be much easier to accomplish and more certain. Ask the students to consider some questions about this, because it would be possible, then, to control not only maladaptive behavior, but <u>any</u> behavior. Is it a good idea to go that far? Can we keep the knowledge for good purposes and keep it out of the hands of manipulators who want to exploit others? Who should decide when and how a therapeutic technique should be used? Who will protect the interests of the mentally ill who could be exploited?

16. **Modifying bad habits or phobias**. Ask students if they know anyone who has had an intense fear or bad habit and has overcome it. See if there were any behavioral principles involved in dealing with the problem. If not, discuss how such principles could have been used.

17. **Teaching behaviors to pets**. Students who have pets that do tricks should be asked how the pet was taught and how the behavior is maintained. You can also emphasize that, according to Skinner, normal and abnormal behaviors are learned and maintained the same way. So, a dog that is well behaved learns that set of behaviors, and a dog that tugs on the leash, gets up on the couch, and begs at the table has also learned those behaviors, although people usually blame the dogs and not themselves!

18. **What makes a good therapist?** Psychoanalysis, behaviorism, humanism, and cognitive therapy all operate on different premises, but success in therapy is related more to the characteristics of the therapist and to the therapist/client fit than to any one particular method. Freud, Rogers, Beck, and Ellis were/are all purportedly excellent therapists. Ask students what makes a therapist effective? Which philosophical underpinnings of various therapies can be universally applied to "competing" therapeutic models? You might also wish to stress that therapeutic models are really not competitive, or mutually exclusive, but rather are complementary. This can lead to a discussion of eclecticism.

19. **What's important in therapy?** Effective therapy is characterized by some basic features, regardless of the particular school of thought. These features are: active listening, clarifying the problem, focusing on feelings, avoiding giving advice, accepting the person's frame of reference, reflecting thoughts and feelings, silence, questions, and maintaining confidentiality. Ask each student to rank these characteristics in order of importance from one to nine, with one being the most important. When they have finished, collect the rankings and tally them to find out which feature, if any, was greatly preferred over the others. Ask students why they think it is the most important, and why the least favorite is seen as less important.

➤ BROADENING OUR CULTURAL HORIZONS

1. **Cultural methods of change.** All societies find some mechanism for facilitating change in others. Compare and contrast the therapeutic role of friends, psychologists, and religious leaders. What might all of these have in common that would help at least some people feel better? When should you see which person?

2. **Psychotherapy in other cultures.** (Internet exercise) Have students research psychotherapy in other cultures. What is the goal of the therapy? What techniques are used? How effective are they? For example, various drugs, herbs, chemicals, and vitamins are used in the Far East to treat "impotence," which is regarded as a psychological problem in about half the cases in America. (See Xu, Shikai, Treatment of Impotence in Traditional Chinese Medicine. Journal of Sex Education and Therapy, 1990,16(3), 198-200.)

3. **What would they think?** If you have students from other cultures, ask them how their culture would likely perceive Freud's ideas of hidden conflicts and unconscious motivation. Do other cultures place more emphasis on the hidden aspects of the personality, or the conscious ones? What is the view of human existence—rational or conflicted?

4. **Behaviors that need to change in different cultures.** Sometimes the purpose of therapy is to change a person's behavior; other times the purpose is to encourage the person to accept aspects of their own behavior more fully. Think about differences between your culture and the culture of your parents (or your children). What behavior patterns do your parents want you to change? What behavior would you want them to accept more readily? What happens when two cultures or two generations clash in terms of whose behavior is supposed to change? How do the politics of power affect the kinds of changes that therapy encourages and the specific groups who are doing most of the changing?

5. **How therapy is viewed in other cultures.** Ask students who are from other cultures how their home cultures view therapy. Is it more accepted, or less? Do people go for therapy when they are troubled, or are there other avenues to improvement? Is it considered acceptable to tell a stranger (a therapist) about all the problems in the family?

6. **Reinforcing culture-specific disorders**. American culture has the highest rates of eating disorders in the world. It also has the highest rates of obesity. Ask students to brainstorm the factors that reinforce these two seemingly inconsistent trends. When they are done, ask what ideas exist in American culture that suggest that these two health issues actually have more in common than they appear to have on the surface.

7. **Culturally-sensitive therapy.** How important is it for a therapist to understand the ethnic group or culture of the client he or she is treating? What kind of cultural or gender differences might make certain kinds of therapy ineffective?

8. **Reinforcements and aversive stimuli in other cultures.** Select a single problem such as alcohol abuse or nail biting. Ask students to interview people from different cultures to find out how they try to deal with these problems. What aversive stimuli might be used? What part do positive and negative rewards play?

9. **My job is making me crazy!** Compared to Europeans, North Americans work longer hours, take fewer vacations, and place more emphasis on work. American workers are also less likely to have health benefits, daycare, and other employee programs. Ask students to identify ways in which corporate employment trends can contribute to higher rates of depression and anxiety. What measures could companies take to help reduce the stress and improve work-related mental health? What, if anything, would workers be willing to give up in order to help change employment trends? Possible changes include job sharing, working fewer hours, flexible work schedules, on-site gyms, etc. Would workers be willing to give up big houses, expensive cars, and some material possessions as a trade-off for a mentally-healthier work environment? Why do we, as a society, value material possessions more than happiness? (Obviously, this discussion applies to cases above the basic level of survival.)

➤ SUPPLEMENTAL ACTIVITIES

Exercise 14.1: Locating Professional Help

This is an enlarged version of an exercise suggested earlier. Its purpose is to give students firsthand experience in locating mental health services in his or her area. This could pay big dividends later. Everyone at some time needs to think about getting or helping someone get professional psychological help. In a crisis or emergency, a person may not have the time or opportunity to do a thorough review of what is available in the area. Being prepared is a great advantage. Students will be surprised, when this project is completed, at the vast number of services available in most communities. There are always many more than people expect.

PROCEDURE

A. Set up one or more scenarios for the students. The following is an example. Each scenario could focus on a different type of problem. This one covers quite a few:

You have a friend who has a serious adjustment problem. It has reached the point where (s)he can no longer do his/her work, is having serious problems with his/her family, and is generally miserable and very anxious. Thoughts of suicide recur, and (s)he has started drinking heavily. (S)He knows you are studying psychology and asks you for some assistance in finding good professional help. The friend indicates that (s)he has some money but is on a limited budget.

B. Distribute **Handout 14.1.** Divide the class into groups of three, asking each group to research the resources that would be available in the city and county to help the friend. They should identify specific sources of help and know something about the kind of assistance that would be provided. This means they should visit the facility, talk to personnel there, read brochures, etc. to become well informed. Provide each student with a worksheet. You may want to modify or add to the sample given.

C. Once the students have completed the research, all groups should report on the same class day. As they give their findings, compile a master list of resources in the area. This could be refined and distributed to the students.

D. Provide some incentives to the class. Give a reward, such as extra class credit, to the groups who bring in comprehensive lists. Be sure that everyone who tried hard is a winner, not just one or two. Another incentive could be having the students, when the comprehensive list is completed, distribute it to places where it could be used like the college counseling office, local churches and clergy, helping agencies in the local government, etc.

522

Exercise 14.2: Behavior Self-Modification

This is an exercise that will get students to think about behavior modification techniques. It is a project that can be done in one class period, as it is described here, or could be more elaborate and done over a whole term. Some modification would be needed, but the basic idea is the same whichever way it is done.

Ask the students to form small groups, three per group would be ideal, and work on a plan to change a behavior. Distribute **Handout 14.2.** Each of the three should have a behavior to change. The group can work on each one. There is an advantage to a group rather than an individual working on the problem because it is more likely to get done if the group works on it. It also gives support to each individual in the planning and executing of the change.

In preparation for this project, you may need to review the basic concepts of operant conditioning to make sure everyone understands them. In particular, go over reinforcement so that they are clear on how it is to be applied.

PROCEDURE

1. Divide the class into groups of three to design and execute the project.

2. Distribute the instructions and worksheets for the exercise and go over them with the students.

3. Ask students to submit their worksheets and a plan of action for your review.

4. If you feel this is worthwhile, ask the students to carry out the plan of action, once it has been reviewed and critiqued by you, and to report back to their group and to you on their progress after a specified number of weeks.

Exercise 14.3: Behavior Modification and Study Habits.
Students often have very limited insight into what motivates and maintains their study habits. **Handout 14.3** asks them to identify the antecedent conditions, set goals, and provide reinforcement.

Exercise 14.4: Our Attitudes Toward Our Brains (exercise and mini-lecture)
This interactive exercise considers the issue of our attitudes toward psychoactive drugs, specifically anti-depressants. It can be also be found in Chapter 2 **(exercise 2.3).**

The brain is an amazing organ, but like any organ, it can malfunction. Neurotransmitter imbalance is one such case. When the brain is "sick," though, people react to the problem much differently (and usually more negatively) than when other organs are "sick." Have students anonymously complete **Handout 14.4.** When they are finished, collect their answers for discussion. You will likely find a number of trends:
  a) A continued expectation that the problem can be fixed without drugs, even though the example said that other alternatives had been exhausted.
  b) A reluctance to seek help, for fear of looking weak.

523

c) A belief that antidepressants are addictive, don't work, or make people worse.
d) A belief that taking antidepressants is "artificial," "unnatural," or a "crutch."

When the students have completed their responses, you can comment on some of their beliefs. Below is a list of some of my favorite quips. It is <u>very</u> important, however, to deliver these sentiments in a way that does not make fun of students' beliefs, or sound at all sarcastic.

You can open the discussion with information about how SSRIs actually work. It is important to acknowledge that we are all uncomfortable with the possibility that the brain might malfunction. We would like to think that the brain is different from other organs. We certainly act as though it is different. But really, it's just an organ. And when it is sick, it needs to be treated. Sometimes therapy works, and sometimes therapy alone is not enough. The stigma attached to mental illness prevents people from seeking the help they need, and makes millions of people suffer needlessly. I am not suggesting that everyone should run out and get a prescription for antidepressants, nor am I "pushing Prozac." But it is important to recognize the biological reality that some people face.

a) If you had chronic chest congestion that would not go away, would you continue to suffer with possible pneumonia, bronchitis, or other ailment, or would you go to the doctor?
b) If you had a broken leg, would you just "tough it out," or would you get a cast on it?
c) If your vision is poor, would you consider wearing glasses to be "artificial" or "unnatural"?
d) If a person had diabetes, would you tell him or her to just "will themselves" to get better, or would you encourage them to remain on their insulin?
e) If a person were on heart medication, and had taken it for a while, would you advise them to stop because they really didn't need it anymore?
f) People on Prozac don't feel the need for a "Prozac fix" if they forget to take a pill *(in response to the fear that antidepressants are addictive).*
g) Some people are allergic to penicillin. Does that make it a "bad" drug? No drug works for everyone. Some of you are probably allergic to penicillin, but penicillin has saved millions of lives *(in response to the inevitable example that "I know someone who took Prozac and they had so many problems with it...").*

Additional facts about antidepressants are listed below:

a) Classes of Antidepressants. There are three major classes of antidepressant drugs: tricyclics, MAOIs (monoamine oxidase inhibitors), and SSRIs (selective serotonin reuptake inhibitors). The SSRIs are the newest, most effective, have the least toxic/fewest side effects and will be the topic of this discussion.

b) *Biology.* People who are depressed have insufficient amounts of the neurotransmitter serotonin, which helps regulate mood. We do not yet know how to add serotonin to the body, but SSRIs work not by adding serotonin, but by regulating the existing supply. In a normal brain, a neurotransmitter is released by the axon terminal, crosses the synaptic gap, activates the receptor site of the adjacent dendrite, and then is "recycled" by the axon. This process of recycling is called reuptake. SSRIs work by slowing down, or inhibiting, the reuptake. This means that the body's own serotonin remains in the synaptic gap longer and therefore "works harder" than it normally would. Although the actual level of serotonin does not increase, it does become functionally more plentiful, with respect to the receiving dendrite.

c) *Side* effects. SSRIs typically have few side effects, and most are not serious enough to discourage ongoing use of the drug. Most people are either not bothered by side effects, or are only minimally bothered. For most people, the benefits greatly outweigh the side effects. Side effects usually occur at the beginning of treatment and dissipate within a few weeks. In addition, many of the reported side effects are not significantly different than the placebo comparison group. The most frequent side effects include: nausea and vomiting, dry mouth, diarrhea, dizziness, and either drowsiness or insomnia.

d) *Contraindications*: Alcohol should be avoided when taking antidepressants, as they reduce the speed at which alcohol is metabolized. This can result in substantial impairment with only minimal alcohol consumption. In addition, MAOIs and some cough and flu medications can cause serious interactions. Pregnant women should discuss possible risks with their doctors.

e) *Prescription issues*. People often conclude that antidepressants are over-prescribed. Some mental health professionals, however, believe that there are many people who would benefit from taking anti-depressants who are not prescribed them for a variety of reasons, including personal resistance. With regard to over-prescribed drugs, tranquillizers, sleeping pills, and antibiotics are more likely to be over-prescribed than antidepressants.

f) *"Normal" people and Prozac*. What happens if a non-depressed person takes an SSRI? Obviously, people who do not need a drug shouldn't take it, but the body will attempt to correct the problem by cutting back on its production of serotonin. It is analogous to non-diabetic taking insulin. There can be side effects to inappropriate use of any drug; however it is much more likely that someone who needs anti-depressants will fail to get them than the reverse.

g) *Will SSRIs help everyone?* No drug is effective for everyone. The particular effectiveness of any drug needs to be monitored and adjusted if necessary. To use another analogy, penicillin is a drug that has saved millions of lives, but some people are allergic to it and should not take it. In contrast, some people are allergic to *macrolide* antibiotics—a penicillin alternative. The particular choice of treatment needs to be tailored for each person individually. Despite personal anecdotes about a given individual's case, the fact remains that millions of people have greatly benefited from this drug.

h)   *Do SSRIs make people suicidal or violent?* Recent research suggests that SSRIs might negatively affect adolescents, and their use in that population is under investigation. In adults, however, SSRIs do not increase the risk of suicide. In determining suicidal risk, one must compare the base rate for suicide among depressed people who are taking SSRIs against the rate of depressed people who are NOT taking SSRIs. Given that depression and suicide are related, one would expect a certain number of suicides among the depressed population to begin with. There is no evidence that SSRIs increase that risk and a great deal of evidence documenting the number of people who have benefited. A revealing discussion of this issue can be found in Peter Kramer's book "Listening to Prozac." The appendix in particular discusses a number of high profile murder cases that were attributed to Prozac, but were later found to be linked to other factors.

Handout 14.1: A FRIEND IN NEED: WORKSHEET

TO THE STUDENT:

You have a friend who has a serious adjustment problem. It has reached the point where (s)he can no longer do his/her work, is having serious problems with his/her family, and is generally miserable and very anxious. Thoughts of suicide recur, and (s)he has started to drink heavily. (S)He knows you are studying psychology and asks you for some assistance in finding professional help. The friend indicates that (s)he has some money but is on a limited budget.

You and your group are to research the area (extend your search to include the whole county) to find all the possible resources that might help your friend.

Complete the following:

1.   Indicate the resources that you have found. Note where you found out about each and how you checked it out.

2.   State briefly what services your friend could expect from each of the resources, who is eligible for the services, and what the fees might be. This will require a personal visit, a phone call, or at least reading some literature provided by the office or agency.

3.   What do you think of the possibilities of your friend getting the kind of help (s)he needs based on what is available in your area? Explain your answer.

Handout 14.2: BEHAVIOR SELF-MODIFICATION: WORKSHEET

TO THE STUDENT:

In this exercise, each student will identify a behavior (s)he wants to change, and the group will help to develop a plan of action to bring this about. You should do the following:

1.　Each person in the group should identify a behavior (s)he would like to change. Keep it simple. Try something like nail biting, smoking, a poor study habit, or overeating. You can certainly think of others.

2.　Use the outline that follows as a guide for developing your program for change. First, you should describe the present situation; then you can work on changes. Keep in mind that you should try to do only what is possible. There is no point in planning what you won't carry out.

I.　**The Present Situation**

　A.　*The problem behavior:* Here you should briefly but clearly state what behavior you wish to change. It should be described exactly as it occurs.

　B.　*The stimulus cues:* These are the stimuli in your environment that have become associated with the behavior you wish to change. An example: smoking while drinking a cup of coffee. If you want to stop smoking, you will have to change that whole behavior pattern because coffee drinking and smoking have become associated. What are all the cues or stimuli that are associated with the undesirable behavior? You should try to identify as many of these as possible. It may be a good idea to do some self-observation, taking notes of the circumstances that surround the behavior you want to change.

　C.　*The reinforcements:* There will be immediate and delayed reinforcements for the behavior you want to change. Be honest about this and try to identify what they are. For example, smoking relaxes you and makes you feel good, you believe it "looks cool", it gives you something to do with your hands, you can blow neat smoke rings, etc.

Handout 14.2: BEHAVIOR MODIFICATION: WORKSHEET (page 2)

II. **Changes That You Plan to Make**

A. *The new behavior that you want to develop to replace the old*: Remember, you can't just stop doing something. You need to do something different in its place. An overeater doesn't stop eating but eats differently! A smoker doesn't stop breathing but inhales differently! Describe the new behavior. It needs to be attainable.

B. *New stimulus cues*: those objects or events you plan to associate with the new behavior to help it become established.

C. *The reinforcements for the new behavior*: These need to be immediate and long range. Plan specific reinforcements and set specific times when they will be received.

III. **Keep accurate and detailed records to chart your progress.** Speak with the instructor about your plan and the progress you are making once you are working on the change.

529

Handout 14.3: BEHAVIORAL MODIFICATION OF YOUR STUDY SKILLS

1.   List at least five things about your studying behavior that need to change.

2.   Identify the antecedent conditions for each studying behavior that you have listed above. Specifically, what things have reward value to get you to study? What aspects of studying are punishing?

3.   Identify other activities that compete with or distract you from your studying behavior. What competing behaviors are rewarded, and how are they rewarded?

530

Handout 14.3: BEHAVIORAL MODIFICATION OF YOUR STUDY SKILLS (cont.)

4.   Indicate how you can change each of your five behaviors.

5.   List ways that you can reward (reinforce) yourself for changing each of your five behaviors.

6.   Specify how your other preferred behaviors can be rearranged so that they will still be rewarded, but will not compete with your studying behavior. Alternately, list the ways that you could make the reinforcements for those other behaviors less immediately available.

531

Handout 14.4: DEPRESSION QUESTIONNAIRE

Please answer the following short answer questions. Do <u>NOT</u> put your name on the sheet.

Suppose that you have been suffering with serious depression. This refers to serious depression, not just a case of "the blues." It is debilitating and lasts weeks or months. You have been suffering from depressive episodes on and off for some time. Things improve, but the depression keeps coming back. You have had some success with psychotherapy/counseling, but the positive results are not enough to eliminate the problem.

1. Would you consider taking an antidepressant?

2. Why or why not? (List as many reasons as applicable.)

3. Have you ever known someone who was seriously depressed?

4. Have you ever known someone who has taken antidepressants? If so, what were the results?

5. Do you understand how SSRIs (Prozac/ Fluoxetine, Paxil/ Paroxetine, etc) work?

➢ JOURNAL QUESTIONS

1. If you have never been in therapy, what feelings do you have about people who go to therapy? What expectations would you have if you went to therapy?

2. Think about some of the ineffective communication or relationship issues in your own family. All families have these issues to varying degrees. Do you ever experience "transference" in bringing these issues into your interactions with people outside your family? Do your friends ever comment on some particular interpersonal habit that you have? Can you trace its origins back to your original family dynamics? Are there any ways that you can overcome this transference and behave in new ways?

3. If you (or a friend of yours) have been in therapy, what encouraged you to seek help? What problem did you bring to the therapy sessions? How did you select the therapist? What therapeutic techniques were used? How did the therapeutic process change you?

4. Keep a dream journal. Explain each dream in terms of the latent and the manifest content.

5. Who in your life seems most genuine, authentic, and empathic in responding to your concerns? Why?

6. Review your listening skills by comparing them to the "basic counseling skills" listed in the textbook. Which ones do you do best? Which ones could stand improvement? How would you go about making those improvements?

7. Think of a problem that your family (or a family you know well) is trying to work through. Would family therapy be helpful? Why or why not?

8. Think of a behavior you would like to change. Would aversion therapy be helpful? Why or why not?

9. Think of a behavior that you would like to change in someone you live with. How could you reinforce the appropriate behavior? How could you discourage the inappropriate behavior? Would tokens be helpful? Why or why not?

10. Which of Ellis's irrational beliefs do you unfortunately believe most strongly? Why?

11. Review a list of irrational beliefs (http://en.wikipedia.org/wiki/Cognitive_distortion). List one irrational thought that you have had in the past week. Now, re-write the thought in a way that provides an alternate interpretation of the thought or event.

12. If you had a major problem, who would you go to for help? What kind of help would be most effective? Why?

13.   You have been deeply depressed for some time, and your therapist has suggested ECT as a treatment. How do you feel about this treatment? What hopes do you have for the outcome of treatment? What fears do you have?

➤ SUGGESTIONS FOR FURTHER READING

American Psychological Association. (2003). Guidelines on multicultural education, training, research, practice, and organizational change for psychologists. *American Psychologist, 58*(5), 377–402.

Corey, G. (2008). *Theory and practice of group counseling* (7th ed.). Belmont, CA: Cengage Learning/Wadsworth.

Ellis, A., & Powers (1998). *A new guide to rational living* (3rd ed.). North Hollywood, CA: Wilshire.

Hall, J. (2006). *What is clinical psychology?* (4th ed.). New York: Oxford University Press.

Frankl, V. (1946/2000). *Man's search for meaning.* Ashland, OH: Beacon Press.

Freud, S. (1988). *Essentials of psychoanalysis.* East Rutherford, NJ: Penguin.

Goldfried, M. & Davidson, G. (1976). *Clinical behavior therapy,* New York: Holt.

Martin, G., & Pear, J. (2010). *Behavior modification: What it is and how to do it* (9th ed.). Upper Saddle River, NJ: Prentice-Hall.

McKay, M., Davis, M., & Fanning, P. (2007). *Thoughts & feelings: Taking control of your moods and your life* (3rd ed.). Oakland, CA: New Harbinger Publications.

Meyers, R., Chapman, L. K., & Weaver, C. M. (2008). *Case studies in abnormal behavior* (8th ed.). Ashland, OH: Allyn & Bacon.

Ormay, T. (2006). Cybertherapy: Psychotherapy on the Internet. *International Journal of Psychotherapy, 10*(2), 51–60.

Prochaska, J. O., & Norcross, J. C. (2010). *Systems of psychotherapy: A transtheoretical analysis* (7th ed.). Belmont, CA: Cengage Learning/Wadsworth.

Rogers, C. (2003). *Client-centered therapy: Its current practice, implication, and theory.* London: Constable and Co.

Spiegler, M. D., & Guevremont, D. C. (2010). *Contemporary behavior therapy* (5th ed.). Belmont, CA: Cengage Learning/Wadsworth.

Watson, D. L., & Tharp, R. G. (2007). *Self-directed behavior* (9th ed.). Belmont, CA: Wadsworth.

Wolpe, J. (1992). *The practice of behavior therapy* (4th ed.). Ashland, OH: Allyn & Bacon.

Yalom, I. D. (2000). *Love's executioner and other tales of psychotherapy*. New York: HarperCollins.

Yontef, G. (2007). The power of the immediate moment in gestalt therapy. *Journal of Contemporary Psychotherapy*, *37*(1), 17-23.

➤ VIDEO SUGGESTIONS

Feature Films

A Clockwork Orange (Malcolm McDowell) Science Fiction. Alex (McDowell) and his "Droogs" terrorize writer Mr. Alexander (Magee) and rape and kill his wife. Alex is later jailed for bludgeoning the Cat Lady to death and submits to Ludovico behavior modification technique to gain his freedom. He is conditioned to abhor violence and even Beethoven. Returned to the world defenseless, Alex is victim to his prior victims. This was a controversial film when produced, but illustrates some extremes to which behavioral conditioning may be taken.

Don't Say a Word (Michael Douglas, Sean Bean, Brittany Murphy), Thriller. Therapist Dr. Nathan Conrad (Douglas) learns that his daughter has been kidnapped by Koster (Bean). Koster is in need of a critical piece of information known only to Elisabeth Burrows, one of his patients. Conrad must unlock the secret stored in Elisabeth's mind, while a detective is close to discovering Conrad's problem. Useful illustrations of personality, disorders, malingering, and treatment.

Girl, Interrupted (Winona Ryder, Angelina Jolie, Clea Duvall), Drama. Nineteen-year-old Susanna (Ryder) commits herself to a mental hospital and spends 18 months exploring her troubled psyche and learning the ways of a mental hospital. She meets several other patients with troubled minds and decides that she must work harder with her psychiatrist in order to get well. Getting out of the hospital is not as easy as getting in, as Susanna quickly discovers.

Educational Films and Videos

Anxiety: Cognitive Therapy with Dr. Aaron T. Beck, (1989), Psychological and Educational Films, 43 min. In this program, Beck discusses his theory of cognitive therapy and presents an assessment outline for the treatment of anxiety. He demonstrates his theory and techniques in a session with a young man whose problems of procrastination are seated in his fears of how other people view him. Beck is a professor of psychiatry, director of the Center for Cognitive Therapy at the Pennsylvania School of Medicine, and the author of several books. This film is an excellent presentation of cognitive therapy and is well produced.

Approaches to Therapy, (1990), Insight Media, 30 min. This video contrasts psychodynamic, humanistic, and cognitive-behavioral approaches to therapy by showing how the same client would be treated by each of the therapies.

Back From Madness: The Struggle for Sanity, (2000), Films for the Humanities & Sciences, 53 min. This program provides a view of the world of insanity that few ever see, following four psychiatric patients for one to two years, from the time they arrive at Harvard's Massachusetts General Hospital. Includes rare archival footage demonstrating how their conditions were treated in the past. An HBO production.

Behavior Modification: Teaching Language to Psychotic Children, (1969), Prentice-Hall, 42 min. This film, based on the work of Ivor Lavaas at UCLA, demonstrates reinforcement and stimulus fading techniques used in teaching language skills to psychotic children. Frequent use of graphs and charts illustrates the effects of the treatment program and rates of improvement.

Bellevue: Inside Out, (2002), Films for the Humanities and Sciences, 76 min. New York City's Bellevue Hospital has a renowned psychiatric emergency center that treats 7,000 men and women annually. This gritty program takes a daunting look at the daily operation of the center by focusing on a handful of people as they struggle with their illnesses. The entire experience is presented, from arrests of the criminally insane and admissions of new patients to long-term treatment and therapy groups. In addition to working with mental disorders, doctors and nurses also confront drug and alcohol addiction in an environment where 50 percent of their patients have substance abuse problems.

Can You Stop People from Drinking? (1992), Nova Videos, 57 min. This video looks at how Russia and the United States are attacking the problem of alcohol abuse. It covers prohibition, hypnotism, imprisonment, surveillance, deception, aversion therapy, and group therapy such as Alcoholics Anonymous.

Carl Rogers Conducts an Encounter Group, (1975), Extension Media Center, 70 min. Carl Rogers discusses factors that he believes are important in successful facilitation of a group. Highlights include Rogers in a group setting interacting with individual members.

Coping with Phobias, (1993), Films for the Humanities and Sciences, 28 min. This program explains why people have phobias and how phobias can usually be overcome. It focuses on fear of flying. The program also visits a speech class to explain the dynamics of this phobia and provide specific suggestions on overcoming the fears involved.

Depression: Old Problem, New Therapy (2002) Films for the Humanities and Sciences, 23 min. In this program, mental health professionals discuss the types, symptoms, and triggers of depression as they relate both to adolescents and to adults. Promising antidepressants such as selective norepinephrine re-uptake inhibitors, Substance P antagonists, and corticotropin-releasing factor receptor antagonists are considered, as are advances in brain scan technology. The value of psychiatric counseling and peer support groups is also stressed.

Depression and Manic Depression, (1996), Films for the Humanities and Sciences, 28 min. Winner of many awards. Depression affects over 17 million Americans each year, and it's been estimated that only one-third of this group gets any treatment, largely because of stigma and fear. The lack of treatment results in a high number of suicides, making this illness as fatal as any other illness and public epidemic. This program from *The Doctor Is In* explains the disease through the experiences of several people, including *60 Min.* host Mike Wallace; Kay Redfield Jamison, psychiatrist and author of a book on her life with manic-depressive illness; artist Lama Dejani; and State Dept. official Robert Boorstin. The program also provides an overview of the medications and therapy currently in use. A Dartmouth-Hitchock Medical Center production.

Don't Panic: The Promise of Intensive Exposure Therapy, (2000), Films for the Humanities & Sciences, 17 min. ABC News anchors Diane Sawyer and Sam Donaldson and correspondent Jay Schadler document a young woman's struggle to overcome the feelings of fear that have reduced her world to the narrow confines of her own home. Through intensive exposure therapy, an alternative to medication and psychotherapy for treating panic attacks with agoraphobia, many patients return to normal living within mere days.

Existential-Humanistic Therapy, (1998), Insight Media, 100 min. Although a bit long for the typical class, this video presents the basic philosophy behind existential-humanistic therapy. It illustrates the approach through the use of a counseling session.

Having Your Cake: Goodbye to Bulimia, (1997), Films for the Humanities and Sciences, 23 min. *"How do you stay so thin?"* In this powerful documentary, four women openly share the details of their personal journeys of self discovery as they battled bulimia. Through intimate interviews, each describes how she first became aware of her self-destructive behavior and how she disarmed it, freeing herself to move forward toward physical and emotional health. The program is currently being used by teachers, therapists, and health professionals as both an early-warning device and an inspirational guide to recovery.

Obsessive-Compulsive Disorder: An Alternative Treatment, (1996), Films for the Humanities and Sciences, 15 min. The startling fact is that 1 in every 40 Americans is affected by OCD to varying degrees. A recently developed program, however, is bringing hope to millions of sufferers. Dr. Jeffrey Schwartz believes that many patients, by gaining self-awareness, can cure themselves. Two patients in this program believe it too, and testify that Schwartz's three-step treatment has helped them to successfully control their obsessive-compulsive behaviors. The patients include a man who compulsively saves newspapers, and a women who counts and recounts the items in her refrigerator. An ABC News 20/20 production.

Health, Mind, and Behavior. (1990) Annenberg/CPB, 30 min. Program 23 in the *Discovering Psychology* series. This presentation discusses the new biopsychosocial model of treating the mentally ill. Host Philip Zimbardo discusses the history of treatments for mental illness and presents a recent model that integrates the traditional biomedical and psychological approaches with a new social awareness that relationships with others can affect our health. This film clearly indicates that the field of psychotherapy is changing and adapting to meet the needs of people in the 21st century.

Locking Up Women, (1993), Films for the Humanities and Sciences, 48 min. This video provides a look inside Britain's Holloway prison, and examines questions about criminality in women.

Mood Disorders: Medication and Talk Therapy, from *The Mind Series Teaching Modules,* 2nd Edition, #33, Worth, 6:08. As this module opens, a female patient suffering from mania discusses her reaction to medication taken for her disorder. The narrator indicates that the medication is beginning to mute her long-term manic reaction. Paul Wender, University of Utah, then distinguishes between the physical and psychological factors responsible for depression. As he talks, we see a bipolar disorder patient named Doug Barton tracing his family genealogy. We learn that Doug's medication has relieved most of his pain. With the aid of an action graphic, the narrator describes where the chemical action of the medication has its effect—at the synapse. Antidepressant drugs seem to alleviate a deficiency of serotonin and norepinephrine in the synapses of depressed patients. Conversely, manic patients seem to have an excess of certain neurotransmitters. For them, lithium dampens or eliminates mania in 80 percent of the cases.

Psychotherapy: Discovering Psychology Series, (1990), Annenberg/CPB, 30 min. In this video from the *Discovering Psychology* series, Dr. Philip Zimbardo discusses the relationship between theory, research, and practice in the treatment of mental disorders. Perhaps the most outstanding feature of this video is its review of the numerous forces (e.g., history and culture) that influence our attitude and treatment of individuals with mental disorders. This program is an excellent preview to the major forms of psychotherapy. It divides psychotherapy into the psychological and the biomedical. Psychosurgery is perhaps the most radical biomedical treatment, with many considering the cure to be worse than the illness. The prefrontal lobotomy can impair memory, emotional expression, and the ability to plan ahead. ECT is also controversial but continues to be used in the treatment of depression. Drug therapy became popular back in the 1950s, with the use of tranquilizers and antipsychotic drugs. Not only do drugs alleviate suffering, they make psychotherapy possible. The program divides the psychotherapies into four categories: psychoanalysis, behavior therapy, cognitive therapy, and humanistic therapy. It provides useful descriptions of the specific treatments, their history, and the kinds of problems that they are most useful for.

Psychotherapy (2001) from the *Discovering Psychology Series,* Annenberg/CPB, 30 min. This video explores the relationships among theory, research, and practice and how historical, cultural, and social forces have influenced treatment of psychological disorders.

Rational Emotive Therapy, (1982), Institute for Rational Emotive Therapy, 29 min. This film overviews "rational emotive therapy" originated by Dr. Albert Ellis in 1955. Interviews Ellis who explains why he rejected traditional therapies and discusses the evolution of RET.

Schizophrenia: Pharmacological Treatment, from *The Brain Series Teaching Modules,* 2nd Edition #28 Worth, 6:06. Two researchers are interviewed, and they talk about how drugs have changed their outlook for actually being able to help people with schizophrenia. Then, a patient named Augustine is interviewed about his reaction to drug treatment for his schizophrenia. Augustine has been on medication for approximately four weeks. He describes how he now looks to the future and the prospect of returning to work. He is much more realistic after four weeks of drug treatment.

The Placebo Effect: Mind-Body Relation, from *The Mind Series Teaching Modules,* 2nd Edition #3 Worth, 6:14. The opening shows an old black and white movie of someone selling Vita-Zone, a so-called cure-all. The narrator indicates that the imagination can work miracles through its faith in anything from voodoo to Vita-Zone. The power of belief, called the placebo effect, has made it more difficult for modern medical researchers to gauge the effectiveness of new drugs. At the same time, it offers the promise that in some cases, the mind can heal the body. Jon Levine, University of California, San Francisco, is shown conducting an experiment designed to study the placebo effect. His male patients have had their wisdom teeth extracted and are administered saline solution in place of a real analgesic. A patient in the recovery area is approached by Levine, who is dressed in a white coat, stethoscope in pocket. Levine injects the contents of a syringe into the patient's I.V. hookup. As he does this, he says he is giving him a shot for the pain and that it will take about 20 min. for it to take effect. Next we see another patient whose saline solution is administered by a computer. The two patients' reactions are dramatically different. The patient who thinks his analgesic was administered by a doctor reports feeling much less pain. The second patient reports that his pain has only gotten worse. The patients' responses indicate that mere belief in the healer and the healing agent can alleviate pain.

538

The Talking Cure: A Portrait of Psychoanalysis, (1988), Insight Media, 56 min. A rare recording of Freud opens this program. Experienced therapists explain and describe what happens in traditional psychoanalysis and how patients commonly respond to the process.

The Human Potential Movement: Journey to the Center of the Self, (1975), Pennsylvania State University, 18 min. This film focuses on the human potential movement and Dr. William Shutz, founder of the Esalen Institute. There are scenes of encounter group sessions emphasizing techniques for releasing aggression.

The World of Abnormal Psychology, #12—Psychotherapies. PBS, 60 min. This program describes the wide range of approaches that therapists use in treating psychological disorders. Therapists demonstrate psychodynamic, cognitive-behavioral, and humanistic strategies in both individual and group therapy sessions.

Therapies (2002) from *Psychology: The Human Experience Series,* Coast Community College District Telecourses, 30 min. This video examines four different styles of therapy treatment for mental disorders and discusses the role of each style of therapy.

Therapy Choices (2002) from *Psychology: The Study of Human Behavior Series,* Coast Community College District Telecourses, 30 min. This video focuses on significant alternatives to traditional individual psychotherapy, group therapy, family therapy, and self-help groups.

Thinking Allowed: Putting Psychotherapy on the Couch, (1988), Thinking Allowed Productions, 30 min. Bernie Zilbergeld expresses his feelings that to achieve personal transformation through psychotherapy one must be motivated to work hard and make difficult and disturbing changes in one's life. He believes that temporary emotional relief does not generally lead to lasting changes.

Token Economy: Behaviorism Applied, (1972), CRM, 23 min. The film begins as B. F. Skinner cites the five classic victims of behavioral mistreatment: old people, orphaned children, prisoners, psychotics, and retardates. He goes on to explain the use of tokens in a program of reinforcement therapy. Finally, to demonstrate Skinner's theories, the film takes the viewer to a facility of the Illinois Department of Mental Health, where the program director explains how token economies are practiced.

Too Much Medicine? The Need for Clinical Evidence, (2000), Films for the Humanities & Sciences, 50 min. This controversial program presents the need for well-designed trials and promotes a spirit of inquiry into the benefits, risks, and ultimate value of medical interventions.

Treating Depression: Electroconvulsive Therapy (ECT), from *The Mind Series Teaching Modules*, 2nd Edition #34 Worth, 5:41. The module opens with a very depressed patient, Mary, being interviewed about her suicide attempts.

Treating Drug Addiction: A Behavioral Approach, from *The Mind Series Teaching Modules*, 2nd Edition # 30 Worth, 5:55. This module examines drug addiction and its treatment.

Treatment Of Disorders (2005) *Psychology Digital Video Library 3.0 Handbook,* from Thomson Higher Education, approximately 30 min. This provides a depiction different mental illnesses with patient interviews.

Treating Phobias, (2002), Films for the Humanities and Sciences, 19 min. This film describes the frequency and the unpredictability of panic attacks for many people. Intervention strategies are described, including "confrontational or supportive exposure," beta blockers, and tranquilizers. The difference between a fear, a phobia, and a panic attack is clarified. Listeners are reminded that it is crucial that people talk about their fears.

Understanding the Brain Through Epilepsy, from *The Brain Teaching Modules,* 2nd Edition #30 (1998), Annenberg/CPB. This video illustrates that drug therapy may be amelioration, and surgery may be a possible complete cure.

What is Gestalt? (1969), Pennsylvania State University, 24 min. This film features a discussion by Fritz Perls and includes an illustration of awareness training.

When Panic Strikes, (1992), Films for the Humanities and Sciences, 19 min. This program begins with a description of how it feels to have a panic attack. The victim found no physician who correctly diagnosed the condition. When she was finally diagnosed as agoraphobic, treatment included medication and exposure therapy. Panic attack patients can lead nearly normal lives with the proper combination of medication and behavioral therapy.

➤ COMPUTER AND INTERNET RESOURCES

PsykTrek 3.0
Unit 14: Abnormal Behavior & Therapy
14d. "Insight Therapies"
14e. "Behavioral & Biomedical Therapies"

INFOTRAC®

Below you will find three journal articles obtained from INFOTRAC® that relate to information contained in this chapter. Instructors should encourage students to utilize this invaluable resource to improve their research skills. Have students locate and read the following articles and answer questions relevant to each article.

American Family Physician, February 15, 2005. **Treatment of panic disorder.**

1.   According to this article, how do panic symptoms develop?

       Answer: Primarily, phobia of internal sensations is thought to drive the patient's avoidance behavior in panic disorder. Some researchers have also proposed a cognitive model, in which patients learn to misinterpret thoughts and emotions as physical symptoms. Yet another theory is that patients escalate otherwise benign body sensations into panic attacks (the behavioral model).

2.   List the four modes of treatment for panic disorder outlined in this article.

Answer: (a) antidepressants, (b) cognitive behavior therapy, (c) antidepressants and CBT combined, and (d) benzodiazepines.

3.   Briefly describe the effectiveness of the four modes of treatment for panic disorder.

Answer: Antidepressants alone are highly effective in reducing attacks and improving function, with SSRIs and TCAs showing equal efficacy. Although long-term data are lacking, it is likely that combining antidepressant therapy and CBT benefits the patient more than either treatment alone and provides the option of discontinuing the antidepressant. Benzodiazepines are effective for short-term stabilization and long-term management of panic symptoms. However, they are inferior to CBT and antidepressants in terms of patient disability and should be used as a bridge to other therapies.

Clinical Psychiatry News, March 2006 v34 i3 p39(1) **Combo tx surpasses fluoxetine or therapy alone, TADS results show. (combined therapy)(Treatment for Adolescents with Depression Study)**

1.   What is TADS and what did it include?

Answer: TADS is Treatment for Adolescents with Depression Study (TADS). The TADS trial included 439 patients aged 12–17 years with major depressive disorder. Patients were randomized to either 12 weeks of fluoxetine alone (10–40 mg/day), cognitive-behavioral therapy (CBT) alone, CBT with fluoxetine (10–40 mg/day), or placebo.

2.   How did combined therapy compare to either cognitive behavior therapy (CBT) or fluoxetine (Prozac) therapy alone? How long did it take for patients to improve?

Answer: After 12 weeks of treatment, the combination therapy was clearly superior to any of the other arms on the basis of these measurements, he said. Average scores on the CGAS improved to 65 in the combination therapy group, 60 in the fluoxetine-only group, and 57 in the CBT-only and placebo groups. The study found that combination therapy reduced the symptoms of depression better than did fluoxetine or CBT alone. But when the main outcome measure was function, rather than symptoms of depression, the results were not as robust, he concluded. "The data seem to show that treatment effects on function lag behind those on symptoms."

3.   How much did adolescents improve during therapy?

Answer: Even with these improvements, however, most patients didn't regain normal function. Only 35 percent of those in the combination therapy group attained a CGAS score higher than 70, representing normal function. In the fluoxetine-only group, only 20 percent of patients attained normalization. The numbers were significantly lower in the other groups—13 percent of those in the CBT-only arm and 19 percent of those in the placebo arm attained normalized function.

Brown University Psychopharmacology Update, July 2005 v16 i7 p9(2) **Clozapine (generic): Clozaril (brand).** (YOUR MEDICATION INFORMATION)

1.   Why are people likely to discontinue taking anti-psychotic drugs, like Clozaril, to treat schizophrenia? What are the side effects that people taking anti-psychotic drugs experience?

Answer: There are dozens of possible side effects, including:

a) Drowsiness or sedation, dizziness, headache, tremor, fainting, fast heartbeat, low blood pressure, excessive salivation, sweating, dry mouth, and fever.

b) Agranulocytosis: The most dangerous potential side effect of clozapine is agranulocytosis, a potentially life-threatening blood disorder in which the white blood cells, needed to fight infections, are decreased.

c) Seizures: Seizures have also been associated with clozapine, especially at higher doses; clozapine should be used with caution in patients with a history of seizure.

d) Myocarditis: Clozapine may also be associated with myocarditis (inflammation of the muscle walls of the heart) and should be discontinued immediately if myocarditis is suspected.

e) Other: Some of the other possible side effects of clozapine include abdominal discomfort or heartburn; akathisia (internal sense of the need to move); blurred near vision; chest pain; chills; confusion; constipation; decreased sexual ability; difficulty breathing; difficulty urinating; high blood pressure; increase blood sugar; increased sweating; increased watering mouth or drooling; insomnia; liver problems (dark urine, decreased appetite, nausea, vomiting, yellow eyes or skin); loss of bladder control; mental depression; nausea or vomiting; low blood pressure when standing up quickly; sore throat; sores, ulcers, or white spots on lips or in mouth; swelling or pain in leg; trembling or shaking; unusual anxiety, nervousness, or irritability; unusual bleeding or bruising; unusual tiredness or weakness; unusually pale skin; weight gain. As with any dopamine blocking agent, there is a risk of tardive dyskinesia, the development of abnormal movements that may not go away when the medication is discontinued, but this risk is smaller with clozapine than with other typical antipsychotic drugs.

2.   Clozapine should not be taken with which other drugs?

Answer: There are many possible drug interaction effects. Clozapine should not be taken with other drugs that can cause low white blood cell counts, such as carbamazepine (Tegretol). Because it has primary effects on the central nervous system (CNS), clozapine should be taken carefully with other psychotropic medications. Taking warfarin (Coumadin) or digoxin (Lanoxin) with clozapine may cause an increase in blood concentrations of those drugs. Cimetidine (Tagamet), erythromycin (E-Mycin) and fluvoxamine (Luvox) may increase blood levels of clozapine. Clozapine may interact with anticholinergics, bone marrow depressants, fluvoxamine, hypotension-producing medications, and lithium.

542

WEB LINKS

Knowledge Builder Links

1) Psychotherapy and Psychoanalysis
   Trephination:
   http://www.neurosurgery.org/cybermuseum/pre20th/treph/trephination.html
   Philippe Pinel: http://en.wikipedia.org/wiki/Philippe_Pinel
   Freud and Psychoanalysis:
   http://www.answers.com/topic/history-and-psychoanalysis?cat=health

2) Insight Therapies
   Carl Rogers: http://psychclassics.yorku.ca/Rogers/personality.htm
   Existential Therapy: http://www.existential-therapy.com/
   Dr. Phil: http://www.drphil.com/

3) Behavior Therapy
   Aversion Therapy: http://www.mhamic.org/treatment/aversion.htm
   Systematic Desensitization:
   http://en.wikipedia.org/wiki/Systematic_desensitization
   Virtual Reality Therapy:
   http://ajp.psychiatryonline.org/cgi/content/full/162/9/1772

4) Operant Therapies and Cognitive Therapies
   Token Economies: http://www.polyxo.com/visualsupport/tokeneconomies.html
   The Beck Institute: http://www.beckinstitute.org
   Albert Ellis Institute: http://www.rebt.org/

5) Group Therapy, Helping Skills, and Medical Therapies
   American Association for Marriage and Family Therapy: http://www.aamft.org/
   American Self-Help Group Clearing House: http://www.selfhelpgroups.org/
   Mental Health Medications:
   http://www.nimh.nih.gov/health/publications/mental-health-
   medications/complete-index.shtml

6) Self-Management and Seeking Professional Help
   Therapy Effectiveness: http://counsellingresource.com/types/effectiveness.html
   Finding a Therapist in Your Hometown:
   http://mentalhealth.about.com/cs/localandregional/ht/htfind.htm?terms=home+to
   wn+health
   Finding a Psychologist: http://www.findapsychologist.org/

543

Additional Web Links

Anti-Depressants
http://depression.about.com/od/depressionmedication1/f/howadswork.htm
http://www.yestolife.com.au/blue_site/3/1g_1d.htm

APA Online
http://www.apa.org/

Cognitive Therapy
http://www.psychologyinfo.com/depression/cognitive.htm
http://cognitivetherapynyc.com/
http://en.wikipedia.org/wiki/Cognitive_distortion

Finding a Therapist
http://www.empowermentzone.com/therapy.txt
http://www.depression.8m.com/therapistrelate.html

Prozac Myths
http://www.depression.8m.com/prozacmyth.html

Psychotherapies for Children & Adolescents
http://www.aacap.org
http://www.clinicalchildpsychology.org/

Psychological Treatments
http://healthinmind.com/english/psychtx.htm
http://www.nami.org (National Alliance on Mental Illness)
http://www.nimh.nih.gov/ (National Institutes of Mental Health)

General
http://www.behavior.net (Forum for Mental Health Professionals)

Self-Help
http://www.mentalhealth.com/
http://www.psychwww.com/resource/selfhelp.htm

PSYCHOLOGY IN THE NEWS

Counseling Resources
http://counsellingresource.com/sitenews/index.shtml
This resource brings you the latest news headlines from around the world in the field of mental health counseling, with links to many resources in mental health news.

Mental Health Net
http://www.mentalhelp.net/
This site provides news, articles, reviewed links, interactive tests, book reviews, self-help resources, and therapist and job listings. Even videos make up the varied content to be found in Mental Help Net's many topic centers.

Mental Health News
http://www.mhnews.org/
This site provides a mental health newspaper for consumers, families, clinicians, providers, and students with topics about mental illness, treatment options, and resources.

Mental Health News Service
http://bubl.ac.uk/link/m/mentalhealthnews.htm
This website provides a collection of articles about mental health, including prevention and treatment of mental health problems.

CHAPTER 15

Social Behavior

Survey Questions
Discussion Questions
Lecture Enhancements

What's attractive?
My ideal date
Defining love
Gender and perception
Role conflicts
Group membership
Countering groupthink
Making attributions
Self-attribution: The self-serving bias
Role-playing assertive behavior
Who's persuasive?
Dissonance reduction after purchases
Are you assertive?
The rumor mill
Frustration and aggression
Defining aggression
Identifying altruism
The decision tree
Will they help?
The bystander effect

Role-Playing Scenarios
Value-Clarification Statements
One-Minute Motivators

King for a moment
How's your love life?
The power of labels
I hate crowds!
Violating social norms
Social exchange
Social comparison
Proximity and liking
Disclosure and reciprocity
Reexamining attributions
Have a "clone" day
Modern day conformity
Will they obey?
When should we protest?
Consumer behavior
Are we all hypocrites?
Would people obey?
Good and bad prejudices
Genetics of aggression
Did you help?

Broadening Our Cultural Horizons	Cultural attitudes
	Role conflicts for immigrants
	Rules for marriage
	Cultural views of love
	Gender and attribution
	Conformity and culture
	Examining our cultural attitudes
	Attribution in individualistic versus collectivist cultures
	Learning about friends' attitudes
	Culture and persuasion
	Affirmative action and cultural diversity
	Sexism and ageism
	Handling international disputes
	Aggressive cues and culture
	Spanking across cultures
	Culture and altruism
	Legislating prosocial behavior
Supplemental Activities	Exercise 15.1: Conformity
	Exercise 15.2: Group Pressure
	Exercise 15.3: Aggression on Television
	Exercise 15.4: Counting Aggression
	Exercise 15.5: The Prisoner's Dilemma
Handouts	Handout 15.1: Conformity: Data Sheet
	Handout 15.2: Student Survey
	Handout 15.3: Aggression on Television: Data Sheet
	Handout 15.4: Counting Aggression
	Handout 15.5: The Prisoner's Dilemma

Journal Questions
Suggestions for Further Reading
Video Suggestions
Computer and Internet Resources

548

➤ SURVEY QUESTIONS

Module 15.1 Affiliation, Friendship, and Love
Survey Questions: Why do people affiliate? What factors influence interpersonal attraction?

Survey Question: How are liking and loving different?

Module 15.2 Groups, Social Influence, Mere Presence, and Conformity
Survey Question: How does group membership affect our behavior?

Survey Question: What have social psychologists learned about social influence, mere presence, and conformity?

Module 15.3 Compliance, Obedience, Coercion, and Self-Assertion
Survey Question: What have psychologists learned about compliance, obedience, and coercion?

Survey Question: How does self-assertion differ from aggression?

Module 15.4 Attitudes and Persuasion
Survey Question: How are attitudes acquired and changed?

Survey Question: Under what conditions is persuasion most effective?

Module 15.5 Prejudice and Intergroup Conflict
Survey Question: What causes prejudice and intergroup conflict?

Module 15.6 Aggression and Prosocial Behavior
Survey Question: How do psychologists explain human aggression?

Survey Question: Why are bystanders so often unwilling to help in an emergency?

Module 15.7 Psychology in Action: Multiculturalism—Living with Diversity
Survey Question: How can we promote multiculturalism and social harmony?

➤ DISCUSSION QUESTIONS

1. From all that you have learned in this class, would you say that the human need to affiliate with others is genetic or learned? What kind of an experiment could you run to test your hypothesis?

2. How has physical proximity influenced your choice of friends?

3. Has the Internet changed the way that people make friends? Do you have any "virtual" friends? Do Internet friendships feel the same as in-person friendships? Is it possible to form long-lasting friendships (or even romantic relationships) over the Internet?

4. It is typical that when a celebrity dies that many people become very upset. Why do you think this is? Is this grief real? Is it possible to have "known" someone you've never met? Is interaction a necessary part of feeling real loss?

5. Think of your closest high school friends. Which theory best explains your relationships: social comparison, social exchange, or the factors underlying interpersonal attraction?

6. Why do people often under-disclose to a friend or spouse and over-disclose to strangers? Explain these behaviors in terms of principles from this chapter.

7. If you were placed in charge of an important decision-making group, what would you do to minimize groupthink? Do you think that some types of committees or groups are especially prone to groupthink? How serious a problem do you think groupthink is in the government? In the military? In business? In schools? In community groups?

8. How do you explain the behavior of the guards in Zimbardo's prison study? What could be done to prevent this from happening in real prisons?

9. Many students hesitate to ask questions in class. How would a student explain this behavior? How would an instructor explain the behavior? How do these explanations relate to attribution theory?

10. Can you think of a recent situation where you made an attribution that turned out to be incorrect? What contributed to your initial assumption? Why did you change your mind?

11. How serious, in your estimation, are problems of conformity, obedience, and passive compliance?

12. Can you think of a personal experience in which you were subjected to group pressures similar to those in the Asch experiment? How did you feel? Did you yield?

550

13. In view of the Milgram obedience experiment, do you think the civil disobedience of the civil rights and antiwar movements was justified? Why or why not?

14. Could what happened in Nazi Germany ever happen here? Why or why not? Are there any events in American history where the government behaved brutally and the population did nothing? (e.g., Native Americans' decimation, slavery, Japanese internment camps, McCarthyism)

15. Is "blind obedience" ever necessary? Explain.

16. Describe the various persuasive techniques for gaining compliance. Under what conditions and in what situations would each technique be most effective? Why does each of the techniques work?

17. Which of the techniques to gain compliance do you find least ethical? Why?

18. How has the antismoking campaign of the American Cancer Society made use of cognitive dissonance to discourage smoking?

19. Name a time when you experienced cognitive dissonance—when your attitude and your behavior didn't match. How did you deal with the inconsistency?

20. In what ways do magazine and television advertisements apply the principles of persuasion? (Consider the communicator, the message, and the audience.)

21. Choose an issue you feel strongly about. State your attitudes concerning the issue. How did you come to hold your present attitudes? What types of experiences or variables influenced you?

22. What are the principles underlying assertiveness training? What procedures are used to teach a person to become more assertive? Under what conditions do you hypothesize (guess) that these procedures are most effective?

23. Reread the experiments performed on passive compliance. What would have been an assertive response to the situations described? An aggressive response?

24. Kenneth Clark has said, "Prejudice is a way that human beings have of betraying the fragility of their egos." What do you think Clark meant? Do you agree?

25. If you consider yourself to be unprejudiced (or low-prejudiced), how do you act if someone tells a racist joke? Do you laugh along with everyone else? Do you ignore it? Do you speak out against it? If you spoke out, how did the people around you react? Discuss this issue in terms of social norms, cognitive dissonance, conformity, and other concepts from this chapter. Is the reaction different if the joke is sexist rather than racist? Why or why not?

551

26.   Is prejudice a personality trait or a group of behaviors? Explain your answer.

27.   What can be done to reduce symbolic prejudice?

28.   Have you ever been a victim of prejudice (including racism, sexism, or other prejudices?) What were the circumstances? How did you respond?

29.   Do you think women are given the same respect, opportunities, and positive treatment as men? Why or why not?

30.   If you were asked to establish a program to end conflict between students attending two rival high schools, what steps would you take?

31.   At what age would you allow your children to begin watching crime dramas or action shows where murders or murder victims are shown?

32.   What do you think are the superordinate goals facing the nation and the world? (To be truly superordinate, a goal would have to be seen as valid by nearly everyone.) Do such goals exist? How could such a goal be converted into greater intergroup cooperation?

33.   What biological and learning factors explain human aggression? Under what circumstances does frustration contribute to aggression?

34.   Studies of capital punishment show that it has either no effect on deterring homicides or that there is a slight decline after it is abolished. How would a social learning theorist explain this decline? If capital punishment does not deter homicides, do you think it can be justified for other reasons? If so, what, in your opinion, are they?

35.   What are the advantages and disadvantages of a free press that allows violence to occur on television?

36.   Describe a situation in which you did or did not offer help to someone who was, or might have been, in need. What influenced your decision? In view of what you know about helping behavior, can you explain why rape or assault victims are advised to shout "Fire!"?

37.   What can be done on your campus to encourage more helping behavior?

➤ LECTURE ENHANCEMENTS

1. **What's attractive?** A good way to introduce the topic of interpersonal attraction is to ask students to make a list of the five characteristics they look for in their friends. In other words, what five factors are most important in determining to whom they are attracted. Student lists will typically include attributes such as honesty, sense of humor, openness, and so forth. Compare the lists produced by students to the factors identified by social psychological research: social comparison, propinquity, physical attractiveness, competence, and similarity.

2. **My ideal date.** Another way to begin discussion of interpersonal attraction is to divide the class into small groups by gender and ask each group to generate a list of characteristics of the ideal person to date. After everyone has finished, ask one person from each group to read their list to the rest of the class while you write it on the board. This generally elicits a great deal of discussion and debate about the attributes that were chosen. There are usually notable differences in the types of characteristics selected by female groups as opposed to male groups. A class discussion could center on possible explanations for this sex difference in preferred characteristics.

3. **Defining love.** As a way of allowing students to explore their own ideas about this subject, they can be put into small groups and asked to write a definition of love on 3" x 5" cards or slips of paper. Then all of the groups should shuffle their cards and place them face down in the center. Each person in turn should select a card, read it aloud, and comment on the definition. After all definitions have been discussed, the groups should be instructed to arrive at one definition acceptable to all of the members. The group definitions should be presented to the class as a whole for discussion and debate.

4. **Gender and perception.** If the class is fairly small, put all the males in one group and all the females in another group. Ask students to discuss things that bother them about the opposite sex. Ask them to select a spokesperson. Bring the groups together. Ask the men to give one example of their major complaints; ask the women to give another example. What you may discover is that both groups are annoyed by similar behaviors. To what extent do men and women misperceive one another? Do many of us have stereotypes and prejudices with respect to the other gender? What are the superordinate goals in male-female relationships?

5. **Role conflicts.** Ask students to write out five roles in their lives (students, employees, roommates, sons/daughters, friends, etc.) Which two of these roles are in the greatest conflict? Which role usually "wins out" and why?

6. **Group membership.** Get students to individually list all the groups of which they are members. Typically, students will not be aware that they are members of many groups. They might, for example, forget to list nationality or gender. Once students have individually listed their groups, brainstorm a list and write it on the board. Students will be amazed at how many groups they belong to!

7. **Countering groupthink.** Demonstrate critical thinking (rather than groupthink) by asking students to work in groups to develop a plan for improving the quality of instruction at your college, or specific actions the community could take to improve the environment. Ask one person in the group to serve as the "designated devil's advocate" (DDA). Ask students to draw up a plan one day and to reevaluate the plan the next day. Did the presence of a devil's advocate add to the quality of the group's solutions?

8. **Making attributions.** Provide students with a list of 20 adjectives, such as honest, courteous, punctual, assertive, generous, shy, frugal, talkative, hard-working, neat, friendly, grumpy, happy, irritable, suspicious, trusting, serious, relaxed, imaginative, and self-assured. Create a column that says "Self" and another column that says "Best Friend." Next to each adjective in each column write either "usually," "rarely," or "it depends." Ask students to hand their sheet to the person next to them and to count the number of times they said "it depends" in each column. The fundamental attribution error predicts that they will describe themselves more often in "it depends" terms than their best friend.

9. **Self-attribution: the self-serving bias**. People typically give themselves above-average ratings, particularly on those characteristics that are the most socially desirable. Write a list of 10 characteristics (below) on the board. Ask students to take out a piece of paper and number 1–10.
   1 or 2 = very below average
   3 or 4 = below average
   5 or 6 = average
   7 or 8 = above average
   9 or 10 = very above average

Tell them to rate themselves on a 10-point scale as to how they compare to their peers (i.e., other students of the same age and class-level as themselves). They should NOT put their names on their paper. When they are finished, collect the papers, shuffle them, and redistribute them. Ask the other students to average the 10 attributes. You will almost certainly get an "average" overall that is significantly higher than the actual average that would be expected in the typical class. You can also ask for a show of hands for the tallies on individual items. You will likely see greater amounts of self-serving bias on intelligence and attractiveness than on punctuality and athleticism, the former being central to self-esteem, and the latter being more peripheral.

Alternatively, you can list 10 "negative" attributes and perform the same procedure. You will find that almost no one is being objective! Point out the value of moderate amounts of the self-serving bias. Specifically, it helps us protect out self-esteem, motivates us, and protects us from depression.

Positive list: intelligent, attractive, cooperative, punctual, generous, popular, ethical, athletic, creative, ambitious

Negative list: unintelligent, unattractive, stubborn, tardy, stingy, unethical, socially alienated, uncoordinated, boring, lazy

10. **Role-playing assertive behavior.** Verbal definitions and discussion of assertive, aggressive, or excessively passive behavior do not necessarily prepare students to make appropriate responses in actual situations. Modeling each type of behavior can be far more effective. A worthwhile demonstration, therefore, is to have students role-play assertive, aggressive, and passive responses to various situations. Excellent sample situations, complete with dialogue, can be found in Chapter 13 of Alberti & Emmons, 2008.

11. **Who's persuasive?** Put students in small groups of ten. Five people will work as a group; the other five will sit behind them observing their behavior. Give the five in the center the following instructions: "You are a committee gathered to develop a list of guidelines on the kinds of social relationships that should and should not take place in a business office. Should single employees be able to date each other? Should supervisors be able to have relatives working under them? If a dating relationship develops between two employees, should one be transferred to a different department?" Give the group 15 minutes to talk. Then ask the observers which group members were most persuasive and why they succeeded in advancing their views.

12. **Dissonance reduction after purchases.** According to dissonance theory, after one has made an important decision, there is a tendency to seek information that bolsters the choice made and to avoid information that contradicts it (due to the dissonance created). Accordingly, it can be very interesting to interview a student who has recently made a major purchase (of an item such as an automobile, stereo, television, etc.). Inquire into the student's information-gathering behavior before the purchase and his or her information exposure after. Typically, people read advertisements for several brands before a purchase but, afterward, only ads for the brand they selected.

13. **Are you assertive?** Ask each student to write on a 3" x 5" card a situation in which they would like to become more assertive. On the back of the card the student should write what they wish they could say in that situation. Either ask the student to read their own card aloud or mix the cards up before distributing them to the class to be read. Then ask each person to repeat the general idea of the card but use his or her own words. Finally, ask students to role-play the entire situation. This can be done in pairs or in small groups.

14. **The rumor mill.** To demonstrate that attitudes can be shaped by both information and misinformation, ask 10 students to help you transmit "information." Begin a "rumor" by selecting from a magazine a photograph of a dramatic event involving several people. Ask the first "assistant" to step outside. Show this student the picture and ask him/her to try to remember as many details as possible. Ask the second "assistant" outside to be told by the first all of the details. The story can be repeated; questions cannot be asked. Once all 10 students have heard what "becomes misinformation," ask the last person to describe what he/she heard. Then present the class with the photograph. What attitudes do students think could be developed in their own lives through misinformation? What can be done to prevent rumors and falsehood from taking place?

15. **Frustration and aggression.** To dramatize the topic of aggression, try beginning this way: Have students stand in pairs, facing one another. Students are then to play a children's game with which they are probably familiar. One player extends his or her hands, palms down, in front of him or herself; the second player places his or her hands, palms up, touching the palms of the first player. The object of the game is for the person with his or her hands on the bottom to quickly move one or both hands over the top of the first player's hands in an attempt to slap them with a downward motion. The first player tries to avoid being slapped by moving his/her hands out of the way at the first sign of motion. If the second player is able to slap the first player's hand(s), he or she continues with hands on the bottom. If he/she misses, the players change roles so that the first player tries to slap the hands of the second. (*Note:* This game has been played by generations of children and poses little risk in class. However, if any student objects, he or she should be excused. Also, it is wise to ask students to remove any large rings they may be wearing.) This game is usually sufficiently frustrating, competitive, and mildly angering to stir up some aggressive feelings in participants. After the game has progressed for a few moments, it becomes interesting to discuss students' reactions and feelings and to ask which views of aggression seemed to relate to their experience.

16. **Defining aggression.** One of the major problems that occur in the study of aggression is how to define it. Although most people seem to know what they mean by the term, when they attempt to define aggression precisely, it becomes less clear. As an example, physical attacks by one individual against another are generally viewed as aggression unless the attacker is in a role for which such behavior is sanctioned (e.g., soldier, police officer). Professional football players are seen as aggressive as are used car salesmen. To highlight this problem for your students, you could give them examples of different behaviors and ask them to consider whether or not they constitute aggressive actions. For example, you could include things like someone being an avid gun collector, a married couple having an argument, and a state executioner pulling the switch on an electric chair. Attempting to decide whether each of these reflects aggression usually results in a fairly heated classroom debate and gives students some idea of the problems involved in defining the concept.

17. **Identifying altruism.** Create a list of situations where people have helped others and indicate whether each of them is altruism. You can offer the choices of yes, no, or maybe. You might also want to introduce the idea of egoism—we help because it benefits us to do so. For each situation, ask students to explain their choice. To get you started, examples might include:

    a.   A lawyer stops to help at the scene of an accident.

    b.   A police officer gives himself as a hostage in exchange for others' freedom.

    c.   A parent runs into a burning house to save his children.

    d.   A person anonymously donates $100 to a charity.

    e.   A teenager stands up to classmates who are bullying a younger student.

    f.   A man stops to help a woman pick up dropped groceries.

18. **The decision tree. (Darley and Latané)** According to John Darley and Bibb Latané, whether or not people will help depends on a five-step process (below). Ask each student to generate a hypothetical or actual helping situation that illustrates each of the steps. Emphasize that although the decision tree is often used to examine why people fail to help in emergencies, it also applies to everyday helping behavior. You can help them get started by providing an example, also below.

Step one: *Noticing*. If a person (bystander) fails to notice that help is needed, then no help will be given. If notice is taken, move on to step two.

Step two: *Interpreting*. If the incident is interpreted as a non-emergency, or as no help needed, then no help will be given. If the situation is labeled as being a case of help needed, then move to step three.

Step three: *Assuming responsibility*. If the would-be helper assumes that others will help (bystander effect/diffusion of responsibility), then no help will be given. If the person assumes responsibility (most likely if no one else is present), then move to step four.

Step four: *Able to help*. If the person is unable to help, no help will be given. If the person is able to help, move to step five.

Step five: *Willing to help*. If the person is unwilling to help, no help will be given. If the person is willing to help, then the person will help or attempt to help.

Example: Someone is drowning at the beach, but you don't notice because you are reading a book and listening to music. You take off your headphones, and notice splashing and yelling. You assume that it is kids "horsing around." Then the screams get louder and you begin to wonder if there is a problem. You look around for the lifeguard, but no one is there. You look to see if anyone else is helping, but they're not. You want to save the person, but you can't swim, or you can swim but you can't leave your toddler unattended. If you can swim and have no toddler, you make a decision about whether you can attempt a rescue safely—is there an undertow? Is the drowning person bigger than you?

19. **Will they help?** A staged "accident" may be used to dramatize research on the inhibition of prosocial behavior. During a lecture have an accomplice drop an armload of books outside the classroom door. This should be accompanied by a crashing sound and then a pained moan. All this should be out of sight of the class but clearly audible to them. Even if students have already read the discussion of prosocial behavior in the text, the majority will not respond to the "emergency." Follow this dramatization with a discussion of student experiences with real emergencies and the inhibiting effects of other bystanders.

20. **The bystander effect.** (Internet exercise) Have students locate news stories of cases where people either failed to help in an emergency, or where they performed feats of heroism. Analyze the situation surrounding the event according to Latané and Darley's decision tree.

➤ ROLE-PLAYING SCENARIOS

1. **Give students a list of achieved roles.** Ask one person to role-play one of them; the class should try to guess the role. Discuss stereotypes with the class using the following examples: student, businessperson, plumber, mother, father, parent, and teacher.

2. **Role-play being a couple in "romantic love."** Then role-play a couple who have been married 15 years and have a companionate love relationship. Is it possible to combine these two styles of love?

3. **Put students in pairs.** They are to discuss what they did last weekend. Decide who is person A. That person will act as the higher-status student. Person B will act as the lower-status student. What behavioral differences take place in the way they converse with each other?

4. **You are a police officer who pulls over your son for speeding.** What do you say? You are at a dance club and you run into your psychology instructor. What do you say?

5. **You just became engaged to a person from a different ethnic or cultural background.** Announce the exciting news to your parents, your closest friends, or your children.

6. **Ask students to stand in a row as if waiting in line.** Ask the student at the end of the line to walk to the front and try to push in front of everyone else. Everyone in line needs to practice assertively saying "No."

7. **You go to a store to purchase a particular sale item, but the salesperson tries to talk you into buying a more expensive version.** How do you resist? What do you say?

558

8. **Practice responding assertively to verbal aggression.** What should you say if a person says to you:
   a. "You are so lazy; you never get your part of the work done."
   b. "For you, this is a great paper."
   c. "Going to school at night and working all day, it is no wonder your house is such a mess."

9. **Road rage and you**. Break students into pairs and ask them to pretend to be in a frustrating situation on the road—the type that often contributes to road rage. One student should be the driver and one should be the passenger. Have each student choose a situation, and then imitate his or her own typical response to it. Then, have them practice the opposite response. When each one is done, have the students switch places. What did they learn while watching each other's angry and calm responses?

10. **How would you deal with each of these situations?**
    a. Your boss inaccurately evaluates you. What would you say to your boss?
    b. You only have money to pay some of your bills. What would you say to a persistent collection agent?
    c. You just received a promotion, but it would entail moving to another city. This would interfere with your spouse's job. How would you tell your boss that you don't want to move?
    d. A large company near you is polluting a nearby river. How would you tell the president that the lake must be cleaned?
    e. Your ex-spouse is behind in the child support payments. What would you say to convince him/her to pay you immediately?

11. **Role-play an interaction between a teenage "bully" and another student.** Practice different responses to verbal aggression, such as ignoring abusive comments and assertively saying, "I'm uncomfortable when you say those things." Why might this be difficult to do?

12. **Ask a student to huddle in a corner of the room and try to look sick or unconscious.** A second student should role-play first a passerby who decides to ignore the "wino" in the corner and then a person who decides to help someone who may be ill or injured. In both cases, the passerby should verbalize aloud the thoughts that lead to a decision to help or to ignore the person in need.

➤ VALUE-CLARIFICATION STATEMENTS

1. Very few people are "real." Most people are phonies who simply play roles.

2. Although we criticize politicians, they still have high status within our society.

3. People make the fundamental attribution error because it's the lazy way out.

4. Conformity is a sign of a weak personality.

5. The people in Milgram's study were basically just sadistic people.

6. Police officers don't have enough power to do their job effectively.

7. It is the instructor's responsibility to prevent cheating.

8. It is impossible for a person to be brainwashed into doing something they don't really want to do.

9. Parents have the right to kidnap their adult children who may become involved in a cult.

10. Most people conform too easily to pressures from others.

11. Most people are never going to change their attitudes.

12. Most people have a lot of racial prejudices, even if they don't realize it.

13. After years of prejudice, it is now time for extra opportunities to be given to minority members.

14. Current hiring practices based on affirmative action have the effect of lowering performance standards.

15. It is impossible for equal-status contact to take place between groups.

16. Democrats and Republicans come from fundamentally different perspectives.

17. It is important for people to act out their aggression rather than hold it inside.

18. Parents should prohibit their children from watching more than two hours of television per week.

19. The government has no business telling parents whether or not they can use physical punishment on their children.

560

20.   People who won't help others even when there is no danger are just selfish.

21.   If a person tries to help, she or he may be sued. Thus, it is dangerous to help in an emergency.

➤ ONE-MINUTE MOTIVATORS

1.   **King for a moment.** Select a person from class to be "King/Queen for the moment." Ask students to demonstrate subtle ways they could defer to this person and confirm this person's high status. Ask students to treat "this high-status person very well" over the next few class periods. At the next class meeting, discuss how it felt to defer to that person. Ask the "King/Queen" how it felt to be treated royally.

2.   **How's your love life?** Ask students to rate their most recent love relationship according to its intimacy, passion, and commitment.

3.   **The power of labels.** Using a pad of yellow "stickums," write "ignore," "praise," and "confront" on alternate pieces of paper. Put one yellow sticky piece of paper on each person's forehead. Ask students to form groups and to discuss what they did last weekend. They need to treat each other according to the roles on each person's forehead. Were they able to guess their role by the way others treated them? How did it feel to be ignored?

4.   **I hate crowds!** Hold class in a large open space like a large auditorium or field bleachers in the parking lot. Make certain that everyone is as spread out as possible. After about 15 minutes, ask students to move in closer. Briefly discuss feelings experienced when distant versus when crowded.

5.   **Violating social norms.** Ask students to violate a social norm. Be careful to stress that these should be minor violations, and nothing illegal or confrontational. They should get your approval before proceeding. For example, they could offer to pay more than the asking price for a quart of milk or offer to help pay for a part of someone else's food while waiting in the cafeteria line. How do others react?

6.   **Social exchange.** Ask students to turn to the two people sitting adjacent to them and to compliment each person for some behavior they observed during the semester. The recipient of the compliment is only allowed to say "Thank you." Discuss social reinforcement and social exchange.

7.   **Social comparison.** Ask students to describe whether they are below average, average, or above average in the following ways: physical attractiveness, friendliness, creativity, athletic ability, sense of humor, height, and weight. Then discuss the concept of social comparison.

8. **Proximity and liking.** Ask students to write the names of people from the class that they didn't know when the class began but they know now. Ask them to swap papers. Does proximity explain who they have gotten to know this semester? (Include proximity outside of class if the students share other classes or live in the same dorm.)

9. **Disclosure and reciprocity.** Put students into pairs. Ask Person A to establish a specific level of disclosure and for Person B to reciprocate. What are the advantages and disadvantages of reciprocity? How should a person go about changing the level of disclosure in a dialogue?

10. **Reexamining attributions.** Have students generate a list of attributions that they have made today. Most will be unaware that they have even made attributions. One example, however, might be some of their attributions about other drivers, someone's behavior on campus, or something in the news. Once you have listed the attributions, identify each one as either an internal or an external attribution. Consistent with the fundamental attribution error, most will be internal attributions. Next, ask students to brainstorm alternative explanations (attributions) for the behaviors listed.

11. **Have a "clone" day.** Ask everyone to wear the same color clothes. Discuss how they felt conforming to this suggestion. Can a person conform without giving up their own individuality? Did students feel a need to distinguish themselves by their choice of clothing within the color constraint?

12. **Modern day conformity.** After students have read about Solomon Asch's conformity experiment, ask them to guess whether the results (one-third conformity overall) would be the same if the experiment were repeated today. Would people today be more conforming, less conforming, or about the same? If they estimate that the rate would be either higher or lower, ask them why. To reduce the effects of social influence, you could ask them to write down their estimate and hand it in. Answer: Similar studies in recent years have yielded results similar to those found in Asch's original study.

13. **Will they obey?** Ask students to perform a series of behaviors: "Would you please: Put your hands on your hips; do three push-ups; move to the back row; sing a song," and so forth. See how long it takes until one student says, "Do I have to?" Answer, "Please participate in this experiment." A few minutes later, ask them why they obeyed. Is their behavior any different from the subjects in Milgram's experiment? Under what conditions should we conform? When should we refuse to obey?

14. **When should we protest?** Give students a sudden pop quiz (especially if that was not a part of the original rules of the class). When someone protests, compliment them on not being a "willing victim." Discuss under what conditions they should passively comply or actively protest.

15. **Consumer behavior.** What is your favorite TV commercial? List the reasons why it is your favorite. In addition to being appealing, did it also persuade you to buy the product? Why or why not? Have you bought any products in the past six months because of the persuasive ad techniques?

16. **Are we all hypocrites?** Ask the class if they are in favor of recycling. Most will agree that they are. Now ask them what they do when they have a non-refundable drink bottle at school. If there is no recycling on campus, ask them if they take it home to recycle. Most will not. Ask them why. The most likely answers are that their attitudes toward recycling are not very strong, and their attitudes toward convenience are very strong. Some will make external attributions (I can't because…) and others will trivialize the issue (It's only one bottle.) Ask them if they are feeling any dissonance because of the poor correspondence between their attitude and their behavior. If you do have recycling on campus, find out how many actually use it. Alternately, choose a different issue that is relevant to your location.

17. **Would people obey?** Before beginning the chapter, explain Milgram's obedience experiment and ask the students to write down their estimate of how far up the shock schedule they personally would go. In addition, ask them to estimate what percentage of people they think would obey all the way to 450 volts. To minimize conformity influence, ask them to write it down individually and hand it in. Note: Those students who already know the answer should be told not to participate. Alternately, ask them to predict the rates of obedience in the follow-up variations of the original experiment.

18. **Good and bad prejudices**. Students should be asked to make two columns on a sheet of paper. In one column, they should list some "good" prejudices that they personally hold, and in the other list "bad" prejudices that they have. Then discuss with the class what prejudice is and whether there can be "good" and "bad" prejudices. Monitor this discussion closely.

19. **Genetics of aggression**. Take a single social trait, such as aggression, and ask the students to trace it in their family tree to see if there is a hereditary pattern. Discuss the possibility that such a trait could be inherited.

20. **Did you help?** Ask students whether they helped the last time they encountered a need. For example, if they saw an accident (more than just a fender-bender) where police or others were not yet helping, did they stop and help? For those who have cell phones, did they call it in? Why or why not?

➤ BROADENING OUR CULTURAL HORIZONS

Students can be reminded that each of us brings a unique "microculture" to our social interactions. These traditions can empower or inhibit us. Emotional discussions can focus on "majority" power, "minority" discontent, the political impact of the new "majority minority," the pain and conflicts of new immigrants, and the complex needs of the "placeless" (often called the "homeless").

1. **Cultural attitudes.** Describe the "traditions" of your home, including favorite holidays, dinner and bedtime rituals, preferred formal language and slang, value and use of money, views toward sex, attitudes toward grandparents, religious values, etc.

2. **Role conflicts for immigrants.** What kinds of role conflicts do you guess that new immigrants experience?

3. **Rules for marriage**. In some cultures, marriages are arranged by relatives rather than being based on romantic attraction. Such marriages are just as likely to last as marriages formed by choice. Why would this be?

4. **Cultural views of love.** All cultures have different approaches to love. Why do you think our culture emphasizes romantic love as the basis for marriage? What other cultural values does this emphasis echo?

5. **Gender and attribution.** Do males and females attribute causation of events in the same way or in different ways? How? Are attributions changing?

6. **Conformity and culture.** If you have students from other countries, ask them whether they think Americans are more individualistic than people from their home countries. Do people from their culture conform more, less, or about the same amount? If there is a noticeable difference, what do they think of it?

7. **Examining our cultural attitudes.** Make a list of 20 different cultural groups. Who would you: Exclude from your country? Leave alone but not want face-to-face contact with? Tolerate face-to-face contact? Enjoy having as an acquaintance? Enjoy becoming close friends with? Admit to marriage within your family? Marry, yourself?

8. **Learning about friends' attitudes.** Ask students to think about how they learned about attitudes held by their friends. How long in the friendship did it take to learn about them? Did friends state them or show them by behaviors?

9. **Attribution in individualistic versus collectivist cultures.** The fundamental attribution error (bias) states that people from individualistic cultures are more likely to make internal attributions than are people from collectivistic cultures. Ask your students why this is true. They will probably not have a ready answer, but encourage them to focus on how Western versus Eastern culture views people and events. (Answer: Western culture emphasizes individual choice, and regards outcomes as the result of things that individuals do, rather than emphasizing the situation. Western culture also emphasizes the idea that anyone can succeed if he/she wants to, and that success or failure is the result of an individual's level of effort, rather than being a function of the situation.)

564

10. **Culture and persuasion.** If you have students from other cultures, ask them how American TV advertising differs from other countries' ads. Is it more conservative? Are there differences in the way the messages are presented?

11. **Affirmative action and cultural diversity.** What are your feelings about affirmative action hiring? In what ways does a more culturally diverse set of employees add to the quality of the decisions made by a company?

12. **Sexism and ageism.** Prejudice and discrimination can take place based on gender and age. Imagine that a person has a brain tumor and goes to a physician for treatment. What kind of treatment would you recommend? What if the person is 40 years old? Would the treatment be different if the person is 65 years old?

13. **Handling international disputes.** Many people have suggested that "economic" warfare should be used during international disputes instead of traditional weapons. Why? What principle of group interaction does this reflect? Is it fair that wealthy nations have a disproportionate amount of economic power during a dispute?

14. **Aggressive cues and culture.** Make a list of all of the aggression cues used by different groups of people. Spend some time researching gangs. What cues do they use to indicate power and to trigger aggression?

15. **Spanking across cultures. (Internet exercise)** Spanking has been used by parents to discipline children. Have students research how individual countries view and respond to spanking. Each student should choose one country and report their findings to the class.

16. **Culture and altruism.** Some cultures encourage more prosocial behavior than other cultures. Did your family stress helping others? Does your general culture suggest that people should go out of their way to help others? Research a culture where strangers are expected to help each other.

17. **Legislating prosocial behavior.** In some countries (e.g., France) failing to help in an emergency is a violation of the law. Are so-called "Good Samaritan" laws a good idea or not? Why?

➤ SUPPLEMENTAL ACTIVITIES

The exercises outlined in this section should help to get students involved in the discussion of social psychology. They should give students an opportunity to see how the concepts they are studying relate to real-life experiences.

Exercise 15.1: Conformity

This is a project that can be done individually by each student. Ask each student to spend an hour at an intersection that has stop signs rather than signal lights. Their task is to observe and record the behavior of the motorists as they reach the stop sign. If it is a four-way stop, the students should be able to collect a lot of data.

Students should be given a data sheet **(Handout 15.1)** to use so they can keep accurate records. It is a good idea to break down the stopping behavior of motorists into all of the likely variations and record each one. The data sheet includes the following:

1.   Coming to a full at the stop sign and then slowly moving up to the intersection if visibility is impaired, as is the law
2.   Coming to a full stop, not at the sign but at the intersection
3.   Rolling to a near stop and moving on
4.   Slowing down, but not stopping, while passing through the intersection
5.   Driving through without slowing down or stopping

When students return to class with their information, you can ask them to work out the percentages for each of the alternative stopping behaviors. It would also be possible to get a set of percentages for the whole class. See if there are differences in different types of neighborhoods and different times of day.

Exercise 15.2: Group Pressure

This exercise involves a mock student survey. Tell them that you are distributing several survey sheets to speed things up, a couple of which were used in a previous class. Start by passing out four sheets, ask them to read the directions, add their opinions, and pass the sheet on to the next person.

Prepare the sheets to be distributed before the class period. All four sheets should be copies of the **student survey** form that follows **(Handout 15.2.)** Two of them should be blank except for the instructions. The other two should already have five signatures on them, each in different handwriting. Next to the signatures should be the following estimates: $75, $80, $60, $75, $65.

After the sheets have circulated throughout the class, collect them. Find the mean for the first four responses on the two blank sheets and the mean for the first four real responses on the two sheets with fake signatures. See if there is a difference between the influenced and uninfluenced groups.

The purpose of the survey should be revealed to the students. Your discussion should center on group pressure and peer influence. However, students may also want to discuss the ethics of fooling them about the real purpose of the survey.

Exercise 15.3: Aggression on Television

Television violence has been a subject of much discussion, and a lot of statistics are quoted for its frequency. Through this exercise, students have an opportunity to concentrate on this aspect of TV programming.

PROCEDURE

A.   Divide the class into small groups of three or four persons.

B.   Ask each group to consider the question of violence on television. Each group should develop a definition of violence. They should then determine what kinds of behavior they would characterize as violent. Both of these should be noted on the student data sheet that is provided at the end of this exercise.

C.   Ask each group to assign members to different shows on television. Each should observe for an hour at a time. They should simply tally the number of violent acts they see for the hour they are viewing.

D.   At the end of a week the students in each group should put their data together, drawing up some statistics for time of day, type of show, etc.

E.   The class discussion should be lively on the day the groups report their findings.

Exercise 15.4: Counting Aggression

As an alternative to Exercise 15.3, have students do a tally of aggressive incidents on their favorite show. **Handout 15.4** is provided.

Exercise 15.5: The Prisoner's Dilemma

TO THE INSTRUCTOR:

A number of interesting variables may be observed when students play the Prisoner's Dilemma game. Within the groups you will see cooperation, and between the groups there will be competition. The students' meanness to opponents will create cognitive dissonance, which will become evident in their descriptions of those against whom they compete.

The students will attempt to deal with the dissonance by referring to their opponents by derogatory or even subhuman terms. In the column where they are asked to describe the other group, students will often use terms such as "fools," "nerds," "idiots," etc.

PROCEDURE

A.   Divide the class into an even number of small groups. Usually three persons to a group would be sufficient.

B.   The game consists of four rounds of play. Two groups will be paired for each round. Change the pairing for each round.

C.   Supply each group with an instruction and payoff sheet and also a record sheet to keep track of each round.

D.   After the game is over, see how each group did to determine who won and by what strategy: cooperation or competition?

E.   An interesting aspect of the game may be the type of descriptive terms used about the opponents. You may want to collect the forms and make a list for the students to reflect on during the next class session.

F.   Students should be given an opportunity to discuss how they felt and why they played the way they did.

568

Handout 15.1: CONFORMITY: DATA SHEET

TO THE STUDENT:

Find an intersection that has stop signs in all four directions. Your task is to observe and record the way motorists behave at the stop signs. You will notice that not all drivers do the same thing. Spend an hour at the location and record all vehicles. Check the appropriate number on the chart using the following criteria. If the intersection is busy, you may need more than one data sheet.

1. Coming to a full stop at the stop sign and then slowly moving up to the intersection if visibility is impaired
2. Coming to a full stop, not at the sign but at the intersection
3. Rolling to a near stop and moving on
4. Slowing down, but not stopping, while passing through the intersection
5. Driving through without slowing down or stopping

TIME OF DAY _____

LOCATION _____

VEHICLE	STOPPING BEHAVIOR					VEHICLE	STOPPING BEHAVIOR				
	1	2	3	4	5		1	2	3	4	5
1						1					
2						2					
3						3					
4						4					
5						5					
6						6					
7						7					
8						8					
9						9					
10						10					

569

Handout 15.2: STUDENT SURVEY

As part of a student survey, your response to the following question is requested.

What do you think is a fair amount for an instructor to require students to spend on books and other materials for a typical college class?

Please write your estimate in dollars, where shown. To authenticate this survey, please write your name in the space provided. Thank you for participating.

NAME   AMOUNT

_____   _____

_____   _____

_____   _____

_____   _____

_____   _____

_____   _____

_____   _____

_____   _____

_____   _____

_____   _____

_____   _____

_____   _____

_____   _____

570

Handout 15.3: AGGRESSION ON TELEVISION: DATA SHEET

Definition of violence:

_____

_____

_____

_____

Some examples of behavior that is evidence of violence on TV:

_____

_____

_____

_____

_____

Make a note of the programs you watched during the week and the number of violent acts you observed.

PROGRAM	DAY	TIME	NUMBER OF VIOLENT ACTS

571

Handout 15.4: Counting Aggression

Name_____

Choose any TV show and tally the number of aggressive incidents as you watch.

Name of show _____

Categories:

1) Lethal violence. Count not only the death, but also the number of counts of violence within that death. (i.e., If the person was shot and stabbed, count that as two cases. For multiple murders, count each victim's violence separately.)

2) Serious physical attacks—with ambulance or hospitalization likely.

3) Physical contact that causes harm but does not require medical attention (e.g., punching, kicking, hitting with objects, tripping, etc.)

4) Attempted physical contact—swings but misses, etc.

5) Threats or posturing (e.g., lunging at another person, spitting, etc.)

6) Serious verbal aggression—threats, etc.

7) Verbal aggression—profanity, insults, "tough talking."

Handout 15.5: THE PRISONER'S DILEMMA

Two prisoners accused of a major jewel theft are isolated from each other and are being pressured to give evidence against each other. Since there is not enough evidence to hold either one, if they both keep silent (cooperate), they will both go free and can split the booty. However, the prosecutor is offering immunity from prosecution as an inducement for one of them to squeal (compete). The squealer then goes free and keeps the jewels all to himself. If both squeal and testify against each other, then both will go to prison.

INSTRUCTIONS

1.   You will play four rounds of this game. On each round, your group will play against one other group.

2.   The goal is to win as many points as possible. During each round, your group must decide whether it will cooperate (be silent) or compete (squeal) with the other group.

3.   The following table indicates your payoff. Remember that the score you get will depend not only on what your group does but also on what the other group decides to do.

4.   After each round, fill in the requested information on the record sheet.

PAYOFF TABLE

WHEN YOUR GROUP:	YOUR PAYOFF IF THE OTHER GROUP:	
	COOPERATES	COMPETES
COOPERATES	+10 POINTS	-15 POINTS
COMPETES	+15 POINTS	-5 POINTS

Handout 15.5: THE PRISONER'S DILEMMA: RECORD SHEET

DIRECTIONS

A.   Select someone in your group to:
  1.   Keep a record of your group's decisions for each round on a piece of paper.
  2.   Fill in the information asked for on the chart below. The information should be entered at the end of each round. The description portion should be a group decision to be sure it expresses the feelings of everyone involved.

B.   Once the round has begun, the recorder should write the group decision on a piece of paper as soon as it is made. When the instructor gives the signal, both groups should reveal their decision at the same time.

C.   At the end of each round, the recorder should enter on the chart:
  1.   The decision of the group to either cooperate or compete
  2.   The number of points won or lost in that round
  3.   Two or three words that describe the members of the opposing group

D.   After the fourth round, the recorder should enter the total number of points earned. Remember to subtract the negative points from the positive ones. It is possible to end up with a negative score.

ROUND	COOPERATE OR COMPETE	POINTS + OR -	DESCRIPTION OF OTHER GROUP
1			
2			
3			
4			

TOTAL POINTS _____

➤ JOURNAL QUESTIONS

1. What behaviors do others expect of you? What "ascribed" roles do you have? What "achieved" roles? When have you experienced "role conflict"? What would happen to your "status" if you violated one of these expectations?

2. How do you feel when someone compliments you? What do you say? What do you do?

3. What do you believe is most important characteristic in selecting a mate? Why?

4. What general topics about yourself would you not be willing to disclose in class? To a few friends? To your best friend? Describe the issue, not the specific information.

5. How have your attitudes changed since high school? What factors explain these changes or a lack of change?

6. Under what conditions, in which situations, or for what behaviors do you most often conform?

7. How conforming are you? Make a list of times in the past week that you have conformed to the ideas of friends, coworkers, and classmates. Make a second list of times when you have not to conformed. Try to be honest—watch out for the self-serving bias!

8. In what situations would you like to become more assertive?

9. When did you first fall in love? Have you ever fell "out of love"?

10. What are your 10 strongest attitudes, in order? Which ones have been consistent since you were a child? Which ones have changed? Why? Which three on the list do you think will be most likely to change as you age?

11. Who do you know who is prejudiced? What is the nature of their prejudice? How do you think it developed? What are the disadvantages of a rigid personality structure?

12. Have you felt discriminated against? What was the situation? How did you react?

13. Describe a time in your life when you were extremely frustrated. Did you consider behaving aggressively? Why or why not?

14. Should TV scenes that merge violence and sexuality be made illegal?

15. Have you ever been in need of help? What happened? What was the situation? Did anyone help you? Why or why not? How did you feel when the problem was resolved?

575

16. Make a list of the situations under which you would and would not be willing to help another person. For example, do you help even when it is inconvenient, mildly dangerous, or when it costs you money? Does it matter who the person is? Make a list of 10 cases where you would help, and 10 cases where you would not.

➤ SUGGESTIONS FOR FURTHER READING

Ajzen, I. (2005). *Attitudes, personality and behaviour* (2nd ed.). New York: McGraw-Hill.

Alberti, R., & Emmons, M. (2008). *Your perfect right* (9th ed.). San Luis Obispo, CA: Impact.

Allport, G. (1958/1988). *The nature of prejudice* (25th anniversary ed.). New York: Perseus.

Aronson, E. (2008). *The social animal* (10th ed.). New York: Worth.

Baron, R. A., Byrne, D., & Branscombe, N. R. (2009). *Mastering social psychology* (12th ed.). Boston: Pearson/Allyn & Bacon.

Baumeister, R. F., & Bushman, B. (2011). *Social psychology and human nature* (2nd ed.). Belmont, CA: Cengage Learning/Wadsworth.

Bonham, V., Warshauer-Baker, E., & Collins, F. S. (2005). Race and ethnicity in the genome era: The complexity of the constructs. *American Psychologist, 60*(1), 9–15.

Cialdini, R. B., & Goldstein, N. J. (2004). Social influence: Compliance and conformity. *Annual Review of Psychology, 55,* 591–621.

Dovidio, J. F., Glick, P., & Rudman, L. A. (Eds.). (2005). *On the nature of prejudice: Fifty years after Allport.* Malden, MA: Blackwell.

Federal Bureau of Investigation. (2009). *Crime in the United States, 2008.* Washington, DC: Federal Bureau of Investigation. Retrieved May 1, 2010, from http://www.fbi.gov/ucr/cius2008/offenses/violent_crime/.

Festinger, L. (1957). *A theory of cognitive dissonance.* Evanston, IL: Row Peterson.

Hall, E. T. (1990). *The hidden dimension.* Garden City, NY: Doubleday, Anchor.

Hyde, J. S., & Delamater, J. D. (2010). *Understanding Human Sexuality* (11th ed.). New York: McGraw-Hill.

Matsumoto, D., & Juang, L. (2008). *Culture and psychology* (4th ed.). Belmont, CA: Cengage Learning/Wadsworth.

Miller, D. T. (2006). *An invitation to social psychology.* Belmont, CA: Wadsworth.

Myers, D. (2008). *Exploring social psychology* (5th ed.) New York: McGraw Hill.

Seifert, K. (1995). *Training for assertiveness*. Burlington, VT: Ash Gate Publishing.

Tal-Or, N., & Papirman, Y. (2007). The fundamental attribution error in attributing fictional figures' characteristics to the actors. *Media Psychology, 9*(2), 331–345.

Zimbardo, P. (2007). *The Lucifer Effect: Understanding how good people turn evil*. New York: Random House.

➤ VIDEO SUGGESTIONS

Feature Films

American History X (Edward Norton, Edward Furlong, Fairuza Balk), Drama. Upon hearing from his younger brother Danny Vinyard (Furlong) that Blacks are breaking into his car, Derek (Norton) gets his gun and shoots the youths dead. Derek is convicted of murder and sent away where his racist attitude changes. Meanwhile, his brother Danny is following in his brother's footsteps. Derek tries to detour Danny away from the group led by a White supremacist.

The Outsiders (Thomas Howell, Matt Dillon, Ralph Macchio), Drama. The movie tells the story of the ongoing conflict between the Greasers and the Socs in rural Oklahoma. Ponyboy (Howell) is the youngest of three orphaned boys and hangs with the Greasers. When Ponyboy and his friend (Macchio) get into a deadly confrontation, the two go on the run from the cops and are faced with growing up very quickly.

Twelve Angry Men, United Artists, 95 min. Henry Fonda stars as a man on a jury who is in disagreement with the other jurors as to the verdict. The film is a powerful demonstration of conformity and social influence.

Educational Films and Videos

A Class Divided, (1985), PBS Video, for the *Frontline* series, 54 min. This is an update of the famous experiment on discrimination based on eye color, constructed in 1968 by Jane Elliott, a third-grade teacher in Riceville, Iowa. The original footage is featured in *The Eye of the Storm* (described later in this listing). This program features interviews with the original students and reviews their reactions to the experiment, as well as the positive changes in attitudes that resulted. It explores these long-term effects through interviews with Elliott and her students.

About (Romantic) Love, (1995), Insight Media, 60 min. This video investigates the connection between love and authentic self-creation. Hosted by Robert Solomon, it offers a rigorous and wide-ranging discussion of the role of love in the formation of human consciousness and individual personality.

Attitudes (2002) from *Psychology: The Human Experience Series,* Coast Community College District Telecourses, 30 min. This video analyzes the formation of attitudes and how they can be turned into prejudice as well as ways to prevent prejudice and appreciate diversity.

Avoiding Conflict: Dispute Resolution Without Violence, (1995), Films for the Humanities and Sciences, 47 min. This program examines remedies to the rising tide of aggression in our schools, playgrounds, streets and homes. It shows ordinary problems that can ignite violence, and how the problems can be resolved. The program focuses on the solutions rather than on the problems and highlights anti-violence programs that teach dispute resolution and conflict avoidance. It focuses on solving problems nonviolently, and averting street violence.

Brother of Mine: Youth Violence and Society, (1993), Films for the Humanities and Sciences, 50 min. By the time most children reach the age of 18, they have seen 28,000 murders on TV. This compelling documentary takes a penetrating look at why children are becoming more violent at home, at school, and on the streets. Interviews with educators, police personnel, psychologists, and the youths themselves—both perpetrators and victims—reveal that violence, accepted as an everyday occurrence, has become a reflection of culture, not a contradiction of it. Proactive school-based programs such as group feedback sessions, student mentoring, and parenting classes demonstrate peaceful conflict resolution.

Cognitive Social Psychology, Discovering Psychology Teaching Module 14, (1990), Holt, Reinhart and Winston, various times. This module from the *Discovering Psychology Teaching Module* series contains several interesting programs addressing several critical aspects of social cognition: 1) a review of the Festinger and Carlsmith study of cognitive dissonance (3:48 min.); 2) historical footage of Jane Elliot's famous "brown-eye" versus "blue-eye" study of discrimination and attitudes (2:00 min.); and 3) a discussion of attitudes by John Mack (3:00 min.).

Conformity, Obedience, and Dissent, (1990), Insight Media, 30 min. This program explores why people conform, obey, and dissent in social situations. It covers Milgram's obedience study, the Asch studies, research on styles of leadership, and the phenomenon of "groupthink."

Constructing Social Reality: The *Discovering Psychology Series,* (1990), Annenberg/CPB, 30 min. This videotape focuses on the power of cognitive control. Our perception and interpretation of reality shape all our social relationships and behavior. Three studies involving young students are used to illustrate the principle. The major focus of the video is on identifying processes that help us become more empathic and independent members of society. In 1968, Jane Elliot, a third-grade school teacher in Riceville, Iowa, used eye color as the basis for discriminating among her students and dramatically altered relationships among them. Robert Rosenthal demonstrated how teachers' expectations shape their students' academic performance. Rosenthal identifies four factors that seem to mediate the effect. Finally, Elliot Aronson and Alex Gonzalez describe how the jigsaw classroom can foster cooperation when students come to see themselves as independent.

Crimes of Hate, (1990), ADL—Anti Defamation League Film Library, 25 min. This video reveals the twisted thinking of perpetrators of hate crimes, the anguish of the victims, and the strategies used by law enforcement officials, community organizations, and individuals to address these crimes.

Dealing with Conflict, (1992), University Film & Video, 20 min. This short video describes the five basic positions people take in conflict and explains the choices people have for constructive or destructive outcomes. It also presents key skills for directing conflict toward positive results. Based on the Thomas-Kilmann conflict mode instrument.

Domestic Violence: Which Way Out? (1994), Filmmakers Library, 30 min. This video deals with a successful treatment program in Bellevue, Washington, that resulted in a low 4 percent repeat offense rate for those completing the intensive treatment. This video could also be used in a Psychotherapy unit, depending on your approach.

Dream Deceivers: The Story Behind James Vance vs. Judas Priest, (1991), University Film & Video, 60 min. On December 23, 1985 two young men in Reno, Nevada, put shotguns to their own heads after drinking alcohol and smoking marijuana as they listened to a record by the rock group Judas Priest. One died, the other was grossly disfigured. Their parents filed suit against CBS Records claiming that subliminal messages mesmerized the young men into their suicide pact. The program examines this tragedy through interviews with the young man who survived, the parents of both men, and members of Judas Priest. This video is meaningful to students who may recall this incident from news stories.

Encounters with Grief, (1992), University Film & Video, 14 min. This somewhat basic video explores the individuality and commonality of grief following a loss and offers perspectives on the process of recovery. It includes interviews with a mother who lost her teenage son, a woman widowed in her 60s, and a man whose wife died at 52.

Eye of the Storm, (1970), ABC, 25 min. This very dramatic and effective film shows the experiment on prejudice performed by grade school teacher Jane Elliot, in which children's eye color becomes the basis for discrimination against them.

Face Value: Perceptions of Beauty, (1995), Films for the Humanities and Sciences, 26 min. This video examines the belief that our perceptions of attractiveness may be universal and biologically programmed and that certain features of the face have an instinctive appeal—large eyes, high cheekbones, smooth skin texture, and a narrow jaw. This video is guaranteed to spark interesting discussion in the classroom.

579

For All Practical Purposes: The Prisoner's Dilemma, (1986), Penn State University, 30 min. (Program 5 in the *Social Choice* series). If you conduct one of the Prisoner's Dilemma exercises in class, this is an excellent video to show the day after the experiment. It illustrates decision-making strategies in games of partial conflict. Prisoner's Dilemma and games of "chicken" are used as primary examples. The program then enlarges its scope to include business-oriented examples, such as negotiations, corporate takeovers, labor relations, and other industrial/organizational examples. This program allows students to see the Prisoner's Dilemma in a broader context.

Frosh, (1993), Insight Video, 98 min. This documentary follows a year in the life of freshman students at Stanford University. It traces the social experimentation and intellectual curiosity, cultural clashes, spiritual cries, academic pressure, and adjustment problems and illuminates the individual self-discovery within a diverse community.

Group Influence (2002) from *Psychology: The Human Experience Series,* Coast Community College District Telecourses, 30 min. This video explains individuality, group behavior, and deindividuation.

Groups and Group Dynamics, (1991), Insight Media, 30 min. This video describes categories of groups and explains how they function, how they differ from other social entities, and how membership is determined.

Helping and Prosocial Behavior (1989) Insight Media, 30 min. Defining reciprocity and social responsibility, this program explores why people help each other and considers the variables that moderate altruistic behavior. It discusses modeling effects and diffusion of responsibility and investigates how mood influences helping.

A History of Social Classes, (2000), Films for the Humanities and Sciences, 52 min. Marx divided the industrial world into two antagonistic classes: the bourgeois and the proletariat. In today's society, this simple dichotomy fails to capture the many segments of a global marketplace. From the communal hunter/gatherers and agrarian cultures to ancient empires and medieval fiefdoms to the technocrats, executives, laborers, and others of the stratified modern world, this program examines how each era has organized its members into social classes. Although the opportunistic meritocracy of the global marketplace has displaced earlier societal models, do older patterns of privilege still linger?

Interpersonal Processes, Discovering Psychology Teaching Module 15, (1990), Holt, Reinhart and Winston, various times. This superior video from the *Discovering Psychology Teaching Module* series contains actual footage from several of the most important social psychological experiments ever conducted. Two of the highlights include: 1) Milgram's obedience experiment (4:29 min.); 2) Zimbardo's prison simulation experiment (6:30); and 3) Aronson's jigsaw puzzle cooperation versus competition study. Additional modules cover topics like the groupthink behavior displayed during the Bay of Pigs incident and a discussion of tactics used by sales people.

580

Media Impact, (1997), Films for the Humanities and Sciences, 28 min. This program emphasizes the seductive nature of films and television. The pervasiveness and sheer volume of electronic images in daily life make it extremely difficult for viewers to discern fact from fiction, as with Oliver Stone's controversial *JFK*. The manufactured reality of films and TV also plays a role in popularizing certain behaviors—some of which are unhealthy or antisocial, like smoking and violence. Studies show that as audiences become saturated with violent images, they can all-too-easily become desensitized to real-life situations. In addition, some suffer from media narcosis, a form of addiction which, when TV is removed from the environment, causes symptoms of withdrawal. This program is an essential component of any course that addresses the importance of critical viewing skills and an awareness of the media's impact on perceptions.

Negotiation and Persuasion, (1989), Insight Media, 30 min. This program demonstrates techniques used to influence attitudes and behaviors, focusing on such elements of nonverbal communication as body language, facial expression, and touch. It discusses persuasive techniques, including ingratiation, supplication, intimidation, foot-in-the-door techniques, door-in-the-face techniques, and the "that's-not-all" technique.

Obedience, (1969), Penn State University, 44 min. Featured in this film are segments of real subjects in Milgram's original obedience experiment. Subjects are shown expressing considerable distress and discomfort as the authority figure commands them to shock the innocent "victim."

Pulling the Punches, (1994), Filmmakers Library, 30 min. This video could be used in a Psychotherapy unit as well as in this social psychology chapter. It provides an intimate view of one man's therapy to control his abusive behavior toward his wife. The patient was treated at Everyman's Center in London. The video goes inside the Center to record his interactions with his counselor.

Quiet Rage—The Stanford Prison Experiment, Insight Media, 50 min. This is the full-length version of the second most controversial experiment in social psychology. It is narrated by Phil Zimbardo, who explains the real purpose of the experiment, shows examples of all the kinds of behavior changes that took place during the experiment, including his own, which he is brutally frank in revealing, and describes precautions taken to prevent harm to his participants, which failed to predict what actually took place. The experiment had been designed to continue for two weeks but had to be discontinued after only six days due to the deterioration of the personalities of the participants, especially those in the role of prisoners. A truly chilling example of just how pliable human behavior is under certain circumstances.

Race And Racism (2001) Insight Media, 60 min. Exploring how the scientific understanding of "race" affects ethical considerations and census questions, this video attempts to define racism. It ponders explanations of racism as an act of will, a disease, a bad habit, or the product of historical economic forces; questions racism as an affront to justice; addresses the social and political status of people of mixed race; and stresses the difficulty of identifying subtly racist assumptions.

Social Behavior, (2006), *Psychology Digital Video Library 3.0 Handbook,* from Thomson Higher Education, approximately 36 min. This unit provides a six-part series on bystander intervention as well as a section on facial analysis and implicit association.

Social Cognition, (2002), from *Psychology: The Human Experience Series,* Coast Community College District Telecourses, 30 min. This video focuses on how people form impressions of others and on how people's behavior is affected by attitudes.

Social Interaction Model, (2001), Insight Media, 60 min. A social interaction model clarifies the dynamics and implications of human social behavior. This video presents a social interaction model designed to elucidate the way people interact in culturally diverse settings. It focuses on the five major components of the model and shows how they overlap.

Social Psychology, (2002), from *Psychology: The Study of Human Behavior Series,* Coast Community College District Telecourses, 30 min. This video shows how people's behavior is influenced by the social roles they play and by the norms or rules governing different roles.

Social Psychology Series, (1989), Pennsylvania State University Audio-Visual Services, 30 min. This eight-part series covers various topics in social psychology, including communication and persuasion, friendship, prejudice, conformity, group decision making, leadership, aggression, helping, and prosocial behavior.

Social Psychology, (1990), Insight Media, 30 min. Social psychology attempts to explain the social forces that influence attitudes and actions. This video discusses studies on stereotyping and prejudice, attribution theory, and the power of social roles. It also analyzes Zimbardo's prison experiment and in-group/out-group experiments.

Street Life: Inside America's Gangs, (1999), Films for the Humanities and Sciences, 46 min. In this program, ABC News correspondent Cynthia McFadden interviews female members of two Los Angeles gangs—the Drifters and Tepa 13—while correspondent John Quinones talks with King Tone, the radical leader of New York City's notorious Latin Kings. In addition, extensive unscripted video footage shot by members of these three gangs provides a glimpse as raw as it is rare of life inside the net that is snaring young people all across the country. Some content may be objectionable.

The Dating Bill of Rights, (1998), Films for the Humanities and Sciences, 26 min. Recommended by *The Book Report* and *Video Librarian.* Dating is an important part of becoming an adult, but it can also be confusing and frightening. This program presents basic guidelines that clarify common myths, such as that "no" really means "yes." Abuse and respect, sexual stereotypes, how to break up, and preventing violence are all discussed, along with what true love is and is not. Skits, dialogue, and quizzes engage the audience and present sensitive material in a very hip format.

The Power of the Situation: Discovering Psychology, Annenberg/CPB Project, 30 min. This program will bolster both students' knowledge of the history of social psychology and their understanding of person/situation interaction as a source of behavior and mental processes. It traces contemporary social psychology back to Kurt Lewin's thesis that behavior is a function of both the person and the environment.

Understanding Prejudice, (1992), Thinking Allowed Productions, 86 min. The demographics of society are forcing us to come to terms with cultural diversity. In this two-part video, Jeffrey Mishlove interviews Price Cobbs, who describes the principles of ethnotherapy, designed to facilitate a deep examination of the ways we think about other groups.

Understanding Prejudice, (2000), Films for the Humanities & Sciences, 50 min. Gold Medal, New York Festivals. A Cambridge Educational Production. Highly recommended by *The Book Report.* This program discusses the nature of prejudice and its effects on individuals and society. The focus is on the following questions: Where does prejudice come from? Why does it exist? Where are we headed as a society? Included are a historical overview of prejudice and definitions of key terms, such as discrimination and bigotry. Interviews illuminate different kinds of prejudices and stereotypes. The timely topics of multiculturalism, homosexuality, "politically correct" language, the role of the media, and religion are discussed. This is an excellent classroom tool for promoting tolerance.

Understanding Race: Race, (1996), Films for the Humanities and Sciences, 52 min. No gene has quantified it, yet it continues to polarize the world's populations like no other concept. This compelling program examines the history and power of the artificial distinction called "race," viewing it within historical, scientific, and cultural contexts. Topics include the anthropological unity of Homo sapiens; sanctioned discrimination, such as segregation cultural biases based on racial stereotypes; and the underlying humanity that inextricably links us all.

Violence: An American Tradition. (2000) Films for the Humanities & Sciences, 55 min. Using archival photos and footage, as well as the words of both historical figures and current experts in sociology, medicine, and history, this program explores the recurring patterns of violence that have emerged in our society as a result of insurrection, anger, prejudice, and ignorance. Hosted by civil rights leader Julian Bond, the program examines many of the most notorious acts of violence that have scarred the American psyche over the past 200 years.

Voices, (1991) Colorado State University, 35 min. Participants from diverse cultural backgrounds discuss how their self-images developed, how they are perceived in our society, and how self-image and image of others combine to affect relationships. This video trains and teaches about intercultural relationships.

➢ COMPUTER AND INTERNET RESOURCES

PsykTrek 3.0
Unit 15: Social Psychology
15a: Attribution Processes
15b: Theories of Love
15c: Attitude Change
15d: Prejudice
15e: Conformity and Obedience

INFOTRAC®

Below you will find two journal articles obtained from INFOTRAC® that relate to information contained in this chapter. Instructors should encourage students to utilize this invaluable resource to improve their research skills. Have students locate and read the following articles and answer questions relevant to each article.

The Psychological Record, Spring 1993 v43 p331 (2) **Social Comparison: Contemporary theory and research.**

1.   Social comparison theory captures what enduring truth about human social life?

   Answer: That other people provide us with important standards for self-evaluation.

2.   What distinguishes contemporary social comparison theory and research from its predecessors?

   Answer: Its emphasis on downward comparison. The basic premise of downward comparison is that subjective well-being can be enhanced through comparison with a less fortunate other.

3.   What is the "uniqueness bias"?

   Answer: The tendency for us to see our own behaviors as at least better than average, given that our standing on the behavior is not strongly constrained by reality. Here, comparison is not so much with a specific less fortunate other as with an imagined inferior constructed for the occasion.

Pediatrics, June 2004 v113 p1771 (5) **Violence and suffering in television news: Toward a broader conception of harmful television content for children.**

1.   The enormous amount of public concern and research effort that has been directed at the prevalence of media violence and at the harmful effects that it may have on children thus far largely has ignored the regularity of real-life violence depicted in television news. List three examples of how this has been ignored according to this article.

Answer: First, large-scale content analyses of media violence that were specifically aimed at detecting harmful television content for children all excluded from their analyses broadcast news programs. Second, legislative proposals that have been put forward to protect children from violent media content all disregard television news. And third, television parental guidelines (V-chip ratings), which were the result of the 1996 Telecommunications Act, are not applied to news and sports programs.

2.   Pediatricians could take action within their own practice, and they could also enhance awareness of the negative consequences of violent news within other domains. List four domains that pediatricians could use to enhance awareness.

Answer: First, families and schools should be informed about the potential negative effects of news violence for children. Secondly, pediatricians could enhance public debate about the suitability of television news for children. Third, pediatricians could promote alternative, special news programs that are tailored to the needs of child audiences. And finally, pediatricians could promote research into the harmful effects of violent news presentations.

WEB LINKS

Knowledge Builder Links

1. Affiliation, Friendship, and Love
       Social Psychology Network: http://www.socialpsychology.org
       Rubin's Love Scale:
              http://psychcentral.com/lib/2007/rubins-love-scale-and-rubins-liking-scale/

2. Groups, Social Influence, and Conformity
       Stanford Prison Study: http://www.prisonexp.org
       Asch's Conformity Experiments:
              http://www.age-of-the-sage.org/psychology/social/asch_conformity.html
       Groupthink: http://en.wikipedia.org/wiki/Groupthink

3. Compliance, Obedience, and Self-Assertion
       Milgram's Obedience Study:
              http://en.wikipedia.org/wiki/Milgram_experiment

Assertiveness:
   http://www.uww.edu/uhcs/brochures/Assertiveness.pdf

4. Attitudes and Persuasion
  Persuasion Techniques:
   http://psychology.about.com/od/socialpsychology/a/persuasiontech.htm
  Cognitive Dissonance:
   http://changingminds.org/explanations/theories/cognitive_dissonance.htm
  Heaven's Gate Cult:
  http://web.archive.org/web/20060907005952/http://etext.lib.virginia.edu/relmove/

5. Prejudice and Intergroup Conflict
  Understanding Prejudice: http://www.understandingprejudice.org/
  Authoritarian Personality: http://www.anesi.com/fscale.htm
  Intergroup Conflict: http://www.cahro.org/html/intergroup_conflict.html

6. Aggression and Prosocial Behavior
  Anger Management: http://www.apa.org/topics/anger/control.aspx
  Frustration-Aggression Hypothesis: http://psychclassics.yorku.ca/FrustAgg/miller.htm
  Media Violence: http://www.media-awareness.ca/english/issues/violence/index.cfm

7. Multiculturalism—Living with Diversity
  Project Implicit: http://implicit.harvard.edu/
  Multiculturalism Guidelines (APA):
   http://www.apa.org/pi/oema/resources/policy/multicultural-guidelines.aspx
  Diversity in College:
   http://www.collegeview.com/articles/CV/campuslife/spice_of_life.html

Additional Web Links

Altruism
http://www.bsos.umd.edu/psyc/sechrist/chapter12.htm

APA Online
http://www.apa.org/

Culture and Society
http://www.nypl.org/locations/schomburg
http://www.socialpsychology.org/cultural.htm
http://dir.yahoo.com/Society_and_Culture/

Crime Statistics/Domestic Violence/Hate Crimes
http://www.fbi.gov/ucr/ucr.htm
http://www.mincava.umn.edu/documents/factoid/factoid.html
http://www.fbi.gov/hq/cid/civilrights/hate.htm

Cults:
http://www.csj.org/

Evolutionary Psychology
http://www.psych.ucsb.edu/research/cep/primer.html

Group Processes
http://www.uiowa.edu/~grpproc/

Kitty Genovese Murder
http://en.wikipedia.org/wiki/Kitty_Genovese
http://www.angelfire.com/comics/mooreportal/kitty.html

Milgram—Obedience
http://en.wikipedia.org/wiki/Milgram_experiment

Pornography—Reports on Pornography and Safety Tips (children)
http://www.pbs.org/wgbh/pages/frontline/shows/porn/
http://www.fbi.gov/innocent.htm
http://www.protectkids.com/dangers/stats.htm

Prisoner's Dilemma
http://serendip.brynmawr.edu/playground/pd.html

Racism and Prejudice
http://www.spssi.org/index.cfm?fuseaction=page.viewPage&pageID=1031&nodeID=1

Research in Social Psychology
http://www.sbp-journal.com/   (Social Behavior and Personality)
http://www.apa.org/journals/psp.html (Personality and Social Psychology)

Social Cognition Psychology
http://www.indiana.edu/~soccog/scarch.html

Social Psychology
http://www.uiowa.edu/~grpproc/crisp/crisp.html

Social Psychology—Societies
http://www.spsp.org/
(Society for Personality and Social Psychology)
http://www.spssi.org/
(Society for the Psychological Study of Social Issues)
http://www.sesp.org/
(Society of Experimental Social Psychology)Social Psychology Links
http://www.socialpsychology.org
http://www.prisonexp.org

PSYCHOLOGY IN THE NEWS

Football Against Racism in Europe
http://www.farenet.org
This link underlines the growing importance of sport in combating racism under the forms of discrimination and encourages grassroots action. Also provides many links to news regarding similar issues.

News and Letters
http://www.newsandletters.org
This link explores racism.

Prejudice in the News
http://www.understandingprejudice.org/teach/assign/news.htm
The goal of this site is to help students see the connection between prejudice and current affairs in nearly all spheres of life.

Racism, No Way
http://www.racismnoway.com.au/news/
This website aims to tackle racism in schools in Australia through providing teachers, students, parents, and governors with games and research.

University of Waterloo
http://www.newsrelease.uwaterloo.ca/archive/news.php?id=120
Search this site for the latest news releases; search by topic and search for experts.

CHAPTER 16

Applied Psychology

Survey Questions
Discussion Questions
Lecture Enhancements

NASA personnel selection
Interpersonal space zones
Elevator rules
My space
This classroom could be better!
Ecological footprint
The commons dilemma
Cognitive maps and behavior

Role-Playing Scenarios
Value-Clarification Statements
One-Minute Motivators

Making career decisions
Interest inventories
Where do I find that?
Personal space
Violating personal space
Testing preferences
What do you want on that test?
Enrichment ideas
Sensory overload
Territory violations
Graffiti board
Crowding
The commons dilemma
Superordinate goals
Interdependence and cooperation
Bad ergonomics

Broadening Our Cultural Horizons

Japanese managerial techniques
Theory X and cultural fit
Multicultural workplaces
Crowding and world view
Culture and personal distance

Supplemental Activity   Exercise 16.1: What Do Psychologists Do?
Journal Questions
Suggestions for Further Reading
Video Suggestions
Computer and Internet Resources

➤ SURVEY QUESTIONS

Module 16.1 Industrial/Organizational Psychology

Survey Question: How is psychology applied in business and industry?

Module 16.2 Environmental Psychology

Survey Question: What have psychologists learned about the effects of our physical and social environments?

Survey Question: What can be done to improve communication at work?

Module 16.3 The Psychology of Education, Law, and Sports

Survey Question: How has psychology improved education?

Survey Question: What does psychology reveal about juries and court verdicts?

Survey Question: Can psychology enhance athletic performance?

Module 16.4 Psychology in Action: Human Factors Psychology—Who's the Boss Here?

Survey Question: How are tools designed to better serve human needs?

➤ DISCUSSION QUESTIONS

1. Under what economic and interpersonal conditions would Theory X management be most successful in encouraging productivity? Under what conditions would Theory Y be most successful?

2. What are the advantages and disadvantages of participatory management? Of management by objectives? Of quality circles?

3. What can employers do to help their employees deal with stress and make appropriate career decisions?

4. Your text points out that psychological efficiency is just as important as work efficiency and includes maintaining good morale, labor relations, and employee satisfaction. What things does the management at your job do to create psychological efficiency?

5. How big a problem do you think the "glass ceiling" is for women? Have you ever seen evidence of this phenomenon at work?

6. If you could change one thing at your current job (besides money), what would it be? What is the one thing that you like best at your current job?

7. In your opinion, what are the advantages and disadvantages of flextime?

8. If you were selecting a person for a job, how would you try to ensure that the person's skills and interests matched those required by the position?

9. Have you ever taken an interest inventory or an aptitude test? Did the results surprise you? Did you answer the questions honestly?

10. How is an aptitude test different from an interest inventory?

11. How do people maintain a sense of distance from strangers when they are in crowded situations that force them into close physical proximity?

12. Being in an elevator forces people to stand closer together than they normally would. How do people compensate for the cramped conditions? What are the "rules" for being in an elevator?

13. Do you enjoy being a part of big crowds? Why or why not?

14. Would you prefer to live in a big city, a medium sized city, or a small city or town? Why?

15. How would you attempt to show that a specific personnel selection technique is both valid and reliable?

16. Why do you think people tend to "mark their territories"? Under what conditions is such marking most important?

17. What can a person do in a densely packed environment to reduce feelings of crowding?

18. Should extra money be spent constructing buildings that accommodate the needs of people or should people learn how to satisfy their own needs within cheaper, more energy-efficient buildings?

19. What social traps can you identify in day-to-day experience? What could be done to change them?

20. Sports psychology, along with other factors, has helped athletes perform better than ever before. Have we reached the maximum level of human performance in sports? Why or why not?

21. Garrett Hardin believes that it is a mistake to send food to countries wracked by famine. According to Hardin, this only allows the population of such countries to expand so that a later, larger disaster becomes inevitable. In your opinion, is it more or less humane to supply food under such circumstances?

22. What kinds of incentives and reinforcers would motivate people to work harder to preserve their environment?

23. If you had an opportunity to go and live on the space station for a month, would you do it? Why or why not?

➤ LECTURE ENHANCEMENTS

1. **NASA personnel selection.** Relatively few psychological problems have manifested themselves among space crew members thus far; however, an analysis of the situation suggests that in the future, more, rather than fewer, psychological problems will arise. This is because, in future missions, the reward/cost ratios will reverse themselves. That is, in the early missions, the psychological and physical costs to the astronauts were quite high, but so were the rewards. However, as space flight becomes increasingly routine, the space missions become longer, and the number of individuals to visit space increases, the external rewards to astronauts will undoubtedly diminish more rapidly than their costs. Therefore, as the extrinsic rewards for space flight wane, it should become increasingly important to select candidates on the basis of positive psychological characteristics. As an interesting illustration of personnel selection issues, you could ask your students to generate a list of attributes that they think the successful astronaut of the future will need to possess. For more information on this subject, see Helmreich (1983).

2. **Interpersonal space zones.** Hall's list of interpersonal space zones relates easily to everyday experience and thus needs little illustration. Just the same, a few quick dramatizations can be worthwhile. To demonstrate the boundary of intimate distance, select a subject, preferably someone slightly shy. Have this person stand with his or her back to the wall. Then arrange four volunteers in a semicircle, five or six feet from the subject and facing him or her. Move the semicircle of people in toward the subject in increments of about six inches. Ask the subject to indicate at what point a noticeable difference in comfort occurs or when (s)he feels that his or her personal space is being invaded.

3. **Elevator rules.** Break students into teams and have them go to a building where there are only a few floors. Station a person near the elevators on each floor. Another student from the team will board the elevator when there is only one other person getting on and violate an "elevator rule," such as not spreading out, staring, getting on the elevator and not turning around, or asking a strange question (e.g., Do you like elevators?). Students should be cautioned NOT to engage in any inappropriate behavior, such as touching. Male students should be particularly careful not to alarm a female rider. When the target

592

person gets off the elevator, one of the other group members waiting on an upper floor should interview the person for his or her reactions, and tell him or her that it was part of a class project. Each team member should take turns being the "rider."

4. **My space.** Even when classroom seats are not assigned, there is a strong tendency for students to select a particular spot at the beginning of the semester and to occupy that place for the rest of the term. While most of them are not conscious of their territorial behavior, they can be made aware of it by being forced to sit somewhere else. At the beginning of class, simply tell the students that you want everyone to sit in a different seat for that day. Instruct the people who typically sit in the back to come up to the front and vice versa. Ask those who usually sit on the left-hand side of the room to move to the right, and so forth. Then proceed with the class as usual. It won't be long before you begin to notice marked changes in the students' behavior. Normally talkative students will seem subdued; those that often ask questions will be quiet; the mood of the entire class will seem altered. Stop at this point and ask the students how they feel. They generally report feeling quite anxious and uncomfortable. This effect is particularly pronounced if it is toward the end of the semester and they have had plenty of time to get used to their seats. (You may even find it necessary to allow them to return to their usual places.) You might like to conclude the demonstration with a discussion of whether human territoriality is innate or learned.

5. **This classroom could be better!** Students could be asked to play the role of an environmental or architectural psychologist and redesign the classroom. It might be useful to begin with their initial perceptions of the environment. Is it seen as a friendly place or cold and forbidding? Is it spacious or crowded? Cluttered or neat? What features contribute to these impressions? Then ask them to come up with modifications in the design of the room that would make it a more comfortable and/or effective learning environment. Have them consider ambient conditions that might readily be altered like lighting, noise level, and temperature as well as the more permanent architectural features like walls, floor, ceiling height, and windows.

6. **Ecological footprint.** (internet exercise) Have students complete the "ecological footprint" exercise at http://www.ecologicalfootprint.org/Global%20Footprint%20Calculator/GFPCalc.html and bring in their results.

7. **The commons dilemma.** Inform students that you are willing to give them extra points on their next test. Students can choose whether they want two points or five points. Assure them that you are not joking, and be prepared to keep your promise. Each student will be given the number of points that he or she chooses. **But, you inform them, there is a catch.** If more that 20 percent of the class chooses five points, nobody gets ANY points. Students may not discuss the situation before writing down their choice. Each student should write down his or her name, along with the choice of points and hand it in. Tally the results. In the unlikely event that fewer than 20 percent choose the selfish

593

option, congratulations! You have a very cooperative class! Although you should not disclose people's identities, some will be willing to volunteer to explain why they chose five points instead of two.

8. **Cognitive maps and behavior.** Geographers have studied cognitive representation of the physical environment for centuries, but it is only recently that psychologists have become interested in cognitive maps and how they influence behavior. Maps are by nature distortions of physical space, and it is thought that these errors reveal important information about the values and interests of the mapmaker. Accordingly, it might be interesting to ask your students to draw a map of their college campus. After they are finished, students can compare maps with one another or you might provide actual copies of a map of the campus. Are there certain landmarks that were included on most students' maps? Were certain parts of the campus overrepresented or more detailed than others (e.g., campus center, gym, and library)? Were there any major aspects of the campus environment that were completely omitted from some students' maps? Do the students agree that a map such as this provides a measure of what is important to them? For an interesting look at how maps reveal what different societies consider important, see B. Nimri Aziz, "Maps and the Mind," *Human Nature,* August 1978.

➤ ROLE-PLAYING SCENARIOS

1. **You are an employer interviewing a new candidate for the position of manager for a videotape rental store.** A "job analysis" has been done, and you are looking for a candidate who can schedule and supervise employees, maintain inventory, anticipate customer rental trends, and interact in a friendly manner with customers. What "critical incidents" would this employee have to cope with? What bio-data would you need?

2. **Imitate the behavior of someone who recently violated your personal space.** How did you deal with it?

3. **You are an employer who believes in Theory X.** You are making your annual report to your employees. What would you say?

4. **A friend of yours has adopted the "complacent" style in selecting college courses.** He/she waits until the last day of registration and enrolls in whatever courses are left. The result is that he/she has taken many courses that may not meet the requirements for a specific major. Figure out a way to motivate your friend to become "more vigilant" in selecting courses and graduating.

5. **You are the chairperson of a new water conservation program.** Give a persuasive speech to the class encouraging them to participate in your program.

➤ VALUE-CLARIFICATION STATEMENTS

1. It costs the employer too much in extra utilities and other overhead to allow flextime.

2. Employers need to pay employees more, even if that means providing fewer psychological benefits.

3. I would be willing to take a lower paying job in exchange for better working conditions and workplace satisfaction.

4. Students and staff should eat in the same area, not in separate areas on campus.

5. Interest inventories and aptitude test don't really help people much in choosing a career.

6. More tax money should be spent building additional prisons as a way to reduce overcrowding among prisoners.

7. The benefits of living in a large city with a lot of activities to engage in outweigh the negative effects of crowding and stress.

8. One day a week all citizens should be required to carpool or use mass transit systems.

9. Fines should be increased for littering.

10. Attempts to protect the environment should not be allowed to endanger businesses, jobs, or the economy.

➤ ONE-MINUTE MOTIVATORS

1. **Making career decisions.** People have different styles when they are making career decisions. See https://career.berkeley.edu/Plan/MakeDecisions.stm. Discuss how you and your friends approach career decisions.

2. **Interest inventories.** Give students a series of interest inventories. Ask them to look at their scores and decide which inventory "best" describes their perception of their interests.

3. **Where do I find that?** Ask students to answer this question: If you wanted to take a series of interest and aptitude inventories, what specific building/service on campus would you go to? Who would you talk to?

4. **Personal space.** If possible, arrange chairs in class very close to each other. Ask students to move their chair to make themselves comfortable. Demonstrate different preferences in personal space.

5. **Violating personal space.** Before class starts, ask a few students to be secret note-takers for a demonstration and one to be a "prop" in a classroom exercise. Ask the "prop" to come up and be part of a conversation with you concerning the physical characteristics on campus. Gradually engage in behaviors that violate personal space, such as moving closer, staring, and so on. (Ideally, the student should eventually run out of room to back up.) The note-takers should record the approximate distance when the person started to react, and what that person did to compensate (e.g., avert eye contact, etc.). When you are done, ask the "prop" student to tell the class what the experience felt like and the note-takers to share their observations.

6. **Testing preferences.** Give students a very short, ungraded pop quiz on the material in the chapter. The next class session, ask them to take a similar quiz in pairs. Which quiz did they prefer? Would it have made any difference if the quiz were actually to count for their grade?

7. **What do you want on that test?** Give students the chance to decide on the kind of a quiz, exam, or written assignment they would like for this chapter. Either students could quickly submit their preferences and you could make the decision based on majority vote or some class time could be spent having students discuss the issue and use consensus for making the decision. Briefly discuss the differences between teaching by objectives prepared by the instructor and teaching by having students participate in developing the goals and the ways to achieve and measure the goals.

8. **Enrichment ideas.** Ask students to write down on a slip of paper something that an instructor (or that you as the instructor) could do to "enrich" this class.

9. **Sensory overload.** Spend five minutes attempting to overload the class with sensory stimulation. You can ask another instructor to class and introduce your double or triple lecture by saying, "Studies show the brain can process twice as much information as it normally processes. Accordingly, Dr. ___ and I will lecture simultaneously. Take notes as well as you can." You also could ask students to bring to class "something that makes noise." The result could be a few tape recorders, radios, flashing lights, buzzers, etc. Ask everyone to "play them" simultaneously. Do people feel overwhelmed? Why or why not? Ask half of the class to take a graded quiz while the other half makes noise. Now do they feel overwhelmed? Why or why not?

10. **Territory violations.** Begin class by using a front desk where a student predictably always sits. Observe the reactions of that student.

11. **Graffiti board.** Bring poster board to class. On the top write "Graffiti Board" and tack the board to the wall. Write something on it. Observe and discuss the graffiti that develops over a week or two.

12. **Crowding.** Hold class in a very small area. Try to lecture as usual. Act a bit surprised when students act restless, uncomfortable, or frustrated. Discuss how it would feel to live in a very densely packed home.

13. **The commons dilemma.** Have students generate a list of examples that illustrate the Tragedy of the Commons. In many cases, students have "taken advantage" of situations that will maximize their own gain while negatively impacting the collective.

14. **Superordinate goals.** Consider coming to class and explaining that you are considering moving the class to meet outside in some uncomfortable area for the rest of the semester. Explain that you want the class to spend a few minutes helping you list reasons why the class should not be moved. Ask them to quickly get into groups and prepare a list of reasons. Then move on to the lecture. The next meeting, mention how unified the class seemed. Discuss both superordinate goals and the ethics of social research.

15. **Interdependence and cooperation.** Assign each person in class a subtopic of this chapter or all of the chapters in the book. Ask each person to develop five objective questions to be used for review for the quiz on this chapter or for the final. Remind students that the entire class is depending on each person. Make a few copies of their questions and put them on reserve to be used for studying for the quiz or final. Discuss mutual interdependence and cooperation.

16. **Bad ergonomics.** Have students tell the class about poor human factors designs in a device that they use regularly, such as their car, cell phone, or work station. Indicate how it could be improved.

➤ BROADENING OUR CULTURAL HORIZONS

1. **Japanese managerial techniques. (internet exercise)** Research Japanese managerial techniques. What are the advantages and disadvantages of the Japanese management style?

2. **Theory X and cultural fit**. Within what kind of a society would Taylor's Theory X be most common? A capitalist, a socialist, or a communist society? Why?

3. **Multicultural workplaces.** Many plants employ a very diverse mixture of people originally from many different parts of the world and cultural backgrounds. What should a plant manager do to try to help this group of people work as an effective team?

4. **Crowding and world view.** How might a person's view of the world be affected by living in a dense and crowded urban environment?

5. **Culture and personal distance.** Some cultures expect personal touching to take place during conversations; others are literally repelled by touch. What does your culture prefer? What would you guess happens when a person from a "touchless" culture contacts a person from a "touchy" culture?

➤ SUPPLEMENTAL ACTIVITIES

This exercise is designed to help students better understand psychology as a profession and to assess its relevance to them as a career choice.

Exercise 16.1: What Do Psychologists Do?

Students have many misconceptions about what psychologists do once they receive their basic education. They also have some erroneous ideas about what it takes to become a practicing psychologist. A beginning course may whet their appetites and make psychology seem like a glamorous career to pursue. Every instructor has experienced students who, after the introductory course, decide to follow a career in psychology. A realistic appraisal of what it takes to become a qualified practitioner and a look at the work done by psychologists may help students to make a better decision regarding the next step in their education.

There are five suggestions here, any one of which could help students along the road. However, some activity along this line would pay dividends.

1. If you are a university or college with a graduate program in psychology, invite faculty and/or graduate students to participate in a panel discussion. Try to get as wide a variety of backgrounds and interests as possible to reflect the diversity in the field. Have the students prepare questions ahead of time so that the time will be spent in a productive, non-repetitive discussion.

598

2. A second type of panel, which though harder to put together may be most rewarding, is to invite a group of practicing psychologists from the community. You should look for persons in school systems, mental health clinics, industry, advertising, social services, research institutes, etc. Speakers should be asked to identify their area of interest and specialization, the kind of work they do, the education required to do the work, the salary range, the career advancement opportunities, etc. Allow students to ask questions. Some questions should be preplanned to be sure pertinent information is elicited.

3. Provide students with an up-to-date list of careers in psychology such as that put out by the American Psychological Association. Ask them to select an area they might be interested in pursuing or that they want to know more about. Send the students to the library, career placement center, or counseling office to gather information on that particular career. They should look for educational requirements, type of work done, salary range, and career advancement opportunities. Students should submit a written report and also report on interesting aspects of their findings to the class.

4. Since most students will not be psychologists, a different approach might be interesting to pursue. Ask students to identify their career goals. Since many will be vague about this, you may have to do some work to get every student to settle on some specific area that is, at least, of interest to them.

5. Now your task is to convince the students that psychologists work in their area of interest either directly or indirectly. For example, if someone says (s)he wants a career in business, you can help them discover that there are psychologists in industry, advertising, personnel selection and training, etc.

6. Once the students have settled on a career choice and identified a psychological service that is provided to people in that field, have them research what the psychologist does. The idea is that they should discover what psychological services they can expect from a psychologist once they enter their career.

7. It may be possible for students with common career goals to work together on this project. Written papers should be submitted and an oral report given to the class.

8. Send some or all of the students to interview some persons who work in psychological careers. The class as a whole should develop questions, and the interviewees should be carefully selected.

➤ JOURNAL QUESTIONS

1.   Make a balance sheet (pros and cons) of the things that you like and don't like at your current job. If you are not currently employed, evaluate your last job.

2.   What hours would you like to work? What hours do you wish your parents or some of your friends worked?

3.   Sketch your spatial bubble. How much distance do you usually place between yourself and others? What situations change the size of your spatial bubble?

4.   Describe the behaviors of your "favorite" and your "most disliked" past employers. Who made you work most efficiently? Who made the job most enjoyable?

5.   What kind of a job would be most satisfying to you? Why? What could your current or a past employer do to enrich your job?

6.   Which coping style have you used thus far in making educational and career decisions?

7.   If you don't live alone, what area in your apartment or home is "yours"? How is this area "marked"? What would you do if your roommate, spouse, child, or sibling invaded your territory?

8.   What social traps are you enmeshed in? How could you try to get out?

➤ SUGGESTIONS FOR FURTHER READING

Aamodt, M. G. (2010). *Industrial/organizational psychology: An applied approach* (6th ed.). Belmont, CA: Cengage Learning/Wadsworth.

Abrahamse, W., Steg, L., Vlek, C., & Rothengatter, T. (2005). A review of intervention studies aimed at household energy conservation. *Journal of Environmental Psychology, 25*(3), 273–291.

Ayman, R., & Korabik, K. (2010). Leadership: Why gender and culture matter. *American Psychologist, 65*(3), 157-170.

Bell, P. A., Greene, T., Fisher, J., & Baum, A. S. (2006). *Environmental psychology* (5th ed.). Mahwah, NJ: Erlbaum.

Bolles, R. N. (2010). *What color is your parachute? A practical manual for job-hunters and career changers*. Berkeley, CA: Ten Speed Press.

Buchanan, M. (2008). Sin cities: The geometry of crime. *New Scientist, 2654* (April 30), 36–39.

Cox, R. (2006). *Sports psychology: Concepts and applications* (6th ed.). New York: McGraw-Hill.

Gill, D. G., & Williams, L. (2008). *Psychological dynamics of sport and exercise* (3rd ed.). Champaign, IL: Human Kinetics.

Helmreich, R. L. (1983). Applying psychology in outer space. *American Psychologist, April*, 445-450.

Hirschhorn, L. (2002). *Managing in the new team environment: skills, tools, and methods*. Lincoln, NE: iUniverse, Inc.

Lamberton, L. (2009). *Human relation: Strategies for success* (4th ed.). New York: McGraw-Hill.

Memon, A., Vrij, A., & Bull, R. (2003). *Psychology and law: Truthfulness, accuracy, and credibility*. Hoboken, NJ: Wiley.

Milgram, S. (1970). The experience of living in cities. *Science, 167*, 1461-1468.

Muchinsky, P. M. (2008). *Psychology applied to work: An introduction to organizational and industrial psychology* (9th ed.). Kansas City, KS: Hypergraphic Press..

Sanders, M. S. & McCormick, E. J. (1993). *Human factors in engineering and design* (7th ed.). New York: McGraw-Hill.

Shapiro, J. M. (2006). A "memory-jamming" theory of advertising. *Social Science Research Network*. Retrieved March 6, 2010, from http://papers.ssrn.com/sol3/papers.cfm?abstract_id=903474.

U.S. Department of Labor (2009). *Job interview tips*. Washington: U.S. Department of Labor. Retrieved May 6, 2010 from http://www.bls.gov/oco/oco20045.htm.

Van Vugt, M. (2009). Averting the tragedy of the commons: Using social psychological science to protect the environment. *Current Directions in Psychological Science, 18*(3), 169-173.

Woods, S. & West, M. (2010). *The psychology of work and organizations*. Belmont, CA: Cengage Learning/Wadsworth.

Wrightsman, L. S., & Fulero, S. M. (2009). *Forensic psychology* (3rd ed.). Belmont, CA: Cengage Learning/Wadsworth.

Zeisel, J. (2006). *Inquiry by design: Environment/behavior/neuroscience in architecture, interiors, landscape, and planning*. New York: Norton.

➤ VIDEO SUGGESTIONS

Applying Psychology in Life, (2001), from *Discovering Psychology Series,* Annenberg/CPB, 30 min. This video discusses some of the innovative ways psychology is being applied to practical situations and professions in areas concerning human factors, law, and conflict negotiation.

Behavioral Sciences, (1991), Films for the Humanities and Sciences, 23 min. Although we are unaware of it, we behave in accordance with some very precise programs that are deeply rooted in our genetic makeup. This program explores three aspects of behavioral sciences: innate as opposed to acquired behavior, social behavior, and behavior in the workplace. In all three cases, scientists have established close links between humans and animals as testimony to the distant origin of some of our behaviors.

Career Evaluation, (1997), Films for the Humanities and Sciences, 15 min. A Cambridge Educational Production. This program shows viewers how to relate their interests, skills, education, training, values, and lifestyle to specific occupations in the world of work. Based on the common-sense notion that you do best at what you really like to do, this video shows you how to find an occupation with job requirements that closely match your interests. Having a close match between your interests and abilities and the requirements of your job results in high job satisfaction. Before making career choices, it is important to know what your career will really be like. It shows you how to research the numerous sources of career information available today.

Inside The Criminal Mind, (2001), Films for the Humanities and Sciences, 45 min. each. This gripping three-part series enters the world of forensic psychology to illustrate how law enforcement officers and mental health professionals get inside the criminal mind. Captivating case studies from the United Kingdom and the United States provide a real-world context for the techniques and processes described.

Kids and Race: Working It Out, (1987), Films for the Humanities and Sciences, 52 min. This film shows how a weekend encounter group can help nine children from diverse backgrounds discuss their feelings about stereotypes and prejudice.

Leadership and People Skills, (1996), Insight Media, 22 min. What is the difference between a leader and a manager? What qualities characterize an effective leader? This program analyzes the particular difficulties that leaders of professionals encounter and examines different approaches and models of leadership. It offers a range of practical ideas for leading professional colleagues.

Making Psychology Part of Your Life, (2002), from *Psychology: The Human Experience Series,* Coast Community College District Telecourses, 30 min. This video examines how psychology can be applied to all areas of our lives.

Organizational Culture, (1999), Insight Media, 12 min. The culture of an organization—its values, attitudes, beliefs, and behavioral standards—develops in the same organic way as the cultures of the individuals who comprise it, and is just as resistant to change. Designed for leaders involved in implementing change, this video teaches how to identify leverage points in the culture of an organization and utilize them to achieve greater efficiency and productivity.

Science in The Arena, (1993), Films for the Humanities and Sciences, 23 min. Since the first Olympic Games 2,600 years ago, the goal of athletes has been to win; however, methods of winning have changed. This program shows three contributions of modern science to the feats of athletes: sports psychology, which uses various psychological techniques, such as autosuggestion, rituals, mental imagery, and relaxation that enable athletes to extend their physical limits; better health through more careful training, with adequate periods of rest and recuperation; and genetics, which can lead to the pre-selection of athletes who are genetically likely to be winners.

Understanding People, (1990), Insight Media, 17 min. This program explains principles of human behavior revealed through Maslow's hierarchy of needs theory, McGregor's X and Y Theory, and the Hawthorne studies. It explores how these principles can be applied in leadership situations to enhance effectiveness.

➤ COMPUTER AND INTERNET RESOURCES

INFOTRAC®

Below you will find two journal articles obtained from INFOTRAC® that relate to information contained in this chapter. Instructors should encourage students to utilize this invaluable resource to improve their research skills. Have students locate and read the following articles and answer questions relevant to each article.

American Journal of Community Psychology, Sept 2004 v34 p129 (17) **Beyond the individual: toward a nomological network of organizational empowerment.**

1.   Define empowerment as outlined in this article.

   Answer: Empowerment is an active, participatory process through which individuals, organizations, and communities gain greater control, efficacy, and social justice.

2.   What was the central goal of this paper?

   Answer: The central goal of this paper is to present a nomological network of organizational empowerment (OE). A nomological network is a theoretical framework that represents the basic features of a construct, their observable manifestations, and the interrelationships among them.

3.   The authors of this article suggest that a conceptual model of empowered organizations include three components. List and briefly describe each of the three.

   Answer: First, the intraorganizational component of OE includes characteristics that represent the internal structure and functioning of organizations. Second, the interorganizational component of OE includes the linkages between organizations. Finally, the extraorganizational component of OE refers to actions taken by organizations to affect the larger environments of which they are a part.

4.   How does OE differ from organizational development and community organization?

   Answer: OE differs because it represents a theoretical construct, whereas organizational development and community organization involve practice techniques that do not have a specific guiding theory.

The Forensic Examiner, Summer 2006 v15 i2 p6(12) **Psychological profiles of terrorists.**

1.   Why do terrorism prevention efforts continue to fall short?

Answer: Intelligence agencies make errors in failing to distinguish between knowledge-based, scientifically-derived preventive efforts and those that are guided by heuristics. They tend to use profiles that are either inaccurate or that are easily changed by terrorists. They fail to use available preventative technology, and continue to have difficulties in effectively collecting, disseminating, and responding to intelligence information.

Intelligence-gathering technology has been designed to deal with Cold-War era ballistic missile threats, neglecting the human-intelligence resources and infrastructures necessary to deal with the threat of terrorism. Commonly-used definitions of terrorism fail to view the world from the terrorists' perspectives.

2.   What is a profile, and what is the profile of a "typical" terrorist?

Answer: The most common misconception regarding profiling is that either race or nationality serves as the only criterion on which to generate a profile. However, there are probably numerous profiles for numerous terrorist targets that vary along ideological lines, technical capacities, and group affiliations. Each target group requires the development of a distinct profile of a likely terrorist based on statistical analyses (not heuristics, nor on purely race/nationality factors) of existing historical data and credible known threats, both from archives and from the intelligence community.

Each profile of a likely terrorist must have as many determinants as possible to facilitate a better match with a real terrorist in future preventive efforts. Possible factors include age range, educational background, ethnicity, socioeconomic status, national origin, psychological makeup, marital status, character type, current economic state, criminal background, religious affiliation, immigration status, and social affiliations.

Determinants extracted from historical data, known threats, and other sources are then rank-ordered according to their relative importance in the generation of a profile. Social and psychological marginality with a negative disposition toward society were also elements common in the American-born and domestic terrorists.

The "typical" terrorist is a narcissistic individual who tends to exhibit a sense of grandiose entitlement, which fits perfectly into the emerging terrorist group's members' belief that they are special in some fundamental way. The pride that develops in such groups gives way to its individual narcissistic members seeing themselves as superior to others (i.e., their rights and needs are more important than those of others), and to them more readily taking offense at others' actions as wrongs against them. In contrast, terrorist leaders often come from relatively privileged life circumstances. Further distinctions exist between field leaders, food soldiers, and suicide bombers/pilots.

3.   What are some of the social and economic factors contributing to terrorism?

       Answer: More often than not, the terrorist is regarded as a mythical figure who represents a messianic being to members of those national groups and social entities, who are disenfranchised by political, religious, or ethnic circumstances.

       In many places where they are entrenched, terrorist organizations employ their financial tools and bureaucratic apparatus to establish schools, infirmaries, and other institutions to benefit the societies in which they are then protected.

       Essentially, in every place where people are in a state of distress (e.g., economic, national, or political) and their plight is not sufficiently noticed, terrorism can get them noticed. Likewise, in every place where peoples' subjective sense of powerlessness is palpable, terrorism will remain a viable option for effective empowerment.

WEB LINKS

Knowledge Builder Links

1. Industrial/Organizational Psychology
   Society for Industrial and Organizational Psychology: http://www.siop.org/
   Women in Management:
        http://www.ilo.org/public/english/bureau/inf/magazine/23/glass.htm
   Job Interview Tips: http://www.bls.gov/oco/oco20045.htm

2. Environmental Psychology
   Ecological Footprint Quiz:
        http://www.ecologicalfootprint.org/Global%20Footprint%20Calculator/GFPCalc.html
   Carbon Calculator: http://www.carbonfootprint.com/

3. The Psychology of Law and Sports
   The Innocence Project: http://www.innocenceproject.org/
   Careers in Psychology and Law: http://www.ap-ls.org/students/careersoverview.html
   Sports Psychology:
        http://sportsmedicine.about.com/od/sportspsychology/Sports_Psychology.htm

4. Human Factors Psychology
   Bad Human Factors Design: http://www.baddesigns.com/
   Human-Computer Interaction: http://old.sigchi.org/cdg/cdg2.html
   International Space Station: http://www.nasa.gov/mission_pages/station/main/

Additional Web Links

Forensic Psychology Links
http://www.psychologyinfo.com/forensic/
http://www.abfp.com/
http://www.psichi.org/pubs/articles/article_58.aspx

Human-Computer Interaction Resources on the Net
http://old.sigchi.org/cdg/cdg2.html

Human Factors Psychology
http://www.psychology.org/links/Environment_Behavior_Relationships/Human_Factors/

Industrial/Organizational Psychology
http://www.siop.org/

Journal of Environmental Psychology
http://www.sciencedirect.com/science/journal/02724944

Scientific Jury Selection
http://psychologytoday.com/articles/pto-20070302-000001.xml
http://en.wikipedia.org/wiki/Scientific_jury_selection

Leadership Styles
http://www.mindtools.com/pages/article/newLDR_84.htm
http://www.nwlink.com/~donclark/leader/leadstl.html
http://www.motivation-tools.com/workplace/leadership_styles.htm

Organizational Psychology
http://www.sosig.ac.uk/roads/subject-listing/World-cat/indpsych.html

Psychology and Law
http://www.apa.org/about/division/div41.aspx

Sports Psychology Web Resources
http://www.fitinfotech.com/books/splinks.html
http://www.apa47.org/

PSYCHOLOGY IN THE NEWS

About.com
http://psychology.about.com/od/branchesofpsycholog1/f/what-is-sports-psychology.htm
This site provides numerous links to related topics in sports psychology as well as articles and links to headline news in psychology.

Industrial/Organizational Psychology Student Association
http://www.gmu.edu/org/iopsa/theion.htm
This site provides current news in the field of I/O psychology, and students can also access news archives.

ABC News
http://abcnews.go.com/Business/FunMoney/story?id=3375623&page=1&CMP=OTC-RSSFeeds0312
This site introduces the field of industrial psychology.

Appendix
Behavioral Statistics

Survey Questions

Supplemental Activities

Exercise A.1: Demonstrating Statistics
Exercise A.2: Distribution of Scores
Exercise A.3: Mean, Median, and Mode
Exercise A.4: The Normal Distribution and IQ
Exercise A.5: What's "Average"?

Handouts

Handout A.1: Means, Medians, and Modes

Suggestions for Further Reading
Video Suggestions
Computer and Internet Resources

➤ SURVEY QUESTIONS

Module A.1 Descriptive Statistics

Survey Question: What are descriptive statistics?

Survey Question: How are statistics used to identify an average score?

Survey Question: What statistics do psychologists use to measure how much

scores differ from one another?

Module A.2 Correlations and Inferential Statistics

Survey Question: How are correlations used in psychology?

Survey Question: What are inferential statistics?

➤ SUPPLEMENTAL ACTIVITIES

Exercise A.1: Demonstrating Statistics

It is possible to demonstrate statistics with a simple classroom exercise. Instruct students to bring a ruler to class the day of the demonstration, along with a used pencil. Have a container of some sort on hand, and have students place all the pencils into the container. Then, individually or in small groups, have students pull 10 pencils at random from the container, measure the length of each of the 10 pencils, and find the mean length. You may plot each student's or group's findings on the board, pointing out how many different means were obtained even though the samples all came from the same population. This activity can be expanded to include measures of variability as well.

Exercise A.2: Distributions of Scores

Another way to demonstrate statistical concepts is to measure the height of the students in the classroom, if time permits. Students can be measured and averaged by rows, and then by more randomly selected samples, and the difference between the two types of samples compared. Plotting the heights on a graph may also lead to a discussion of the normal curve.

Exercise A.3: Mean, Median, and Mode

Handout A-1 gives students some basic practice in calculating means, medians, and modes. One of the examples intentionally requires a bit of extra thought. Their ability to deal with exceptions should make their level of understanding clear.

The answers are:
#1 mean =74.3   median = 77   Mode = 78
#2 mean =$45,556   median = $35,000   Mode = $20,000 and $50,000

Exercise A.4: The Normal Distribution and IQ

Draw a normal distribution for IQ scores on the board. Explain how the mean and the standard deviation allow us to predict the percent of people who have various IQ scores. You will have to spend some time helping them make the calculations.

Set facts:
Mean = 100
Standard deviations: 1 s.d. = 68% of the population (rounded off)
(normal curve)   2 s.d. = 95% of the population
                         3 s.d. =99% of the population

Standard deviation – WAIS = 15 IQ points; Stanford-Binet = 16 IQ points

610

Ask students:
What percent of people have an IQ above 145? (1/2 of one percent)
What percent of people have an IQ above 70?   (97.5%)
What percent of people have an IQ between 70 and 115? (81.5%)
Make up your own additional questions.

Exercise A.5: What's "Average"?

Students often have trouble with the concept that the mean is not always the best average measure of central tendency. Have students, individually or in groups, create a number of situations where the mean, median, or mode is each a poor example. Here are a few cases to get them started:

1. Improper use of the mean: Bill Gates (and his billions) move to a farming town of 10,000 people. What is the best measure of central tendency of income?
2. Improper use of mode: A small college town's population is approximately one-fourth students. Most of them have an income of about $10,000 per year. What is the best way to calculate the average income of the people in the town?
3. Improper use of median: Mr. and Mrs. Johnson have one 12-year-old daughter. Mr. and Mrs. Johnson never watch TV, but their daughter watches about 10 hours per week. What is the average amount of TV watching in the Johnson home?

➤ SUGGESTIONS FOR FURTHER READING

Gonick, L., & Smith, W. (1994). *The cartoon guide to statistics.* New York: Harper-Collins.

Gravetter, F. J., & Wallnau, L. B. (2010). *Statistics for the behavioral sciences* (8th ed.). Belmont, CA: Cengage Learning/Wadsworth.

Heiman, G. W. (2011). *Basic statistics for the behavioral sciences* (6th ed.). Belmont, CA: Cengage Learning/Wadsworth.

Huff, D. & Geis, I. (1993). *How to lie with statistics.* New York: Norton.

Pelham, B. W. (2007) *Conducting experiments in psychology: Measuring the weight of smoke* (8th ed.). Belmont, CA: Cengage Learning/Wadsworth.

Stanovich, K. E. (2010). *How to think straight about psychology* (9th ed.). Boston: Allyn & Bacon.

➤ VIDEO SUGGESTIONS

The Scientific Method: Processes and Investigations (Films for the Humanities & Sciences, 2000, CD-ROM). An engaging blend of animations, photographs, diagrams, video, and audio, this stimulating CD-ROM challenges students to investigate meaningful scenarios in the same way that professional scientists seek to understand the world. Highly interactive, available for both Windows and Macintosh users.

Statistics and Psychology (Films for the Humanities & Sciences, 2000, 25 min.) A look at how to statistically test the relationship between experimental data and reported historical findings. Clear illustrations are given of the use of correlation and other statistical approaches.

Why Use Statistics? (Films for the Humanities & Sciences, 2000, 20-25 min.) This four-part series includes *Handling Variability, Describing Data, Using Samples,* and *Bivariate Data: When y Depends on x.* May be purchased separately or as a set.

➤ COMPUTER AND INTERNET RESOURCES

PsykTrek 3.0
Unit 1: History & Methods
1c. "Statistics: Central Tendency and Variability"
1d. "Statistics: Correlation"

WEB LINKS

Knowledge Builder Web Links

1. Descriptive Statistics
    Frequency Distribution of Tossing Coins and Dice:
        http://teacherlink.org/content/math/activities/ex-randomevents/guide.html
    Measures of Central Tendency: http://cnx.org/content/m11061/latest/
    Descriptive Statistics: http://www.socialresearchmethods.net/kb/statdesc.htm

2. Inferential Statistics
    Concepts and Applications of Inferential Statistics:
        http://faculty.vassar.edu/lowry/webtext.html
    Scatter Diagram: http://www.asq.org/learn-about-quality/cause-analysis-
        tools/overview/scatter.html
    Correlations: http://www.statsoft.com/textbook/stbasic.html

Additional Web Links

APA Online
http://www.apa.org/

Resources for Teaching Statistics:
http://it.stlawu.edu/~rlock/tise98/onepage.html

Statistics Courses, Handouts, and Exercises
http://www.roma.unisa.edu.au/10920/links/link_2.htm
http://www.mste.uiuc.edu/hill/dstat/dstat.html

Handout A.1: MEANS, MEDIANS, AND MODES

For each of the following, calculate the mean, the median, and the mode. For each example, show your work.

Example #1: The recent results of your psychology test for your class of 21 students were: 68, 89, 54, 61, 78, 82, 65, 78, 93, 61, 77, 90, 64, 88, 74, 78, 87, 90, 46, 75, and 63.

Mean =

Median =

Mode =

Example #2: In a small town, four families have an income of $20,000, five have an income of $30,000, three have an income of $40,000, four have an income of $50,000, one has an income of $70,000, and one has an income of $200,000.

Mean =

Median =

Mode =

Which of mean, median, and mode represents the best expression of the "average" income for this village, and why?

614